NICARAGUA
Managua
San José
COSTA RICA
Panama City
PANAMA

Caracas
Port of Spain
TRINIDAD & TOBAGO
VENEZUELA

Magdalena
Orinoco
GUIANA HIGHLANDS
Bogotá
Georgetown
GUYANA
Paramaribo
SURINAME
FR.
Cayenne
GUIANA

COLOMBIA

Equator

Equator

Quito
ECUADOR
Napo
Jupará
Negro
Amazon

Ucayali
AMAZON BASIN
Purus
Madeira
Tapajos
Xingu
São Francisco

BRAZIL

PERU
Lima
ANDES MTS.
Araguaia
BRAZILIAN HIGHLANDS

La Paz
BOLIVIA
Brasília

Paraná

ATACAMA DESERT
Tropic of Capricorn
Tropic of Capricorn

Isla San Ambrosio
(CHILE)

PARAGUAY
Asunción

Paraná

Archipélago
Juan Fernández
(CHILE)
Santiago
Colorado
PAMPAS
Buenos Aires
URUGUAY
Montevideo

ARGENTINA

SOUTH

CHILE
Negro
ANDES MTS.
ATLANTIC

OCEAN

PATAGONIA

Strait of
Magellan
Stanley
Falkland Islands
(UK)

South Georgia &
South Sandwich Islands
(UK)

# THE GREENWOOD
## ENCYCLOPEDIA OF
# WORLD
## POPULAR CULTURE

# The Greenwood Encyclopedia of World Popular Culture

*General Editor*

GARY HOPPENSTAND

*Volume Editors*

MICHAEL K. SCHOENECKE, North America

JOHN F. BRATZEL, Latin America

GERD BAYER, Europe

LYNN BARTHOLOME, North Africa and the Middle East

DENNIS HICKEY, Sub-Saharan Africa

GARY XU and VINAY DHARWADKER, Asia and Pacific Oceania

# THE GREENWOOD
# ENCYCLOPEDIA OF
# WORLD
# POPULAR CULTURE

## LATIN AMERICA

Gary Hoppenstand
*General Editor*

John F. Bratzel
*Volume Editor*

GREENWOOD PRESS
Westport, Connecticut • London

Library of Congress Cataloging in Publication Data

The Greenwood encyclopedia of world popular culture / Gary Hoppenstand, general editor ; volume editors, John F. Bratzel ... [et al.].
    p. cm.
 Includes bibliographical references and index.
 ISBN-13: 978-0-313-33255-5 (set : alk. paper)
 ISBN-13: 978-0-313-33316-3 (North America : alk. paper)
 ISBN-13: 978-0-313-33256-2 (Latin America : alk. paper)
 ISBN-13: 978-0-313-33509-9 (Europe : alk. paper)
 ISBN-13: 978-0-313-33274-6 (North Africa and the Middle East : alk. paper)
 ISBN-13: 978-0-313-33505-1 (Sub-Saharan Africa : alk. paper)
 ISBN-13: 978-0-313-33956-1 (Asia and Pacific Oceania : alk. paper)
 1. Popular culture—Encyclopedias. 2. Civilization, Modern—Encyclopedias. 3. Culture—Encyclopedias. I. Hoppenstand, Gary. II. Bratzel, John F. III. Title: Encyclopedia of world popular culture. IV. Title: World popular culture.
HM621.G74   2007
306.03—dc22    2007010684

British Library Cataloguing in Publication Data is available.

Library of Congress Catalog Card Number: 2007010684
ISBN-13: 978-0-313-33255-5 (Set)
ISBN-10: 0-313-33255-X

ISBN-13: 978-0-313-33316-3 (North America)
ISBN-10: 0-313-33316-5

ISBN-13: 978-0-313-33256-2 (Latin America)
ISBN-10: 0-313-33256-8

ISBN-13: 978-0-313-33509-9 (Europe)
ISBN-10: 0-313-33509-5

ISBN-13: 978-0-313-33274-6 (North Africa and the Middle East)
ISBN-10: 0-313-33274-6

ISBN-13: 978-0-313-33505-1 (Sub-Saharan Africa)
ISBN-10: 0-313-33505-2

ISBN-13: 978-0-313-33956-1 (Asia and Pacific Oceania)
ISBN-10: 0-313-33956-2

First published in 2007

Greenwood Press, 88 Post Road West, Westport, CT 06881
An imprint of Greenwood Publishing Group, Inc.
www.greenwood.com

Printed in the United States of America

The paper used in this book complies with the Permanent Paper Standard issued by the National Information Standards Organization (Z39.48–1984).

10  9  8  7  6  5  4  3  2  1

For my happy and beautiful granddaughter,
Myra Lacy

# CONTENTS

*FOREWORD: POPULAR CULTURE AND THE WORLD*
  Gary Hoppenstand                                              ix

*INTRODUCTION: POPULAR CULTURE IN LATIN AMERICA*               xi
  John F. Bratzel

ARCHITECTURE                                                    1
  Patrice Elizabeth Olsen

ART                                                            23
  Braden K. Frieder

DANCE                                                          51
  John Charles Chasteen

FASHION AND APPEARANCE                                         75
  Regina A. Root

FILM                                                           93
  Randal P. Garza and Lúcia Flórido

FOOD AND FOODWAYS                                             115
  Jeffrey M. Pilcher

LITERATURE                                                    139
  Daniel J. Nappo

LOVE, SEX, AND MARRIAGE                                       171
  Linda A. Curcio-Nagy

MUSIC                                                         195
  Peter Manuel

PERIODICALS                                                   217
  Robert T. Buckman

RADIO AND TELEVISION                                          249
  Leonardo Ferreira

SPORTS AND RECREATION                                         271
  Joseph L. Arbena

# CONTENTS

THEATER AND PERFORMANCE   307
*Kristen McCleary*

TRANSPORTATION AND TRAVEL   345
*John F. Bratzel*

*GENERAL BIBLIOGRAPHY*   379

*ABOUT THE EDITORS AND CONTRIBUTORS*   381

*INDEX*   385

# FOREWORD

## POPULAR CULTURE AND THE WORLD

## POPULAR CULTURE AND THE WORLD

### GARY HOPPENSTAND

Popular culture is easy to recognize, but often difficult to define. We can say with authority that the current hit television show *House* is popular culture, but can we say that how medical personnel work in hospitals is popular culture as well? We can readily admit that the recent blockbuster movie *Pirates of the Caribbean* is popular culture, but can we also admit that what the real-life historical Caribbean pirates ate and what clothes they wore are components of popular culture? We can easily recognize that a best-selling romance novel by Danielle Steel is popular culture, but can we also recognize that human love, as ritualistic behavior, is popular culture? Can popular culture include architecture, or furniture, or automobiles, or many of the other things that we make, as well as the behaviors that we engage in, and the general attitudes that we hold in our day-to-day lives? Does popular culture exist outside of our own immediate society? There can be so much to study about popular culture that it can seem overwhelming, and ultimately inaccessible.

Because popular culture is so pervasive—not only in the United States, but in all cultures around the world—it can be difficult to study. Basically, however, there are two main approaches to defining popular culture. The first advocates the notion that popular culture is tied to that period in Western societies known as the Industrial Revolution. It is subsequently linked to such concepts as "mass-produced culture" and "mass-consumed culture." In other words, there must be present a set of conditions related to industrial capitalism before popular culture can exist. Included among these conditions are the need for large urban centers, or cities, which can sustain financially the distribution and consumption of popular culture, and the related requirement that there be an educated working-class or middle-class population that has both the leisure time and the expendable income to support the production of popular culture. Certainly, this approach can encompass that which is most commonly regarded as popular culture: motion pictures, television, popular fiction, computers and video games, even contemporary fast foods and popular fashion. In addition, this approach can generate discussions about the relationship between popular culture and political ideology. Can popular culture be political in nature, or politically subversive?

Can it intentionally or unintentionally support the status quo? Can it be oppressive or express harmful ideas? Needless to say, such definitions limit the critical examination of popular culture by both geography and time, insisting that popular culture existed (or only exists) historically in industrial and postindustrial societies (primarily in Western Europe and North America) over the past 200 years. However, many students and critics of popular culture insist that industrial production and Western cultural influences are not essential in either defining or understanding popular culture.

Indeed, a second approach sees popular culture as existing since the beginning of human civilization. It is not circumscribed by certain historic periods, or by national or regional boundaries. This approach sees popular culture as extending well beyond the realm of industrial production, in terms of both its creation and its existence. Popular culture, these critics claim, can be seen in ancient China, or in medieval Japan, or in precolonial Africa, as well as in modern-day Western Europe and North America (or in all contemporary global cultures and nations for that matter). It need not be limited to mass-produced objects or electronic media, though it certainly does include these, but it can include the many facets of people's lifestyles, the way people think and behave, and the way people define themselves as individuals and as societies.

This six-volume *Encyclopedia of World Popular Culture* then, encompasses something of both approaches. In each of the global regions of the world covered—North America, South America, Europe, the Middle East, Sub-Saharan Africa, and Asia—the major industrial and postindustrial expressions of popular culture are covered, including, in most cases, film; games, toys, and pastimes; literature (popular fiction and nonfiction); music; periodicals; and radio/television. Also examined are the lifestyle dimensions of popular culture, including architecture; dance; fashion and appearance; food and foodways; love, sex, and marriage; sports; theater and performance; and transportation and travel. What is revealed in each chapter of each volume of *The Greenwood Encyclopedia of World Popular Culture* is the rich complexity and diversity of the human experience within the framework of a popular culture context.

Yet rooted within this framework of rich complexity and diversity is a central idea that holds the construct of world popular culture together, an idea that sees in popular culture both the means and the methods of widespread, everyday, human expression. Simply put, the commonality of national, transnational, and global popular cultures is the notion that, through their popular culture, people construct narratives, or stories, about themselves and their communities. The many and varied processes involved in creating popular culture (and subsequently living with it) are concerned, at the deepest and most fundamental levels, with the need for people to express their lifestyle in ways that significantly define their relationships to others.

The food we eat, the movies we see, the games we play, the way we construct our buildings, and the means of our travel all tell stories about what we think and what we like at a consciously intended level, as well as at an unintended subliminal level. These narratives tell others about our interests and desires, as well as our fundamental beliefs about life itself. Thus, though the types of popular dance might be quite different in the various regions of the world, the recognition that dance fulfills a basic and powerful need for human communication is amazingly similar. The fact that different forms of popular sports are played and watched in different countries does not deny the related fact that sports globally define the kindred beliefs in the benefits of hard work, determination, and the overarching desire for the achievement of success.

These are all life stories, and popular culture involves the relating of life's most common forms of expression. This *Encyclopedia of World Popular Culture* offers many narratives about many people and their popular culture, stories that not only inform us about others and how they live, but that also inform us, by comparison, about how we live.

# INTRODUCTION

## POPULAR CULTURE IN LATIN AMERICA

### JOHN F. BRATZEL

Latin America is a geographic concept rather than a cultural one. The region is referred to as "Latin America" because the two main languages of the region, Spanish and Portuguese, have their basis in the Latin language. Although the geography of the region is important, to appreciate the people and events of the region, the culture of Latin America has to be understood. If there is a single word to describe that culture, it is "diverse."

Each nation is an amalgam of various ethnicities, customs, and traditions. Generally speaking, the indigenous cultures of Latin America mixed with the Spanish and Portuguese culture in varying degrees to create distinct societies. But any discussion of culture in Latin America cannot ignore the African contribution to the region. It must be remembered that the majority of slaves that were brought to the New World went to Latin America. In places, African forms continued and flourished and eventually became part of the larger culture. Finally, other cultures from Asia and Europe settled in Latin America and contributed to the diverse mix of Latin America.

Within these diverse peoples, history, economics, geography, and political factors then joined to determine the culture of the particular nation. Moreover, within nations, culture is also varied so that one country can have multiple customs and traditions. Finally, cultural forms arrive through travel and the media. Television, movies, and books from other nations, such as the United States, also add to the various national and regional cultures of Latin America.

This volume concentrates on "Popular Culture," the culture of everyday life in Latin America. The goal is to look at the world of the vast majority of Latin American citizens in contemporary times rather than the high culture of mostly the upper classes. This is not an easy task considering the size and diversity of Latin America. Each of the chapters could easily be a whole book, but even then, they still could not completely deal with the subject. Nevertheless, this volume offers a window through which to understand Latin American culture and provides a good general overview. Depending on the subject and the nature of the information, some chapters are arranged topically and some are arranged geographically by culturally related groups of countries (for example, Mexico and some Central American countries) or by geography alone (roughly from north to south). Each chapter concludes with a useful selected resource guide for additional sources of information, including print resources, Websites, videos, and recordings related to the chapter's topic.

## THE CHAPTERS IN THIS BOOK

Patrice E. Olsen is a historian who specializes in the history and development of **Architecture** in Latin America. In her chapter she details the major developments of the last 50 years as the nations of Latin America blended both internal and external forms to create an architectural landscape. The architecture that each nation created acts as a record of the people, but this record changes quickly as new architectural forms appear.

Cities, in particular, have undergone major rebuilding. In many cities, for example, new International Style buildings have replaced some of the older colonial architecture, although this trend has slowed. The Brazilian government created the completely new city of Brasília, which was intended to open up the interior of Brazil.

Even as cities have changed and been created, they have had to deal with an enormous rate of growth and the problems such growth brings. Latin American cities have to deal with massive urban sprawl, which has created huge rings of poverty and slums around many of these locales. Today this sprawl also includes new American-style shopping malls, which erode the importance of the city center.

Latin American architecture is becoming more eclectic with multiple styles and forms, many having their roots in differing national and international styles. According to Olsen, the "dynamism and creativity" that defines Latin American architecture will continue as will the tension of competing styles and forms.

**Art** comes in many types, from paintings, to sculpture, to photography. Braden Frieder analyzes these forms and places them in their national and international context. It is clear that art in Latin America took styles from a variety of cultures, blended them, and produced unique and fascinating new forms and images.

In his chapter, Frieder looks at each nation and writes about the development of art in each. Mexico, for example, built on its indigenous cultural roots, but it was painters such as Diego Rivera who helped define Mexico. Rivera painted large murals celebrating the Mexican Revolution. In them he showed the noble Indian and the rapacious European, but he also showed the blending of the two races.

In Guatemala in the 1960s, expressionism, abstract painting, and social realism were the main emphases. The fighting that plagued the nation for many years brought about Vértebra Group, which created protest art. Peru emphasized social realism, modernism, and indigenous subjects and forms in its art. Brazil's indigenous population was destroyed or marginalized early in its history, and as a result, African influences, from the many slaves brought to Brazil, have influenced Brazilian art. Contemporary Brazilian artists became known worldwide as they "helped shape the development of conceptual and performance-based art in the 1960s and 1970s." Argentina was most influenced by Europe, in particular by cubism and surrealism.

The well-known author and historian John Chasteen writes on **Dance** in Latin America. He points out that, while it is difficult to identify a national dance for the United States, dance has considerable significance in Latin America. Many countries have national dances that are central "to dominant nationalist ideologies . . . as well as a powerful symbol, of collective identity."

Europeans coming to the New World brought with them the dance of two; a dance that imitated courtship. While the style was European, African influences, particularly in the body movements, were added. These dances emphasized the mixing of the two cultures, although Africans, before the end of the slave trade, also continued to perform separate African dances. At independence, new forms of dance that emphasized the identity of countries such as the *Jarabes, Huapangos, Joropos, Lundus, Bambucos,* and *Zamacuecas* served to define the new nations. The quest for modernity, mixed with racism, eventually allowed new European forms to gain popularity over national dances.

In the final section of the chapter, Chasteen examines the history of dance for a number of countries. He emphasizes the significance of dances such as the Tango and the Samba, as well as salsa dancing and the *Merengue.*

What is defined as attractive changes over time and among societies and cultures. Regina Root's chapter on **Fashion and Appearance** describes and analyzes Latin America and offers insights and ideas concerning this ever-changing reality. Fashion has often been overlooked by scholars, but what a person or a group wears often tells a great deal about their social standing, political ideas, and identity.

So important was dress in maintaining the social order that the Spanish crown adopted laws about who could wear what types of clothing. Indians or mestizos could put on Spanish clothing and indicate where they saw the future for themselves, but if an individual wore certain upper-class fashions, the law often stepped in to ensure that people of lower status did not overstep their bounds.

The rise of shopping centers and international retail stores has tended to homogenize clothing, but many nations still cling to elements of their native dress. This is particularly true at festival times. Often nationalists will avoid contemporary Western dress to indicate their origins and their opposition to hegemonic powers. At another level, Latin American clothing has found its way into the mainstream, from Clark Gable's Panama hat of the 1930s to the contemporary Cuban *guayabera* shirt for men.

Fashion will continue to change in Latin America, but it can be viewed as markers for the present and harbingers of the future.

One of the best gauges of popular culture is found in the **Film** industry. To earn money, films have to appeal to a wide popular audience. Randal P. Garza and Lúcia Flórido point out that although Hollywood films have dominated the market in Latin America, the region has always had its own film producers and that recently, more and more films shown in Latin America are of Latin American origin.

Mexico, Brazil, and Argentina have the largest film industries, and the chapter focuses on these nations, but other nations are producing film as well. Starting in 1941, the Mexican government supported its film industry, but although the effort resulted in Mexican films, they were not of particularly high quality. With the advent of NAFTA money flowed into film production, and Mexico is now producing high-quality movies. Brazil's early film efforts were also eclipsed by Hollywood, but the economic upturn of the nation allowed for more productions. The seizure of the Brazilian government by the military, slowed the development of movie production, but today more Brazilian studios are producing more films in and about Brazil. Argentina's film industry did not develop after World War II, for economic and political reasons. It is only in the last few years, through co-productions with other media, that the Argentine cinema has begun to rebound.

One of the most significant markers of popular culture is **Food and Foodways.** Everyone has to eat, but what they eat, how, and when are set by the culture. In Latin America there has been a blending of foods, just as there has been in other parts of the cultures.

Historian Jeffrey Pilcher, in his examination of Latin America, points out that when the Spanish arrived, the staple foods of the region were corn, potatoes, and manioc. Among other things, the Spanish brought wheat, cows, pigs, and goats. Spanish cuisine did not overpower indigenous favorites, and over time there was a combining of cuisines with the addition of tastes and forms from Asia and Africa.

Since before independence, Mexico has seen the arrival of numerous culinary trends from France, from the Middle East, from Asia, and from the United States. Each has had an effect on Mexican cuisine, but in most cases the resulting foods have been hybrids. Foods arriving from other areas are modified to fit Mexican sensibilities.

Brazil and the Caribbean were both heavily influenced by African cooking and African food such as yams, okra, cowpeas, and numerous greens. As in other regions, there was a combination of various foods. Peru's also saw a blending of European and indigenous foods, but "everyday foods in the Andes show less commonality between elites and commoners than do other regions of Latin America." Finally, in Argentina and Chile, indigenous forms had less influence than in any other region. Still the arrival of immigrants changed the cuisine of the region, creating a European blend.

**Literature** has an important place in Latin American society, and while it is sometimes difficult, as Daniel J. Nappo explains, to define the boundaries between "fine" literature and "popular" literature, "popular literature can perhaps be given a working definition of texts that are intended to inform—or more commonly, to entertain—the most inclusive grouping of readers in a given society." Ultimately, popular literature, in whatever form, is significant because of its ability to transmit culture, ideas, and dreams to wide segments of each society.

Popular literature owes much to poetry, which historically was both read and recited. In much the same way, popular literature also includes the spoken word such as the Mexican *corrido*, because this genre is offered orally to a mass audience. Novels were late in developing in Latin America because of the large illiterate population and various Spanish prohibitions against publishing.

After independence, however, novels grew in significance and the melodramatic romance novel became popular. Photonovels, which as the name implies, mix the visual with the written word, have produced a form that is both accessible and cheap for a mass readership. In Brazil, in much the same way as photonovels, the *literatura de cordel* proved to be accessible also.

Despite trends to the contrary, the Latin American family is still central to the society. War, political unrest, and economic problems have often unsettled the institution, but it is still strong in Latin American culture.

Linda Curcio-Nagy begins her discussion of **Love, Sex, and Marriage**, with the pre-Columbian world in which men and women were supposed to play different, but complementary roles. This was true, with a few exceptions, in religion, in the political sphere, in inheritance, and in other social spheres.

The arrival of Europeans fundamentally changed society. As a result of liaisons and marriages between Europeans and indigenous people, a whole class of mestizos was created. Moreover, European culture was far more patriarchal, which altered the parallel male and female relationships of indigenous culture. The Spanish also ended polygamy, which was practiced within the pre-Columbian societies.

Following independence, the new nations adopted laws that legalized the existing European social structure. Women were defined as obedient to their husbands and as mothers and homemakers. Men were supposed to be masculine and virile, dealing in the economic and political sphere. Beginning in the 1960s, however, women began to assert themselves more and with the growing need for both husband and wife to work, women gained position in the society. A higher level of equality was achieved, but traditional demands still exist. Young people today "must negotiate between tradition and changing perceptions about gender roles" in Latin American society.

The **Music** of Latin America has influenced the world's music and is some of the most popular music in the world. In his chapter, Peter Manuel notes that Latin American music is "uniquely modern and expressive" and suggests that the "power of the region's musics has derived from their inherently creole nature, as the product of peoples at once liberated from Old World traditions—both African and European—but able to draw extensively from them."

The music of the Caribbean has an influence out of proportion to the region's population. Slaves brought African forms which emphasized rhythm, call-and-response singing, and rhythmic syncopation. When combined with European music, the amalgamation created a uniquely Caribbean sound. This sound developed over the years and in Cuba was eventually combined with the big-band sound and transported to the United States. In recent years, Caribbean music has continued to change with the development of both the merengue and reggae music. In the non-Spanish Caribbean, the creole population created calypso music and developed the steel band.

Argentina is best known for the development of the tango. Led by individuals such as Carlos Gardel, the tango eventually became the national music of that country. Similarly, in Brazil, samba music, an outgrowth of African and European forms, eventually gained status in that country. The music of both nations has enjoyed wide international popularity.

When an individual thinks of popular culture, **Radio** and, particularly, **Television** immediately come to mind. Millions of people all over Latin America tune in regularly to watch their favorite shows, thereby helping to define what shows are aired, but also taking from the programs new ideas and views of life. The rise of television and radio in Latin America has not always been an easy one. Professor Leonardo Ferreira, however, supplies the context to begin to understand this most important popular culture field.

Radio broadcasting began in the 1920s, but a clear sense of where it fit in society did not come about until the 1930s, when laws began to be passed by Latin American governments to organize and regularize it. While officially defined as a medium for the public good, Ferreira points out that the old elites often dominated control of radio.

Television broadcasting followed the model of radio in that it was dominated by large commercial interests often owned by one family. Moreover, these individuals in many cases worked closely with the government, which limited the potential of television as an independent voice. During its growth, Latin American television, however, also developed new broadcasting programs. Among the most significant was the *telenovela*.

Thousands of cheering fans in the stadium, millions more watching on television, countless newspaper and magazine articles, coupled with lunchtime analysis all mark **Sports** today. Sports are very much part of the mainstream of popular culture, and Latin America is no exception.

Historian Joseph Arbena points out that sports existed in Latin America before the arrival of Europeans and was an important part of life in pre-Columbian times. The ball game *ulama* (or *ulamaliztli*) was "America's oldest sport" and had strong "ritualistic and religious meaning"—so much so that the Spanish attempted to suppress the game. During the colonial period, the Spanish brought horse racing, cockfighting, and bullfighting as well as other games.

The single most dominant sport in Latin America is soccer, whose popularity is simply enormous. The game was largely imported by the British and found a ready home in the region. Latin America has won the World Cup nine times and has an enviable record in the competition.

Other sports have also done well in Latin America, such as baseball and basketball. Boxing and track and field have also had a significant presence, as have tennis and golf. Today, automobile racing, particularly NASCAR, is growing in popularity.

Women have also entered sports in Latin America, most notably in soccer where countries now support women's teams in international competition. The rise of women in sports seems likely to continue.

**Theater and Performance** constitute an important means of defining popular culture, and because of its power, Latin American governments have often tried to control the medium. While elite theater has existed since the arrival of Christopher Columbus, the low cost of popular theater means that it has considerable influence on the society. In Latin America, over the last few decades, theater has often had political motives and, on occasion, been sponsored by governments.

Kristen McCleary, the author of the chapter, also points out that Carnival is theater and that it has changed significantly over the years. In some nations, Carnival emphasizes the society's indigenous roots, while in other nations such as Brazil and Cuba, African forms are clearly evident. At times, the dominant society has attempted to extirpate indigenous and African strains, but Carnival demonstrates "a remarkable legacy of cultural resistance, transformation, and adaptation."

Argentina's early history can boast of nomadic circuses which the elite saw as a barrier to their goal of being wholly European. Argentine theater also suffered repression during the 1970s which forced many playwrights into exile and also saw the burning of theaters.

Despite the introduction of theater to Brazil in the colonial period by the Jesuits, Brazil has not had a strong theater tradition. Brazil is much better known for its carnivals, which vary depending on the region. Some emphasize the nation's African heritage, while others are more European in their style.

**Transportation** is a requirement in every society both for people and goods. John F. Bratzel, however, notes that transportation is more than simply moving things around; how items and people are transported is also part of the popular culture.

If there is a single dominant people-mover in Latin America, it is the bus. Virtually every nation has both first-class buses and second-class buses. The latter go to every small town and cater to those individuals who are less well off. Often these buses are decorated and stylized, emphasizing religious and sports motifs. Buses need roads, and while some nations have well-developed road systems, others do not. Virtually all nations have benefited from the Pan American Highway, which runs from Alaska to southern Chile.

In Latin America, railroads were once the sign of modernity, and nations worked hard to lay track. Most railroads today, however, have been abandoned, and only tourist trains, taking advantage of the scenery, still exist.

International air travel is available in all nations from national and international airlines. Depending upon topography and distances, local internal airlines also operate in Latin America.

In almost every case, coastal nations have resorts based on beaches and water sports. Other vacation spots take advantage of the dramatic terrain and scenery found in Latin America.

# ARCHITECTURE

PATRICE ELIZABETH OLSEN

In general terms, architecture is a means of enclosing space to fulfill the need for shelter; to conduct the functions of government, trade, and commerce; and to provide the space for social gatherings and entertainments. Architecture can be seen as an artifact created by people, and as a social action, as it results from the collaborative efforts of individuals, government, and the private sector, encompassing on occasion innovative technologies and approaches to building. Architectural historian Spiro Kostof, writing of architecture in general, perceived architecture as "a human artifact as well as a social act, the outcome of teamwork, used by individuals, business, as well as the nation as a whole." The meaning of each building is contained in its form—thus, to study architecture allows one to develop insights into the social, political, intellectual, economic, and technological history of a given era. When seen collectively, in a city skyline or in a neighborhood, architectural features indicate changes in what a society prioritizes, what it aspires to, and what it values. Architecture, in sum, communicates a great deal as a record of the culture that produced it.

Popular architecture incorporates vernacular architecture, that is, the architecture built without involvement of architects. It is the market, or humble *abarrote*, found in a venerable colonial-era building in Mexico City or Guatemala City "recycled" by new occupants. It is the boutique or expensive shop in Miraflores, Lima, or in the Recoleta neighborhood of Buenos Aires. Popular architecture also encompasses the larger-scale works executed by the state to fulfill its functions of governing, the postmodern office buildings and hotels, and the mansions in exclusive neighborhoods. It often involves the translation of exotic styles or cultural imports, fusing them with indigenous forms. Popular architecture in Latin America also involves the creation of new building forms, exterior ornamentation, and new interior patterns and layouts. Significant elements in the popular architecture, when they are truly functional, fuse respect for the site, and its unique climatological and topographic features, with the needs of the clients. Such works can be of any scale: from the *bohios* of palm thatch and wood of the Caribbean to São Paulo's forty-story curvilinear Copan skyscraper by Brazilian architect Oscar Niemeyer.

Achievements in contemporary Latin American architecture have brought the region's architects international renown. They have received the highest awards given to architects by

1

the American Institute of Architects (AIA), as well as the Pritzker Architecture Prize. Pritzker recipients include Brazilian architects Oscar Niemeyer (1988) and Paulo Mendes da Rocha (2006) and Mexican architect Luis Barragán (1980). Ricardo Legorreta, whose impressive, diverse works range from hotels to factories to residences, was awarded the AIA's Gold Medal, the highest honor bestowed upon an architect by that association, in 2000. Efforts by the Office of the Historian of the City of Havana were recognized in 2001 by the Philippe Rotthier European Prize of architecture for work in the reconstruction of the city's oldest quarter. Recognition of these outstanding achievements brought further attention to the world-class architecture created in Latin America, and to efforts in the preservation of historical integrity of its cities. Juries recognized the singularity of achievements, as architects created for their own environments and made important contributions to architecture as an art, as well as to the built environment. Their unique solutions and expressions have made an impact on the theory and practice of architecture throughout the world. In many cases they adapted exotic styles to meet local needs. In attempting to express a new national or regional identity in architecture, they also forged a new mission for architecture and architects: to put architecture in the service of social justice. Simply stated, many architects throughout Latin America, imbued in this spirit, sought to build for and with the people. The built environment throughout Latin America records their successes.

## GENERAL THEMES

To speak of contemporary popular architecture in Latin America is generally to speak of cities and towns. Recent data from the Inter-American Development Bank (IADB) indicates a pattern of considerable urban growth. The percentage of Latin America's population living in urban areas has continued to grow. Approximately 64 percent of the population in Latin America lived in urban areas in 1980; by 1990 this had increased to 72 percent, and just 7 years later, the number had increased to 78 percent. Further, IADB data indicates that in every nation in Latin America the urban population exceeds 50 percent. The populations of Argentina, Brazil, Chile, Colombia, Mexico, Nicaragua, Peru, Uruguay, and Venezuela are even more urbanized. At least 70 percent of the people in these countries live in urban areas, with Venezuela having the highest urban concentration at 94.7 percent. The capital cities continue growth rates often reported as "alarming." Of the 20 largest cities in the world, 4 are in Latin America: Mexico City[2] with a metropolitan population of 18,131,000; São Paulo [4] with 17,711,000; Buenos Aires [10] with 12,431,000; and Rio de Janeiro [19] with 10,556,000.

The physiognomy of Latin American cities is diverse, and at first impression it would appear difficult, if not reckless, to draw generalities among sites as distinct as Mexico City, Havana, or Santiago, or Caracas, or Brasília. Yet significant commonalities do exist in the architectural history of Latin American cities and in trends in urban growth and responses to that growth by architects, planners, governmental agencies, and other organizations, as well as initiatives by the private sector.

### Commonalities

#### The Importation and Adaptation of Foreign Styles

New World cities of today are a product of the Conquest. The Spaniards created an architecture of awe, and their power is represented in the landscapes of Mexico City, Lima,

Havana, Cartagena, San Luis Potosí, and many others. This is apparent in the city layout, the grid-plan, stipulated by royal edict issued in 1573. Philip II's 178 Ordinances went further, in regulating building height and materials, the size of plazas, and the orientation and placement of civic and religious structures. The first colonial structures, few of which remain in any of the first cities, were of a sober, classic architecture. This architecture was "popularized" over time, as local craftsmen embellished interiors and exteriors, creating a New World baroque, the Churrigueresque, Latin America's first truly popular architecture.

The importation of foreign styles continued following independence. The mid- and late nineteenth century witnessed various significant changes in the cityscapes throughout Latin America. Elites throughout the region vied to have their city labeled "the Paris of Latin America," which was the shorthand for cultural attainment adopted by many commentators to represent the nation's emergence out of the chaos and instability of caudillo rule. The stereotyped disorder was replaced by another image of progress, order, and refinement (if only superficially). Popular taste included neo-Gothic, neo-Tudor, and Italian Baroque styles, and various permutations of anything perceived as French, particularly the mansard roof. Elites and governments building in such fashions sought to emphasize their cultural refinement, modernity, and civic virtue. In Argentina, Sarmiento's critique of civilization versus barbarism was continually debated. Elites turned to the French beaux arts style to represent their cultural progress, as seen in the Anchorena Palace (1909, Alexander Christopherson, today the Palace of Foreign Affairs). Chile too found the beaux arts an ideal vehicle to convey a modern image, seen in residences and institutions, particularly the Catholic University in Santiago (1914). In Mexico, from 1877 through 1910, President Porfirio Díaz attempted to give the nation a modern image that could propel it to a higher standing internationally. He popularized the French beaux arts style in civic and private buildings. Prominent foreign architects received the most important government commissions. Italian architect Adamo Boari designed the new neo-Gothic Post Office Building (1907) and the beaux arts and art nouveau Teatro Nacional (now the Palacio de Bellas Artes, completed in 1934). French architect Emile Bernard designed the neoclassic Palacio de Poder Legislativo, intended as both a governmental building and monument to Porfirian greatness (1900, completed as the Monument to the Revolution, 1937). Similarly, in Rio de Janeiro, affinity for Gallic culture led to the adoption of French neoclassical architecture, as in the Teatro Nacional (1906).

Soon, however, architects and builders sought cultural and artistic independence from Europe and what they perceived to be the facile emulation of imported styles. In Mexico, the revolution of 1910 provided the opportunity to sever these connections and to create a new style, more representative of the nation. In 1925 an invitation by the AIA to participate in an international exposition on architecture and planning offered Latin American architects the opportunity to participate in discussions on styles as well as to consider their roles within society: not only fulfilling material needs but discerning and expressing their nation's fundamental, ethical, and aesthetic values. The search for modernity would lead in coming decades to the employment of styles as diverse as neocolonial, California colonial, art deco, neo-indigenist, functionalist, nationalist, International, and postmodern, each used for utilitarian as well as aesthetic needs.

Popular architectural expressions throughout Latin America in the 1920s and 1930s illustrated the tensions inherent in efforts to create a cohesive expression of identity. In these years, the neo-colonial style was employed widely, given the perception that the Hispanic past had to be honored. This influence is apparent in Buenos Aires' Cervantes Theater (1922, Aranda and Repetto) and the Bank of Boston (1924, Paul Bell Chambers and Louis Newberry Thomas). In Rio de Janeiro, José Mariano Filho employed forms borrowed from the eighteenth-century baroque style. Numerous neo-colonial projects were developed in

Mexico under the sponsorship of Education Secretary José Vasconcelos, who believed it the perfect stylistic expression for the "cosmic race," a fine example of which is Carlos Obregón Santacilia's design for the Benito Juárez School (1927).

In 1925 the International Exhibition of Decorative Arts was held in Paris. The focus on stylized, geometrized ornamentation would quickly become popular in Latin America. Deco details are seen in every building type, from banks, to offices and apartments, to theaters and garages. Deco is often fused with indigenous elements recalling the pre-Hispanic past, as in the Police and Fire Station in Mexico City (1928, Vicente Mendiola and Guillermo Zárraga), the Finance Ministry Building in Santiago (1930, Smith Solar and Smith Miller), and in Buenos Aires in the Santander Bank (1926) and House of Theater (1927, both by architect Alejandro Virasoro). Perhaps the most lyrical example is the landmark Cristo Redentor statue in Rio de Janeiro.

## Modernity: Functionalism and the Influence of Le Corbusier

Perhaps the most significant, durable influences in modern Latin American architecture in the twentieth century have been modernism and the application of the ideas of Swiss architect Le Corbusier (Charles Edouard Jeanneret-Gris). In many countries, the first applications of Le Corbusier's path-breaking work *Vers une Architecture* [Toward a New Architecture] were manifest in Latin American functionalism.

Functionalism involved a new conception of building that corresponded to the new technology of the age. Its advocates claimed it was based on local realities and unencumbered by previous architectural practices. Functionalist structures were to be of geometric shapes and have plain surfaces; architects perceived that the more simple the lines and form, the better such buildings could symbolize the modern machine age. Functionalist practice also insisted that "dishonest" elements be eliminated, particularly ornate capitals and false fronts. Unnecessary ornamentation concealed the building's true social and physical reality and impaired its function. Moreover, embellishments obscured the true social and physical reality of the society that built the structure.

Architects who sought alternatives to such ornamentation followed Le Corbusier's dictums closely. As he explained in the influential *Vers une Architecture,* a house was a machine for living. By extension, offices were machines for work, as were factories. Constructing simply, with steel and concrete or iron skeletons, or with buildings supported by *pilotis* (reinforced concrete stilts), walls were no longer load bearing. Exterior walls could be thin skins of glass or stucco, and windows were positioned to allow more natural light and ventilation.

Le Corbusier's writings bore fruit almost immediately following their publication in Latin America in the late 1920s. Their significance lay not only in providing the impetus for creating new building forms, but also in changing architectural training and architects' perceptions of their roles and missions in modern society. His works held the promise of reconstruction and affirmed that sound, functional design should and would improve societies. If one perceived, as did Mexican architects Juan O'Gorman, Juan Legarreta, and Alvaro Aburto and others of the socialist vanguard, that the problems of their nation were social and the answers to these problems were structural, one found much in Le Corbusier's writing to apply. Basing construction on local realities meant liberation—the discarding of past tendencies of facile copying of European styles. They could again borrow solutions, but with liberty to adapt them to their own environment.

Le Corbusier's proclamations held the promise of reconstruction and served as a symbol for a new faith stronger than that existing in the profession before: the affirmation that good design could change societies for the better. In proclaiming architecture to be "one of the most urgent needs of man," Le Corbusier provided his Latin American audiences with an appealing message.[1] If his prescription that buildings could only be white "by law" seemed too restrictive, one could still be inspired by his rejection of slavish reproduction of styles: "the styles of Louis XIV, XV, XVI or Gothic are to architecture what a feather is on a woman's head; it is sometimes pretty, though not always, and never anything more."[2] Le Corbusier provided architects throughout Latin America who were already seeking simplicity in their work with additional support for their stance with his counsel to design in accord with the "true and profound laws of architecture which are established on mass, rhythm and proportion" and not in terms of "parasitic" styles.[3] In his lectures in Buenos Aires in 1929, Le Corbusier liberated architects from past copying of French or other styles, a freedom that would allow them to assert their own identity in architecture.

His impact on the built environment has been profound. Although Le Corbusier did not visit Mexico or provide plans for development or construction within that nation, his work inspired many to adopt his credo of "the house as machine for living" and become vocal opponents of the prevailing design in Mexico, the neocolonial. In their assessment, this style did not resolve spatial problems or make use of the advantages of new materials, nor did it constitute a reflection of social changes. Neocolonial buildings such as Rafael Goyeneche's Hotel Majestic (1925) represented the persistence of archaic, wasteful, irrelevant design and a Mexican identity derived from colonial exploitation. These disciples of Le Corbusier viewed failure to act progressively as denying the nation access to the modernity that the revolution had promised; Le Corbusier had cautioned, "We are dealing with an urgent problem of our epoch, nay more, with *the* problem of our epoch. The balance of society comes down to a question of building. We conclude with these justifiable alternatives: Architecture or Revolution."[4]Functionalist architects built a great deal, most often under government contract, such as in the University of Chile's Law School (1934, J. Martínez) and the Oberpauer Building (1929, Sergio Larraín). Their talents extended to private-sector developments as well, notably in Buenos Aires in the thirty-story Kavanagh apartment building (1936, Sánchez Lagos, and De la Torre), the Grand Rex Cinema (1937, Alberto Prebish), and the Comega Building (1932, Enrique Couillet and Alfredo Joselvich). Their dedication to the construction of hospitals, schools, and popular housing throughout the 1930s arose from their functionalist convictions, as well as their advocacy of professional teaching and technical preparation to reflect this new agenda.

In 1930, Lúcio Costa became director of the National School of Fine Arts (ENBA) and instituted radical changes in the architecture curriculum, incorporating Le Corbusier's concepts. Although he was replaced after 11 controversial months, the new ideas proved durable as the next generation of architects, known later as the *carioca* school (including Oscar Niemeyer), began building. Their output was prodigious and included Rio's ABI Building (1935), the Santos Dumont Airport (1944), the Boavista Bank (1946), and their collaboration with Le Corbusier on the Brazilian Ministry of Health and Education (1936), to name but a few. At this time, the faith of the new architects in technology and progress was absolute. Solutions inevitably followed correct statements of problems, regardless of scale, ranging from the problem of the house, to the problem of the city, to the problems of the nation.

Throughout Latin America, however, questions remained. Could architecture truly include all those who had been excluded from full social, economic, and political participation for centuries? Could better, more inclusive design rectify long-standing social inequities? Functionalism involved sweeping, untested professions of faith in progress, technology, standardization, and the machine—and an interpretation of function in terms not only of structure but also of performance. Derived from the machine, this interpretation of function was a restricted one. Yet functionalism quickly proved practical because the construction of functional designs was consistently less expensive than other styles. Governments and the private sector built schools, housing, factories, office buildings, and other facilities quickly and on limited budgets, such as Legarreta's Minimalist Workers Houses in Mexico City (1934) and later, in Caracas, in public housing done by the Talle de Arquitectura del Banco Obrero (TABO) at Cerro Grande (1955) and El Paraíso (1957). But perhaps just as significant was the hope implied in functionalist theory. Its powerful, creative declarations of architecture's practical aspects appealed to idealistic young architects such as O'Gorman, Aburto, and Legarreta of the *Liga de Escritores y Artistas Revolucionarias* (League of Revolutionary Artists and Writers) and the Austral Group in Argentina. These artists saw the continued suffering and injustice in the capital and wanted to ameliorate the conditions of poverty and misery "at minimal cost and with maximum efficiency." They believed what they had discovered was nothing less than a formulation of revolutionary ideals to construct a new society.

## International Style

From 1940 to 1950, a different approach to design evolved— the International Style. Like functionalism, this style excluded ornamentation; its emphasis on volume instead of mass yields structures that appear lighter and more graceful than functionalist designs. Simplicity of structure is promoted in cubes and glass boxes; modernity is expressed via sleek glass and steel curtain walls. Such architecture is a popular expression of the energy perceived by many in those years of the "Mexican Miracle" or the "Brazilian Miracle," a period in which rapid economic growth brought unprecedented wealth to these nations. This growth meant prosperity for some: the glass box appeared on Mexico City's skyline; in the city's first condominiums, designed by Mario Pani and Salvador Ortega (1955), and sophisticated office buildings, notably Juan Sordo Madaleno's Seguros Anahuac building (1958) and Augusto H. Álvarez's Edificio Castorena (1957). Government buildings, such as Pani and Enrique del Moral's Secretaría de Recursos Hidrúaulicos building (1950); Augusto Pérez Palacios and Raúl Cacho's Secretaría de Comunicaciones y Obras Públicas (1953); and Enrique de la Mora, Francisco López Carmona, and Félix Candela's Bolsa de Valores building (1953–56), manifested Mexico's rise out of revolutionary turmoil and the centralization of its political power.

Mario Pani also designed the city's first *multifamiliares* (multifunction housing projects, or "cities-within-cities," with their own markets, clinics, schools, and nurseries) in the Centro Urbano Presidente Alemán (1950) and the Centro Urbano Presidente Juárez (1952). These pathbreaking housing projects for government workers, adaptations of Le Corbusian concepts, dramatically extended state responsibility for the provision of housing for its workforce. These projects later proved insufficient to meet the demands for hygienic housing for the hundreds of thousands of capital city residents lacking these things.

By the 1980s, the International Style had been adopted with the same sort of enthusiasm and ambition as functionalism had been before it. In this period, official architecture stressed monumentality, within this style representing the power that the state sought to possess. The optimism inherent in this style is apparent as the government reasserted the image of the state as the guarantor of development and the provider of education, health care, and housing via more monumental projects. In Mexico such projects include the Centro México Nacional (1961) by Yáñez, José Villagrán García, and others, and museums that conserve and celebrate Mexico's cultural heritage, notably the Museo de Arte Moderno

(1964) and Pedro Ramírez Vázquez's magnificent Museo Nacional de Antropología (1964). In Buenos Aires, significant works include the Argentina Televisora Color Building (1978, Manteola, Sánchez Gómez, and others). In Santiago many examples indicate the popularity of curtain wall high-rises, often featuring mirror glass: the Estado 10 Building (1982, Borquez, Paredes, and Sotomayor), the Catedral Building (1982, Enchenique, Cruz, Bolsier, and Dunner), the Shell Building (1989, Asahi and Associates), and the Consorcio Nacional de Seguros-Vida Building (1992, Huidobro, Brown, and Judson).

## Urban Growth and the Shantytown

The squatter settlements and slums on the periphery of Latin American cities carry a variety of names: *favelas* (Rio de Janeiro and São Paulo), *mocambos* (Recife), *palafitas* (Salvador da Bahia), *collampas* (Santiago de Chile), *villas miseries* (Buenos Aires), *ranchos* (Caracas), *barriadas* (Lima), and *ciudades perdidas* (Mexico). According to data collected in 2005 by the United Nations Economic Commission for Latin America and the Caribbean (ECLAC), 40 percent of the urban population live in squatter settlements or unsafe settlements, generally in peri-urban areas. What has driven and continues to propel this urban growth? Conflict and drought account for this in part. In Mexico migration from rural to urban areas accelerated during and after the revolution of 1910, as many sought refuge and opportunity in cities. In Brazil, peasants fleeing the droughts of the sertão region of the northeast similarly sought better lives in the cities on the coast. More recently, demands for labor increased dramatically in the 1950s and 1960s as Latin American nations embarked on import substitution industrialization programs. At the beginning of the 1950s, approximately 50 percent of urban population growth in Venezuela, Nicaragua, Colombia, and El Salvador was due to rural migration. Conditions facing these migrants were dismally similar throughout the region: acute housing shortages and impeded access to steady employment. Classic works in Latin American literature and scholarship detail this life on the margins, from anthropologist Oscar Lewis's studies in Mexico City (*Children of Sánchez*), to Carolina Maria de Jesus's memoirs (*Child of the Dark*), to journalist Alma Guillermoprieto's accounts (*The Heart that Bleeds*), and Mike Davis's analyses (*Planet of Slums*). Some would find shelter in the *vecindades* (tenements) of Mexico City, as Lewis's respondents did. These tenements were old, two-story, crumbling brick or concrete structures lacking adequate ventilation, water, and waste disposal. Others looked to the city's margins to find a home and occupied vacant land on hillsides, as de Jesus did, constructing her first shelter of scavenged tar paper, cardboard, and scrap metal. Such "invasions" of unoccupied land continued through the last four decades as *paracaídistas* (literally, "parachutists") or squatters occupied marginal lands without services such as sanitation, utilities, or paved roads. They built rudimentary shelters from found materials and began to form communities. Gradually, as residents' financial situations improved as a result of their work as laborers, street vendors, domestics, and so forth), the settlements improved and became working-class *barrios*. Residents' initiatives and pressures on city governments resulted in paved roads, sewer lines, electricity, and other services. "Self-help" housing has replaced the drafty shacks: the architecture of these new barrios is crafted by the residents themselves, generally they are concrete and cement, one-story houses, often with rebar protruding from the roof, indicating the owner's intend to expand. Yet the migrations continue, and as one settlement is "regularized" with titles to land and utilities provided by the state to owners, precarious, unregulated settlements continue to grow. One of the largest of these in the Americas, Ciudad Nezahualcóyotl, constructed on the drained bed of the former Lake Texcoco in Mexico City, had a population

## A DIFFERENT SHANTYTOWN—SÃO PAULO'S PRESTES MAIA BUILDING

Urban homelessness presents a grave problem throughout the developing world, says Mike Davis in his recent work *Planet of Slums*. In São Paulo, a new group, the *Movimento Sem-Teto do Centro* (MSTC, Downtown Roofless Movement), has occupied and restored derelict buildings in the city center, providing an alternative to makeshift housing in peripheral slum areas. According to its Website (http://www.mstc.org/br.movimento.php), MSTC seeks to unite individuals and associations to build a single strong social movement "to attack the causes of misery, struggling for effective urban reform." Through collective direct action—that is, the invasion of abandoned structures—they pressure the city, state, and national governments to recognize and alleviate urban poverty.

MSTC's longest occupation to date has been that of the twenty-two-story Prestes Maia building, long abandoned, infested with vermin, and a haven for criminal activity. In 2002, 468 homeless and low-income families occupied the building and cleaned and restored the structure. In doing so, they created a new community with safe and affordable housing, workshops, classrooms, a library, and social and cultural activities. The building is governed by residents, who meet weekly to discuss tenant issues and responsibilities. Residents pay approximately $10 per month toward upkeep of the building. Despite such initiatives, residents now face eviction. The MSTC has successfully appealed eviction orders issued by the city government in January 2006, asserting that the building had been abandoned for many years and should be claimed as public property in accordance with Brazilian law. The movement continues to grow and at one time occupied 13 buildings in São Paulo.

of 1.2 million in 1990; largely without municipal services, it is the poorest part of the city.

## The "Malling" of Latin America

Another significant trend throughout Latin America is the rise of the shopping mall. This development involves changes in consumption patterns and cultural life, changes brought about in part by rising incomes of the upper-middle class and upper class over the past 30 years. Historically cities such as Guadalajara, Mexico City, or Lima had distinct areas where particular goods were sold and occupations concentrated; shopping was distinctly a social endeavor, providing the opportunity for diverse peoples to mingle on the streets and in the markets. Civic improvements in the 1930s and 1940s replaced the centuries-old, often unsanitary open-air markets with new indoor municipal markets. Department stores such as Havana's El Encanto and Mexico City's Puerto de Liverpool offered the latest in fashion and furnishings to the carriage trade. In the 1930s the first United States chain stores, among them Sears and Piggly Wiggly, made their appearance, marking another invasion, this time commercial, in the august historic centers of Latin American cities.

Perhaps it is not surprising that innovations in U.S. retailing have been disseminated in Latin America, or that Latin America's status-conscious people would welcome the establishment of Cartier and Chanel boutiques in the 1970s and 1980s along the "better" streets of Santiago or São Paulo. The new shops closely resembled their counterparts on New York's Fifth Avenue and Chicago's Magnificent Mile and reaffirmed local elite self-perceptions. Further, the "invasion" of franchise food establishments, such as McDonald's and Pizza Hut, seemed to follow logically; such stores were often based in venerable buildings in the city centers. The cityscapes seemed to absorb such intrusions without much dissent. These new establishments were located "downtown" and were a part of the urban fabric and street life.

The new malls are manufactured environments. Removed from the street and its inconveniences and nuisances, the malls are located some distance from city centers. Accessible chiefly by automobile and with difficulty via public transportation, the malls serve to separate classes further. The malls bear close resemblance to their U.S. counterparts in many ways: from commodious parking lots to the ubiquitous food courts and movie theaters. Architecture may borrow from local or regional identity, as entrances are marked with friezes depicting heroic aspects of national history or beautiful flora and fauna. Interior courts may contain works of local artists. Yet a sameness persists: inside it is difficult to discern whether one is at the Centro Andino in Bogotá or the Mall del Centro in Santiago de Chile. The most recent trend is toward offering consumers the superlative. For example, Rio de Janeiro's São Conrado Fashion Mall, opened in 2002, offers the latest European fashions. And Caracas may now boast of Latin America's largest shopping mall. Opened in 1998, the modernist Sambil Shopping Mall has 500 stores on its five floors, as well as performing arts space and amusement park rides.

## New Monumentality

Contemporary Latin America popular architecture also encompasses monumental or "signature" projects. These are ambitious projects, involving great amounts of resources and talent. As a result of such commitment of resources by governments and the private sector throughout the past 50 years, new building forms and new expressions of identity have emerged.

### *Brasília*

In 1955, Brazilians elected Juscelino Kubitschek as president. Promising "fifty years of progress in five," he embarked on an ambitious program to develop the country's interior. For centuries, Brazilian political and economic activities were concentrated along the Atlantic coast. Developing the interior was a symbolic as well as pragmatic act, a rejection of European dominance that had created coastal cities for easy extraction and transport of wealth, and a turn inward, to develop vast resources as part of the industrialization program. With aspirations of *grandeza,* Kubitschek decided to relocate the capital to the vast *planalto central* in the state of Goiás, 746 miles from Rio de Janeiro. The new city, Brasília, would thus symbolize modern Brazil: its vigor and modernity clearly articulated in the built environment. The new city could also function as a model; built on virgin land, it would contain a new social order, without class barriers or the patterns of inequality that had evolved over time in cities such as Recife, Rio de Janeiro, and São Paulo. In sum, Brasília offered the idealistic architect and planner the opportunity to create from a blank slate, to realize modernist ambitions that better design could produce a more egalitarian society.

Although Le Corbusier's influence in contemporary architecture is seen throughout Latin America, nowhere have his ideas been so clearly developed as in Brasília. Here his ideas would be applied on an unprecedented scale and with rapidity; Kubitschek could serve one 5-year term. The city had to be completed within that time. The myriad functions and activities of a capital—offices for each branch of government and the bureaucracies, as well as housing, schools, and other necessities—had to be developed; this would prove an epic adventure in city planning and in the realization of that plan.

In March 1957, Brazilian architect Oscar Niemeyer headed a jury to determine the commission for the city's master plan. This was a national competition; the exclusion of foreign planners was deliberate, in keeping with the spirit of nationalism infusing this project. The jury selected a simple and elegant design by Lúcio Costa. It featured two intersecting 7-kilometer-long monumental axes, connected via a wide highway. To some these axes resembled a drawn bow; to others, they resembled the outstretched wings of an aircraft—the perfect metaphor for a modern, machine-age city. Costa envisioned the city with broad roads and highways, minimizing the congestion that plagued other Brazilian cities. The results would be monumental, truly representative of Brazilian *grandeza*. Niemeyer's designs for the government buildings are among the most dynamic statements of modernism in the hemisphere. His idealism is apparent in the way he sought to bring people, architecture, and the environment together. Notable too is his attention to geometric forms and volumes.

The city's political center is the Plaza of the Three Powers, with the refined, understated Palacio de Planalto across the plaza from the Supreme Court. Pilasters used to support each building lend stylistic unity and lighten the masses of the buildings. Extending from this plaza, the central axis contains the National Theater and the Metropolitan Cathedral, Nossa Senhora Aparecida, the latter a dramatic conical structure supported by pilasters, with stained glass between the concrete supports. At the end of the plaza is the magnificent Congress Complex. Perhaps the purest representation of Niemeyer's vision of Brazilian nationalism and pride, the complex is immense but does not overwhelm. Two slim towers arise from a broad horizontal base, connected via skywalks at the sixteenth and seventeenth stories; the Senate and Chamber of Deputies chambers are in two parabolic dishes, one inverted, on either side of the towers. The Alvorada Palace, set apart from other governmental buildings, is the presidential residence. Here too concrete pilasters are used, shaped as an inverted colonnade and set in a reflecting pool. The building is imposing, an indelible statement of executive power.

In terms of housing, Costa's master plan placed residential sectors perpendicular to the monumental axis, on the second bowed axis. Government employees and officials were to reside in the *supercuadras,* three- to six-story apartment buildings with pristine facades of white concrete and large expanses of glass. In each supercuadra grouping would be schools, clinics, and shopping and recreation facilities. Social conflict due to residential design was evident; contractors raced toward preparing the city for its inauguration on April 21, 1960. Niemeyer and others had not planned for the working class, the *candangos,* or laborers who had built the city, to remain—they presumed that many of those who had migrated from the sertão or other desperately poor areas would leave following the city's completion. In these brief, intense years of construction, however, the laborers had gained a sense of belonging in the city. In the end, their rough quarters on the margins of Brasília's master plan would be "regularized," and the patterns of social stratification of the country's coastal cities would be reproduced in Brasília as the city grew. Originally planned for 500,000 people, its population in 2004 was estimated at 2.2 million.

## MEXICO CITY—POSTMODERNISM IN THE MEGALOPOLIS

Diverse currents, often contradictory, characterize contemporary Mexican popular architecture. Trends in design for and by the upper classes continue patterns of the 1930s and 1940s in terms of residential segregation and conspicuous displays of wealth. Examples include the well-to-do *colonias* of Lomas de Chapultepec and Los Altos, joined more recently by Santa Fe and others. The developments do not match the creativity and originality Luis Barragán's achievement in the lava gardens of Pedregal de San Ángel, or at Ciudad Satélite

(1957), the latter with abstract entrance towers by Matías Goeritz. A notable trend is movement back to the city center as gentrification progresses, guided by Carlos Slim's Historic Center Foundation and the federal district government. The upwardly mobile now have options to purchase condominiums in renovated buildings; this gentrification has also invigorated the center in other significant ways. Government actions in improving infrastructure, lighting, street cleaning, and policing have made this area more inviting for tourists and residents.

The city continues to grow, horizontally and vertically. Horizontal growth has pushed the Federal District's population over its boundaries into the State of Mexico; the Metropolitan Zone now encompasses an area of roughly 1,489 square kilometers. The city is growing taller, too, albeit hesitantly. This is a seismically active area. The most recent severe earthquake on September 19, 1985, devastated the city center. The forty-two-story International Style Torre Latinoamericana (1948–56, architect Augusto H. Álvarez; engineer Adolfo Zeevaert) of aluminum and glass curtain wall withstood the earthquake. Innovations in structural engineering have made possible the recent construction of more *rascacielos,* among them the Pémex Tower (1984, Pedro Moctezuma Díaz Infante), and the fifty-story World Trade Center (1996, Gutíerrez Cortina Arquitectos).

Contemporary architecture in Mexico also illustrates the tensions and diversity in Mexican society, as well as continued foreign influences. Mexico City, in particular, is frequently labeled by critics as "chaotic," a jumble of architectural styles with little cohesion that manifests no rational plan. Others more kindly call the city's mixture of functionalism, International Style, brutalism, and postmodernism "pluralist," evidence of the city's cosmopolitanism. Similar situations exist in other large cities such as Monterrey and Guadalajara, yet stylistic confusion is more muted in each of these cities due to the dispersion of modern construction to newly developed areas and lower densities of land use. Perhaps the "chaos" is the inevitable and even praiseworthy result of a culture that cannot be expressed by a single national style (as proponents had sought years earlier). Instead what has evolved is a diverse architecture: at times monumental, as in the Colegio de México building (1975, Abraham Zabludovsky and Teodoro González de León), or rationalist, as in the Loteria Nacional building (1981, Ramón Torres), or embodying plastic integration as in the INFONAVIT building (1975, Zabludovsky and González de Léon). Architects still find inspiration in pre-Hispanic forms, as seen in Agustín Hernández and Manuel González Rul's designs for the Colegio Militar (1976). Monumental architecture is in demand, beautifully rendered in the Basilica de Guadalupe by architects Pedro Ramírez Vázquez and others (1976).

Postmodernism appears as well; it is most apparent in the hotels constructed from the early 1990s to the present. Hotels such as the Fiesta Americana and Gran Melia loom above Chapultepec Park, along the Paseo de la Reforma. Bearing little relationship to the landscape or to nearby structures, they appear more as corporate symbols, as one would see in Houston, Los Angeles, or Atlanta. Perhaps the most glaring postmodern addition to the cityscape is the new Sheraton Centro Histórico on Avenida Juárez opposite the Alameda Park. Built on the site of the former Hotel del Prado (a casualty of the 1985 earthquake), its dark tinted-glass façade soars 27 stories, perhaps a massive equivalent to Obregón Santacilia's functionalist Guardiola Building (1938) 2 blocks east, but it is no match for the beaux arts Palacio de Bellas Artes, adjacent to the Alameda. This hotel, like the others, does not possess the creativity or the awareness of Mexican culture of other hotels designed with greater care, such as those by Ricardo Legorreta. In his use of color, form, light, and shadow, Legorreta was able to express Mexican vitality and culture, particularly in his design for the Sheraton María Isabel (1961). Contemporary Mexican architecture, as practiced by Legorreta, Enrique Norten, Alberto Kalach, and Juan José Díaz Infante, among others, indicates that postmodern sterility need not dominate the landscape.

## UNIVERSITY CITIES

The ability of popular modernist architecture to represent progressive ideals is clearly demonstrated in the monumental projects for new university campuses in Mexico and Venezuela. Both the Universidad Nacional Autónoma de México (UNAM, National Autonomous University of Mexico, 1949–53) and the Universidad Central de Venezuela (UCV, Central University of Venezuela, 1944–77) serve as dramatic symbols. Both contain some of the best works of national architects in highly functional solutions to the challenge of meeting rising demands for higher education.

The venerable UNAM was founded in 1553, making it the second oldest university in the Americas. Classes were held in various buildings to the north and east of Mexico City's central plaza, the Zócalo. Spatial constraints placed limits on growth; overcrowding and difficulties in coordinating university activities were noted in the 1920s. At the end of 1940, the Cárdenas government sponsored studies that recommended the construction of a new campus on vacant land in the southwest area of the city. Over the next several years, the government acquired a 7 million-square-acre site in the Pedregal de San Ángel. In 1949 José Luis Cuevas, Mario Pani, and Enrique del Moral developed the master plan for Ciudad Universitaria. The creation of a new campus was a strong statement of the government's adherence to ideals of social justice voiced in the Constitution of 1917. Education would be accessible to all Mexicans. The master plan expressed that accessibility; buildings were set apart on park-like open spaces. Attention to circulation provided further opportunity to highlight the setting; curved campus roads opened views to the solidified lava-bed landscape and many gardens.

A team of 150 architects contributed to the design of the 30 initial campus buildings, generally large-scale horizontal and vertical volumes. Their use here recalls similar monumental volumes at pre-Hispanic sites such as Teotihuacan and Uxmal. The complexity of Mexican identity is beautifully represented in 3 campus buildings: the Rectory, Central Library, and University Stadium. The Rectory tower, containing the university's administrative offices, is divided horizontally by a mural by David Álfaro Siqueiros. Juan O'Gorman took the concept of plastic integration further, as his stone mosaics cover the library's entire façade. The mosaics depict scientific themes and Mexican history in the style of the pre-Hispanic codices. The University Stadium, constructed for the 1968 Olympic Games, has a mural by Diego Rivera at the entrance depicting the evolution of sports in Mexico. Other structures exemplify the innovative approaches in design and technological advances by Mexican architects and engineers, particularly Félix Candela's Cosmic Rays Pavilion, featuring an ultrathin (1.5-centimeter) hypar shell form.

Throughout the past 40 years, periodic protests at the UNAM campus proclaim, "*La educación sera para todos*" (education will be for all). Originally meant to serve 25,000 students and staff when it opened in 1953, UNAM's current enrollment is approximately 300,000, challenging both governmental commitments to higher education and the abilities of the campus to meet the educational needs of this growing city and nation.

The new campus of the Central University of Venezuela is also a monumental work, perceived by many architectural historians to be the country's most significant example of modernist architecture. Built in four stages over the course of 33 years, the campus plan and buildings, although they were inspired by Le Corbusier, also express a uniquely Venezuelan identity, particularly in terms of plastic integration. The campus was planned by Venezuelan architect Carlos Raúl Villanueva, with monumental axes to structure the campus and symmetric placement of buildings. Among the first structures, the University Hospital (1944) and Olympic Stadium (1950) are noteworthy for the plastic use of reinforced concrete.

Given climatic conditions, Villanueva altered the campus plan in later construction phases, adding more covered spaces and walkways. A nearly 1500-meter-long sidewalk links campus zones and ends at the center of campus in the Plaza Cubierta. Here the architecture meets popular culture. The sculptures and murals by Venezuelan artists Mateo Manaure, Pascual Navarro, and Carlos González Bogen, made of glass, bronze, ceramic, aluminum, and stone, are placed in a beautiful setting of tropical foliage. The nearby amphitheater, with repeating wing-shaped sections that rise from the roof line, appears prepared to take flight. Interior acoustic panels by Alexander Calder, "Nubes Acústicos" or "Acoustic Clouds" (also called "Platillos Voladores" or "Flying Saucers") further represent this theme. A fine synthesis of architecture and art, a plastic integration, exists here. This created a precedent for public art throughout Caracas, along highways and in subway stations, plazas, and buildings.

Like Mexico City's UNAM, the new campus of the UCV was to represent and promote progress and modernity. It too faces enrollment pressures. Intended to serve from 4,000 to 5,000 students, the current enrollment is approximately 50,000 on this 504-acre campus.

## CUBA, THE REVOLUTION, AND ARCHITECTURE

Popular architecture in Cuba follows a different trajectory than elsewhere in the hemisphere. Whereas utopian or idealistic Mexican and Brazilian architects of the 1930s believed that design should serve the interests of the collective, the countries' capitalist development programs and the actions of the private sector heavily impacted their cityscapes. Socialist Cuba, conversely, has consistently placed architecture in the service of societal needs for housing, health care, education, governmental and office space, and industrial production. Yet its architects did not possess a blank slate upon which they could create a new spatial arrangement for revolutionary society. And Cuba, like other Latin American countries, would not be immune to further foreign cultural penetration. As a former Spanish colony, Cuba's popular architecture contains elements similar to that of other former colonies in the Caribbean. Houses, whether detached or row houses, typically have tall ceilings for heat to escape, covered balconies and arcades, and louvered windows. Such designs are found in cities and towns throughout the island, a functionality in domestic architecture attained centuries ago and replicated throughout the Caribbean. Concern for function (defense of the city) dictated Havana's shape. It was protected by fortifications and high, stone city walls until 1863, when the walls were breached to allow further growth. A Spanish–Creole culture flourished, with taste favoring neo-baroque facades painted cream or blue; a similar gentility prevailed in provincial capitals such as Santiago, Bayamó, Santa Clara, and Trinidad.

Once Havana's walls were breached, new land could be developed to meet the needs of the growing middle and upper classes. Vedado (literally "forbidden," given its location outside the walls) soon had residences in the latest mode: beaux arts, neocolonial (often with Moorish influence), and art nouveau. U.S. cultural influences, unsurprisingly, grew stronger due to its military occupation of Cuba in 1898. Along with dramatic improvements in public works (particularly roads, sanitation, disease eradication, and school construction), the occupation provided a means for new architectural influences to enter Cuba. This is clearly seen in the construction of the Capitolio (completed 1926, Raúl Otero and others), modeled after the U.S. Capitol Building, and the Presidential Palace (1913–30, Paul Belau and Carlos Maruri). Such neoclassic works appeared to be fitting symbols of sovereignty for the new republic and were considered as such by elites of the day, the Platt Amendment and other aspects of Yankee influence notwithstanding.

U.S. influences continued to dominate Cuban popular architecture in the following 40 years, to the revolution's end in 1959. In this manner cityscapes throughout Cuba manifested continued evidence of U.S. economic interests. In Havana, the neocolonial Hotel Nacional (1930), an immense beige stone building along the Malecón, was designed by the prominent American firm McKee, Mead, and White. It would be joined later by hotels built for the booming tourist trade. The new hotels of the late 1940s and 1950s were executed in the International Style, with flourishes reminiscent of art deco Miami Beach properties, among them the seventeen-story Riviera (1950) with its cantilevered curvilinear balconies and the boxlike Capri (1958). The twenty-seven-story Havana Hilton, completed in 1958 (Nelson Beckett and Associates) was the latest in International Style. Its mosaic-tiled entrance depicting stylized ocean waves is one of the few elements that distinguish it from other modernist properties developed by the company in those years. Such influence is also seen in apartment building, notably the huge FOCSA Building (1956, Ernesto Gómez Sampera and Martín Domínguez). Built of reinforced concrete and steel, the broad, flat Y-shaped building has thirty-nine floors and a singularly cold façade, a stark contrast to the surrounding eclectic architecture.

It is difficult to overstate the impact of the revolution of 1959 on Cuban society. Popular architecture provides valuable insights into this process of revision from capitalism to socialism. Following their arrival into Havana on January 1, 1959, revolutionary brigades were quartered in the Hilton (amid confused but photo-snapping tourists); within a year, the hotel would be expropriated and rechristened the *Habana Libre* (Free Havana), its casinos shut, as were all others. Architecture— privately held structures and new developments— were to serve the collective. Buildings themselves would communicate the values of revolutionary society; the most blatant example of this is the Ministry of the Interior building in the Plaza of the Revolution, just a few blocks up from the Habana Libre, with its four-story portrait of Che Guevara, suitably illuminated in red. In the new revolutionary discourse, there was no place for the vocabulary of art deco, nouveau, or neoclassical. All were symbols of excess, of the exploitation by one class of another. Revolutionary philosophy required a different style—functional, simple, rational. The inspiration would come from their new ally, the Soviet Union. From 1960 to the mid-1980s, the Soviet International Style would be employed in large-scale construction throughout Cuba.

This style, notable for its emphasis on pure functionality, is heavily influenced by Le Corbusier. As housing is considered a basic civil right, the government constructed over a million new housing units under Soviet sponsorship. Throughout Cuba these concrete prefabricated units are seen; anonymous and characterless, they appear to be warehouses for a designated population, their severe exteriors softened only by bright paint. The largest project built, Alamar, has 100,000 units. Located on Havana's outskirts, it is a planning failure, lacking human scale and amenities, as well as necessities such as schools, clinics, and markets.

Other housing solutions were found in the expropriation of properties previously held by the elites. Such homes, often of lavish scale and decoration, were subdivided with space allocated to the new occupants based on family sizes. Although the Cuban government states that there are no significant housing problems or homelessness due to such initiatives, severe problems exist due to the continual lack of resources for maintenance and repair. Recent studies undertaken by the Office of the Historian of the City of Havana (OCHC) have determined that two-thirds of housing is in poor condition and 30 percent is substandard. A few initiatives have begun to address this problem, most notably those taken by the Centro Memorial Dr. Martin Luther King Jr., in the working-class neighborhood of Marianao. Residents of this neighborhood are provided training and building materials donated by various foreign non-governmental organizations (NGOs) and churches to repair their dwellings. This initiative has increased community ties and creative expression in architecture. Following Havana's designation as a World Heritage Site by the United Nations Educational, Scientific and Cultural Organization (UNESCO), the OHCH has undertaken other reconstruction projects, using funds derived from tourism. These include the Malecón restoration project, renovating the apartment and office buildings along the sea wall, and the renovation of Plaza Vieja and the San Isidro neighborhood. Colonial-era churches have also been restored and secularized; most notably, the seventeenth-century baroque San Francisco de Asís now serves as a concert hall.

Following the collapse of the Soviet Union, efforts to promote tourism increased dramatically. The OCHC has restored a large area of Habana Vieja, from the Castillo de la Real Fuerza to Plaza Vieja. Narrow streets—Obispo, Mercaderes, La Lamparilla—beckon the tourists, as do venerable restaurants El Bodeguita del Medio and La Floridita. Artisans in the new workshops painstakingly restore the stained glass *media lunas* (fan lights), symbols of old Havana's gracious buildings. Yet the modern, or postmodern, intrudes: the edgy façade of the Benetton shop stands out from the stately colonial architecture of Plaza Vieja; the new Sol Melia and Golden Tulip hotels contain scant revolutionary messages. Cuban identity and culture depicted in this area are decidedly neutral. The image of Cuban nationalist José Martí is permitted, and a mural along Mercaderes Street depicts colonial ladies and gentlemen in their Sunday-best top hats and parasols. A few blocks away, however, socialist Cuba reappears; what little signage exists reaffirms the revolution, the most incendiary reserved for the spaces flanking the approaches to the International Style U.S. Interests Section.

Cuba's recreational and ecotourism developments have been less confrontational but still possess a political impact. Sites such as Hanabanilla (Las Villas province) and Pinares de Mayarí, in the Sierra Maestra are dedicated to providing all-inclusive, inexpensive vacations for Cubans. At Las Terrazas, in the province of Pinar del Rio, guests see reforestation projects, organic farms, and a restored coffee plantation; its Moka Hotel is a green building, a model for alternative energy and low-impact design. Its red-tiled roof and white stuccoed walls evoke popular architecture throughout Central America.

The collapse of the Soviet Union provided an opportunity for a new architectural paradigm, postmodernism, to enter Cuba. Two of the most cited examples postmodernism are seen in Santiago. In 1991 Cuban architect José Antonio Choy designed the Santiago Hotel and Santiago Train Station. The two bold works mark a dramatic departure from the Soviet International Style and its rigid, massive forms. The hotel features bold use of color and mirrored blue glass façade; its form, a composite of solids terminating in a staggered series, dominates the landscape. The train station appears to be inspired by the works of architect Frank Gehry, with its use of corrugated metal and unusual elements such as a functionless bridge, and large metal blocks scattered at random at the building's entrance. It is a stark contrast to other structures in the region and to past representations of Cuban identity on the landscape. Given such developments, it appears that the expressions of Cuban popular architecture in coming years will be pluralist, with no one vision prevailing.

## SUMMARY

Latin American popular architecture is marked by dynamism and creativity with impressive constructions. Given their rapid population growth, many Latin American cities are surrounded by "belts of misery"—substandard housing and squatter settlements occupied by those on the margins of economic development programs. But even on the margins there is a vitality, the will to survive, and to succeed—the rebar marking the second or third story-to-be, aspirations fulfilled by the second or third generation of migrants. Cultural penetration continued to be prominent in popular architecture and is perhaps inevitable in this era of globalization. The ubiquitous glass box of the International Style, however, is gradually receding on skylines, supplanted by postmodern hybrids containing local references. The built environment indicates that this tension between the local and globalized styles will persist.

## SKYSCRAPERS

Since the sixteenth century, urban growth in Latin America has been horizontal, given its abundant land. In the United States and Europe, technological advances in architecture of the early twentieth century, as well as new building materials such as structural iron and steel, enabled property owners and developers to build high-rises. Yet this form was not adopted quickly in Latin America, not until limitations posed by the environment (such as poor subsoil and seismic activity) were overcome by structural engineers and architects. More challenging were limitations presented by zoning or tradition: colonial-era structures in city centers remained highly significant in terms of local or national identities and were also important as tourist attractions. Yet skyscrapers carry immense symbolic meaning, representing progress, modernity, and prosperity. Their adoption to symbolize these traits in Latin America was inevitable.

Over the past 30 years, the skyscraper has been adopted in all Latin American cities with the exception of Havana. Travel writers frequently note the uneasy juxtaposition of "parades of glittery high-rises" that shadow colonial plazas in La Paz, Bolivia, Lima's combination of "sleek modern skyscrapers and elegant if faded colonial architecture," and Caracas' "jumble of skyscrapers and undisguised hovels." A vigorous race to build the tallest building in Latin America, or South America, is on: in Santiago Cesar Pelli designed what might be the tallest skyscraper in South America, providing sixty floors of office space in the Gran Torre Costarena (to be completed in 2009). Joining it will be the fifty-two-story Titanium La Portada, only 200 meters away (to be completed in 2010). The tallest building in Latin America will most likely be Panama City's 104-story hotel and apartment/condominium Ice Tower, designed by Panamanian architects Pincon, Lozano, and Associates. Other new construction in that city includes the sixty-two-story Trump Ocean Club and the ninety-three-story Palacio de la Bahía, designed by Jesús Díaz and Associates, on Panama Bay. Such buildings, dazzling in form and construction, have irrevocably altered city skylines. The product of both national and foreign architects and engineers, their forms frequently evoke other lofty achievements elsewhere, further evidence of the globalization of architecture.

# RESOURCE GUIDE

### PRINT SOURCES

Aja, Marisol. "Juan O'Gorman." Pp. 9–48 in Alejandrino Escudero (ed.), *Apuntes para la Historia y Crítica de la Arquitectura Mexicana del Siglo XX: 1900–1980,* vol. 2 . México, D.F.: Secretaria de Educación Pública, Instituto Nacional de Bellas Artes, 1982.

Aldrich, Richard. *Style in Mexican Architecture.* Coral Gables, FL: University of Miami Press, 1968.

Alvarez Checa, José, and Manuel Ramos Guerra. *Obra Construida, Luis Barragán Morfín 1902–1988.* Seville: Consejería de Obras Públicas y Transportes, Dirección General de Arquitectura y Vivienda, 1991.

Anda Alanis, Enrique X. de. *Evolución de la Arquitectura en Mexico: Epocas Prehispanica, Virreinal Moderna y Contemporanea.* México, D.F.: Panorama Editorial, 1987.

———. *Cuidad de México: Arquitectura 1921–1970.* Sevilla: Consejería de Obras Públicas y Transportes and México, D.F.: Gobierno del Distrito Federal, 2001.

Arana, Mariano, and Lorenzo Garabelli. *Arquitectura Renovadora en Montevideo 1915–1940.* Montevideo: Fundación de Cultura Universitaria, 1991.

Bayon, Damian, and Paolo Gasparini. *The Changing Shape of Latin American Architecture: Conversations with Ten Leading Architects.* Translated by Galen D. Greaser. Chichester, NY: Wiley, 1979.

Bethell, Leslie, ed. *A Cultural History of Latin America: Literature, Music, and the Visual Arts in the 19th and 20th Centuries.* Cambridge, UK, and New York: Cambridge University Press, 1998.

Born, Esther. *The New Architecture in Mexico.* New York: Architectural Record and W.W. Morrow, 1937.

Brand, Stewart. *How Buildings Learn, What Happens After They Are Built.* New York: Penguin Books, 1994.

Brillembourg, Carlos, ed. *Latin American Architecture, 1929–1960: Contemporary Reflections.* New York: Monacelli Press, 2004.

Bullrich, Francisco. *New Directions in Latin American Architecture.* New York: George Braziller, 1969.

Burian, Edward R., ed. *Modernity and the Architecture of Mexico.* Austin: University of Texas Press, 1997.

Cetto, Max. *Modern Architecture in Mexico.* Translated by D. Q. Stephenson. New York: Praeger, 1961.

Collado, Ramón, Clara Iliana Robaina, Manuel Coipel, Madeline Menéndez, Azalia L. Arias, and Alejandro Ventura. *San Isidro, The New Image, A Social Project for the Total Revitalization of a Havana Neighborhood.* Navarra, Spain: Ediciones Boloña, Colección Arcos, 1998.

Crouch, Dora B., and June G. Robinson. *Traditions in Architecture: Africa, America, Asia, and Oceania.* New York: Oxford University Press, 2000.

Damaz, Paul F. *Art in Latin American Architecture.* New York: Reinhold, 1963.

Davis, Mike. *Planet of Slums.* New York and London: Verso, 2006.

Dietz, Henry. *Urban Poverty, Political Participation, and the State: Lima, 1970–1990.* Pittsburgh: University of Pittsburgh Press, 1998.

Doblado, Juan Carlos. *Arquitectura Peruana Contemporánea, Escritos y Conversaciones.* Lima: Arquidea Ediciones, 1990.

Evenson, Norma. *Two Brazilian Capitals: Architecture and Urbanism in Rio de Janeiro and Brasilia.* New Haven: Yale University Press, 1973.

Foster, David William. *Buenos Aires, Perspectives on the City and Cultural Production.* Gainesville, FL: University Presses of Florida, 1998.

Fraser, Valerie. *Building the New World, Studies in the Modern Architecture of Latin America 1930–1960.* London: Verso, 2000.

García Fernández, Emilio, José Ramón Moreno García, Angel Sánchez González, Maria Teresa Padrón Lotti, and Eugenio Casanovas Molleda. *The Havana Malecón, A Transformation and Cooperation Process.* Navarra, Spain: Ediciones Boloña, Colección Arcos, 1998.

Gasparini, Graziano, and Luise Margolies. *Arquitectura Popular de Venezuela.* Caracas: Fundación Eugenio Mendoza, 1986.

Gilbert, Alan, ed. *The Mega-City in Latin America.* New York: United Nations University Press, 1996.

González Cortazar, Fernando, ed. *La Arquitectura Mexicana del Siglo XX.* México, D.F.: Consejo Nacional para la Cultura y las Artes, 1994.

Guillermoprieto, Alma. *The Heart that Bleeds, Latin America Now.* New York: Vintage, 1995.

Gutiérrez, Ramón, Marcelo Martín, and Alberto Petrina. *Otra Arquitectura Argentina, un Camino Alternativo.* Bogotá, Colombia: Scala, 1989.

Hardoy, Jorge E. *Urbanization in Latin America: Approaches and Issues.* New York: Doubleday, 1975.

Hitchcock, Henry-Russell. *Latin American Architecture Since 1945.* New York: Museum of Modern Art, 1955.

Holston, James. *The Modernist City: An Anthropological Critique of Brasilia.* Chicago: University of Chicago Press, 1989.

Jeanneret-Gris, Charles Edouard (Le Corbusier). *Towards a New Architecture.* Translated by Frederick Etchells. New York: Dover, 1986.

Jesus, Carolina Maria de. *Child of the Dark, the Diary of Carolina Maria de Jesus.* Translated by David St. Clair. New York: New American Library, 1962.

Joseph, Gilbert M., and Mark D. Szuchman, eds. *I Saw a City Invincible, Urban Portraits of Latin America.* Wilmington, DE: Scholarly Resources, 1996.

Kandell, Jonathan. *La Capital: The Biography of Mexico City.* New York: Random House, 1988.

Kappe, Shelley, ed. *Modern Architecture, Mexico.* Santa Monica, CA: SCI-ARC Press, 1981.

Katzman, Israel. *La Arquitectura Contemporanea Mexicana, Precedentes y Desarrollo.* México, D.F.: Instituto Nacional de Antropología e Historia, 1963.

King, John, ed. *The Cambridge Companion to Modern Latin American Culture.* Cambridge: Cambridge University Press, 2004.

Kostof, Spiro, with Greg Castillo. *A History of Architecture, Settings and Rituals.* 2nd edition. New York: Oxford University Press, 1995.

Le Corbusier—see Jeanneret-Gris, Charles Edouard.

Lemos, Carlos. *História da Casa Brasileira.* São Paulo: Editora Contexto, 1989.

Lewis, Oscar. *The Children of Sanchez, The Autobiography of a Mexican Family.* New York: Random House, 1961.

Liernur, Jorge Francisco. *Arquitectura en la Argentina del Siglo XX: La Construcción de la Modernidad.* Buenos Aires: Fondo Nacional de las Artes, 2001.

López Morales, Francisco Javer. *Arquitectura Vernácula en México.* México, D.F.: Editorial Trillas, 1987.

Low, Setha M. *On the Plaza, The Politics of Public Space and Culture.* Austin: University of Texas Press, 2000.

Llanes, Llilian. *The Houses of Old Cuba.* New York: Thames & Hudson, 1999.

Moreno, Juan. *Monumentos Históricos Nacionales.* Caracas: Instituto del Patrimonio Cultural, 1998.

Morse, Richard M., and Jorge E. Hardoy, eds. *Rethinking the Latin American City.* Washington, DC: Woodrow Wilson Center Press, 1992.

Neuwirth, Robert. *Shadow Cities: A Billion Squatters, A New Urban World.* New York: Routledge, 2004.

Oficina del Historiador de la Ciudad de la Habana. *Challenge of a Utopia, A Comprehensive Strategy to Manage the Safeguarding of Old Havana.* Navarra, Spain: Ediciones Boloña, Colección Arcos, 2001.

Opher, Philip, with Xavier Sanchez Valladares. *Mexico City, A Guide to Recent Architecture.* London; Ellipsis, 2000.

Pick, James B., and Edgar W. Butler. *Mexico Megacity.* Boulder, CO: Westview Press, 1997.

Roca, Miguel Angel, ed. *The Architecture of Latin America.* London: Academy Group, 1995.

Rodríguez Alomá, Patricia. *Viaje en la Memoria, Apuntes para un Acercamiento a la Habana Vieja.* Navarra, Spain: Ediciones Boloña, Colección Arcos, 1996.

Rojas, Eduardo. *Urban Heritage Conservation in Latin America and the Caribbean: A Task for All Social Actors.* Washington, DC: Inter-American Development Bank, Sustainable Development Department, 2002.

Schaedel, Richard P., Jorge E. Hardoy, and Nora Scott Kinzer, eds. *Urbanization in the Americas from Its Beginnings to the Present.* The Hague and Paris: Mouton Publishers, 1978.

Scarpaci, Joseph, Roberto Segre, and Mario Coyula. *Havana: Two Faces of the Antillean Metropolis*, rev. ed. Chapel Hill, NC: University of North Carolina Press, 2002.

Segawa, Hugo M. *Arquitectura Latinoamericana Contemporánea.* Barcelona: Gustavo Gili, 2005.

Segre, Roberto. *Arquitectura y Urbanismo de la Revolución Cubana.* Havana: Editoria Pueblo y Educación, 1989.

———, and Fernando Kusnetzoff, eds. *Latin America in Its Architecture.* New York: Holmes & Meier, 1981.

Slesin, Suzanne, Stafford Cliff, Jack Berthelot, Martine Gaumé, and Daniel Rozensztroch. *Caribbean Style.* New York: Clarkson N. Potter, 1985.

Suzuki, Makoto, ed. *Modern Mexican Architecture.* Tokyo: Process Architecture, 1983.

Trebbi del Trevigiano, Romolo. *Arquitectura Espontanea y Vernacula en América Latina, Teoría y Forma.* Santiago, Chile: Ediciones Universitarias de Valparaíso, 1985.

Underwood, David Kendrick. *Oscar Niemeyer and the Architecture of Brazil.* New York: Rizzoli, 1994.

Ward, Peter. *Mexico City, the Production and Reproduction of an Urban Environment*, 2nd ed. New York: Wiley, 1998.

## PERIODICALS

*A + T* Bilingual review of architecture and technology.
*AIA* Paraguay Review of architecture, art, and engineering.
*ARARA: Art and Architecture of the Americas* (online) http://www2.essex.ac.uk/arthistory/arara/.
*Arquine.* International review of architecture.
*Arquitectura en México.*
*Arquitectura y Humanidades* Mexican quarterly journal on architecture and the humanities.
*Boletín IFA.* Bulletin of the Instituto de Investigaciones de la Facultad de Arquitectura, Universidad de Zulia, Venezuela.
*Construyendo.* Argentine magazine for the construction industry.
*Cuadernos de Arquitectura y Urbanismo.* Universidad de Chiapas, Mexico.
*El Constructor.* Uruguayan journal on construction techniques and architecture.
*Obras.* Mexican journal of architecture and construction.
*Opus Habana.* Review of architecture and art published by the Office of the Historian of the City of Havana.
*Portaplanos.* Journal of the Facultad de Arquitectura y Urbanismo, Chile.
*Revista Ambiente.* Argentine journal of ethics and aesthetics for the built environment.
*Revista de Arquitectura.* Journal of the Facultad de Arquitectura y Urbanismo, Universidad de Chile.
*Summa +.* Bimonthly review of architecture and design.
*Tecnología y Construcción.* Venezuelanjournal of architecture and design.
*Urbe.* Online bulletin on architecture, Universidad de Concepción, Chile.
*WAM:* Web Architecture Magazine. Bilingual online publication. http://www.arranz.net/web.arch-mag.com/welcome.html.

## VIDEOS/FILMS

*Americas: Vol 3: Continent on the Move* (Mexico, 1993). Annenberg/CPB project.
*City Life.* (Brazil, 2001). Bullfrog Films.
*Doing the Right Thing.* (Brazil, 2001). Bullfrog Films. *Escaping from History.* Mexico, 1994). Bullfrog Films.
*Imagining New Worlds.* (Mexico, 1996). Annenberg/CPB Collection. *Life and Death in Rio.* (Brazil, 1985). Media Guild.
*Life and Debt.* (Brazil, 1992). Bullfrog Films.
*Megacities.* (Mexico City), 1998). Lotus Film<s?>.
*Mexico City, the Impossible City.* (Mexico, 2005). Films for the Humanities & Sciences.
*Pavements of Gold.* (Peru, 2001). Bullfrog Films.
*Parque Central.* (Venezuela, 1991). First Run Icarus Films.
*San Juan: Ciudad de Todos.* (United States, 2000). Puerto Rico, ], Tropical Visions Entertainment Group.
*Slums/A Documentary.* (Brazil, 1991). Cinema Guild
*Sustainable Urban Living.* (Brazil, 2003). Insight Media.
*Urban Design and Planning in Havana, Cuba, an Historical Perspective.* (United States, 2001). Virginia Tech University.

## WEBSITES

*Architecture of South and Central America.* http://www.greatbuildings.com/places/south_america.html.
Arquitectura.com. 2006. *Arquitectura en Linea.* http://www.arquitectura.com.
Brown, Jeanne. *Architecture and Building: Resources by Topic.* University of Nevada, Las Vegas. Accessed August 16, 2006. http://library.nevada.edu/arch/rsrce/webrsrce/contents.html.
*DatArq.* http://www.datarq.fadu.uba.ar. Database for modern architecture.
Inter-American Development Bank (IADB). http://www.iadb.org.
International Union of Architects [UIA]. Accessed February 8, 2006. http://www.uia-architectes.org.

Latin American Network Information Center (LANIC). http://lanic.utexas.edu/la/region/architecture/.

Matthews, Kevin. *Caribbean Architecture and Urban Design.* Artifice, Inc. 2006. Accessed 2006. http://www.periferia.org.

*SPIRO— Architecture Visual Resources Library Image Database.* University of California at Berkeley. www.mip.berkeley.edu/spiro.

United Nations Economic Commission for Latin America and the Caribbean. http://www.un.org/popin/regions/eclac.html.

United States Agency for International Development, *Making Cities Work.* http://www.making citieswork.org/urbanWorld/latin-america-caribbean.


## ORGANIZATIONS

### General

American Institute of Architects (AIA), The American Institute of Architects,
1735 New York Ave. NW,
Washington, DC 20006-5292,
http://www.aia.org.

Taller Internacional de Urbanística Latinoamericana. http://www.tiul.org.ar/.


### Argentina

AIE—Asociación de Ingenieros Estructurales, H. Yrigoyen 1144 1º Of. 2, (C1086AAT), Ciudad Autónoma de Buenos Aires, Argentina. http://www.aiearg.org.ar/.

Colegio de Arquitectos de la Provincia de Buenos Aires, Boulevard 53 nº 320—La Plata, Buenos Aires, Argentina, http://www.capba.org.ar/.

Federación Argentina de Entidades de Arquitectura—FADEA, Buenos Aires, Argentina. http://www.fadea.org.ar/.

Sociedad Central de Arquitectos, Buenos Aires, Argentina. http://www.socearq.org.


### Brazil

Associação Brasileira de Arquitectos Paisagistas (ABAP), Rua Campevas 115 cj. C- Perdizes 05016-010, São Paulo, Brazil. http://www.abap.org.br.

Associação Brasileira de Escritórios de Arquitectura (AsBEA),Rua Tabapuã, 479–Cj 62 Itaim Bibi, 04533011– São Paulo, Brazil. http://www.asbea.org.br.

Fundaçao Oscar Niemeyer, Rio De Janeiro, Brazil. http://www.niemeyer.org.br.

Instituto do Patrimônio Histórico e Artístico Nacional (IPHAN), Brasília, Brazil. http://www.iphan.gov.br/.


### Chile

Colegio de Arquitectos de Chile, Avenida Lib. Bernardo O'Higgins 115, Santiago, Chile. http://www.colegioarquitectos.com.


### Colombia

Sociedad Colombiana de Arquitectos, Bogotá, Colombia. http://www.sociedadcolombianade arquitectos.org.

## Costa Rica

Cámara de Consultores en Arquitectura e Ingeniería, San José, Costa Rica. http://www.ccai.co.cr/.
Cámara Costarricense de la Construcción,
Barrio Francisco Peralta, 150 Oeste de la Casa Italia.
San José, Costa Rica,
www.construccion.co.cr/.
Colegio Federado de Ingenieros y Arquitectos (CFIA), San José, Costa Rica. http://www.cfia.or.cr.

## Cuba

Oficina del Historiador de la Ciudad de La Habana, Havana, Cuba. http://www.historiadordela
habana.cubasi.cu/.

## Ecuador

Colegio Nacional de Arquitectos del Ecuador, Quito, Ecuador. http://www.cae.org/ec.

## El Salvador

Asociación Salvadoreña de Ingenieros y Arquitectos, 75 Av. Norte No. 632, Col. Escalón, Apartado
Postal: 743, San Salvador, El Salvador. http://www.asiasv.org.
Facultad de Arquitectura, Universidad Politécnica de El Salvador, San Salvador. http://www.upes.edu/
sv/facultades/arquitectura.html.

## Honduras

Colegio de Arquitectos de Honduras, Junto al Col. San Miguel, Col. Payaqui, Tegucigalpa, Honduras.
http://www.e-cah.org.

## Mexico

Centro de la Vivienda y Estudios Urbanos A.C., Mexico City. http://www.cenvi.org.mx.
Colegio de Arquitectos de la Ciudad de México, Sociedad de Arquitectos Mexicanos, Mexico City.
http://www.camsam.org.
Federación de Arquitectos de México, A.C., Luis Cabrera #68, Col. San Jerónimo Aculco, c.p. 10400,
Del. Magdalena Contreras, México D.F. http://www.fearm.org.mx.
Instituto Mexicano del Edificio Inteligente, Av Paseo de la Reforma No. 505, Piso 9, Suite A, Col.
Cuauhtémoc, C.P. 06500, Edificio Torre Mayor, Mexico, D.F. http://www.imei.org.mx.

## Panama

Sociedad Panameña de Ingenieros y Arquitectos, Panama City. http://www.spiachiriqui.com.pa.

## Peru

Colegio de Arquitectos de Perú, Av. San Felipe 999 Jesús Maria, Lima 11, Perú. http://www.cap.org.pe/.

## Puerto Rico

Colegio de Arquitectos y Arquitectos Paisajistas de Puerto Rico, San Juan, Puerto Rico. http://www.caappr.com/enlaces.cfm.

## Uruguay:

Facultad de Arquitectura, (FARQ), Universidad de la República, Bulevar Artigas 1031– C.P. 11200, Montevideo, Uruguay. http://www.farq.edu.uy/.
Sociedad de Arquitectos del Uruguay (SAU),Gonzalo Ramírez 2030,
CP 11200, Montevideo, Uruguay. http://www.sau.org.uy.

## Venezuela

Arquitectos Venezolanos, Urb. Santa Juana, Vda. C-1 Casa #43, Mérida, Edo. Mérida, Venezuela. http://www.arquitectosvenezolanos.com.
Colegio de Ingenieros de Venezuela, Caracas, Venezuela. http://www.civ.org.ve/.

# NOTES

1. Jeanneret-Gris, 1986 (in Resource Guide), p. 13.
2. Ibid., p. 25.
3. Ibid., p. 236.
4. Ibid., p. 265.

**ART**

BRADEN K. FRIEDER

Latin America is one of the most culturally diverse parts of the world. In the early modern period, most of Latin America was ruled by Catholic Spain (except for Brazil, ruled through most of its colonial history by Portugal, also Catholic), which imposed a basic unity of language and religion on this vast region. Spanish colonial civilization, however, was thinly spread over a multitude of indigenous cultures, each with its own artistic traditions, forming nations within nations even after independence from Spain. One would hardly expect unity from such variety, but art in Latin America today is tied together by a continuing search for identity. Latin American artists have always been keenly aware of artistic developments across the Atlantic, but they have always actively transformed their European models, creating an art that is uniquely their own. Artists in Latin America also share a concern for creating socially conscious art. And, everywhere in Latin America, artists have an enduring faith in folk traditions and popular culture, which form an ongoing dialogue with ideas from abroad.

## MEXICO

Mexico has perhaps the richest and most varied artistic tradition in Latin America. Archaeologists believe human beings were living in Mexico as early as 10,000 BC, with village life appearing around the second millennium BC. Mexico's first advanced civilization, the Olmec, developed in the Formative or pre-Classic period around 1500 BC. In the Classic period, the Maya civilization flourished in what is now southern Mexico. Migrations of warlike tribes characterized the post-Classic period, culminating in the conquests of the Aztecs, whose military empire included most of Mexico and parts of Central America. Following the Spanish conquest in 1521, European art and technology were grafted onto native traditions, producing a strong and distinctive artistic heritage that is uniquely Mexican. In the modern era, Mexican artists have made important contributions to world art with the muralist movement. Traditional arts and crafts also remain particularly strong in Mexico today. Mexican popular art is known for its vibrant color, and it is often touched by a macabre sense of humor.

ART

## RELIGIOUS ART IS INDEED POPULAR

The image of the Virgin of Guadalupe is encountered in Mexican popular art and religious memorabilia from religious statuettes and medals to posters, T-shirts, and coffee mugs. Pictures of the Virgin, often surrounded by flashing lights, are placed in taxis and buses to protect travelers. Popular religious artworks in Mexico are made in a variety of media, including oil paintings on tin and copper sheet, a holdover from the Colonial era. Niches or wall altars of embossed metal enclosing paintings for private devotion are hung in many homes. Prayer cards and colored candles in tall glasses decorated with pictures of Catholic saints are commercially produced and are used in Mexican churches and private homes for vigils, votive offerings, and *novena* (nine-day) prayers for those in need. These candles are sometimes called "novena lights." Popular subjects include St. Martin of Tours, who brings wealth and success, and the Holy Child of Atocha, who protects people who are in prison or living under harsh political conditions. Placards with pictures of saints known for the holiness of their lives are placed next to doorways to forbid entry to the devil. In colonial times, and in small villages today, painters of saints and other religious subjects in a popular style are called *santeros* (saint makers).

In ancient times, the walls of Mexican temples and palaces were decorated with sculptures and colorful murals depicting creation stories of the gods and the exploits of rulers. The primary subjects of pre-Columbian art were transformation, sacred warfare, and captive sacrifice. Small figurines and personal adornments were made from a wide variety of materials, most often jade, although other stones, beads, feathers, and even human bone were also used. Images of pre-Columbian deities are still found in popular religious art in Mexico today, including illustrations of *La Santísima Muerte* or Holy Death, an Aztec goddess of the underworld who ensures male fidelity for women. Popular Aztec legends are illustrated on calendars hung in restaurants and private homes. Perhaps the most famous pre-Columbian image found in Mexican art today is an eagle perched on a cactus holding a serpent in its claws. The eagle and serpent refer to an omen sent by the gods, who told the Mexicans to settle on the island that is now downtown Mexico City. The eagle and serpent are encountered everywhere in Mexican popular art and occupy the center of the full version of the Mexican national flag. Little ceramic whistles, similar to ocarinas, in the shape of animals have been discovered in 2,000-year-old Maya graves. These instruments are still made in Mexico and are sold to tourists visiting pre-Columbian archaeological sites.

During the Colonial period, Indian artists embellished churches with reliefs and murals in a mixed Hispano-Indian style. Young Indians and *mestizos* (people of mixed European and Indian blood) were taught to illustrate Christian subjects by Spanish priests at monastery schools, despite the fact that Indians were technically prohibited from making religious artworks. One of the most enduringly popular images in Mexico today is the Virgin of Guadalupe, believed to have appeared to an Indian shepherd named Juan Diego in the sixteenth century. The Virgin of Guadalupe is always shown with brown skin, and she is surrounded by a flaming aureole or *mandorla*. Her image appears in Mexican art from the Colonial period to the present, and she is considered the patron saint of Mexico.

Sculpture in colonial Mexico was primarily religious. Many of these sculptures were designed to be carried in church processions and are still in use today, especially during Holy Week or *Semana Santa* (the week before Easter Sunday). Most processional sculptures are made of wood, although some Mexican folk sculptures are made of lighter corn pith (*pasta de caña*). These sculptures were made as lifelike as possible in order to remind ordinary viewers of the Passion of Christ. Processional sculptures of Christ, the Virgin, and the saints are sometimes dressed in actual clothes, or are decorated with real hair, glass eyes, bone teeth, and even dried animal blood to enhance their realism. Others are simple armatures for clothing made especially for the figures, although they have lifelike faces and hands. In Mexico and Central America, roadsides are sometimes decorated with homemade shrines to the saints.

The first national art school in Mexico, the Real Academia de San Carlos in Mexico City, was founded in 1785. Courses were taught by Spaniards, although provisions were made for the instruction of poor Mexican boys. Major changes appeared in Mexican art during the Independence era. Few, if any, formal portraits of the Mexican liberator Miguel Hidalgo were made in his lifetime, although popular prints showing him with cross and battle gear were published by Claudio Linati. Small commemorative medallions in colored wax were made of José María Morelos, who carried on the struggle for independence from Spain. Agustín de Iturbide, the first emperor of Mexico, was immortalized in anonymous popular paintings imitating the French academic style, in which the white creole ruler appears like a miniature Napoleon. By the middle of the nineteenth century, subjects drawn from American and national history began to appear in Mexican painting. Juan Cordero (1824–84) and José María Obregón (1832–1902) painted romantic images of Christopher Columbus as the discoverer of America. Félix Parra (1845–1919) and Leandro Izaguirre (1867–1941), on the other hand, emphasized the brutality of the Spanish conquest and the benevolence of the padres who befriended the Indians. José María Jara (1866–1939) painted atmospheric genre paintings (scenes from everyday life) featuring Mexican subjects. European traveler-reporter artists, such as Alexander von Humboldt (1769–1859) and Frederick Catherwood (1799–1854), documented folk costumes and pre-Columbian ruins, and their work was widely distributed in the form of popular prints. Mexican painter José Agustín Arrieta (1802–74) painted still lifes with native fruits, market scenes, and picturesque local people wearing traditional dress (*costumbrismo*). The most popular Mexican artist of the nineteenth century was the landscape painter José María Velasco (1840–1912). Velasco's favorite subject was the Valley of Mexico, whose sweeping vistas he painted in a style reminiscent of the Barbizon school. Velasco achieved international renown, and his landscapes were shown in Philadelphia and Paris. Alongside academically trained artists, folk artists also produced art, especially *ex-votos,* small religious paintings designed for household shrines as thank offerings to the saints for healing and other miracles. Sculpture did not play a major role in Mexican art of the Revolutionary period. In the decorative arts colonial styles continued, although images of revolutionary heroes occasionally are found on popular ceramics from the Independence period.

Mexico also has made significant contributions to the graphic arts. Satirical illustrations with a popular bent first appeared in newspapers and broadsheets in the mid-nineteenth century and were consumed by an avid public. Although they were frequently illiterate, working-class Mexicans were eager for news and are sometimes shown enjoying illustrated newspapers on the streets in early photographs. Mexican popular prints poked fun at the clergy, the professional elite, and middle-class pretenders to higher social status. Others directly attacked government abuses, and many early Mexican printmakers remained anonymous to avoid prosecution. In spite of strict censorship, particularly under the regime of Porfirio Díaz, satirical newspapers and periodicals were the major outlet for popular liberalism in modern Mexico. Part of the appeal of satirical prints was that they could be cheaply produced, making them available to all social classes. Foremost among Mexican printmakers was José Guadalupe Posada (1852–1913). Posada's lithographs satirized everything from the Revolution to child abuse. Posada worked mainly for the "tabloid" press of his day, and his illustrations featured accidents, executions, freaks, popular heroes and villains, suicides, and other lurid subjects, accompanied by snippets of text explaining each image. Posada often illustrated *corridos,* satirical street songs that were published and enjoyed a wide distribution. Posada's prints frequently include the laughing skeleton or *calavera,* a Mexican satirical motif with roots in both Gothic Spain and pre-Columbian art. Posada's presention of humorous social commentary in a simple and dramatic visual language proved enormously popular and was imitated by the printmakers of the Taller de Gráfica Popular and the Mexican muralists. Like Posada, these artists were searching for a way to express the values and problems of revolutionary Mexico in a new modern style.

Modern art in Mexico drew on Indian cultural traditions (*indigenísmo*), but was shaped by the European avant-garde. Gerardo Murillo or "Dr. Atl" (1875–1964) arranged exhibitions of folk art and painted sweeping vistas in homemade colors that emphasized the dramatic power of the Mexican landscape, but he distanced himself from the more radical developments in European painting. Diego Rivera (1886–1957) visited Europe as a young man, where he absorbed the ideas of Picasso and the avant-garde artists. Rivera's early paintings combined synthetic cubism with native Mexican subjects, although he soon abandoned these preliminary studies and returned to Mexico, where he joined the muralist movement. The Mexican muralist movement produced the greatest public art of the twentieth century. José Vasconcelos, minister of education under President Obregón, was committed to a program of socially conscious art to spread the ideals of the Mexican Revolution to ordinary people. The Mexican muralists revived the tradition of large-scale wall painting and drew on a wide variety of historical styles, from the Italian Renaissance to the brawny heroism of popular comics. Rivera was commissioned to decorate several major public buildings in Mexico City, including the Ministry of Education (1926–28) and the Palacio Nacional (1929–30; 1950). Indigenism assumed a primary place in Rivera's luminous and imposing cycles on the history of Mexico in the Palacio Nacional, which highlighted the technical accomplishments of the Indians while disparaging the abuses of the Spaniards and modern capitalism. While he was still working on the Ministry of Education murals, Rivera completed a stunning series of murals at the National Agricultural School in Chapingo (1926–27). Here he combined allegorical images of Mother Earth with portraits of Emiliano Zapata and other popular revolutionaries, whose buried bodies are shown fertilizing the land. Returning to Mexico City after a visit to Moscow, he completed the Ministry of Education murals, which are tied together by a banderole bearing the words of a Mexican *corrido* or popular song. Rivera was invited to the United States, where he completed easel paintings and murals celebrating American industry, although his left-wing politics alienated some of his patrons. Although he criticized the industrialists, he was an advocate of modern science and technology, which he believed would play important roles in the coming socialist utopia. José Clemente Orozco (1883–1949) painted murals whose political content was more ambiguous and universal. Orozco's *Christ Destroying His Cross* (1943) was so shocking it was defaced by angry students of the National Preparatory School. Like Rivera, Orozco also worked on mural projects in the United States. His paintings at Dartmouth College celebrate the achievements of American public education, while lampooning the moribund faculty at institutions of higher learning. David Alfaro Siqueiros (1898–1974) was the most intellectual of the Mexican muralists, painting scenes of the Revolution in a more abstract and expressive style. His series of historical murals in the Museo de la Historia, Mexico City (1957), are his best-known works. Other important muralists were Fernando Leal (1900–64) and Juan O'Gorman (1905–82).

With their large-scale and public locations, Mexican murals presented the promises of the Revolution and keep them alive for Mexicans today, whatever their political and economic realities. The Mexican muralist movement also had a lasting impact on the international art scene, especially in the southwestern United States, where many Mexican immigrants live. Latino artists decorate public spaces in urban Los Angeles and other

American cities, using a type of popular imagery shaped by the Mexican muralists to address the social concerns of the postmodern world.

Frida Kahlo (1907–54) introduced an alternate reality to Mexican art with her intense and highly personal paintings, whose principal subject was the physical pain she endured from injuries suffered in a bus crash as a teenager. Her work was admired by the European surrealists, who considered her one of their own. Kahlo drew on a wide variety of sources, from Mexican folklore and *ex-votos* to the sensationalist prints of Posada. Frida Kahlo was also the wife of Diego Rivera, and she shared her husband's political beliefs. Kahlo's art has grown in popularity today, and her paintings are reproduced everywhere from college art classes to Mexican postcards. Other Mexican artists explored surrealism in a more abstract style that deemphasized political content, especially the painter Rufino Tamayo (b. 1899), whose art is on public display in a museum dedicated to him in Mexico City. Other Mexican surrealists were Leonora Carrington (b. 1917) and Remedios Varo (1908–63), whose paintings are reproduced on the covers of Mexican schoolbooks. Surrealist art in Mexico is sometimes called magic realism.

Sculpture has played a secondary role to painting in modern Mexican art. Geometric abstraction and proto-minimalism were introduced to Mexico by the German sculptor and architect Mathias Goeritz (1915–90). Goeritz was an academic theorist who envisioned a synthesis between large outdoor sculpture and urban planning, although his preoccupation with aesthetics was criticized by the Mexican muralists. Goeritz founded the El Eco Experimental Museum in Mexico City in 1952, primarily as an exhibition space for his sculptures. Goeritz also intended the Eco to be a popular space and a challenge to the institutional museum, and he organized public performances by modern dance groups there. In spite of his rejection by the muralists, Goeritz's famous *Five Towers* in the suburb of Satelite are today one of Mexico City's most popular landmarks.

The tradition of satirical Mexican prints was continued by the printmakers of the Taller de Gráfica Popular, founded by Leopoldo Méndez (1902–69) and Pablo O'Higgins (1904–83), an American artist who had settled in Mexico. The Taller de Gráfica Popular provided work spaces, facilities, and basic instruction for artists who otherwise had no access to printmaking equipment and techniques. Méndez and O'Higgins celebrated the labor of Mexican peasants but sometimes showed them as victims of powerful forces beyond their control. Activist prints were also produced for the periodical *El Machete,* which was taken over by the Communist Party in 1924. Isidoro Ocampo (1910–83), a cofounder of the Taller de Gráfica Popular, created political prints attacking Spanish fascism, and also papier-mâché objects inspired by Mexican folk art. Alberto Beltrán (1923–2002), another member of the Taller de Gráfica Popular, studied printmaking at the Academy de San Carlos and made linocuts showing heroic Mexican workers. Other printmakers associated with the Taller were Angel Bracho (b. 1911) and Alfredo Zalce (1908–2003). Galo Galecio (1906–93), a painter and printmaker from Ecuador, studied at the Taller de Gráfica Popular and made woodcuts showing peasant religious beliefs (see the section on Ecuador in this chapter). José Chavez Morado made leftist wood engravings that were more ambiguous and fantastical, inspired by Picasso's prints attacking Spanish dictator Francisco Franco. The prints of the Taller de Gráfica Popular were publically distributed in the form of posters and broadsheets, and the artists of the Taller were actively involved in the literacy campaigns of the Mexican government from 1944 onward. Simpler printing methods such as woodcutting and linocutting were preferred because they were cheap and more readily available to artists and the public.

Mexican photographer Manuel Alvarez Bravo (1902–2002) explored surrealism and social realism in his silver-gelatin prints. Alvarez Bravo's work was exhibited in Paris and was admired by surrealist writer André Breton. Alvarez Bravo met the French photographer Henri

Cartier-Bresson in Mexico and exhibited with him at the Palacio de Bellas Artes in Mexico City, an important public venue for art, in 1935. Alvarez Bravo's work typically features street scenes and still lifes of Mexican subjects, in which ordinary objects become sinister and threatening when removed from their everyday context. Bravo also exhibited photographs with political overtones, such as *Murdered Striking Worker* in 1934. Along with other Mexican artists, Bravo's work figured prominently in the Exposición Internacional del Surrealismo held in the Galería del Arte Mexicano in 1940. The exhibition also showcased examples of Mexican popular art, including Colima pottery and dance masks from Guerrero and Guadalajara.

Among many significant contemporary artists in Mexico, the work of Oaxacan artist Francisco Toledo (b. 1940) is especially noteworthy. Toledo combines images of Mexican plants and animals with ideas from pre-Columbian myth in watercolor and gouache. Toledo is also a printmaker and ceramicist. Painter and printmaker José Luis Cuevas (b. 1933 or 1934) was instrumental in the break from muralism in contemporary Mexican art and has exhibited in Europe and the United States. Among his many influences are Spanish baroque painting, Goya, Picasso, and the writings of the Marquis de Sade. Cuevas has also written a book called the *Cuevário*.

Many traditional arts and crafts techniques are still practiced today by artists throughout Mexico. Traditional Mexican pottery is sometimes made without the use of a true potter's wheel, which was introduced after the Spanish conquest. Pottery in Mexico is often fired outdoors in large open-air kilns, especially in the Yucatán. The facades of local churches may be decorated with colorful glazed tiles, made using techniques brought from Spain during the Colonial period, and brightly colored streamers are suspended from the towers of churches on holy days. Colonial-style ceramics, a specialty of Puebla, are collected by Mexicans and tourists alike. Mexican metalworkers continue to make Spanish-style wrought iron, and the silversmiths of Taxco and other areas have preserved colonial metalsmithing traditions. Folk artists in Mexico make knives, jewelry, and other metal objects decorated with silver and coral. Artisans in Puebla make elaborate cutouts from colored paper, which are hung in interior spaces and in some cases are still used for spiritual healing and other magic rituals. Traditional fig-bark paper or *papel de amate* is used for folk paintings in many parts of Mexico. Even food is used as a medium for visual art in Mexico. Decorated loaves of bread are made for the *Día de los Muertos* (Day of the Dead) celebrations in November, and the antics of sugar skeletons in marzipan graves enliven the windows of candy stores. In restaurants on Independence Day, *enchiladas* are served in the three colors of the Mexican flag. Gum or *chicle* is used for playful small-scale sculptures, which are often brightly painted and suggest continuity with an ancient tradition. Gourds are hollowed and painted with ornate silhouette designs in black and red lacquer. In many areas, folk costumes are worn as a part of everyday dress, especially by older people in isolated communities. For example, the *huipil*, a Maya female garment worn in pre-Columbian times, is still worn in parts of the Yucatán and Central America. The pre-Columbian backstrap loom, in which tension is maintained on the warp threads by rocking motions with the hips, is used in some villages. Most impressive are the hand-carved and brightly painted wooden masks worn for folk dances in traditional communities throughout Mexico. Many of these have their origins in pre-Columbian masks, especially the jaguar masks of central Mexico and the Gulf Coast, although other types were introduced during the Colonial period. Mexican masks and dance costumes often display a clever mixture of traditional and modern decorative methods. In the Gulf Coast region, for example, old Coca-Cola bottles are dipped in wet ashes and applied to the bodies of boy dancers to transform them magically into spotted jaguars and other fierce animals. Throughout Mexico, folk artists continue local traditions and are valued members of their communities.

# BELIZE

In ancient times, Belize (formerly British Honduras) was inhabited by the Maya people, whose civilization is now believed to have originated in what is now Belize and northern Guatemala. Since gaining independence from Britain in 1981, Belize has also begun to contribute to the world art scene.

Art in Belize during the Colonial period closely followed British examples. In 1974 Philip Lewis formed Soul to Art in Belize and began holding regular exhibitions. In the 1980s, the art of Michelle Perdomo began to move away from the British model. Other significant contemporary artists in Belize include Rachel Heusner, Kenneth Oliver, Terryl Godoy, Pen Cayetano, and Benjamin Nicolas. Popular Belizean sculptors often use native hardwoods, especially ziricote and mahogany, for their work. Noteworthy sculptors in wood are George Gabb and Ignatius Peyrefitte Jr., who sculpts madonnas. The Garcia sisters emphasize the Maya heritage of Belize in their art.

# GUATEMALA

Guatemala was the cradle of the Classic Maya civilization. In the Colonial period, Guatemala was an important province of the Viceroyalty of New Spain, producing sculptures of sufficient quality to be exported to Mexico City and Spain. Modern Guatemala is witnessing a renaissance of Maya culture following a devastating 36-year guerrilla war, which ended in 1996.

During the Independence era, Francisco Cabrera was a noted miniaturist and engraver in the neoclassical style. Printmaker Julián Falla produced etchings and lithographs of revolutionary themes. In the 1890s, Guatemala City was rebuilt in the fashionable French style. Expatriate European artists, mostly Italians, settled in Guatemala and influenced the development of the arts there. Venezuelan sculptor Santiago Gonzalez also settled in Guatemala and began training local artists. Gonzalez especially encouraged study abroad. Noteworthy painters from this period were Rafael Iriarte (1876–1962), Humberto Garavito (1887–1990), and Alfredo Gálvez Suárez (1879–1946). Important sculptors were Rafael Rodríguez Padilla and Rafael Yela Günther.

The Escuela de Artes Plásticas was established in Guatemala City in 1920. Artists at the school, especially Andres Curruchic (1891–1969), explored issues of national identity via impressionism, scenes of Indian life, and primitivism. Carlos Mérida, of Quiché Maya descent, went to Europe at age seventeen, where he met Picasso, Modigliani, and other artists living in Paris. His paintings were exhibited at the Academy of Fine Arts in Mexico City in 1920. In 1922 he met Diego Rivera and assisted him with the first murals for the National Preparatory School in Mexico City. Government support for the arts in Guatemala, however, did not begin until 1945. Guatemala opened itself to artistic influences from Mexico, the United States, and Europe. Modernism and formalist concerns were explored by Guillermo Grajeda Mena and Roberto Osage. Dagoberto Vázquez studied art in Chile. Roberto González Goyri studied in the United States, and Adalberto Leon went to France. As in Mexico, between 1955 and 1980, artists were hired by the government to decorate public buildings, although in Guatemala most of these artists were sculptors. They typically worked in large dimensions in concrete.

Expressionism, abstract painting, and social realism were the main preoccupations of Guatemalan artists in the 1960s. During the guerrilla war the Vértebra Group produced protest art, especially Elmer Rojas, Marco Augusto Quiroa, and Roberto Cabrera. Noteworthy modern photographers include Juan J. Yas, Domingo Noriega, and Valde Arellano. Much of contemporary art in Guatemala is concerned with the widespread massacre of Indians there in the 1980s.

## EL SALVADOR

The cultural history of El Salvador is complex and little known outside Central America. Olmec carvings from Mexico have been found as far south as the Pacific coast of El Salvador. In the Classic period the Maya civilization also extended into El Salvador as far as the River Lempa, although other peoples contributed to the artistic development of the country farther to the south and east. What is now El Salvador was added to the Aztec empire by the conqueror Ahuítzotl in the fifteenth century. Earthquakes and volcanic activity devastated the region in colonial times, and much of the art in the Spanish settlements was lost. In 1992 government and leftist forces signed a peace treaty guaranteeing political reform, ending a 12-year civil war that cost nearly 75,000 lives.

Francisco Cisneros is reputed to be an important artist from the early Independence period, although not many of his remaining works can be securely identified. Other significant nineteenth-century artists were Pascasio González (1848–1917) and his pupils. The Escuela Nacional de Artes Gráficas was founded in San Salvador by Carlos Alberto Imery (1879–1949). Important modern artists in El Salvador include Mauricio Aguilar (1919–78) and Benjamin Cañas (1933–89). Sculptor Valentín Estrada (1902–84) explored realism and national traditions.

## HONDURAS

Honduras marked the southernmost extension of the Maya civilization into Central America. The Chorti Maya are their modern descendants. Other indigenous groups were the Miskito, Pech, Tawahka, Tolupan (Jicaque), and Ahuas. The most important ethnic group when the Spanish arrived was the Lenca, although there are few material remains of their earlier culture. Honduras is also home to the Garífuna, the descendants of African slaves who survived a shipwreck in 1635. The Garífuna mixed with the island Caribs and maintained a precarious independence until their surrender to the British in 1796. In the Colonial period, Honduras was a center for mining precious metals, and wealthy mining towns such as Tegucigalpa boasted handsome churches and cathedrals. In modern times Honduras has seen mostly military rule, although free elections were held in 1982.

Political instability after 1838 led to a decline in the traditional arts in Honduras, as did the spread of photography and lithography. Toribio Torres and Toribio Pérez worked in a late Colonial style, completing portraits of bishops and important families. History painting and heroic portraiture in the French academic style also appeared in Honduras at this time. Most of the sculptors working in Honduras in the nineteenth century were Europeans. In the twentieth century, Honduran artists were mostly trained in Europe, especially in Italy. Pablo Zelaya Sierra (1896–1933) was an early modernist interested in cubism. Confucio Montes de Oca (1896–1925) and the portrait painter Carlos Zúñiga Figueroa (1892–1964) were inspired by impressionism and Spanish baroque painting. Maximiliano Euceda (1891–1986) shows the influence of Sorolla. In 1940 the Escuela Nacional de Bellas Artes opened, bringing large-scale mural painting on the Mexican model to Honduras. Honduran muralist Miguel Angel Ruiz (b. 1928) worked with Diego Rivera and Juan O'Gorman.

Painting in Honduras since 1940 shows the influence of surrealism, naturalism, and primitivism. Beginning in the 1990s, Honduran artists began to make an impact on the international art scene. Painter Santos Arzú Quioto (b. 1963) has exhibited his work throughout Latin America and in the United States, and his work was awarded the gold medal by the Dominican Republic in 2000. Arzú's work was featured in the 48th Venice Biennale in 1999 and also at the Tapei Musuem of Fine Arts.

## NICARAGUA

At the time of the Spanish conquest in 1523, Nicaragua was home to two somewhat mysterious tribal groups: the Chorotega of the Pacific coast and the Guetar of the mainland and Caribbean drainage. The Chorotega may have been related to the ancient Nicoya culture of the Pacific coast of Costa Rica, whose ceramic remains are similar. The development of art during the Colonial period was slow, and at any rate much of it was destroyed by volcanic activity, earthquakes, and the depredations of pirates. In modern Nicaragua, the arts enjoyed little support under the Somoza regime, although the Sandinista revolution encouraged protest art in the 1980s.

Prominent artists of the nineteenth century in Nicaragua were Julio Toribio Jerez (active ca. 1850) and Adolfo León Caldera (active 1864–74). Artists on the threshold of modernism were Juan Bautista Cuadra (1877–1952), Antonio Sarria de Masaga, and sculptor Jorge Naros. Still lifes and landscapes were painted by Alejandro Alonso Rochi (1898–1973) and Roberto de la Selva, both of whom achieved success outside Nicaragua. Important modern artists include Pedro Ortiz de Masaga, Rubén Cuadra de León, and Ernesto Brown, the latter of whom founded the Círculo de Bellas Artes in 1937. Modern Nicaragua has also produced several prominent women artists, most notably Asilia Guillén, who explored painting and embroidery in a primitivist style. Armando Morales mixed abstract and figurative elements and achieved an international reputation. At the Escuela de Bellas Artes, founded in Managua in 1939, students studied both realism and abstraction. In the 1960s, the Praxis Group painted abstract landscapes and also actively opposed the Somoza regime. Artists of the Solentiname Commune explored primitivism and national themes. The Sandinistas renewed government sponsorship of the arts in the 1980s. The Union Nacional de Artistas Plásticas painted public murals and also made significant contributions to the development of the graphic arts in Nicaragua.

## COSTA RICA

The Spanish conquest of what is now Costa Rica began in 1509 and was completed around 1521. At the time of the conquest, the Guetar, a Chibcha-speaking people of South American origin, occupied the mainland and Caribbean coast. Between about 500 and 800 AD, another relatively advanced culture was centered on the Nicoya peninsula, whose descendants may have been the Chorotega groups living in Costa Rica and Nicaragua at the time of the Spanish conquest. Little if any art from the Colonial period made in Costa Rica has survived, and most artwork was imported from abroad. Since the 1940s, Costa Rica has had a stable economy and has experienced none of the political upheavals of its northern neighbors.

In the Colonial period, the majority of painting and sculpture in Costa Rica was imported from Ecuador, Guatemala, and Mexico. A local sculptural tradition first appeared in the nineteenth century with the work of Fadrique Gutierrez (1841–97). Juan Mora González (1862–95) produced portraits and statues of colored wood. Regular exhibitions were held in the 1920s and 1930s, and a debate commenced between modernists and academics. In the 1960s, the Grupo Ocho experimented with nonrepresentational art. Other progressive groups were the Grupo Taller and Grupo Totem. Juan Luis Rodríguez made significant contributions in the graphic arts. Of the modern movements, surrealism has had a lasting impact on the work of artists in Costa Rica.

## PANAMA

The pre-Columbian cultures of Panama were generally more advanced than their neighbors to the immediate north and produced sophisticated metalwork and pottery using techniques and designs imported from South America. Colonial art in Panama, however, was generally unexceptional, and most of the artists are anonymous. Artists working in Panama during the early Independence era were mostly foreigners, although the pace of artistic development accelerated in Panama after independence from Colombia in 1903. Modern and contemporary artists from Panama have made significant contributions to painting and the graphic arts.

Most of the artists working in Panama after independence from Spain in 1821 were foreigners interested in landscape and folk customs (*costumbrismo*). A Panamanian tradition in the arts did not develop until after the country gained independence from Colombia in 1903. Manuel Amador, Roberto Lewis, and Humberto Ivaldi painted portraits, still lifes, and the local landscape. The French academic tradition alternated with modernism. In 1913 the first national art school, the Academia Nacional de Pintura, was established. The school later split into the Escuela Nacional de Pintura and the Escuela Nacional de Artes Plásticas. Realism, expressionism, abstraction, and nationalist themes were explored by Juan Manuel Cedeño (b. 1940), Alfredo Sinclair (b. 1915), Eudoro Silvera, and Ciro Oduber (b. 1921). Public murals were painted by Juan Bautista Jenine (1922–82) and Issac Leonardo Benítez (b. 1940s). In 1950 the international avant-garde movement arrived in Panama, and local artists began to study abroad. Returning students introduced the arte informel movement from Spain, and pop art was introduced by Coqui Calderon. Julio Zachrisson was an important printmaker. Overall there has been very little interest in sculpture in modern Panama and a general lack of interest in performance, conceptual, and "earth" art, with the exception of Emilio Torres (b. 1944). Contemporary Panamanian artists are exploring themes from pre-Columbian myth, the Spanish heritage, religion and race, and the tropical landscape.

## COLOMBIA

The Spanish conquest of Colombia was particularly rapid and destructive, and little is known for certain about the artistic history of ancient Colombia. Surviving examples of pre-Columbian goldwork, however, show that Colombia was home to several advanced civilizations that flourished prior to the Spanish conquest. Major ethnolinguistic groups in Colombia were the Arawak, Carib, and Chibcha. In the 1530s, Spanish conquistadors scrambled for Colombian gold and emeralds as they searched for El Dorado, a fabled land of riches. Colonial Colombia was part of the Kingdom of New Granada, one of the wealthiest Spanish colonies, and handsome churches filled with paintings and sculptures were built in the larger cities and towns. Following independence from Spain, the liberator Simón Bolívar established Colombia as the center of a republic covering large parts of Central and South America, the Federation of Gran Colombia, which included the present countries of Colombia, Venezuela, Ecuador, and Panama. The federation broke up into 3 countries in 1830, and Panama finally broke off from Colombia in 1903. Colombia entered the twentieth century with progressive reforms but has suffered from chronic political instability from the 1950s to the present. In spite of these obstacles, Colombian artists have made important contributions to the visual arts.

Colombia played a major role in the struggle of South America for independence from Spain. In 1819, Pedro José Figueroa painted a portrait of Simón Bolívar as Liberator and Father of the Nation. The Neoclassic style, however, did not arrive in Colombia until after the 1830s, and it was based on European models other than the Spanish style. Battle scenes and heroic portraits were the order of the day. José Gabriel Tatís painted his large cycle known as the *115 Portraits* in watercolor in 1853. Epifanio Garay Caicedo and other anonymous painters immortalized the Colombian heroine Policarpa Salvarrieta, who was executed by Spanish soldiers in 1817. Colored lithographs were also distributed showing idealized images of a young-looking Simón Bolívar. In photography, García Heria (1816–87) introduced the daguerreotype to Colombia. Ramón Torres Méndez (1808–85) captured local dress and customs in his *Costumbres Neogranadinas.* Foreign traveler-reporter artists also documented local culture. Between 1850 and 1859, the Comisión Corográfica made maps and watercolor illustrations of Colombian culture and ethnology, led by Venezuelan Augustín Codazzi. The first national academy, the Escuela Nacional de Bellas Artes, was founded at Bogotá in the late nineteenth century. The French academic style was taught by Epifanio Garay, known primarily for his upper-class portraits. José María Espinosa (1796–1883) was a history painter and recorded incidents during his military service under General Narino.

In the early twentieth century, a school of landscape painting based on the English romantic tradition developed in Colombia, though Colombian painting was tempered by both Spanish realism and the plein-air method of the Barbizon school. The Colombian school was called the Escuela de la Sabana for its preference for views of the Sabana de Bogotá, a picturesque part of Colombia. Principal painters were Eugenio Peña (1860–1944), Roberto Parámo (1841–1915), and Ricardo Borrero Alvarez (1874–1931). Andrés de Santa María (1860–1945) was inspired by the French impressionists. Beginning in the 1930s, the Bachué Group rejected academicism and foreign subject matter. Native themes were emphasized, especially indigenous mythology. As in Mexico, Colombian muralists such as Pedro Nelgómez aimed their art at the popular community. Débora Arango addressed the status of women and social themes, although her art was initially rejected as immoral and obscene. Marco Ospina (1912–83) explored abstraction, whereas painter, printmaker, and sculptor Eduardo Ramírez Villamizar (b. 1923) introduced constructivism. Armando Villegas (active 1950s) was an abstract expressionist, although he also painted metal sculptures in the constructivist style. Edgar Negret (active 1950s) has a museum dedicated to his work. Figurative painter and printmaker Alejandro Obregón made political art in response to the massacre of Colombian students in the 1950s. In the 1960s, geometric abstraction was explored by Carlos Rojas (b. 1933), Manuel Hernández (b. 1928), and Omar Rago (b. 1928). Women artists such as Olga de Amaral (b. 1936) made engravings. Pop art also came to Colombia in the 1960s. Colombian pop artists were Bernardo Salcedo (b. 1939), Hernando Tejada (b. 1944), Beatriz González (b. 1938), Santiago Cárdenas (b. 1937), and Ana Mercedes Hoyos (b. 1942). Figurative art returned to Colombia in the 1970s, side by side with an interest in conceptual art. By far the most important contemporary artist in Colombia is Fernando Botero. Botero achieved an international reputation for his satirical vignettes of the important social classes in Colombia, whose massive figures recall both pre-Columbian statuettes and folk paintings from the Revolutionary period. Other important modern Colombian artists are Santiago Cárdenas (b. 1937) and Juan Camilo Uribe (b. 1945).

## VENEZUELA

Prior to the Spanish conquest, Venezuela was home to four major ethnolinguistic groups: the Arawak, Carib, Chibcha, and Paezan. Venezuela was also a crossroads between the ancient cultures of the northern Andes and groups living along the Caribbean coast. As in Colombia, examples of advanced goldwork suggest a sophisticated level of technical development. Venezuela was ravaged by German explorers and Spanish conquistadors in the 1530s who were searching for El Dorado, a mythical land of untold riches. The inhabitants of Venezuela mounted a strong resistance against the invaders, however, and Spanish settlement at first was slow. An indigenous people, the Tairona, led revolts against the Spanish crown in the Colonial period. Independence from Spain in the nineteenth century ushered in a series of military despots, and military rule has continued on and off in Venezuela to the present day. Venezuelan artists have made particularly important contributions to architecture and the visual arts in the twentieth century, especially in the area of nonrepresentational art.

Colonial art in Venezuela presumably followed traditional European models. Artistic development nearly ceased altogether at the beginning of the nineteenth century due to earthquakes and the chaos caused by power struggles following independence from Spain. Juan Lovera, a native painter from the Colonial period, made portraits of independence heroes. Prints glorifying the achievements of Simón Bolívar were made in Caracas, although other prints satirized the attempt to impose French revolutionary ideas on the social realities of colonial America. Other significant artists from the early Independence period were Hilarion Ibarra (active 1798–1854) and sculptor José de la Merced Rada (active 1797–1855). The Academia de Dibujo y Pintura opened in Caracas in 1835. Many of the artists working in Venezuela, however, were traveler–reporters from abroad, especially from Britain. Most of these artists were also portrait painters. Camille Pisarro briefly came to Venezuela at the age of twenty-two; he made drawings and paintings of the coastal and interior landscapes in the company of another foreign artist, the Danish painter Fritz Georg Melbye. There were also a few native Venezuelan artists. Martín Tovar y Tovar painted heroic portraits and *The Battle of Carabobo,* physically the largest painting in Latin America. Other significant artists were the teenaged prodigy Arturo Michelena, who studied in Paris, and Cristóbal Rojas.

Artistic activity in Venezuela accelerated rapidly after 1900. Tito Salas (1888–1974) was influenced by the Spanish painter Sorolla. The Círculo de Bellas Artes in Caracas, which included artists Manuel Cabré and Antonio Edmondo Monsanto, rebelled against the imported academic style. Painter Emilio Boggio lived in Paris and absorbed impressionism. Venezuela's first great painter was Armando Reverón (1889–1954). Reverón was initially influenced by the impressionists, but soon began producing highly original landscapes in a monochromatic style, based on a special color theory invented by the artist. Reverón was patronized by the wealthy elite in Caracas, but, like Gauguin, he shunned society and moved to a small seaside village in 1921, where he spent the remainder of his life. Other early twentieth-century painters were Federico Brandt, Luis Alfredo López Méndez, Rafael Monasterios, portrait and still-life painter Marcos Castillo, and Francisco Narváez.

Oil wealth and democracy brought sweeping social changes to Venezuela after 1936. Artists still studied in Paris, but many went instead to Mexico and the United States. Héctor Polo explored surrealism. Jacopo Borges initially studied cubism but later worked in an expressionist style. Luis Guevara Moreno and Oswaldo Vigas drew their inspiration from pre-Columbian art, as did pop artist Marisol, who has gained an international reputation. Notable printmakers were Luisa and Alivio Palacios. Bárbaro Rivas, who had no formal training, painted native scenes. Avant-garde groups also appeared in Venezuela: the Taller Libre de Arte, Los Disidentes, Pez Dorado, and Presencia 70. Venezuelan artists were influenced by European and American avant-garde movements, but mixed them freely and were never dominated by a single movement. In the second half of the twentieth century, Venezuela experienced exciting and original developments in nonrepresentational and conceptual art. Alejandro Otero (b. 1921) was initially shaped by Picasso, but he later became interested in the purely formal art of Mondrian, and his paintings changed to rhythmic bars of color on a plain white surface. Jesús Rafael Soto (b. 1923) explored the relationships between physical and pictorial space by superimposing two-dimensional patterns painted on transparent Plexiglas. Carlos Cruz-Diez (b. 1923) created interesting perceptual experiments by assembling boxes filled with cardboard louvers painted in different colors, which created shifting patterns depending on the viewer's position. Apolinar (b. 1928), a self-taught artist, produced a series of imaginative books, booklike art objects, and mixed-media compositions. Marisol Escobar (b. 1930) has continued to make headlines in the postmodern art world. Marisol was born in Paris of wealthy Venezuelan parents and studied art in Paris and New York. Marisol creates flat "sculptures" in plywood and paint, sometimes arranged in life-size scenes. Her *Self Portrait Looking at the Last Supper* (1982–84) sets up a playful visual dialogue between the viewer/artist and the Renaissance masterpiece.

## ECUADOR

Ancient Ecuador was home to several pre-Columbian cultures, whose artifacts show surprising similarities to Mexican art. Prior to the Spanish conquest, Ecuador was made a part of the great empire of the Incas, of which it formed a part of the northern quadrant, or Chinchayasuyu. Colonial Ecuador was immensely rich in emeralds and developed its own school of religious art, examples of which were exported throughout the Spanish colonial world. Modern Ecuadorian artists turned inward for inspiration and made significant contributions to the development of surrealism in Latin America.

Ecuadorian artists began to paint outside of religious traditions in the early nineteenth century. An anonymous Ecuadorian artist painted *The Execution of the Heroine Rosa Zarate and Nicolas de la Peña in Tumaco* in 1812. Other anonymous painters made portraits of military leaders in oil on traditional tin sheet. Antonio Salas (1795–1860) began as a late Colonial painter in Quito, but also portrayed heroes and leaders of the revolution, especially Simón Bolívar. After 1838 he returned to religious works and painted scenes from the life of the Virgin for the Augustinian order. His son Ramón Salas (ca. 1815–80) was also a painter. Nineteenth-century Ecuadorian art swung between romanticism and realism, and produced a number of paintings in the *costumbrismo* tradition (paintings of regional people and customs). Painters were Juan Agustín Guerrero, Rafael Troya (1845–1920), and *costumbrista* painter Joaquín Pinto. Sculpture did not develop as rapidly during this period.

In 1912 European art teachers began to arrive in Ecuador. The Escuela Nacional de Bellas Artes was founded in Quito. Ecuadorian artists in the 1930s explored issues of national identity but remained open to the ideas of the European avant-garde. The failure of the liberal revolution begun in 1895 ushered in the socialist ideals of the Mexican muralists. Notable painters were Camilio Egas, Oswaldo Guayasamín, a mestizo artist who experimented with expressionism and cubism, Manuel Rendón Seminario, and Araceli Gilbert. Galo Galecio

(b. 1912) was a printmaker who went to Mexico to study at the Taller de Gráfica Popular (see the discussion of Mexico). Galecio was also a mural painter, and he collaborated with Oswaldo Guayasamín on monumental murals in Quito and Tulcán. A reaction to national themes appeared in the 1960s, replaced by a preference for pre-Columbian themes treated in an international style. Enrique Tábara explored surrealism and symbolism. Ramiro Jácome and Washington Iza founded Los Quatro Mosqueteros, an "anti salon" group. Oswaldo Viteri (b. 1931) established an international reputation with his assemblages, in which he attached found objects to his canvases. In the 1970s, an oil boom brought sweeping changes to Ecuador. Mauricio Bueno engaged conceptual ideas about art and postmodernism, whereas other artists drew on neo-nationalist themes. Primitivism and magic realism were explored by native Quechua painters, including Gonzalo Endara Crow and Jaime Andrade. Etcher Nicolas Svistoonoff represented the graphic arts in Ecuador.

## PERU

Civilization developed somewhat earlier in Peru than in Mexico and Central America. Large ceremonial centers from as early as 2,500 BC have been excavated in Peru, along with examples of highly advanced textiles, some of which were woven without the aid of looms. Later Peruvian civilizations also boasted adept metalworkers and ceramicists. Spectacular discoveries in the 1980s revealed the splendor and technical skills of the Moche, a lost civilization that flourished along the coasts of central Peru from about 100 AD to 750 AD. A succession of military states arose after 500 AD, whose far-flung conquests incorporated large parts of highland and lowland Peru. The last of these was the mighty Inca empire of the Quechua people, which stretched from Ecuador to Chile and was the largest empire in ancient America. Much was lost during the Spanish conquest, which began in 1532 but was not completed until the end of the sixteenth century. The descendants of the Inca staged episodic revolts against the Spanish crown until Peru finally gained independence from Spain in the nineteenth century. Peru produced important art during the Revolutionary era, and modern Peru continues to make significant contributions to the arts.

Colonial painters in Peru often combined devotional pictures of the Virgin with images of Pachamama, the Inca mother goddess. These paintings are still in place in older churches, and sculptures from the Colonial period are used for religious processions. José Gil de Castro (1785–1841), a mulatto painter, was the most important artist working in Peru during the struggle for independence from Spain. His early training is unknown, but presumably he was apprenticed to a late Colonial master in Lima. Castro's canvases show heroes of the revolution in a manner recalling paintings of religious martyrs from the Colonial period and often use the same iconography. His *Portrait of the Martyr Olaya* from 1823 is one of the most famous images from revolutionary Latin America. In it the Peruvian patriot is shown wearing white clothes indicating his innocence. Castro also completed a well-known *Portrait of Simón Bolívar in Bogotá* in 1823, in a manner recalling French academic portraits of Napoleon Bonaparte. Painter Pancho Fierro was a self-taught mulatto and was known mostly for his satirical vignettes of contemporary life. Other significant painters of the nineteenth century were Ignacio Merino, Francisco Lazo, José Correia de Lima, and Teófilo Castillo, who moved away from academicism toward realism. The Escuela Nacional de Bellas Artes was founded in 1919.

Between 1922 and 1950, Peruvian artists advocated *indigenísmo*. Many writers and artists in Peru shared the ideas of Peruvian Socialist Party leader Mariategui and contributed to his vanguard review *Amauta,* which advocated a return to the communelike society of the Incas. Enrique Camino Brent and Mario Urteaga Alvarado made art in a social realist style. Others were interested in European modernism, including Sabino Springuett, a follower of the Fauves, and Carlos Quispe Asin. Other modernists were Juan Manuel Ugarte Eléspuru and Macedonio de la Torre. Modernism and indigenism are blended in the work of Sérvulo Gutiérrez Alarcón and Fernando de Szyszlo, who investigated abstraction and pre-Columbian myth and helped form the Grupo Espacio. Other artists, including Victor Humareda, remained within the figurative tradition. Murals were painted by Teodoro Núñez Ureta. Other important Peruvian modernists were José Milner Cajahuaringa and Alberto Guzmán, who created geometric metal forms and hybrid creatures from old machine parts.

## BOLIVIA

The high mountain plateaus of Bolivia were home to several advanced civilizations prior to the rise of the Inca, who incorporated Bolivia into their vast South American empire. Indeed, many social and artistic practices once thought to be Incan are now believed to have originated in the earlier civilizations that developed in the area of Lake Titicaca in Bolivia. The major indigenous group in Bolivia is the Aymara. In colonial times, Bolivia produced enormous wealth from the great silver mines at Potosí. The mines once produced so much ore that the Spanish authorities had trouble producing coins of acceptable quality on time from the huge quantity of metal flowing into their coffers. The fronts of colonial palaces in Bolivia were reportedly covered in sheets of solid silver and gold. Since gaining independence from Spain in 1825, Bolivia has experienced nearly 200 military coups and countercoups, although civilian rule was finally established in 1982.

The quality of art in Bolivia entered a steep decline after independence in 1825. French academic art provided the main model for painters, although Colonial traditions were maintained by Manuel Ugalde. A painter known as Borda completed landscapes and portraits. Melchor María Mercado painted watercolors of Indians and mestizos in the *costumbrista* manner. The ideas of the European avant-garde entered Bolivia in the 1920s and 1930s. In Sucre, the Anteo Group painted murals and fantasies inspired by pre-Columbian art. The Salón Romero introduced abstract expressionism and the ideas of the New York School. Social and indigenist themes have dominated Bolivian art since the 1930s, especially in the work of artists of the Generación del '52. Since the 1980s, Bolivian artists have dealt primarily with popular urban themes: loss of identity, the politically oppressed, students, prostitutes, and drug dealers and addicts. Important modern Bolivian artists are Roberto Valcaral (b. 1951) and Fernando Rodríguez-Casas, a formalist interested in problems of space and perspective.

## GUYANA

The indigenous people of Guyana were the Warrou. Major linguistic groups were Arawak and Carib. Guyana was colonized by the Spanish, French, Dutch, and English, although the majority of the colonial settlements in the seventeenth century were Dutch. Indigenous peoples in Guyana still practice traditional crafts in use from before contact with Europeans, although the visual arts were not encouraged among the Dutch settlers. The abolition of slavery in 1834 led to waves of immigrant workers from India, which added a strong Asian component to the African and European cultural heritage of the country. In the twentieth century, small artistic communities appeared in Georgetown, the largest colonial city and now capital of the independent Republic of Guyana. What was then called British Guiana was a crown colony until 1953, when Guyana was granted home rule.

In 1931 the Arts and Crafts Society put on the first art show in Guyana in Georgetown. The Guyana Art Group was formed in 1944. The first native Guyanese artist to achieve critical attention was Samuel Horace Broodhagen (1883–1950). Aubrey Williams (1926–90) painted in an abstract expressionist style; his intense tropical colors recall Paul Gauguin. Oswald Hussein (b. 1954) carves wood sculptures inspired by Arawak mythology. In 1970 a group of radical artists founded the Expressionova Group, which was interested in surrealism. Contemporary artists in Guyana are rejecting academic concerns.

Basketry, featherwork, and weaving are still practiced by all the indigenous peoples of Guyana. Ceramics are divided into two main styles: the Mabaruma and Karinga styles. Mabaruma ceramics are characterized by modeling in low and high relief with red or white slips. Karinga ceramics are characterized by red or black geometric bands on white, sometimes with dots. Mention must be made of the magnificent feather crowns of the Waiwai. Feathers are also woven into the hair in many regions. Guyana is also home to sophisticated basketry, including a unique type of manioc press whose workings are said to resemble the digestion of an anaconda snake.

## SURINAME

Suriname (formerly Dutch Guiana) gained its independence in 1975 and has experienced socialism, military coups, and civilian rule in the meantime. Suriname is one of the most ethnically diverse countries in South America, with peoples of African, Indian, Indonesian, and European origin. Major ethnolinguistic groups at the time of European contact were Arawak and Carib. The Dutch colonists did not encourage the development of the arts, but the indigenous peoples of Suriname today have found a lively market for their traditional handicrafts among tourists. A small artistic community exists in Paramaribo, the capital of Suriname.

Protestant Dutch settlers brought no real artistic tradition to Suriname, although lithographs were made depicting life in the colony, along with a few landscapes in watercolor. Such art was mostly the work of Dutch and European amateurs. Venezuelan painter Pedro Lovera visited Suriname in 1885. Alphonse Favery (1900–79) introduced impressionism in the early twentieth century. Sculpture existed, but it was imported mostly from Italy to decorate colonial gardens. Erwin de Vries (b. 1929), however, has experimented with abstract sculpture. Another noteworthy modern artist working in Suriname is Stuart Robles de Medina (b. 1930). Decorative arts in Suriname are mostly imported from Europe, with the exception of crafts practiced by indigenous peoples.

Traditional palm baskets from Suriname are painted red or black. Wooden benches are also carved in the shapes of jungle animals. Indigenous peoples wear necklaces made from seeds and animal teeth, with feather rings or crowns on their heads. Earthenware pottery is made by coiling; it is then decorated with parallel lines in brown and black and motifs of snakes, frogs, and human faces. Suriname pottery is still fired in open-air kilns. Traditional ceramic drinking bowls are especially sought after by modern collectors.

## FRENCH GUIANA

The Department of French Guiana is the only nonindependent state in South America; it officially remains an overseas department of France. French Guiana was inhabited by Arawak-speaking and other groups prior to European contact. The French colony was first settled in 1604. In modern times, French Guiana was known mostly for its notorious penal colony, the prison on Devil's Island, which operated until 1951. The artistic heritage of French Guiana is unique for its employment of prisoner-artists, who completed several major artistic commissions on the mainland. Today French Guiana has a small but active community of artists.

A distinctive type of gold jewelry inspired by convicts' chains was formerly worn in French Guiana. French Guiana also produced several prisoner-artists of note. François La Grange painted the interior of the chapel of Isle Royale between 1938 and 1941, and also completed works in oil on canvas following his release. Mangipulo was a native (Galibi) artist. Jone Lie A Fo (b. 1945) came from Suriname and settled in French Guiana and has had exhibitions in the Netherlands, Venezuela, and the Caribbean. Artists' groups include Mi Wani Sabi (I Want to Know), the Association des Artistes de Guyane (1979), and the Association des Artistes Peintres (1980), who are primarily avant-garde in nature. Art students from French Guiana are currently studying in Europe and the United States.

In traditional arts and crafts, the forest environment is the main source of artistic imagery. Feathers are worn as headdresses and on the body. Live birds are sometimes injected with pigments to produce entirely new colors of feathers. Tattooing and other forms of body adornment are also practiced. Bead jewelry is made from shell, glass, seeds, and stones. Traditional basketwork from French Guiana features geometric or animal-shaped ornaments that are woven directly into the functional parts of the basket. Pottery is also made (primarily for tourists) in red, white, and black wares.

## BRAZIL

Modern Brazil is the largest and most populous country in South America. From the earliest European explorations of Brazil in 1500 to the twentieth century, however, the indigenous people of the region are estimated to have declined in number from about 3 million to 200,000. In spite of this, the profound geographic isolation of much of the interior of Brazil allowed many indigenous cultures to survive more or less intact, until penetration by logging interests in the late twentieth century. At the time of European contact, the indigenous inhabitants were mostly nomadic Tupí-Guaraní Indians. In the colonial period, Brazil's position as Portugal's most important territory in America put a distinctively west Iberian stamp on the art, language, and society of this part of Latin America. Due to the large number of African slaves brought to the Caribbean and Brazil, African culture also had a greater impact on the development of popular art in Brazil than in most other Latin American countries. Brazil in the twentieth century experienced both civilian and military rule. Modern Brazil has made great contributions to the arts, and not only in Latin America: Brazilian artists helped shape the development of conceptual and performance-based art in the 1960s and 1970s in the United States and Europe.

The Academia Imperial das Bellas Artes opened in Rio de Janeiro in 1826, bringing the French academic style to Brazil. Neoclassical ideas gave way to romanticism in the 1830s. Foreign traveler-artists also worked in Brazil, most notably Jean-Baptiste Debret (active 1816–31), who was court painter to the Braganzas in Brazil and the founder of the Academia Imperial. He is best known for his prints showing Brazilian jungle landscapes and indigenous tribes of the interior. These are ostensibly realistic, but are tinged with a certain romantic spirit. Brazilian art was unusually conservative for the remainder of the nineteenth century.

Modernism arrived in Brazil with the Semana de Arte Moderna in Sâo Paulo in 1922, co-organized by painter Emiliano de Cavalcanti (1897–1976). Contributing painters included Anita Malfatti, who introduced avant-garde ideas to Brazil and also contributed to popular American magazines such as *Vogue* and *Vanity Fair*. Malfatti was interested mostly in cubism and futurism, but also expressionism. A monthly revue of modern art appeared in São Paulo in 1922, the futurist-inspired *Klaxon*. Tarsila do Amaral studied in Barcelona and Paris and was initially interested in the ideas of Fernand Léger, but also in primitivism and surrealism. Back in Brazil she associated with various modernist groups and contributed illustrations to the modernist manifesto *Revista de Antropofágica*, so called because its aim was to "devour" the art of the colonizer and appropriate his virtues in cannibal fashion, thus reconciling foreign and native traditions. The ideas of the Bauhaus and constructivism also had an impact in Brazil, especially on the decorative arts and design. Brazilian artists of the 1930s and 1940s, addressed social and labor themes, especially Eugênio de Proença Sigaud (1889–1979), José Antonio da Silva (b. 1909), and Cándido Portinari (1903–62). Da Silva was a rural laborer in São Paulo for many years and painted scenes of the working class in the area.

Like Mexico, Brazil has a strong and continuing tradition of popular prints. Sheets or pamphlets of popular stories and verses called *cordeles* were made with woodcuts on the cover. These could be cheaply reproduced and were often collected by ordinary Brazilians and kept in suitcases. The 1950s saw the establishment of Brazilian printmaking clubs, the Clube de Gravura de Porto-Alegre and the Clube de Gravura de Baje, both with a popular leftist slant. Vasco Prado (b. 1914), a co-founder of the Clube de Gravura de Porto-Alegre, advocated social realism and produced prints showing gauchos and herdsmen of the prairies of Rio Grande do Sul. Henrique Oswald produced aquatints, etchings, and drypoint drawings with more ambiguous subjects, although they had provocative titles such as *Inflation* (1944–50). Newton Cavalcanti (b. 1930) made woodcuts and wood engravings showing traditional religious beliefs. Lasar Segall (1891–1957) was a Russian Jew who visited Brazil in 1912 and focused on Brazilian themes in his paintings and prints. In Europe he met Otto Dix and George Grosz and joined the German expressionists. Segall made woodcuts and drypoints with social themes, including prostitutes and other outcasts.

In the 1950s and 1960s, Brazilian artists explored abstraction, constructivism, concrete and neo-concrete art, informal art, kinetic art, optical art, and process art. None of these artists, however, belonged entirely to these movements. Brazilian artists were among the first to move away from a strictly visual experience of art to art that engaged the entire human being. Lygia Clark (1920–88), a practicing psychologist as well as an artist, produced organic shapes from sheet metal and rubber that she called "bugs" and "grubs," which the artist or viewer could manipulate and rearrange in an endless variety of spatial permutations. These artworks effectively broke away from the limiting idea of the picture within a frame and the static conception of traditional sculpture. Clark later went on to further experiments in viewer participation with abstractions created from elastic bands attached to the bodies of a group of participants, creating a web of geometric possibilities that was constantly changing, in which the motion of each participant affected all the others. Hélio Oiticica (1937–80) was also interested in the arrangement of surfaces, but in a more geometric style. "Nuclei" and "spatial reliefs," flat pieces of wood or metal whose shapes could be rearranged, were suspended in space or over mirrors. His later "bolides" were containers of various sorts with moveable parts, painted in colors and designed to present a variety of spatial experiences to the viewer. Oiticica was also interested in public interaction with his artworks, and people were photographed dancing next to his portable bolides, which could be placed on sidewalks. In 1970, Oiticica installed a series of "nests" at the Museum of Modern Art in New York as small unrestricted leisure spaces to be occupied and shaped by the public. Lygia Pape (b. 1929) created moveable fundamental shapes as part of her *Book of Creation,* in which the intellectual progress of the human species was presented as a series of unfolding abstractions, which she and a companion then photographed in various outdoor settings. Pape also staged outdoor performances in which crowds were invited to put their heads through holes cut in a colossal piece of fabric, creating a complex fluid surface that was constantly changing. In addition to their democratic approach to art-making, Brazilian artists of the 1960s and 1970s subverted the idea of the museum or monument as the only places where people can see and experience art. Sergio Camargo (b. 1930) has made a significant impact on the international art scene. His constructivist-inspired wooden reliefs, painted in monochromatic colors, explore the full spatial potentials of simple two-dimensional shapes: rows of circles, for example, become complex assemblies of tubelike extrusions that curve outward in a multiplicity of directions. Mira Schendel (1919–88) was raised in Italy but moved to Brazil in 1949, where she began painting with the encouragement of Sergio Camargo. Schendel went on to create interesting and unusual graphic artworks by making scratches on inked glass and then transferring them to thin Japanese paper. She also made flexible "sculptures" from knotted pieces of paper, which could be rearranged in any way the artist or viewer chose. More recently, artist Zé Caboclo has attracted attention with his brightly painted groupings of small ceramic figures, which are based on genre subjects and themes drawn from popular culture, such as doctors and their patients, soccer teams, and so on.

## POPULAR ART BY NATIVE PEOPLES IN BRAZIL

Many tribal groups in Brazil have retained their indigenous craft traditions. The abundance of plant materials in the rain forest led to many distinctive and sophisticated styles of basket and cloth weaving, especially among the Timbira, Kayabi, Xavante, Desana, Tukuna, and Paresi peoples. Featherwork, body painting, and masks for tribal dances are also highly developed art forms in Brazil, especially among the Xingu, Kadiwéu, and Kaapor, the latter group making particularly outstanding objects from feathers. Other forms of body art and deformations such as head flattening are also practiced. The Yanomamo wear necklaces made from animal claws.

## CHILE

The northern half of modern Chile was once part of Collasuyu, the southern quarter of the Inca empire. The Quechua-speaking groups living there were linguistically related to the Incas. Central and southern Chile was inhabited by the Araucanian Indians (who call themselves the Mapuche). The Mapuche lived in both nomadic and settled communities and strongly resisted both the Incas and the establishment of Spanish authority after 1541. During the struggle for independence in Latin America, the Mapuche briefly forced Spain to acknowledge the autonomy of their Kingdom of Arauco. The Araucanians were not completely subjugated until 1880, and the descendant of the king of Araucania still lives in exile in France. Modern Chile has produced art of international stature.

Peruvian painter José Gil de Castro (1785–1841; see the discussion of Peru) accompanied General Bernardo O'Higgins on the campaign for Chilean independence. Castro painted society portraits in Chile as well as the revolutionary heroes O'Higgins and San Martín. During his stay in Chile, art moved away from colonial traditions toward revolutionary subject matter. European artists also settled in Chile. The Academia de Pintura was founded in 1849. The school produced primarily landscape painters: Pedro Lira, Juan Francisco González, and Alfredo Helsby. Sculptures in a neoclassical style were produced by Rebeca Matte, who immortalized the heroes of the War of the Pacific against Peru and Bolivia (1879–83).

Arturo Gordon and the "Generación del Trece" broke with the academic tradition at the beginning of the twentieth century. In the 1920s, the Grupo Montparnasse pushed forward the break with naturalism, importing ideas from the Fauves. Chilean artists, including Pablo Burchard, studied in Europe. The Grupo Rectángulo, a group interested in abstract art, competed with other imported ideas from Arte Informel, constructivism, and geometric abstraction. Social realism, often combined with discarded or found objects, predominated in Chilean art after the 1960s. Significant artists include José Balmes (Grupo Signo) and especially Roberto Matta Echaurren (b. 1911). Matta traveled to Europe as a young man and joined the surrealists in 1938. Matta's surrealist paintings explore different levels of reality, using the surrealist practice of automatism, in which artistic forms are left to develop freely by the subconscious mind. Paintings like *Invasion of the Night* (1941) incorporate biomorphic abstractions in a manner reminiscent of Arp and Joan Miró. Matta is also one of a few surrealist artists to deal directly with political themes. Matta has shown in New York, Mexico, Rome, and Paris. Printmaking in Chile was represented by the Taller 99, active in the 1940s and 1950s.

## PARAGUAY

Indigenous peoples of Paraguay included the Chaco and the Guaraní, the main culture of the region. Most were hunter-gatherers, although some were farmers. From 1608 until their expulsion from Spanish America in 1767, the Jesuits strongly established themselves in south and east Paraguay, building missions in even the most isolated areas of the country. Following independence from Spain, Paraguay experienced a massive loss of human life in wars with neighboring Uruguay, Brazil, and Argentina. The political situation in Paraguay was particularly unstable after World War II; nonetheless Paraguay has made significant contributions to Latin American art.

Colonial traditions in popular art from Paraguay continued long after independence from Spain. During the War of the Triple Alliance (1864–70), lively and humorous wood engravings were published in the newspapers *El Cabichuí* and *El Sentinela*. Academic naturalism, however, was the rule in the fine arts. Paraguayan artists in the nineteenth and early twentieth centuries studied abroad in Rome, Spain, and France. The influence of Cézanne and the Fauves appeared in the 1920s in the work of Julián de la Herrería, who trained in Madrid, and Jaime Bestard. In 1954 the Arte Nuevo Group was founded. Olga Blinder was an important artist associated with the group. Paraguayan art of the second half of the twentieth century has experimented with the ideas of the European avant-garde alongside figuration, but also with cubism, expressionism, art deco, and Mexican muralism. Osvald Salerno (b. 1952) has made significant contributions to the progressive art scene in Paraguay. American popular culture and a certain cult of American modernity have also played a significant role in Paraguayan art after mid-century. Alternatively, the work of artist Carlos Colombino addressed human rights violations by Paraguayan regimes. Another movement, Re-Figuración, explores the nature of pictorial signs.

## URUGUAY

Prior to European contact, Uruguay was inhabited by the Guaraní, the Chanae, and the Charrúa, who were the largest indigenous group. Spanish explorers were the first Europeans to visit Uruguay, but the country was colonized instead by the Portuguese. After a prolonged struggle, Spain finally obtained Uruguay in 1778, although by this time most of the indigenous peoples had been driven off, sold into slavery, or exterminated. Uruguay was reconquered by the Portuguese from Brazil in 1817, although independence was finally achieved in 1825 with help from Argentina. Modern Uruguay has become one of the most prosperous countries in South America and has experienced both socialism and military rule. A civilian government was restored in 1984, although the electorate has rejected proposals to open the state oil monopoly to foreign investors. Uruguayan artists have made important contributions to modern Latin American art, especially in the graphic arts and sculpture.

Artistic production in colonial Uruguay was extremely limited. Traveler-reporter artists descended on Uruguay in the nineteenth century, however, and made drawings and lithographs of contemporary life. The most notable of these was Conrad Martens, an Englishman who had accompanied Charles Darwin to South America. The first important native artist was Juan Manuel Blanes (1830–1901). Blanes left school at an early age but managed to teach himself to draw. Later he studied in Italy, where he learned portraiture and history painting. Blanes traveled throughout southern South America, painting mostly historical allegories and portraits of military heroes. He eventually returned to Italy in 1898, where he spent the remainder of his life. Noteworthy Uruguayan sculptors around the turn of the century included Juan Manuel Ferrari, a disciple of Rodin.

Modernism arrived in Uruguay with Carlos Federigo Saez, although amateur painter Gustavo Lazarini (b. 1918) painted society portraits in watercolor in a traditional style until the 1940s. Impressionism was introduced, although somewhat belatedly, by Pedro Blanes Viale. The Círculo de Bellas Artes was founded in 1905. Pedro Figari (1861–1938) was a post-impressionist painter who depicted the contemporary life of blacks, creoles, and gauchos. Figari was initially trained as a lawyer, and as the director of the School of Fine Arts and Crafts in Montevideo, he introduced radical reforms in educational practices and the arts. In 1924 he helped found Amigos del Arte, a group dedicated to the defense of modern art. Modern printmaking in Uruguay was represented by Carlos González (b. 1905) and Rafael Barradas (1890–1929). González, a self-taught printmaker, made wood engravings of the lives of the *campesinos* (peasants), including expressive renderings of duels between peasants and of funeral processions. Barradas traveled to France, Italy, and Switzerland, but eventually settled in Spain. He was initially attracted to futurism, but later developed his own styles of expression, which he called "vibracionismo," "clownism," and "mystic" painting. Cubism and the avant-garde were introduced in the 1930s and 1940s by the Taller Torres García in Montivideo, headed by artist Joaquín Torres-García (1874–1949). Torres-García published theoretical books on art and also founded several other influential art groups prior to the establishment of the Taller Torres García. Torres-García erected his *Cosmic Monument,* a freestanding wall covered with glyphlike symbols, in the Parque Rodo in Montevideo. He considered this sculpture to be a compendium of his ideas about art. Another important modern Uruguayan sculptor is Gonzalo Fonseca. Arden Quin (b. 1913) was born in Uruguay but went to Argentina and cofounded the important movement Arte Concreto-Invención in Buenos Aires (see the discussion of Argentina). On the contemporary art scene in Uruguay, Luis Solari makes drypoint etchings and animal masks based on indigenous mythology.

## ARGENTINA

There is very little material evidence for the pre-Columbian inhabitants of Argentina, probably because the region was sparsely inhabited prior to European contact. Main indigenous groups were the Guaraní and Diaguita. Spanish settlement was slow, and Argentina remained largely empty until well into colonial times. Modern Argentina's contributions to the arts, however, are impressive, in spite of prolonged periods of authoritarian rule and severe economic crises. Argentinian artists founded important movements in modern Latin American art and are especially prominent in the areas of abstraction, surrealism, and nonrepresentational art.

Artistic activity during the colonial period in Argentina was extremely limited, more than in any other Latin American country. There were far fewer gold and silver mines in Argentina than in Mexico or Peru, although there was a steady flow of imported metalwork through Argentina because of its location astride an important trans–South American trade route. Decorative objects from colonial Argentina include special cups for drinking local *mate* tea, usually gourds or polished nuts with silver mounts, including a small silver straw. This unique tea service is still used in Argentina today.

European artists began visiting Argentina regularly after 1816. Painter Cándido López portrayed the War of the Triple Alliance (1865–70) against Paraguay. Prilidiano Pueyrredón painted portraits and nudes. A national school for the arts, the Escuela Nacional de Bellas Artes, was founded in 1878. Eduardo Sívori was a prominent artist at the beginning of the twentieth century. Argentina's contributions to modern art are impressive by any standard. Emilio Pettoruti introduced cubism with his interior views and still lifes painted in a precise analytical cubist style that was still partly representational. The door was opened to avant-garde ideas from Europe, especially arte informel and abstraction. Xul Solar (born Alejandro Solari, 1887– 1963) traveled to Europe and returned to Argentina to paint mystical landscapes, imaginary cities, and dancing figures in a style influenced by both cubism and surrealism. Painter Batlle Planas and especially his pupil Roberto Aizenberg (b. 1928) were more directly influenced by surrealism, though on highly individualistic lines. Aizenberg was familiar with the surrealist concept of automatism, but his painting style is closer to de Chirico and Picasso. His early figures in empty landscapes recall Dalí, although his later work focused on Babel-like towers, sexual symbols that also represented accumulated culture and tradition.

One of the most creative periods in Latin American art began in 1944 with the publication of *Arturo* in Buenos Aires. The avant-garde review only ran one issue but gathered together artists who later formed two highly influential movements: Arte Concreto-Invención and Arte MADI. Arte Concreto-Invención held only two exhibitions, but the same group went on to form Arte MADI (an acronym that can be interpreted alternately as Movimiento de Arte De Invención or MAtérialisme DIalectique). These artists were inspired by constructivism, Dada, and Mondrian, but all of them vigorously rejected surrealism and automatism in favor of nonrepresentational artworks that were carefully thought out beforehand. Sculptor Gyula Kosice (b. 1924) was born in Hungary but settled in Buenos Aires. Kosice created articulated wood sculptures called "Royi," composed of abstract shapes joined by turn pins that could be repositioned by the artist to form various combinations. In addition to his kinetic sculptures, Kosice was also probably the first artist in the world to experiment with "light" sculptures made from sections of glowing neon tubes. Diyi Laañ (b. 1927), Juan Mele (b. 1923), and Juan Bay (b. 1892) created paintings composed of broad geometric areas of color arranged in relation to each other rather than to the square and rectangular shapes dictated by the traditional picture frame, which was considered limiting and irrelevant. Arden Quin (b. 1913), originally from Uruguay, created articulated paintings in which the various abstract forms are separated but can be repositioned in relation to each other on a framework of interconnecting struts. Enio Iommi (b. 1926) created small-scale sculptures in which more delicate geometric shapes were carefully placed in relation to each other, then connected by slender metal rods. Argentinian artists were represented in the Realités

Nouvelles installation in Paris in 1948, introducing the ideas of Arte MADI to the art world outside Latin America.

## THE CARIBBEAN

The Caribbean was probably settled several times in prehistory by separate but related groups of migrating peoples, mostly from the area of Venezuela and the Guianas. The last wave of immigrants prior to European contact took place perhaps between the twelfth and fourteenth centuries of the Christian era. These were mostly Arawaks and Caribs, although the Arawaks living in the Caribbean have always called themselves the Taíno. The Taíno spread throughout the Greater Antilles and were probably the people who greeted Columbus when he arrived at the end of the fifteenth century. The Taíno were mostly a peaceful people who survived by hunting and fishing, but they also raised simple crops. The Caribs, on the other hand, were fierce warriors and cannibals and raided both Taíno and later Spanish settlements for prisoners. The Taíno were forced to labor for the Spaniards and quickly fell prey to overwork and European diseases against which they had no immunity. At the end of the sixteenth century, a Spanish priest counted only sixty Taíno left in the Caribbean. To make up for the deficit caused by the loss of Indian labor, Spanish colonists began importing large numbers of African slaves to the Caribbean, and African culture has made a deep and lasting impression on Caribbean art, music, and religion. The Caribbean islands changed hands several times during the colonial period, and the Spanish, French, English, Dutch, and Americans have all at one time laid claim to various islands. In spite of political unrest and widespread poverty, modern Caribbean artists have made very important contributions to the visual arts, both in Latin America and the wider world.

The first Spanish settlers in the Caribbean brought Spanish and Flemish religious paintings with them from Europe. There were some sculptures in churches and official buildings. Most were brought from Seville, although some were imported from Mexico. Local folk artists also carved painted wooden figures of saints and other Christian subjects called *santos.* Most of these so-called "primitive" *santos* were heavily influenced by African culture because Taíno artistic traditions had largely disappeared by 1550. Traditional *santos* are still produced by folk artists in many Caribbean villages today. Fanciful prints depicting the Caribbean landscape and its inhabitants were made as early as the sixteenth century by Dutch printmaker Theodore de Bry. These fine prints were widely known in Europe, and they helped construct Western ideas of the "noble savage." Colonial art in the seventeenth and eighteenth centuries was limited primarily to Dutch and English engravings showing Caribbean ports and towns. Official portraits were also painted for the colonial authorities.

The search for national identity in Caribbean art began in the 1930s. Art academies were founded in Cuba and Haiti. Art, however, was still mostly based on European examples until well into the twentieth century. Modernism, including realism, neo-impressionism, and the ideas of the avant-garde, came to the Caribbean from Europe. After 1940, Caribbean art developed rapidly on its own. The art addressed social problems, mostly the balance of colonial power and dependence on foreign wealth. Philomé Obin (1892–1984) represented the Caribbean's first independence leader in *Toussaint l'Ouverture Receives the Letter from the First Consul* (1945). Other Caribbean artists turned inward, drawing on the rich Afro-Caribbean spiritual tradition for inspiration. In Caribbean *vodoun* (voodoo), Catholic saints had long been identified with Yoruba gods from Africa. Haitian painter Hector Hippolyte (1894–1948) was initiated as a voodoo priest, and he painted representations of voodoo divinities such as *Agoué and His Consort* (1945–48). Hippolyte was greatly admired by surrealist poet André Breton, and the painter's work was included in the first surrealist exposition in Paris after the war in 1947. Rigaud Benoit (1911–86), a disciple of Hippolyte, painted scenes of Caribbean life and folk customs in oil on Masonite. Georges Liautaud (b. 1899) and Wilson Bigaud (b. 1931) also drew on voodoo traditions: Liautaud made totemic sculptures from iron (a metal endowed with spiritual power in Africa), whereas Bigaud painted Caribbean folk life, including scenes of animal sacrifice. The most influential artist to emerge from the Caribbean in the twentieth century was Cuban painter Wifredo Lam (1902–82). Lam spent a long time in Paris, where he absorbed ideas from the surrealists. He returned to Cuba in 1941 and began painting subjects drawn from the world of *santería,* the Cuban equivalent of *vodoun.* Lam's paintings are done in a monochromatic cubist style, and they often incorporate abstracted images of horned and masked magical beings. Lam's work has been influential abroad and has inspired the work of African American artists in the United States. A lively folk art tradition continues in the Caribbean today. Contemporary Rastafarian artists, for example, decorate entire automobiles with found objects and trash, sometimes even stacking old cars on top of each other.

# RESOURCE GUIDE

## PRINT SOURCES

Ades, Dawn. *Art in Latin America.* New Haven: Yale University Press, 1989.

Angulo Iñiguez, D. *Historia del Arte Hispanoamericana.* Vol. 3. Barcelona: Salvat, 1956.

*Arte Argentina: Dalla Independenza ad Oggi, 1810–1987.* Exhibition catalog, Rome, Instituto Italiano-Latino Americano, 1987.

Arellano, J. E. *Pintura y Escultura en Nicaragua.* London: Oxford, 1985

Argul, J. P. *Pintura y Escultura del Uruguay: Historica Crítica.* Montevideo: Publicación de la Revista del Instituto Histórico y Geográfico del Uruguay, 1958.

*Art in Latin America: The Modern Era 1820–1980.* Exhibition catalog by D. Ades and others, London, Hayward Eli Gallery, 1989.

*Arte Plumaria del Brasil.* Exhibition catalog by S. F. Dorta and L. H. Velthem, Mexico City, Museo Nacional de Antropología, 1982.

Baltra, Eli, ed. *Crafting Gender: Women and Folk Art in Latin America and the Caribbean.* Durham, NC: Duke University Press, 2003.

Bayon, Damian, ed. *Casasola: Tierra y Libertad: Photographs of Mexico 1900–35 from the Casasola Archives, Museum of Modern Art. Arte moderno in América Latina.* Madrid: Taurus, 1985.

Belbenoit, René. *Dry Guillotine; Fifteen Years Among The Living Dead by René Belbenoit, Prisoner No. 46635.* Illustrations by a fellow prisoner, with an introduction by William La Varre. New York: Blue Ribbon Books, 1938.

Calzadilla, Juan. *Movimientos y Vanguardia en el Arte Contemporáneo en Venezuela.* Caracas: M. Barquin, 1978.

Carmen Ramírez, Mari. *Cantos Paralelos: La Parodia Plástica en el Arte Argentino Contemporáneo (Visual Parody in Contemporary Argentinean Art).* Austin, TX: The University of Texas, Jack Blanton Museum of Art, and Buenos Aires: Fondo Nacional de las Artes, 1999.

Chase, G. *Contemporary Art in Latin America.* New York: Free Press, 1970.

Damian, Carol. *The Virgin of the Andes: Art and Ritual in Colonial Cuzco.* Miami Beach, FL: Mellen Press, 1995.

Damian, Carol, and Steve Stein, eds. *Popular Art and Social Change in the Retablos of Nicario Jiménez Quispe.* Lewiston, NY: Mellen Press, 2004.

Dark, Philip J. C. *Bush Negro Art: An African Art in the Americas.* London: Academy Editions, 1973.

Eléspuru, J. M. *Pintura y Escultura en el Perú Contemporáneo.* Lima: Peruarte, 1970.

Everard, Sir Ferdinand Im Thurn. *Among the Indians of Guiana*. New York: Dover Publications, 1967.

García Esteban, F. *Artes plásticas en el Uruguay en el siglo XX*. Montevideo: Universidad/Publicaciones, 1970.

Grenand, P., and F. Grenand. "Les Amerindiens de Guyane Française Aujourd'hui: Elements de Compréhension." *Journal de Société des Américanistes* 64 (1979): 361–82.

Grizzard, Mary. *Spanish Colonial Art and Architecture of Mexico and the U.S. Southwest*. Lanham, MD: University Press of America, 1986.

Herrera, Hayden. *Frida: A Biography*. New York: Harper & Row, 1983.

Kubler, George. *The Art and Architecture of Ancient America*. New Haven : Yale University Press, 1990.

Kunzle, David. *The Murals of Revolutionary Nicaragua, 1979–1992*. Berkeley: University of California Press, 1998.

Lemos, Carlos, José Roberto Teixeira Leite, and Pedro Manuel Gismonti. *The Art of Brazil*. New York: Harper & Row, 1983.

Miller, Mary Ellen. *The Art of Mesoamerica, from Olmec to Aztec*. London: Thames & Hudson, 1986.

Museum of Modern History. *Twenty Centuries of Mexican Art*. New York: Museum of Modern Art, 1940.

Pagano, J. L. *Historia del Arte Argentino Desde los Aborígenes Hasta el Momento Actual*. Buenos Aires: L'Amateur, 1944.

Pan American Union. *Modern Artists of Costa Rica: An Exhibition of Paintings and Sculpture Assembled by the Group of San José*. Exhibition catalog Washington, DC: Pan American Union, 1964.

Plá, J. *Arte Moderno del Paraguay: Nuestro Retrospectiva*. Asunción, 1964.

Poupeye, Veerle. *Caribbean Art*. New York: Thames & Hudson, 1998.

Price, Sally and Richard. *Maroon Arts: Cultural Vitality in the African Diaspora*. Boston: Beacon Press, 1999.

Rochfort, Desmond. *The Mexican Muralists: Orozco, Rivera, Siqueiros*. London, Lawrence King, 1993.

Rodríguez Prampolini, Ida. *El Surrealismo y el Arte Fantástico de México*. Mexico City: UNAM, 1983.

Sanz y Díaz, J. "Pintores Salvadoreños Contemporáneos." *Ars* 8 (1957): 53–69.

Stephens, John. *Incidents of Travel in the Yucatán* (with prints by Frederick Catherwood). New York: Harper & Brothers, 1843.

Stone-Miller, Rebecca. *Art of the Andes from Chavín to the Inca*. London: Thames & Hudson, 1995.

Sullivan, Edward, ed.. *Brazil: Body & Soul*. New York: Guggenheim Museum, 2001.

Tamayo, Rufino. *Rufino Tamayo: 70 Años de Creación*. Mexico City: Museo de Arte Contemporáneo Internacional Rufino Tamayo, 1987.

Thompson, Robert Farris. *Face of the Gods: Art and Altars of Africa and the African Americas*. New York: Museum for African Art and Munich, 1993.

Toledo Museum of Art, *Chilean Contemporary Art*. Toledo, OH: Toledo Museum of Art, 1942.

Traba, M. *Historia Abierta del Arte Colombiano*. Cali: Instituto Colombiano de Cultura, 1974.

Turner, Jane, ed. *The Dictionary of Art*. New York: Grove's Dictionaries, 1996.

Tyler, Ron, ed. *Posada's Mexico*. Washington, DC: Library of Congress, 1979.

Zamora, Martha, and Marilyn Sode Smith. *Frida Kahlo: The Brush of Anguish*. Seattle: Chronicle Books, 1990.

## MUSEUMS AND ART COMMUNITIES

### Mexico

Museo Nacional de Historia, Primera sección del Bosque de Chapultepec, Colonia Chapultepec Polanco, México 11580, México. http://www.cnca.gob.mx/cnca/inah/museos/munh.html. Art of the Independence era, including murals by Siquieros.

Palacio de Bellas Artes, Avenida Juárez y Eje Lázaro Cárdenas, Centro Histórico, México 6050, México. www.conaculta.gob.mx/palaci/index.htm. Murals by Rivera and Siqueiros, also regular art exposiciones.

Palacio Nacional and Ministry of Education, Avenida Pino Suarez, Corregidora esquina Guatemala, Zócalo de la Ciudad de México, México 6060, México. www.shcp.gob.mx/dgpcap. Murals by Diego Rivera.

Museo Casa de Frida Kahlo, Londres 247, Colonia del Carmen, Coyoacán (México), México. www.cnca.gob.mx/cnca/inah/monuhis/fazul.html. Frida Kahlo's family home in Coyoacán, now a museum. Folk art collected by Kahlo, also artworks by Diego Rivera and Frida Kahlo.

Mercado el Parián, Puebla, México. Puebla's crafts district, featuring traditional Mexican ceramics and other decorative arts.

Museo Rafael Coronel, Ex-Convento de San Francisco s/n, Centro, Zacatecas, México. Large collection of Mexican masks and other popular crafts.

## Belize

Bliss Gallery, Bliss Centre for the Performing Arts, 2 Southern Foreshore, Belize City, Belize.

Museum of Belize, Belmopan, Belize. http://www.belize.gov.bz/features/museum/welcome.html.

## Guatemala

Museo de Santiago/St. James Museum, 4th Calle Oriente, Palacio del Ayuntamiento, Antigua, Guatemala. Silverwork, pottery, crafts.

Museo Nacional de Artes e Industrias Populares, 10a Calle 10-72, Guatemala City 01001, Guatemala. Contemporary painting and sculpture, also portraits, flags, photographs, and maps.

Museo Ixchel del Traje Indígena, 6a. Calle Final, Zona 10 Centro Cultural, Campus de la Universidad Francisco Marroquín, Guatemala City, Guatemala. http://www.museoixchel.org/. Folk costume.

## El Salvador

Museo Nacional David J. Guzmán, San Salvador, El Salvador. http://www.4elsalvador.com/museo%20nacional.htm. A museum is being planned for archaeology, ethnography, and history.

## Honduras

Galeria Nacional de Arte, Plaza de la Merced, Calle Bolivar, Francisco Morazán, Tegucigalpa, Honduras. Art from prehistoric to colonial times, also modern art, especially magic realism.

## Nicaragua

Museo de Arte de las Américas (Museo del Arte Moderno de América Latina), Managua, Nicaragua. Considered by many to be the best art museum in Latin America. Works donated by Wifredo Lam, Roberto Matta, and Jesús Rafael Soto in support of the Sandinista opposition to American intervention in Nicaragua.

## Costa Rica

Museo de Arte Costarricense, Parque Metropolitano de La Sabana, Apartado 378, FECOSA 1009 San José, Costa Rica.

## Panama

Museo de Arte Contemporaneo, Avenida San Blas, Panama City, Republica de Panama. http://www.macpanama.org/index.html.

## Colombia

Museo Nacional, Carrera 7, Calles 28 y 29, Bogotá, D.C., Colombia. http://www.museonacional.gov.co/home.html.

Museo de Arte Moderno, Calle 24 6-00, Bogotá, D.C., Colombia. http://www.cybercol.com/colombia/museos/museoamoderno.html.

Museo de Artes y Tradiciones Populares, Carrera 8, No. 7-21, Bogotá, D.C., Colombia. Popular arts and crafts from around Colombia.

Museo de Arte Moderno La Tertulia, Avenida Colombia No. 5-105 Oeste, Cali, Colombia.

Museo de Arte Moderno, Medellín, Colombia.

Museo de Antioquía Francisco Antonio Zea, Medellín, Colombia. http://www.museodeantioquia.org/paginas/mus_01.html.

## Venezuela

Museo de Bellas Artes, Plaza Morelos Parque Los Caobos, Caracas 1010, Venezuela. http://www.mipunto.com/venezuelavirtual/temas/1er_trimestre02/bellasartes.html.

## Ecuador

Museo Municipal, Sucre, entre Pedro Carbo y Chile, Guayaquil, Ecuador. http://www.guayaquil.gov.ec/147.gye, Guayaquil.

Museo de Arte e Historia de la Ciudad, Espejo 1147, Apartado 399, Quito, Ecuador. http://www.quito.gov.ec/museociu/museo.htm.

## Peru

Museo de Arte, Paseo Colón 125, Lima 1 (Cercado), Parque de la Exposición, Lima, Peru. http://museoarte.perucultural.org.pe/.

## Bolivia

Museo Nacional de Arte, Calle Comercio y Socabaya, Casilla: 11390, La Paz, Bolivia. http://www.mna.org.bo/. Early through contemporary art.

Museo Virtual de Arte Boliviano, http://www.bolivianet.com/arte/index.htm. Virtual gallery of contemporary Bolivian art.

## Guyana

Walter Roth Museum of Anthropology, 61 Main Street, Georgetown, Guyana. http://www.sdnp.org.gy/wrma/index.html.

## Brazil

Museu de Arte Moderna, Av. Infante Dom Henrique 85, Parque do Flamengo, Rio de Janeiro 20021-140, Brasil. http://www.mamrio.com.br/.

Museu de Arte de São Paulo, São Paulo, Brasil. Museu Paulista da Universidad de São Paulo, São Paulo, Brasil.

## Chile

Museo Nacional de Bellas Artes (formerly Museo de Pinturas), Parque Forestal s/n, Casilla 3209, Santiago, Chile.

Museo de Arte Contemporáneo, Parque Forestal s/n, frente a calle Mosqueto (ver plano), Santiago, Chile.

## Uruguay

Museo Nacional de Artes Plásticas, Museo Nacional De Artes Visuales, Julio Herrera y Reissig esq. Tomás Giribaldi, s/n, Parque Rodó, CP: 11300, Montevideo, Uruguay. http://www.mnav.gub.uy/.

## Argentina

Museo Nacional de Bellas Artes, Av. Del Libertador 1473, Capital Federal, Buenos Aires, Argentina. http://www.mnba.org.ar/.

## Caribbean

Centro de Desarrollo de las Artes Visuales, San Ignacio No. 353, esq. Teniente Rey, Plaza Vieja, La Habana Vieja, Havana, Cuba. http://www.universes-in-universe.de/car/habana/ort/e-centro-desarrollo.htm.

Centro de Arte Contemporaneo Wifredo Lam, San Ignacio No 22, Esquina Empedrado, Habana Vieja, Havana, Cuba.

Museo Nacional de Bellas Artes, Havana, Cuba.

Museo de Arte de Puerto Rico, San Juan, Puerto Rico.

# DANCE

JOHN CHARLES CHASTEEN

The best known popular dance traditions of Latin America—from Salsa and Meringue to Samba and Tango—present an image of dizzying variety, but they are ramifying branches of one main trunk that sprouted on the Atlantic shores of America but with tap roots reaching to Europe and Africa. Dance is among the most pervasive and persuasive representations of Latin America's basic foundational trope, its prime nationalist touchstone—the idea that Latin American nations were founded on a process of racial mixing. Mythic resonances give Latin America's popular dance traditions considerable cultural significance. National dances are central to dominant nationalist ideologies. Deep historical resonances have made Latin American popular dance an effective agent as well as a powerful symbol of collective identity.

The Latin American emphasis on national dances seems surprising from a U.S. perspective. After all, what could be considered the national dance of the United States? None is formally so designated, of course. Nor does any immediately suggest itself, except perhaps the Square Dance because of its associations with the historical narratives of cowboys and pioneers. Or could it be Swing because of its intense and broad popularity during the mid-twentieth century? There is no consensus or even a notable debate because the entire question of a national dance is unfamiliar in the United States.

In Latin America, on the other hand, people generally have ready answers when asked about the national dance. That does not mean that everyone agrees what it is or what it should be. In the case of the Brazilian Samba, for example, the status of national dance is official—it is subsidized in the form of government support for Rio de Janeiro's dancing Samba-parade competition. Yet the Samba danced at carnival in Rio de Janeiro and televised throughout Brazil is a style not often danced in the rest of the country. In northern and northeastern Brazil, people identify with local styles of carnival dancing that are no less Brazilian. Still, they recognize the Rio Samba as the official national dance in the eyes of the world. Argentine Tango, another example, clearly stands out as the national dance when viewed from abroad. Within Argentina, however, Tango dancing is emblematic of the city of Buenos Aires rather than of the country as a whole.

The question of a national dance is, of course, political. In the two cases previously mentioned, the national dance recognized outside of the country originated in the national capital. A confluence of influence, resources, talent, and international exposure gave the Samba and the Tango national preeminence and international projection, reducing competitors to the status of regional folk dances. Most of the time, a national dance does not arise to predominate over all others in spontaneous popularity but is forged as part of a nationalist project. Yet politics is not the whole story. Colombia and Cuba offer examples of national dances associated with regions far from the country's levers of power.

For centuries Latin America has been filled with dances that could compete for the laurels of a national dance. During the 1800s, they were all national dances in one sense, reflecting the distinctive customs of poor, predominantly rural, populations, such as the peasant dances studied by European folklorists of the period. These dances were understood to be representative of an authentic identity, a distinctive national spirit. Ironically, however, although they stand for national uniqueness, these peasant dances show a powerful family resemblance.

## NATIONAL DANCES

### Origins

In the beginning, there was the Dance of Two, the basic archetypal form from which Latin America's national dances all stem. In its basic choreography, a man and woman face without touching, in attitudes of courtship: he imploring and insisting, she avoiding and resisting. The dancing couple is often encircled by participant spectators, who sing and clap and, in turn, enter the circle as dancers. But it is in the type of movements that Latin American dance differs from European dance. In Latin American dance, the bodies of both men and women move with hip-driven undulations. This movement has many names in Spanish and Portuguese (especially including forms of the verbs *quebrar* or *requebrar*, also *menear, contonear,* and *gingar*), which can be used to trace its presence in written documents. These basic elements of the Dance of Two appear in a thousand variations, accompanied by many different sorts of music and rhythm, from a strongly percussive Cuban rumba to an old-fashioned Chilean *cueca*, performed by women in long skirts with fluttering handkerchiefs. In the simplest forms of the Dance of Two, spectators surround the dancers and provide the music themselves by clapping and singing ribald lyrics.

The Dance of Two stood out from the gamut of American dance practices early in the era of Spanish colonization. Two well-known sixteenth-century versions, the Chacona and the Zarabanda, became lightening rods for criticism in both America and Europe. A piece of Mexican zarabanda music that was written, according to Inquisition records, in 1556 is the earliest known composition for this popular Latin American dance. Zarabandas and Chaconas were being danced in Peru by 1598. African slaves, plebeian Spaniards, and people of mixed descent were apparently the principal dancers. By all indications, indigenous people living in their own communities maintained separate dance traditions and contributed less to the formation of the Dance of Two. Sugar plantations in Brazil and the Caribbean do not appear to have been the crucial venues for the genesis of this tradition, which later spread throughout Latin America. Urban settings predominated, especially the fluid and diverse social milieu of Atlantic ports. Seville, Spain's designated port for shipping to and from colonial Spanish America, became the scene of Europe's first "Latin dance craze" around 1600.

The Dance of Two was clearly born of a cultural encounter—its courtship choreography unmistakably European, its style of body movement unmistakably African. Therefore, the Dance of Two and its progeny made compelling representations of the idea of racial mixing, or *mestizaje,* a concept to which national ideologies throughout Latin America assigned special importance in the twentieth century.[1] National dances are explicitly defined as *mestizo* (meaning "mixed race") dances, and children at patriotic school pageants generally dance costumed as mestizo country people. In addition, racial mixture of another sort frequently figures in the imagery surrounding the Dance of Two. Male and female dancers may be presented with contrasting racial identities—most frequently, a lighter-skinned man with a darker woman. This pairing can be viewed both as a convivial sign of interracial socializing and as an interracial union. Either way, the result is patriotic because a transcendence of difference contributes to national unity.

The political potency of Latin American popular dance derives precisely from its role as a symbol of mixture. The combination of basic European and African elements in the Dance of Two made it into a New World creation, something that already separated Americans from Europeans in the 1600s. Various regional versions or derivations of the Dance of Two became prominent symbols of American identity during the 1700s. Precisely for the same reason, Latin America's independence movements adopted the many variations in the 1800s, and, in the 1900s, they became self-conscious emblems of mestizaje.

In addition to strong racial overtones, Latin America's national dances embody certain social processes surrounding their emergence. European and African influences met and mingled, not just at a moment of mythic genesis, but constantly over several centuries. How these influences met and on what basis they mingled, somehow bridging the inevitable divide between the enslaver and the enslaved, requires considerable explanation. However it happened, the result is unquestionable. One way or another, all of Latin America's national dances have African roots somewhere.

After all, Latin America was the primary destination of the Atlantic slave trade from the beginnings of the trade in the 1500s to its end around 1850. Most slaves labored in plantation agriculture, but both the Spanish and Portuguese also used large numbers of slaves for domestic service and artisan trades in colonial cities. In fact, all important cities—even in parts of Latin America where the present population of African descent is small, such as Lima and Mexico City—were full of slaves in the colonial era.

Urban environments encouraged dancing. Dance traditions can be expressed only in a group. A successful social dance requires partners, musicians, and spectators, all sharing a certain understanding of what they are doing. Enslaved Africans came from many, widely separated cultures. To dance (and to carry on other aspects of their social lives), they preferred others who shared their language and religious beliefs as well as their dance traditions. Africans who shared an affinity created diasporic social organizations that were usually called "nations" (*naciones* in Spanish, *nações* in Portuguese). Because urban slaves generally enjoyed greater freedom of movement and association, they had more opportunity than their rural brethren to belong to an active African nation. These nations existed in all of Latin America's important urban areas, sometimes under different names. In Havana, Cartagena, and Lima, for example, they were called *cabildos de nación.* In addition, nations were often more or less subsumed into Catholic lay brotherhoods, called *cofradías* in Spanish America, or *irmandades* in Brazil, where this sort of organization was especially common.

African nations functioned somewhat like mutual aid societies. Nations took responsibility for providing proper burial, for example, something slaves could not trust their masters to do. This function meshed strongly with that of the cofradías and irmandades, which arranged for burial of their members in Catholic rites. It says something about the power of African dance traditions, however, that dancing together was the black nations' salient act of self-definition and self-expression. Nations sometimes owned a house devoted especially to their dances. When they did not have their own dance house, people from the nations danced in the plaza, on the edge of town, or on the beach. There, on Sundays and holidays, the people of the nations would be arrayed in large circles, each centering on dancers. The accompanying music would be mostly percussive; each nation tended to have its own distinctive rhythm.

Recreating social relations remembered from an African homeland was a natural impulse in the black nations. Yet a permanently ongoing process of energetic adaptation was required of enslaved Africans in America. Not only had they landed in an unfamiliar environment, but even their companions in bondage were unfamiliar in their own way. Many nations in America had distinct minority groups within them. African nations therefore expressed their will to unity partly by forgetting diverse African origins and creating a shared identity in their American present.

Their dancing (or at least, the dancing that Europeans were allowed to see) was based on the distinctively American Dance of Two. The point merits emphasis because written evidence—whether produced by travelers, journalists, or government officials—so insistently refers to the dancing of the nations as "savage" and "African." The following description of Cuban dancers is by Swedish traveler Fredrika Bremer in 1854.

> [The dancers were] between forty and fifty Negroes, men and women, all in clean attire, the men mostly in shirts or blouses, the women in long plain dresses. I here saw representatives of the various African nations—Congoes, Mandingoes, Luccomées, Caraballis, and others dancing in the African fashion. Each nation has some variations of its own, but the principal features of the dance are in all essentially the same. The dance always requires a man and a woman, and always represents a series of courtship and coquetry, during which the lover expresses his feelings, partly by a tremor in all his joints, so that he seems ready to fall to pieces as he turns round and round his fair one, like the planet around its sun, partly by wonderful leaps and evolutions, often enfolding his lady with both arms, but without touching her; yet still, as I said, this mode varied with the various nations.[2]

After the slave trade ended in the early to mid-1800s, the African nations in Latin America began to fade away. American-born slaves seldom participated, so the passing of the African-born generation heralded the closing of their meeting houses, and, by the 1900s, the African nations of Latin America were mostly a memory. The impulse to sociability lived on, however, in various sorts of clubs, associations, and festive societies, especially carnival-parading societies. Overall, the African nations and the social organizations that evolved from them maintained a constant presence in Latin American cities during 3 formative centuries, and during that time they provided a continuous source of inspiration for the region's popular dance culture. In sum, Africans put the "Latin" hip movement in Latin America's national dances. But in what sorts of historical situations did people who were not of African descent learn to move their hips?

## Development

The interface between the black nations and the wider colonial milieu was a two-way street. The development of Latin American popular dance includes the waves of dance fashion that radiated through the Atlantic world from European centers of imperial expansion such as Madrid, Lisbon, and, later, Paris.

European influence on Latin American popular dance arrived in consecutive waves defined by basic patterns of choreography. The earliest wave, characteristic of the 1500s and 1600s, was defined by the *open-couple* choreography of the Dance of Two. The next wave, in the 1700s, was defined by an open-couple refinement called the *Minuet* and, more important, by the emergence of *interdependent-couple* choreography in contradance and its many variations. Interdependent-couple dances involved several couples interacting and changing partners in complex ways, as in square dancing, for example. The 1800s saw a third wave, the *close-couple* dances, such as the Waltz and the Polka, in which the dancers embrace. These dance fashions, in turn, moved through Europe and, with a time lag of no more than a few years, arrived in Latin American cities, where they began to interact with the dancing of the black nations.

Of course, European dance ideas did not arrive in the abstract. Nor, for the most part, did they arrive in dance manuals. Instead, European dance ideas, like African ones, were carried to the New World in people's heads. European musical theater troupes, especially Spanish ones, became prime transmitters of new music and dance fashions. Many of the sources for documented accounts of early Latin American popular dance are theatrical. The Spanish theatrical tradition that emerged more or less simultaneously with the colonization of America always included a great deal of dance—so much so that a typical troupe had more dancers than actors. Dance figured in the plots of comedies, reappeared in the frequent musical interludes called *entremeses,* and normally closed an evening's program. Furthermore, Spanish theatrical dance tended to be popular in style, rather than ballet-related. Musical theater troupes toured Latin American cities routinely in the nineteenth century, connecting their repertoires not only to Europe, but also to each other across national boundaries. These theatrical personnel suffered the social stigma that plagued their counterparts throughout the Atlantic world. Unfettered by a bigoted respectability, they freely entered into fruitful contact with musicians and dancers of African descent.

Latin American popular dance culture continued to absorb influences from Europe via the musical theater through the nineteenth and early twentieth centuries. Latin America's black musicians played an outstanding role in the resulting process of transculturation. This was true in the colonial period, when many musicians were slaves, and it was true after independence, when military bands proliferated and black men filled armies throughout the region. Because black musicians were so common in nineteenth-century Latin America, they became musical mediators, playing for a European light opera company at a fancy downtown theater one night and at a family member's birthday party the next night. It was common for black musicians, when playing for themselves, to apply syncopated rhythms to the melodies they had learned at work, suiting the new melodies to the sort of dancing their friends wanted to do.

Celebrations of the Catholic Church constituted another, critically important factor in the diffusion of African moves in Latin American popular dance. By definition, church celebrations included the whole society, humble and powerful, enslaved and free. During the 3 centuries of colonial rule, the African nations danced exclusively on Sundays and church holidays. In addition to providing free time, some church holidays specifically called for celebratory activities, prominently including dance. The Feast of the Epiphany was often accompanied by street dancing, and so was the Feast of Corpus Christi. In preparation for these holidays, as well as many others, lay brotherhoods could do church-sanctioned fundraising and meet periodically for practice sessions that had a time-honored way of becoming parties in themselves. The sacrament of marriage called for a wedding dance. Baptisms were also celebrated with dancing, as were "saint's days," usually synonymous with birthdays. In addition, the local recognition of patron saints and particular religious devotions associated with each parish church were celebrated with dancing. One way or another, the Church sanctioned or sponsored most of the dancing that occurred in colonial and nineteenth-century Latin America.

Church sanction and sponsorship of popular dance may seem odd. The Dance of Two and its progeny, with their coquetry and liberation of the lower body, were notably transgressive by any strict interpretation of Catholic standards. Clerics fulminated against them. The Church had struggled for centuries in medieval Europe against pagan dances and yet often appropriated them because an all-embracing religion cannot afford to allow the expression of greatest joy to be unsanctioned and sub-rosa. Significantly, among the most common generic names the Spanish gave to the dancing of African slaves in colonial Latin America was *calenda,* the name of pagan dance celebrations in early medieval Spain. In the New World, Catholic proselytizers found dance to be a tool too valuable not to use when evangelizing the indigenous people.

Popular dance in the setting of Church-sponsored celebrations never became totally sanitized. A clear tension persisted between the profane spirit inevitably suggested by the Dance of Two and the ethereal spirit that was more conventional in European religiosity. Among the chief forms of documentary evidence concerning popular dance in the sixteenth thorough the eighteenth centuries were the periodic denunciations by churchmen who were convinced that dancing in religious pageants or processions or celebratory gatherings had gone too far. Not until the nineteenth century, and then only gradually, did the Church purge popular dance from its Latin American liturgy. By that time, however, various other venues for popular dance were opening up, and energies formerly expressed within a church framework flowed into them.

As far back as the 1600s, the black nations had a powerful connection to a particular spot on the Catholic calendar, January 6, the Feast of Epiphany. This twelfth day of Christmas, commemorating the Magi's adoration of the Christ child, was a focus of intense popular festivities in medieval Europe. Spanish and Portuguese versions of the festivities prominently included shepherd carolers and figures representing the 3 kings who offered gifts to the baby Jesus. Traditionally, one of these kings, usually Balthazar, was presented as African. So central were these figures to popular imagining of Epiphany in the Iberian world that the colloquial term for the occasion was "the day of kings."

Throughout Latin America, the day of kings became an occasion for the black nations to carry out their most crucial and most potentially threatening political act—choosing their own symbolic kings. Sometime before 1600, Epiphany became the great occasion for the public meetings of black nations, who chose and crowned leaders in connection with Epiphany pageants that reenacted the adoration of the baby Jesus by non-European potentates. In that context, the appearance of hundreds of slaves gathered around their own kings became acceptable to Spanish and Portuguese authorities, symbolizing black obeisance to the state religion of these strongly theocratic empires.

As dancing at Epiphany pageants declined in the late nineteenth century, the energies of black dancers were transferred to a nearby spot on the Catholic calendar, one that many viewed as a pagan survival. That is why *carnestolendas* or carnival, the last 3 days before Lent, became so salient in the history of Latin American popular dance. The eve of Lent was a moment when various transgressive activities were permitted, a kind of "last hurrah" of carnal pleasures preceding weeks of austerity and self-denial. Until the later nineteenth century, popular dance had not figured importantly among the activities associated with carnival. Instead, people had marked the occasion with practical jokes, especially those between men and women. But the festival's penchant for the risqué, as well as its timing at the conclusion of the Christmas holiday season, made it a natural home for the rowdy energies of popular dancers no longer welcome at the Feast of Epiphany. As a result, carnival became the great occasion for popular dance in cities such as Rio, Havana, and Buenos Aires by 1900.

Carnival celebrations were partly segregated by class, with the wealthy often reveling in private clubs, surrounded by their social equals. But carnival celebrations also included spaces notorious for their cross-class and cross-racial mixing. Street reveling naturally involved such mixing. In addition, theaters held inexpensive public dances, which were often costume balls that revelers attended in disguise—a circumstance that further facilitated heterodox encounters. Such venues were well known for promiscuous contacts involving "slumming" males of superior social status and women of the popular class. Overall, carnival's "anything goes" ethos created an ambience made to order for white experimentation with dance styles created by blacks. This role of carnival, best known in Brazil, is a general Latin American phenomenon.

Next, red-light districts and seedy music halls also figured prominently as popular dance venues. The frequent mention of prostitution in early lore surrounding the Tango constitutes only one particularly well-known example of this phenomenon. Red-light districts played a similar role, circa 1900, in many Latin American locales, and even in North America in New Orleans, with its Storyville district, the cradle of jazz. In such settings, men of middle-class status or better frequently danced with women of radically different social origins.

Private parties, which tended toward class segregation, were also a venue for the development of popular dance genres. At the pinnacle of the nineteenth-century social hierarchy, rich and powerful families met at elaborate galas, for which newspaper columnists began to provide elaborate coverage. Their dance programs were entirely European, with few exceptions. Middle-class soirées called *tertulias,* warmly remembered in many nineteenth-century memoirs, combined dance with other activities. Although straight versions of current European dance fashions dominated in such locales, national dances might appear at particular moments, particularly late in the evening, or during carnival season, when a generally transgressive mood encouraged them. The mestizo poor also celebrated at humble parties of their own, often in the open air. National dances constituted the main fare at the gatherings of the poor, but imitations of current (or recently passé) European forms appeared as well. Given an opportunity, dancers at even the humblest of mid-nineteenth-century assemblies might try a Minuet. From Epiphany pageants to carnival balls, a particular matrix of cultural activities and social relations in the 1700s and 1800s constituted the interface between European dance fashions and African-inspired dance traditions, which is where Latin America's national dances were born, or at least conceived. No wonder these dance traditions have served as such appropriate symbols of national identities that claim to transcend race and class.

## PATRIOTIC CONSECRATION

To speak of the Dance of Two and its progeny as national dances became a commonplace during the Wars of Independence, 1810–25, an era which was truly a watershed in the history of Latin American popular dance. In those years Mexican Jarabes and Huapangos, Venezuelan Joropos, Colombian Bambucos, Brazilian Lundus, and Chilean and Peruvian Zamacuecas came to figure as parallels of the national folk dances that East European nationalists, for example, were making into symbols of shared ethnicity during the same period. The tendency to associate collective identities with particular dances seems almost universal in human history. World historian William McNeill has speculated that dance—along with other coordinated rhythmic exercises, including military drill—produces feelings of collective solidarity through an innately human process he calls "muscular bonding." Whether or not that is true, dance unquestionably played a powerful part in the formation of social identities in Latin America.

African traditions, such as those maintained and transformed by Latin America's black nations, provide a clear illustration of the role of dance in forming group identities. The dance history of Spain and Portugal is rife with further examples. In the 1490s Spanish regional dances were used at the court of Fernando and Isabel to symbolize the diverse provinces of a newly unified Spain. Both the Portuguese and the Spanish monarchies orchestrated public dancing for their dynastic celebrations, and the various constituent ethnicities of these multicultural Iberian societies were often asked, or even commanded, to represent their collective identity choreographically, with the Moors dancing as Moors, the Jews dancing as Jews, the African slaves dancing as Africans. The adoption of the Feast of Epiphany as the occasion for elections of black kings, with their attendant coronation dances, forms part of this overall pattern.

The struggles for independence from Spain and Portugal in 1810–25 channeled these energies in a slightly new direction. Rather than displaying the diverse cultural identities of a monarch's subjects, the Jarabes, Huapangos, Joropos, Lundus, Bambucos, and Zamacuecas were used to mark and to express membership in an emerging national community defined largely by American birth. To enjoy national dances—or, even more persuasively, to participate in them—was to assume a cultural distance from Spain and Portugal. Various versions of the Dance of Two and its spin-offs performed this function effectively because, for many generations, they had been understood as something specifically non-European, something American. Broadly shared among the American born, the Dance of Two was particularly associated with the salt of the earth, conferring on them a powerful aura of folk authenticity. The national dances became directly associated with the patriot armies themselves. Argentina's Montonero Minuet, which combined slow and stately sections with sprightly Dances of Two, arose in the insurgent ranks, as the name Montonero implies. The Zamacueca had parallel origins and associations in Chile and Peru. In combating the Mexican insurgency, the viceregal government cracked down harshly to prevent Jarabes from being danced on stage in Mexico City. This wartime affirmation of native identities through dance, understood as folk dance, expressive of traditional rural customs, was paralleled precisely in Spain and Portugal, then fighting their own wars of independence against occupying Napoleonic armies.

The rise of Latin America's national dances expressed a persuasive connection with Enlightenment and Romantic ideologies. The crisis of Latin American independence went in tandem with political crises in Spain and Portugal, where modern republican ideas took root for the first time. The most basic of these ideas was the right to self-government, usually referred to in Latin America as popular sovereignty. In this measure, Latin America was going through its own version of Europe's "Age of Revolution," following the young United States along that path. Latin America's independence movements contained diverse currents, absolutely all of which waved the banner of popular sovereignty during their struggles. Some of this early vogue of Latin America's national dances was therefore the top-down project of an often upper-class patriot leadership that was eager to garner wide support. On the other hand, Latin Americans responded warmly overall to the new patriotic glamour of their national dances. And why shouldn't they? After all, they had stubbornly cultivated and identified with these forms for generations, despite ecclesiastical disapproval and periodic official crackdowns against them. The independence movements made the colonialist's "dirty dancing" into the patriot's badge of honor.

The independence-era vogue of Latin America's national dances was driven partly by ideology, partly by popular approval, and partly by political necessity. After all, the national dances were strongly associated with people of mixed race, against whom many among the patriot leaders harbored strong prejudice. They surely would have preferred not to confer patriotic prestige on "vulgar" popular dance styles, and, as soon as independence was won and as soon as the need passed, they recoiled from the vulgarity. Overall, the early vogue of Latin America's national dances had evaporated by the 1840s. Exceptions to this pattern only confirm the rule. In Argentina, for example, the vogue of national dances did not recede until after the fall of strongman Manuel de Rosas, who continued to use them as a nativist cudgel to pummel political enemies who were associated with Europe. Cuba presents an instructive case. Cuba sat out the wave of independence struggles that swept over the continent between 1810 and 1825. Cuba's national dances then rose in prominence after 1850, along with its own independence movement, when national dances on the continent were in full decline.

The nationalist prestige of Latin American popular dance thus showed a clear ebb and flow in the nineteenth century, and similar long-term fluctuations have characterized the twentieth century as well. The flood tide occurred in the 1930s, when nationalist ideologies of various stripes held sway in much of the world. In addition, clear political necessity was at work internally in Latin America. Landowning oligarchies that had held power during decades of booming agricultural exports were losing economic and political clout. New, more urban-based nationalist coalitions struggled to replace them with mass-based political parties. Nationalists appealed directly to the interests and sentiments of their potential supporters—peasants, workers, and the urban middle class—and one element of their appeal was a renewed celebration of national culture. Versions of the Dance of Two and its spin-offs returned to the spotlight during the surge of Latin America's artistic nationalism. The Cuban Rumba and the Brazilian Samba, both classic Dances of Two, became informal national symbols in these years, as did the Argentine (and Uruguayan) Tango. All of these dances gained international projection through the cinema.

Latin America's national dances became firmly institutionalized in the mid-twentieth century. Schools taught them, civic festivals and Sunday television programming featured them, and most people became quite familiar with them as spectators, if not as participants. In varying degrees, national dances gained expanded popularity as social dances in the 1940s and 1950s. Latin America had folk revivals in the 1960s. Dance genres that derived directly from national traditions maintained their dynamism in a manner that correlated with the presence of people of African descent, most notably in the circum-Caribbean region and in northern Brazil. Dances originating in these places circulated within Latin America. In the 1950s, simplified versions of the Colombian Cumbia, another classic Dance of Two, began to spread everywhere from Mexico to Argentina, but in a class-stratified manner, as the social dance of poor urban people and rural-urban migrants. In the 1960s, Cuban traditions of son music were modified in New York to produce salsa music, which recordings and touring musicians carried immediately throughout the Caribbean basin. Salsa music and dance found an avid audience and developed regional centers in cities such as Miami, Caracas, and Cali. The Dominican Merengue underwent a similar geographic expansion in the 1980s and 1990s.

## NATIONAL CASE STUDIES

After independence, Latin America's national dances evolved within national frameworks. A number of Latin American popular dance traditions—those of Cuba, Colombia, Brazil, and Argentina, especially—rose to national prominence and international projection. On the other hand, the dances of Mexico and the Andes provide a look at indigenous traditions.

### Mexico and the Andes

Mexico and the Andes have national traditions stemming from the Dance of Two, but they also have contrasting indigenous-inspired traditions. In both areas, the Dance of Two received the patriotic consecration of the independence era, producing national dances—the

Mexican Jarabe and the Peruvian Zamacueca—that held sway through the 1800s. Meanwhile, indigenous-inspired traditions with pre-Columbian roots continued to grow and develop in a thousand villages in both regions. Until the twentieth century, these dances expressed local, indigenous identities rather than national ones. Finally, in the 1920s, village dances were put forward as national dances, ones that better reflect the importance of the indigenous heritage in Mexico, Ecuador, Peru, and Bolivia.

Latin America's indigenous dance traditions, dating from before the European invasion, were infinitely variable in their details, but they shared broad characteristics. They followed the global norm in that they were mostly choral dances—that is, danced by groups as opposed to individuals or couples. In notable contrast to African traditions, indigenous Americans danced mostly with arms and legs, not the torso. Men were the principal dancers. Women danced much less frequently. War, hunt, and harvest constituted important occasions for local communities to dance. Totemic dances mimicking animal behavior were especially common. Dancers very often sang while they danced, thereby learning and relaying the collective memory of these oral cultures. Often the dancers used alcohol and other mind-altering drugs. A dance group might include dozens of inebriated men in a line, elbows locked, taking two steps forward, one step back, to the left, to the right, for hours, singing an anthem of identity, while moving with precise synchronization. In the 1500s, the Caribbean variant of such a dance was called an Areito, the Mexican variant, a Mitote, and the Andean variant, a Taqui.

Ancient Aztec dancing included many totemic and social themes. In one, participants formed concentric circles according to age and social class, reflecting the highly stratified character of Aztec society. There was a dance "of old men," in which the dancers wore masks and bent over with a hand on their aching backs, as in a folk dance often taught to children in Mexico today. Some Aztec dancing was performed by a class of specialists who executed rituals so strictly choreographed that a misstep might be punished by death. As with indigenous dance overall, Aztec dance was mostly masculine. And not surprisingly, given the intensity of the Aztec warrior cult, war dances loomed large. Aztec dancing also appears to have been particularly enthusiastic, a trait that Spanish missionaries found a useful tool in their spiritual conquest.

Likewise, Inca practice in the pre-Columbian Andes included many animal dances and dances that reflected the social order, such as one in which the participants used their tools to represent agricultural labor and another one performed only by Inca nobility before the throne of the emperor. Inca practice also included dances that marked the winter solstice, as well as dances with priestly functions, such as exorcism. Interestingly, the Inca's subject peoples also used dances to represent themselves as part of the pageantry of a multiethnic empire, a phenomenon exactly parallel to the Iberian pattern previously discussed. This parallelism no doubt facilitated the indigenous people's symbolic integration into Spanish political rituals. The chronicler Bernabé Cobo described seeing 40 such dances in a Corpus Christi procession, performing exactly the same function as the dances of Moors, Jews, or Africans in the Corpus Christi processions of the Iberian Peninsula.

But if the Spanish sometimes turned indigenous dances to their own purpose, indigenous traditions also functioned as vehicles of resistance against the political and cultural incursions of outsiders. In fact, indigenous dance movements served on several occasions as the focus of armed rebellion against Spanish colonizers, sometimes with millenarian overtones reminiscent of the indigenous Ghost Dancers on the U.S. Great Plains in the 1880s. The importance of dance in the Taqui Onkoy uprising, one such dance-centered resistance movement in the colonial Andes, is signaled by the name of the dance, Taqui, in the name.

When sedentary indigenous communities came under Spanish colonial control, Catholic missionaries used dance in their proselytization. The predominant framework of this participatory catechism seems to have been Spain's own Moros y Cristianos (Moors vs. Christians), a dance representing choreographed a mock battle commemorating the Christian reconquest of Iberia, completed in 1492. Moros y Cristianos was both more and less than a dance, in the normal sense. No particular music or movements defined it. Some Moros y Cristianos performances were elaborately staged mass spectacles involving horses, lots of clanging swordplay, a specially constructed Moorish castle to be captured and set afire, and even a simulated naval battle. The performance included various dramatis personae—the mounted, Moor-slaying Santiago, Spain's patron saint, being the most prominent—scripted dialogue, and stirring speeches. In simpler versions, costumed dancers in contrasting colors engaged in a more stylized conflict. The conflict itself (and the certainty of Christian victory) defined the performance, which was extremely popular in both Spain and Portugal during the 1500s.

With their appealing music and pageantry, Moros y Cristianos performances constituted an ideal packaging for the object lesson of Christian supremacy over conquered non-Europeans. Indigenous villagers were encouraged to make the performance part of the annual fiestas honoring each village's patron saint. They were most successful in Mexico, where a pre-Columbian tradition rich in war dances had prepared the way. In the 1700s, when Moros y Cristianos performances were disappearing from Mexican cities, indigenous villagers preserved them and made them their own. Colonial authorities then began to prohibit the performances as having strayed too far from their original purpose, but the prohibitions failed. During the 1800s and into the 1900s village festivals descended from Moros y Cristianos were performed annually throughout much of indigenous Mexico. These performances developed many names and truly myriad local varieties. Some became Danzas de la Conquista, which actually dramatize the victory of Cortés over Montezuma. Others jettisoned the old scenario, preserving only the figure of Santiago and, especially, his horse. A particularly interesting variant, called Concheros, took hold in Mexican cities in the mid-twentieth century and recruited participants principally among rural-urban migrants. Concheros reversed the ideological polarity of Moros y Cristianos to celebrate an indigenous heritage.

Despite their enormous variety, Mexican indigenous traditions, like those throughout Latin America, have a unifying theme: community. Village performances have always been community efforts. In colonial days they were staged by Catholic lay brotherhoods and later by village authorities or annually selected sponsors—called *padrinos* or *funcionarios* among other names. Along with the honor of sponsoring the performance, wealthier families within the community accept a heavy financial burden and, by hosting their village fiesta, share the wealth with villagers unable to contribute. Moreover, the village pageant is a permanent institution, not just an annual event. Players normally retain their roles from year to year and often maintain elaborate costumes for the purpose. Concheros who dance in Mexico City plazas have transferred this emphasis on community to a new environment, forming a tight-knit hierarchical social organization that integrates its members year-round. These patterns exactly parallel the manner in which people of African descent have used Epiphany performances, Catholic lay brotherhoods, and, eventually, carnival organizations such as Rio's *escolas de samba*.

In the Andes, a dance of indigenous people has recently been the subject of anthropological scholarship: the musical Comparsas, danced in the street in various religious celebrations and also at carnival. These Comparsas are clearly descended from the dances staged in colonial religious processions, such as the Corpus Christi procession. Highly stylized dramatic interaction is central to these dances, which involve costumed choruses of men and women along with various figures, such as the landowner, who represent nonindigenous authority. This is precisely the form that was adopted by the street dancers of the fading black African nations, although with an entirely different style of body movement. The Comparsas of Cuzco, Peru, and Oruro, Bolivia, are hardly pure in the sense of lacking nonindigenous influences. The dancers affirm their own indigenous identity, or perhaps disown it, or, more ambivalently, impersonate it. One way or another, however, indigenous identity is always somehow at issue in these dances.

Peruvians today agree that Huayno is their national dance. *Huayno* means, in the Quechua language, a dance for men and women in couples. Huayno music is clearly of indigenous inspiration, as is the dancers' immobile torso. Huaynos are basically line dances, a very common pre-Columbian form. Yet, couple dances played almost no part in pre-Columbian traditions. Thus, the twentieth-century Huayno is clearly an adaptation of indigenous tradition to satisfy the current expectation that a national dance should be danced by both men and women. Overall, the status of Huayno as Peru's national dance is due almost totally to the efforts of anthropologists, intellectuals, community leaders, educators, and nationalist politicians, who created a national dance suitable for a nation that only in the twentieth century truly began to valorize its indigenous roots. Most Peruvians are exposed to Huayno, as dancers, only in school and as spectators at folk-dance presentations.

In the 1800s, Peru had a different national dance, one descended from the Dance of Two. Variants of the Dance of Two, always associated with the black population of coastal Peru and Lima, traveled by many names on the Pacific coast of South America during the nineteenth century. The version usually called Zamacueca was notable primarily in its extensive use of handerchiefs by the male partner, who spends much of the dance twirling his handkerchief in the air. In the mid 1820s, when Lima was occupied by patriot armies from Venezuela, Colombia, Chile, and Argentina, Zamacuecas were the spice of the patriots' late-night carousing, especially associated with Lima's black neighborhood "below the bridge" across the Rimac river. After the final defeat of Spanish arms in the Peruvian highlands, patriot soldiers returned home—especially, it seems, to Chile—whistling the music of Zamacuecas.

For 3 centuries Chile had been strongly linked to Lima by patterns of colonial administration and trade. The wars of independence had seen the creation in Santiago of popular gathering places called *chinganas,* devoted to wine, national dances, and various forms of veiled prostitution. Chinganas often operated in the open air and always under Chile's new republican flag. If not Zamacuecas, various other closely related Dances of Two were doubtless danced around Santiago, with its appreciable black population, before the final patriot victory of 1824. Still, the arrival of Peruvian Zamacuecas with the lingering prestige of Lima boosted the popularity of the dance in Santiago.

In a common pattern repeated throughout Latin America, Zamacueca's patriotic aura faded in Chile as dreams of post-independence prosperity were realized only slowly in the 1830s and 1840s. Still, the dance exemplifies the irrepressible popularity of the African-influenced tradition in the period. A Polish traveler who saw Zamacuecas danced at the annual celebration of Chilean independence in 1838 (a natural extension of dancing for royal birthdays in colonial days) testified that all social classes danced it in Chile, "from the peasant's hut to the most elegant salon." Domingo Faustino Sarmiento, the Argentine writer and statesman, lived in Santiago during these years and wrote about the Zamacuecas. "It is the only point of contact of all social classes. Rich and poor dance it, the lady and the washerwoman, the gentleman and the *roto*," he concluded, using the distinctively Chilean word for ragged person. The Zamacueca had become a powerful symbol of Chilean identity. By the twentieth century it was folkloric, no longer the stuff of nightlife, but still standard in civic celebrations, its name shortened to Cueca. It is one of the most emblematic Dances of Two, described by a French traveler to Chile on the eve of the twentieth century:

> The dancing woman waves a handkerchief in one hand and, with the other, gathers her petticoats frivolously before the advances of her partner. He, left hand on his hip, twirls a hand-kerchief over his head and, with rhythmic step, twirls around his partner trying to capture her attention. But she lowers her gaze resolutely and tries to evade him. He insists, pursues her, besieges her, cuts off her retreat, yet she escapes. He loses patience, deploys all his attractions, redoubles his daring, struts and undulates, stamping his feet to the music. She gazes dreamily at the tips of her shoes. The music, the singing, the rhythmically clapping hands spur her pursuer, whose hopes rise when the fleeing figure gives signs of weakening. Finally, she looks up, and the meeting of their eyes decides the double victory or double defeat.[3]

The basic scenario of this description, paralleled by Dances of Two all over Latin America, shows how school children have learned to perform gender roles in the course of learning national dances.

Meanwhile, in Peru as well, the patriotic glow of the Zamacueca dimmed after independence. Curiously, however, war with Chile provoked a comeback and a change in name for the Peruvian national dance. The change happened because, ironically, among the several versions of Zamacueca danced in Lima during the 1870s, one of the most currently fashionable was a Chilean variant called Chilena. Obviously, the name rankled once Peru and Chile went to war in 1879. To solve the dilemma, a Peruvian journalist suggested a new name for the national dance, Marinera, a name that would patriotically commemorate the feats of the Peruvian navy, which had recently gained a modest but much-prized victory against the Chileans. Besides, pointed out the journalist later, the nautical reference worked well for the swaying hips and the dance's characteristic "movement of the poopdeck."

The name change stuck, but Marinera had a fatal flaw as a national dance in Peru. It was strongly associated with the country's narrow Pacific coastal region and with Lima, where the population was more black and white than indigenous. Marinera held little appeal for the huge majority of Peruvians, the indigenous masses of the highlands. During the nineteenth century that mattered little, because Lima could afford to ignore the highlands. The guano exports that funded the Peruvian state and afforded Lima the trappings of progress in the mid-nineteenth century came from the coast, from offshore islands, in fact. In the twentieth century, however, as Peruvians began to understand Peru as an essentially indigenous and Andean country, the Huayno displaced the Marinera as the national dance for that reason.

The evolution of Mexico's national dances has a similar trajectory. Independence-era Dances of Two—Jarabes, Jaranas, and Huapangos—continued to exist, but mostly in rustic and folkloric versions by the twentieth century. These dances corresponded to a mestizo Mexican culture in which people of African descent still played an important part. But over time, as Mexico's population of African descent dwindled and the country discovered its rural roots, the Dance of Two lost its political charm in Mexico just as it had in Peru. However, when the triumph of the 1910 Revolution raised Mexico's indigenous folk culture to nationalist prominence, no single national dance emerged to represent it. Instead, Mexico's twentieth-century search for national authenticity, overseen by the Institutional Revolutionary Party, produced a catalog of regional folk dances to keep the school children busy on national holidays. Some of the folk dances were Dances of Two, but others came from the indigenous tradition. All were more folkloric productions rather than spontaneously popular social dances, however. Twentieth-century Mexicans dancing on a Saturday night were more likely to dance something Cuban or Colombian in origin, although the music was played and even composed by Mexicans.

## Cuba

Latin American countries with large indigenous populations have tended to outgrow their first national dances, deriving from the Dance of Two, replacing them with folkloric dances of indigenous origin, whereas countries with large black populations have produced new national social dances in an evolving succession, changing choreography but preserving an African-influenced style of body movement. Cuba's national dances confirm that pattern.

Cuba's large population of African descent makes its cultural legacy comparable to Brazil's. Unlike Brazil, however, Cuba did not become independent between 1810 and 1825. Well-garrisoned, booming economically, and isolated from the major independence movements on the mainland, Cuba played the part of "Ever Faithful Isle" until the 1860s, when its own struggles for independence finally started. By the 1860s, open-couple formations had become totally passé dances from an older generation. Instead, interdependent-couple formations, in which couples went through complicated evolutions and—a new titilation—often changed partners, dominated dance floors in the Atlantic world. So, when the nationalist spirit associated with independence struggles swept over Cuba in the mid-nineteenth century boosting popular dance to patriotic status, it was an interdependent-couple form, Contradanza Cubana, that became the national dance.

Contradanza Cubana, or Danza for short, differed from straight contradance in its subtle rhythms. Cuba's African nations were among the most vigorous in Latin America in the mid-nineteenth century, and Cuban musicians already had an international reputation. The rhythmic excitement that they put into their Danza made it vastly popular on the Caribbean island at all social levels, from the salons of polite society in Havana to the humble dwellings of enslaved people. Descriptions of Danza show a grounded shuffle, with strong lateral movement of the hips. A century and a half ago, the fervor of Cuban popular dance already stood out for world travelers such as the Colombian Tanco Armero:

> [Cuba's] dominant passion, of course, is dancing. Everybody dances in Havana, people of whatever age, class, or condition, from toddlers to old women, from the Captain General to the least of the public employees. They dance the same dances in the palace and in the thatched-roofed huts of the blacks, and even cripples who cannot get up from their seats still move their bodies to the beat of the music. You can hear danzas playing all day long, both in people's houses and by organ grinders in the street, where even pedestrians go dancing by.[4]

From other stops on his world tour, Tanco Armero recalled the singing street vendors, but only in Cuba had he ever seen street vendors dance.

The dance programs of middling and wealthy Cubans were unlike their counterparts elsewhere in Latin America of the 1800s because they privileged a national dance at mid-century. The powerful mid-century vogue of Danza coincided with the onset of Cuba's on-again, off-again independence wars. In the 1880s (an off decade, without fighting but not without tensions) a new national dance, called Danzón, arose from within the tradition of Danza. Like the Brazilian Maxixe, which appeared in the same years, the Danzón began as a new way of dancing the existing repertoire. Contradanza Cubana, like many interdependent-couple dances, included a "swing-your-partner" moment when partners briefly closed couples. Danzón made this moment the main part of the dance, and, to swing their partners, Cuban dancers went into close embrace and synchronized their hips, just as Maxixe dancers did. Here was the same volatile combination that made Maxixe off limits for the middle class except at carnival. In Cuba, though, the nationalist spirit of the 1880s and 1890s seems to have trumped middle-class prudery when it came to Danzón. With a rapidity that astounded observers and confounded journalistic attempts to stem the tide, the sons and daughters of Havana's privileged famous surrendered themselves to Danzón, which reigned as Cuba's national dance until the 1920s.

Son, the father of Salsa, originated in eastern Cuba, far from Havana. Like early Samba, Son had rustic associations. The music was played by small string bands and the lyrics tended toward nostalgia for the countryside. As a social dance, Son was a simple and relatively unadorned closed-couple form with subtle lower-body movement. The Son tradition took Havana by storm in the 1920s and got considerable international exposure in the 1930s and 1940s. By the 1950s in Havana and then in New York, certain musicians working within the Son tradition had developed the musical characteristics basic to Salsa. At that point, the story becomes notably international, and the question of Cuba's national dance gets a bit muddy.

A relatively unnoticed early act of Fidel Castro's revolutionary government was to make Danzón, by then a dignified dance of elders, the official national dance. Perhaps seniority was a plus, because, despite Che Guevara's pronouncement that Cuba had a "revolution with *pachanga*," the revolutionary government at first tried to dampen the rowdy dance fervor of the island's nightlife. A dampening did occur in the 1960s and 1970s, but since then various styles in the Cuban national tradition have interacted with international music influences—including rock, salsa, and hip-hop—to reinvigorate the island's vibrant social dance culture. The current manifestation of that trend is called Timba. Meanwhile, the political kudos of national dance accorded by the Castro government have been accorded to a folkloric performance that is never danced socially, the Rumba. Note that this is not Rhumba, misspelled with an "h" in the mid-twentieth-century United States to described various imported versions of the Son tradition. Rumba in its folkloric form is a classic Dance of Two in a strongly African mode, with percussive and voice accompaniment only. Government endorsement of Rumba as Cuba's national dance was clearly a gesture of official patronage for Afro-Cuban culture, paralleling the regime's tolerance of Afro-Cuban religion, *santería*. These racial politics plainly reflect the continued emigration of white Cubans, whose departure has gradually changed the demographics of the island's population.

## Brazil

In Brazil, nationalism and enduring popularity combined to create "the kingdom of Samba." The Samba began as a classic Dance of Two, Samba de Roda, a recreation of Rio de Janeiro's African nations that led a second life in dancing processions like those of Epiphany. During the mid-twentieth century, the Samba enjoyed wide popularity as a social dance in Brazil. Today Rio's Samba parades at carnival every year symbolize the participation of people of African descent in the Brazilian nation, a gesture of inclusion basic to contemporary Brazilian political culture.

Two previous national dances in the same Afro-Brazilian tradition preceded the Samba in the limelight. The first was the Lundu, a Dance of Two that emerged in the 1780s. Never declared the national dance by government edict, the Lundu acquired the title by clear Brazilian consensus during the independence period. Although the struggle involved limited bloodshed and was in no way comparable to what occurred in Spanish America, Brazil's fight for independence in the 1820s brought a surge of national feeling, and dancing the Lundu was a way to affirm one's patriotic spirit. The Lundu was danced on stages and in taverns, in public squares and private homes. A distinctive aspect of the Lundu was the raised arm position, reminiscent of Spanish Flamenco. The often romantic and sometimes off-color song lyrics were always in Portuguese to a thrumming guitar accompaniment. And of course, the Lundu included lots of hip and pelvic movement, too. European travelers thought it deplorably African. Once the Portuguese had recognized Brazilian independence, the nativist vogue for Lundu dancing waned, however. During the mid 1800s, the Brazilian elite wanted above all for Brazil to become more like Europe.

Beginning in the 1870s, a new Brazilian national dance began to emerge. Maxixe ("xixe" sounds like "she she") seems to have gained its momentum not from any political program, but from a general effervescence of urban popular culture that occurred in much of the Atlantic world at that time. To dance the Maxixe, the dancing couple embraced as for the Waltz or the Polka, but they moved their hips as in the Lundu. The Maxixe started as a new way of dancing to the music of the existing international repertories, music that Brazilian musicians were subtly transforming with syncopated rhythms and local percussion instruments. Synchronized hip movement in a close embrace made the Maxixe highly transgressive by nineteenth-century standards. Occasionally the woman even straddled her partner's leg, as in the late twentieth-century Lambada. Poor urban Brazilians danced the Maxixe at any time of year, but middle-class Brazilians did so mostly at carnival or, in the case of men, on slumming expeditions to Rio's red-light district. By 1900, the Maxixe had become the proverbial national dance, and its vogue lasted for decades.

The Samba replaced the Maxixe as Brazil's national dance around 1930. The difference was subtle at first. The collective composers of the canonical first musical recording of samba discography, *On the Telefone* (1917), could not quite agree, for example, on whether the composition was samba or maxixe. During the decades-long reign of maxixe at Rio carnival, the name Samba had sometimes been used as a synonym for maxixe, especially when the dancers switched to the open-couple formation of the old Dance of Two and a circle of onlookers gathered around them. The name Samba implied a variety of virtuosic steps for showing off and had rural associations and deep resonances in Afro-Brazilian folklore, highlighting African roots. In the 1920s, a new generation of Rio carnival revelers from the poor black invasion neighborhoods called *favelas*, formed carnival parade groups called *escolas de samba*, or Samba schools. The processional dancing of the Samba schools drew on deep traditions, and the "Sambistas" adopted an increasingly percussive accompaniment also intended to highlight those roots. The flowering of the Samba schools in the 1930s was simultaneous with a flowering of musical compositions that found wide circulation in radio and cinema. A closed-couple form of the Samba was danced socially. The popularity of the Samba was already moving it toward the status of national dance when state and national governments decided to endorse and even subsidize it. A new nationalist spirit was afoot, and the Samba became its emblem.

The Samba's nationalist spirit in the 1930s and 1940s reflected the independence-era phenomenon of a hundred years prior, with some important differences. Once again, Brazilian popular dance was politically engaged to represent popular sovereignty. The Brazilian nation was being reinterpreted to become more racially inclusive, at least at the symbolic level. During these years intellectuals, led by the influential anthropologist Gilberto Freyre, elaborated and expounded a racial ideology privileging the idea of racial mixture. The adoption of the ideology was not paralleled by any notable diminishment of the disadvantages of color in Brazilian society, so this was a hollow victory in terms of direct material results. Yet, in purely ideological terms, the transformation was positive, and the carnival Samba was its official emblem. The ideological work done annually by Rio carnival has given the Samba impressive staying power as a national symbol, even though its popularity as a social dance waned in the second half of the twentieth century.

## Colombia

Colombia's national dances, like Cuba's and Brazil's, have drawn vigor from the country's large population of African descent, about a quarter of the total. The Bambuco, the first Colombian national dance, arose during the independence era. The military bands of Bolívar's patriot armies could clearly play Bambucos, although it may not be true that they played one during the patriot charge at the decisive final battle of Ayacucho in 1824.

The Bambuco is a standard Dance of Two. Colombians of the mid-1800s believed that blacks from the southwest Cauca region of the country were the creators of the Bambuco. By that time, however, it was danced throughout Colombia, in hot lands and highlands, by mestizos, whites, and indigenous people as well. The Bambuco's popularity at mid-century was probably fueled by the country's high level of popular political mobilization. The Cauca region and the people of African descent were at the center of that mobilization. An article on the Bambuco in 1868, for example, ties it to freed slaves and freeborn mulatto artisans.

By the early twentieth century, the Bambuco had become established as national folklore, with a substantial following in the urban middle class. At the same time, the origins of the dance were obscured by the evolution of living traditions. Just as U.S. blacks stopped playing the banjo in the twentieth century, allowing the memory of the instrument's African origins to flicker out, Colombian blacks ignored the folkloric Bambuco and turned to other dances, leaving twentieth-century folklorists to define the Bambuco mistakenly as essentially European or mestizo in origin. Ironically, the Bambuco's dissociation from people of African descent became one of its main attractions to folklorists who were eager to downplay Colombia's African heritage. Colombia is an intensely regionalized country, and Colombians historically have understood their regions partly through racial stereotypes. In this scheme, the Bambuco represented the country's mestizo Andean regions in explicit contrast to its Afro-Colombian coastal regions.

The Colombian coast got its revenge in the 1950s, when the Cumbia became a popular dance sensation, spontaneously "invading" the dance floors of the country's Andean region. The exciting new social dance abruptly eclipsed the folkloric Bambuco in the national imagination. By 1960, Colombians unanimously claimed the Cumbia as their new national dance. In its folkloric form, the Cumbia is a Dance of Two that is not so different from the Bambuco, but an accompaniment of strongly African percussion made it more in tune with the mid-twentieth century's international social dance genres, especially those emanating from Cuba. Danced socially, the Cumbia became a closed-couple dance that, like other twentieth-century dances with powerful rhythms, was perceived as liberating and modern—just the thing for the ethos of the 1960s. However, during the 1980s, the popularity of the Cumbia declined in Colombia, where it competed with the Salsa, the Merengue, and several new national genres, such as the Vallenato, for space on dance floors. Today Cumbias are rarely played in a Colombian discoteque. Still, international fame and several decades of quasi-official status make the Cumbia the national dance in the minds of most Colombians. In addition, the carnival celebration of Barranquilla, regional capital of Colombia's Caribbean coast, has grown in importance over several decades, and the Cumbia is the official rhythm of its parades.

The Cumbia also developed an enduring following in other Latin American countries. It is easier to dance than many Cuban rhythms, which perhaps accounts for its rapid spread in

## HIP-HOP AND OTHER INTERNATIONAL INFLUENCES

Latin Americans have always danced many international styles in addition to their national dances. Minuets, Quadrilles, Waltzes, and Polkas found favor in the 1800s. International styles, from Jazz Dancing to the Twist, became even more accessible in the 1900s because of the advent of radio, record players, and the cinema. In general, people at the top of the social hierarchy responded most quickly to international styles. Some countries, notably Brazil and Argentina, developed their own rock music industries in the 1980s, although, as in the United States, dancing was not the principal purpose of that music.

In the 1990s U.S. hip-hop music became quite popular and spawned a number of vigorous Latin American offshoots. In Brazil, for example, hip-hop recordings based on sampling of older recordings and electronic drum tracks were locally produced under the name *funk* and galvanized young dancers in a number of major cities. Interestingly, Funk Dancing (and dancing to U.S. soul or Motown music, as well) became a focus of black racial identity among Brazilians of African descent, whereas Brazilian dance traditions (with obvious African roots of their own) had normally been viewed as emblems of mixed-race (i.e., national) identity. Reggae music from Jamaica attracted many Brazilian dancers and inspired local imitators as well.

In the Caribbean region, Jamaican reggae and dancehall music fused with U.S. hip-hop influences (and possibly with local Panamanian and Puerto Rican influences as well) to produce *reggaeton*. Reggaeton music is, for the most part, electronically synthesized and is always based on electronic drum tracks. Reggaeton is also strongly reminiscent of hip-hop in that the lyrics are recited or "rapped" rather than sung. Although reggaeton is principally dance music, the dancing that it accompanies is, for the most part, quite simple, without fancy steps or turns in the manner of the Salsa or the Merengue. A notorious exception is the *perreo* or "doggy" maneuver, in which a dancing couple rubs their lower bodies together. In a final similarity with hip-hop, reggaeton has occasionally inspired a reaction critical of the lyrics' disparaging attitude toward women.

areas without vital African-influenced traditions, first in highland Colombia and then internationally. Today local dance bands produce and record cumbia music in Mexico, Peru, and Argentina, and the genre has shown considerable staying power in those places, where its practice now spans several decades, although only occasionally does it escape its reputation as a lower-class dance.

## Argentina and Uruguay

Latin America's predominantly white countries (or those with this perception) also have national dances descended from the diasporic Dance of Two. Both the Argentine capital at Buenos Aires and the Uruguayan capital at Montevideo, its much smaller twin across the Río de la Plata estuary, were about one quarter black in the early nineteenth century. Both cities had substantial African nations that modernized their names after independence to become

African Associations and transformed their kings into presidents. The African Associations of the Río de la Plata retained their strong attachment to the Feast of Epiphany, a particular time for their public dances, which were called *candombes.*

Candombe sounds enough like *candomblé* (the Afro-Brazilian religion of Yoruba origin, similar to Cuban santería) that there must be a connection of some kind. However, the words refer to quite distinct phenomena. The African Associations of the Río la Plata in the 1800s, like black nations throughout Latin America, had ceremonial functions and religious practices that we know little about. But their candombes were public affairs full of white spectators. They were occasions for the Dance of Two, eventually adding fashionable contradance motifs, not venues for spirit possession and trance dancing, as in candomblé. Candombes were held on Sundays in vacant lots on the edge of town and in public squares on Epiphany and, especially, at celebrations and holidays associated with national independence. Black participation as patriots in the wars of independence led to gradual abolition of the candombes, which was complete by the mid-1800s. Unfortunately, black military service also decimated the male population. After 1880, inundation by mass European immigration completed the whitening of Buenos Aires and Montevideo.

Nonetheless, Argentina's and Uruguay's national dances constituted perfectly recognizable specimens of larger Latin American patterns. In the independence period, the national dance was the Montonero Minuet, mentioned earlier as a example of the frequent association between national dances and patriot armies. The Montonero Minuet was followed by a national dance of the mid-century, an interdependent-couple variety, called the Pericón. Energetic political uses of popular dance continued in Argentina and Uruguay after independence because populist political mobilization extended for decades under the polarizing leader, Juan Manuel de Rosas. But the Río de la Plata's real popular dance furor still lay in the future, far from politics, in the poor neighborhoods of Buenos Aires and Montevideo, where people of African descent still lived in the 1880s and 1890s. They were the creators of the Milonga, the progenitor of the twentieth-century Tango.

The Milonga was the exact analog of the Maxixe and the Danzón, a late nineteenth-century national dance of close embrace and marked hip movement. Like the Maxixe and the Danzón, the Milonga began as a new way of dancing the existing repertoire. Milonga choreography involved *cortes y quebradas*—quebradas being the familiar reference to swiveling hips, *cortes* being sudden stops or changes of direction. It was "cut-and-break dancing," so to speak. Interestingly, the sort of music that lent itself best to the new style was *habanera,* an international form of Cuban danza that had spread throughout mid-nineteenth-century Latin America thanks to touring Spanish musical theater. The Milonga's rise in popularity occurred in the 1880s, in perfect synchrony with the emergence of the Maxixe and the Danzón. But a contemporary dictionary of Argentine expressions defined the Milonga as a dance "exclusively of the lower orders." The middle class kept its distance for more than a decade, leaving the Milonga for hoi polloi. Young men of wealth did experiment with the Milonga in the brothels that loom prominently in early Tango lore, however, and many public dance halls became venues for commercial sex. Eventually, the lure of the Milonga's close embrace, synchronized hips, and cut-and-break choreography began to attract the curiosity of more middle-class youth, just as the Danzón was already doing in Havana and the Maxixe in Rio. The tipping point happened in 1900 during the big carnival balls given all over Buenos Aires that week. The newspaper reporting on these events proclaims the advent of Tango Criollo, which was nothing more than Milonga-style cutting-and-breaking with a new name.

The Tango was born of the Milonga in somewhat the way that rock and roll was born of rhythm and blues—by crossing a color line and a division between social classes. To rebaptize Milonga dancing as Tango helped remove the stigma attached to the style. In the ear of white Buenos Aires, Milonga sounded like a pastime of pimps and whores and unappealing lowlife. Tango, on the other hand, had an alluringly naughty ring. Its most immediate referent in 1900 was a blackface carnival caricature, something whites did in the spirit of cross-dressing.

The word "tango" has had so many meanings. It was used all over Latin America, in the 1800s, to refer to the dancing of slaves. In Buenos Aires, houses belonging to the African Associations had sometimes been called tango houses. Blackface performances reminiscent of U.S. minstrel shows were called tangos in the second part of the century. Lyrics for such performances were often written in mock black dialect, switching r's and l's to represent the fractured Spanish of African slaves. Such lyrics made any sort of music a tango, and Spanish musical theater performed many habaneras (of Cuban descent, after all) as tangos. Tangos in mock dialect were very often sung at carnival in Buenos Aires and Montevideo by parade groups of white males in blackface. White imitation of blacks under the name tango, in 1900 in Buenos Aires and Montevideo, was a well-established convention that absolutely everyone understood.

So when a few daring dancers showed off Milonga moves at public Buenos Aires carnival balls, the electrified crowd and newspaper chroniclers hailed the cutting-and-breaking discretely as the Tango. The new name helped make the point that Milonga-dancing pimps and whores were (supposedly) not in attendance. To further clarify the point and, perhaps, to specify the absence of undesirable immigrants as well, the newspaper chroniclers added the adjective "criollo" for good measure, but it did not last. The name that the whole world came to know for Latin America's most famous dance ever was simply the Tango.

In the early twentieth century, the Tango became a truly global phenomenon. The initial, crucial step was from Buenos Aires to Paris, on the eve of World War I. The Tango's Parisian vogue eased acceptance of the new national dance by the Argentine and Uruguayan middle classes and launched the dance internationally as well. International acceptance of Tango dancing (and middle-class acceptance at home) was facilitated by the evolution of the style. The upbeat, funky Tango of 1910 slowed and changed mood entirely by 1930. The lyrics changed from off-color ditties to bitter ballads of unrequited love. The hunched shoulders and marked hip movement of the early Tango disappeared—or, rather, was preserved only in a style called, once again, the Milonga, which became a "retro" subgenre within the Tango repertory. What people in Buenos Aires and Montevideo danced socially in the mid-twentieth century was the Tango *liso*, or plain Tango, with less mobile hips and without fancy footwork. The Tango's association with black people faded in the 1930s and 1940s when it became fully established as the Argentine and Uruguayan national dance. In its current form, the dance preserves nothing of its African roots except the mark of their erasure. Those roots have, in fact, been largely forgotten, even on the streets of Buenos Aires and Montevideo.

Nor are African roots evident in international forms of the Tango. When the dance first made a hit in Paris a hundred years ago, European dancers adapted it to fit their own aptitudes and abilities. The dance was "bleached and ironed," made more balletic, standardized, and codified into specific steps that could be taught by the numbers. Dance instructors who learned to dance the Tango in Paris created instruction manuals and literally traveled around the world teaching from them. The international Tango craze peaked in the 1920s, when Rudolph Valentino danced it on screen and the Tango-curious could be found on dance floors from Des Moines to Shanghai. This form of the dance, the one still practiced today in international ballroom dance competitions, soon lost the key improvisational dimension of Tango dancing and, by the substitution of set steps and theatrical attitudes to be practiced in advance, resulted in something that Argentines and Uruguayans find almost unrecognizable.

At home and internationally, the Tango declined in popularity as a social dance from the 1950s until the 1990s. In Argentina and Uruguay, the national dance was upstaged on dance floors by folkloric competitors, by rock music (emanating from abroad and, eventually, locally produced), and by an itinerant version of the Cumbia. In the 1990s, however, Tango dancing experienced a revival that was driven, at least in part, by an extensive international circulation of Argentine and Uruguayan instructors. Today, most metropolitan areas in Europe and the United States have clubs of Tango enthusiasts who cultivate a version of the dance more closely in touch with Buenos Aires.

## Epilogue

In the late twentieth century, the Salsa and the Merengue, Salsa's first cousin from the Dominican Republic, became international phenomena, danced in Europe and the United States as well as in some urban areas of Asia and Africa. The profusion of turning figures that can be used in both dances shows their descent from contradance. But the two dances are rhythmically quite dissimilar, the Merengue being much more straightforward and therefore easier to learn than the Salsa. That advantage seems to have contributed to the popularity of the Merengue, which overtook the Salsa on international dance floors in the 1990s.

In addition, by the end of the twentieth century, a rhythmically stripped-down form of the Cumbia has become perhaps the most important social dance of poor urban people in Spanish American countries outside the Caribbean basin, who adopted it as their own. The melodic influence of Andean music makes the Peruvian Cumbia distinctive, whether as highly produced "tecno-cumbia" or down-home *chicha*. Meanwhile, long-haired Argentines and Uruguayans play and sing (and compose) their own versions of cumbia music. Mexico's local versions constitute the cumbia music that is probably most danced in Mexico and among Mexican inhabitants of the United States as well. The music of the Tejana singer Selena, for example, was cumbia-based.

Overall, however, the prestige and popularity of Latin America's various national dance traditions ebbed in the late twentieth century. Except for the Caribbean genres that expanded internationally, most national dances were gradually relegated to the status of folklore, rather like Square Dancing in the United States—something danced not in most social settings, but rather by groups of aficionados or by school children. In southern Brazil, for example, the Samba, the great popular music and dance of the 1930s and 1940s, is now practiced mostly at carnival, struggling to find any space on dance floors (or in radio play lists) at any other time of the year. Various regional genres of northeastern Brazil retained true popularity as social dances, but rock and funk music, both imported and homegrown, have made enormous inroads, as have new popular genres, such as *música sertaneja*, or "country music."

The very concept of national dance has lost some currency in Latin America since 1950. Probably that loss of currency reflects, at least in part, the post-cold war eclipse of nationalism throughout the continent in recent years. In addition, some Latin American countries have outgrown old national dances that reflect an earlier sense of self. Millions of Latin American still experience a lot of patriotic pride in their national dances, but none seems forcefully articulated to a contemporary political movement. Perhaps that is just as well, but it is certainly not permanent. The political energies that can be engaged by national dances are too powerful in Latin America to lie dormant forever.

# RESOURCE GUIDE

## PRINT SOURCES

Austerlitz, Paul. *Merengue: Dominican Music and Dominican Identity.* Philadelphia, PA: Temple University Press, 1997.

Boggs, Vernon W. *Salsiology: Afro-Cuban Music and the Evolution of Salsa in New York City.* Westport, CT: Greenwood Press, 1992.

Browning, Barbara. *Samba: Resistance in Motion.* Bloomington and Indianapolis: Indiana University Press, 1995.

Castro, Donald S. *The Argentine Tango as Social History, 1880–1955.* Lewiston, NY: The Edwin Mellen Press, 1991.

Chasteen, John Charles. *National Rhythms, African Roots: The Deep History of Latin American Popular Dance.* Albuquerque: University of New Mexico Press, 2004.

Collier, Simon, and Susana Azzi. *Tango: The Dance, the Song, the Story.* London, UK: Thames and Hudson, 1995.

Daniel, Yvonne. *Rumba: Dance and Social Change in Contemporary Cuba.* Bloomington: Indiana University Press, 1995.

Delgado, Celeste Fraser, and José Esteban Muñoz, eds. *Everynight Life: Culture and Dance in Latin/o America.* Durham, NC: Duke University Press, 1997.

Fryer, Peter. *Rhythms of Resistance: African Musical Heritage in Brazil.* Hanover, NH: Wesleyan University Press, 2000.

Gillmor, Frances. *The Dance Dramas of Mexican Villages.* Tucson: University of Arizona, 1943.

Guillermoprieto, Alma. *Samba.* New York, NY: Vintage Books, 1990.

Johnson, Edith. *Regional Dances of Mexico.* Skokie, IL: National Textbook Company, 1974.

Manuel, Peter, Kenneth Bilby, and Michael Largey. *Caribbean Currents: Caribbean Music from Rumba to Reggae.* Philadelphia, PA: Temple University Press, 1995.

McNeill, William H. *Keeping Together in Time: Dance and Drill in Human History.* Cambridge, MA: Harvard University Press, 1995.

Mendoza, Zoila S. *Shaping Society through Dance: Mestizo Ritual and Performance in the Peruvian Andes.* Chicago and London: University of Chicago Press, 2000.

Murphy, Joseph M. *Working the Spirit: Ceremonies of the African Diaspora.* Boston, MA: Beacon Press, 1994.

Pacini Hernández, Deborah. *Bachata: A Social History of a Dominican Popular Music.* Philadelphia, PA: Temple University Press, 1995.

Savigliano, Marta. E. *Tango and the Political Economy of Passion.* Boulder, CO: Westview Press, 1995.

Shaw, Lisa. *The Social History of the Brazilian Samba (1930–1945).* Aldershot (Hampshire, UK): Ashgate Publishing Ltd., 1999.

Sloat, Susanna. *Caribbean Dance from Abakuá to Zouk: How Movement Shapes Identity.* Gainesville: University Press of Florida, 2002.

Taylor, Patrick. *Nation Dance: Religion, Identity, and Cultural Difference in the Caribbean.* Bloomington: Indiana University Press, 2001.

Vianna, Hermano. *The Mystery of Samba: Popular Music and National Identity in Brazil.* Translated by John Charles Chasteen, ed. Chapel Hill: University of North Carolina Press, 1999.

Wade, Peter. *Music, Race, and Nation: Música Tropical in Colombia.* Chicago: University of Chicago Press, 2000.

Waxer, Lise A. *The City of Musical Memory: Salsa, Record Grooves, and Popular Culture in Cali.* Middletown, CT: Wesleyan University Press, 2002.

## WEBSITES

*Current Argentine Tango:* http://www.totango.net/ttindex.html.
*Hispanic Heritage Resource Site:* http://www.gale.com/free_resources/chh/.

*History of Dance Index:* http://www.centralhome.com/ballroomcountry/history.htm.
*Insider's Guide to Rio:* http://www.ipanema.com/carnival/samba.htm.
*London School of Samba:* http://www.londonschoolofsamba.co.uk.
*Merengue and Bachata from the Dominican Republic:* http://home.tiscali.nl/pjetax/htmlfile/indexpage.html.
*Reggaeton in the United States:* http://www.barrio305.com/.
*Salsa in the United States:* http://www.salsaroots.com/.

# NOTES

1. The Portuguese word *mestiçagem* and its adjective form *mestiço* are used in a parallel way in Brazil. This article uses the Spanish words for the sake of uniformity.
2. Fredrika Bremer, *The Homes of the New World: Impressions of America* (New York: Harper and Brothers, 1853), 2:38–49.
3. André Bellesort, *Le jeune Amérique, Chili et Bolivie* (Paris, 1897), quoted by Pablo Garrido, *Historial de la cueca* (Valparaíso: Ediciones Universitárias de Valparaíso, 1979), 64.
4. Tanco Armero, *Viaje de Nueva Granada* (doc. 456) in Gustavo Eguren, *La fidelísima Habana* (Havana: Editorial Letras Cubanas, 1986).

# FASHION AND APPEARANCE

REGINA A. ROOT

What is Latin American fashion? This question is addressed in the pages of *The Latin American Fashion Reader*, published in 2005, which brought together the work of an international group of scholars whose research integrates the study of dress into the workings of culture, identity formation, and social change in Latin America. In search of an answer, these scholars have looked to the transformative qualities of dress, arguing that fashion in Latin America has always been "a profoundly social experience that invites individual and collective bodies to assume certain identities and, at times, also to transgress limits and create new ones."[1] Such an approach never fully answers the question, of course, for it is expected that the realm of the "profoundly social" looks something like the images in a kaleidoscope—multifaceted and constantly remade in the face of image and pleasure, beauty and transgression, elite and everyday patterns of consumption.

A student of popular culture must establish the context from which a given style emerges, paying attention to the social, political, and historical forces that inform its making. In today's Argentina, for example, long hair and a stylized image of revolutionary Che Guevara stamped on a red T-shirt—which would no doubt have been perceived as an overtly rebellious statement when worn in that country some 20 years ago—seem perhaps less menacing these days than short hair and a designer suit. What makes for such a dramatic shift in representation? Why would one be more acceptable than the other in multiple contexts? To understand this more fully, one would have to consider very carefully Argentina's legacy of authoritarianism, its transition to democracy, and the economic crises that debilitated the stability of its governing structures in the early part of the twenty-first century. Further consideration would unravel the cultural significance of the fashion icons in question, including the implications of revolutionary legacies, such as Che Guevara's, in the Latin America of the post–Cold War period, and the impact of donning an elegant, foreign-made suit at a moment of political corruption and economic crisis. At the same time, in the context of an interpretive global community of consumers for whom clothes and appearance reflect the "aura" of celebrity, both the wearers of the T-shirt and the suit might ultimately be bound to the same machine of mass production and consumption. Finally, such fashion icons project another message altogether if placed in the context of El Alto, Bolivia, where some young Aymara men sport Che Guevara tattoos and don baggy pants and baseball caps, having appropriated the look from black urban America, as they blend native music rhythms and rap tunes to protest their marginalization from society.[2]

Such contrasts often receive a great deal of attention from the international press as demonstrated by the discussion of the casual dress of the region's "indigenous Che Guevara," Bolivian president Evo Morales, who defies conventions by not wearing a suit. Although he celebrated his inauguration in elaborate indigenous dress, at a later meeting with international leaders Morales appeared sporting a striped, earth-toned sweater but forgoing a business tie. On the world stage, it would appear that such dress calls into question the power of traditional status markers and their representatives, perhaps connecting in some sartorial manner the desire for socioeconomic revolution in Bolivia with a larger hemispheric struggle against what are perceived as the forces of cultural imperialism. Latin American fashion thus circulates broadly as containing a meaning, allowing individuals and groups to make choices for themselves, and sometimes their families, as they contemplate triumphs and plot challenges in their everyday lives.

*Fashion Theory: The Journal of Dress, Body and Culture*, which canonized the field of fashion studies in the mid 1990s, defines fashion in its editorial policy as "the cultural construction of the embodied identity."[3] In the Latin American context, fashion has often been viewed as a cultural process in which individual and collective bodies assume, alter, or transgress certain identities. To fully appreciate fashion's transformative qualities, therefore, it is important to remember that the concept itself is grounded in particular social frameworks that are temporal, sensory, and spatial in nature. Someone must decide what is fashion and who is fashionable, and another must convince the public that such declarations only follow an obvious cultural logic. In everyday life, one's identity is thus culturally fashioned and made. Because there is a great deal of variety in early twenty-first-century dress and style, what one wears generates meaning, and the individual exerts some control over her or his image, whether "dressing for success" or plotting alternative styles.

In the realm of popular culture, appearance involves an outward sign, a prevailing behavior revealed, and a public act that manifests itself in everyday life. Here the question of appearance is linked to commonly accepted ideals of beauty and style, the trends that challenge these ideals, and the community-based or national expressions of ideal appearance. Although such expressions are certainly evident in everyday life, this discussion must also depend on those historical representations—such as images found in art, photography, literature, and other texts—which have survived time and are used by scholars to articulate general trends. When considering artistic portraits of the urban-based elite, for example, it is important to remember that such projections exalted certain features or behaviors and sometimes served as visual registers to discriminate against those who did not possess a similar social ranking. While most contemporaries emphasize that one should not judge a person by her or his appearance, such a standard has not always existed in times past. Dress and appearance in Latin America were often the source of hot debates that sought to determine the rank and role of different social groups at given historical moments.

## THE COLONIAL LEGACY

In 1492 Christopher Columbus claimed what are today the islands of Cuba, the Dominican Republic, and Haiti for Spain and initiated the conquest of the indigenous populations in the region known today as Latin America. One of the first images of the landing, a 1493 wood engraving that was used to illustrate a letter regarding the discovery to a king's representative, reveals a robed King Ferdinand with a crucifix on his crown on one side of a shore and Columbus in a dark admiral's hat beside his crew on the other. The American natives, their inordinate size allowing them to tower over Columbus and his crew, stand in stark contrast. Without returning the gaze of these Spanish representatives of an historic mission, the members of the native community represented walk away, as if unaware that their long hair and "nakedness" would produce bewilderment. Spanish literature from this early colonial period reveals much about the sense of awe experienced by the first colonizers, and the marvel with which they viewed material goods such as cotton, intricate feather work, and woven cloth. Shortly thereafter, the "New World" provided Europe with material goods as varied as silver, gold, sugar, chocolate, textiles, and dye. Portugal, motivated by its own interests for colonial power, successfully challenged Spain for control of the region that makes up today's Brazil. As Spain and Portugal quickly established colonial governments, native populations suffered the effects of brutal conquest, pandemic illness due to unfamiliar pathogens, and tortures aimed to force conversion to Christianity. The term "black legend," coined by Friar Bartolomé de Las Casas to describe the exploitative practices of settlers, included those who had turned to slavery and other forms of violence to establish ranches, mines, and textile industries in the New World.

Dress served as an important visual register in the construction of cultural, racial, and ethnic differences in the colonial period. Mariselle Meléndez argues that, in the early part of the sixteenth century, depictions of nakedness served to justify notions of European "superiority."[4] Such images privileged the powerful, "civilized" colonizers and marked indigenous people as "barbarians" in need of governance. Catholic missionaries often targeted the clothing of peoples from more tropical regions and insisted that they cover themselves. Many women continued to wear ethnic clothing, although colonial administrators often debated the appropriateness of certain native garments such as the *anacu*, a tunic-style dress worn in the Andes, believing that its sides should not reveal the legs.[5] Women in Michoacán lengthened their skirts and appropriated the *toca*, or wimple, to cover their heads.[6] For native men, on the other hand, the change was more noticeable, as colonial powers dictated that they wear Castilian shirts and white cotton trousers of Flemish origin (popularly used in Spain) and crop their long hair.[7] Other garments in use included ponchos, locally produced hats, and sometimes sandals finished the costume. While European-style dress was certainly promoted by colonial authorities, the excessive borrowing of styles was strongly discouraged. While some *caciques*, or noble Indians, distinguished themselves from common Indians by wearing shoes instead of sandals, dressing in silk or armor, and carrying arms, local authorities sometimes stripped those imitating Spanish dress too closely.[8]

Prior to colonization, dress and textiles served as indicators of social and religious identity and as mediums of exchange. The installation of colonial regimes, with the subsequent clashes in the symbolic system of goods, dictated what people wore and ate, where they lived, and how they interacted in public spaces. For many, things had changed very little. Arnold Bauer writes that "throughout the colonial period and beyond, native men and women, in diminishing numbers, to be sure, continued to dress in homespun and home-woven cloth and to depend primarily upon the ancestral diet of native foods."[9] The terms of textile production in some regions, however, would change dramatically with the introduction of steel shears and European methods involving spinning and rotary wheels, eventually substituting for obsidian instruments, the drop spindle, and the arduous backdrop loom.[10] Some religious orders, private investors, and even indigenous communities established textile workshops, or *obrajes*, but these faded into colonial history with the emergence of alternate markets for cotton in the eighteenth century and the influx of goods from Asia brought to Latin America by the Spanish Empire's Manila galleons.[11]

By this time, the caste system that had been imposed to maintain a sense of hierarchy that privileged Europeans and to respond to racial mixing, or *mestizaje*, was increasingly being called into question. From the onset of colonization, natives and African slaves had been forced to wear Western styles of dress, a system that reinforced the authority of the Spanish and Portuguese, and over time, of their Creole descendants. Decrees prohibited the use of certain textiles by those whom the caste system deemed inferior, thus leading to the prohibition of velvet, taffeta, or silk for specially fashioned Incan *unkus*, or tunics, in the Andean region and the *rebozos*, or intricately woven scarves, commonly worn by women in Mexico. A few of those marginalized by this lack of special privileges did issue complaints, and court records throughout the region included statements that challenged the inability to access European goods. Archeologists are still in the process of compiling records of colonial material culture; when it comes to the realm of fashion, it sometimes appears that there may have been great movement across ethnic lines.

Because the caste system could not be enforced completely, prominently displayed visual registers of racial mixing known as *casta* paintings used conventions in dress as worn by couples and their offspring. Light-skinned *mestizos* (a term that was used to identify people of European and indigenous descent) sometimes imitated the consumption patterns and styles of more socially preferable castes in order to be mistaken for one of them. Since cultural hybridity had become a fact of daily life, many mestizos could cut their hair and turn away from the hues of local dyes to distinguish themselves from Indians and thereby identify with higher castes with greater privileges.[12] It appears that visible social groups of the seventeenth and eighteenth centuries manipulated dress codes in order to challenge a caste system that seemed only to expand with increasingly hostile labels for the lower castes, such as *coyote* and *lobo* [wolf].[13] Responding to a perceived threat, the Spanish crown issued a series of statements to emphasize the delineations of dress according to caste hierarchies, denouncing the ostentatious dress on the part of *mestiza* women but not the luxurious presence of clergymen. While those who transgressed were at times punished publicly, there is not enough evidence to indicate whether or not such actions were commonly enacted. Once racial miscegenation had challenged the very categories of the caste system, however, it is clear that the aura of colonial power began to disintegrate. Disruptive performances of dress, therefore, served as early indicators of a cultural crisis that would bring about the subsequent fragmentation of the Spanish Empire.

## FASHIONING INDEPENDENCE

By the early nineteenth century, the region experienced several calls for independence from Spain and Portugal that deeply affected the way people consumed fashion. For Cuba and Puerto Rico, this struggle for independence would not materialize until the end of the nineteenth century, although the description of fashion and dance in several literary works began to foreshadow the demise of Spanish rule and construct alternate political identities. Under the colonial caste system, Creole descendants of Europeans had been designated as being of inferior social status, although some boldly dared to appropriate subtle details in order to imitate their Spanish superiors, such as the use of gold and silver threads or of special fabrics in the construction of outfits.[14] As rivalries increased between factions and civil wars ensued, Creoles moved to Parisian styles that symbolized the legacy of "Liberty, Equality, and Fraternity" espoused by the French Revolution and advocated a society based on merit rather than inherited privilege. Such ideas even made their way into women's fans of the period, which sometimes depicted portraits of distinguished political leaders or challenged prevailing authority figures. Portraits of Simón Bolívar of Venezuela and José de San Martín of Argentina in uniforms of their own design circulated in lithograph form and in official documents, although it would be impossible to distinguish the patterns from Spanish designs were it not for the particular uses of color. By the late nineteenth century, the garments of founding fathers would appear represented in illustrated magazines throughout the region without any hint of the owner, as if the aura of the garments now on display for the national community represented some higher truth (see, for example, the renditions published by the *Papel Periódico Ilustrado* from late nineteenth-century Colombia). Visions of women who took on the male uniform in order to fight Spanish oppression, as exemplified by Juana de Azurduy of Bolivia and by Josefa de Tenorio, a slave from Argentina who argued that she merited equal status in postcolonial society, survive in popular poems and the archives. The record is silent about the responses of most women, who were often called upon to piece together and sew the accessories of war during the struggle for independence.

Fashion, whether in print or in practice, would emerge as an important metaphor for political change and renovation. Men's top hats could contain a political message that another would see only if saluted by the wearer. Despite the occasional flourish, urban men's fashions remained somber and much less remarkable than those of their female counterparts, in part because these were conventionally associated with the "civilized" aristocracy of European nations. Children throughout the region went to school in uniforms. Most women's styles were subject to continuous transformations, with corseted waists and the extremes of layered body dressing appropriated from European dress.

By the end of the nineteenth century, Clorinda Matto de Turner of Peru and Juana Manuela Gorriti of Argentina advocated dress reform in the push for female emancipation. The affordability of the sewing machine (often driven by a foot treadle) now allowed the consumer to choose between homemade or ready-made clothing. Transatlantic fashion magazines such as *La Torre de Oro*, with main offices in Sevilla and Buenos Aires, would suggest that the initial gap between Iberian and Latin American dress codes had waned. The advent of comfortable textiles, the use of built-in bustles, and the rejection of the crinoline skirt helped women feel a bit more comfortable in their dresses. Lengthened bodices, uncorseted waists, and deep, jewel-like tones surfaced in urban areas, revealing a more relaxed appearance and contrasting dramatically with the dress of rural communities. Alongside the onslaught of economic transformation brought about by bureaucratic modernization in the late nineteenth century, fashion and appearance continued to register innovative styles with modern sentiments.

## FASHION AND NATIONALISM IN THE TWENTIETH CENTURY

At the beginning of the twentieth century, despite calls for consumer nationalism, the inventories of stores in most of Latin America differed little from those of Europe and the United States. In fact, foreign goods abounded despite a proliferation of images of "national" types such as the Venezuelan *llanero*, the Argentine gaucho, and the Mexican *charro*, or cowhands. Increasingly in the cities, fashion and appearance were connected to a feeling of "modernity," and consumers desired to purchase and wear items made in Europe. British department stores such as Casa Mappin in downtown São Paulo, Brazil, or Harrods in Buenos Aires, Argentina, marketed to a steady flow of consumers who desired to infuse their day with "Englishness." In more rural areas, many shed their traditional garments for cotton shirts, pants, and sandals. With the proliferation of mass-produced patterns that could be constructed with a sewing machine, Arnold Bauer writes that "even the lower-class men wore clothing tailored in a modern Western style."[15] Cultural movements such as *indigenismo* in the Andes and *negritude* in the Caribbean, in addition to resisting the terms of political underdevelopment in the 1940s and 1950s, brought to the fore highly individualized styles that contrasted greatly with those that could be purchased in the department stores of urban areas.[16]

At this same time, these elements of Latin American dress began to inspire the fashions of Europe and the United States, from the woven leather sandals of Mexico called huaraches to the blouse with ruffles of lace inspired by the Afro-Cuban Rumba. In the first half of the twentieth century, North Americans returned home after working on the Panama Canal and, later, Clark Gable and the "gambler" style helped make the "Panama" hat, actually made in Ecuador, immensely popular. In *Vogue* and *Look* magazines, visions of haute couture looked to the celebrity of Eva Perón of Argentina and Frida Kahlo of Mexico. Some young women of the working classes dyed their hair blond and painted their lips with bright lipstick to look like Perón, a former actress who would become a populist leader and the first lady of Argentina. The mestiza heritage of surrealist painter Kahlo, who asserted a postrevolutionary cultural identity through the use of traditional Mexican costumes, inspired many to integrate native designs and brightly colored accessories into their wardrobes. By the end of the twentieth century, the very image of prominent Latin American celebrities such as Perón and Kahlo, in addition to the likeness of Che Guevara, would be screen printed on everything from handbags to T-shirts. María Claudia André believes that the appropriation of such "Latin American icons for export"—and the subsequent erasure of their cultural significance—has much to do with the increasingly complex global fashion system that has reconfigured symbols of national and Latin American identity to create a kind of logo to which a celebrity-focused public subscribes.[17] The messages and meanings of most fashions, and these cases would certainly seem to prove it, are subject to numerous reinventions and displacements, a process that can also be seen when a young Cuban American dons the *guayabera*, a lightweight, embroidered cotton shirt worn outside the pants throughout the Caribbean, or a teenage club kid wears Inca-techno styles at a rave.

In the second half of the twentieth century, the revolutionary movements of Cuba (1959 to the present) and Nicaragua (1979–90) signaled turns toward socialist anti-fashion, which represented the pursuit of luxury as affiliated with capitalist domination and its exploitation of the working classes. In Cuba mini-skirts were perceived as counterrevolutionary when "a Chinese style system of uniforms" was instituted following the Revolution.[18] Distinguished Nicaraguan poet Ernesto Cardenal, wearing a peasant *cotona* shirt almost daily, suggested that all citizens wear such a uniform as a "symbol of a new equality."[19] Many of the multinationals in the garment industry outsourced the production of their goods, relying on the cheap labor of workers in Latin America to weave, assemble, and sew garments. The *maquiladora* industry, or export-processing zones such as the one established in the 1960s between Mexico and the United States, has been the source of several human rights violations that, on occasion, have led to consumer boycotts. The United Nations currently assists a few projects that have fueled the growth of more socially conscious textile and fashion industries, such as the Rocinha Cooperative of Women's Artisans and Seamstresses—women who live in the shantytowns of Rio de Janeiro who have worked with Carlos Miele of Brazil on haute couture designs that are sold throughout the world. In recent years, even the most revolutionary of leaders—including Fidel Castro of Cuba— have occasionally shed their deep-green combat fatigues for designer wear. Some current presidents, such as Luiz Inacio Lula da Silva of Brazil, and other political leaders don suits that have been fashioned only in their countries, symbolic of their allegiance and support for what each nation produces.

## THE INTERNET AGE

By the end of the last century, at a time when shopping malls and Wal-Mart Super Centers began to dot the map of the region, it was not uncommon to talk about purchasing clothes using English terms, from *American style* to *bluyeans*. Despite the fact that poverty remains a critical issue for the region, and much disparity exists between those who have purchasing power and those who experience extreme poverty, many are quite adamant about having access to specific labels and logos that are advertised on television and the Internet. Real and counterfeit goods—whether sneakers, baseball caps, purses, or scarves— have saturated department stores, kiosks, and the popular marketplace. Brazilian Avon ladies sell makeup to members of the indigenous tribes in the Amazon, some of whom have indicated that they prefer the brand to natural products that have been used for centuries, and elite urban women alike. In many regions, the poor use secondhand clothing from other parts of the world; however, members of the more privileged classes shun the concept of high-priced vintage clothing popular in Europe and the United States and prefer luxury brands to denote "status." The images broadcast in Hollywood films and music videos further the demands for particular styles, influencing the choice of color, style, or application technique. Overall, clothing produced in China, Taiwan, Korea, and the Philippines, writes Mike González, has "supplanted, by the even more profound exploitation of their labour, many of the sweatshop industries that produced cheap clothing in Latin America through the 1960s and 1970s."[20]

With this influx of global goods, it is usually impossible to distinguish the nationality of most Latin Americans by their dress alone. A few regional differences still exist, especially in rural communities, but even the local artisans who market clothing and wares that replicate "authentic" garments or styles for the tourists are often dressed in Western-style clothing. Anthropologists focused on this remaking of the local marketplace into a world market emphasize the influences that an individual designer, artisan, or community navigate when attempting to preserve the sacred attributes of traditional garments. Without question, accelerated modernization, tourism, and globalization have significantly altered the ways in which fashion is created, consumed, and marketed. Indigenous communities in Central America and the Andes sometimes work with foreign-based companies to produce garments that are a version of "native costume." Global competition is also quite fierce, creating challenges for small collectives. Manos del Uruguay, for example, decided to expand its local worker base drastically to create a national network of knitters who could help produce enough garments when substantial orders came in from Banana Republic and other well-known clothing companies. Given the opportunities created by the global market, many Latin American universities are expanding their offerings in fashion design, which have often emerged from existing programs in architecture and urbanism. In 1999 Hispanic designers Carolina Herrera (Venezuela) and Oscar de la Renta (Dominican Republic), with the assistance of Beth Sobol (United States) and Victoria Puig de Lange (Ecuador), formed the Council of Latin American Fashion Designers to establish a platform for designers that is showcased in the Fashion Week of the Americas, based in Miami. To address the transnational qualities of fashion design within Latin America, in 2004 designers Laura Novik of

Argentina and Celaine Refosco of Brazil formed *Identidades latinas,* an organization that facilitates transnational collaborations in an expanding fashion marketplace and which is quickly providing an important professional network for designers throughout the region. Supermodels Valeria Mazza (Argentina) and Giselle Bündchen (Brazil) became prominent figures on the catwalks of haute couture houses, while still being connected to designers and clothing lines in their native countries.

## MEXICO AND CENTRAL AMERICA

With the purchasing power parity of over a trillion dollars, a significant upper middle class has emerged in Mexico despite economic crisis. At the same time, 40 percent of this nation lives in poverty, particularly in the rural areas. In Mexico City, department stores sell a myriad of "status" goods that one might find in any major metropolitan area in the United States. Although a thin figure is desired and is more acceptable in the city, obesity resulting from malnutrition has been on the rise throughout the country—over a third of the population, according to the World Health Organization—as diets high in fat and sugars replace more traditional ones. Although data on body image appear to be limited for the entire region, one recent assessment of adolescent men and women of both high and low socioeconomic backgrounds in Guatemala City, Guatemala, and Panama City, Panama, indicates that they are on the whole dissatisfied with their current physiques, with young female participants in the study more likely to choose undernourished silhouettes as ones depicting good health, choices perhaps related to the influx of advertisements on television and in magazines that promote lean and sculpted bodies.[21]

Of the Central American countries, Costa Rica and Panama are the more economically developed. Quite a few, like Nicaragua, are in the midst of rebuilding their economic infrastructures following years of civil war and crisis. Dire poverty remains a significant problem for the region, with over half of all Central Americans unable to satisfy the most basic needs. Scholars have sometimes traced the roots of poverty to the protagonists of the Spanish conquest who capitalized quickly on forced indigenous labor when the Spanish Crown granted *encomiendas,* or land for service, and thereby also enslaved native peoples of the region. Early Spanish accounts, such as those by conquistadors Hernán Cortés and Bernal Díaz del Castillo, marveled at the luxurious dress and possessions of indigenous nobility. Cotton cloth had served in pre-Hispanic times as *quachtli,* a tribute to indigenous nobility and medium of exchange. Imperialist expansion brought about a shift in material culture throughout the region, however, with Spanish mercantilist trade routes transporting cotton from India, silks from the Philippines, and porcelain from China to the main ports.

Today as in the past, indigenous communities of Mexico and Central America have given voice to their history and religious beliefs with intricate color-coding systems and sacred symbols in woven textiles. In Guatemala, over 150 indigenous communities maintain their traditional dress. The rainbow-colored *huipil* of Guatemala and the highlands of Mexico once placed deities of the sun and the underworld in dialogue with the Christian faith espoused by colonial authorities. This blouse-like garment, part of the *traje* ensemble worn today by traditional Mayan women, reveals a great deal of information about a wearer's heritage, status, and personal beliefs. A Mayan Indian woman's dress, while an emblem of pride in the rural community in which she lives, might become the source of discrimination against her in more urban areas. Mike González writes that when Nobel Peace Prize recipient Rigoberta Menchú wears the huipil and *pollera,* or full skirt with gathers, it registers an opposing stance to that of the Westernized *ladinos* of her native Guatemala.[22] Scholars are looking at the way in which indigenous beauty queen contests, which usually highlight some of the most elaborately designed ethnic garments, have created a space for political discussion in the region; winners of these contests sometimes used their status to voice political opposition during and following the atrocities of Guatemala's civil war.[23] Yet, in the twenty-first century, many of the children of ethnic communities have adopted Western-style dress in order to assimilate themselves into mainstream culture.

Despite the push toward homogenization, religious festivals and rites continue to attract people who are dressed in more traditional garments and, when appropriate for popular celebrations, use costumes that incorporate masks and straw hats in order to represent magic, nostalgia, and the rhythm of daily life in the community. In Mexico some women wear braids and ribbons, dried palm hats with flowers, rebozos or hand-woven shawls, beaded necklaces, embroidered blouses, pleated skirts, and leather or rope sandals to these festive events; their younger daughters wear smaller versions of the same style. Several family workshops throughout the region, some of which cater to tourists, create intricately embroidered garments with narratives that represented the sights of daily life: flowers, birds, animals, and human customs. During rural festivals, a few dress as the charros, or cowhands, once did, with silver-plated accessories and wide sombreros, in order to celebrate an important symbol of national identity.

## STATUS AND WESTERN STYLES IN MEXICO AND CENTRAL AMERICA

While the colonial caste system was abolished after independence, those who had less status continued to suffer discrimination and abuse. Even today, indigenous people in ethnic dress have at times been denied access to public buildings or transportation because of their appearance. The pressure on young people to adopt Western styles is often driven by a desire for social acceptance beyond his or her community. Pamela Scheinman has studied the abandonment of indigenous dress in the region through the analysis of *ixcacles*, handmade agave-fiber sandals that Nahua society invests with magical powers in curing rituals and for walking into the afterlife.[24] While traditional wearers still abound, young people have discarded these sandals in favor of more modern—and less indigenous—styles. Craftspeople thereby regularly modify their designs to appeal to tourists who will use them as beachwear or as a souvenir, which helps perpetuate the craftsperson's income and the larger cultural heritage. In Costa Rica, a more multicultural feel permeates dress, with the multicultural influences of Rastafarian culture along the Caribbean coast as well as those of the seminomadic Ngöbe, who make their way to and from Panama with *polleras*, or full skirt with gathers; patterned *chacaras*, or bags woven with agave fibers; and colorful *chaquira*-bead necklaces.

Throughout the region, a young woman usually wears a new dress designed for a community festival or for her *quinceañera*, an elegant celebration of her fifteenth birthday. In some families, the young woman wears the *china poblana* costume, which refers to the servant dress of a woman from Puebla and evokes the image of the legendary Asian woman brought to Mexico as a slave in the seventeenth century. Over the centuries, embroidery and sequins were added to this often white, peasant-style blouse and red skirt that would come to represent a national archetype of femininity in dress. Today, this costume often incorporates the colors or emblems of the Mexican flag. In the United States, the queen who presides over the Cinco de Mayo festivities often wears china poblana to celebrate her Mexican-American heritage.

## THE CARIBBEAN

Beyond the Central and South American coast, in the islands of the Caribbean, multi-cultural influences prevail. In the context of Puerto Rico, cross-cultural fusions became quite apparent in women's dress following the Spanish American War of 1898. In their analysis of fashion magazines, photographic images of women, and records of imports to the island, Dilia López-Gydosh and Marsha Dickson have discovered that the women of Puerto Rico discarded Spanish fashions in favor of those of the United States to push for their suffrage.[25] While some forms of Spanish dress persisted through the early part of the twentieth century, such as eyelet lace and the "untucked" shirtwaist, most fashions on the island reflected the push toward cultural assimilation. Eventually, however, the only remnant of Spanish colonialism found in women's dress was the *porta-abanico*, a long necklace that carried a folded fan, which women waved as they engaged a subtle language of resistance. In today's Puerto Rico, a formality prevails in religious contexts, with men taking off their hats when entering a church and some older women using parasols to walk to church on a sunny day.

Following the end of Spanish colonialism in Cuba, the rhetoric of fashion provided a forum for discussions on the configuration of national identity, even if that identity came to the shores of the island from afar. In the 1920s renowned author Alejo Carpentier penned articles under the female pseudonym of Jacqueline in the pages of Havana's *Social* magazine. The writings of Jacqueline, who most readers associated with a fashionable French or U.S. identity, were immensely popular. While Cuban fashions were central to the creation of national identity, these columns asserted that the appropriation of foreign models would facilitate the island's cultural development.[26] A more collective vision of Cuba's cultural identity is represented by the *guayabera*, which Marilyn Miller believes "invests its wearer with Cubanness" and is associated with the *guajiros*, or people from rural areas on the island.[27] Following the revolution of 1959, Fidel Castro and other political figures adopted the shirt with simple lines—at times with intricate embroidered detail along the front—as a kind of relaxed uniform that contrasted sharply with the fashions of Havana's elite. Today, the folkloric garment is used mostly by those on the island who cater to foreign tourists and Hispanics living in the United States. Designers inspired by the colors and customs of the Caribbean include Oscar de la Renta of the Dominican Republic, who markets his elegant designs from New York City; Meiling of Trinidad, noted for upscale street wear; and Sylma Cabrera of Puerto Rico, known for her whimsical children's clothing.

## SOUTH AMERICA

From Punta Gallinas, Colombia, to Cape Horn, Chile, the South American continent is home to many cultures. Since the nineteenth century, immigration has brought people from many parts of Asia, Europe, and the Middle East, adding to the proliferation of styles worn in urban and rural communities. Although almost a third of the continent's peoples make a living from subsistence agriculture and are more likely to maintain traditional rural customs, two-thirds of the continent's population lives in urban centers such as Buenos Aires, Bogotá, São Paulo, and Santiago. In urban areas there are department stores, boutiques, and local markets where clothing is sold and exchanged. Marketing research from Cotton Incorporated reveals a diverse set of purchasing trends, with Brazilians preferring to shop for clothes in small, independent stores, and Colombians opting for U.S.-style department stores.[28] Both groups normally buy as a response to store displays and not because of television marketing or catalogue announcements. While multinational marketing firms have begun to pay more attention to this region's shopping trends, the statistics are not always widely available. It is apparent that the history of high inflation in much of the region has impacted a consumer's ability to purchase fashion, cosmetics, and perfumes, although most urban areas have available to them a host of designer goods, and consumers are, on the whole, adamant about having access to the latest styles. *Elle*, *Vogue*, and other fashion magazines have their own editions in some countries, and images of popular culture from U.S. magazines like *Rolling Stone* and *People* are widely available in the numerous kiosks found in urban centers. Seminudity in fashion magazines is widely accepted, distinguishing many of these magazines from their counterparts in the United States. Young people will sometimes imitate the provocative styles showcased in fashion centers with few alterations, a fact that has caused alarm and even the creation of laws. In the Buenos Aires province of Argentina, parental pressure resulted in the "Sizes Law," which mandated that stores targeting adolescents offer merchandise in all sizes. Prior to this law, some stores did not carry anything past a size 3, and considered 4 an oversize. Many blamed this practice for the unusually high rates of anorexia and bulimia in the nation: one in ten adolescents suffers from these illnesses.[29] A new fashion police, with its professed "measuring tape in hand," currently plans to target stores that purposefully sell incorrectly sized garments. The deaths due to anorexia of Uruguayan Luisel Ramos and Brazilian Maria Carolina Reston Macan in 2006, or what Brazilian psychologist Dr. Marco Antonio De Tommaso termed the "dictatorship of beauty," has also forced the global fashion industry to debate the demands placed on models amidst calls for regulating the health of models.[30]

## Attention to Appearance

Obesity, eating disorders, and plastic surgery rates are on the rise throughout the region. The World Health Organization estimates that 30 to 40 percent of the population of Brazil, Peru, Chile, and Colombia are overweight, while only 2 to 8 percent are underweight; research suggests that the increase in obesity can be explained, in part, by demographic and socioeconomic changes in these countries.[31] Although thin bodies are deemed attractive in urban areas, female plumpness has sometimes been interpreted as a sign of tranquility in rural communities. In Brazil, a woman with B-cup-size breasts may consider very strongly the need for a breast reduction procedure; others seek buttock implants in order to flaunt string bikinis on the beach. And Hollywood stars still flock to the office clinic of Ivo Pitanguy in Rio de Janeiro, established by the retired plastic surgeon internationally renowned for his innovative procedures. Even during its economic crisis, the *Observer* reports, Argentina imported more silicone implants per capita than any other country in the world.[32] Some psychologists blame the region's machismo, or the domination of women, for this obsessive pursuit of a more fashionable body; while others, including most plastic surgeons, argue these new technologies have made beauty accessible to those who insist on undergoing these procedures. In Venezuela, the country that has produced the most Miss Universe and Miss World winners and is the biggest spender on cosmetics in the region, plastic surgery is a goal for which even the economically disadvantaged attempt to save. Apparently, it is also not uncommon for a young teenager in Venezuela to receive a plastic surgery gift certificate at her quinceañera party to help "improve" her body image. When Hugo Chávez addressed the United Nations with his call for a "socialist revolution" in his country, the *Associated Press* wrote that hundreds of citizens banged pots and even fired gunshots outdoors when his televised comments interrupted the 2005 Miss Venezuela beauty pageant for 15 minutes.[33]

Increasingly, it is clear that men also elect plastic surgery with regularity. Argentine President Carlos Menem, known for his poncho and sideburns in his first presidential campaign, later transformed his look to complement the neoliberal economic policies he espoused, wearing Versace suits and boasting higher cheekbones and a surgically moved hairline.

## Dress Codes in Cultural History

The history of the South American continent shares its colonial legacy with the nations of Mexico, Central America, and the Caribbean. During the colonial period, when a caste system prevailed, songs and images prescribed appearances and etiquette along racial lines. In Colombia, a dress code emphasized the individual's ethnic background, with certain colors or hues required of each caste.[34]

In other parts of the Andes, upper-class natives wore crossover styles that combined Old World and New World designs. Although a noble Incan of Peru might have worn an unku with knee breeches and stockings, Spanish authorities for the most part insisted that indigenous peoples continue to dress as they had in times past. Lynn A. Meisch writes that "the government of Peru prohibited the wearing of the headband, tunic, mantle, and other insignia of the Incas including jewelry engraved with the image of the Inca, or sun" following the indigenous rebellions of the late eighteenth century.[35] Today, there is still a great deal of social polarization along racial and ethnic lines. Indigenous styles, while symbolically poetic for the wearer in Bolivia or Peru, imply a low social status; Western-style dress tends to grant the wearer a higher status. Although there are certainly outside influences affecting the creation and consumption of indigenous styles, such as tourism and multicultural trends in urban areas, many indigenous garments are fashioned only for special festivals, periods of mourning, and the projection of indigenous identity.

Following the retreat of Spanish colonialism, popular dress sometimes revealed seminomadic indigenous origins, but subsequent appropriations transformed these styles into symbols of national identity. Gauchos, or rural workers who roamed the pampas of Argentina, adopted the indigenous poncho. In the Southern Cone, the poncho became an icon of cultural integration, a fact that seems lost in the recent global fad for poncho-style capes and gaucho-like pants. Although rural costumes were certainly prevalent in urban areas during the nineteenth century, and typically worn by street vendors, city dwellers quickly moved away from indigenous, rural, and Spanish styles in order to profess their allegiance to the interests of emerging nation-states. In Buenos Aires, for example, women transformed the Spanish *peineta*, or hair comb made of tortoiseshell and worn atop the head, into the three-foot-by-three-foot *peinetón*. This exuberant hair comb also came to represent the politically conscious woman who sought recognition in public and representation in government.

Following the consolidation of nation-states in the region, many countries experienced an increase in immigration and foreign investment capital. Foreign department stores, such as Harrods in Argentina (1912) and the Mappin Stores in Brazil (1913), marketed a vision of sophistication that relied on class-based hierarchies. Novelists in the region were quick to capture the proliferation of publics in city life and the discomforting role that luxury played when an employee could dress the same way as his millionaire employer. Rita Andrade argues that department store fashion marketing campaigns were so successful because they prescribed distinctiveness at a moment of urban expansion and massive immigration.[36] Displays of affluence throughout the region set apart *la gente decente*, who made up a minute percentage of the total population, from the growing middle class and *la gente de pueblo*, or the working classes. With the arrival of new immigrants, the styles and black mourning dress that had prevailed in the cityscape of the nineteenth century gave way to a myriad of foreign styles. Intellectual dandies such as José Asunción Silva of Colombia flaunted European-style tuxedos and white gloves while tending to the finer details of etiquette. The dandies of today, largely an executive class, travel to Brazil's Daslu, a luxury mall with black-suited guards posted outside, which is accessible by helicopter.

## A "Copacabana" Way of Life

Similar dynamics govern the consumption of clothing, cosmetics, and fragrances in South America today. In the media and on tourist postcards, attention to a stereotypical "Copacabana way of life" projects an ideal that few can afford. The stress on bodily freedom at the beach in Brazil, which became a form of resistance to the sexual, racial, and political divisions imposed on Brazilians during military dictatorship from 1965 to 1984, has given way to a more fragmented set of leisure styles.[37] The relaxed styles of youth culture contrast sharply with those of previous decades. In the second half of the twentieth century, many countries witnessed a backlash against democracy and installed military governments. In countries such as Argentina, Chile, and Uruguay, strict gender codes imposed clean-cut looks for men and feminine styles (skirts, dresses) for women. During the recent dictatorship in Argentina, the Mothers of the Plaza de Mayo in Argentina began protesting human rights abuses and searching for information about their "disappeared" family members while wearing white shawls, in reality their children's cloth diapers, on their heads. What became their emblematic shawl has the name of a disappeared loved one embroidered on it. In the early part of the movement, the Mothers wore morning robes and house slippers to their weekly gatherings, as if to register that they no longer had anyone to care for at home. Following the economic crisis in Argentina, many students and human rights protesters have worn *Arte y Confección* T-shirts and other clothing produced in abandoned factories such as Brukman, which its workers seized and have run ever since. In contemporary Argentina, young males wear long hair and women wear jeans. Transvestites, known for their seductive haute couture styles in the 1990s, now "dress without glamour, like any other sweaty worker in the streets."[38] Those who wear European fashions go against the trend, for symbols of "status" are regarded by the majority with suspicion, as if such clothes reflect allegiances to those forces blamed for the economic disenfranchisement of others. Indeed, prominent political leaders have moved to local and regional designs to support the development of emerging textile and fashion industries.

Into the twenty-first century, several fashion houses continued to gain prominence abroad, including Laurencio Adot of Argentina; Alexandre Herchcovitch, Ronald Fraga, and Carlos Miele of Brazil; Rubén Campos of Chile; Silvia Tcherassi and Amelia Toro for women's wear, and Lina Cantillo and Ricardo Pava for men's wear in Colombia; Sitka Semsch in Peru; and Angel Sánchez in Venezuela.

## CONCLUSION

As is to be expected with any segment of world popular culture, the dress and appearance of people living in Mexico, Central America, the Caribbean, and South America have produced a wide array of messages and possible meanings. Overall, the fashion of this region reflects larger cultural processes at work. At various times, the textiles, adornments, and styles of Latin America have represented a host of social and political identities. As suggested in *The Latin American Fashion Reader*, "Fashion interprets the present and plots the future."[39] Scholars of popular culture will no doubt continue to register this pulse of daily life in order to fully comprehend a history in the making.

# RESOURCE GUIDE

## PRINT SOURCES

Arenas Abello, R. "La moda en la Colombia de ayer." Pp. 12–20 in A. Wild (ed.), *La moda en Colombia*. Santa Fé de Bogotá, Colombia: Ediciones Alfred Wild, 1996.

Bauer, A. J. *Goods, Power, History: Latin America's Material Culture.* New York: Cambridge University Press, 2001.

Carrera, M. M. *Imagining Identity in New Spain: Race, Lineage, and the Colonial Body in Portraiture and Casta Paintings.* Austin: University of Texas Press, 2003.

Durbin, P. "Manos del Uruguay: The Bottom Line." *Grassroots Development: Journal of the Inter-American Foundation* 26.1 (2005): 18–25.

"Fashion Police Target Rake-Thin Teens: Argentina Seeks to Tackle Anorexia, Bulimia." *Reuters* (2005, July 2, 7:41 p.m.).

Femenías, B. *Gender and the Boundaries of Dress in Contemporary Peru.* Austin: University of Texas, 2004.

Forero, J. "El Alto Journal: Young Bolivians Adopt Urban U.S. Pose, Hip-Hop and All." *New York Times* (2005, May 26): A4.

González, M. "Clothing and Dress." Pp. 371–373 in D. Balderston, A. López, and M. González (eds.), *Encyclopedia of Contemporary Latin American and Caribbean Cultures.* London: Routledge, 2000.

Hendrickson, C. *Weaving Identities: Construction of Dress and Self in a Highland Guatemala Town.* Austin: University of Texas Press, 1995.

Holland, N. "Fashioning Cuba." Pp. 147–156 in A. Parker, M. Russo, D. Sommer, and P. Yeager (eds.), *Nationalisms and Sexualities.* London: Routledge, 1992.

Lescano, V. *Followers of Fashion. Falso diccionario de la Moda.* Buenos Aires: Interzona Editora, 2004.

Logan, I., et al. *Rebozos de la Colección Robert Everts.* Mexico City: Museo Franz Mayer and Artes de México, Colección Uso y Estilo, 1994.

Mc Arthur, L. H., D. Hobert, and M. Peña. "An Exploration of the Attitudinal and Perceptual Dimensions of Body Image among Male and Female Adolescents from Six Latin American Cities." *Adolescence* (Winter 2005). Available at http://www.findarticles.com/p/articles/mi_m2248/is_160_40/ai_n15969840.

Meisch, L. "America, South: History of Dress." Pp. 45–49 in V. Steele (ed.), *Encyclopedia of Clothing and Fashion.* Detroit: Thomson Gale, 2005.

Murrieta, R. O. "Colonial Attire in New Spain." in Paloma Garostiza (ed.), *Baroque Mystique: Women of Mexico-New Spain Seventeenth and Eighteenth Centuries.* Monterrey: Museo de Historia Mexicana en Monterrey and San Antonio: Instituto Cultural Mexicano, 1994.

Obiko Pearson, N. "Beauty Obsession United Divided Venezuela." *Associated Press* (2005, December 30, 3:18 p.m.).

Orlove, B., ed. *The Allure of the Foreign: Imported Goods in Postcolonial Latin America.* Ann Arbor: University of Michigan Press, 1997.

Phipps, E. "Textiles as Cultural Memory: Andean Garments in the Colonial Period." Pp. 144–156 in D. Fane (ed.), *Converging Cultures: Art and Identity in Spanish America.* New York: Brooklyn Museum/Harry N. Abrams, 1996.

Root, R. A., ed. *The Latin American Fashion Reader*. Oxford: Berg, 2005.

———. "Searching for the Oasis in Life: Fashion and the Question of Female Emancipation in Late Nineteenth-Century Argentina." *The Americas: A Quarterly Review of Inter-American Cultural History* 60.3 (2004): 363–390.

Savigliano, M. E. "Evita: The Globalization of a National Myth." Pp. 344–360 in J. Abbasi and S. L. Lutjens (eds.), *Rereading Women in Latin America and the Caribbean: The Political Economy of Gender*. New York: Rowan & Litfield, 2002.

Sayer, C. *Costumes of Mexico*. Austin: University of Texas Press, 1985.

Schevill, M. B. "America, Central, and Mexico: History of Dress." Pp. 37–42 in V. Steele (ed.), *Encyclopedia of Clothing and Fashion*. Detroit: Thomson Gale, 2005.

———, J. C. Berlo, and E. Dwyer eds., *Textile Traditions of Mesoamerica and the Andes: An Anthology*. Austin: University of Texas Press, 1996.

Tranberg Hansen, Karen. "The World in Dress: Anthropological Perspectives on Clothes, Fashion, and Culture." *Annual Review of Anthropology* 33 (2004): 369–392.

"T-Shirts Celebrate Mexico's Tacky Side," *Associated Press* (2005, July 14).

Zorn, E. *Weaving a Future: Tourism, Cloth and Culture on an Andean Island,* Iowa City: University of Iowa Press, 2004.

## WEBSITES

*Cotton Incorporated.* http://www.cottoninc.com/TextileConsumer. With offices worldwide, this U.S.-based corporation has its headquarters for Latin America in Mexico City. Summaries of its marketing and textile research on consumer practices and attitudes are often available online. See, in particular, Volume 15 of *Textile Consumer.*

"The Developing World's New Burden: Obesity." *The International Obesity TaskForce.* Food and Agriculture Organization of the United Nations. http://www.iotf.org/popout.asp?linkto=http://www.fao.org/FOCUS/E/obesity/obes1.htm.

*Inexmoda.* http://www.inexmoda.org.co/. This Colombian organization promotes national designs abroad and analyzes ways in which to market future trends from Latin America.

*Moda Brasil.* http://www2.uol.com.br/modabrasil/. Edited by Kathia Castilho Cunha and Carol Garcia, this online fashion news source has columnists, links to the Portuguese-language *Fashion Theory Brazil*, and a virtual museum of clothing and appearance in Brazil and the rest of the world.

*São Paulo Fashion Week.* http://spfw.uol.com.br/. *São Paulo Fashion Week* was created by Paolo Borges in 1996 to rival those of London, Paris, Milan and New York. The publicity generated by the São Paulo catwalks has, in turn, inspired fashion weeks in other Latin American cities such as Buenos Aires and Bogotá.

## VIDEOS/FILMS

*Camila* (Argentina, 1984). Directed by María Luisa Bemberg. Set designer Esmeralda Almonacid accurately depicts the fashions and material culture of the period of Juan Manuel de Rosas (1829–52).

*Estética* (Cuba, 1984). Directed by Enrique Colina. A documentary that analyzes individual style in socialist Cuba. Available in the United States through Cuban Cinema Classics, http://www.wm.edu/cubancinemaclassics/about.htm.

*Evita* (United States, 1994). Directed by Alan Parker, starring Madonna as Eva Duarte. This musical drama, based on the stage production by Andrew Lloyd Webber and Tim Rice, tells the riveting political love story of President Juan Perón, his wife Eva (1919–52), and the Argentine people. This film inspired several fashions in Latin America and the United States in the mid-1990s.

*Frida* (United States, 2002). Directed by Julie Taymor. Based on the biography by Hayden Herrera, this film reconstructs the costumes worn by surrealist artist Frida Kahlo (1907–54) in her paintings and in real life.

*Miss Universo en Perú* (Peru, 1985). Directed by Grupo Chaski. Filmed by a revolutionary collective that advocated women's equality and indigenous rights, this documentary juxtaposes the interests that created the 1982 Miss Universe beauty pageant in Peru with the views of feminists, who protested the event, and those of the mostly indigenous women who watched the event on television and reflected on its material excess.

*Real Women Have Curves* (United States, 2002). Directed by Patricia Cardoso. While working at a sewing factory in Los Angeles, a first-generation Mexican-American teenager finds herself caught between the traditions of her family and a strong personal ambition to seek a university education.

*Ropa Americana* (Canada, 2003). Directed by Monica Veiga. This documentary follows the story of an old purple T-shirt donated to Goodwill by a Toronto housewife. From there, the shirt falls into the hands of a textile company representative, who then sells it to a second-hand store in Costa Rica. The old purple T-shirt ultimately ends up in the Ropa Americana shopping bag of a Costa Rican housewife.

## ORGANIZATIONS/MUSEUMS

The Costume Collection at the Smithsonian National Museum of American History, Behring Center, Washington, DC, tel. 202-633-1000. http://americanhistory.si.edu/collections/hispanicdesigners/. This comprehensive, historical collection includes the work of Hispanic designers living in the United States.

The Costume Institute at the Metropolitan Museum of Art, New York, NY, tel. 212-570-3908. http://www.metmuseum.org/Works_of_Art/introduction.asp?dep=8. The Costume Institute boasts a historical collection of 80,000 costumes and accessories from around the globe. Its Latin American collection includes haute couture pieces by internationally renowned designers such as Carolina Herrera (Venezuela), Carlos Miele (Brazil), and Oscar de la Renta (Dominican Republic).

Council of Latin American Fashion Designers. http://www.miamifashionweek.com/html/council.html. Established in 1999, this organization, founded by Carolina Herrera, Oscar de la Renta, and Beth Sobol, showcases Latin American designers at the annual Fashion Week of the Americas, based in Miami, Florida.

Fowler Museum of Cultural History at the University of California–Los Angeles, Los Angeles, CA, tel. (310) 825-4361. http://www.fowler.ucla.edu/incEngine/. Thanks in large part to the legacy of Patricia Anawalt, the extensive collection of this museum includes Guatemalan costumes, Peruvian textiles, and Mexican masks. See, in particular, the research from the museum's Center for the Study of Regional Dress.

Museo de las Américas, San Juan, Puerto Rico, tel. 787-724-5052 http://www.prtc.net/~musame/. Some popular garments used in religious rites and celebrations.

Museo Ixchel del Traje Indígena, Guatemala City, Guatemala, tel. 502-331-3622. http://www.ixchel friends.org/. Collection of Mayan garments used by men, women, and children as well as traditional textiles.

Museo Nacional de Arqueología, Antropología e Historia del Perú, Plaza Bolívar s/n Pueblo Libre, tel. 4-63-50-70. http://museonacional.perucultural.org.pe/textiles.htm. From wigs to tunics, this museum possesses one of the most important collections of indigenous Andean textiles spanning 2,500 years.

Museo Nacional de la Historia, Castillo de Chapultepec, Mexico, tel. 50-61-92-17. http://www. mnh.inah.gob.mx/colecciones/coleccion_indumentari.html.An extensive collection of Mexican garments and accessories from the eighteenth through the twentieth centuries.

Museo Nacional del Traje, Buenos Aires, Argentina, tel. (11) 4343-8427. http://www.funmuseodel traje.com.ar/. Contains over 8,000 pieces from eighteenth-century to present-day Argentina.

The Museum of Fine Arts, Houston, TX, tel. (713) 639-7300. http://www.mfah.org/. This museum focuses on textiles and costumes of Western Europe and the Americas from the last two centuries.

The Textile Museum, tel. (202) 667-0441, http://www.textilemuseum.org/. This museum has acquired major collections of Ecuadorean, Peruvian, and Bolivian textiles and costumes. There is also a collection of Mexican materials from the postrevolutionary period.

# NOTES

1. Root 2005 (in Resource Guide), p 1.
2. Forero 2005 (in Resource Guide).
3. "Aims and Scope," *Fashion Theory: The Journal of Dress, Body and Culture* 10.4 (December 2006), p. 402.
4. See M. Meléndez, "Visualizing Difference: The Rhetoric of Clothing in Colonial Spanish America," in Root 2005 (in Resource Guide), pp. 29–30.
5. Phipps 1996 (in Resource Guide), p. 153.
6. Bauer 2001 (in Resource Guide), p. 71.
7. Ibid., pp. 71–73.
8. Ibid., p. 110. Bauer cites the *Archivo General de Indias*, Quito, leg. 211, fol. 73.
9. Ibid., p. 12.
10. Ibid., pp. 105–108.
11. See A. Tinajero, "Far Eastern Influences in Latin American Fashions," in Root 2005 (in Resource Guide), pp. 67–68.
12. Bauer 2001 (in Resource Guide), p. 111.
13. Carrera 2003 (in Resource Guide), pp. 22–105.
14. Bauer 2001 (in Resource Guide), p. 112.
15. Ibid., p. 170.
16. Ibid., pp. 179–181.
17. See M. C. André, "Frida and Evita: Latin American Icons for Export," in Root 2005 (in Resource Guide), p. 248.
18. González 2000 (in Resource Guide), p. 372.
19. Ibid.
20. Ibid., p. 373.
21. See Mc Arthur et al. 2005 (in Resource Guide).
22. González 2000 (in Resource Guide), p. 372.
23. See p. 281 of Jon Schackt's article on "Mayahood Through Beauty: Indian Pageants in Guatemala," *Bulletin of Latin American Research* 24.3 (2005): 269–287; and "Protesting Panzós: Community Queens and Indigenous Opposition to the State in Guatemala, 1970–1978" or pp. 129–168 of Betsy Konefal's "May All Rise Up: Highland Mobilization in Post-1954 Guatemala," University of Pittsburgh, available at http://etd.library.pitt.edu/ETD/available/etd-08112005-100651/unrestricted/konefal_dissertation_2.pdf.
24. See P. Scheinman, "Ixcacles: Maguey-fiber Sandals in Modern Mexico," in Root 2005 (in Resource Guide), pp. 79–92.
25. See D. López-Gydosh and M. A. Dickson, "Every Girl Had a Fan Which She Kept Always in Motion: Puerto Rican Women's Dress at a Time of Social and Cultural Transition," in Root 2005 (in Resource Guide), pp. 198–210.
26. See James Pancrazio, "Transvestite Pedagogy: Jacqueline and Cuban Culture," in Root 2005 (in Resource Guide), pp. 232–246.
27. See M. Miller, "*Guayaberismo* and the Essence of Cool," in Root 2005 (in Resource Guide), pp. 213–231.
28. *Cotton Incorporated* (in Resource Guide).
29. "Fashion Police Target Rake-Thin Teens: Argentina Seeks to Tackle Anorexia, Bulimia" 2005 (in Resource Guide).
30. See Tom Phillips, "Everyone Knew She Was Ill. The Other Girls, the Model Agencies . . . Don't Believe It When They Say They Didn't," *Observer* (2007, January 14), available at http://observer.guardian.co.uk/magazine/story/0,,1987928,00.html.
31. "The Developing World's New Burden: Obesity," *The International Obesity TaskForce* (in Resource Guide).

32. See John Carlin, "High-flying, adored and siliconised," *Observer* (2006, February 12), available at http://observer.guardian.co.uk/woman/story/0,,1705316,00.html.
33. Obiko Pearson 2005 (in Resource Guide).
34. R. Arenas Abello, "La moda en la Colombia de ayer," in Wild 1996 (in Resource Guide), p. 14.
35. Meisch 2005 (in Resource Guide), p. 48.
36. See R. Andrade, "Mappin Stores: Adding an English Touch to the São Paulo Fashion Scene," in Root 2005 (in Resource Guide), pp. 183–184.
37. See Nizia Villaça, "As She Walks to the Sea: A Semiology of Rio de Janeiro," in Root 2005 (Resource Guide), p. 191.
38. See F. Forastelli, "Scattered Bodies, Unfashionable Flesh," in Root 2005 (in Resource Guide), p. 286.
39. Root 2005 (in Resource Guide), p. 13.

**ARCHITECTURE:** Aerial view of Rio de Janeiro, with the famous *Cristo Redentor* [Christ the Redeemer] statue overlooking the city. © Marcaux / Dreamstime.com.

**ARCHITECTURE:** The Palacio de Bellas Artes, designed in the Beaux-Arts style, in Mexico City. Courtesy of Shutterstock.

**ART:** Floral trinket boxes for sale on the street in the city of Taxco, Mexico. These type of souvenirs are very popular for tourists throughout Mexico, with the price about $1.00 to $2.00 each. © Richard Gunion / Dreamstime.com.

**ART:** *Five Women of Guaratingueta* (1936) by the Brazilian artist Emiliano di Cavalcanti, who lived from 1897–1976. The Art Archive / São Paulo Art Museum Brazil / Dagli Orti.

# DANCE

**DANCE:** Tango dancers in the streets. Courtesy of Shutterstock.

**DANCE:** Alessandra Mattos, queen of Estacio de Sa Samba School drum section, dances during the carnival parade in Rio de Janeiro. AP Photo/Victor R. Caivano.

# FASHION AND APPEARANCE

**FASHION AND APPEARANCE:** Peruvian woman in local traditional wool clothing. Courtesy of Shutterstock.

**FASHION AND APPEARANCE:** Model Naomi Campbell and Brazilian designer Carlos Miele walk the runway during a Spring 2005 collection showing. AP Photo/Jennifer Graylock.

# FILM

FILM: Mexican actress Salma Hayek (as Frida Kahlo) in Julie Taymor's *Frida* (2002). Hayek was also one of the producers of this movie about the Mexican artist. Courtesy of Photofest. Copyright © Miramax.

FILM: *The Motorcycle Diaries* (2004), also known as *Diarios de motocicleta*, directed by Walter Salles. Shown on left in background: Argentinian actor Rodrigo De la Serna (as Alberto Granado); on right in foreground: Mexican actor Gael García Bernal (as Ernesto 'Che' Guevara de la Serna). Courtesy of Photofest. Copyright © Focus Features.

**FILM:** A street vendor sells copies of bootleg music CDs and movie DVDs in Lima, Peru, 2004. Fake products in Peru go well beyond discs to include designer clothing, liquor, books, passports, university diplomas, and even plastic plumbing. Lenient sentences to counterfeiters only reinforce the commonly held attitude that access to counterfeit goods is a fundamental consumer right for poor and rich Peruvians alike. AP Photo/Martin Mejia.

# FOOD AND FOODWAYS

**FOOD AND FOODWAYS:** In South America, *carne asado* is typically a large section of beef roasted over an open fire. Courtesy of Shutterstock.

**FOOD AND FOODWAYS:** A favorite drink of Argentinian gauchos, mate is a tea traditionally brewed and drunk from a gourd. Here is a yerba mate ceremonial gourd and *bomballis* [straw]. Courtesy of Shutterstock.

**FOOD AND FOODWAYS:** Colorful vegetables in the street market in Peru. © Kamchatka / Dreamstime.com.

# LITERATURE

**LITERATURE:**   In the late 1800s and into the twentieth century, one of the most popular non-fiction books circulating in Mexico was a prophetic dream book, published on a yearly basis, called *El Nuevo oráculo* [The New Oracle]. Courtesy of Daniel J. Nappo.

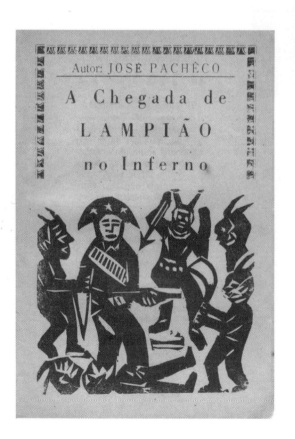

**LITERATURE:**   Based on the life of folk hero Lampião, *Lampião no inferno* [Lampião in Hell] by José Pacheco describes some of Lampião's greatest exploits and escapes. Courtesy of Daniel J. Nappo.

# FILM

## RANDAL P. GARZA AND LÚCIA FLÓRIDO

When in an average video store in any major Latin American city, one might be surprised to find out that most of the available movies are Hollywood products, which come with subtitles and are released only a month or so after their U.S. release date. Despite the growing popularity of national cinema in countries such as Brazil, Argentina, and Mexico, made-in-America movies still remain extremely common, representing the majority of titles available. However, over the past decade, Latin American cinema has gained support at home and abroad as its quality has substantially increased. Latin American actors and actresses are recognizable faces and draw crowds to the theaters. Some titles, such as the Brazilian *City of God* (2003) or the Mexican *And Your Mother Too* (2002), have been in contention for Oscars, becoming sudden box office hits and cult movies. If the international success of Latin American film is not really a recent phenomenon (because of some 1950, 1960, and 1970 titles that made history abroad), one can surely state that the 1990s and the early years of this century mark the beginning of a new era: a time for international outreach and stabilization in relation to the powerful European and American publics.

Even if new titles are easily accessible and plenty of information about them is available, a study of Latin American film is still quite an arduous task because of a lack of proper and organized documentation. Moreover, the scope of the cinema industry (and its national and international presence) varies from strong to almost nonexistent in the different countries of the region. Finally, when compared to the relatively numerous critical resources such as encyclopedias, journals, and databases commenting on films produced in the United States, encompassing guides of that sort are still unfortunately lacking for most Latin American films. While the situation is improving, with national *cinematecas* (film libraries) now being the norm in practically every Latin American country, the information available in them is frequently limited and difficult to access. As in much of the world, there is a growing movement throughout Latin America to preserve the records of older films in electronic format. The regional cinematecas devote a greater percentage of their resources to establishing a Web presence that can promote their nation to the rest of the world rather than focusing on maintaining physical centers, usually visited only by locals. Thus, it is often far easier to access information from researching the Internet than it is to work with such centers directly; they typically have limited hours, staff, and other necessary resources such as computers and video viewing equipment dedicated to public use. It is unquestionable that the technological revolution of the late twenty century deeply changed the face of the Latin American movie scene, although not necessarily for the better, especially in countries such as Mexico, Brazil, and Argentina.

Another interesting point regarding the availability of new technologies is the influence of digitized media. With the lower production costs associated with digitized media, both foreign and independent national film companies no longer necessarily need the immense capital previously required for movie production and distribution. On the other hand, the widespread adoption of new technologies has also hurt the U.S. movie industry abroad by facilitating piracy. Illegal copies of American DVDs are usually the only film-related items that can be found in the open markets of the region, while films made nationally are nearly impossible to acquire. The legally produced versions are sold in retail outlets only. For example, even before the worldwide opening of widely anticipated films such as *Terminator 3: The Rise of the Machines* or *Finding Nemo*, it was possible to purchase a copy of *La rebelión de las máquinas* or *Buscando a Nemo* in the streets of most large Latin American cities for a mere fraction of the price of the movie ticket.

Such technologies, however, have not led to a dramatic increase in the accessibility of Latin American films. The simple fact that almost every illegal copy for sale in the streets or available for download is of an American film confirms this point. While it is relatively easy to find titles by world-renowned Mexican directors such Alfonso Cuarón and Alejandro González Iñárritu, the same cannot be said of the great majority of less popular or older films. To illustrate this point, it is currently extremely difficult to find a copy of the Mexican landmark *Rojo amanecer* (1989), directed by Jorge Fons, even on VHS. Despite the fact that it portrays the student massacre of October 2, 1968, in Mexico City and is traditionally shown every year on this date throughout Mexico, it has yet to be converted to DVD and offered for worldwide purchase. Copies of older titles are only in VHS format or, even worse for those who own NTSC machines, in PAL-formatted VHS. Amazon.com, Barnes and Noble, and Facets Multimedia offer an ever-increasing list of more modern Latin American titles that are often complete with foreign audio tracks and subtitles. The catalog of older Latin American titles, however, is sparse at best, with the majority of titles limited to those that have the greatest probability of maximizing revenue.

The history of film in Latin American is not a uniform topic since the development of cinema has not enjoyed the same level of sophistication across all cultures. For example, in 2007, the Internet Movie Database listing of recent films produced or co-produced in Latin America showed an astounding disparity: Mexico (14,817), Argentina (6,919), Brazil (5,609), Cuba (1,285), Chile (1,028 ), Venezuela (785), and Colombia (769), just to mention the most important markets, since all others listed have generated fewer than 500 titles. Since the production of the top three—Mexico, Brazil, and Argentina—is so much greater than that of the next highest, Chile, this chapter will focus primarily on the three top-producing countries.

## MEXICO

Since its inception, Mexican commercial cinema has enjoyed money-making success in the United States; nevertheless, the vast majority of American citizens are amazingly unaware of its existence. This ignorance is partially the result of the English-Spanish language barrier. Mexican cinema follows the tradition of most Latin American film: until the early 1990s, films were produced almost exclusively with the domestic audience in mind.

Today, Mexican cinema has reached out and caters to both national and international publics. The Mexican film industry is in many ways similar to its American counterpart; the difference is that financial resources are limited in Mexico. In any major Mexican city, the movie-watching pattern mirrors that of the United States: multiplexes are everywhere, with small theaters either suffering from the competition or being used mostly as special viewing locations geared toward an intellectual crowd that favors cult and off-the-beaten-path movies. Small towns have fewer multiplexes, if any at all, and prices vary slightly from one city to the other, depending on the economic situation of any given group of citizens.

A movie ticket costs an average of US$5 to US$7 in Mexico City, but not as much in less-cosmopolitan or rural areas. Since the price of a ticket is quite high, taking into account the average minimum wage, going to the movies is not as common a pastime as it is in the United States. Renting a DVD or a video is far more affordable as a family activity, and most middle-class homes have a DVD player or a VCR. A few low-income families also have access to VCRs, but in a very limited number.[1] The same phenomenon happens in other Latin American countries. The lower classes still see an outing to the movies as a special weekend activity, perhaps because the ticket prices are perceived as being quite high given their earnings. The majority of movies watched in Mexico (as well as in Brazil and Argentina) are made in America, and these are popular with all age groups. With the growing number of high-quality Mexican productions, though, the tendency of preferring Hollywood to national cinema will most likely decrease.

The history of the Mexican movie industry happened in parallel with the advancement of film technologies in other countries. Some 8 months after Louis and Auguste Lumière made their pioneering commercial film debut to a small Parisian audience in March 1895, this novel form of entertainment arrived and enjoyed immediate success in Mexico. Thus, the minidocumentaries of the Lumière brothers mark the beginning of popular cinema in the Americas. The Mexican film industry began as a propaganda tool with which to put forth the idealized views of the nation and, more specifically, the dictatorship of Porfirio Díaz. Having such a practically exclusive purpose for producing documentary films separated early Mexican cinema from what was being done in other countries at the time. Bernard and Veyre, the representatives of the Lumière brothers charged with demonstrating and promoting their new technology in Mexico, made some 35 films in Mexico City, Guadalajara, and Veracruz; the first starred Díaz himself: *El presidente de la república paseando a caballo en el bosque de Chapultepec* [The President of the Republic Horseback Riding in Chapultepec Forest] (1896).

The Mexican Revolution (1910–20) only added to the demand and subsequent production of such documentaries as Mexicans flocked to salons in hopes of keeping up-to-date with the developments of the conflict via newsreels. One of the more notable filmmakers to capture the events of the war was the engineer Toscano Barragán (1872–1947) who, by then, had already made a name for himself as a pioneer in the industry, having directed and exhibited a number of both short and feature-length films. However, by the revolution's end, the tide had clearly turned; the population grew increasingly tired of the fight and, consequently, of documentary films about it.

Fiction films, alongside documentaries, also had an early start. In 1896 Bernal and Veyre filmed the short *Un duelo a pistola en el bosque de Chapultepec* [A Pistol Duel in Chapultepec Forest]. Despite the notice that the events of the plot were a reenactment of the actual duel, the public outcry was enormous. Unable to separate reality from fiction, early audiences simply assumed that everything shown on the screen must have been captured by filming real-life events. In 1898 Toscano Barragán was credited with creating Mexico's first fiction films. The short *Don Juan Tenorio* starred the popular actor Paco Gavilanes. Other fiction titles produced during this period included *El san lunes del valedor* or *El san lunes del velador* (1906), directed by Manuel Noriega, and the first scripted film longer than one reel: *Aventuras de Tip Top en Chapultepec* [Adventures of Tip Top in Chapultepec] (1907).

The years from approximately 1915 to 1923 are considered the Golden Age of silent movies in Mexico. In 1916 the closing years of the Mexican Revolution saw the production of the first full-length (60 minutes) film from the city of Mérida in the Yucatán: *1810 o los libertadores de México* [1810 or the Liberators of Mexico]. However, *The Fire* (shown for the first time in Mexico in 1915), *La luz, tríptico de la vida moderna* [The Light, Triptych of Modern Life] (1917) often claims the title of being the earliest full-length Mexican film since it was produced in Mexico City and not in the Yucatán. Despite the fact that it was an almost exact copy of the plot of the Italian *Il fuoco*—except for the Mexican setting—this film was hailed for its technical sophistication as well as for having identified the first true Mexican silent screen starlet, Emma Padilla Rosales (1900–66).

The years 1915 to 1923 mark the end of a period when filmmakers in Mexico were just beginning to familiarize themselves with this new medium and move to more sophisticated forms of cinematographic narrative. With the end of the Mexican Revolution, and faced with both political and economic uncertainties at home, Mexican studios made efforts to challenge the ever-increasing dominance of Hollywood movie houses by producing films with topics that gave form to an emerging national identity. Following norms established by both Hollywood and European producers, Enrique Rosas introduced the twelve-part original serial known as *El automóvil gris* [The Grey Automobile] (1919). It was hailed as the prototypical example of Mexican narrative film. Uniquely blending reality and fiction, the plot tried to recreate the actual events surrounding a 1915 group of bandits' thievery in Mexico City.

In the 1920s the industry also suffered from the exodus of many Mexican actors who left the country in order to learn new techniques of artistic expression abroad. Of the more notable figures to seek fame in Hollywood during this period were Lupita Tovar (b. 1911), Lupe Vélez (c. 1908–44), Ramón Novarro (1899–1968), and Dolores del Río (c. 1904–83). The precocious teen Lupe Vélez reached celebrity status as soon as she arrived in Hollywood. Similarly, Dolores del Río enjoyed immense fame in the United States, with a career that spanned some 50 years. First appearing in silent films such as *All the Town is Talking* (1925), *Upstream* (1926), *Resurrection* (1927), *Ramona* (1928), and *Evangeline* (1929), del Río became one of the few early Mexican performers who went on to do what many iconic early American actors could not: make an effortless transition from the silent film era to the "talkies." Despite reaching international renown as her U.S. career developed, few people knew of del Río's Mexican heritage early in her career. With xenophobia at an all-time high in the United States, del Río was often credited as having less-menacing Spanish origins. She would only make her Mexican debut in Roberto Gavaldón's (1909–86) *La otra* in 1946.

The advent of sound in the 1930s brought with it a renewed attention to national filmmaking as Mexican studios continued to promote the country's interests through cinema. The burgeoning film industry of the 1930s encouraged directors and actors who sought to break the perceived cultural imperialism of film coming from Europe and the United States and, thereby, promote a uniquely Mexican national identity. Cinema had one major advantage in that it could employ new sound technologies that married image to dialogue in order to literally speak to moviegoers. Hollywood, where the most important movie houses had by then taken to producing features with sound, was at a distinct disadvantage in the Latin American markets since its films were recorded in English; the attempt to include Spanish subtitles was only met with frustration from a largely illiterate Mexican population. The subsequent attempts by Hollywood to recapture a Spanish-speaking audience by making films in Spanish and starring Spanish actors likewise suffered initial failures. Furthermore, by the time of the first "talkies," Mexicans had already become accustomed to seeing their favorite foreign film actors on screen and did not readily accept these substitutes.

Mexico's first movie with sound was the eighty-one-minute *Santa* (1932), directed by Antonio Moreno (1887–1967) and starring Lupita Tovar. Despite being billed as a purely Mexican production, the majority of the technology, actors, and crew were from other countries. While not praised as a masterpiece of Mexican cinema—in fact, it was and is often criticized as being an Hispanic imitation of Hollywood—*Santa* is recognized as one of the first Mexican feature films to use sound, and it was also one that introduced the popular stereotype of the idealized prostitute. Based on a Frederico Gamboa novel, *Santa* narrates the life of the protagonist who, by a series of unfortunate events, is forced from the bucolic countryside of her birth to work as a prostitute in the seedy city. As the plot suggests, although she might indeed lose her virtue, she never loses her idealism, even when she develops cancer and eventually dies in surgery. A film that would be remade some four times (a silent version in 1918, *Santa* in 1931, and two more in 1943 and 1968), it proved that this stereotype continued to impact Mexican films.

Although 1932 saw the production of only a handful of Mexican titles, subsequent years witnessed an explosion in both the number of films produced as well as in their critical acclaim. One of the first directors able to fully capitalize on the enormous potential of sound in movies was the celebrated filmmaker Fernando de Fuentes (1894–1958). This author and pioneer of Mexican cinema is best remembered for having directed three classic films: *El compadre Mendoza* [My Buddy Mendoza] (1933), *Vámonos con Pancho Villa* [Let's Go with Pancho Villa] (1935), and *Allá en el Rancho Grande* [Over on the Big Ranch] (1936). The first two, along with an earlier one titled *Prisionero 13* [Prisoner Number 13] (1933), constitute what is known as de Fuentes's "revolutionary trilogy." A huge international success in its day, *Allá en el Rancho Grande* helped solidify Mexico's place as one of the most important filmmaking countries outside the United States. In it, Fuentes delighted audiences with the image of the singing cowboy or *charro*—a character that would be played many times over by the beloved actors Jorge Negrete (1911–53) and Pedro Infante (1917–57). To this day, the works of de Fuentes continue to be shown around the globe, and he continues to be heralded worldwide as the first important Mexican filmmaker.

The World War II years (1939–45) corresponded to a capital moment in Mexican cinema when President Manuel Ávila Camacho made the decision to ally his country with the United States against the threat from Germany, Italy, and Japan. The consequences for the film industry included continued access to the materials for film production, such as raw film, cameras, and editing equipment. Although the United States still maintained its place as the world's main producer—and, more importantly, distributor—of feature films, Mexico also saw a number of its actors recognized nationally and internationally. In genres ranging from social commentary and drama to comedy and musicals, many directors made household names out of Pedro Infante (1917–57), Germán Valdés's "Tin Tan" (1915–73), Mario Moreno's "Cantinflas" (1911–93), and María Félix (1914–2002), or "La Doña" as she was called. With her celebrated performance in *Doña Bárbara* (1943), Félix broke the stereotype of how Mexican women were traditionally portrayed in film by interpreting her roles with a toughness never before seen in female characters. Likewise, the actor-singer-comedian Tin Tan—often appearing with his guitar-playing sidekick, El Carnal Marcelo—made a number of films that led to the popularity of a type of clothing and slang known as *pachuco*.

Melodrama, the style of choice for prominent post-World War II Mexican directors, came to the fore as a form of popular tragedy established in its own historical context. This genre clearly dominated Latin American filmmaking of the 1940s and 1950s and also, unfortunately, led to the common American stereotype of Mexican film as being a poor-quality imitation of Hollywood features. It is for this reason, though, that while enjoying stellar popularity in Latin America, the names of classic stars such as María Félix, Mario Moreno Reyes, Silvia Pinal (b. 1931), and Pedro Infante are virtually unknown in the United States. Cantinflas, who made over fifty feature films in both Mexico and the United States, even had the honor of a word created after him appear in the dictionary. Thanks to his unique style of speech in such comedic masterpieces as *Ahí está el detalle* [Here is the Point] (1940), *El analfabeto* [The Illiterate One] (1960), and *Su excelencia* [Your Excellency] (1967), to "cantinflear" was defined as "to babble or talk gibberish." Although he would appear in a number of films and television programs in the United States, it is precisely this ingenious crafting of wordplay that prevented many of his early titles from being released to an American audience unable to grasp his linguistic twists and double entendres.

Similar to other countries in Latin America, the postwar Mexican film industry suffered a general decline in the quality and quantity of titles produced. Thanks to more aggressive marketing in Latin America by Hollywood, film production fluctuated greatly in Mexico after World War II. Beginning in 1941, the Mexican government initiated protectionist policies that imposed the showing of national films in national theaters and, in 1942, the Banco Cinematográfico or "Film Bank" was created with the purpose of lending both private and public support of national films. Although the Film Bank began as a private institution, enjoying substantial governmental support, by 1947 it had been transformed into an entirely state-run enterprise. While this change resulted in the increased production of national films—some of which were certainly noteworthy—for the most part, this reorganization had generally negative long-term consequences. With profit in mind, many of the movies produced in the decades that followed seemed to display entirely forgettable plots derived from equally formulaic scripts. Private producers largely abandoned the government-run film industry until about 1977 because of the lack of support for creativity and freedom of expression in filmmaking. In 1979 the Banco Cinematográfico was officially dissolved and, although it took some years to recuperate, the industry has since enjoyed the economic recovery typically associated with free-market capitalism.

In recent times, Mexican cinema has experienced a small boom, having produced a number of films that have met with critical acclaim and commercial success internationally. Often called *El nuevo cinema mexicano* (New Mexican Cinema), this renaissance began with the tumultuous rise to power of President Salinas de Gortari (1988–94), a leader who, as many believed, had illegally taken power by means of election fraud in 1988. Recognizing the need to jump-start the Mexican economy, Salinas moved to enter into the North American Free Trade Association (NAFTA) with the United States and Canada. As a prerequisite to Mexico's participation in this agreement, some previously state-run industries were necessarily opened up to privatization. This posed an interesting problem as Salinas still wanted to cultivate the artistic development of the country, especially the movie-making arena. The result was an economic model that attracted the financial backing of both domestic and foreign sources for a select number of films that eventually proved to be highly successful. Starting with Alfonso Arau's (b. 1932) interpretation of Laura Esquivel's (b. 1950) novel *Como agua para chocolate* [Like Water for Chocolate] (1992), Mexican filmmakers went on to create three more internationally celebrated titles. *Amores perros* [Love That Betrays] (2000), by Alejandro González Iñárritu (b. 1963), starred the critically acclaimed young actor Gael García Bernal (b. 1978) and went on to receive both the Academy Award and Golden Globe 2001 nomination for Best Foreign Film. Following on this success, Bernal also starred in Alfonso Cuarón´s (b. 1961) *Y tu mamá también* [And Your Mother Too] (2001). Another example is Carlos Carrera's (b. 1962) controversial *El crimen del Padre Amaro* [The Crime of Father Amaro] (2002) that details the illicit sexual relationship between a priest and one of his parishioners. Taking into account the recent triumphs of the industry and the explosion of the Spanish-speaking population throughout the world, Mexico is clearly well situated to enjoy future achievements in the field of cinema.

A new generation of Mexican movie stars appeared in the mid- and late 1990s, arriving in Hollywood soon after. Among the most internationally recognizable names are Diego Luna (b. 1979), the above-mentioned Gael García Bernal, and Salma Hayek (b. 1966). Luna and Bernal starred together in the controversial *Y tu mamá también* [And Your Mother Too]. Since then, Bernal has played in the international box office hits *Motorcycle Diaries* (2004) and *Bad Education* (2004). With four new movies on the way, Bernal has now also taken on the roles of director and producer. His first film (produced with Diego Luna), *Déficit*, is expected to be completed in 2007. Some of Luna's most popular works by American production companies are *The Terminal* (2004) and *Dirty Dancing: Havana Nights* (2004); recent titles include *Un mundo maravilloso* (2006) and *Sólo Dios sabe* (2006), which he also produced. Salma Hayek's prominence on the U.S. movie scene has proved so strong that to many in the younger public her Mexican nationality is not even evident: many think that she is American. With over 30 movies under her belt, her most successful titles are *After the Sunset* (2004), *Once Upon a Time in Mexico* (2003), *Frida* (2002), and *Traffic* (2000).

## BRAZIL

It is possible to list two dates for the beginning of Brazilian film history. For some, it started on May 1, 1897, in the city of Petrópolis, State of Rio. At that time, Petrópolis was a summer haven for upper-class Brazilians, who preferred the cooler climate of the mountains to the heat of coastal cities. There, in the Teatro Cassino Fluminense, the Italian businessman Vittorio di Maio created the *cinematógrafo* (a rudimentary projector) as a means of entertaining the vacationers. The first movie-goers marveled at the new invention, imported straight from Europe where the brothers Lumière had originally demonstrated it in 1895. This new audience had the opportunity to watch some European documentaries and four short movies produced in Brazil. The subjects of these Brazilian productions were taken straight from daily life: a circus woman on a trapeze, children playing at school, people coming in and out of streetcars in Rio, and the arrival of a train in Petrópolis. Despite the down-to-earth choice of topics, it is indisputable that Brazilian cinema at its debut catered mostly to a privileged group of viewers.

The other version of Brazil's movie history has its beginnings in 1898, when the Italian-Brazilian Affonso Segreto made available the first devices that would allow for rudimentary moviemaking. Segreto was responsible for the earliest showing of the Lumière brothers' work in the city of Rio in 1896. In subsequent years, Segreto recorded and showed moments of Brazil's public life: celebrations, carnivals, political events, and the like were his favorite topics. Movie showings, however, were sparse and accessible almost exclusively by the elites (as in the Petrópolis case). At that time, electricity was not readily available, even in the capital, Rio de Janeiro. As an immediate result of the expansion of electrical services in big cities, movie theaters, or showing rooms, started appearing everywhere. Brazilian cinema gained a vital impulse with the opening of so many new rooms. As a result, the movie industry, invested in the development of films that dealt with Brazilian culture and life and aimed at bringing a more economically diverse population to the movies, was able to dramatically increase the number of movie-goers. It took many more years, though, to drastically transform the socially selective aspect of movie watching in Brazil and to open the doors to the general public.

The first decade of the twentieth century was quite prolific, and Brazilian movies far outnumbered foreign productions. On the average, 100 movies were made every year, indicating that Brazilian cinema had parted from its elitist origins to become an entertainment for the masses. Movies dealt mostly with current affairs, such as local and national news, but also explored gruesome or unsolved criminal activity, the crowd's favorite. Comedies, soccer-inspired documentaries, and carnival-based story lines also abounded. The year 1908 was said to be the beginning of the Golden Age of Brazilian cinema, thanks to the release of immensely popular titles such as *The Stranglers*, *The Sinister Suitcase*, and *Mr. Anastácio Arrived from a Trip*, Brazil's first comedy. Affonso Segreto, Antônio Leal, and Alberto Botelho were among the most inspired and well-known producers of the decade. With the growing market for movies, the stages of production, distribution, and exhibition gained structure and became quite efficient.

The Golden Age of Brazilian film ended around 1911 when a group of American movie executives visited Brazil and decided to invest in the nation's fast-growing market. Without laws to restrain the importation of films, Brazilian productions were soon obliterated by North American and European movies, whose quantity and technical superiority rendered a fair competition virtually impossible. Moreover, foreign films, mass-produced in countries where the movie industry was already all powerful, were less expensive to acquire, and consequently easier to distribute, than ones made in Brazil. A few native filmmakers survived the foreign invasion, managing to remain intellectually creative despite of financial difficulties. For example, Luis de Barros, from Rio de Janeiro, focused his efforts on the adaptation to film of well-known Brazilian novels by José de Alencar, an admired nineteenth-century Romantic writer. *The Little Widow*, *Iracema*, and *Ubirajara* (produced between 1914 and 1919) coexisted with newsreels and political propaganda films. Since their quality was quite debatable, they did not receive much consideration from motion-picture reviewers. Brazil's first woman director, Carmen Santos, was also one of the rare entrepreneurs who decided to face the growing foreign pressure in the 1920s. Although she began as an actress, she also produced and directed her own movies early in her career. In the 1930s Santos founded the studio Brasil Vita Filme, through which she would later act in, direct, script, and produce *Conspiracy in Minas* (1948). Also in the 1930s, Gilda Abreu, another woman moviemaker of renown, wrote, sang and acted in, directed, and produced a number of films.

The contribution of Italian immigrants to the history of Brazilian cinema has yet to be given full credit. From its beginnings to the years of foreign supremacy in the national movie scene, Italian Brazilians played an undisputable role in keeping alive the "seventh art." Gilberto Rossi, among others, was part of a movement to revitalize the national movie industry, providing technical education and creating the Azzuri School of Cinematic Arts, the first movie-making institute in the country. Besides caring for the practical aspects of the film industry, such as the training of skilled professionals, Rossi and his partner José Medina produced a number of movies considered, by today's critics, to be of superior intellectual quality. Some of their titles, *Redeeming Example* (1919), *Perversity* (1921), *The Fault of Others* (1922), and *Fragments of Life* (1929), became the first dramas made in Brazil to achieve national notoriety. Some Italian-American producers from the 1920s, nonetheless, betrayed their origins and fully surrendered to foreign themes. Eugenio Centenaro, for example, filmed numerous westerns under the name of E. C. Kerrigan. This tendency toward Americanization, or to the concealment of one's identity under the mask of a phony foreign producer, revealed the tendency to view whatever was made abroad as automatically better than national products.

Nonetheless, foreign influences in Brazilian cinematic tradition were not necessarily negative. European avant-garde moviemakers, for instance, exerted quite a beneficial influence, fostering the creative impulse of some Brazilian producers. Inspired by Walter Ruttmann's *Berlin, Symphony of a Great City* (1927), Adalberto Kemeny and Rodolfo Lustig created *São Paulo, Symphony of a Metropolis* (1929); and Humberto Mauro made *Minas Blood* (1930), about Cataguases, a city in the State of Minas Gerais. It is within the context of avant-garde inspiration that *Limit* appeared. This movie by Mário Peixoto, with photography by Edgar Brazil, premiered in 1930 to a very small audience, never reaching the commercial circuit. The young director, in his twenties at the time, along with Edgar Brazil, was recognized by national and international critics, who praised the film's unique technique and unprecedented style. The movie soon became a legend; its reputation was enhanced by the fact that it remained Peixoto's only work. By 1980s, *Limit* found a definitive place among viewers, being readily available in video stores and movie theaters, and on television. By the end of the twentieth century, it had already achieved the status of the best Brazilian movie ever made, according to a research done in 1995 by the newspaper *Folha de São Paulo*.[2]

When sound was added to the movies, Brazilian producers believed that they could finally prevail over the growing popularity of foreign film, most markedly American film. The first movie with sound in Portuguese, *Lips without Kisses* (1930), was, nonetheless, the work of Wallace Downey, an American. The Cinédia Studios were founded in the 1930s as an outcome of this confident outlook for the future of the nation's film industry. The *chanchada*, a Brazilian concept in which music and dance enhance a comical story line having as a typical background the sunny city of Rio de Janeiro, instantly took over the market. *Alô, Alô, Brasil* (1935) and *Alô, Alô, Carnaval* (1936), chanchadas by the director Adhemar Gonzaga starring Carmen Miranda, were extremely successful, helping to launch the actress's career in Hollywood. Chanchadas were widespread among national audiences for over 30 years, and they were partially responsible for creating the stereotypical image of Brazilians as a lighthearted, life-loving, sensuous, and easygoing people. It is unquestionable, however, that the chanchadas reconnected Brazilians with their movie industry.

Another variety of Brazilian movie appeared with the advent of Vera Cruz Films, founded by Francisco Matarazzo Sobrinho in the 1940s. Based in São Paulo and having as its main goal the making of movies more consequential than the chanchadas, the studio produced a few excellent works, such as *The Cangaceiro* (1953), but went bankrupt a year later. Vera Cruz Films played a critical role in the Brazilian movie industry by introducing foreign standards of technical and intellectual quality to the national market. On the other hand, it was also criticized for trying to portray an image of the country that was artificial and mostly Hollywood inspired, fast becoming the reverse of the chanchada in its choice of subject matter. Vera Cruz Films was replaced by Brasil Films, which generated, on its turn, a wide variety of movies, many of them also opposing the spirit of the chanchadas and dealing with serious social topics. In a way, São Paulo moviemakers fought against Rio's comic verve by transforming themselves into masters of severity. Chanchadas remained, however, very well liked by viewers, falling slowly into oblivion only when television arrived in Brazil at the end of the 1950s.

The next step in Brazilian cinematic history, the Cinema Novo (New Cinema), brought international recognition to the country's unstable movie industry. The Cinema Novo came as a direct effect of fiscal prosperity, social vitality, and a widespread desire for progress among Brazilians of all classes. As a general rule, the movement preached against Hollywood and its idea of commercial filmmaking. They also opposed movies made in Brazil that followed the same capitalist philosophy and fought against the notion that art was for sale by powerful movie studios. Distancing themselves from the idea of consumerist filmmaking, these new writers and directors aimed at making independent movies with strong sociopolitical content. They avoided using professional actors, filmed on location (not in studios), and treated exclusively Brazilian serious subjects of interest, such as the contrast between rich and poor in underdeveloped, rural areas of the country. Some of the most prominent titles of this phase are *The Hustlers* (1962), by Rui Guerra; *Ganga Zumba* (1963), by Carlos Diegues; *Barren Lives* (1963), by Nelson Pereira dos Santos; and *Black God, White Devil*

(1964), by Glauber Rocha. These directors have remained influential creative forces throughout their careers.

From 1964 until 1968, with the advent of another military coup that initiated a period of intense political persecution in the country, Brazilian cinema reflected its unstable surroundings through movies that dwelled more on mental reactions to the crises than on actions to reverse those crises. The loss of freedom to protest powers in place, the annihilation of leftist parties, and, in a certain sense, the end of idealism were all portrayed in movies that had as background Brazil's big cities. The films from the second phase of Cinema Novo dealt, mainly at a philosophical level, with the subject of disappointment and alienation in the face of a reality that seemed too surreal to be real. Works that best exemplify the struggles of a generation of intellectuals living under dictatorship are *The Challenge* (1966), by Paulo Saraceni; *Land in Anguish* (1967), by Glauber Rocha; and *The Brave Warrior* (1968), by Gustavo Dahl.

A third moment of the Cinema Novo tried to bring together the idea of film as art form and political instrument with the desire to reach a larger public. While the Cinema Novo prior to 1969 appeared to frown on the need for a mass audience, directors filming during and after 1969 saw a larger number of viewers and, consequently, the economic success that would generate, as a sign that their political beliefs were going further than ever before. They thought that once the leftist principles behind the movies were made available to the general public, the chances of actually producing drastic social changes would be enhanced. Moreover, in order to fight Hollywood and its extremely effective movie distribution industry, the leaders of Cinema Novo had to create their own system of production, distribution, and advertising, somewhat inspired by the same American movie industry they condemned. The names of Luíz Carlos Barreto and his distribution company, Difilm, remain strongly related to this moment in Brazilian cinema. *The Girl from Ipanema* (1967), by Leon Hirszman, was the first color movie produced in the country. Well accepted by public and critics alike, it simultaneously exploited and distorted stereotypes in order to reveal the reality behind the fiction of an idealized femininity. However, it was *Macunaíma* (1969), by Joaquim Pedro de Andrade, the first Brazilian feature film produced under the auspices of the Cinema Novo, that brought big crowds to the theater and resulted in substantial profit.

Without selling itself out to foreign interests and still remaining faithful to its fundamental leftist ethics, this third phase of the Cinema Novo incorporated into the Brazilian market whatever they found of use in American cinema and consumed it without guilt or shame. This approach reflected, in many ways, the philosophy of two inseparable cultural movements created by the nation's intellectual elite: Canibalismo and Tropicalismo. To summarize both concepts, the "cannibal" artist wisely selects and makes good use of whatever is valuable in foreign cultures without surrendering to them, as in the case of filmmakers from the third generation of Cinema Novo. The "tropicalist" plays with the idea of Brazil as a sultry dreamland, where eternally cheerful people sing and dance all year long, such as the life portrayed in Carmen Miranda's movies and in many chanchadas. Since this third phase corresponded to a moment of intense political persecution in Brazilian history, moviemakers, in order to evade the traps of censorship, had to find ways to voice their criticism and inform the viewers of their projects. Canibalismo and Tropicalismo proved to be effective means of communication between artist and public. As a result, the main characteristics of works from this phase were the use of metaphors and allegories under which writers and directors camouflaged their attacks on the military establishment. Unfortunately, when censorship became too severe, hampering creativity and putting the lives of movie directors in danger, many fled to Europe in search of intellectual freedom and a more auspicious artistic environment.

If censorship in Brazil under the military rule was often fierce, it concentrated its efforts mainly on condemning movies with sociopolitical content. This being the case, films with a hidden subversive message existed side by side with a flourishing industry based exclusively on low-quality eroticism with a comic twist—the widespread Pornochanchada. These works, produced mainly at the early 1970s and popular among a public that sought an inconsequential movie-going experience, dealt with sexual stereotypes, perpetuating a womanizing and homophobic point of view. Thus, when it came to purpose and attitude, the Pornochanchada, drastically dissimilar from the Cinema Novo or even the Udigrudi, or underground, films, left no significant mark on the cinematographic history of Brazil. Moreover, it is not surprising that the peak for the making of Pornochanchadas corresponded to a moment of vacuum in Brazilian artistic and intellectual productions as a whole.

From 1972 to 1980, Brazilian cinema underwent an astonishing revival. Following a weakening of the military government and, consequently, of censorship, many of the writers, directors, and producers of the Cinema Novo who had been in exile returned to the country, bringing to the screen a fresh approach to old themes and a new wave of creativity. The most celebrated titles from the 1970s were the outcome of this new-found inspiration. *The Amulet of Ogum* (1974) and *Tent of Miracles* (1977), by Nelson Pereira dos Santos; *Xica da Silva* (1976) and *Bye, Bye Brasil* (1980), by Carlos Diegues; and *All Nudity Shall be Punished* (1973), by Arnaldo Jabor, are only some of the many well-known titles presented during this period. Another important fact that stirred the movie industry was the hands-on instruction that these seasoned directors provided to their successors in the field. Once these returning filmmakers resumed their work, they also brought to the scene a group of young directors who followed in their footsteps and contributed immensely to the rebirth of the cinematographic industry in Brazil. One of these was Bruno Barreto, who remains one of the greatest names in Brazilian cinema. His *Dona Flor and Her Two Husbands* (1976) was a national and international hit and coincided with the new phase of Embrafilme.

By the mid 1970s, Brazil was producing about 100 movies a year, all of them displaying new standards of technical quality and most dealing with nationalistic subjects, which remained a perennial point of contention among more progressive, antipopulist critics. The year 1975, however, was a definite marker for the industry. Under new management, Embrafilme, founded in 1969 by the military leadership, began sponsoring, promoting, and protecting the cinematographic arts in the country as it had never done before. The creation of the Concine in 1976 also assisted the mission of endorsing the country's film industry. Rules were set in place with the sole objective of preventing American cinema from drastically overshadowing Brazilian cinema. For example, by law, all foreign films had to be preceded by a national short-length production, and theaters were mandated to exhibit a minimum of 133 Brazilian movies each year. In the years to come, Embrafilme helped guarantee an average of 40 percent of the market exclusively to national motion pictures.[3] During this period, a focus on history prevailed in movies such as *Alleluia Gretchen* (1976), by Silvio Back; *The Fall* (1976), by Ruy Guerra and Nelson Xavier; and *Colonel Delmiro Gouveia* (1978), by Geraldo Sarno.

In the 1980s, however, Brazil went through yet another acute economic crisis, and the funds previously reserved for running Embrafilme were no longer available at the same level. Moreover, internal dissention on how to run the government-sponsored company led to its inevitable decline. Gradually, foreign film and, more specifically, American cinema took over the slice of the market once reserved for national movies. The convergence of many detrimental factors almost resulted in the extinction of Brazilian film production during the 1980s. Based on the individual effort of writers, directors, and creators, however, some masterpieces managed to find their way to the theater. Amid the crisis, *Pixote* (1980), by Hector Babenco; *They Do Not Wear Black-Tie* (1981), by Leon Hirszman; *Ahead, Brazil!* (1982), by Roberto Farias; and *Hour of the Star* (1985), by Suzana Amaral, kept the besieged industry alive, projecting the country abroad and bringing home numerous international

## CONTEMPORARY BRAZILIAN CINEMA

Since 1994, Brazilian cinema has encompassed a variety of themes, diversified its focus, and ceased to have dominant phases, as had occurred during the three moments of the Cinema Novo, in which certain issues were constantly revisited. Contemporary movies deal with diverse subject matters. If themes characteristic of the Cinema Novo, such as class conflicts, still remain quite popular, they appear from a new perspective. Works dealing with topics as diverse as national and personal identity exist side by side with films portraying the draught in the Northeast or those reviving nationalistic symbols. Others explore the eternal problematic issue of urban versus rural, and still others focus on political satire. The topics of violence in Brazilian big cities, life in the slums of Rio, and the division between rich and poor, seem to be the ones that reach the foreign public with greatest pungency. Documentaries treating the same subjects also abound, and many have been recognized nationally and internationally. Since comedy is such an important aspect of Brazil, numerous current movies explore humorous subjects.

awards. Despite occasional hits, however, the 1980s were a period of serious struggle for the Brazilian motion-picture industry. Curiously, the transition from dictatorship to democracy in Brazil, which in principle should have propelled a renaissance of the arts, led to diminishing production in most artist fields. Once the government reduced its financial support to the cinema industry, it could not stand on its own resources.

In 1990 Fernando Collor de Mello, the first president elected by direct vote since 1960, introduced drastic economic measures to contain inflation, reduce external debt, and curb internal spending. Many public servants were fired, and governmental agencies were closed. Both the Embrafilme and the Concine became extinct. Brazilian intellectuals, who, with the election of a young, popular president, were hoping for an exciting moment in the artistic field, soon realized that the road ahead would be grimmer than ever before. As a direct consequence of Collor's actions, Brazil produced an average of ten movies a year between 1991 and 1994. The reduction in the number of films was accompanied by a remarkable decrease in the number of movie theaters as well. From over 3,000 showing rooms in 1975, fewer than 1,000 remained 15 years later. In 1980 Brazilian productions had accounted for 35 percent of the national market; by 1991, they totaled only 1 percent.[4] In 1992 Fernando Collor was impeached, but the country's motion picture industry took 2 years to start recovering from the setbacks forced on it by the "Plan Collor."

In 1993, under the presidency of Itamar Franco, a new set of regulations giving fiscal breaks to enterprises sponsoring cultural ventures were created with the purpose of energizing Brazil's film production. Thanks to the "Audio-visual Law," Brazilian movies started to find a new ground for development. The first movie to be made under the auspices of the Audio-Visual Law was Carla Camurati's *Carlota Joaquina, Princess of Brazil* (1995).

Another interesting aspect of recent Brazilian cinema is the existence of many women writers, directors, and producers. Among many, Carla Camurati, Bia Lessa, Sandra Werneck, and Daniela Thomas continue to be the most active in the industry.

The mid-1990s and the first years of the twenty-first century remained exceedingly fertile when it comes to offering examples of movies that have made cinematic history, bringing Brazilians back to the theater and also conquering the foreign market. Some of these were *High Art* (1991), by Walter Salles; *The Oyster and the Wind* (1997), by Walter Lima Junior; *Central Station* (1998), by Walter Salles Jr.; *Possible Loves* (2000), by Sandra Werneck; and *Me, You, Them* (2000), by Andrucha Waddington. Most recently, with Brazilian movies arriving more quickly in international markets and finding larger, more enthusiastic audiences, titles such as *Carandiru* (2002), by Hector Babenco; *City of God* (2002), by Fernando Meirelles; *God Is Brazilian* (2003), by Carlos Diegues; *The Man Who Copied* (2003), by Jorge Furtado; and *Olga* (2004), by Jayme Monjardim, have achieved great triumphs. As an article on the number of movies produced nationally states, the percentage of spectators increased from 0.1 percent in 1993 to 21 percent in 2003, a noteworthy achievement.[5] If numbers are healthier nationally, the country, however, still has a long way to go in order to fully reach the foreign market, which is more competitive and more culturally diversified each year. Moreover, the influence of new technologies and the end results of their growing availability in Brazil remain to be fully investigated. Quality television programming and streaming video, in conjunction with the rapid release of movies as DVDs and the increasing number of satellite services, will definitely offer new challenges to the Brazilian cinematographic industry.

Some of Brazil's top movie stars have entered the U.S. market and have become recognizable faces outside their home country. For example, Fernanda Montenegro (b. 1929), one of the most traditional actresses of the modern cinema, was nominated for an Oscar thanks to her outstanding performance in *Central Station* (1998). She also starred in *Pixote* (1981). Sonia Braga (b. 1950) is another staple of Brazilian cinema. She became famous by appearing in the adaptations of Jorge Amado's *Dona Flor and Her Two Husbands* (1976), *Gabriela* (1983), and *Tieta* (1996). Braga has taken part in numerous American sitcoms and films. She has starred in *Alias*, *Sex in the City*, *George Lopez*, *American Family*, and *CSI*, among others. More recently, Glória Pires (b. 1963) has contributed immensely to Brazil's film industry. A child star, she started acting at the age of five and has been thriving since then. Famous for her portrayals of evil women on television soap operas, she has branched out to play all sorts of characters, both on television and on the big screen. Her most recent films are *The Inheritance* (2001) and *If I Were You* (2006). A young Brazilian actress who has become a strong performer in Latin America is Luana Piovani (b. 1976). Piovani is, for the most part, a television artist who has just started to venture into film with *The Man Who Copied* (2003). Lima Duarte (b. 1930), a soap opera star and director, has played most recently in *Magic Mirror* (2005) and *After the Ball* (2005). Antonio Fagundes (b. 1949), another household name, has performed in many television series and movies, including *God is Brazilian* (2003). Rodrigo Santoro (b. 1975) has made an international career starring in movies such as *Charlie's Angels 2: Full Throttle* and *Love Actually*. He also had main roles in *Abril Despedaçado* [Behind the Sun], nominated as Best Foreign Film for the 2002 Golden Globes. Santoro is known to take up challenging roles such as in *Carandiru* (2003), by the well-known Hector Babenco, where he appears as a transvestite. Most Brazilian actors and actresses started their careers in television, playing in the famous Rede Globo miniseries and soap operas. The transition from small screen to big screen is thus a natural movement, and many stars will take parts in both universes, remaining accessible to moviegoers and non-moviegoers alike.

## ARGENTINA

Similar to that of Mexico and Brazil, the history of film in Argentina began in 1896 with the first public exhibition of the revolutionary Lumière projector in Buenos Aires by Francisco Pastos and Eustaquio Pellier. Not even a year later, Eugene Py—a Frenchman living in Buenos Aires—produced a film called *La bandera argentina* [The Argentine Flag] (1897) and introduced it to an enthusiastic society that was already caught up in a period of great economic development and growth. This initial work was followed by a series of short reality films such as those by Dr. Alejandro Posadas, who recorded his own surgeries. By 1900 special movie houses had been established in Buenos Aires for the sole purpose of showing the short films and newsreels of the time. In 1910 *La revolución de mayo* [The May Revolution] became the first Argentine movie produced with professional actors.

When World War I essentially closed down European film exports, national producers stepped in to try to fill the void. In 1914 Argentina produced its first feature film, *Amalia*. This was followed a year later with the box office smash *Nobleza gaucha* [Gaucho Nobility] (1915), based on the national figure of the gaucho, or idealized Argentine cowboy. The promise of capital gain served as the inspiration for the making of the world's first animated film, *El apóstol* [The Apostle] (1917), by the Italian-born Frederico Valle (1880–1960). An estimated one hour in length, it took some 12 months to be completed and was seen by some as a clandestine attack on the political milieu of the time. Despite having generated over 200 silent titles, the nascent industry was never organized, and as a result, many of these early films were never properly preserved and are now unfortunately lost.

As in Mexico and Brazil, cinema in Argentina only emerged as an industry with the advent of sound in 1930. The initial attempts were of inferior quality when compared with films produced in Mexico and the United States, and it was not until 1933, when film studios such as Argentina Sono, Tango, and Lumiton were founded, that the country's industry began to take shape. From the beginning, nonetheless, Argentine cinema faced serious problems because of competition from foreign films as well as because of its own underdeveloped distribution system. Although both Mexico and the United States tended to provide more protectionist support of their national cinemas, Argentina, for the most part, left private filmmakers to fend for themselves in terms of distribution and price negotiation. Thus, while the years from 1930 to 1936 can be described in general terms as a period of expanding film production, it was primarily on the domestic level since Argentine filmmakers were not able to fully compete with the technological advancements of foreign movie producers until about 1937.

By the latter half of the 1930s, Argentina had solidified its place as a national and international producer of quality films with over 20 studios generating hits that would help regain some of the foreign market. For example, *Ayúdame a vivir* [Help Me to Live] (1936), directed by José Agustín Ferreyra (1889–1943), was the first of such films to gain international attention, thanks in part to the performance of the rising star Libertad Lamarque. *Mujeres que trabajan* [Working Women] (1938), directed by Manuel Romero (1891–1954) was one of many films that attracted audiences who wanted to see the stars actually perform their beloved tangos. Voted one of the best Argentine films of all time, *Prisioneros de la tierra* [Prisoners of the Earth] (1938) was director Mario Soffici's (1900–77) masterful brooding drama, a mix of complex character development and cinematographic expertise. Finally, *La guerra gaucha* [The Gaucho War] (1942) emerged as a result of the association of four movie actors, a director, and a producer, who formed the studio Artistas Argentinos Asociados. Directed by Lucas Demare (1910–81), it remains one of the best examples of the country's Golden Age of cinematic history. Surpassing even the enormous box office take of *Gone with the Wind* (1939) in Argentina, *The Gaucho War* touched on the national identity in portraying Leopoldo Lugones's vision of the heroic battle of the gauchos during the 1814–18 war for independence from the Spanish in northern Argentina.

Although the nation experienced relative success in the early years of national cinema, all this changed with the coming of World War II. Because of Argentina's position of neutrality during the war, an act seen as almost pro-Axis, national movie producers found themselves cut off from the raw supplies needed for filmmaking by the United States, which supported the film industry of the pro-Allies Mexico. The lack of raw celluloid, combined with Argentina's inability to produce it, led to tight state control of the limited quantities of virgin film available. Consequently, production levels plummeted, and by 1946, when the supply was reestablished, Mexican titles had almost all but eliminated Argentine films in the

Spanish-speaking world. Furthermore, while Mexican cinema flourished under the technical guidance and economic backing of the United States during this time, Argentina's limited production led to the failure of many movie houses and to the stagnation of the developing international system of distribution. Although the close of the war once again freed up the raw materials needed for film production, the national industry was then faced with serious setbacks that would not be addressed until the Perón dictatorship.

Beginning in 1944, General Juan Domingo Perón (who effectively ruled from 1943–55), began a series of programs in which he sought to protect Argentina's film industry by subsidizing production and establishing new measures for viewing and distribution. The protectionist strategy had mixed results. While pro-Perónists, such as director Hugo del Carril (1912–89), were granted permission and the celluloid needed to produce films such as *Las aguas bajan turbias* [Troubled Waters] (1952), many other titles never came to be. Similarly, with production houses competing for their share of state funds, the market became saturated with formulaic movies, whose only purpose was to satisfy the requirements necessary to receive a governmental subsidy. Perhaps the most detrimental policy, though, was Perón's system of economic reciprocity. This program, which generally provided that Argentina would only import a quantity of foreign goods equal to its own exports, had negative repercussions in dealings with countries such as Mexico and the United States since they preferred to operate under a system of free trade. The overall result was a decline in the number of films released between 1950 and 1953 in Argentina.

Forced into the untenable position of having to earn more money from fewer national movies, many production companies went bankrupt. It was only with Perón's overthrow in the coup of 1955 that foreign investment was once again welcome in Argentina. Although the revocation of the protectionist revisions opened the country once again to a glut of works from Hollywood and Europe, it had a negligible effect on domestic filmmaking. In 1957 new interest in national cinema fostered the establishment of the National Film Institute, an entity designed to help promote domestic production through loans, subsidies, and protectionist policies. Despite all these attempts, the Argentine film industry did not experience a period of growth between 1956 and 1981, turning out a mere thirty films each year.

Compared to the relatively positive outlook with regard to the modern film industries of Mexico and Brazil, Argentina has suffered a number of setbacks that have affected both the quality and quantity of national films. From 1930 to 1989, Argentina could be described as being highly isolationist in its politics—especially regarding its Latin American neighbors. Fiscal deficits increased annually, which, in turn, led to a state of hyperinflation mixed with recession that came to a head in the middle of 1989. President Carlos Saúl Menem (b. 1930) was elected in 1989 (he ruled until 1999) and almost immediately began one of the most rapid programs of privatization in the history of the world. Similar to Brazil in the 1990s, Menem tried to curb the country's economic difficulties by pegging the Argentine peso one-to-one with the American dollar and opening up most previously state-run agencies, such as the post office, utilities, and communications, to foreign investment. The worldwide reaction in terms of foreign investment was massive and swift. However, although it was initially successful, this fiscal policy eventually proved to be unstable as the rising American dollar, rampant unemployment, and enormous national debt all converged, producing dire consequences for the country. Despite a series of substantial loans from the International Monetary Fund (IMF), Menem's fiscal policy had to be abandoned, resulting in even greater economic hardships for the country. All of this took its toll on the production of national cinema since many producers were dependent on state subsidies. On the other hand, there were masterpiece titles produced during this era—*Camila* (1984), *Dark Side of the Heart* (1992), and *Yo, la peor de todas* [I, the Worst of All] (1990)—the majority co-produced by foreign filmmakers.

Currently, the movie industry of Argentina has placed its hopes in the 1995 "New Act," which forced national video and television companies to help subsidize the production of feature films. Combined with the continued trend of foreign co-production, this new source of investment has led to a renaissance of the seventh art. Although Argentine filmmakers have yet to reach the level of investment and maturity found in Mexico and Brazil, creative young Argentine directors have often worked with modest budgets to continue the great tradition of films that enjoy worldwide distribution and, consequently, critical acclaim. For example, *Nueve reinas* [Nine Queens] (2000), written and directed by Fabián Bielinsky (b. 1959), has won numerous international awards. The director Marcelo Piñeyro (b. 1953), who produced the 1986 Oscar-winning Best Foreign Language Film, *La historia oficial* [The Official Story] (1985), scored another hit when he directed popular actress Cecilia Roth (b. 1956) in *Plata quemada* [Burnt Money] (2000). *Roma* [Rome] (2004), by Adolfo Aristarain (b. 1943), has received accolades for the production team as well as for actress Susú Pecoraro (b. 1953). *Los diarios de motocicleta* [The Motorcycle Diaries] (2003), based on the journal of the iconic Ernesto "Che" Guevara, won an Oscar in 2005 as well as other important awards. *Los diarios*, in particular, illustrates the current trend in Argentine cinema. Credited with having been produced by Argentina in association with the United States, Peru, Chile, Germany, France, and Brazil, the film by the Brazilian Walter Salles (b. 1956) exemplified an international effort built on a national base.

Among the internationally recognizable Argentine actors are Ricardo Darin (b. 1957), Norma Aleandro (b. 1936), and Ines Esteves (b. 1964). Darin's most recent work is *The Education of Fairies* (2006); he has also starred in, among other titles, *Sammy and Me* (2002) and *Son of the Bride* (2001). Aleandro, a household name in her native country, has an extensive filmography, with a television and movie career spanning over 50 years. Her later roles included Beba in *Live in Maid* (2004), Norma in *Son of the Bride*, and Gloria in *Only Human* (2004). Esteves has taken part in popular television miniseries, but her roles on the big screen made her famous outside Argentina. Two of her works are *Eva* (2004) and *Four Friends* (2001). The young director Alejandro Agresti (b. 1961) was responsible for the cult film *A Less Bad World* (2004), *A Night with Sabrina Love* (2000), and *The Lake House* (2006), which promises to become a classic of Argentine cinema.

## OTHER LATIN AMERICAN COUNTRIES

### Overview

While Mexico, Brazil, and Argentina have substantial film industries, the remaining countries in the region have not yet established niches in the national and international markets. In Central America, for example, perennial economic and political crises hamper producers in their efforts to develop movie-making traditions. If the first showings happened as early as 1910, the seventh art never quite had a solid career in countries such as Costa Rica, Honduras, and Panama. Since the majority of people in Third World countries struggle to survive and lack the basics for a decent living, it is not surprising that making movies or going to the cinema remain activities that not many can afford. Moreover, since governments in the region lack the funds to assist the poor even in the most rudimentary ways, no one can blame them for not sponsoring a film industry.

Despite the numerous economic and social difficulties most Latin American countries experience, there are some excellent works, products of tenacious directors who fight for the few subsidies still available. In Costa Rica, thanks to its relative stability, great titles were turned out in the 1990s, among them *Bajo el Límpido Azul de tu Cielo* (1997) and *Florencia de los Rios Hondos* (1999). El Salvador has a movie history closely related to its revolutionary past. The Revolutionary Film Institute was created in 1980 with the purpose of supporting the industry and making the country's art known abroad. With the assistance of the Institute, *Carta de Mozaran* (1982) and *Tiempo de audacia* (1983) were produced. These titles, among others, deal with the country's revolution and document the historical moment. The first Salvadorian movie, however, had been produced some 20 years previously. The director Alejandro Cotto was responsible for *El Rostro* (1960), and in 1994 Guillermo Escalon made *Alejandro* in honor of Cotto's role in Salvadorian cinematic history. Nicaragua's film history is similar to that of El Salvador. The INCINE, a film institute inaugurated in 1979, followed the model of the Cuban ICAIC (Instituto Cubano del Arte y la Industria Cinematográficos) and produced many documentaries on the subject of the revolution. The documentary tradition started with young directors and producers such as Martha Clarissa Hernandez and Maria Jose Alvarez. Currently, a few Nicaraguan titles have been shown abroad, attracting a small but faithful group of followers.

## Cuba

Different from cinema in the countries mentioned above, Cuban cinema has maintained a stable place in the movie-making business, reaching international markets and increasing its popularity despite the U.S. embargo. Since the inception of ICAIC in 1959, the revolutionary theme has been a staple, but this gives outsiders a chance to understand Cuban history from a Cuban perspective. Cuban cinema reached its maturity with the making of *Memorias del Subdesarollo* (1968). *Memorias* was directed by Tomás Gutiérrez, finding a place among the 100 best films of all time list (International Federation of Film-Clubs). Recent films such as *Strawberry and Chocolate* (1993), *Guantanamera* (1995) and *Havana Blues* (2005) marked the beginning of a certain popularization of Cuban cinema. Showings of Cuban titles take place in university cities and cosmopolitan centers in the United States. VHS tapes and DVDs of new works can be found in selected U.S. video stores.

## Colombia

Colombia's film industry has produced internationally celebrated works, such as *Maria Full of Grace* and *Additions and Subtractions* (both in 2004). These became box office hits in the United States, creating a place for a new group of actors, directors, and producers. Catalina Sandino Moreno (b. 1981), for example, was nominated for an Oscar in the Best Actress category for her role in *Maria Full of Grace*. Drug trafficking and violence remain constant subjects, but they are presented through a humane, socially committed point of view, in which the thin line between right and wrong is constantly held in check. Other important works by Colombian moviemakers are *The Rose Seller* (1998) and *Under the Antioquian Sky*, a silent film from 1925.

## Chile

In recent years, Chilean cinema has experienced a boom and promises to become the next stronghold in the Latin American film industry. With titles that were instant hits nationally, this new age of Chilean movies has opened the doors to talented young actors and directors. *Coronation,* directed by Silvio Caiozzi, came out in 2000 and recounted the history of an influential Chilean family. A co-production with Sweden, *Bastards in Paradise* (2000) takes place in Stockholm, where Chilean immigrants face the hardships of living abroad. One of the biggest hits in the history of Chile's filmography is *The Sentimental Teaser* (1999), by Cristian Galaz. Other recent titles include *Pretiendo,* (2005), by Claudio Dabed; *In Bed* (2005), by Matias Bize; *Sacred Family* (2004), by Sebastian Campos; and *Play,* by Alicia Scherson (2005), Chile's Oscar nominee for Best Movie. While support for Chilean cinema is steadily growing, most movies, even more recent and very successful ones, face distribution problems when they reach the international markets and are often restricted to small showing rooms and selected video stores.

## Bolivia

Compared to of the rest of Latin American, Bolivia has produced the fewest movies in recent history. For many years, no movies were produced, and pessimism seemed to haunt Bolivian moviemakers. Bolivia's project for a local cinemateca was abandoned because of economic problems. As of 2004, there were only fifteen movie theaters playing new titles, and even in big cities, showing rooms were scarce. In 1995, for example, five movies came out, among them *Sayari,* by Hugo Ara, and *La Oscuridad Radiante,* by Marcos Loayza. The year 2003, however, produced more important titles, such as *El Atraco,* by Paolo Agazzi, and *Hombre Llorando,* directed by Angelino Jaimes. Actors from the country usually work in co-productions, perhaps the best route to reach to a larger public.

# RESOURCE GUIDE

## PRINT SOURCES

*Latin American Cinema*

Burns, E. Bradford. *Latin American Cinema: Film and History.* Los Angeles: UCLA Latin American Center, 1975.
Gabriel, Teshome H. *Third Cinema in the Third World: The Aesthetics of Liberation.* Ann Arbor, MI: UMI Research Press, 1982.
Hart, Stephen M. *A Companion to Latin American Film (Monografías A).* Woodbridge, Suffolk: Tamesis Books, 2004.
King, John. *Magical Reels: A History of Cinemas in Latin America.* London: Verso, 1990.
Martin, Michael T. *New Latin American Cinema.* Detroit: Wayne State University Press, 1997.
Noriega, Chon A., and Ana M. López, eds. *The Ethnic Eye: Latino Media Arts.* Minneapolis: University of Minnesota Press, 1996.
Pick, Zuzana M. *The New Latin American Cinema: A Continental Project.* Austin: University of Texas Press, 1993.
Schwartz, Ronald. *Latin American Films, 1932–1994: A Critical Filmography.* McFarland, 2005.
Stock, Ann Marie, ed. *Framing Latin American Cinema: Contemporary Critical Perspectives.* Minneapolis: University of Minnesota Press, 1997.
Usabel, Gaizka S. de. *The High Noon of American Films in Latin America.* Ann Arbor, MI: UMI Research Press, 1982.

## Brazilian Cinema in English

Foster, David William. *Gender and Society in Contemporary Brazilian Cinema.* Austin: University of Texas Press, 1999.

Hollyman, Burnes Saint Patrick. *Glauber Rocha and the Cinema Nôvo: A Study of His Critical Writings and Films.* New York: Garland, 1983.

Johnson, Randal. *Cinema Novo X 5: Masters of Contemporary Brazilian Film.* Austin: University of Texas Press, 1984.

Johnson, Randal, and Robert Stam. *Brazilian Cinema.* New York: Columbia University Press, 1995.

Nagib, Lúcia, ed. *The New Brazilian Cinema.* London/New York: Palgrave Macmillan, 2003.

Stam, Robert. *Tropical Multiculturalism: A Comparative History of Race in Brazilian Cinema and Culture.* North Carolina: Duke University Press, 1997.

West, Dennis. *Contemporary Brazilian Cinema.* Albuquerque, NM: Latin American Institute, 1984.

Xavier, Ismail. *Allegories of Underdevelopment: Aesthetics and Politics in Modern Brazilian Cinema.* St. Paul: University of Minnesota Press. 1997.

## Brazilian Cinema in Portuguese

Augusto, Sérgio. *Este mundo é um pandeiro: A chanchada de Getúlio a JK.* São Paulo: Companhia das Letras, 1989.

Bernardet, Jean Claude. *Historiografia clássica do cinema brasileiro: Metodologia e pedagogia.* São Paulo: Annablume, 1995.

Borges, Luiz Carlos R. *1960–1980, o cinema à margem.* Campinas: Papirus Livraria Editora, 1984.

Costa, João Bénard da, and Maria José Horta Paletti, eds. *Ciclo de cinema brasileiro: Apresentado por Cinemateca Portuguesa e Fundação Calouste Gulbenkian em Colaboração com Fundação Cultural Brasil Portugal, com o alto patrocínio da Embaixada do Brasil: Grande Auditório da Fundação, Sala Dr. Félix Ribeiro (Cinemateca Portuguesa): Lisboa, abril/junho 1987.* Lisbon: Fundação Calouste Gulbenkian: Cinemateca Portuguesa, 1987.

Empresa Brasileira de Filmes. *Guia de filmes produzidos no Brasil entre 1897–1910.* Rio de Janeiro: Empresa Brasileira de Filmes, 1984.

Hollanda, Heloísa Buarque de, Ana Rita Mendonça, and Ana Pessoa, eds. *Realizadoras de cinema no Brasil, 1930–1988.* Rio de Janeiro: CIEC/Escola de Comunicação/UFRJ: Museu da Imagem e do Som do Rio de Janeiro, Secretaria de Estado de Cultura, Fundação de Artes do Rio de Janeiro: Livraria Taurus-Timbre Editores, 1989.

Miranda, Luiz Felipe. *Dicionário de cineastas brasileiros.* São Paulo: Secretaria de Estado da Cultura: Art Editora, 1990.

Moreno, Antônio. *Cinema brasileiro: História e relações com o estado.* Niterói, Brazil: EDUFF/Goiânia, Brazil: Editora UFG, 1994.

Moura, Roberto, et al., eds. *História do cinema brasileiro.* São Paulo: Art Editora, 1987.

Paiva, Salvyano Cavalcanti de. *História ilustrada dos filmes brasileiros, 1929–1988.* Rio de Janeiro: F. Alves, 1989.

Simis, Anita. *Estado e cinema no Brasil.* São Paulo: Annablume: FAPESP, 1996.

Viany, Alex. *Introdução ao cinema brasileiro.* Rio de Janeiro: Alhambra: Embrafilme, 1987.

## Mexican Cinema in English

Foster, David William. *Mexico City in Contemporary Mexican Cinema.* Austin: University of Texas Press, 2002.

Mora, Carl J. *Mexican Cinema: Reflections of a Society (1896–1980).* Berkeley: University of California Press, 1982.

Mosier, John. "Film." Pp. 173–189 in Harold E. Hinds Jr. and Charles M. Tatum (eds.), *Handbook of Latin American Popular Culture.* Westport, CT: Greenwood Press, 1985.

Noriega, Chon A., ed. "Introduction." *Visible Nations: Latin American Cinema and Video*. Minneapolis: University of Minnesota Press, 2000.

Ramírez Berg, Charles. "*El automóvil gris* and the Advent of Mexican Classicism." Pp. 3–32 in Chon A. Noriega, ed. *Visible Nations: Latin American Cinema and Video*. Minneapolis: University of Minnesota Press, 2000.

Schnitman, Jorge. *Film Industries in Latin America: Dependency and Development*. Norwood, NJ: Ablex, 1984.

Stavans, Ilan. *The Riddle of Cantinflas: Essays on Hispanic Popular Culture*. Albuquerque: University of New Mexico Press, 1998.

## Mexican Cinema in Spanish

Agrasánchez, Rogelio Jr. *Bellezas del cine mexicano/Beauties of Mexican Cinema*. Mexico City: Archivo Fílmico Agrasánchez/Agrasánchez Film Archive, 2001.

Ayala Blanco, Jorge. *La aventura del cine mexicano*. Mexico City: Ediciones Era, 1968.

———. *La búsqueda del cine mexicano (1968–1972)*. 2 vols. Mexico City: UNAM, 1974.

Ciuk, Perla. *Diccionario de directores del cine mexicano*. Mexico City: Consejo Nacional para la Cultura y las Artes (CONACULTA) y Cineteca Nacional, 2000.

Dávalos Orozco, Frederico. *Albores del cine mexicano*. Mexico City: Editorial Clío, 1996.

Galindo, Alejandro. *Verdad y mentira del cine mexicano*. Mexico City: Katún, 1981.

García, Gustavo. *No me parezco a nadie: la vida de Pedro Infante*. Mexico City: Editorial Clío, 1994.

García Riera, Emilio. *Breve historia del cine mexicano, primer siglo: 1897–1997*. Mexico City: Ediciones MAPA, 1998.

Infante Quintanilla, José Ernesto. *Pedro Infante, el máximo ídolo de México*. Monterrey: Ediciones Castillo, 1992.

Pérez Medina, Edmundo. *Cine confidencial: charros del cine nacional*. Year 1, N. 6 (November 1999). Mexico City: Mina Editores, 1999.

Ramírez, Gabriel. *Crónica del cine mudo mexicano*. Mexico City: Cineteca Nacional, 1989.

## Argentine Cinema in English

Barnard, Timothy, and Peter Rist. "Argentina." Pp. 3–81 in Timothy Barnard and Peter Rist (eds.), *South American Cinema: a Critical Filmography (1915–1994)*. Austin: University of Texas Press, 1996.

Costello, Tom, ed. *International Guide to Literature on Film*. London: Bowker-Saur, 1994.

Elert, Nicolet V., Claire Lofting, Laurie Collier Hillstrom, Aruna Vasudevan, and Leander Shrimpton, eds. *International Dictionary of Films and Filmmakers*, 3rd ed. 5 vols. Detroit: St. James Press, 1996.

Nowell-Smith, Geoffrey, ed. *The Oxford History of World Cinema*. Oxford: Oxford University Press, 1996.

Schnitman, Jorge. *Film Industries in Latin America: Dependency and Development*. Norwood, NJ: Ablex, 1984.

Slide, Anthony. *The International Film Industry: A Historical Dictionary*. New York: Greenwood Press, 1989.

Williams, Gayle, comp. "Film: Bibliography." Pp. 559–568 in Paula H. Covington, David Block, Dan Hazen, Peter Johnson, and Barbara Valk (eds.), *Latin America and the Caribbean: A Critical Guide to Research Sources*. New York: Greenwood Press, 1992.

## Argentine Cinema in Spanish

Centro de Investigaciones Literarias Españolas e Hispanoamericanas. *Quién es quién en el teatro y el cine español ehispanoamericano*. 2 vols. Barcelona: Centro de Investigaciones Literarias Españolas e Hispanoamericanas, 1990.

Fundación Cinemateca Argentina. *El Cine Argentino* (CD-ROM). Argentina: Fundación Cinemateca Argentina, 1997

Trelles Plazaola, Luis. *Cine sudamericano: diccionario de directores*. Río Piedras: Universidad de Puerto Rico, 1986.

## WEBSITES

*Brazilian Cinema.* Updated 2003. Consulate General of Brazil in San Francisco. http://www.brazilsf.org/culture_cinema_eng.htm.

*Brazilian Cinema Promotion.* Updated 2005. Grupo Novo de Cinema e TV. http://www.gnctv.com.br/braziliancinema/index.jsp.

*Cinema Brasil Na Internet.* Updated 2000. Fibre Cine Video Producing Company. http://cinemabrasil.org.br/site02/index.html.

*Cineteca Nacional.* Updated August 2006. Fideicomiso para la Cineteca Nacional. http://www.cinetecanacional.net.

Drummond, Marcelo. Updated 2005. *Adoro Cinema Brasileiro.* http://www.adorocinemabrasileiro.com.br/. A complete site on Brazilian cinema from its beginnings to most recent releases. Site is in Portuguese.

España, Claudio. Updated November 2002. "Argentina Fathers and Sons: The Revival of Argentinean Cinema." *3continents.com/Centre de documentation cinématographique.*

Farber, Mario and Irene Raizboim. Updated 2002. *Historia del Cine Argentino.* http://surdelsur.com/cine/cinein/index.html. Argentine cinema history. www.3continents.com/cinema/infos_diverses/eng_argentina.html.

*Film Listings Archive: Brazilian Cinema.* Pacific Cinematheque. http://www.cinematheque.bc.ca/archives/brazil_ma99.html.

*Latin American Cinema.* Updated May 5, 1997. Zona Latina. http://www.zonalatina.com/cinema.htm. A list of Websites, movie sites, online articles, and other related information.

*Latin American Cinema Guide.* Updated November 18, 2005. Emory University. http://web.library.emory.edu/subjects/studies/latinamerica/latinamericancinema.htm. Compilation of sites dealing with Latin American cinema.

*Latin American Network Information Center—Cinema.* Updated 2006. University of Texas–Austin. http://lanic.utexas.edu/la/region/cinema. The most complete Website on Latin American cinema. It lists many other links on the subject, all separated by categories and countries.

*Latin American Studies.* Updated April 2005. New York University Libraries. http://www.nyu.edu/library/bobst/research/soc/lat-am/lavid.htm.

*Latin American Video Archives.* Updated 2005. http://www.latinamericanvideo.org.

Maza, Maximiliano. *Más de Cien Años de Cine Mexicano.* Updated July 24, 2006. http://cinemexicano.mty.itesm.mx/front.html.

*Mexican, Caribbean, and Latin American Cinema: A Bibliography of Materials in the UC Berkeley Library.* Updated June 13, 2006. University of California–Berkeley. http://www.lib.berkeley.edu/MRC/LatinAmFilmBib.html.

Villaça, Pablo. "Voices: A Brief History of Recent Brazilian Cinema." *MCN—Movie City News.* Updated August 30, 2005. http://www.moviecitynews.com/voices/2005/Villaca1.html.

## FESTIVALS

### Latin American Film Festivals

*Festival Internacional del Nuevo Cine Latino-Americano.* http://www.habanafilmfestival.com/.
*London Latin American Film Festival.* http://latinamericanfilmfestival.com/laff15/en/about/.
*Los Angeles Latino International Film Festival.* http://www.latinofilm.org/.
*Providence Latin American Film Festival.* http://www.murphyandmurphy.com/plff/.
*San Diego Latino Film Festival.* http://www.sdlatinofilm.com/.
*Vancouver Latin American Film Festival.* http://www.vlaff.org/.

### Brazilian Film Festivals

*Brazilian Film Festival of Miami.* http://www.brazilianfilmfestival.com.
*Festival de Gramado—Cinema Brasileiro e Latino.* http://www.festivaldegramado.net/festival/1986?.
*Festival do Rio.* http://festivaldorio.com.br/.

*Festival de Brasília do Cinema Brasileiro.* http://www.cinemando.com.br/200306/festivais/brasilia.htm.
*Mostra do Audiovisual Paulista.* http://www.mostraaudiovisual.com.br/.
*Prêmio ABC de Cinematografia.* http://www.abcine.org.br/.
*Semana do Cinema: Brasil e Independentes.* http://cf.uol.com.br/cinemascopio/noticia.cfm?CodNoticia=15.

## Mexican Film Festivals

*Festival Expolocaciones México 2001.* http://www.conafilm.org.mx.
*Festival Expresión en Corto, Guanajuato y San Miguel de Allende.* http://www.expresionencorto.com/.
*Festival Internacional de Cine Contemporáneo de la ciudad de México.* http://www.ficco-mex.com.
*Festival Internacional de Cine y Video Voladero.* http://www.voladero.com.
*Festival Internacional de Cine de Morelia.* http://www.moreliafilmfest.com/.
*Festival Internacional de Escuelas de Cine (CCC).* http://ccc.cnart.mx.
*XIX Muestra de Cine Mexicano e Iberoamericano de Guadalajara.* http://www.guadalajaracinemafest.com.

## Argentine Film Festivals

*Asociación de Críticos Cinematográficos de Argentina.* http://www.cronistasdecine.org.ar.
*Festival Internacional de Cine de Mar del Plata.* http://www.mardelplatafilmfest.com.
*Festival Internacional de Cine Independiente—Buenos Aires.* http://www.bafici.gov.ar.
*Festival Uncipar— Jornadas Argentinas de Cine y Video Independiente.* http://www.solocortos.com/uncipar.

## AWARDS

### Latin American

*Buenos Aires Latin American Film and Video Festival.* http://www.festlatinoba.com.ar/.

### Brazilian

*Brazilia Festival of Brazilian Cinema.* http://www.candango.com.br/.
*Festival de Cinema de Gramado.* http://www.festivaldegramado.net/.

### Mexican

*Ariel Awards: Mexico.* http://www.academiamexicana.com/.
*Mexican Cinema Journalists.* http://www.pecime.com.mx/.

### Argentine

*Argentinean Film Critics Association Awards.* http://www.cronistasdecine.org.ar/.

# NOTES

1. Roland Soong, "VHS and DVD Buyers in Latin America," *Zona Latina*. Updated June 30, 2002. Accessed February 21, 2007. http://zonalatina.com/Zldata243.htm.
2. *Mário Peixoto.* Accessed February 21, 2007. http://www.mariopeixoto.com/biografia.htm.
3. For more information on the Embrafilme see Villaça 2005 (in Resource Guide, Websites).
4. See Villaça 2005 (in Resource Guide, Websites).
5. See GloboFilmes, *About Us.* Accessed February 21, 2007. http://globofilmes.globo.com/GloboFilmes/0,,5367,00.htm.

# FOOD AND FOODWAYS

JEFFREY M. PILCHER

Mexican philosopher José Vasconcelos may well have had culinary inspiration for his early vision of globalization, articulated in 1925, that the people of Latin America represented a "cosmic race" unifying civilizations and heralding the future of humankind. The daily bread of the region comprised Native American corn tortillas, potatoes, and manioc as well as European wheat bread. Three centuries of slavery brought a wealth of African foods, particularly to the Caribbean and Brazil. When slavery was finally abolished in the mid-nineteenth century, Asian indentured servants offered a new source of labor for tropical plantations as well new flavors to regional cuisines. And although Vasconcelos opposed the twentieth-century arrival of industrial foods from the United States such as Coca-Cola, this latest wave of globalization had followed patterns of cultural contact established in earlier times.

Geography set an appropriately dramatic stage for the people of Latin America. Rugged mountain chains with extensive highland plateaus make up two core regions: Mesoamerica, encompassing present-day Mexico and Central America, and the Andes Mountains, here limited to the chain of countries from Colombia to Bolivia. Although these zones are located mainly in the tropics, altitude makes them cooler and drier than the islands and coastal plains of the Caribbean, a third distinct region of Latin America, which also can be extended to the tropical rainforests and heavily eroded mountains of Brazil's Atlantic coast. The temperate plains of South America's "southern cone" constitute a fourth basic zone, the only one with a climate ideally suited to European foodstuffs. The cuisines of these regions overlap considerably; for example, many people living along the Pacific coasts of tropical South America and Mesoamerica eat a diet more closely resembling that of the Caribbean than that of the neighboring highlands. As a result of the tremendous variety of microclimates, the cuisine of any given valley differs, at times radically, from the foods eaten on mountain slopes a short distance away.

Native Americans took full advantage of their abundant natural resources, and where staple foods could support high population density, they built great civilizations. Maize, a sturdy grain that produces high yields in diverse climates, became the foundation of Mesoamerican civilizations, including the Maya and the Aztec Empire. Potatoes, a nutritious root crop domesticated in the Andean region, likewise supported diverse civilizations,

115

culminating in Pre-Hispanic times with the Inca Empire. Another prolific root, manioc, provided the staple food source in the tropical lowlands of the Caribbean and Brazil, where Taino, Carib, and Tupi-Guarani peoples formed village-based chieftainships. By contrast, the thick grasses of the pampas precluded large-scale agriculture before the advent of heavy iron plows, and therefore hunting and gathering predominated in the Southern Cone. The three basic staples, corn, potatoes, and manioc, can be divided botanically into countless local varieties, which provided genetic diversity to ensure against famine and plague. With their prolific yields, these crops subsequently spread around the world as part of the Columbian Exchange, eventually joining a handful of Afro-Eurasian domesticates to become mainstays of modern agriculture.

Iberian cuisines emerged from a historical succession of settlers in the peninsular crossroads between Europe and Africa. In classical times, Phoenician, Greek, and Roman colonists had implanted the staples of the Mediterranean diet: wheat bread, olive oil, and grape wine. The Moorish occupation of Spain, from 711 to 1492, introduced the fragrant spices and elaborate sauces of the Middle East. Livestock raising, particularly sheep, was another mainstay of the peninsular economy throughout the Middle Ages. Conquistadors sought to transplant these foods to the Americas but met with mixed success, depending on the vagaries of climate and the reception of indigenous farmers and cooks. European settlers also established the legal mechanisms for regulating food supplies in Latin America, although they often drew upon indigenous customs for ensuring public welfare. These Iberian institutions included public granaries (known in Spanish as *alhóndigas*), semiprivate meat monopolies (*abasto de carne*), and municipal oversight of guilds and markets.

As a general rule, Iberian foods and dietary practices form the common basis for a unified Latin American cuisine, whereas indigenous traditions, along with African and Asian introductions, provide the spice of regional diversity. Scholars have debated the relative success of the conquistadors in transforming their American colonies into replicas of the Old World, but one cannot deny the tremendous variety of mestizo cuisines, reflecting centuries of cultural blending.

Beginning in the nineteenth century, new culinary influences spread through Latin America. French haute cuisine, along with its continental counterparts from Germany and Italy, became fashionable among the elites of the region during the belle époque around the end of the nineteenth century. Populist politicians of the twentieth century often rejected French food in favor of Spanish and even indigenous dishes, as more authentic expression of their national culture. But this gentrification of local foods clashed with the social hierarchies of Latin America, and a new set of imported fads—industrial processed foods from the United States—spread through the region. In contrast to their downscale image in the United States, McDonald's hamburgers became an icon of wealth throughout Latin America. At the same time, more modest snack foods and soft drinks permeated all levels of society. Nevertheless, these new forces of standardization have produced new mestizo variants, reflecting the ongoing dialectic of local and global influences.

## MESOAMERICA

### Mexico and Highland Central America

Vasconcelos had a tumultuous career as revolutionary, educator, and presidential candidate, and his ideal of *mestizaje* reflected a similar ambivalence about cultural and social blending within Mesoamerica, a region encompassing Mexico and highland Central America. Native

American civilizations devised elaborate cuisines, but the Spanish conquistadors were determined to eradicate them in favor of Mediterranean foods. Throughout the colonial era, the indigenous cuisine of corn remained a sign of social inferiority, while wheat bread was a mark of elite status. In the nineteenth century, mestizo elites used the nascent science of nutrition to explain the failure of development, but using cultural rather than racial arguments. The problem lay not with any genetic flaws but rather in the supposed dietary inferiority of corn. Only in the second half of the twentieth century, a time of rapid urbanization and declining agrarian reform, did the middle classes accept corn-foods as part of their national identities. Yet even today, wheat bread is never missing from any table of distinction.

The native civilizations of Mesoamerica developed an essentially vegetarian but nevertheless well-balanced diet, based on maize, beans, squash, and chiles and complemented by a variety of regional foods. Corn may have supplied up to 80 percent of the ordinary peasant diet, but when it was supplemented with protein-rich beans, the two offered complementary amino acids that ensured adequate nutrients. Squash, meanwhile, provided minerals and helped to store water, which was vital in the arid climate of Mesoamerica. With more than 80 different varieties, chile peppers contributed to the enormous regional variation in cooking styles. Other important vegetables were tomatoes, avocados, and diverse greens known in Spanish as *quelites.* In pre-Hispanic times, the only domesticated animals were turkeys and small dogs, but a variety of other game, birds, fish, and shellfish, and even insects offered additional protein. Cacao, domesticated in Central America, was boiled and drunk as *chocolatl,* but it was bitter, often flavored with chile peppers. Native Americans also fermented the sap of the agave plant to make *pulque*, a highly nutritious alcoholic beverage.

The preparation of tortillas, the cornerstone of Mesoamerican corn cuisine, was extremely labor intensive, which may have contributed to the burden of patriarchy. The first essential step was to make *nixtamal,* by simmering the kernels in a solution of mineral lime, which loosened the indigestible husk and heightened the nutritional value. Without this calcium bath, vitamin $B_3$ (niacin) was chemically bound, and people who ate a predominantly corn diet in Europe and the U.S. South often suffered from the debilitating disease pellagra. The next step in making tortillas was to grind the wet dough on a *metate,* a three-legged, basalt grinding stone. After this backbreaking chore, women patted the tortillas out by hand into thin disks, and cooked them briefly on an earthenware griddle. Nixtamal was also the essential ingredient for festival foods such as tamales and gorditas.

Native civilizations developed elaborate cuisines for religious celebrations and to achieve social distinction. In many ancient cities, well-fed nobles grew taller than commoners, thanks to their better access to animal protein. A terrible famine in the year One Rabbit (1454), in the early stages of Aztec imperial expansion, focused attention on food supplies for the island capital of Tenochtitlán. At the time, Moctezuma the Elder used canoes to distribute maize to starving people, and in later years, the Great Feast of the Lords recalled this imperial beneficence through ceremonial handouts of tamales (maize dumplings) from canoes. The Aztec empire demanded tribute of food and other goods from subject peoples, especially in the productive raised fields of Lake Chalco-Xochimilco. Among the warrior elite, civic and religious banquets assumed a competitive nature, with each host attempting to serve the finest chile pepper stews, tamales, and hot chocolate. Spanish conquistadors spoke with awe about the hundreds of lavish dishes served daily to Moctezuma the Younger.

Discussions of Aztec feasts invariably turn to cannibalism, which some scholars have attributed to protein hunger, but this crude materialist theory fails to account for the ritual consumption of flesh from sacrificial victims. Noble priests and warriors, who partook of this ceremonial communion, already had access to animal protein from fish and game. Nor did the Maya resort to cannibalism despite comparable nutritional circumstances. The ideal of reciprocity offers a more persuasive cultural explanation. According to myth, the gods sacrificed their own blood to create maize, and humans had a responsibility to feed the gods in return.

Quite apart from the question of cannibalism, mutual disgust marked the culinary encounter between Spaniards and Native Americans. Moctezuma's emissaries compared European bread with dried maize stalks, and the codices ranked pork fat among the plagues brought by the conquistadors. Later Spanish settlers expressed indignation when indigenous beggars turned up their noses at bread, a common form of alms in Europe. The Spaniards were equally dismissive of native foods, and complained bitterly about the tortillas that served as rations during the conquest. Even the elite food of chocolate seemed bitter and disagreeable at first, perhaps especially when spiced with chiles. Catholic missionaries attempted to propagate wheat in order to replace maize gods with the Holy Eucharist, but peasants found the European grain unproductive, expensive to grow, and prone to disease, although some entrepreneurial natives cultivated it for sale to urban Hispanic markets. As a result, wheat bread and maize tortillas became status markers within the racial hierarchy called the system of castes.

## Culinary Blending

Notwithstanding the racial boundaries of colonial society, culinary blending took place along with other forms of biological and cultural mestizaje. The Mexican national dish, *mole poblano*, illustrates the incorporation of chile peppers and cacao into the heavily spiced Arabic dishes of medieval Spain. Hot chocolate, sweetened with sugar, was a favorite drink of *criollo* elites (that is, people of pure Spanish descent but born in Mexico), who had to pay dearly for imported wine. At the same time, indigenous cooks gradually learned to beat pork fat into tamales, giving the dumplings a lighter texture and richer flavor. European distilling technology also transformed the fermented native pulque into distilled tequila.

Nor were the new influences on Mesoamerican cuisine limited to Hispanic settlers. French foods began to arrive already in the eighteenth century, when the Bourbon dynasty claimed the Spanish throne. The elite desire for French cuisine became even stronger in the nineteenth century, although the French-imposed Emperor Maximilian, who ruled from 1864 to 1867, ironically developed a taste for mole poblano and other local foods. This New World belle époque reached its pinnacle under the dictatorship of Porfirio Díaz (1876–1911). Restaurants run by such celebrated French chefs as Sylvain Daumont hosted exclusive banquets for political and financial elites, who guzzled endless bottles of Mumm champagne. Middle-class Mexicans meanwhile purchased cookbooks with which they sought to reproduce *bistec à la Chateaubriand* and other elaborate dishes. Despite fantasies of continental sophistication, recipes were often "Mexicanized" to suit local tastes—for example, through the use of chile peppers—making them very different from Parisian dishes of the same name.

Italian, German, Chinese, and Lebanese migrants added their own foods to the mix. Italian restaurants, beer gardens, and even chop suey joints opened in Mexico City during the Porfirian era. In some border towns of Sonora and Baja California, the finest restaurants in town serve Chinese food—a legacy of the large numbers of immigrants who sought to cross the U.S. border in violation of the Chinese Exclusion Act but instead settled in northwestern Mexico. In the early twentieth century, large numbers of Lebanese came to Puebla and Yucatán. Their pita and kabobs fitted easily into the local taco culture, and an adaptation of gyros cooked on a vertical rotisserie became widely popular under the name *tacos al pastor*.

Yet these immigrants never came in sufficient numbers to satisfy Porfirian intellectuals, who believed that progress would only come by diluting the relative weight of Native Americans within Mexican society. Indians living in subsistence villages were considered to be incapable of participating in the market economy or national life, although large numbers of these rural folk were actually mestizos, and even monolingual Indians often engaged in market-oriented agriculture. In any event, the mestizo elite made their argument based not on the genetic qualities of the indigenous masses but rather on the newly developed science of nutrition. If an inferior grain, maize, was the cause of their backwardness, then national redemption would come from the adoption of a supposedly superior staple, wheat. This conclusion was based more on cultural stereotypes than on experimental data, but there was an element of validity to the argument. Corn was an ideal subsistence crop, sturdy and capable of supporting a community in the most difficult times. Wheat, by contrast, was a risky market crop with high potential profits but subject to drought and disease. If the rural population could be moved from subsistence agriculture to wage labor, the Porfirian ideal would be realized.

## Mexico and Tortillas

This goal was indeed ultimately achieved, not through the replacement of maize in the diet but rather through the industrialization of tortilla production. This uniquely Mexican undertaking proceeded in three distinct stages around the beginning, middle, and end of the twentieth century. The arduous task of hand-grinding maize on the metate was first replaced by forged steel mills capable of grinding wet nixtamal. These new machines arrived in Mexican cities by the late nineteenth century but took decades to spread through the countryside, in part because of concern among women about their position within the family. The ability to make tortillas was long considered essential to a rural woman seeking marriage, and any who neglected the grinding stone risked unfavorable gossip. But by mid-century, corn mills had arrived in virtually every community in Mexico, transforming social relationships and helping to incorporate rural dwellers into the monetary economy. At that point, new technology had been developed to automatically press out and cook tortillas, which facilitated the spread of small-scale tortilla factories throughout the country. Finally, the industrial production of dehydrated *masa harina* (tortilla flour) allowed the vertical integration of food processing under Grupo Maseca, which dominated corn markets throughout Mexico by the end of the twentieth century.

The industrialization of other foods likewise began around the turn of the century. For many peasant women in Central America, roasting and grinding coffee beans was a time-consuming daily task, on top of making tortillas. The spread of mechanical coffee mills likewise allowed free time for women to engage in economic activity outside the home, helping to transform gender relations. In major cities, beer and soft drink manufacturing, along with the canning and bottling of foods, became important industries. Yet markets for modern commodities such as refrigerated meats, canned vegetables, comestible oils, and bottled drinks depended primarily on the growth of incomes and infrastructure.

In Mexico, the Revolution of 1910 first disrupted the development of the food industry through a decade of warfare, then provided a powerful impetus for its growth through the creation of a revolutionary food welfare program. This agency, founded in 1937 by President Lázaro Cárdenas, was originally intended to help the beneficiaries of agrarian reform to compete in the marketplace. Yet political crises, particularly urban inflation and food shortages, disrupted these rural development plans. Bureaucrats purchased staple crops from a few commercial growers in the Pacific Northwest and imports from the United States rather than from large numbers of small *ejidos* (communally owned farms) in central and southern Mexico.

The construction of grain storage facilities around urban centers and in ports on the Gulf of Mexico perpetuated this bias in the 1950s. The agency, known at its peak by the acronym CONASUPO, provided cheap food to the cities in order to win populist political support while at the same time containing union demands for higher wages, thereby indirectly subsidizing private industry. For example, bureaucrats supplied low-cost corn to the politically powerful *nixtamal* millers in Mexico City, who then sold tortillas to the public at fixed prices, gaining substantial profits for themselves in the process. By the 1960s, decades of official neglect led impoverished farmers to begin taking up arms and demanding a return to agrarian reform. The government responded by repressing the rebels and then extending the welfare programs to supply industrial processed food to the countryside as well. This expansion into food processing to provision the new rural stores prompted cries of socialist intervention by business leaders, who nevertheless continued to profit from the welfare agency's supplies of subsidized raw materials for their own factories.

A dual system of food distribution developed in Mexico. Supermarket chains such as SUMESA and Aurrera, opened in the 1940s and 1950s, but even today they remain concentrated in upper-middle-class neighborhoods. Foreign restaurants, from Aunt Jemima pancake houses in the 1950s to McDonald's hamburgers in the 1990s, were likewise aimed at the wealthy. Manufactured foods reached the rest of the population through small-scale grocers, often in municipal markets, and ambulant vendors. These merchants depended on corporate distributors for credit as well as business supplies such as display cases and refrigerators. Rural stores established in the 1960s and 1970s by CONASUPO stocked products such as animal crackers and soft drinks, either produced by state factories or purchased from private groups, thereby helping to incorporate rural consumers into larger national markets. Financial crisis and neoliberal reform in the 1980s and 1990s led to the abrupt privatization of the state welfare agency. The abolition of food subsidies and the fire sale of state firms allowed private manufacturers to collect windfall profits as the price of corn and beans rose dramatically for the poorest consumers.

Culinary modernity and increased incomes have not always resulted in improved nutrition. Studies by anthropologists and public health authorities from the 1960s to the 1990s have documented a fundamental trend toward the replacement of corn and beans by sugar and fats. Well-to-do peasants and working-class urban residents both derive an average of 20 percent of their calories from processed foods including soft drinks, beer, chips, and candy. The rural poor, unable to afford such snacks except on special occasions, dump heaping spoons full of sugar into weak coffee. As a result, increasing numbers of people have encountered an epidemiological trap, falling victim to the dietary diseases of the rich world without escaping the nutritional deficiencies of the poor world. Serum cholesterol levels among residents of the wealthy, meat-consuming areas of northern Mexico average higher than those in the United States. Heart disease has become a serious problem throughout Mesoamerica, and ranks as a leading cause of death even among Maya peasants. Excessive sugar consumption has meanwhile created an epidemic of diabetes, while hypoglycemia, hypertension, arteriosclerosis, and various forms of cancer have likewise grown more common. These diseases seemed all the more tragic given the continuing prevalence of serious malnutrition in the region.

## National Cuisines in Mexico and Central America

Even as imported processed foods have become more common, many have sought to preserve and in some cases actually invent national cuisines. In Mexico, beginning in the 1920s after the revolution, mole poblano was depicted as the epitome of culinary mestizaje.

According to one popular tale, the dish was invented in the seventeenth century by cloistered nuns, who combined Old World spices with indigenous chile peppers for a visiting archbishop, thus providing divine sanction for the Mexican nation. The colonial convent where this supposedly happened was even refurbished as a tourist attraction. A leading figure in the creation of Mexico's national cuisine was Josefina Velazquez de León (1899–1968). The author of more than 150 cookbooks, she traveled throughout Mexico teaching classes, collecting recipes, and helping to spread knowledge of the diverse regional cuisines of Mexico. Other foods have likewise been embraced as national icons, for example, pupusas in El Salvador and coffee in Costa Rica. Such everyday connections to the nation have been particularly important for migrants working abroad.

The everyday foods of Mesoamerica reflect the mestizaje that permeates the culture of the region. Rural workers eat a largely indigenous daily round of tortillas and beans with a bit of salsa before and after work, but it is generally washed down with a weak coffee and sugar, which were Old World imports. European influences are more prominent in the diets of urban workers, who typically eat a lunch of *tortas* (sandwiches) or tacos accompanied by a soft drink. For middle-class families, the main meal of the day comes around 2 o'clock and follows a pattern of wet soup of chicken broth, a drier soup of rice or pasta, a main meal such as *puchero* (a Mexican version of pot-au-feu), beans, and dessert. Breakfast consists of chocolate and a bit of bread, while a light supper of tacos or enchiladas might round out the day. Those who cannot make it home in the afternoon for *comida* often go to a small *fonda,* where they are served a fixed menu, while supper is often taken at a street-corner taco shop. Meanwhile, exclusive restaurants serve nouvelle cuisine to wealthy natives and tourists.

The majority of festival foods correspond to the Catholic calendar. Day of the Dead (All Souls' Day) is the most memorable celebration, with its candy skulls and black *mole* sauce. The Christmas season is traditionally marked by parties in which families make hundreds of tamales and give them to friends and relatives. Indigenous communities maintain more exotic festival foods, often consumed in honor of the town's patron saint or for a family celebration such as weddings. For example, in Veracruz, some communities will cook a Zacahuil, an enormous pit-cooked tamale that can feed the entire town.

Throughout history, the incorporation of successive new influences has been a hallmark of Mesoamerican cuisine. The arrival of industrial processed foods in the twentieth century followed patterns of culinary change established earlier. Perhaps the most revolutionary culinary change of the twentieth century was not the arrival of foreign foods such as McDonald's hamburgers or Coca-Cola but rather the mechanization of tortilla making, which freed peasant women from long-hours of labor and allowed them greater access to public life.

## THE CARIBBEAN AND BRAZIL

The greatest African influences on the cuisines and cultures of Latin America took root in Brazil and the Caribbean, including Cuba, the Dominican Republic, Puerto Rico, Haiti, and Lowland Central America and Venezuela. In contrast to Mesoamerica and the Andes, the indigenous peoples of this lowland tropical region practiced a less intensive horticultural regime, which was largely supplanted after the Conquest by sugar plantations. Asian cooking practices, introduced on a small scale during the colonial period, gained greater importance through the influx of indentured servants and other migrants in the nineteenth century after the abolition of the slave trade. The twentieth-century growth of tourism, particularly in the Caribbean, prompted the invention of an haute cuisine based on fresh seafood and fruit, but these dishes had little connection to the actual diets of the people.

## MOORISH HEN

Take a raw hen and divide in pieces. Then prepare a pan with two spoons of butter and a little slice of bacon. Place the hen within it and allow it to brown. Cover the hen with enough water to cook it. When the hen is almost cooked, take green onion, parsley, coriander, and mint, chop everything finely and put it in the pot, with a little lemon juice. Finish cooking the chicken very well. Then take bread crumbs and spread them over the bottom of a tureen and arrange the hen on top. Cover with poached egg yolk and powdered cinnamon.[1]

Both the Taino and the Caribs, who migrated from coastal Venezuela up through the littoral of Caribbean islands, as well as the Tupi-Guarani people of Brazil, combined horticulture with hunting and gathering to maximize the dietary value of local resources. Because the soils were generally poor, farmers usually practiced swidden (slash-and-burn): cutting down large plants, burning them to release nutrients, and then planting with a digging stick instead of a plow. After a few years, when the soil had been exhausted, the people moved on and prepared new garden plots. Hunting and gathering also contributed significantly to indigenous diets, and all available protein was eaten, including rodents, fish, shellfish, and insects.

The staple food source throughout the region was a root plant known as manioc, cassava, and yucca respectively in the Tupi, Taino, and Carib languages. It has two varieties, sweet and bitter, and was domesticated in South or Central America, or possibly the sweet variety originated in Central America and the bitter in northern South America. The former grows more quickly, reaching maturity in six to nine months, can be eaten like a potato without elaborate preparation, but rots quickly if left too long in the ground. The bitter variety can be stored underground for months after reaching maturity, which takes from 12 to 18 months. The leaves of both are edible, resembling spinach. The bitter manioc root contains toxic chemicals and must be processed by grating and soaking. To drain the hazardous liquids, indigenous people strained the pulp through a *tipiti,* a long cylindrical basket made of palms and hung from a tree branch, which is still used in many parts of the Caribbean and South America. Boiling detoxified the juice and provided the basis for a manioc beer. The pulp was meanwhile formed into flat breads and baked on a griddle, or else dried and made into a coarse meal, called *farinha de mandioca* in Brazil.

Native people supplemented the staple manioc with a wide variety of other nutritious foods. They raised maize in garden plots but did not make tortillas, instead typically roasting or boiling corn on the cob. Other important food sources were sweet potatoes, arrowroot, beans, gourds, and palms, along with peanuts, brazil nuts, and cashews. Indigenous fruits included pineapple, papaya, guava, and mamay. Chile peppers and achiote flavored the starchy diet. The Tupi and Caribs may also have practiced cannibalism, at least according to the conquistadors. Iberian sources must be read with caution, however, since the enslavement of Indians was forbidden by royal edict except in the case of cannibals. Whatever such practices did exist probably were motivated more by ritual than by hunger.

As in Mesoamerica, Iberian settlers found local foods distasteful at first and sought to implant familiar Mediterranean staples, although only with partial success, thereby establishing new criollo cuisines. Manioc, in particular, was described as insipid, sour, and with a texture like sawdust. Unfortunately for the newcomers, wheat grew poorly in the tropical lowlands, and they had to rely on expensive imported grain or sailor's hardtack. Most settlers eventually acquired a taste for the nutritious local bread, and farinha de mandioca pastries called *beijú* have become popular favorites with all classes in Brazil. On the other hand, citrus fruit, originally domesticated in South Asia, grew prolifically in the Americas.

Lime juice became a widespread condiment, squeezed over virtually anything, and a pickle of vinegar and lime called *escabeche,* from the Arabic word *sebech* or "acidic food," was commonly used to preserve seafood, meat, and vegetables. Most European livestock, except for sheep, were also successfully introduced to the Antilles. Hogs adapted particularly well to the new environment, and in the early days of exploration, sailors left breeding pairs on each new island so that shipwreck survivors would have access to a familiar food, pork.

The most important crop introduction for the future of the Caribbean and Brazil was sugarcane. Brought to the Mediterranean from South Asia by Arabs, sugar had been planted on Madeira and the Canary Islands in the fifteenth century. Spaniards established the first sugar mill in Hispaniola in 1515, but by the end of the century the rapidly growing European market had fallen to Portuguese planters in Brazil. Caribbean exports regained prominence in the mid-seventeenth century after the British and French claimed Barbados, Saint-Domingue (later Haiti, the western third of Hispaniola), and other islands. Sugar remade the region ecologically, because all suitable land was cleared and planted in the profitable crop. Even greater social transformations resulted from the plantation system. Enslaved Native Americans worked the crop at first, but disease and neglect decimated their numbers, and within a century they had been replaced by African labor. In all, more than ten million African slaves were transported to the Americas, the vast majority to work and die on sugar plantations.

Slave diets varied depending on the nature of the landscape and the economic interests of the masters. In places such as Barbados, where virtually the entire island was suitable for sugar cultivation, owners found it more profitable to cultivate sugar alone and import food for the slaves. Such rations usually consisted of starchy grains, cornmeal or occasionally rice, supplemented by salted cod or dried beef. An alternative was allowing a free day for the slaves to cultivate their own garden crops. Known as the "Brazilian plan," it was adopted most commonly in areas where plenty of marginal land that could not be cultivated in sugar was turned over to manioc and other staples. The two systems were seldom mutually exclusive, and imported salt meat and cod often supplemented slave provision grounds. Mercantilist policies dictated that slaves should be provisioned from within the empire, and slaves in the Spanish Caribbean ate cod caught by Basque fishermen off Newfoundland and beef salted by gauchos on the Argentine Pampas.

The nutritional value of slave diets has inspired controversy among both contemporary reformers and modern-day scholars. One interpretation holds that plantation workers actually ate better than those who escaped slavery in Africa, but this seems unlikely except in the case of local famine. Another debate concerns the relative nutritional value of provision grounds and slave rations. Some have argued that slaves working under the "Brazilian plan" lacked sufficient free time to feed themselves, while other studies have pointed to the low nutritional content of most rations. In any event, malnutrition contributed to the high mortality and low reproductive rates of slaves. Disorders that contemporaries described as "dropsy" or the French "*mal d'estomac*" may have been the vitamin deficiency diseases beriberi and pellagra. Malnutrition also contributed to chronic stillbirths, infant mortality, and perhaps the widespread geophagy (dirt eating) among slave women.

Notwithstanding the poor quality of the typical slave's diet, African cooks took a significant role in shaping the development of Caribbean and Brazilian cuisine. Their influence can be seen first in the large number of African foods that enriched the regional diet. Bananas, domesticated in the Pacific and carried to Africa by Arab traders, were subsequently transported to the Americas to help feed slaves. Indigenous African foods that feature prominently in the diet include yams, okra, pigeon peas, cowpeas, blackeyed peas, malaguetta peppers, ackee fruit, and numerous greens. Palm oil, called *dendê* in Brazil, is an indispensable ingredient

123

in such popular dishes as *vatapá*, a puree of dried shrimp and coconut milk, flavored with garlic and malaguetta peppers, and served over rice. Caribbean specialties such as the thick, starchy *ajiaco* stew likewise demonstrate African influence. Runaway slaves formed their own mestizo blends with Native American cooking traditions, for example, the *gadámalu* tamales made of manioc, corn, and often coconut, steamed in banana leaves by the Garifuna living along the Caribbean coast of Central America.

New migrants from Asia enriched the foods of the region in the nineteenth century. Each success in the abolition of Caribbean slavery, from the British islands in 1838 to Cuba in 1886, brought new waves of indentured servants to work the sugar fields. Until the system ended following World War I, about 500,000 Indians and 125,000 Chinese had made the trip. Although planters sought to repatriate workers when their terms of service ended, considerable numbers succeeded in establishing themselves on the land or as merchants. By the turn of the twentieth century, the Barrio Chino, Havana's Chinatown, was crowded with restaurants, grocers, and other businesses. Unlike other migrants, relatively little culinary mixing took place; instead, Cuban–Chinese restaurants usually offered two separate menus of Cuban and Chinese dishes. Indian specialties such as curry were adopted more widely in the Caribbean, especially in Trinidad, where the greatest number of migrants settled.

The abolition of Brazilian slavery in 1888 coincided with a shift from sugar to coffee as the predominant crop, prompting the government to encourage free labor migrants instead of indentured servants. Along with Italians, Lebanese, and other migrants, about 190,000 Japanese settled in Brazil, bringing with them a taste for miso soup, pickles, and other traditional dishes. As early as 1914, they had begun to manufacture soy sauce locally, but Brazilian influences did creep into their cooking, they took up drinking coffee instead of tea, and cooking rice with pork fat.

The export boom of the late nineteenth century meanwhile allowed elites to share in Latin America's Francophone belle époque. The nouveaux riches of Rio de Janeiro indulged in French-style banquets or English tea and sandwiches at the Derby Club, the Café Mourisco, and the numerous teahouses and cafes of the exclusive *cidade velha* (old city). Havana's elite *tertulias* (cafe societies) were interrupted briefly by the Cuban struggle for independence (1895–1898), but the postwar revival of sugar exports introduced another source of conspicuous consumption: investors and tourists from the United States, eager for luxury while visiting the tropical island.

These elite indulgences laid a heavy burden on workers in the agriculture industry and on all people dependent on the ecologically impoverished landscape. Brazil's Atlantic rainforest, once comparable to the great forests of the Amazon, was largely cleared to plant coffee, even as the Amazon itself was invaded by rubber harvesters. Migrant workers in both regions earned only a pittance, while merchant houses and multinational companies profited from European and North American demand for coffee and automobile tires. Bananas offered another lucrative export crop throughout the Caribbean, including large parts of Central America. Aspiring planters from the United States bought up huge tracts of land, which were eventually consolidated through mergers into the United Fruit Company. Plantations operated as isolated enclaves, run by North American managers and engineers, and relying on poorly paid itinerant local labor. The boom and bust of commodity exports continue to dominate Latin American economies into the twenty-first century. Brazil's remote Mato Grosso is on the brink of becoming one of the world's largest sources of agricultural exports, thanks to genetically modified (GM) crops and heavy inputs of fertilizer and irrigation. This boom promises needed foreign exchange in the short run, but the longer-term legacy threatens to repeat the tragedy of Green Revolution agriculture in large parts of Africa, baking the fragile soil into permanently sterile brick.

Over the course of the twentieth century, industrial foods made inroads into even the most isolated communities, where they gained prestige value among impoverished people. Imported food and drinks arrived first in the export enclaves of fruit and mining firms, which shipped them as a convenience to expatriate managers on the return passage of otherwise empty cargo hulls. Local workers purchased cans of soda and boxes of crackers at company stores, thereby passing a taste for the exotic luxury along to their neighbors back home. Because they could only be consumed on rare festive occasions, the highly sweetened treats held special allure for children, helping to draw them into the cash economy.

Not all forms of culinary modernity were embraced with equal fervor. New methods of processing the staple manioc met with the same skepticism that corn mills originally produced in Mesoamerica. A pedal-powered grater, for example, promised to reduce the laborious task of grinding the root crop, which had traditionally been done with a hand rasp made of wood with sharp stones embedded. Yet this new technology conflicted with cultural expectations. Men not only began to question the fidelity of their wives if they neglected the labor-intensive kitchen work; they also took over the work themselves when it offered cash wages instead of merely contributing to household subsistence.

Ultimately, the arrival of industrial processed foods did little to improve poor diets and may well have exacerbated the problems of nutritional health in the Caribbean and Brazil. The United Nations Food and Agriculture Organization has warned of serious malnutrition throughout the region. A majority of childhood deaths on the islands are nutrition related, and a full third may have resulted directly from malnutrition. Haiti, in particular, has one of the highest levels of infant mortality rates in the world. Malnutrition is also a serious problem in the urban *favelas* (shantytowns) and among landless rural workers in Brazil. In Cuba, the Communist government of Fidel Castro dedicated itself to overcoming the inequalities of health that had plagued the island prior to the 1959 revolution. The socialist medical system indeed responded to the needs of ordinary workers, but the U.S. trade embargo caused serious shortages, undermining nutritional health. For decades, the Cuban people subsisted largely on subsidized foods from Communist countries, particularly rice from China and Vietnam, but the collapse of the Soviet Union led to brutal hardships beginning in the 1990s. Puerto Rico has been largely exempt from regional hunger thanks to the U.S. food stamp program. Nevertheless, nutritious traditional dishes have increasingly been replaced by junk foods.

The staple, everyday food throughout Brazil and the Caribbean, served on elite and popular tables alike, is the nutritionally balanced combination of rice and beans. Regional variations abound, from the *moros y cristianos* ("Moors and Christians") of Cuba, where black beans are most common, to the red beans and rice favored in Puerto Rico. Indigenous starches are likewise consumed across the social spectrum, ranging from fried plantain chips, called *patacones* in coastal Colombia, to the thick *sancocho* stew, a typical recipe for which includes pumpkin, squash, potato, sweet potato, yam, plantain, and yautía (another tuber), along with a little meat and chile pepper. Middle-class families supplement these starches with daily portions of meat and vegetables, cooked in traditional dishes such as *ropa vieja* ("old laundry," a stew of shredded lean meat), or *asopao,* a more soupy stew with chicken or seafood. Perhaps surprisingly, seafood does not constitute a large part of the everyday diet in the islands of the Caribbean. The local catch was long disdained by Iberians, who preferred imported salt cod to local lobsters. More recently, seafood harvests have been served to tourists or exported to Europe and North America. Nevertheless, some local favorites using fresh fish and shellfish include Puerto Rico's fried *mojo* and the Brazilian *vatapá.* As in Mesoamerica, street foods are the most common way of eating out, often starchy dishes such as *mofongo* (plantain cooked with pork cracklings), or cassava pastries.

More formal establishments, for example, Brazilian *confeitarías* and Cuban-Chinese restaurants, serve a range of social classes, while exclusive resort hotels cater to tourists and wealthy residents.

Festival foods of the region recall the diverse origins of the inhabitants. Spanish and Portuguese influences are apparent in the New Year's Eve tradition of serving *bacalao* (salt cod), either as fritters or a main dish. The Cuban *lechón de navidad* consists of a whole hog pit-roasted and served at Christmas. *Bolinhos,* deep-fried rice balls, also a Sicilian treat, are devoured during the Brazilian Festa de São Benedito. Meanwhile, Caribbean curries attest to the presence of Asian immigrants, and African influences can be seen in the peanut sauce of *xinxim de galinha,* a chicken and shrimp dish served with rice and cassava meal. The blending of these various traditions can be seen most clearly in Brazil's weekend *feijoada,* an enormous meal combining black beans (feijoa) with rice and manioc meal, collard greens, beef jerky, pig's feet, and sausages.

The coexistence of culinary modernization with continued malnutrition prompted a search for national cuisines as a source of comfort in difficult times. Brazilians have come to see the feijoada as a national dish representing the blending of African, Portuguese, and Native American cuisines. Cuba's most celebrated cookbook author, Nitza Villapol (1923–98), was treasured for her work collecting traditional recipes and helping cooks cope with food shortages. Throughout the Caribbean, people embraced local dishes as an alternative to tasteless factory foods from the United States. These local, peasant foods were eclipsed in foreign eyes by a new pan-Caribbean haute cuisine invented in tourist hotels by classically trained chefs who had little use for the starchy staples of the islands and instead relied on imported ingredients and fresh seafood unavailable to most residents. Globalization thus reproduced inequalities of class, but without fundamentally transforming the diets of ordinary people.

## THE ANDES: COLOMBIA, ECUADOR, PERU, AND BOLIVIA

The geographic extremes of the Andes Mountains, including modern-day Colombia, Ecuador, Peru, and Bolivia, posed challenges and opportunities for indigenous civilizations and for Spanish conquistadors alike. The wide range of climates yielded a wealth of foodstuffs and encouraged trade between different production zones. Such exchange was facilitated by the presence of domesticated livestock, unique to the Americas. The settlers also took advantage of these diverse climates to produce a range of Mediterranean foods that were scarce in other parts of the Spanish empire. Nevertheless, the formidable landscape also allowed Native Americans greater opportunities to preserve their culture unaffected by colonial rule. As a result, divisions between indigenous and Spanish cuisines are often greater in the Andes than in other parts of Latin America.

The northern Andes form a double range of mountains with a broad central plateau, in contrast to the more narrow chain that stretches the length of Chile to the south. At about 10,000 feet above sea level, the highlands have a wet and cold climate ideal for growing potatoes and other tubers. Midrange valleys offer a drier, warmer climate suited to the Mesoamerican staples maize, beans, and squash, as well as a local grain, quinoa. Mountain peaks rising above 16,000 feet provide pasture for native camelids: the llamas and alpacas. The Pacific Coast is extremely arid as a result of cold ocean currents, which bring fog but no rain, along with abundant supplies of fish and shellfish. The eastern slopes of the Andes, descending into the Amazon basin, is the source for coca leaves, which are chewed as a stimulant by people living at higher altitudes.

The range of foods available to Andean peoples in pre-Hispanic times provided a sound basic diet. The staple potato is extremely well-rounded nutritionally, with high quantities of protein, carbohydrates, and a variety of vitamins and minerals. Andean farmers complemented the white potato with numerous other tubers. The *oca* came in two varieties, one highly sweet and the other bitter, which was rendered edible through a process of freeze-drying. The relatively insipid *ulloco* was often fermented to give it more taste. Still another type, the *maca,* grew at high altitudes and in barren soils. Quinoa, which at 13 percent contains the highest quantities of protein of any of the major grains, was often ground into flour for making flat bread. The greens of the various tubers and of quinoa were also eaten. Maize was not made into tortillas but rather boiled, roasted, or made into porridge. Perhaps the favorite method for preparing the Mesoamerican grain was by fermenting it into an alcoholic beverage called *chicha,* although a variety of tubers and fruits could also used in this fashion. Andean farmers also cultivated most of the foodstuffs found in Mesoamerica and the Caribbean including manioc, sweet potatoes, avocado, and cacao. Moreover, local inhabitants had greater access to animal protein in the form of llamas, alpacas, and guinea pigs. Unlike other pastoralists, Andean peoples did not consume the milk of camelids, either raw or in processed form.

Achieving nutritional health in such an extreme environment demanded great ingenuity. Coastal dwellers devoted scarce irrigation water not to food crops but rather to cotton, which was woven into nets to harvest the rich seafood available from the Pacific. Residents of the altiplano learned to make freeze-dried potatoes, called *chuño,* by exposing the tubers alternately to temperatures above and below freezing, them trampling them underfoot for more convenient storage. Another form of dehydrated potato involved an initial boiling and then drying in the sun. Indeed, methods of preservation often overlapped with cooking techniques, thereby facilitating trade between different climate zones. Fish from the Pacific coast and llamas from mountain peaks were both salted and dried. The latter dried meat, called *charqui,* was the source of the English word "jerky."

Andean principles of social reciprocity and good governance likewise contributed to general levels of nutritional health. Local notables (*kurakas*) organized labor and redistributed production for the benefit of the entire community. The Inca Empire (1438–1532) in particular sought to maximize the efficiency of this system by maintaining enormous granaries, both as military depots for their expansionist policy and as distribution centers to ensure against famine. The ideal of equality notwithstanding, Andean nobles ate far more meat than did commoners. Moreover, to provide greater quantities of chicha beer for Inca ceremonial purposes, the empire resettled entire highland villages at lower elevations in order to increase maize production. Another consequence of this agricultural shift was that maize porridge became a more important source of nutrition for both elites and commoners alike.

The conquistadors rapidly subdued the indigenous highland empire, but notwithstanding the success of mining towns such as Potosí, Spanish settlement remained largely anchored along the coast. Agriculture helped account for this preference, since Mediterranean crops were more successful in irrigated fields along the coast than in the cold, damp altiplano. Wheat was planted to make bread for the Holy Eucharist, as was that other basic staple of Catholicism, the vine. The grapes proved better for making brandy than for wine; indeed, the Pisco Valley grew into such an important producer that South American brandies became known generally as *pisco.* Sugar plantations became another mainstay of the colonial economy, prompting the importation of large numbers of African slaves to Peru. Citrus also flourished along the coast and gave rise to a distinctive Peruvian version of escabeche, shortened to *ceviche,* which involved "cooking" seafood in the acid of lime juice.

## THEOLOGICAL SOUP

There it goes, to appear in the awaited *Eclectic Cuisine,* the tastiest and most substantial confection that has emerged from the hands of a chef.

An integral part of the sumptuous meals with which the Augustine Friars of Lima fed the guests invited to theological conferences, from which it takes its name, it consists of a broth made with the meat of turkey, hen, pigeons, beef, lamb, and head and feet of the same, and a handful of garbanzos: all of this, with salt to taste, cooked at a slow fire in a pot with a lid.

Arrange in the soup plates beforehand, pieces of bread cut in the form of fingers and fried in pork fat or butter; carrots, green peas, cabbage (all of this, cooked earlier in a separate broth); onions soaked in salted hot water. In addition, all of the parts of the birds that have been put in the broth: livers, hearts, and gizzards, cut into small pieces, adding strips of boiled eggs.

Put all of this in the broth, boiling well, and replace the lid, allow to rest ten minutes, then serve.

This nutritive food, in which the liquid part is so fortifying that it refreshes the brains of those illustrious men, to investigate the nebulous of science—such a saintly name, and nevertheless so vain—circling, like flies, without comprehending, around the eternal light: God.

Meanwhile, please make use of this powerful life-giving agent, in order to return with me to the Lima that loves you and misses you.

Clorinda Matto de Turner
(Lima)[2]

Potatoes, like other native staples, were unappealing to Europeans at first, but settlers in the predominantly indigenous highlands often ate them of necessity. Even the Marquesa de Cayara, Doña Josepha de Escurrechea, living in opulent Potosí, included potato soup (*locro*) and tamales with potatoes added to the corn in her cookbook of 1776. Indigenous dishes also found their way into elite banquets alongside Hispanic salt cod, beef tongue, empanadas, candies, and custards.

At the same time, Native Americans incorporated many European foods into their repertoire. After the conquest, large herds of llamas died from an indigenous disease (*caracha*), which had formerly been controlled by Inca officials, who culled infected animals. Andean shepherds often tended cattle and sheep instead, developing a taste for beef and mutton as a result. Grilled beef hearts (*anticuchos*) have become a favorite street food in native barrios. Another European introduction that fit well into native agriculture was barley, a hearty grain that was adapted to cold and high altitude and did not compete with potatoes for soil and irrigation. Spanish friars also convinced their indigenous charges to grow small amounts of wheat, and little impetus was needed to add European fava beans to the native frijoles. In addition to the exchange of European and American foods, other new culinary blends resulted from increased contact between different indigenous civilizations; for example, South American tamales and *humitas* may have been introduced from Mesoamerica after the conquest. Thus, Doña Josepha's potato tamales took mestizaje to new levels of complexity.

In the colonial era, foods helped define regional and ethnic differences between the largely Hispanic lowlands and the more indigenous altiplano. Yet this was not always based on the origins of foods. Although wheat bread and rice were markers of the European elite, another Old World crop, barley, became associated with the native lower classes. Stews were a common food of all, but in contrast to the Hispanic *puchero* brimming with meat and vegetables, the indigenous *chupe* or *locro* often contained little more than potatoes with onion for flavoring.

New spaces for food consumption and sociability began to herald the arrival of modernity in Andean cities in the late eighteenth century. Cafes had become centers of Enlightenment discussion in Lima several decades before independence, in the 1820s. Another popular innovation in the early nineteenth century, *picanterías*, served spicy local foods along with chicha to a cross section of society. Social divisions became more apparent over the course of the nineteenth century, as middle-class fondas offered a more respectable venue for dining out. The mid-century export boom, based on the valuable fertilizer guano, made it possible for elites to import French chefs. Two of the most popular restaurants in Lima were the Maison Dorée, owned by one J. Créton, and Prospere Chevalier's Lion d'Or. At the same time, French pastry chefs began to profit from the Hispanic sweet tooth, which had been satisfied earlier by the candied fruits and custards of colonial nuns.

For the working classes, who perceived the nineteenth-century economic boom as a source of inflation and growing inequality in food distribution, Peruvian Chinese restaurants, called *chifas*, offered a cheap source of nourishment. Founded by indentured servants in the late nineteenth century, these establishments served both local foods as well as Chinese dishes, like their counterparts in Havana's and San Francisco's Chinatowns. By the 1920s, some chifas had attained a reputation for excellence that attracted diners from all levels of society.

Modernity also led to the industrialization of Andean food supplies. Already in the colonial period, corn mills had been imported to Cochabamba for large-scale chicha production. In the late nineteenth century, the native beverage had to compete with beer, made by German immigrants using the abundant highland barley production. Regional breweries included Cervezeria Bavaria in Colombia and the Paceña Brewery of La Paz, Bolivia. Even indigenous coca growers were drawn into the global economy by the advent of Coca-Cola. The Atlanta-based corporation bought up plantations in Peru to ensure steady access to raw materials. As the U.S. image of cocaine changed from middle-class wonder drug to dangerous contraband in the early 1900s, Coca-Cola established a New Jersey factory to remove the cocaine chemically before adding the leaves to its secret formula. A Peruvian rival called Inka Cola was founded in 1935 and competed successfully with Coke in the domestic market. Other coca-based drinks, such as the recently introduced KDrink, have been banned outside the Andes, although they do not contain any narcotics. If legalized, such drinks could offer poor farmers an alternative market to their usual dependence on the illicit drug trade.

Cookbooks provided nineteenth-century Andean women with a socially acceptable space for literary production, which had formerly been a largely male prerogative. One of the foundational texts, published by Juana Manuela Gorriti (1819–92), was entitled *La cocina ecléctica* [Eclectic Cooking] (1877). The recipes indeed were drawn from acquaintances throughout Spanish America, and Gorriti herself had been born in Argentina, had married a future president of Bolivia, Manuel Belzú, then had run a women's school in Lima after their separation before returning to Buenos Aires toward the end of her life. The book, sold through subscription, created an international community of cooks that helped instill in its contributors and readers a continental vision reaching far beyond the domestic space of the family kitchen and national borders. Gorriti also took an interest unusual, for criollas, in Native American civilizations, and the book introduced some indigenous recipes into a primarily Hispanic repertoire. Nevertheless, long after the bloody Túpac Amaru rebellion (1780–83) fears of racial conflict impeded the development of a self-conscious mestizo ideology or cuisine.

Populist governments in the Andes finally began to address the problems of hunger, inequality, and discrimination against indigenous peoples in the second half of the twentieth century. The Bolivian Revolution of 1952 carried out large-scale agrarian reform while also seeking to incorporate Native Americans into the national life. The outcome of the reforms varied; in some regions, where land recipients had access to credit and markets, productivity expanded as a result of the breakup of landed estates. Even in those areas where output declined, the peasantry may have benefited from greater equality in distribution. In 1968, the Peruvian revolutionary regime of Juan Velasco implemented an ambitious food welfare program in its efforts to improve living standards. The government diverted production of fish meal exports from Europe, where they had been used as chicken feed, to supply hungry people living in the highlands. Unlike the more permanent land reform of Bolivia, the welfare program proved too fragile for the changing political climate. Refrigerated depots for distributing the fish had closed within a decade, and economic crises of the 1980s brought poor Peruvians in both the city and the countryside to the brink of malnutrition.

Everyday foods in the Andes show less commonality between elites and commoners than do other regions of Latin America. For indigenous highlanders, daily meals consist of thin gruels of barley or potato, supplemented perhaps with some onions. Seasonal foods add some variety to the diet, for example, when fava beans are harvested. The primary source of animal protein comes from hard-boiled eggs and *cuy* (guinea pigs) raised in the home. Urban workers supplement this basic subsistence with rice, wheat bread, and some meat, as well as treats of anticuchos, *choclos* (grilled corn), or *churros* (crullers), purchased at night from a street-corner vendor. By contrast, the elite of coastal Lima dine in exquisite establishments that are comparable to the finest international restaurants. For the midday meal, cevicherías are a favorite location for fresh seafood, while in the evening, upscale chifas offer Chinese dishes that rival the cuisine of Beijing or Shanghai.

In contrast to cosmopolitan restaurants, the festival foods of the region rely on more traditional Andean and Hispanic recipes. Native American religious celebrations still survive in the Peruvian highland festival of Pachamanca, deriving from Quechua terms for earth and pot, and consisting or pit-roasted cuy, potatoes, and other indigenous ingredients. Hispanic dishes include *seco de chivo*, a thick goat stew, and *turrón de Doña Pepa*, an almond sweet associated with the image of Christ of the Miracles in Lima.

In the Andes, as elsewhere in Latin America, the wealthy have reaped the benefits of globalization. Peru has led the way in exploiting tourist markets, both by encouraging cooking schools in Lima and by offering government support for Peruvian restaurants abroad. Outbreaks of cholera brought fears for the ceviche market, but tourist restaurants in Lima were able to obtain supplies of fresh seafood, even as poor barrios suffered from contamination. These class divisions were equally apparent in the southernmost nations of the continent, historically the wealthiest region of Latin America.

## THE SOUTHERN CONE: ARGENTINA, CHILE, BRAZIL, AND URUGUAY

The cuisines of Argentina, Chile, and Uruguay, along with neighboring southern Brazil, reveal most clearly the European heritage of Latin America. In part, this regional distinctiveness resulted from the temperate climate, which facilitated the production of European foodstuffs. The presence of nomadic Indians rather than settled, agrarian civilizations limited race mixture and, in many areas, completely prevented the colonization of Europeans until the latter part of the nineteenth century. Finally, the Southern Cone became the preferred destination for workers during the great proletarian migrations of the nineteenth and twentieth centuries. Although Native American, African, and Asian peoples and foods also left their mark on the region, their influences are less pervasive than in other parts of Latin America.

Pre-Hispanic peoples of the Southern Cone were generally not agriculturalists, except for the Araucanians living in the Chilean Andes, who shared elements of highland culture with their Inca neighbors to the north. In the littoral plains to the east, grasslands extended from Rio Grande do Sul in modern-day Brazil through Uruguay and the Argentine pampas.

Without heavy steel plows, indigenous peoples could not cultivate the dense sod of native grasses and instead practiced hunting and gathering. Armed with the bola, a weapon consisting of two or three stones roped together, they would run down rhea (American ostrich) and guanaco (wild ancestral llamas), entangling their legs of their prey in the missile's leather straps. Guaraní living along the rivers in the vicinity of modern Paraguay supplemented their gathering activities with abundant fish and shellfish. The fishing folk on the Pacific Coast ate an almost exclusively seafood diet including seabirds, the occasional beached whale, and, in Patagonia, seals.

Despite fierce Araucanian resistance, Spaniards gradually settled Chile's fertile valleys, which proved ideally suited to Mediterranean agriculture. The province became a major exporter of wheat within the empire, supplementing the smaller harvests of Peru. Olive trees, which are slow to mature and require a very particular climate of winter rains and summer drought, also took root in central Chile, providing oil, which is a second basic requirement of proper Spanish cooking. Finally, vineyards planted in the foothills on both sides of the Andes yielded excellent wine, unlike the rough liquid distilled into pisco farther north. Livestock was also raised in the early years of the colony, but as Peru's growing European population demanded ever-greater quantities of wheat, grazing land was increasingly turned over to the plow. Thus, Chilean cooks were best able to reproduce the diet of their Spanish homeland.

The grasslands of the pampas meanwhile became a major center of livestock production. Following Hispanic patterns, the land was divided into vast estancias in which cattle grazed under the supervision of gaucho horsemen. Like the vaqueros of northern New Spain and the gauchos of the Venezuelan llanos, these early cowboys were of mixed European, African, and Indian origin. Jerked beef, called *charqui* after the Andean product, found only minor export markets, and the hides and tallow were the most profitable export commodities. As a result, the gauchos had access to unlimited quantities of beef, either roasted over an open fire as a simple *asado* or a more elaborate *carne con cuero,* with the cowhide still attached to preserve the natural juices. The gaucho's other staple was strongly caffeinated *mate* tea, imported from the plantations of Paraguay. Brewed in small gourds, mate was drunk through a communal silver straw (*bombilla*). On festive occasions the gauchos ate corn mush, either sweetened with sugar and honey (*mazamorra*) or in a savory mix of meat and spice, called *locro,* but quite different from the indigenous vegetables stews of the same name in the Andes. Gauchos generally scorned vegetables and consumed them only in a more Hispanic *caldo* (soup).

Industrial food-processing technology brought new wealth to the pampas in the nineteenth century. As European factory laborers began to gain more purchasing power in the second half of the century, large-scale meat salting plants (*saladeros*) were established to supply their demand for beef. In Buenos Aires, this industry centered in the district of Nueva Chicago, named after the North American meatpacking capital. Yet Latin Americans did not simply import technology from the United States; Uruguayan physician Francisco Lecoq performed early experiments with refrigerated transport in the 1860s. A decade later, in 1876, Charles Tellier successfully shipped a cargo of meat from Argentina to France. Developing regular markets took time, however, because early freezing methods significantly degraded the quality of meat. South American producers did not enter European markets on a large scale until after 1900, when improved refrigeration allowed chilled but not frozen meat to arrive in good condition. Also around the turn of the century, landowners on the pampas made significant investments to improve the quality of the cattle, importing prized European breeding stock and shifting to new forage crops: alfalfa and maize. As production grew rapidly on the eve of World War I, Chicago firms led by Swift and Armour bought out the initial British and South American investors. Fears of a monopoly by the "Big Five" led to calls for nationalization in the 1920s, but the industry continued under U.S. domination for decades thereafter.

Notwithstanding the profits from chilled beef exports, pampas land was increasingly converted to the production of wheat in the late nineteenth century. Once again, European factory workers provided the consumer demand, as new milling technology transformed white bread from an expensive luxury into an affordable staple. To facilitate cheap grain shipments, British investors helped finance the construction of railroad lines linking pampas farms to the port of Buenos Aires. Multinational grain merchants such as the firm of Ernesto Bunge and Jorge Born soon came to dominate these markets through their access to credit and storage facilities, squeezing the profits of small farmers. Nevertheless, those who adopted an efficient system of mixed production, sharing the land between ranch and farm, could compete successfully with North American and Australian exporters.

The production of wine, as with meat and grain, underwent a process of rapid modernization in Europe and the United States, and South American vintners adopted the latest technologies. Formerly Chilean wines had been made exclusively with the *país* grape, an old Spanish variety introduced in the sixteenth century. While this continued to be the source of pisco in the north, in the valleys around Valparaiso and Santiago, vintners began to replant in the 1850s and 1860s with Cabernet Sauvignon and Merlot grapes, the noble varietals of Bordeaux. Leading vineyards such as Macul and Concha y Toro improved the quality of their wines by modernizing their grape presses and fermenting barrels. Meanwhile, in Mendoza, Argentina, Italian immigrants began to plant the Malbec, an obscure grape from Bordeaux, which came into its own in the Andean foothills. Germans and Italians also began making wines, sparkling wines, and liquors for local markets in Uruguay and Brazil. Brewing offered another business opportunity for German newcomers, who founded the Cervecería Quilmes in Buenos Aires and Antárctica in São Paulo.

The ability to produce and consume greater quantities of familiar European foods and drinks attracted large numbers of migrants to the Southern Cone, which also enriched the local cuisine. In Argentina alone, about six million people arrived between 1870 and 1914, primarily Italian and Spanish, although only about half settled permanently. The working classes of Argentina found they could add more meat to their *puchero* and *carbonada* stews than had been available in the old country, and Chilean *cazuelas* were often enriched by the addition of beaten eggs. Immigrants also brought new methods of cooking foods such as the *milanesa,* a Milanese beef cutlet that became popular throughout Latin America. Italian macaroni, polenta, and *ñoquis* (gnocchi) also became commonplace, as did fresh green salads dressed in olive oil. Germans meanwhile brought their elaborate sausage, potato, and sauerkraut dishes. Over time, agricultural exports to Europe undermined the purchasing power of ordinary workers, reducing their access to meat and other luxuries. Rural workers in Chile often continued to subsist on rations of *harina tostada* (toasted gain).

The elite used their profits from the fin de siècle export boom to share in the conspicuous consumption of European cuisine. Already in the mid-nineteenth century, sidewalk cafes had become prominent along Avenida de Mayo in Buenos Aires, where all classes gathered to consume either the traditional mate or the novelty coffee. Beginning in the 1880s, wealthy *porteños* began to frequent the chic Florida Street, with its exclusive clubs and department stores, including a branch of the London establishment, Harrods. Chilean landowners, not to be outdone, constructed imitation chateaux to mirror their ambitions for Bordeaux-style wines.

The outbreak of World War I crippled the export boom, and francophone liberal oligarchs soon lost power to a new generation of populist politicians. In Chile, these cultural nationalists replaced French banquet menus with criollo dishes such as *pastel de choclo* made of chicken, corn, and olives baked in an earthenware pot. Argentines meanwhile invented a gaucho national identity based on elaborate *asado* grills. Self-styled gauchos in southern Brazil had a similar version called *churrasco*. So important was the asado to Argentine identity that Juan Perón's populist government (1946–54) subsidized beef to garner support and avoid unrest among the urban workers who formed his base of power. With the encroachment of urban modernity, cooking on grills in the city became a way of creating nostalgia for a mythical past of gaucho masculinity.

Women also mediated social change through foods by, for example, employing new technology to prepare labor-intensive traditional recipes. Home economist Petrona Carrizo de Gandulfo (1898–1992) exemplified the purported goal of easing the domestic burdens of middle-class Argentine women. An immigrant from the provinces, she found work in Buenos Aires during the 1920s giving cooking demonstrations for a British gas company. These early lectures on the benefits of reliable gas appliances over temperamental

## TUCUMÁN EMPANADAS

Cut a kilogram of veal, without veins, in small pieces; boil it in water, then drain and set aside, seasoning it with fine salt.

Put in a skillet 300 grams of beef fat, place on a fire and brown two white onions and four green ones, well chopped; next add a tablespoon of sweet pepper, one of ground hot pepper, and fine salt; allow to boil a minute, remove from the fire and allow to cool a bit; add the meat, a tablespoon of vinegar and mix well; put also some raisins, chopped hard-boiled egg, and mix all together, allowing to cool until the fat is congealed.

Make a dough: put on the table a kilogram of flour, form a space in the middle and put a little water with salt, 100 grams of beef fat, and mix all together forming a dough; add 150 grams more of fat and continue to knead until it is quite smooth; cut it in pieces, form small balls, and roll out; on each one put a little of the stuffing, moisten the edges and close. Cook in an oven at a hot temperature.[3]

wood-burning stoves set the tone for a long career as a cooking teacher. In 1934, she published *El libro de Doña Petrona*, which became the most successful cookbook in Latin American history. The volume offered the growing ranks of middle-class housewives access to classical French and Italian dishes, but these recipes were nevertheless adapted to criollo tastes and combined with traditional Argentine favorites such as empanadas and *dulce de leche* (milk caramel). Newspaper and magazine columns and radio broadcasts allowed Carrizo de Gandulfo to reach a broader audience, and with the advent of television in the 1950s, she began a popular show that lasted for more than two decades. Doña Petrona and other cooking teachers thus helped to bring modernity to Latin American women, while still reinforcing the idea that the woman's rightful place was in the kitchen.

Everyday foods of the Southern Cone give prominent place to meat, especially beef. Empanadas are stuffed with *picadillo* (chopped beef), steaks are cooked over improvised grills, and meatballs are served in thick sauces. Seafood has a place on the menu, particularly in Chile, with its long coasts and rich harvests. Even urban workers have come to expect meat as a supplement to bread and other starches, although recurring economic crises often make it difficult to obtain. In contrast to North American preferences, all parts of the cow are relished across the social spectrum, and *riñones* (kidneys), *mollejas* (sweetbreads), and *morcilla* (blood sausages) will be found on elite tables. The influx of European immigration has also left an important mark on the everyday diet, as pasta will often be served as a first course before the arrival of meat. Restaurants, not surprisingly, feature steaks, and often allow customers to cook their own at a tableside *parrilla* (grill).

Festival foods likewise emphasize meat, and a favorite way of celebrating any event, from a wedding to a religious holiday, is with an asado. This masculine ritual could be a simple affair for workers, who would grill a steak on wire lattice set above a fire, and eat it accompanied by a bottle of local wine and bread. More elaborate urban picnics required a full-scale parrilla, consisting of a shallow pit covered by an iron grate. While men cooked a variety of sausages, innards, and steaks, women prepared salads, vegetables, and sauces such as *chimichurri*, a spicy vinaigrette flavored with herbs and chile peppers. Chileans also have their own versions of a clambake, called a *curanto*, to celebrate the abundant shellfish along the coast.

The nations of the Southern Cone have developed profitable food exports toward the end of the twentieth century. Chile led the way in gaining markets in the United States and Europe for table fruits that were unavailable in the winter months of the Northern Hemisphere. Chile has also competed successfully for international wine markets with technologically advanced vintners in California, Australia, and Europe. Argentina, which long had a reputation for making cheap table wines, has meanwhile established the malbec as a noble grape varietal worthy of attention by wine connoisseurs. Moreover, despite recurrent economic crises, Argentina can still make a valid claim to having the best steak restaurants in the world.

## CONCLUSION

The importance of food in human health and in social and cultural relationships has attracted a wide range of scholars. Indeed, the connections between nutrition and identity call out for interdisciplinary approaches. This conclusion will seek to summarize briefly the historical development of food studies in Latin America and to identify the main debates that have arisen within the field.

An essential first step for scholars was simply to untangle the complex origins of Latin American staple foods. Russian botanist Ivan Vavilov, leading a worldwide survey of plant origins in 1920s, identified the Andes and Mesoamerica as two of eight primary hearths of domestication. Archaeologists in Latin America pioneered stratigraphic research methods, most notably in Mexico, where Manuel Gamio mapped the ancient city of Teotihuacan in the 1920s and Richard McNeish traced the evolution of maize in the Tehuacán Valley in the 1950s. Continued improvements in the technology of carbon dating, such as Lawrence Kaplan's investigations of fossil beans, have refined these sequences of domestication, although the precise origins of many plants remain elusive.

The cultural development of cooking has been an even more intractable problem, since ethnographic descriptions, not to mention historical recipes, are scarce and often misleading. Geographer Carl O. Sauer first outlined the regional nature of Latin American material culture in the 1920s. Early anthropologists often assigned pre-Hispanic origins to the cuisines of what were then considered relatively pristine indigenous villages. Margaret Park Redfield, for example, conducted important early field work on domestic life in the town of Tepoztlán, Mexico. In the 1940s, George Foster sought to redress this situation by noting the uniform importance of Iberian culture ever since the conquest. Sociologist Gilberto Freyre, in his groundbreaking 1930s study of Brazilian plantation society, emphasized the complex blending of African, Portuguese, and Native American cultures and cuisines. Alfred Crosby pioneered the study of demographic and cultural consequences of what he called the "Columbian Exchange." Contemporary studies of culinary exchange have often focused on the "biographies" of individual plants. Sidney Mintz innovatively connected the rise of sugar plantations and slavery with European consumption patterns and the origins of industrialization. Mexican anthropologist Arturo Warman adopted an equally global vision of the history of corn and capitalism.

Nutrition has been an ongoing concern for scholars and public health officials alike in Latin America. The nineteenth-century origins of nutritional science have been linked to social Darwinist theories about the inferiority of non-Western diets and, hence, civilizations. National nutrition surveys of the 1930s were often surprised to discover the basic soundness of vegetarian peasant diets. Nevertheless, archaeologists have found subclinical levels of malnutrition among skeletal remains of pre-Hispanic urban dwellers. The nutritional consequences of the conquest have also been a crucial part in debates of historical demographers. The boom of export monoculture may well have made farm workers of the nineteenth century into some of the worst-fed people in Latin American history. Medical anthropologists such as Guillermo Bonfil Batalla, Ellen Messer, and Kathleen DeWalt have demonstrated that addressing health problems requires a level of respect for existing culinary cultures. Moreover, public health efforts are increasingly stymied by the spread of industrial processed junk foods.

Recent research has also focused on the social connotations of food in constructing class, gender, and ethnic identity. Mary Weismantel's detailed ethnographic study of highland Ecuador has shown the racialized and gendered nature of foods, which reinforce the inferiority of women and Native Americans, while enticing young people into a Hispanic modern society. Enrique Ochoa's work on the politics of food welfare in Mexico likewise demonstrates the hegemonic power of food in supporting an authoritarian one-party state. A dissertation in progress by Rebekah Pite examines the twentieth-century transformations of middle-class gender roles in Argentina through the life and works of Doña Petrona Carrizo de Gandulfo.

National cuisines have also been an important focus of scholars in the region. Rosario Olivas Weston's comprehensive research into the history of Peruvian food has uncovered vital documentary sources. Patricia Vega Jiménez's work on coffee and national identity in Costa Rica offers insightful comparative perspective for students of consumer culture in Europe and the United States. Aníbal Arcondo, by contrast, has posed the question of why Argentina does not have more of a national cuisine, concluding that the sheer abundance of raw materials obviated the need for elaborate cooking techniques, when a simple asado would suffice. Finally, Jeffrey Pilcher has examined the ongoing struggle between indigenous corn tortillas and Hispanic wheat bread in the formation of Mexican identities.

Yet too sharp of a focus on national cuisines risks ignoring the globalizing trends that increasingly shape the foods and lives of Latin Americans. Arnold Bauer's comprehensive account of material culture provides essential historical context for any such study. The importance of foreign agribusiness in the region has been examined by many fine works, most recently, Steve Striffler and Mark Moberg's edited volume on the banana. Meanwhile, Mexican anthropologist Ivonne Vizcarra Bordi has demonstrated how the spread of genetically modified corn has allowed marginalized indigenous women to earn a living making tortillas for middle-class consumers, thus demonstrating the power of food to connect macroeconomic trends to the everyday lives of ordinary people. As this recent proliferation of research shows, food has become an important subfield of Latin American studies.

# RESOURCE GUIDE

## PRINT SOURCES

Arcondo, Aníbal. *Historia de la alimentación en Argentina, desde los orígenes hasta 1920.* Córdoba: Ferreyra Editor, 2002.
Bauer, Arnold J. *Goods, Power, History: Latin America's Material Culture.* Cambridge: Cambridge University Press, 2001.

Bolívar Aróstegui, Natalia, and Carmen González Díaz de Villegas. *Mitos y leyendas de la comida afrocubana.* Havana: Editorial de Ciencias Sociales, 1993.

Coe, Sophie D. *America's First Cuisines.* Austin: University of Texas Press, 1994.

Derby, Lauren. "Gringo Chickens with Worms: Food and Nationalism in the Dominican Republic." Pp. 451–493 in Gilbert M. Joseph, Catherine C. Legrand, and Ricardo D. Salvatore (eds.), *Close Encounters of Empire: Writing the Cultural History of U.S.-Latin American Relations.* Durham, NC: Duke University Press, 1998.

Drinot, Paulo. "Food, Race and Working-Class Identity: Restaurantes Populares and Populism in 1930s Peru." *The Americas* 62:2 (2005, October): 245–270.

Fleites-Lear, Marisela. "Mirrors in the Kitchen: The *New Cuban Woman* Cooks Revolutionarily." In Jeffrey M. Pilcher (ed.), *From "Hoppin' John" to the "Spotted Rooster": Food and Memory in the Carolina Lowcountry and Caribbean.* Columbia: University of South Carolina Press, forthcoming.

Freyre, Gilberto. *The Masters and the Slaves: A Study in the Development of Brazilian Civilization,* translated by Samuel Putnam. New York: Alfred A. Knopf, 1946.

Fry, Peter. "Feijoada e soul food: Notas sobre a manipulaçao de símbolos étnicos e nacionais." *Ensaios de Opinião* 2.2 (1977): 44–47.

Funes, Fernando, ed. *Sustainable Agriculture and Resistance: Transforming Food Production in Cuba.* Oakland: Food First, 2002.

Gade, Daniel W. "South America." Pp. 1254–1260 in Kenneth F. Kiple and Kriemhild Coneè Ornelas (eds.), *The Cambridge World History of Food,* Vol. 2. Cambridge, UK: Cambridge University Press, 2000.

Juárez, José Luis. *La lenta emergencia de la comida mexicana, ambigüedades criollas 1750–1800.* Mexico City: Editorial Porrúa, 2000.

Long, Janet, ed. *Conquista y comida: Consecuencias del encuentro de dos mundos.* Mexico City: Universidad Nacional Autónoma de México, 1996.

Lovera, José Rafael. *Historia de la alimentación en Venezuela.* Caracas: Monte Avila Editores, 1988.

Mayer, Enrique. *The Articulated Peasant: Household Economies in the Andes.* Boulder, CO: Westview Press, 2002.

Mintz, Sidney W. *Sweetness and Power: The Place of Sugar in Modern History.* New York: Viking Penguin, 1985.

———. *Tasting Food, Tasting Freedom: Excursions into Eating, Culture, and the Past.* Boston: Beacon Press, 1996.

Morales, Edmundo. *The Guinea Pig: Healing, Food, and Ritual in the Andes.* Tucson: University of Arizona Press, 1995.

Ochoa, Enrique C. *Feeding Mexico: The Political Uses of Food since 1910.* Wilmington, DE: Scholarly Resources, 2000.

Olivas Weston, Rosario. *La cocina en el virreinato del Peru.* Lima: Escuela Profesional de Turismo y Hotelería: Universidad de San Martín de Porres, 1996.

———. *La cocina cotidiana y festiva de los limeños en el siglo XIX.* Lima: Escuela Profesional de Turismo y Hotelería: Universidad de San Martín de Porres, 1999.

Peloso, Vincent C. "Succulence and Sustenance: Region, Class, and Diet in Nineteenth-Century Peru." Pp.46–64 in John C. Super and Thomas C. Wright (eds.), *Food, Politics, and Society in Latin America.* Lincoln: University of Nebraska Press, 1985.

Pilcher, Jeffrey M. *¡Que vivan los tamales! Food and the Making of Mexican Identity.* Albuquerque: University of New Mexico Press, 1998.

———. *The Sausage Rebellion: Public Health, Private Enterprise, and Meat in Mexico City, 1890–1917.* Albuquerque: University of New Mexico Press, 2006.

Redfield, Margaret Park. "Notes on the Cookery of Tepoztlan, Morelos." *American Journal of Folklore* 42.164 (1929, April–June): 167–196.

Remedi, Fernando J. *Los secretos de la olla. Entre el gusto y la necesidad: la alimentación en la Córdoba de principios del siglo XX.* Córdoba, Argentina: Centro de Estudios Históricos, 1998.

Rossells, Beatriz. *La gastronomia en Potosí y Charcas: Siglos XVIII y XIX, 800 recetas de la cocina criolla.* La Paz: Editora "Khana Cruz," 1995.

Schávelzon, Daniel. *Historias del comer y del beber en Buenos Aires: Arqueología histórica de la vajilla de mesa.* Buenos Aires: Aguilar, 2000.

Striffler, Steve, and Mark Moberg, eds. *Banana Wars: Power, Production, and History in the Americas.* Durham, NC: Duke University Press, 2003.

Super, John C. *Food, Conquest, and Colonization in Sixteenth Century Spanish America.* Albuquerque: University of New Mexico Press, 1988.

Vega Jiménez, Patricia. *Con sabor a tertulia: Historia del consume del café en Costa Rica (1840–1940).* San José: Editorial de la Universidad de Costa Rica/Instituto del Café de Costa Rica, 2004.

Vizcarra Bordi, Ivonne. *Entre el taco mazahua y el mundo: La comida de las relaciones de poder, resistencia e identidades.* Toluca, México: Editorial Emahaia, 2002.

Warman, Arturo. *Corn and Capitalism: How a Botanical Bastard Grew to Global Dominance.* Translated by Nancy L. Westrate. Chapel Hill: University of North Carolina Press, 2003.

Weismantel, Mary J. *Food, Gender, and Poverty in the Ecuadorian Andes.* Philadelphia: University of Pennsylvania Press, 1988.

Wheelock Román, Jaime. *La comida nicaragüense.* Managua: Hispamer, 1998.

Wilk, Richard. *Home Cooking in the Global Village: Caribbean Food from Buccaneers to Ecotourists.* London: Berg, 2006.

## ENGLISH-LANGUAGE COOKBOOKS

Aboy Valldejuli, Carmen. *The Art of Caribbean Cookery.* Garden City, NY: Doubleday, 1957.

Andrade, Margarette de. *Brazilian Cookery: Traditional and Modern.* Rutland, VT: Charles E. Tuttle, 1965.

Bayless, Rick, with Deann Groen Bayless. *Authentic Mexican: Regional Cooking from the Heart of Mexico.* New York: Morrow, 1987.

Harris, Jessica B. *Tasting Brazil.* New York: Macmillan, 1992.

Kennedy, Diana. *The Art of Mexican Cooking: Traditional Mexican Cooking for Aficionados.* New York: Bantam Books, 1989.

Kijac, Maria Baez. *The South American Table: The Flavor and Soul of Authentic Home Cooking from Patagonia to Rio de Janeiro, with 450 Recipes.* Boston: Harvard Common Press, 2003.

Ortiz, Elisabeth Lambert. *The Book of Latin American Cooking.* New York: Alfred A. Knopf, 1979.

Quintana, Patricia. *The Taste of Mexico.* New York: Stewart, Tabori, and Chang, 1986.

Rojas Lombardi, Felipe. *The Art of South American Cooking.* New York: HarperCollins, 1991.

## WEBSITES

*ElGourmet.com.* http://www.elgourmet.com. Website of an Argentine food magazine featuring news, recipes, restaurant reviews, and cooking schools throughout Latin America.

*Food and Nutrition in Latin America.* http://www1.lanic.utexas.edu/la/region/food/. University of Texas at Austin compendium of links to Websites and recipes.

Institute for Food and Development Policy. *Food First.* http://www.foodfirst.org/. NGO concerned with hunger and the ecology, particularly in Latin America.

*Latin American Food & Cooking.* http://www.carnegielibrary.org/subject/food/latin.html. Carnegie Library of Pittsburgh links to websites and recipes.

*Tequila Aficionado.* http://www.tequilaaficionado.com/. News of the industry and tasting events.

*Vino! Chilean Wineries.* http://www.vino.com/wines/country.asp?CID=3. Links to prominent winemakers and map of Chilean wine regions.

## VIDEOS/FILMS

*Black Sugar* (United States, 1989). Directed by Michael Regier.

*Gabriela* (1983). Directed by Bruno Barreto, starring Sonia Braga, Marcello Mastroianni.

*The Last Supper* (Cuba, 1976). Directed by Tomás Gutiérrez Alea. Instituto Cubano de Arte e Industria
   Cinematográficos.
*Like Water for Chocolate* (1992). Directed by Alfonso Arau, starring Marco Leonardo, Lumi Cavazos.

# NOTES

The publisher has done its best to make sure the instructions and recipes in this book are
correct. However, users should apply judgment and experience when preparing recipes,
especially parents and teachers working with young people. The publisher accepts no
responsibility for the outcome of any recipe included in this volume.

1. *Um tratado da cozinha portuguêsa do século xv* (Lisbon: Instituto Nacional do Livro, 1963), p. 141.
2. Juana Manuela Gorriti, *La cocina ecléctica,* edited by María Rosa Lojo (Buenos Aires: Aguilar, 1999
   [1877]), pp. 30–31.
3. Petrona Corrizo de Gandulfo, *El libro de Doña Petrona* (Buenos Aires: Cía. Gral. Fabril Financiera,
   1949), p. 261.

# LITERATURE

DANIEL J. NAPPO

Popular literature is the most widely read and beloved of all the varieties of literature existing in Latin America. Some evidence of its enormous popularity is provided by the Chilean author Ariel Dorfman. After explaining to a young Peruvian woman who lived in the slums that he believed her favorite *fotonovelas* (photonovels) were "a hazard to her health and her future," he was abruptly told, "'Don't do that to us, *compañerito* (little friend). . . . Don't take my dreams away from me.'"[1] What could this literature possibly be that lets the most marginalized Latin Americans dream? The many genres of popular literature—ranging from oral poetry to best-selling novels—also make such a definition exceeding difficult to ascertain.

And yet, if we are to determine which texts from the rich and varied Latin American tradition may be selected and offered as examples of the genre, there must be some workable definition of popular literature. Jean Franco has provided a definition of popular culture that, while doing nothing to narrow our focus, may provide a key term or two that would help us to understand the nature of popular literature:

> My own preferred definition would be the broadest possible and would include a spectrum of signifying practices and pleasurable activities, most of which fall outside the controlling discipline of official schooling. . . . [it is] the area . . . traversed by class stratifications and subtle subcultural distinctions acquired largely in a noninstitutional setting.[2]

The terms "official" and "noninstitutional" broaden our understanding of the topic in the sense that the preference for this kind of literature is not instilled in the classroom or in any other setting where a small, elite group within society has sanctioned its content, production, and distribution. There are indeed groups that benefit (economically and politically) from the production and distribution of popular literature; however, the taste for this material existed long before anyone sang its virtues or tried to profit from it.

Some have attempted to define popular literature only in reference to the market: if its purpose is strictly entertainment, and the text is mass produced and widely sold, it is therefore an example of popular literature.[3] This variety of popular literature is best exemplified by pulp paperbacks and cheap books that interpret dreams, predict the future, and offer self-help or spiritual advice. However, there are countless examples of rare or unique texts of

139

popular literature (that is, not mass produced), and others that have never been sold because they have never made the transition from oral performance to the printed page.[4]

Popular literature can perhaps be given a working definition of texts that are intended to entertain—and less frequently, to inform—the most inclusive grouping of readers in a given society. So inclusive is this group of readers that often they cannot even read the texts, but come to interpret them through the use of illustrations, photographs, or oral renditions. Furthermore, the entertainment is of a variety that is not endorsed by the official classes and institutions of a given society but often seen as being in poor taste, insipid, or even lowbrow. This is not to say that popular literature cannot be celebrated or even co-opted by the affluent or hegemonic classes, but that it usually begins in obscurity, beyond the pale of what is normally considered acceptable by those in control. Comic books in Latin America are a thriving example of popular literature. Unlike their counterparts in the United States, Latin American comic books transcend class boundaries and are read by young and old alike.

In spite of the more standard meaning of the word *popular* as common or mainstream, it is important to remember that the term also refers to the people: that is, popular literature represents texts produced by the people for the people. A Mexican *corrido* (historical ballad) from the Revolutionary period (but recorded in 1930) evokes this idea when the performer sings, "Perhaps this corrido has only one positive quality; from the soul of the people it comes, and to the soul of the people it goes."[5] Given this admittedly idealized description of popular literature, we may be inclined to believe that such texts provide a much more reliable index of what the vast majority of people really had on their mind in a given time and place. As such, popular literature can be an invaluable resource for historical and cultural studies.

However, as one might suspect, the means of popular literary production have very rarely been in the hands of the common people, even though they are invariably the intended audience. This is especially true when one considers the importance of printing, for unless one happens to be at the right place and the right time to catch an oral performance, the printed version of a popular text is likely the most readily available resource. This brings us to one of the great ironies of popular literature: in order to be transmitted to the most people possible—that is, to become popular on the widest scale—the text must in some sense lose some of its vitality or even become corrupted by those who control the means of publishing it.

Popular literature has often served the purpose of inscribing the values of the dominant class on the much larger and occasionally insurgent classes of citizens. Some of these values include the necessity of hard work, obedience, veneration of national leaders, and pie-in-the-sky millennial belief. Apart from political considerations, popular literature—for having such an immense readership—naturally exhibits many commercial tendencies: that is, what is actually printed may not actually serve the people by helping to inform them (as many examples of the Mexican corrido or, to a lesser extent, the Brazilian *literatura de cordel* [literature on a string] do) but may be merely entertaining or sensational material intended to be sold quickly. Entertainment, then, is generally the purpose of popular literature. "Photonovels, comics, soap operas, popular fiction, cinema, dance, music festivals, fashions, and everyday life may represent attempts at control but they also have to meet the real desires and needs of the people. Above all, they have to entertain."[6] Occasionally, what appears to be popular literature of the most obvious variety is in fact intended to be read only by a small sector of society. Jeffery M. Pilcher, who has studied Mexican cookbooks extensively, notes that most published examples from the Frenchified pre-Revolutionary era "had little room for the corn cuisine of the street,"[7] which demonstrates that even this eminently popular variety of text was hardly popular at all. It also suggests that when a text is labeled as popular, consumers may be more inclined to purchase it, believing that they are part of the national mainstream or, even better, more authentic citizens.

Out of the necessity to analyze representative traditions in depth, the present survey must have some parameters. A further consideration is to provide representative examples from all Latin American countries, including Brazil and the Greater Antilles. Unfortunately, such an endeavor would prove exceedingly difficult in a multivolume work, let alone a single chapter. The fact that many forms of popular literature in the smaller countries are oral poetry (either sung or recited) and not fixed to the printed page makes any treatment of them here virtually impossible. For that reason, the popular literature to be examined in this chapter has generally appeared in printed form. Historically, the distribution of the Latin American printing industry has been centered in certain cities: Mexico City, Lima, Bogotá, Caracas, Rio de Janeiro, and Buenos Aires.[8] This fact, coupled with the virtual invisibility of many forms of popular literature, compels us to focus our attention on the major cities and the largest countries.

Although this examination of popular literature must favor examples that feature the written word, the spoken word will be examined in the treatment of the Mexican corrido; the genre is less music than it is an oral rendition of stories and themes that interest the people. The illustrations or photos that accompany some popular literature texts, to help surmount the illiteracy that existed in many of the countries being studied, will not prohibit the examination of them. The following major genres will be explored: the corrido, the popular novel, the photonovel, the comic book, and the Brazilian literatura de cordel. Because of space constraints and the fact that the focus in this chapter is on the most popular genres from the late nineteenth century to the present, popular poetry will not be discussed, though resources are provided at the end of the chapter. In general, what will be examined will be the most distinctive and well-known of all the myriad forms of popular literature existing in Latin America. By focusing on the major forms of popular literature in the largest countries, we can also illuminate corresponding, lesser-known examples from smaller countries—for example, Paraguay, Honduras, or the Dominican Republic.

## POPULAR LATIN AMERICAN LITERATURE IN HISTORICAL PERSPECTIVE

Latin America provides an especially rich tradition of popular literature because of the tradition of rigid class distinctions, uneven development, and low rates of literacy. The first printing press in the Americas was established in Mexico City in 1535 (the second in Lima in 1583), and the Spanish Crown strictly controlled what materials were printed and circulated during its 300 years of colonial domination; these presses were established largely to produce works of devotion and manuals for preachers.[9] However, the geographical distance of Spain from her colonial holdings permitted much laxity in the enforcement of censorship laws.

Popular literature begins to appear consistently in the period shortly before independence, when popular dissent could be expressed as a result of the spread of print technology and the development of the colonial capitals as large, viable centers of cultural production distinct from the European centers. The Mexican José Joaquín Fernández de Lizardi (1776–1827), the author of the text traditionally recognized as the first Latin American novel, began his literary career writing popular verses that were sold on the streets of the capital as pamphlets.[10] His popular series of sociopolitical writings, *El pensador mexicano* (1812), which provoked the colonial authorities to imprison him for 2 years, are not unlike the early journalistic endeavors of the American Benjamin Franklin (1706–90) in that they articulated concerns and values that were not shared by Europeans.

After independence in the nineteenth century, the predominant literary movements—Indianism, Romanticism, *costumbrismo* (literally "custom-ism," prose describing the culture and landscape in the Americas), Realism, and Modernism—featured writers from generally upper-class or aristocratic backgrounds. These major movements, with the exception of Modernism, sought to present native cultures and (to a greater or lesser extent) articulate a regional voice. Nevertheless, most literature of the nineteenth century was not popular by any stretch of the imagination. With few exceptions, including the romance novel *María* (1867) by Jorge Isaacs (Colombia, 1837–95), the verse of Jose Martí (Cuba, 1853–95), and, of course, the great narrative poem *Martín Fierro* (Argentina, 1872, 1879) by José Hernández (1834–86), the literature of the nineteenth century failed to strike a chord with the masses.

However, this would change with the cultural and political revolutions of the twentieth century. A prominent example is post-Revolutionary Mexico (c. 1920–40), where the new government sought to define what it meant to be Mexican in terms of indigenous (rather than European) culture. It is in this period that important scholars, generously supported by the government, began their fundamental studies of Mexican oral poetry, popular music, dance, archeology, and folklore.[11] Although such investigation has done much to establish the scholarly fields of popular culture and folklore, it has also served to confuse our definitions, because many of these scholars proceeded in a manner that was politically motivated (and part of a larger nation-building project) rather than objective.

Critics and investigators today, living in an age far removed from the Industrial Revolution and low literacy rates, often struggle to identify historical examples of popular literature. Apart from the texts produced by cultural elites that were clearly aimed at the same class (an obvious example would be the many Latin American novels modeled on European trends, which had their vogue at the turn of the twentieth century), in some ways almost anything could be viewed as popular. Compounding the difficulty is the vast diversity between and within each national tradition of popular culture. As Harold E. Hinds, Jr. and Charles M. Tatum point out:

> While most Latin American countries share, in a very general sense, a common history and culture, the evolution of their diverse forms of popular culture is often not at all uniform. This is due to many factors, such as the rate of economic development, which in some countries has had a direct bearing on the establishment and development of popular culture industries.[12]

Literacy, of course, is an important factor in any consideration of a national literature. Today most industrialized Latin American nations can boast of literacy rates comparable to those of the United States, Canada, and many European nations. For example, as of 2004, most of the Latin American and Caribbean region has literacy rates above 80 percent, with many countries, such as Uruguay, Mexico, and Brazil at 90 percent or more.[13] As of 2000 three of the four largest Latin American nations had figures for daily newspapers, circulation, and readership that put them ahead of the vast majority of nations in the world: Brazil (465 different daily newspapers; 45.9 printed copies per thousand inhabitants); Mexico (311; 93.5); Argentina (106; 40.5); Chile (53; data not available); Ecuador (36; 98.2); Uruguay (4; data not available).[14] Nearly all Latin American nations have national libraries, some of which have several points of service located in the largest cities. In the early 1990s the national library of Brazil contained over 5 million volumes; Chile, 3.5 million volumes; Colombia, 463,000 volumes; Perú, 3.8 million volumes; Venezuela, 3.6 million volumes.[15] Public libraries, on the other hand, are not nearly as prevalent in the region, nor are their holdings as extensive. Argentina had the largest public system, with 1,545 libraries and 13.4 million total volumes; Chile had 289 public libraries with 1.1 million volumes; Venezuela had 23 public libraries with 3.2 million volumes.[16] In regard to the libraries of institutions of higher education, as of 1996 Mexico had 1187 libraries and a total of 14 million volumes.[17] Total number of books according to UDC (Universal Decimal Classification)[18] data show that by the mid-1990s Brazil had by far the largest registry of books (104 million), followed by Argentina (39.6 million), Colombia (11.3 million), Uruguay (1.9 million), and Perú (1.8 million).[19]

Although much popular literature is oral or printed on small presses, publishing in Latin America is also an important consideration. The publishing industries of Latin America largely serve the people within the particular nation or, to a lesser extent, the wider Latin American region. Nevertheless, Latin American countries still import many more books than they export—a situation that undoubtedly diminishes the production of autochonous, popular literature. In 1997, for example, Mexico exported 112 million books and imported 247 million (134 millon deficit); Argentina (47.6 million, 91.8 million, 44.2 millon deficit); Brazil (12.2 millon, 247 million, 235 million deficit); Chile (1993: 25.2 millon, 30.7 million, 5.5 million deficit).[20] The nations of the region with the most dynamic publishing industries are (in order) Brazil, Argentina, Mexico, and Colombia. However, in recent years Mexico and Colombia have seen a decline in title production. In regard to bookstores, Brazil has an estimated 1,200 bookstores for its total population of 170 million people.[21] Argentina has approximately 1,500 bookstores throughout the country, a figure that is quite impressive given its smaller population.[22] There are 500 bookstores serving a population of 100 million in Mexico; compare these figures with those for Spain, which has 3,500 bookstores serving 40 million inhabitants.[23] Figures for Colombia are not available, but it is reported that Bogotá has numerous bookstores that sell titles in Spanish, French, English, and Japanese.

At the beginning of the twenty-first century, popular literature is still the most prevalent literature in Latin America. The sheer number of texts sold in urban centers—often hundreds of thousands of copies in a single day—makes the success of the latest bestseller by Carlos Fuentes or Mario Vargas Llosa (which are usually published by one of the enormous Spanish publishing companies) seem trifling. Latin American popular literature does not exist in the richly appointed parlors or the syllabi of the major universities, but around the entrances of the overcrowded subway systems, at the bus stops, in the markets, and any place an ambulatory musician can capture the attention of large groups of people, some of whom will give him or her a few spare coins.

## THE MEXICAN *CORRIDO*

The Mexican corrido is one of the most well-investigated and recognized forms, because many of its essential characteristics can be found in other traditions of oral, lyric poetry found throughout Latin America. Corridos or corrido-like compositions can be found, for example, in Nicaragua, Venezuela, Colombia, Chile, and Argentina.[24] The corrido also raises questions that are crucial toward understanding the phenomenon of popular literature. For example, when does a literature cease to be popular, and how does the identity of a text change when it is transmitted into print? The term *corrido* probably refers to the poet's tendency "to run" (*correr*) through a narrative in an improvisational manner, with little concern for elegant literary embellishments. The greatest investigator of the Mexican corrido, Vicente T. Mendoza, famously defined it as an "epic-lyric-narrative genre" that relates events that "powerfully affect the sensibilities of the masses."[25] As this concise definition suggests, the importance of the corrido as a vehicle for popular expression cannot easily be disputed. Because many corridos were written *in situ*—for example, immediately after a battle—they often provide an invaluable perspective of historical events. Scholars of the Mexican corrido have been nearly unanimous in identifying the genre as a reliable source of popular memory and expression.[26]

## Early Versions of the Corrido

Although it is difficult to ascertain, most investigators of the Mexican corrido believe the form descended from the Spanish *romance*, which was imported to Mexico with the Conquistadors, probably in the sixteenth or seventeenth century. While forms of music such as the *romance*, *décima*, and *copla* were widespread in colonial Latin America, they were probably far from being popular forms.[27] Daniel Castañeda, a folklore scholar of the post-Revolutionary period, argued that there is evidence of corridos as early as the seventeenth century.[28] Mendoza, on the other hand, felt that the corrido was a relatively recent development of the later half of the nineteenth century.[29] The most famous corrido scholar, Américo Paredes, agreed with Mendoza in regard to the relatively recent, mid-to-late nineteenth-century origin of the corrido; by focusing on the border tradition, Paredes postulated that settlers to Nuevo Santander (the region of northern Mexico and the U.S. Southwest) brought décimas, romances, and coplas with them, forms that would eventually produce the corrido.[30] The corrido became a particularly Mexican form of oral literature near the end of the nineteenth century, especially in the northern areas of Mexico and the border region, and saw its greatest development during the Mexican Revolution (1910–20). Corridos were published and sold in Mexico City quite prolifically during this same period, but many examples (for reasons soon to be explained) are not authentic corridos but products of the popular journalism industry.

Primordially, the corrido is an oral literature. For this reason, the vast majority of all the ballads ever composed have been lost. This is especially true since the typical *trovador* or *corridista*—the musician who performed the corrido, normally with a guitar or harp—was often illiterate. Most researchers (with the notable exceptions of Mendoza, Paredes, Strachwitz, and Wald) have depended on the popular broadsheet (*hoja suelta*) form of the corrido, which were mass produced in the capital and circulated throughout the country. In the decades before and during the Revolution, these broadsheets often featured the marvelous graphic art of Manuel Manilla (1830–95?) and José Guadalupe Posada (1852–1913) and were sold on street corners with corridistas providing accompaniment. Many investigators have assumed these corridistas to be real composers putting the latest news to music, rather than hired musicians calling attention to the stacks of *hojas sueltas* being sold at their feet. But it is no coincidence that the period from approximately 1880 to 1920, when Mexico City's popular press was a burgeoning industry, is also regarded as the apogee of the corrido.[31] Rather than being authentic corridos from the provinces, these printed corridos were often composed by *letristas* (professional lyric writers) based in Mexico City and expressed sentiments that can only be described as strongly opposed by the Mexican people. Some of these printed corrido broad sheets may be attempts to curry favor with the Revolutionary or counter-Revolutionary regime in temporary control of the capital. There are, for example, printed corridos voicing enthusiastic support for the presidency of General Victoriano Huerta, a cruel military strongman who assassinated the elected president and ruled the capital like a Mexican Caligula from February 1913 to July 1914. Other broadsheet corridos refer to the popular Revolutionary Emiliano Zapata (1879–1919) as "the Attila of the South"; this description had first appeared in *El Imparcial*—a daily newspaper that supported the dictator—in 1910.

## Getting the News from the Corrido

It is therefore necessary to view the corrido of this period not entirely as a popular form of oral literature but as a medium for bringing the news to the largely illiterate public. (Being viewed as news, the corrido is therefore subject to all the same pressures and propagandistic motives that any journalist or newspaper would experience.) In 1895, only 14 percent of Mexicans could read and write; by 1910, the year of Francisco Madero's presidential bid and the start of the Revolution, the figure rose to about 20 percent.[32] By 1921, only 72 percent of the national population remained illiterate.[33] The latest news was often circulated on broadsheets featuring three principal parts: an eye-catching illustration, a standard block text description of the event, and a series of rhymed verses, usually arranged in four-line stanzas and only occasionally referred to as a corrido. The purpose of such a layout was to make the news more appealing to more people, both those who could read and those who could not. The largest headlines and most unforgettable graphics represent a precursor of the modern *nota roja* (200-point print) news headline that is still seen on papers sold on corners, bus stops, and metro entrances in the largest cities. These stories are often scandalous or graphic; occasionally they serve as exemplary tales of what could happen to people when they sinned or, in the case of the executed bandit, challenged the government.

The popular press was an important component of daily life in the capital, especially as the technocrats of the Porfirio Díaz dictatorship (1876–1910) used whatever means were available to stay in power. Although not exactly the same as newspapers, the widely circulated corrido broadsheet undoubtedly provided turn-of-the-century Mexicans insights (however contrived) into the political and moral values of their fellow citizens. If the political message and values were favorable to Díaz and his leadership, Mexicans would be inclined to continue supporting the regime, or at the very least to feel that their personal disaffection was an isolated case. This may seem like a generalization, or imply a "false consciousness" that turn-of-the-century Mexicans never really entertained,[34] but if thousands of broadsheets were circulated in the streets the day after the dictator won yet another rigged election, and these corridos (that supposedly came from the "soul of the people") lent their support unconditionally to Díaz, who would deny that the result would be a population less inclined to protest?

Corrido broadsheets were circulated on street corners, in front of churches, at train stations, and in similar locations where large numbers of people passed; the broadsheet hawker would often be accompanied by a musician who would attract attention as he or she put the verses to music. The simple, almost monotonous music of the corrido was well suited for the transition from oral performance to mass publication and distribution with musical accompaniment, because no guitarist had to read notes or learn the melody from another musician. This dubious transition between the oral performance of the corrido and its preservation in print leads to the important yet often overlooked distinction between corridistas and the professional letristas, who would put an account of current events into verse and then circulate the lyrics as an a source of news. Many of the most famous printers working in the capital before and during the Revolution occasionally printed the lyrics of corridos they learned from rural musicians; these ballads often chronicled the deeds of outlaws or reported accidents such as train derailments and natural disasters such as floods and droughts. More often, however, someone among the printing staff would improvise rhymed stanzas after reading a provocative story in the latest newspaper or after speaking to journalists. Among the employees of the popular printer Antonio Vanegas Arroyo (1852–1917) were several reporters and professional writers, including Arturo Espinoza and Constancio Suárez.[35] The printer Eduardo Guerrero was a prolific letrista; during the second half of the Revolution his vividly colored, more standardized corrido broadsheets would come to saturate the market once dominated by the more personal and stylized work of Vanegas Arroyo. While all this publication was occurring in the capital, there were countless corridos being produced by poet-musicians to the north and south, most of which narrated the exploits of Revolutionary leaders such as the general Felipe Ángeles (1869–1919) and the archetypal social bandit, Francisco "Pancho" Villa (c. 1887–1923).[36]

## Recording Corridos

The 1920s and 1930s saw a degeneration of the corrido as a result of the advent of commercialization and the recording industry. As we have seen, the corrido had been commercialized previously, to the extent that its lyrics were printed and sold on the streets of the capital, but this new decadent phase occurred largely because fewer new corridos were being produced (thanks in no small part to the end of the Revolution and the demise of many of its charismatic leaders), and because recording studios usually requested performances of earlier ballads rather than new ones. Yet another reason was the virtually anonymous character of oral renditions and the less subversive nature of printed (or in this case recorded) versions of corridos. As James C. Scott explains, "Oral traditions, due simply to their means of transmission, offer a kind of seclusion, control, and even anonymity that make them ideal vehicles for cultural dissidence."[37] As an example of how the corrido became co-opted by commercial interests, the Mexican film industry produced many *comedia ranchera* (singing cowboy) movies in the 1940s that were based on corridos; these films turned actors such as Pedro Infante and Jorge Negrete into cultural icons.[38] Many of the first commercial corridos were recorded in studios along the U.S.–Mexico border and sold to Mexican families living in the Southwest.[39] In spite of the often healthy sales of recorded corridos, the folk music researcher Chris Strachwitz notes:

> All the while the popularity of true *corridos* apparently continued as a vibrant folk tradition in many regions of México and along the *frontera* [the U.S. border] but were rarely recorded on the Mexican side because the audience for that type of balladry had no buying power or the texts were not politically correct! . . . the *corrido* genre was commercialized to the hilt and every pseudo "story" song was labeled as a "*corrido.*"[40]

It is for this reason that recorded corridos, including the examples recorded by U.S. companies that traveled to Mexico for material, were intended for sale in the relatively more prosperous market consisting of Mexicans living north of the border. As if this were not enough evidence of the decline of the corrido as a popular form in this period, the *corrido culto* (erudite corrido) began to appear. These texts were long, epic poems written in book form by intellectuals; thematically, they tended to glorify important events of the Revolution. These corrido cultos were never meant to be put to music and, in fact, found little audience among the literary elites who produced them.[41]

## The Narcocorrido

After several decades of little activity, the corrido re-emerged, thanks to a handful of inspired corrido composers and a change of subject matter that can only be described as a return to origins: the depiction of modern social bandits, in this case the *narcotraficantes* (narcotraffickers) who import or grow heroin, cocaine, and marijuana in western Mexico and smuggle it into the United States. The narcotrafficker, of course, has much popular appeal because he usually comes from very humble origins; furthermore, when he makes a fortune selling illegal drugs, as a matter of procedure he invests money into his community, often helping to build schools, financing low-interest loans, and providing many of the sundry public services the state and federal governments seem incapable of providing. Whereas the earliest corridos celebrated the exploits of bandits such as Heraclio Bernal, Valentín Mancera, and Ignacio Parra, the modern narcocorrido offers stories about notorious drug traffickers (many of whom were from Sinaloa) such as Félix Gallardo, Rafael Caro Quintero, Ramón Arellano Félix, and Amado Carrillo Fuentes.

Although there had always been corridos about the illegal importation of products to the United States, including everything from candle wax to alcoholic beverages during Prohibition (1919–33), the trafficking of drugs represents the most popular theme of the modern corrido. As early as the 1940s, corridos such as "Carga Blanca" [White Cargo] put to lyrics the perils and violence associated with such commerce. This period corresponded with the emergence of *norteño* (northern) music, featuring "close harmony singing, solid rhythmic accompaniment on the low-tuned twelve-string guitar . . . and sprightly accordion breaks."[42] Some of the most important corrido composers of this era include Ángel González (who wrote the romantic narcocorrido "Contrabando y Traición" [Smuggling and Betrayal]), Paulino Vargas, Rosalino "Chalino" Sánchez, and Mario Quintero Lara from Los Tucanes del Norte [The Toucans of the North], who wrote the famous narcocorrido "Tres animales" [Three Animals].[43]

Undoubtedly, the most famous narcocorrido performers are Los Tigres del Norte [the Tigers of the North], a group from Sinaloa that also performs *ranchera* (country), *norteño*, and other traditional forms. The founding members are the three Hernández brothers—Jorge, Raúl, and Hernán—and their cousin, Óscar Lara. The Tigres launched their career in the late 1960s, but they had their first hits in the early 1970s with the narcocorridos "Contrabando y Traición" and "La Banda del Carro Rojo" [The Red Car Gang] (the latter composed by Paulino Vargas). In the past three decades they have sold millions of recordings and are among the wealthiest recording artists in Mexico. Teodoro Bello, the Tigres' principal songwriter in the 1990s, helped to reestablish the popularity of the group with corrido-style compositions such as "Jefe de Jefes" [Boss of Bosses] and "El Mojado Acaudalado" [The Wealthy Wetback]. From the point of view of a classicist, it is difficult to describe the Tigres, multimillionaires with luxury homes in Mexico and other desirable areas, as modern corridistas, but they are the most prolific performers of the genre and have done much to articulate the problems of modern Mexico, as well as to promote corrido studies. For example, in 2000 the Tigres donated $500,000 to the University of California, Los Angeles to help establish the largest collection of Spanish-language folk music in the world.[44] The Tigres, thanks to their success, have run their own recording company, Fonovisa, for several years and are under little pressure to produce hit singles and thus compromise the integrity of their work. The Tigres have recorded fifty-five albums and posted more than $32 million in sales; they have also won 130 platinum and 125 gold records in the course of their 30+ year career.[45] It would seem that whatever they record is quickly bought up by the masses, especially in northern Mexico and the southwestern United States. In spite of their unparalleled success, and the fact that much of their music has nothing to do with narcotrafficking, Elijah Wald notes that most educated Mexicans dislike the narcocorrido—and by extension the Tigres—because they "bemoan" the decline of the corrido "as a once noble form."[46] This statement, perhaps, is a testament to the popular nature of the modern, recording-studio corrido, and especially the narcocorrido.

## THE POPULAR NOVEL

That the novel was slow to develop in Latin America is a standard assertion among scholars of literature. Many factors contributed to this late development, not the least of which was the Spanish crown's prohibition of the circulation of novels in 1531, the widespread illiteracy of the colonial period, and the pyramidal social structure, in which those at the pinnacle looked to Europe for new literature rather than to the colonial capitals where they lived. Furthermore, Spanish writers of the colonial period did not have much interest in writing novels, nor did the reading public have any desire to read books that "reflected [the] trivial circumstances of Spanish life."[47] Given this, it is often difficult to encounter examples of Latin American novels prior to the 1840s, let alone popular novels. When the novel finally began to flourish in the second half of the nineteenth century, the popular novel also emerged. This variety of novel features many subgenres, including the detective, romance (often called *novela rosa*), spy, fantasy or science fiction, adventure, and historical. Often an orderly classification is next to impossible because a historical novel, for example, can have features of the romantic novel, or an adventure novel can have features of the spy novel.

## The Romance Novel

In the tradition of the Latin American popular novel, however, the romance subgenre has enjoyed preeminence, for a number of social and historical reasons. The region, being such an amalgam of different cultures, ethnicities, and borders, has had an affinity for romance because, in a few words, stories that overcome cultural, ethnic, or geopolitical boundaries—or simply flirt with them—produce a very compelling read. Every Latin American nation, of course, has experienced the marginalization of the native peoples to some degree, as well as the institution of slavery. Bearing this in mind, Doris Sommer has written that the romance novel offers readers an allegory of the nation that produces it: "[There is] a contagious desire for socially productive love . . . when they end in satifying marriage . . . happiness reads like a wish-fulfilling projection of national consolidation and growth, a goal rendered visible."[48]

One consistent characteristic of the popular novel is that it tends toward the melodramatic: that is, the plot develops in a sensational or improbable manner, less development is observed in regard to characterization, and the endings are usually excessively happy or tragic. For this reason, the romance novel is especially susceptible to the charge that it represents a kind of escapist literature.[49] This assertion may be overly critical. However, it is no coincidence that one reliable test for the popularity of a twentieth-century novel is the period of time it takes before it is made into a feature-length film: the shorter the period between the initial publication and the film premiere, the more popular it tends to be.

Naturally, the main difficulty in discussing novels is that, unlike other genres of popular literature, these texts can easily lend themselves to an appraisal that no longer views them as popular but as more highly esteemed works of literature. For example, although Rómulo Gallego's *Doña Bárbara* (Venezuela, 1929) was made into a popular film, abridged to fit into comic books, and transmitted to television screens all over Latin America as *telenovelas* (prime-time soap operas), it ranks quite high on the list of indispensable works of Latin American literature taught at universities and included on doctoral program reading lists. For this reason some investigators have used terms such as *semipopular* to describe works such as José Joaquín Fernández de Lizardi's novel, *El periquillo sarniento* (1816, 1831), which was written by an author who was not from the underprivileged classes but, with a prodigious talent for gauging popular taste, managed to produce a text that appealed to both the masses and more privileged groups of readers.[50] The history of the Latin American novel essentially begins with this work.[51]

One of the earliest romance novels was produced by the Cuban Cirilo Villaverde (1812–94), *Cecilia Valdés o la loma del ángel* [Cecilia Valdés or the Angel's Hill] (1839, 1879).

This two-part novel concerns a romance between a beautiful *mulata* (a female with parents of African and European ancestry) named Cecilia and a young master named Leonardo, who is white. The protagonists do not know that they are sister and brother. When Leonardo is preparing to marry another woman more suitable to his class, Cecilia provokes an admirer of hers to kill the young master. Such a plot—the impossible romance that ends in tragedy—occurs repeatedly in the Latin American romance novel.

One of the most famous and critically acclaimed romantic novels was Gallegos's *Doña Bárbara*. So well known is this novel that its popularity led to a film version produced in Mexico (1943), and helped to propel its author to the Venezuelan presidency (1959–64). The novel concerns a female political boss (*caudilla*), a "devourer of men" who is eventually tamed by the civilized man who ventures to her ranch in the middle of the *llana,* the barren and forbidding Venezuelan wild. Although the allegorical names of the characters border on the obvious—Bárbara (barbaric), Santos Luzardo (*Santa Luz y Ardor,* or saintly light and zeal), the American industrialist Mr. Guillermo Danger—Gallegos crafted the rest of the novel with more subtlety. Some aspects—for example the chapter entitled "La bella durmiente" [The Sleeping Beauty]—invoke the fairy tale. Doris Sommer has written that *Doña Bárbara* is arguably the "national novel" of Venezuela.[52]

A lesser-known popular novelist is Benito Lynch (Argentina, 1880–1951). Enrique Anderson Imbert writes that in his many novels Lynch "cuts out a piece of land, populates it with men and women, invents a plot rich in human and psychological conflicts, and then makes us believe that what he is relating is real."[53] Lynch's most celebrated novel is *El inglés de los güesos* [The Englishman of the Bones] (1924), the story of which concerns an English anthropologist who visits the pampa to investigate the pre-Conquest civilizations. While the Englishman stays at the humble ranch of a hardworking laborer, the laborer's daughter falls in love with him. The foreigner and the young woman enjoy a passionate romance, but when the cool, selfish anthropologist finishes his investigations, he takes his leave of the pampa and the girl. She commits suicide. In 1940 the novel was made into a highly successful film by the Argentine director Carlos Hugo Christensen.

In the second half of the twentieth century, the popular novel continued its growth. The detective novel has seen much development in particular, and the preeminent author of this subgenre is Paco Ignacio Taibo II (b. 1949). Although Taibo was born in Spain, he came to Mexico at the age of ten and has worked as a professor of history and anthropology. Taibo is an extremely prolific author and has written for comic books and newspapers and has published important historical essays and books dealing with anarchism, Mexico's 1968 student movement, and the revolutionary Ernesto "Che" Guevara (1928–67). Among his most famous novels are *La vida misma* [Life Itself] (1987), *Cuatro manos* [Four Hands] (1991), *La bicicleta de Leonardo* [Leonardo's Bicycle] (1994), and *Regreso a la misma ciudad y bajo la lluvia* [Return to the Same City] (1996). Taibo's novels usually take place in the megapolis of Mexico City and feature elaboratedly constructed plots, with crimes meticulously unraveled by protagonists such as José Daniel Fierro, an inquisitive crime writer, and the one-eyed detective Héctor Belascoarán Shayne. This second protagonist—Mexico's version of Auguste Dupin or Sherlock Holmes—proved so popular that Taibo brought him back for *Regreso a la misma ciudad* after he (like Holmes) had been killed in an earlier novel.

## Brazilian and Mexican Popular Fiction

Although it is by far the largest Latin American nation, Brazil was among the last to receive the printing press, which finally arrived in Rio de Janeiro and Salvador in 1808.[54]

These first presses were used primarily to publish newspapers; consequently, many of the earliest Brazilian novels of importance were published in serial form. In spite of these relatively inauspicious beginnings, according to the Brazilian Consulate General, Brazil currently provides about half of the total literary output of Latin America in terms of titles and total number of books.[55]Considering such a statistic, it is not surprising that Brazil has produced many significant popular novelists.

One of the greatest was José de Alencar (1829–77), a romantic who investigated popular ballads and folklore in order to write allegorical novels about the origins of Brazilian culture and society.[56] As Afrânio Coutinho explains, writers of Alencar's era began "[a] search for local color" that led to "an understanding of popular literature . . . which the romantics felt was the original character of literary creativity."[57] *O Guaraní* (1857) and *Iracema* (1865), his two most famous novels, are thoroughly popular and narrate the story of what happened when whites, Indians, and mestizos became lovers in nineteenth-century Brazil. *O Guaraní* was published as a serial in what was then Brazil's largest newspaper, *O Diário do Rio de Janeiro*, and has since been adapted for feature-length films several times.[58] *O Guaraní* is a complex story of parallel relationships between a European soldier and a hot-blooded *mestiza* (a woman with Indian and European parents) and between a noble Indian king and a blonde, blue-eyed daughter of a landed family. *Iracema* is about a beautiful Indian princess who falls passionately in love with a blonde soldier named Martim. After Iracema becomes pregnant, Martim—assuming the "white man's burden" of civilizing savage lands—leaves her to wage war for extended periods of time, effectively all but abandoning her. When Iracema gives birth to their mestizo child, she dies and Martim returns sadly to her side. Realizing what he has lost, he and his son leave to recruit settlers to populate the land where Iracema is buried. Alencar's novels, in the words of Doris Sommer, provided Brazilians just what they longed for in the middle of the nineteenth century: "an undeniably local cast to the founding moment of Brazilian history."[59] It is for this reason that *Iracema*, much like *Doña Bárbara* in Venezuela, is viewed as Brazil's national novel.

In the twentieth century, Brazil produced yet another popular novelist of world renown: Jorge Amado (1912–2001). Of Amado's twenty-two novels, most have gone through dozens of editions in his native country; several have also been made into popular films and been translated in most of the world's major languages. In addition to novels, Amado also wrote biographies, travel guides, and children's literature. Early in his career, Amado revealed that he hoped to produce a novel with a "minimum of literature" that would portray people as they really were.[60] Perhaps his best-known work, *Dona Flor e seus dois maridos* [Dona Flor and Her Two Husbands] (1966), is also his most popular because it deals with death, romantic love, fidelity, and *candomblé*, an Afro-Brazilian popular religion. These popular themes, combined with the fantastic events of the novel (the spirit of Dona Flor's deceased, philanderous husband returning to their marriage bed, in spite of the presence of her new, hardworking yet boring husband), lead to a work of literature that is as interesting to the literary critic as it is to the waitress or bus driver. The novel was made into a highly successful film in 1978, featuring the well-known Brazilian actors Sonia Braga and José Wilker.[61] As a testament to Amado's unrivaled popularity, a later novel, *Tereza Batista, cansada de guerra* [Tereza Batista, Home from the Wars] (1972), became the inspiration for Brazilian *literatura de cordel*.[62]

Today the best-selling Brazilian author is undoubtedly Paulo Coelho (b. 1947), a virtual mass culture phenomenon. Since the beginning of his career in the late 1980s, he has written numerous bestsellers, and his philosophical novels have been translated into over sixty languages. Coelho's most famous novel, *O alquimista* [The Alchemist] (1988), describes the spiritual maturation of a Spanish boy named Santiago who travels to North Africa in search of treasure. The author's official Website indicates that *O alquimista* alone has sold approximately eleven million copies throughout the world.[63]

One final example of the popular novel comes from Mexico: *Como agua para chocolate* [Like Water for Chocolate] (1989) by Laura Esquivel (b. 1950). Taking place in northern Mexico in the years preceding and during the Revolution, this romantic novel tells the story of a young woman named Tita who is not permitted to enjoy herself or marry but, being the youngest of several sisters, is forced to care for her domineering and hypocritical mother. As proof of its popular character, the title of the novel comes from a popular expression,[64] and between the chapters readers find recipes for delicious Mexican dishes. The relationship between these recipes and the plot of the novel cannot be underestimated; as Pilcher points out, "[a]ttempts by Mexican patriots to forge a national cuisine reflected the deep historical connections between food and identity."[65] The novel has gone through numerous editions and was made into a highly-successful film in 1992. As this recent example suggests, the popular novel is as commercially successful as it ever was and will probably continue to entertain many more readers than any Nobel laureate could hope to with his or her work.

## THE *FOTONOVELA* (PHOTONOVEL)

The *fotonovela* (photonovel) represents a genre of popular literature centered on entertainment rather than on the circulation of

### WHICH NONFICTION IS POPULAR IN LATIN AMERICA?

Given that the essential purpose of popular literature is to entertain, it comes as no surprise that in comparison to the quantity of fictional works (of all genres) there are not nearly as many nonfiction texts. It is also difficult to determine what would be a popular, nonfictional text, given that the possibilities would include religious manuals, self-help or philosophical books (the universally famous texts of liberation theology would be included here),[66] psychology studies, and other topics. In terms of mass-produced texts in the public domain (for example, kiosks, public transportation, and popular markets), there has been a long history of books and pamphlets dealing with the interpretation of signs, the zodiac, indigenous religions, and the meaning behind cataclysmic world events such as earthquakes, world wars, and volcanic eruptions. Rural Latin America has been the setting for countless messiahs, folk saints, and popular manifestations of spiritualism; much of this popular belief can be seen in the other genres of popular literature in this survey, especially the corrido and the Brazilian *literatura de cordel*. In the late 1800s and into the twentieth century, one of the most popular books circulating in Mexico was a prophetic dream book, published on a yearly basis in the manner of a farmer's almanac, called *El nuevo oráculo* [The New Oracle].[67]

information such as the latest news. The typical photonovel is about the size of a thick magazine, but rather than being composed of text, the story is conveyed by photograph panels with narrative explanations and ballon-caption dialogue between characters. More than a literature that appeals to the semiliterate population, the photonovel is instructive in a sense that, like the comic book, it can help people learn to read because of the close correlation between the photos and printed dialogue and narration. The photonovel is also appealing to literate people who wish for a quick, entertaining read of what is occasionally spicy subject matter. (However, many people who purchase photonovels would be ashamed if they were caught reading one.) Cornelia Butler Flora contends that this genre of popular literature, next to the comic book, represents "the most widely distributed printed material in Latin America."[68]

The origin of the photonovel is not easy to trace. Some have pointed to nineteenth-century France, when, following the invention of photography, *Les Mésaventures de Jean-Paul Choppart* [The Misadventures of Jean-Paul Choppart] (1834) appeared in Paris. The text used captioned photographs to tell a romantic story.[69] Following its success many more photonovels appeared, until by the end of the century examples were circulating in the Americas.[70] By the late 1920s, when the largest Latin American countries had followed Hollywood's lead and established their film industries, motion pictures helped to increase the production and distribution of the photonovel. According to Butler Flora, the first commercial photonovel was adapted from the 1932 Hollywood movie *Grand Hotel* and sold in Italy by the Del Duca brothers' publishing company: "The first number sold fifty thousand copies the first week; the one million copies of the second number published next week were also sold out."[71] In this period photonovels were often called *cine-novelas* (film novels) or *cine de bolsillo* (pocket cinema). The motion picture industry, seeing an opportunity to cash in, quickly co-opted the photonovel to help promote their latest films, circulating these short texts with selected scenes either before the premiere or shortly thereafter. This close relationship between cinema and the photonovel may be seen as a reversal of what was previously described in the examination of the popular novel, where the printed text became celluloid.

German Mariño Solano argues that the photonovel developed after World War II, first in Italy and then in France, as a result of the development of the film industries of these countries.[72] Italian production companies continued to promote the photonovel, and by the late 1940s and early 1950s photonovels were being sold throughout Latin America; this period of course corresponds to the golden age of several Latin American cinema traditions, most notably the Mexican and the Argentine. In Argentina photonovels—those promoting a new motion picture and others telling an original story—became so widespread that singers and other performers began appearing in them as models in order to promote their careers.[73] Romantic photonovels also emerged, often recycling a plot concerning a poor, attractive girl of high moral standards who finds herself among wealthy people who share none of her scruples. Today the photonovel remains more prevalent in the countries with the most highly developed film industries: Mexico, Argentina, and Brazil. However, photonovels have also been produced in response to especially popular radio programs.[74] Photonovels are often produced by a handful of large publishing firms, sold in the capitals, and then whatever is left after the first few weeks on the market is distributed in more rural areas, or even in other countries.

In the most detailed and humorous examination of the photonovel to date, Fernando Curiel de Fossé identifies four identifying features of the genre: (1) the bubble caption for dialogue; (2) onomatopoeia, especially in regard to nonverbal utterances and sound effects; (3) visualized metaphors such as hearts with arrows driven through them; and (4) kinetic figures, such as lines that follow a fired bullet to its target, or an explosive image when a fist strikes another person.[75] None of these features is as highly developed as they are in the comic book, mainly because the latter medium is drawn (rather than assembled from a series of photographs), so more artistic expression and invention are possible.

Like the motion picture, the photonovel has melodramatic tendencies. The transgression of social or class boundaries, usually to pursue a romance, is a recurring theme. Some examples that are not linked to a particular mainstream film tend to exhibit an excess of violence or even soft-core pornography. Characterization usually amounts to a handful of stock stereotypes: women are spoiled, materialistic, but often victimized by sexual blackmail; men are boorish and abusive; sons are reckless spendthrifts; and fathers are as domineering and shortsighted as those in Shakespearean tragedies.[76]

The photonovel is veritable phenomenon of publishing. In the largest cities of Latin America, it is not uncommon for thousands of copies of a new edition to sell out in a few days. Limiting his investigation to a single work week (August 15–19, 1977), Curiel de Fossé discovered that the Mexican romantic photonovels *Cita* [Date], *Ternura* [Tenderness], *Chicas* [Girls], and *Cita de lujo* [Luxury Date], sold a total of 960,000 copies. All of these titles were produced by a single publishing business, Ediciones ELE, with releases on different days (*Cita* on Tuesday, *Ternura* on Wednesday, etc.). The record for the most copies sold in a single day—360,000—belonged to *Novelas de amor* [Novels of Love].[77] Today, in the large metropolitan centers of Latin America, photonovels continue to sell extremely well. They are, however, less connected with motion pictures and remain something of a literature of the street; the most reputable Latin American bookstores do not stock them, and they are normally sold at newspaper or magazine stands located at subway entrances or on street corners.

## THE COMIC BOOK

Latin America's comic book (*historieta*, or "little story") tradition is quite extensive and has produced many characters and series of enduring popularity. Only within the past 25 years have comic books received serious attention from researchers, many of whom refer to these texts as "graphic novels." This term distinguishes comic books from the photonovel in at least one important way: their narrative is presented through illustrations rather than photographs. Illustrations may be drawn, painted, or produced with computer images and be either black-and-white or color (most comic book covers, however, are color). In most other respects—the size, pagination, use of bubble captions for dialogue, onomatopeia, a narrative sustained by illustrative panels—the comic book is quite similar to the photonovel. For its physical characteristics and the manner in which it is sold, the comic book is not to be confused with a comic strip, which appears on a daily or weekly basis in newspapers or periodicals. The comic book is an independent, popular text that provides entertainment.

The origins of Latin American comic books date from about the middle of the nineteenth century, when political caricatures and cartoons were printed in daily newspapers or supplemental sections. The Italian Angelo Agostini (1843–1910) produced many pioneering cartoons in Brazil, the most notable of which was called *As aventuras de Nhô Quim ou Impressões de uma Viagem à Corte* [The Adventures of Nhô Quim or Impressions of a Journey to the Court]. Started in 1869, *Nhô Quim* is the first known comic strip with a recurring character.[78] Later, these more sporadically printed comics evolved into Sunday editions (*dominicales*) in the early twentieth century, where cartoonists were alloted more space and could develop recurring characters. Many of these characters, however, were the protagonists of imported U.S. strips. Dominicales were less political and, like the Sunday "funnies" in the United States, were usually directed at children. By the 1920s and 1930s, when a number of characters from dominicales became popular, they spun off from their newspapers to become the protagonists of the first comic books. Although U.S. characters such as Donald Duck and Archie have enjoyed much success in the Latin American market, innumerable characters—some with publication histories of more than 50 years—have originated in the lands south of the Río Grande and north of the Tierra del Fuego.

Like other genres of published popular literature discussed here, Latin American comic books have tended to originate in the major urban centers of the largest countries and spread centrifugally to the smaller communities and rural areas. Although all Latin American nations have produced comic books, the ones with the most extensive traditions are Mexico,

Argentina, Brazil, and Cuba. Comic books are usually published on a weekly basis by large publishing companies, but monthly and even daily schedules are not uncommon. Some of the largest companies include Grupo Editorial Vid, Editorial Argumentos, and Novedades Editores, all located in Mexico City; others are Ediciones de la Urraca, located in Buenos Aires; and Editora Brasil America Ltda (EBAL), which was one of the biggest South American publishers for 30 years. In Mexico, during its Golden Age of comic books (from the early 1930s to the mid-1950s), the pages usually measured 7$\frac{1}{2}$ by 10$\frac{1}{2}$ inches.[79] However, Latin American comic books generally tend to be smaller than their U.S. counterparts, usually measuring approximately 5$\frac{1}{2}$ by 7$\frac{3}{4}$ inches. Smaller comic books, often of a soft- or hard-core pornographic nature and referred to in Mexico as *libros vaqueros* ("cowboy books") or *libros policíacos* ("detective books"), are sold in public areas such as bus stations, subway entrances, and newspaper kiosks. Most other Latin American countries have similar genres.

## Mexican Comic Books

According to the researcher Adriana Malvido,[80] Mexico is the largest per capita producer and consumer of comic books in the world, with approximately 40 million copies of new historietas circulated per month (this figure includes weekly publications). Although recent decades have witnessed a decline in sales, as late as the 1990s eight of the ten best-selling periodicals were comic books.[81] The reason for the unparalleled success of comic books in Mexico is twofold: thanks to the relative political stability and economic growth after the Revolution, Mexicans generally had more money and leisure time than other Latin Americans; furthermore, the post-Revolutionary government's aggressive educational programs helped to raise literacy rates and to create a readership for all varieties of reading material.[82]

While Mexican comic books also originated from the tradition of political caricature and cartooning, and later from dominicales, the cigarette brand El Buen Tono began inserting small historietas into packs of their product in the 1880s. About the same time the great Mexican popular artist José Guadalupe Posada created a recurring character known as Don Chepito Mariguanero Charrasca y Rascarrabias, an unwieldy name loosely translated as "Sir Joey Pothead Switchblade Sourpuss."[83] A prototype of later historieta characters, Don Chepito was no hero by any stretch of the imagination but a dandy who behaved inappropriately in highly public situations. Don Chepito's antics were narrated in verse, and turn-of-the-century Mexicans bought his broadsheets along with corridos, Day of the Dead calaveras, and important news stories.

Anne Rubenstein writes that the first Mexican comic book was *Adelaido el Conquistador,* which ran for 100 weekly issues in 1932–33.[84] Some of the most popular early examples include *Pepín* [Joey] (1936–55) and *Chamaco* [Brat] (1936–55), both of which predate the earliest U.S. comic book, which appeared in 1937. *Pepín* was so popular in the mid-1940s that it was sold eight times per week (with two editions on Sunday).[85] According to Hinds and Tatum, *Chamaco* was the first daily comic book in the world.[86] Another important early comic book was *Paquín* [Little Francisco], produced by the Spanish publisher Francisco Sayrols in 1934, which is considered by at least one investigator to be the first Mexican comic book.[87] From those beginnings, and coupled with the economic prosperity of Mexico in the 1940s and 1950s, the industry grew enormously.

To monitor content of the millions of historietas circulating in Mexico, the post-Revolutionary government established the *Comisión calificadora de periódicos y revistas* (Newspaper and Magazine Reviewing Commission) in 1944. This relatively small agency has the responsibility of "protecting the populace . . . from the influence of morbid contents in frankly anti-educational publications."[88] Although the Commission attempted to exercise control over content, nothing really approaching censorship was ever achieved, because of the popularity and persistence of the genre as well as the fact that some of the Commission's laws were unenforceable. The most notable Mexican comic books from the postwar era include José Guadalupe Cruz's *Adelita* (a story taking place during the Mexican Revolution), Joaquín Cervantes Bassoco's *Wama: El hijo de la luna* [Wama: The Son of the Moon], Adolfo Mariño Ruiz's *El charro negro* [The Black Cowboy], and Germán Butze's *Los supersabios* [The Wise Guys].[89] Among the many publications of Yolanda Vargas Dulché (1926–99), *Lágrimas, risa y amor* [Tears, Laughter, and Love], stands as the most popular and—with forty-plus years of publication—the most enduring romance comic book in Mexico.

Kalimán—a master of science, metaphysics, and hypnosis—is an extremely popular superhero in Mexico with readership throughout Spanish America. Also known as "el hombre increíble" ("the Incredible Man"), Kalimán is a superhero raised by Tibetan lamas who pursues justice the world over; his name is a combination of *Kali*, the Hindu goddess, and *man*, which recalls Superman.[90] Kalimán began as the protagonist of a Mexican radio program in 1963 until his creators, the Cuban exile Modesto Vázquez González and the Mexican Rafael Cutberto Navarro, began publishing stories in a weekly comic 2 years later. By the 1970s, Kalimán comics were published by Promotora K, a publishing firm created by Vázquez González and Cutberto Navarro. The principal illustrators for the series were Leopoldo Sea Salas and Cristóbal Velasco. By the late 1970s, between 3 and 7 percent of the Mexican public had purchased copies of *Kalimán*.[91] The comic book spawned a highly successful series of films (with accompanying photonovels) that set several box office records in the 1970s. According to Adriana Malvido, late-1980s editions of his exploits sold two million copies per week in Mexico.[92] Although the series ended in 1991, new editions of *Kalimán: El hombre increíble* appeared in the fall of 1998.

Another extremely popular comic book is Gabriel Vargas's *La familia Burrón* (*The Burrón Family* or, depending on one's interpretation of *Burrón*, "The Big Dumb Family"), which features an urban, working class family who try to make ends meet in their humble barrio. Of all the comic books under examination here, *La familia Burrón* is the most recognizably Mexican because of its setting and the values of its characters. Vargas (b. 1918) has endeavored to provide Mexican readers situations and customs that they can identify as their own, as well as reflect changes in Mexican urban society.[93] The conflicts and adventures of the Burrón family and their neighbors are the subject matter of the series. The principal character is Borola, an energetic woman who is married to Don Regino, the neighborhood barber. Borola is domineering and capricious, often doing outrageously foolish things in order to appear as if she belongs to the upper class. The clever dialogue and wordplay of Vargas has encouraged some academics—including the great Mexican writer Alfonso Reyes—to declare that he deserves a place in the Academy of the Spanish Language.[94] *La familia Burrón* has been published weekly, with only one interruption in the late 1970s, for nearly 60 years. Vargas has been awarded numerous prizes for his lifetime of creativity, including the Mexican National Science and Arts Prize (2003). Recently the prestigious press Editorial Porrúa has begun publishing collections of classic episodes.

One of the most important Mexican cartoonists is Ríus, who was born Eduardo del Río in Michoacán state in 1934. His career as an artist and political commentator began in 1954 when his single-panel cartoons began to appear in the magazine *Ja-já*. In subsequent years, Ríus's cartoons have appeared in just about every major Mexican newspaper and throughout Latin America. Ríus created the strips *Los supermachos* [The Supermachos] and *Los agachados* [The Downtrodden] to criticize Mexican political leadership in the 1960s and 1970s.

## MEMÍN PINGÜÍN

Memín Pingüín, who first appeared in 1943, is an extremely popular character in Mexican *historietas*. A Cuban–Mexican child who is consumately devoted to his mother, Memín Pingüín behaves in a comic, self-deprecating manner against the backdrop of the soap opera–like activities of an astonishingly white, upper-class family. He speaks in a kind of Caribbean-influenced Spanish slang, often providing witty or scandalous observations much to the embarrassment of his hosts. Memín Pingüín is the invention of Yolanda Vargas Dulché, the most famous and prolific author of comics in Mexico, and has been drawn since the mid-1960s by Sixto Valencia Burgos (b. 1934). When a commemorative series of six Memín Pingüín stamps was produced by the Mexican postal service in June 2005, the governments of the United States and Mexico briefly traded accusations of racism because of the highly stereotypical physical characteristics and behavior of the beloved character.[96]

According to the cartoonist, *Los supermachos* was discontinued in 1968 because of pressure—and later intimidation—generated by Luis Echeverría, Mexico's Minister of the Interior in the late 1960s and later president (1970–76).[95] Although Ríus has worked predomininantly in comic strips, his work has been celebrated and anthologized to such an extent that not to mention it would be a mistake. The same holds true for Quino (born Joaquín Salvador Lavado, 1932), the Argentine cartoonist, who produced perhaps the most famous cartoon in all of Latin America, *Mafalda*, which details the adventures of an unusually ironic and precocious little girl. Quino is also very well known for his political cartoons, most of which are no longer than a single panel.

### Argentinian Comic Books

Argentina has also had a prolific history of comic book publication, although its development has been sporadic. Like Mexico, by the 1920s and 1930s Argentina had many popular comic strip characters, such as the Cisco Kid and the Indian Patoruzu (created by the pioneering Dante Quinterno, 1909–2003). By 1928, the first magazine devoted to comics, *El Tony*, was published. Early comic books were often printed by the same Italian publishing firms that produced photonovels, leading to a situation in the 1940s in which comic books scripted and drawn by Europeans dominated the Argentine market. In 1947, for example, the Italian publisher Cesare Civita launched the highly successful adventure comic book *Salgari*, which was produced largely by Italian writers and illustrators.[97]

But Argentines would soon reclaim their market with an explosion of creativity and innovation. In the mid-1950s, Héctor Germán Oesterheld (1917–77), who abandoned geological studies to become a writer of short stories and comic book serials, established Editorial Frontera and helped to launch a resurgence of Argentine comic books. Oesterheld was an astonishingly prolific writer who was able to produce engrossing tales in the genres of science fiction, surrealism, western, combat, and adventure. With Editorial Frontera, Oesterheld surrounded himself with a truly outstanding group of artists to illustrate his stories; more importantly, he gave these artists—Francisco Solano López (b. 1928), Hugo Pratt (1927–95), and Alberto Breccia (1919–93), among others—enough freedom to develop characterization over action and, more generally, to revolutionize the conventions of their panel-based art form. The most famous Oesterheld titles include *Hora cero* [Zero Hour], *Frontera* [Frontier], *Misterix, Supermisterix, Mort Cinder*, and the "El Eternauta" series. This brilliant collaboration, unfortunately, was not to last. Once the talent of his illustrators (and especially of Breccia) became internationally recognized, European and U.S. comic book publishers lured them away from Buenos Aires. Sadly, Oesterheld's involvement with the Montoneros (a guerrilla movement opposed to old-guard Peronists), led to his capture and "disappearance" in 1977 during the military dictatorship of General Jorge Videla.

The work of Alberto Breccia merits special attention. Born in Uruguay, Breccia's graphic work was published regularly in comic strips such as *Tit-Bits* as early as 1939, but it wasn't until his collaboration with Oesterheld that his talent began to blossom fully. Like Oesterheld, Breccia was an avid reader, which gave his stories and illustrations a sophistication that drew praise normally reserved for works of literature. Visually, his art evolved from standard line and shading techniques (as in "Kid, de Río Grande" from *Tit-Bits*, 1942), to a style less dependent on line but more experimental with regard to light and darkness ("Mort Cinder. En la penitenciaría" [In The Penitentiary] from *Supermisterix*, 1964), and then to a virtually surrealistic representation with ample brushstrokes ("Perramus" from *Fierro*, 1985).[98] In order to avoid the same fate as Oesterheld, Breccia had to destroy the original pages of *Ché*, a comic book detailing the career of the famous revolutionary; he nevertheless buried a copy in his garden and, after the fall of the military dictatorship in 1983, produced "Perramus," a comic book that was highly critical of the regime.[99]

The early 1980s and the 1990s witnessed a decadence in Argentine comic books, due in no small measure to the military dictatorships and economic instability of the nation. One of the most famous comic book heroes of recent years is Cazador (Hunter), who appeared for the first time in the late 1980s but did not have his own comic series until 1990. The creator of Cazador, Jorge Luis Pereira (also called Lucas, b. 1963), took the name Robert Howard for his protagonist in honor of the American creator of Conan. In point of fact, Cazador is like an urban Conan; in each subsequent series of his adventures the physical size and grotesqueness of Cazador have become more pronounced. Recent artwork, as with other comic book series, features more of an airbrushed quality reminiscent of the influential Animé designs imported from Japan. In spite of the ups and downs, Argentina remains a nation with many comic book dealers and annual conventions.

## Brazilian Comic Books

Although Brazil is also among the leading producers of comic books (histórias em quadrinhos) in the world, generally there has been much more U.S. (and now Japanese) influence there than in other markets. The first prototypes appeared in the mid-1930s with the *Suplemento Juvenil* [Youth Supplement], which was published as a weekly tabloid by the daily newspaper *A Nação* [The Nation]. In 1939 the daily *O Globo* began publishing *Gibi* [The Little Black Boy], which was the most popular Brazilian comic until 1950. This particular series dominated the market to such an extent that the word *gibi* still serves as slang for comic books.[100] A national comic book industry first started to develop in the 1940s, especially with the establishment of Adolfo Aizen's (1907–91) Editora Brasil America Ltda (EBAL). More comic book publishers soon followed, including Editorial Abril, Globo Editorial, and Circo Editorial. In spite of this growth, there was still much foreign influence; Disney comics in particular dominated the Brazilian market in the 1940s and 1950s. U.S. companies such as Marvel and Fawcett sold many of their texts in Brazil through the forementioned publishers, often exporting their most popular characters: Pafuncio ("Bringing Up Father"), Capitão Marvel (Captain Marvel), and Homem-Borracha (Plastic Man). However, many Fawcett stories "were redrawn by Brazilian cartoonists and there were some original stories written and illustrated by local artists."[101]

In the 1960s, following the cultural nationalism of the previous decade and in conjunction with new directions in music (*bossa nova*) and cinema (*cinema novo*), Brazilian comics also began to reflect indigenous culture.[102] The most important title of this period is *O Pererê* by the author and cartoonist Ziraldo (b. 1932), which featured Brazilian folklore and sold very well during its four-year run. Comic books by Maurício de Souza (b. 1935) also continued to enjoy much success in this period. His most famous title is *Turma da Mônica* [Monica's Class], a children's comic book. The later half of the 1960s witnessed a surge in horror comics, with titles such as *Drácula*, *O Estranho Mundo de Zé do Caixão* [The Strange World of Joseph of the Coffin], and *Sexta-Feira 13* [Friday the 13th] dominating the market. Since horror comics also enjoyed much popularity in the United States during the 1950s, this trend in Brazil should also be seen as further example of foreign influence.

Even into the 1970s and 1980s, when Brazilian artists enjoyed more opportunities to produce original material, U.S. influence continued. Brazilian underground comic books (also known as *udigrudi*, a Brazilian adaptation of "underground") designed for adults, often show the influence of the American cartoonist Robert Crumb.[103] In 1989, when the Hollywood motion picture *Batman* was released, Batman comic books were revived in Brazil and promoted with a considerable multimedia campaign, selling about 300,000 copies.[104] Some of the most popular adult comics of this period include *O Balão* [The Balloon], *Chiclete com Banana* [Chewing Gum with Banana], *Circo* [Circus], and *Porrada!* [Slap Down!]. Brazilian adult comics in the 1980s, as pointed out by Nadilson M. da Silva, grew from the growing counterculture scene but also demonstrated strong commercial aspirations, much like the United States' *Mad* magazine.[105]

One example of a truly underground author is Alcides de Aguiar Caminha (1921–92) who, for approximately 40 years, sold pornographic comic books in São Paulo and Rio de Janeiro under the pseudonym of Carlos Zéfiro. Aguilar Caminha was obliged to hide his identity because he worked for years as a civil servant in the Brazilian Department of Labor. Calling his comic book series *Os Catecismos* [The Catechisms], and selling them clandestinely to only a limited number of people from the 1940s to the 1970s, Aguilar Caminha finally revealed his identity in a *Playboy* interview a year before his death. Although his *quadrinhos* were rare, they were highly sought after. Aguilar Caminha was not a particularly skilled artist, but his interesting biography and persistence have made the name Carlos Zéfiro legendary among aficionados of Latin American comic books.

Since 1998, a Brazilian comic book called *Spirit of the Amazon* has combined entertainment with social activism. The creator, Orlando Paes Filho (b. 1962), is a very popular science fiction and fantasy novelist who, when he was only sixteen, conceived the idea for *Spirit of the Amazon*: six extraterrestrials who come to Earth determined to save the planet's fragile ecosystem by combating greedy executives and their corportations. Indigenous people call on these extraterrestrials to save them and their way of life, but believe them to be spirits. According to Michael Dobran, *Spirit of the Amazon* was outsold only by the enormously popular U.S. comic *X-Men*.[106]

## BRAZILIAN LITERATURA DE CORDEL

Brazil, for its size and the rich diversity of its culture, has undoubtedly witnessed the development of every form of popular literature treated in this chapter. In addition, ever since colonization in the sixteenth century, Brazilian society has been highly stratified with clearly defined upper and lower classes—conditions that facilitate the development of an authentic popular culture. However, to add something above and beyond what has already been said of the previously discussed examples of popular literature, the focus here will be the genre that is perhaps the most uniquely Brazilian: *literatura de cordel*, "literature on a string."

In spite of the fact that Brazil is the largest country in South America, its popular culture and literature are often left outside surveys such as this one because of its relatively unique historical development and the fact that its national language is Portuguese rather than Spanish. Nevertheless, Brazil shares many characteristics with the largest Hispanic American nations, one of the most important being the demographic and cultural differences between its largest centers of population (the metropolitan centers of the coast, also known as the *litoral*) and the more rural and underdeveloped regions in the interior and northeastern states. This division, of course, is reflected throughout Latin America: Mexico (Mexico City and the rural north and south); Argentina (Buenos Aires and the pampa); Perú (Lima and the interior regions); Venezuela (Caracas and the llana). Today most literatura de cordel is produced in the more underdeveloped regions, while its sale and institutionalization occur in the metropolitan centers.

Literatura de cordel (also known by the term *folhetos,* or "little books") consists of small, cheaply produced books made of newspaper-weight paper, usually measuring about $4\frac{1}{2}$ by $6\frac{1}{2}$ inches. Folhetos commonly have eight, sixteen, thirty-two, or (less commonly) sixty-four pages because the paper used to make them is printed on both sides, folded in two, and then inserted one into the other.

The text consists of verses that usually have six lines to a stanza, and although different rhyme schemes are occasionally employed, the most common is a-b-c-b-d-b. To prevent plagiarism and unauthorized printing, cordel poets often craft an acrostic into the last stanzas of their poems so that their name will read vertically, top to bottom, with the initial letters of each line. The printing technology that has been traditionally used to produce folhetos is the manual press; however, in recent years poets have increasingly come to depend on larger publishers where they are often contracted for 10 percent of the profits but lose all legal right to future editions.[107] Because of the rural origins of this literature, folhetos are usually sold in country markets; they are displayed by hanging them over strings, in the manner of a towel on a clothesline (hence the name),so that buyers can see the title, the author's name, and the block print artwork on the cover. The market for this literature includes "illiterate and semiliterate individuals . . . who appreciate the simple language, the decorative cover, and the accessible price . . . as well as their appealing subjects."[108] However, largely because of their stylized and often charming artwork, there are now people interested in purchasing folhetos the world over. While other nations have traditions of literatura de cordel, most notably Chile, the genre is almost universally recognized as Brazilian.

In regard to these general characteristics, literatura de cordel recalls the corrido broadsheet. However, some investigators see not only the Iberian romance as a primary source, but also the European chapbook tradition. As the pioneering researcher of this genre explains, literatura de cordel represents "stories in verse [and] the world's richest and most varied heirs to a centuries-old ballad and chapbook tradition once embracing most of Europe."[109] Moreover, literatura de cordel began in earnest in the mid-nineteenth century, when an influx of capital in rural Brazil (thanks in part to the relocation of American cotton producers who wished to continue using slaves) made the purchase of manual presses possible. This mid-nineteenth century origin is yet another point of comparision with the Mexican corrido.

However, whereas the corrido represents a clear example of what was once an oral tradition, with generations of musicians who played what they composed and never committed their lyrics to the printed page, the Brazilian literatura de cordel is more closely associated with printed, popular verse—even though many poets often sell their texts by reading or singing their works in front of their place of business. Singing cordel poets and vendors are known as *repentistas* (related to the Portuguese noun *repente*, meaning "burst" or "gust").[110] It is also true that folheto poets often read to one another, in much the same manner as Argentine *payadores* exchanging verses, employing a style of recitation known as *toada*. While reciting the toada, the poets utilize a particular type of chant (which at times sounds similar to rap) that permits the voice to carry farther. Nevertheless, "a number of today's . . . authors have never performed aloud their own or other's verses" and "[t]oday the practice of reading *folhetos* aloud is less common . . . [still occurring] however, in the South and in smaller Northeastern fairs."[111] Examples of the genre are found throughout Brazil, but most investigators feel that the folheto originated in the northeastern coastal states of Pernambuco, Paraíba, Rio Grande do Norte, and Ceará.[112]

Clearly, the investigation of this genre of popular literature could focus on any number of topics: the poetry, the poet, its production/distribution, its oral recitation, or the distinctive graphic art of its cover. The subject material of these little books is generally stories and current events that greatly interest the masses. Folhetos draw heavily on the Bible, the lives of saints, and fairy tales and often venture into the *exemplum*—the medieval genre of literature that featured simple, engaging stories with a clearly illustrated moral, such as filial obedience or the importance of charity. "At heart, a *cordel* story is a moral question whose answer becomes evident through a largely ritual narrative process."[113] The relationship to medieval literature is an important distinguishing characteristic of the folheto.[114] Two reasons for this persistence of medieval stories and forms could be the considerable isolation of the Brazilian Northeast from the southern *litoral* metropolises (where new trends are imported and produced), and the fact that most of the first major colonial centers (Fortaleza, Recife, Pernambuco), as well as the capital (Salvador), were located in the Northeast. When the colonial center moved south in the middle of the eighteenth century, one result was the petrification of some aspects of the Northeastern culture that had been imported there in the sixteenth century.

Literatura de cordel can also be instructional, teaching readers how to accomplish certain jobs or how to have a happier household. In recent years the Brazilian government has utilized the folheto to promote programs such as AIDS and sexually transmitted disease prevention, traffic safety, and political awareness.[115] Often they provide the latest news stories, which, when adapted to popular tastes by the poet and occasionally crafted to highlight a particular moral, become a fascinating synthesis of journalism and fiction. New and interesting folhetos appeared, for example, shortly after the 9/11 terrorist attacks in New York City and Washington, D.C.[116] In the course of her extensive research, Candace Slater discovered that folheto poets and the people that sell their work often market their texts to particular audiences. In what could be something of a blueprint for popular literature marketing the world over, she noted that "[o]ld women, for instance, are known to like prophecy and religious themes; young men favor adventure stories and plenty of humor; teenage girls prefer tales of love and suffering."[117]

To the extent that this genre of popular literature has been co-opted by privileged classes, or to the degree in which it is an authentic expression of the people, we see that many of the same factors that influenced the production and distribution of the Mexican corrido are in evidence here. Mark Dinneen, in his study of popular culture in the northeastern region of Brazil, notes that the literatura de cordel developed in an "area of conflict" created by the dominant classes, which seek "to appropriate popular cultural practices and expressions and incorporate them into a broad scheme of national culture," and the popular classes, which resist by means of the "social forces behind their practices and expressions."[118] Within this arena of conflict, the individuals who have had an interest in controlling the popular classes have been known to read selected texts to their largely illiterate workers, and through these means maintain a controlling hand in agricultural production, as well as an unofficial censorship.[119] But when the most disaffected classes choose to be entertained, it is their particular worldview that must be reflected in their literature, and in this literatura de cordel has been and continues to be very successful. It would be fair to say that throughout its history the folheto has been more consistently produced by the people for the people than many other forms of popular literature. Slater notes that while some of the most successful poets come from relatively privileged households, the vast majority trace their roots to the "subsistence farmer class."[120]

The first and perhaps greatest folheto poet, Leandro Gomes de Barros (1868–1918), grew up in Teixeira (Paraíba), where as a boy he listened to the narrative ballads of popular singers. More than a thousand different folhetos are attributed to Gomes de Barros.[121] Possibly the best-selling example of literatura de cordel is *O Pavão Misterioso* [The Mysterious Peacock] by João Melquíades Ferreira, which tells the story of two lovers who, recalling Shakespeare's *Romeo and Juliet*, are not permitted to marry because of the girl's father. When the young man obtains an incredible mechanical peacock, he whisks her away and they elope. Another famous folheto, *Côco Verde e Melancia* [Green Coconut and Watermelon] by José Camelo de Melo Resende, narrates the romantic adventures of a couple named Watermelon and Green Coconut.

The narratives of cordel literature often feature a predictable, six-step structure, not unlike the recurring structure of the folktale.[122] First, the story begins with "a state of *harmony* (1)" where moral and material obligations are met; the *test* (2) occurs when a character is challenged and the initial harmony is in danger of being disrupted; the character's *response* (3) follows, and it may be "right or wrong"; this response generally elicits a *counterresponse* (4) from another character; the climax of the narrative is achieved with the judgment (5), "when right is rewarded and wrong punished"; finally there is a *reaffirmation* (6) of the original harmony.[123] Divine intervention, beneficent or misguided monarchs, and great disparities between rich and poor are common situations. By working with such exemplary characters and exaggerated situations, the texts are able to convey morality much more forcefully. "*Cordel* stories deal with values as much as or more than facts, acting not as a mirror but as a purposely distorted lens designed to create a particular vision."[124]

Another common topic of cordel literature is the social bandit. Like Robin Hood, the social bandit steals from the wealthy and, if not giving everything to the poor, usually manages to win their admiration in a region where there is little law and order. Of all the social bandits who have operated in Brazil, undoubtedly the most famous is Lampião (Virgolino Ferreira da Silva, 1898–1938), who eluded the authorities for nearly two decades until he was hunted down and killed in northeastern Brazil. *Lampião no inferno* [Lampião in Hell] by José Pacheco describes some of Lampião's greatest exploits and escapes; countless other folhetos have depicted his childhood and his demise and have even speculated on his activities in the afterlife. As noted earlier in the description of the corrido and narcocorrido, bandits and outlaws as subject matter constitute one of the most common themes of all popular literature.

Only in the past few decades has the simple, attractive artwork of folheto covers begun to attract much attention. Using nothing more than woodblocks and knives, the cordel artists (many of whom are poets) create lasting, distinctive images that can sell for less than $10 in the market but for several hundred dollars in the United States or Europe. The most famous living artist, José Francisco Borges (b. 1935), of Bezzeros (Pernambuco), has seen his art exhibited in the Louvre and the Smithsonian Institution.[125] Today literatura de cordel is no longer frowned upon by the intellectuals and privileged classes of the metropolis. Although some point to foreign fascination with the genre for its widening appeal, the little books and artwork are sold throughout the largest cities of Brazil.

Now that esteem for the folheto has crossed class and cultural boundaries, some of the inventive nature of the genre has been lost; many folhetos are now mass-produced for sale to tourists, and some can even be purchased online. Even one of the folheto's original purposes—providing the latest news to the mostly illiterate population living in the vast, relatively inaccessible Northeast—has become largely unnecessary because of increased literacy and the advent of more sophisticated communication technology. Nevertheless, the popular preference for news presented in an appealing fashion has not become outdated. In Slater's words:

> The *cordel's* transformation or, in some cases, disappearance, for instance, cannot be credited exclusively or even primarily to competition from the mass media. Radio and television per se have not affected the course of popular poetry as much as have the larger social and economic changes of which they are both agent and reflection. Indeed, the great majority of new *cordel* stories in both the Northeast and the South are based on journalistic themes gleaned in part from newspapers, radio, and television.[126]

In spite of the advent of communication technology and more reliable means of keeping informed of world events, the future of literatura de cordel, as well as of popular literature in general, seems bright. Like the Peruvian woman who upbraided Ariel Dorfman, we do not always look to literature for self-improvement or to learn the latest news, but simply to be entertained. While the story found in a folheto (or in a photonovel, popular novel, or comic book) may seem predictable or even hackneyed to some, "[t]he fact that a reader knows that good will triumph does not diminish his interest in the particulars of the struggle, which serves to reaffirm a spiritual order, of which most persons find little proof in daily life. . . . The folheto appeals to the buyer largely because it offers him a world at once familiar and happily different from the one he knows."[127] In other words, popular literature was never intended to be a mirror of society, but rather a rose-colored lens through which people could see their reality in a much more entertaining and reaffirming manner. Curiel de Fossé tells his reader that to admit that the photonovel is an opium for the masses, rather than napalm, represents a significant improvement in terms of its reception.[128] Rather than condemnation, popular literature perhaps deserves more in the way of objective scholarship and assessment, particularly because its finest examples are so highly compelling. To learn about a people, an investigator can do no better than to look at what they actually read.

# RESOURCE GUIDE

## PRINT SOURCES

Accorsi, Andrés. "Argentine Comics: History." Pp. 25–46 in John A. Lent (ed.), *Cartooning in Latin America*. Cresskill, NJ: Hampton Press, Inc., 2005.

Anderson Imbert, Enrique. *Spanish American Literature: A History.* Translated by James V. Falconieri. Detroit: Wayne State University Press, 1963.

Appendini, Guadalupe. "A manera de prólogo." Pp. v–viii in Gabriel Vargas, *La familia Burrón*, Vol.1. México, D.F.: Editorial Porrúa, 2000.

Barriga, Patricio, and Rodrigo Villacis. *Fotonovela.* Technical Note 13. Amherst, MA: Center for International Education, University of Massachusetts, n.d.

Barros-Lémez, Álvaro. "Los orígenes del folletín." Pp. 71–90 in *Paralaje y circo: ensayos sobre sociedad, cultura y comunicación*. Montevideo, Uruguay: Monte Sexto, S.R.L., 1987.

————. "Algunas reflexiones acerca de la influencia de las historietas." Pp. 179–187 in *Paralaje y circo: ensayos sobre sociedad, cultura y comunicación.* Montevideo, Uruguay: Monte Sexto, S.R.L. 1987.

Bartra, Armando, and Gisela Gil-Egui. "Dawn, Noon, and Dusk of a Tumultuous Narrative: The Evolution of Mexican Comic Art." Pp. 253–278 in John A. Lent (ed.), *Cartooning in Latin America.* Cresskill, NJ: Hampton Press, Inc., 2005.

Batista, Sebastião Nunes. *Antologia da literatura de cordel.* Natal, Brazil: Fundaçião José Augusto, 1977.

Beezley, William H. *Judas at the Jockey Club and Other Episodes of Porfirian Mexico.* Lincoln: University of Nebraska Press, 1987.

————, and Linda A. Curcio-Nagy, eds. *Latin American Popular Culture: An Introduction.* Wilmington, DE: Scholarly Resources, Inc., 2000.

Brunori, Vittorio. *Sueños y mitos de la literatura de las masas. Análisis crítico de la novela popular.* Translated by Joan Giner. Barcelona: Editorial Gustavo Gili, S.A., 1980.

Bueno, Eva P., and Terry Caesar, eds. *Imagination Beyond Nation: Latin American Popular Culture.* Pittsburgh: University of Pittsburgh Press, 1998.

Burns, E. Bradford. *A History of Brazil,* 3rd edition. New York: Columbia University Press, 1995.

Butler Flora, Cornelia. "The *Fotonovela* in Latin America." *Studies in Latin American Popular Culture* 1 (1982): 15–26.

————. "Photonovels." Pp. 891–892 in Harold E. Hinds, Jr., and Charles M. Tatum (eds.), *Handbook of Latin American Popular Culture.* Westport, CT: Greenwood Press, 1985.

Castañeda, Daniel. *El corrido mexicano. Su técnica literaria y musical.* México, D.F.: Editorial Surco, 1943.

Coutinho, Afrânio. *An Introduction to Literature in Brazil.* Translated by Gregory Rabassa. New York: Columbia University Press, 1969.

Curiel de Fossé, Fernando. *Fotonovela rosa/fotonovela roja. Textos de difusión cultural, Serie Diagonal.* México, D.F.: UNAM, [1978] 1990.

Curran, Mark J. *Literatura de cordel.* Recife: Universidade Federal de Pernambuco, 1973.

Da Silva, Nadilson Manoel. "Brazilian Adult Comics: The Age of Market." Pp. 101–118 in John A. Lent (ed.), *Cartooning in Latin America.* Cresskill, NJ: Hampton Press, Inc., 2005.

Dinneen, Mark. *Listening to the People's Voice: Erudite and Popular Literature in North East Brazil.* New York: Kegan Paul International, 1996.

Dorfman, Ariel. *The Emperor's Old Clothes: What the Lone Ranger, Babar, and Other Innocent Heroes Do to Our Minds.* Translated by Clark Hansen. New York: Pantheon Books, 1983.

Foster, David William. *From Mafalda to los Supermachos: Latin American Graphic Humor as Popular Culture.* Boulder, CO: Lynne Rienner Publishers, 1989.

Franco, Jean. *An Introduction to Spanish-American Literature.* London: Cambridge University Press, 1969.

————. "What's in a Name?: Popular Culture Theories and Their Limitations." Pp. 169–180 in Mary Louis Pratt and Kathleen Newman (eds.), *Critical Passions. Selected Essays.* Durham, NC: Duke University Press, 1999.

Frank, Patrick. *Posada's Broadsheets: Mexican Popular Imagery, 1890–1910.* Albuquerque: University of New Mexico Press, 1998.

Gamboa, Fernando. "José Guadalupe Posada: The Man. His Art. His Times." In *Posada: Printmaker to the Mexican People.* Chicago: Lakeside Press, 1944. Accessed August 8, 2005. http://muertos. palomar.edu/posada/posadalife.html.

García Canclini, Néstor. *Hybrid Cultures: Strategies for Entering and Leaving Modernity.* Translated by Christopher L. Chiappari and Silvia L. López. Minneapolis: University of Minnesota Press, 1997.

Galeano, Eduardo, and José Francisco Borges. *Walking Words.* Translated by Mark Fried. New York: Norton, 1997.

Goidanich, Hiron Cardoso. *Enciclopédia dos quadrinhos.* Porto Alegre: L&162, 1990.

Gretton, Thomas. "Posada and the Popular: Commodities and Social Constructs in Mexico before the Revolution." *Oxford Art Journal* 17.2 (1994): 32–47.

Hernández, Guillermo E., ed. *The Mexican Revolution: Corridos about the Heroes and Events 1910–1920 and Beyond! A Four CD Set.* Accompanying book. El Cerrito, CA: Arhoolie Folklyric, 1996.

Hinds, Harold E., Jr. "Comics." Pp. 81–110 in Harold E. Hinds, Jr., and Charles M. Tatum (eds.), *Handbook of Latin American Popular Culture*. Westport, CT: Greenwood Press, 1985.

———, and Charles M. Tatum, eds. 1985. *Handbook of Latin American Popular Culture*. Westport, CT: Greenwood Press.

———, and Charles M. Tatum. *Not Just for Children: The Mexican Comic Book in the late 1960s and 1970s*. Westport, CT: Greenwood Press, 1992.

Irwin, Robert McKee, Edward J. McCaughan, and Michelle Rocío Nasser, eds. *The Famous 41: Sexuality and Social Control in Mexico, c. 1901*. New York: Palgrave MacMillan, 2003.

King, John, ed. *The Cambridge Companion to Latin American Culture*. Cambridge, UK: Cambridge University Press, 2004.

Knight, Alan. *The Mexican Revolution*, 2 vols. Lincoln: University of Nebraska Press, 1986.

Lara, Jesús, ed. and trans. *Quechua People's Poetry*. Translators Maria E. Posner and James Scully. Willimantic, CT: Curbstone Press, 1986.

Lent, John A. "Latin American Comic Art: an Overview." Pp. 1–24 in John A. Lent (ed.), *Cartooning in Latin America*. Cresskill, NJ: Hampton Press, Inc., 2005.

López Casillas, Mercurio. *José Guadalupe Posada, Ilustrador de cuadernos populares*. Mexico City: Editorial RM, 2003.

Lowenthal, Leo. *Literature, Popular Culture, and Society*. Palo Alto, CA: Pacific Books, 1961.

Ludmer, Josefina. *The Gaucho Genre: A Treatise on the Motherland*. Translated by Molly Weigel. Durham: Duke University Press, 2002.

Malvido, Adriana. "La industria de la historieta mexicana o el floreciente negocio de las emociones." *Revista mexicana de comunicación* (Sept.-Oct. 1989). Accessed September 12, 2005. http://www.mexicanadecomunicacion.com.mx/Tables/FMB/foromex/industria.html.

Mariño Solano, Germán. *Fotonovelas. Una aproximación desde los cuentos de hadas y el melodrama*. Bogotá: Enda América Latina, 1990.

McDowell, John H. *Poetry and Violence: The Ballad Tradition of Mexico's Costa Chica*. Urbana-Champaign: University of Illinois Press, 2000.

Mendoza, Vicente T. *El romance español y el corrido mexicano*. México, D.F.: UNAM, 1939.

———. *El corrido mexicano*. México, D.F.: FCE, [1954] 1984.

———. *El corrido de la Revolución mexicana*. México, D.F.: INEHRM, 1956.

———. *Glosas y décimas de México*. México, D.F.: FCE, [1957] 1995.

Meyer, Jean. "Revolution and Reconstruction in the 1920s." Pp. 201–240 in Leslie Bethell (ed.), *The Cambridge History of Latin America: Mexico Since Independence*. New York: Cambridge University Press, 1991.

Minc, Rose S., ed. *Literature and Popular Culture in the Hispanic World: A Symposium*. Gaithersburg, MD: Ediciones Hispamérica and Monclair State College, 1981.

Monsiváis, Carlos. *Mexican Postcards*. Translated by John Kraniauskas. London: Verso, 1997.

Paredes, Américo. *With a Pistol in His Hand: A Border Ballad and Its Hero*. Austin: University of Texas Press, [1958] 2000.

———. *A Texas-Mexican Cancionero. Folksongs of the Lower Border*. Austin: University of Texas Press, [1976] 1995.

———, and Richard Bauman, eds. *Toward New Perspectives in Folklore*. Reprint, Bloomington, IN: Trickster Press, [1972] 2000.

Pilcher, Jeffrey M. "Many Chefs in the National Kitchen: Cookbooks and Identity in Nineteenth-Century Mexico." Pp. 123–141 in William H. Beezley and Linda A. Curcio-Nagy (eds.), *Latin American Popular Culture: An Introduction*. Wilmington, DE: Scholarly Resources, Inc., 2000.

Rodríguez Demorizi, Emilio. *Poesía popular dominicana*. Santo Domingo, Dominican Republic: UCMM, 1973.

Rubenstein, Anne. *Bad Language, Naked Ladies, and Other Threats to the Nation: a Political History of Comic Books in Mexico*. Durham, NC: Duke University Press, 1998.

Sandoval, Juan Ventura. "La literatura culta y la literatura popular: Regiones en desencuento." Pp. 71–82 in *México: Literaturas regionales y nación*. Xalapa, Veracruz, Mexico: Universidad Veracruzana, 1999.

Scott, James C. *Domination and the Arts of Resistance: Hidden Transcripts.* New Haven, CT: Yale University Press, 1990.

Secchia, Ofelia, and Carlos Alberto Moyano, eds. *Argentina—poética gauchesca: antología de la poesía y refranero gauchesco.* Buenos Aires: Docente, 1984.

Simmons, Merle E. *The Mexican Corrido as a Source for Interpretive Study of Modern Mexico (1870–1950).* Bloomington: University of Indiana Press, 1957.

Slater, Candace. *Stories on a String: The Brazilian Literatura de Cordel.* Berkeley: University of California Press, [1982] 1989.

Sommer, Doris. *Foundational Fictions: the National Romances of Latin America.* Berkeley: University of California Press, 1991.

Spina, Vincent. "'Useless Spaces' of the Feminine in Popular Culture: *Like Water for Chocolate* and *The Silent War.*" Pp. 210–226 in Eva P. Bueno and Terry Caesar (eds.), *Imagination Beyond Nation: Latin American Popular Culture.* Pittsburgh: University of Pittsburgh Press, 1998.

Tyler, Ron, ed. *Posada's Mexico.* Washington, DC: Library of Congress/Amon Carter Museum of Western Art, 1979.

Ubidia, Abdón, Mario Razzeto, et al. *Poesía popular andina: Ecuador, Perú, Bolivia, Chile.* Vol. 2. N.p.: IADAP., 1982.

UNESCO. *UNESCO Statistical Yearbook 1999.* Montreal: UNESCO Institute for Statistics, 1999.

Vergueiro, Waldomiro C. S. "Brazilian Superheroes in Search of Their Own Identities." Pp. 119–132 in John A. Lent (ed.), *Cartooning in Latin America.* Cresskill, NJ: Hampton Press, Inc., 2005a.

———. "Brazilian Pornographic Comics: Eroticism in the World of Carlos Zéfiro." Pp. 133–142 in John A. Lent (ed.), *Cartooning in Latin America.* Cresskill, NJ: Hampton Press, Inc., 2005b.

Wald, Elijah. *Narcocorrido: A Journey into the Music of Drugs, Guns, and Guerrillas.* New York: HarperCollins, 2001.

Williamson, Edwin. *The Penguin History of Latin America.* London: Penguin Press, 1991.

## WEBSITES

ABGRA. *Access to Information in Latin America. Workshop Seminar. National Report: Argentina.* 1999. Asociación de Bibliotecarios Graduados de la República Argentina. Accessed January 7, 2007. http://www.ifla.org/VI/2/conf/argentina-e.pdf.

Cabás, Ramiro. *Martín Fierro: El Libro.* Accessed August 16, 2006. http://webs.satlink.com/usuarios/c/cabas/mfierro/mfierro.htm. Complete text of the Argentine epic by José Hernández.

*CCQ Humor.* Accessed August 10, 2006. http://www.ccqhumor.com.br/index.htm. An extensive Website featuring articles about and samples of Brazilian comic books, including the work of Carlos Zéfiro.

De Moya, Álvaro. "Historias en Viñetas." Accessed August 14, 2005. http://www.mre.gov.br/cdbrasil/itamaraty/web/espanhol/comunica/quadrin/apresent/apresent.htm. A good survey of Brazilian cartooning and comic books.

*Emiliano Zapata, 1909-1919.* Accessed August 15, 2006. http://members.tripod.com/~pacogaray/. A comprehensive Website with dozens of corridos written about the Mexican revolutionary.

*Kalimán; El hombre increíble. Official Site.* Accessed August 12, 2005. http://www.kaliman.net/. Includes history, trivia, forums, and artwork from popular issues.

"Lira popular o literatura de cordel." *Nuestro.cl. El sitio del patrimonio cultural chileno.* Accessed September 10, 2005. http://www.nuestro.cl/biblioteca/textos/lira/lira.htm. Outstanding site dedicated to the Chilean tradition of this popular literature.

Pulido, Marcelo. *Historieteca: Historieta argentina.* Accessed July 20, 2006. http://www.historieteca.com.ar/historieteca.htm. A comprehensive site with information on Argentina's rich comic book tradition; also has dates and locations of conventions.

University of New Mexico Library. *Mexican Popular Prints: José Guadalupe Posada.* Accessed August 17, 2005. http://elibrary.unm.edu/posada/. An excellent resource for viewing Posada's turn-of-the-century broadsheets.

Victtor, J., and Paula Schuabb. *Academia Brasiliera de Literatura de Cordel.* Accessed September 16, 2005. http://www.ablc.com.br/. Outstanding site with much information about cordel.

# NOTES

1. Dorfman 1983 (in Resource Guide, Print Sources), pp. 3–4.
2. Franco 1999 (in Resource Guide, Print Sources), p. 179.
3. See, for example, C. Hugh Holman and William Harmon's *A Handbook to Literature*, 6th ed. (New York: MacMillan, 1992), p. 368: "Writing in one of the commercially viable modes, especially prose fiction. This literature is valued on a strictly quantitative basis—number of copies sold."
4. Vivian Schelling has recently discussed the nature of popular culture in an illuminating manner by dividing the subject into three main approaches: popular culture as folklore, as "mass" culture, and finally as a medium utilized in power relations. See her chapter "Popular Culture in Latin America" in King 2004 (in Resource Guide, Print Sources), pp. 171–201.
5. "Este corrido quizá ésto sólo bueno tiene: del alma del pueblo viene y al alma del pueblo va." From "The Corrido of Ortiz Rubio," composed by E.G. Sandoval and performed by La Bella Netty and Jesús Rodríguez (recorded San Antonio, Texas, March 1930, Vocalion 8325) and cited in Hernández 1996 (in Resource Guide, Print Sources), p. 141.
6. Franco 1999 (in Resource Guide, Print Sources), p. 177.
7. Pilcher 2000 (in Resource Guide, Print Sources), pp. 126–127.
8. As of 1998 Brazil accounted for 54 percent of the total book production in the Latin American region, according to CERLACL (Regional Center for the Promotion of Books and Reading in Latin America and the Caribbean). The production of the remaining, Spanish-speaking nations is presented in pie graph form in ABGRA 1999 (in Resource Guide, Websites), p. 6.
9. Williamson 1991 (in Resource Guide, Print Sources), p. 149.
10. Anderson Imbert 1963 (in Resource Guide, Print Sources), p. 146.
11. Important examples include Rubén M. Campos's *El folklore literario y musical de México* (Mexico City: Secretaría de Educación Pública, 1929), and the studies of the corrido by Castañeda (1943) and Mendoza (1939, [1954] 1984, 1956, [1957] 1995) listed in the Resource Guide.
12. Hinds and Tatum 1985 (in Resource Guide, Print Sources), p. xi.
13. United Nations Development Programme, *Human Development Report* (2004).
14. United Nations, *Statistical Yearbook* (2003–04), pp. 92–93.
15. UNESCO 1999 (in Resource Guide, Print Sources), p. IV-20.
16. Ibid., p. IV-40.
17. Ibid., p. IV-58.
18. The Universal Decimal Classification (UDC) is the world's foremost multilingual classification scheme for all fields of knowledge. See UDC Consortium, *About Universal Decimal Classification and the UDC Consortium,* http://www.udcc.org/about.htm.
19. UNESCO 1999 (in Resource Guide, Print Sources), p. IV-92.
20. UNESCO 1999 (in Resource Guide, Print Sources), pp. IV-138–IV-140.
21. See Iosif Landau, "How I Wrote a [*sic*] (Almost) Bestseller at 70," *Brazzil Magazine* (2002, November 1). Accessed January 7, 2007. http://www.brazzil.com/content/view/7049.
22. ABGRA 1999 (in Resource Guide, Websites), p. 13.
23. Euromonitor International. Accessed August 15, 2005. http://www.euromonitor.com/Books_and_Publishing_in_Mexico.
24. Slater [1982] 1989 (in Resource Guide, Print Sources), p. 4.
25. Mendoza [1954] 1984 (in Resource Guide, Print Sources), p. ix.
26. Mendoza, for example, writes that under normal circumstances, when the *corridista* can freely perform, his poetry represents "the most genuine expression of the people's feelings" (Mendoza 1956, in Resource Guide, Print Sources, p. 9). Merle E. Simmons, the American scholar who has written the most comprehensive study of the corrido to date, writes that, more than a "significant historical document," the corrido reflects "with a high degree of fidelity what the *pueblo*" is thinking at a given historical moment (Simmons 1957, in Resource Guide, Print Sources, pp. 36–37).
27. Mendoza [1957] 1995 (in Resource Guide, Print Sources), p. 7.

28. Castañeda 1943 (in Resource Guide, Print Sources), p. 12.

29. Mendoza [1954] 1984 (in Resource Guide, Print Sources), p. xiv.

30. Paredes [1958] 2000 (in Resource Guide, Print Sources), p. 129.

31. Mendoza [1954] 1984 (in Resource Guide, Print Sources), pp. xxxv–xlii.

32. Knight 1986 (in Resource Guide, Print Sources), p. 41.

33. Meyer 1991 (in Resource Guide, Print Sources), p. 208.

34. Scott 1990 (in Resource Guide, Print Sources), pp. 71–73.

35. Carlos Cedeño, "Don Antonio Vanegas Arroyo: Voz e imagen del pueblo mexicano," *El Gallo Ilustrado* (Sunday supplement to *El Día*) (1980, March 9): 6.

36. The social bandit is a Robin Hood figure who often comes to embody popular disaffection before or during a social or political revolution. The best examination of the social bandit belongs to historian Eric J. Hobsbawm in his seminal study, *Primitive Rebels: Studies in Archaic Forms of Social Movement in the 19th and 20th Centuries* (New York: Norton, 1965), pp. 13–28.

37. Scott 1990 (in Resource Guide, Print Sources), pp. 140, 160.

38. Chris Strachwitz, "A History of Commercial Recordings of Corridos," in Hernández 1996 (in Resource Guide, Print Sources), pp. 15–16.

39. During the San Antonio, Texas, recording of the famous blues musician Robert Johnson (1910?–38), there were two Mexican *conjuntos* (music groups)—Hermanas Barraza con guitarras and Andrés Berlanga y Francisco Montalvo—and the singer Eva Garza, scheduled to make recordings during the same ten-day period, November 21–30, 1937.

40. Strachwitz, "A History of Commercial Recordings of Corridos" (see n. 38), p. 16.

41. Outstanding examples of the corrido culto include Francisco Castillo Nájera's "El gavilán (corrido culto)" (1939), Daniel Castañeda's "Gran corrido a la Virgen de Guadalupe" (1941), and Celedonio Serrano Martínez's "El coyote: Corrido de México" (1951). The authors of these last two examples were notable scholars of the corrido and of folklore.

42. Wald 2001 (in Resource Guide, Print Sources), p. 14.

43. The "three animals," a recurring symbol of the narcocorrido, represent the three major drugs smuggled into the United States: the parakeet (cocaine), the rooster (marijuana) and the goat (heroin). Wald 2001 (in Resource Guide, Print Sources), p. 28.

44. See http://www.chicano.ucla.edu/research/lostigres.html.

45. See http://www.hispaniconline.com/hh03/mainpages/culture/music_tigres.html.

46. Wald 2001 (in Resource Guide, Print Sources), p. 4.

47. Anderson Imbert 1963 (in Resource Guide, Print Sources), p. 78.

48. Sommer 1991 (in Resource Guide, Print Sources), pp. 6–7. Conversely, the detective novel is not nearly as prevalent in Latin America; the spy novel is even more unusual. This may be because of a pervasive skepticism in the state's ability to establish law and order, and the lack of a tradition of foreign involvement or imperialism as seen in the nations that have produced the most spy novels: England and the United States. The relative infrequency of the fantasy or science fiction novel in Latin America may have something to do with the prevalence of such literary tendencies as magical realism, but this is purely speculative.

49. Brunori 1980 (in Resource Guide, Print Sources), p. 45.

50. Sandoval 1999 (in Resource Guide, Print Sources), p. 81.

51. It is worth mentioning that some scholars view the Brazilian Nuno Marqués Pereira's text, *Compêndio narrativo do peregrino en América* (1728), as the first Latin American novel. See, for example, Eugenio Chang-Rodríguez's *Latinoamérica: su civilización y cultura*, 3rd edition (Boston: Heinle, 2000): 111.

52. Sommer 1991 (in Resource Guide, Print Sources), p. 274.

53. Anderson Imbert 1963 (in Resource Guide, Print Sources), p. 311.

54. Burns 1995 (in Resource Guide, Print Sources), pp. 111, 115.

55. See Consulate General of Brazil, San Francisco, *Literature*. Accessed January 8, 2007. http://www.brazilsf.org/culture_literature_eng.htm.

56. José de Alencar, *O nosso cancioneiro, Cartas ao Sr. Joaquim Serra* (Rio de Janeiro: Livaria São José, 1962).

57. Coutinho 1969 (in Resource Guide, Print Sources), p. 145.
58. Sommer 1991 (in Resource Guide, Print Sources), pp. 140–41.
59. Ibid., p. 144.
60. From the prefatory notes of *Cacau* (Rio de Janeiro: Ariel, 1933). Cited in Bobby J. Chamberlain's *Jorge Amado* (Boston: Twayne, 1990), pp. 23–24.
61. *Dona Flor e seus dois maridos* was later remade as a Hollywood film, *Kiss Me Goodbye* (1982), which starred Sally Field and James Caan.
62. Slater [1982] 1989 (in Resource Guide, Print Sources), pp. 148–49.
63. See *Sitio Oficial Paulo Coelho*. Accessed January 8, 2007. http://www.paulocoelho.com/espa/des.shtml.
64. Although an exact translation is impossible, the saying *Como agua para chocolate* refers to the process of cooking pure chocolate over flame and, in the instant it is about to burn, sprinkling some water on it to cool it off and give it a liquid consistency. The expression could be used whenever problems or (in the case of the novel) sexual passion reaches an intolerable point and must be resolved or alleviated in some way.
65. Pilcher 2000 (in Resource Guide, Print Sources), p. 124.
66. For a history of liberation theology, see Leonardo and Clodovis Boff, *A Concise History of Liberation Theology*. Accessed January 8, 2007. http://www.landreform.org/boff2.htm.
67. See Paul J. Underwood, *The Power of God against the Guns of Government: Religious Upheaval in Mexico at the Turn of the Nineteenth Century* (Stanford, CA: Stanford University Press, 1998), p. 56.
68. Butler Flora 1985 (in Resource Guide, Print Sources), p. 151.
69. Ibid.
70. Curiel de Fossé [1978] 1990 (in Resource Guide, Print Sources), pp. 29–31.
71. Butler Flora 1985 (in Resource Guide, Print Sources), p. 152.
72. Mariño Solano 1990 (in Resource Guide, Print Sources), p. 99.
73. Butler Flora 1985 (in Resource Guide, Print Sources), p. 153.
74. Mariño Solano 1990 (in Resource Guide, Print Sources), p. 100.
75. Curiel de Fossé [1978] 1990 (in Resource Guide, Print Sources), pp. 43–46.
76. Ibid., p. 100.
77. Ibid., p. 22.
78. Vergueiro 2005a (in Resource Guide, Print Sources), p. 120.
79. Hinds and Tatum 1992 (in Resource Guide, Print Sources), p. 10.
80. Malvido 1989 (in Resource Guide, Print Sources).
81. Rubenstein 1998 (in Resource Guide, Print Sources), p. 8.
82. Ibid., pp. 3–4.
83. Frank 1998 (in Resource Guide, Print Sources), p. 194.
84. Rubenstein 1998 (in Resource Guide, Print Sources), p. 18.
85. Lent 2005 (in Resource Guide, Print Sources), p. 1.
86. Hinds and Tatum 1992 (in Resource Guide, Print Sources), p. 3.
87. Bartra and Gil-Egui 2005 (in Resource Guide, Print Sources), p. 257.
88. Rubenstein 1998 (in Resource Guide, Print Sources), p. 2.
89. Hinds and Tatum 1992 (in Resource Guide, Print Sources), pp. 3–4.
90. Ibid., p. 34.
91. Ibid., p. 33.
92. Malvido 1989 (in Resource Guide, Print Sources).
93. Hinds and Tatum 1992 (in Resource Guide, Print Sources), p. 161.
94. Appendini 2000 (in Resource Guide, Print Sources), p. viii.
95. Lent 2005 (in Resource Guide, Print Sources), p. 17.
96. See James C. McKinley, Jr., "New Racial Gaffe in Mexico; This Time It's a Tasteless Stamp Set," *The New York Times* (2005, June 30).
97. Accorsi 2005 (in Resource Guide, Print Sources).
98. See the series of illustrations at La Historieta Argentina, *Alberto Breccia*. Accessed January 8, 2007. http://www.buchmesse.de/comic-argentina/ebrecciaf.htm#1.

99. Lent 2005 (in Resource Guide, Print Sources), p. 17.

100. Ibid., p. 7.

101. Ibid.

102. Da Silva 2005 (in Resource Guide, Print Sources), p. 102.

103. Ibid., pp. 105–6, 110.

104. Ibid., p. 112.

105. Ibid., p. 117.

106. Michael Dobran, "Pow! Wow! The Spirit of Brazil," *Brazzil Magazine* (2003, June). Accessed January 8, 2007. http://brazzil.com/2003/html/news/articles/jun03/p141jun03.htm.

107. Slater [1982] 1989 (in Resource Guide, Print Sources), p. 26.

108. Ibid., p. 7.

109. Ibid., p. xxi.

110. Ibid., p. 273.

111. Ibid., pp. xix, 29.

112. Slater writes (ibid., p. 9): "No one knows exactly when, in what quantity, and under what conditions these booklets entered colonial Brazil. It is probable that they, like their Spanish counterparts, arrived with the first settlers, but this is difficult to prove. There is evidence that the Rio de Janeiro branch of the Livarie Garnier, one of the important publishers of the French chapbooks known as the *littérature de colportage*, began importing quantities of Portuguese pamphlet literature toward the middle of the nineteenth century. The old stories about Charlemagne, the Princess Magalona, and the Gambler Soldier were readily available to Brazilian readers at that time. Although it is likely that both oral and written versions of these stories circulated in Brazil much earlier, it is certain that the Northwestern *folheto* draws heavily on these nineteenth-century imports." See also Dinneen 1996 (in Resource Guide, Print Sources), pp. 18–26.

113. Slater [1982] 1989 (in Resource Guide, Print Sources), p. 216.

114. During a recent conversation with a Brazilian colleague, I was told that medieval verse could be sung to the standard melody of the repentista without any difficulty making the verses or meter fit.

115. See Larry Rohter, "The Troubadours of Brazil's Backlands," *New York Times* (2005, June14).

116. See Candace Slater, "Terror in the Twin Towers: The Events of September 11 in the Brazilian *Literatura do cordel*," *Latin American Research Review* 38.3 (2003, October): 37–59.

117. Slater [1982] 1989 (in Resource Guide, Print Sources), p. 29.

118. Dinneen 1996 (in Resource Guide, Print Sources), p. 14.

119. Slater [1982] 1989 (in Resource Guide, Print Sources), pp. 1–2.

120. Ibid., p. 23.

121. Ibid., p. 24.

122. The principal study of narrative structure in the folktale is Vladimir A. Propp's *Morphology of the Folktale* (Austin: University of Texas Press, 1968).

123. Slater [1982] 1989 (in Resource Guide, Print Sources), p. 59.

124. Ibid., p. 211.

125. Larry Rohter, "From Brazil's Backlands, a Master of a Folk Tradition," *New York Times* (2002, March 27).

126. Slater [1982] 1989 (in Resource Guide, Print Sources), p. xix.

127. Ibid., p. 216.

128. Curiel de Fossé [1978] 1990 (in Resource Guide, Print Sources), p. 19.

# LOVE, SEX, AND MARRIAGE

LINDA A. CURCIO-NAGY

Throughout history, marriage has been a defining moment for most individuals, marking their permanent entrance into adulthood. Men and women, socialized from an early age, expected to form unions and have children. The family became the institution that sheltered and supported the individual, serving as a buffer against the vicissitudes of life. Family also shaped individual behavior and conditioned his or her interaction with larger societal expectations. Sexual relations were obviously linked to marriage and the creation and strengthening of the family, but not necessarily so. Individuals viewed their sexual selves in unique ways that sometimes reflected societal norms and expectations regarding marriage and family. On other occasions, individuals sought to negotiate or deviate from established beliefs and customs. These norms in turn were affected by political, economic, and cultural changes that impacted the family and ideas about gender roles, sexuality, and marriage practices.

During the last 500 years, Latin America experienced profound changes that impacted all areas of society. Amerindian civilizations fought against and lost their battle against European invaders searching for riches, lands, and new converts. Indigenous and European values clashed, and the resultant conflicts fostered new traditions regarding marriage, sexuality, and the family. The nineteenth century ushered in independence without altering societal norms but devastated families, victims of constant political unrest. However, new perceptions, modes of production, and technologies and medicines would increasingly challenge traditions, behaviors, and societal norms dating from the colonial era. However, although definitions may adapt to changing circumstances, most Latin Americans see the family as the bulwark of their society.

## HISTORICAL INFLUENCES

Amerindian civilizations at the time of the arrival of Europeans were extremely diverse. They ranged from the highly organized Incan empire to the Aztec imperial confederation, the Mayan city-states, semi-sedentary Chichimec in northern Mexico, and the Tupi-Guarani in Brazil, among many others. Linguistically and culturally distinct, these civilizations were the latest in a long line of indigenous groups dating thousands of years before the birth of Christ. Given this tremendous diversity, it is difficult to provide a complete and thorough description of marriage and sexual customs for the pre-Hispanic era. In addition, archaeological remains, our primary source of information about pre-Columbian societies before 1500, shed very limited light on intimate customs and beliefs about marriage and sexuality. However, in the case of the Aztecs and the Incas, archaeological evidence has been augmented by information provided by Spanish and indigenous sources, albeit biased and impacted by Conquest events and issues. Although the information is incomplete, documents do provide a fascinating glimpse of the Aztec and Incan family.

## Gender Parallelism in Pre-European Times

Gender parallelism, a method of organizing religious and social elations in which the universe is divided into two interdependent sexually linked spheres, defined both Incan and Aztec society. Men and women were thought to have different tasks and roles, neither one necessarily subordinate to the other. Male and female were conceptualized into complementary forces that impacted all aspects of life. Deities were thought to have masculine and feminine characteristics, and one god could manifest multiple gender characteristics or manifestations. For example, Viracocha, the principal Andean god, had both male and female characteristics, and he produced a set of male and female deities who in turn created men and women. The Aztecs believed that an omnipotent couple, Ometeotl, created the gods, who then created humanity. All men and women viewed the gods as their ancestors and maintained a filial relationship to them. Continuing the inheritance pattern, men and women inherited properties and status along gender lines, women from their mothers, and men from their fathers. Religious ritual also was determined by parallelism. Both the Incas and the Aztecs had gender-specific religious specialists. In the Andes, women were dedicated to the worship of female deities. Under the Aztecs, temples were staffed by both male and female priests, but certain duties were specifically the domain of each sex.

Gender parallelism also impacted the political sphere as elite men and women ruled their respective gender realms. Under the Inca, the Coya (the sister/wife of the emperor) ruled over the empire's women and administered them with the aid of ranked female officials. In the case of the Aztecs, ruling noblemen and their wives appeared to share parallel terms of office. At the local kinship level (the *calpulli*), female officials administered the community activities of women.

Gender parallelism created highly distinct roles for men and women that were based on heterosexuality. Homosexuality during the pre-Hispanic period has been the subject of some study and speculation given the paucity of sources. In general, European accounts of indigenous sexuality are not reliable historical sources, because it was useful for Spaniards to label indigenous males as "sodomites" (sexually perverse) and "effeminate" in their rhetoric of conquest. Notwithstanding Spanish bias, pre-Columbian society in general does not appear to have prescribed alternative sexualities or to define sexuality in rigid terms. Homosexual activities were represented on pottery and other artifacts, although it is unclear whether these images depict actual (ritual) acts or the mythological actions of deities connected to masculinity and fertility (as most of the images focus on the phallus). At the time of the Conquest, European explorers claimed that they encountered men who dressed and acted as women. They may have witnessed the tradition later known as *berdache* among some indigenous peoples, in which select males took on the characteristics and gender of female as part of rituals or as a permanent transgender lifestyle. Clear prescriptions of homosexuality were only evident among the Aztecs.

## The Aztecs

Aztec commoners generally engaged in endogamy—that is, marriage within their calpulli, a group of apparently related individuals who shared rights and responsibilities, from specialized artisanal knowledge to rights to work certain lands. To the Aztecs, marriage was the natural state for men and women; so much emphasis was placed on marriage that men who were not married by their early twenties were mocked by their peers and neighbors. Sex was considered one of the most pleasurable aspects of life, when done in moderation; and, in particular, premarital sex was common unless a young person was dedicated to temple service. Virginity held no special place in Aztec society and, as a consequence, did not impact one's social status or suitability for marriage. Many couples formed consensual unions and officially married only after they had a child. However, the elite generally did not have sexual relations before marriage, in an effort to set themselves apart from commoners. However, elite males engaged in polygamy and could also have several concubines in addition to more than one official wife. These marriages formed alliances between different noble houses or ethnic groups, strengthened one's legitimacy and prestige, and expanded one's economic and political influence. Whether elite or commoner, divorce was possible in Aztec society; if such was mutually agreeable, the couple could split apart and the individuals could marry others.

The official marriage process itself was complex and involved a series of rituals and deliberations. The groom's parents approached the prospective bride's family and expressed their desire for a marriage between the families. In most cases, parents contacted an official matchmaker who knew all the families and individuals involved. The matchmaker also officiated at the ceremony, at which both the bride and the groom appeared in their finest garments. The bride's mother gave a cape and breechcloth to the groom, while the groom's mother gave the bride a shift (long tunic) and a skirt. The matchmaker tied together the shift and the cape. The couple then was escorted to a bedroom where they were placed in the beds. There they were to pray and fast for four days without moving. The matchmaker then searched the room looking for a sign of the viability of the union. If she found corn, it was a fortuitous marriage; coal foretold trouble that required more fasting, rituals, and if necessary, the dissolution of the proposed marriage.

Generally men married between 20 and 22 years of age. The bride was usually younger, averaging between 16 and 18 years. Most brides sought to marry slightly down on the social ladder, because they would then carry a more elevated status in the home of their mothers-in-law, as the newly married first resided in the groom's household compound. Most household compounds were joint residences shared by paternal families. For example, the families of an uncle and his nephew, the families of two brothers, or the families of a father and son would live together. Such joint residences could contain two to six nuclear families. After many years and many children, nuclear families might leave and build their own compound to live, for example, with their married son and his family. Thus, a young wife with limited status would spend many years under the tutelage of her husband's mother, aunt, or sister. Otherwise, a young woman could gain status in her household only after having four children.

Once married, a young couple's life revolved around several activities. Males concentrated on farming or the familial trade and serving the state in the Aztec army. Women worked in the home and sought to have at least four children. Women's activities complemented those of their husbands. Keeping hearth and farming were related activities cosmologically. Farming required slash-and-burn agricultural techniques, irrigation, and proper rituals to the fertility deities, especially Tlaloc, the god of rain. From tilling and planting, farmers called upon the fertility of the earth to sustain life. Household duties also had religious significance. Sweeping, weaving, and cooking were conceptualized as a cosmic battle in which wives waged war, because dirt and impurity upset the balance between order and chaos. From disorder—dirt, cotton threads, and unprocessed corn—wives created order—a clean house, woven material, and tortillas or corn dough for tamales. The ability to perform these daily tasks well reflected the piety, character, and sexual standing of women. For example, a woman with a reputation as a good cook was also seen as pious in her daily activity. Weaving in particular had sexual connotations, such that women renowned for weaving were also thought to be highly fertile. Consequently, girls were not allowed to weave an entire piece of cloth until puberty, when they could also become sexually active. Highly skilled embroiderers were thought to be very lusty and passionate women by nature because of the delicate and detailed designs they produced on cloth. Women had to guard their brooms because it was believed a woman could not resist the sexual advances of a man who collected twenty straws from her broom.

The activities of wives and husbands were so linked that husbands at war or away from their home on trade business feared for the safety of their wives because they believed that events at home could impact their activities while abroad. This relationship between female activity at home and male activity away from home was particularly important when husbands went to war. Wives maintained the household altar and cooked special tortillas and toasted maize in imitation of the soldier rations carried by their spouses. Women also had to sweep more often and do so following the sun's path across the sky. If a wife failed to sweep properly, maintain the rituals at the altar, and cook according to the necessary specification, she could cause her husband to be injured on the battlefield.

Conversely, wives gained status when their husbands succeeded on the battlefield by capturing an enemy warrior for sacrifice to the Aztec patron deity, Huitzilopochtli. The greatest prestige lay in capturing four enemy captives. Such an accomplishment granted the husband the right to wear more distinguished clothing in public and to participate in an honored position during certain festivals, especially the one in which his captive or captives were sacrificed. Generally a warrior received a part of the body of his deceased captive, which was hung outside the doorway of his home to demonstrate his martial prowess and to honor his household. Successful warriors also engaged in a type of ritual cannibalism with the meat of the sacrificial victim prepared in a stew. This meal was ritually shared with many family members to increase the power, prestige, and piety of the household and the calpulli.

Although wives shared in their husband's success on the battlefield and aided them by performing rituals well on the home front, women also were thought to wage their own brand of warfare each time they became pregnant. The Aztecs recognized that men and woman had sex and produced children, but they also believed that the gods rewarded a woman with a child because she had been diligent and dedicated with her pious devotions. Aztec society highly valued children, and a woman's social reputation increased with each successful birth. Women who were unable to conceive found their moral and religious character questioned by their family and neighbors.

Aztec triage and obstetrics at the time of the Conquest were far superior to that practiced by Europeans. Midwives successfully performed caesarian births. However, birthing still was the most common reasons for female mortality. Death in childbirth elevated the deceased woman to divine status, just as death on the battlefield honored her husband. Before cremation, she was laid out, and her corpse had to be closely guarded because male warriors and shamans coveted her hair and fingers as talismans against disorder and misfortune.

Gender socialization for the healthy baby began almost immediately. During the bathing ceremony, the midwife gave a formal religious speech, the words of which depended upon the sex of the child. Girls were forewarned that their life would be one of toil and exhaustion. They were warned that they would not wander because their place was at the hearth. To emphasize this point the placenta and umbilical cord of females were buried at the household hearth. Girl babies were also given miniature tools for weaving, indicating their future tasks. Boy infants were informed that their place was not at home but out fighting like the eagle and jaguar (for which the Aztec elite military organizations were named). Their umbilical cord was buried on a battlefield, and they were given miniature weapons.

Children were assigned chores beginning at age five and were expected to perform them and to act respectfully to all elders. Children were segregated by sex and learned tasks from their respective parents. Children could be dedicated to a temple, but generally girls remained at home, learning household skills from their mothers and other female relatives. Boys followed their fathers into the fields or trade workshops. When fathers were away, other male relatives tutored and watched over boys. At approximately 12 years old, children entered schools based on their gender and class. Elite male children entered the *calmecac*, where they learned reading, writing, mathematical and scientific knowledge, and religion. Commoner boys attended the *telpochcalli*, connected to their neighborhood and calpulli. They learned martial arts necessary to succeed in battle and rituals, songs, and dances to please the many deities in the Aztec pantheon. Girls, whether commoner or elite, attended special schools that emphasized religion and proper performance of rituals at home and in larger public festivals. Once schooling was completed, young people were expected to marry and have children.

## The Incas

For ancient Andean society, the tradition of gender parallelism appears to have been even more pronounced and pervasive in society than for the Aztecs. Religiously, the most important deities of the pre-Columbian Andean area were Pachamama and Illapa, and it was believed that males and females descended in parallel lineages from these two deities. Pachamama controlled the powers of the earth and especially fertility. Pachamama was worshipped by both women and men, but women were considered her descendents who therefore had a special relationship to her. Offerings to this mother goddess included *chicha* (an alcoholic beverage made from corn) and coca leaves. Pachamama was also the goddess of midwives, a position in society that was considered a religious vocation. Individuals were contacted by the goddess in their dreams and consequently were called to her service. Birthing a special child (particularly beautiful or intelligent) was a sign of being chosen by Pachamama as a midwife. Women in general were thought to have a close relationship to the earth deity and in essence represented their household to Pachamama. So important was this relationship that during the sowing of agricultural fields, men and women had to work side by side, because although men tilled the field and prepared the planting rows, only women could place the seed in the ground. To do otherwise was to court disaster. The devotion to Pachamama was closely linked to that of one of her daughter goddesses, Saramama, the diety of corn. The devotion to Saramama was administered by women exclusively. Special fields and herds were worked specifically for her cult, and women organized and hosted village festivals to her at which men were limited participants and spectators.

Illapa, the thunder god and a manifestation of Viracocha, was associated with the skies, mountains, and rain. He was also seen as the ancestral father of the heroic founders of the most important *ayllu* (kinship group) in a given village, and was connected to conquest and warfare. His shrines were located on mountaintops, and only men worshipped at these sacred locations, because they were thought to be his descendents. Pacamama and Illapa complemented each other and together made agricultural success possible. However, Illapa's connection to conquest and political authority and power injected hierarchy into gender relations. This complementarity and hierarchy can be seen in the way that the Inca empire was governed. The Incan sun god, Inti, personified by the emperor, ruled over the empire with his sister, the moon goddess or the Coya, who was his complement, but not his equal. She did not possess the same amount of authority or power as the emperor.

Parallelism was also evident at the individual level for commoners. Andean society highly valued marriage and viewed it as the joining of two equals. This emphasis on balance translated to other areas in life, including agriculture, where it was customary for men and women to work together. Most religious rituals called for men and women to share responsibilities (other than those dedicated specifically to Saramama and Illapa) and perform rites as a couple. Although men, at least during the time of Inca rule, were the public spokespersons for their family, it was clear that women were consulted and impacted the decision-making process with great authority.

Andean society strongly supported monogamy in marriage. To commit adultery was thought a grave offense that brought dishonor not only to the individuals involved but to the entire community. However, when marriage became too abusive or the spouses proved highly incompatible over time, women abandoned the home and returned to their family, thereby effectuating a divorce. Premarital sexual relations were expected and, in some sense, encouraged, because sexual experience was valued by society. Virginity was essentially seen in a negative light, as the lack of sexual experience devalued one's attractiveness as a marriage partner. Trial marriage was practiced widely, could last from 3 months to 3 years, and usually led to formal marriage. If a trial marriage failed, any children resulting from the union were to be accepted by society.

Although most Andean peoples valued sexual experience before marriage, the Incas sought to reinforce Andean maleness and increase gender hierarchy at the expense of parallelism. The Incan emperor, the living embodiment of the sun, claimed all Andean women in the empire as his sisters, thereby taking upon himself the right to determine the marital status of his female subjects. Consequently, once a year representatives from the imperial capital, Cuzco, would visit communities and select girls between the ages of 10 and 12 who were thought to be the most beautiful. These young women were taken to Cuzco and became *acllas*, or wives of the sun. Acllas were no longer tied to their communities of birth. Their labor and their ability to marry and form alliances at the local level would be lost to their villages and kinship group. Acllas had to be virgins and remain so under penalty of death unless otherwise designated by the emperor. An aclla was destined to serve the emperor in several ways: as his personal concubine; as a marriage partner to reward a worthy official or forge an alliance on behalf of the empire; as a celibate priestess devoted to a sun temple either in a provincial capital or in Cuzco; or as a sacrificial victim whose spirit then guarded imperial lands (usually those of her home province). The creation of the aclla class institutionalized virginity at the imperial level but did not appear to affect more popular and local ideas, which continued to place little value on virginity.

## Colonial Latin America

The arrival of Europeans and the subsequent military conquest of indigenous nations would have a profound effect on Native American society. The warfare, disease and forced labor, and relocation of indigenous communities during the sixteenth century disrupted marriage traditions. Commoners increasingly had to marry outside of their group in order to locate suitable partners. This in turn impacted descent and inheritance patterns. It made it especially challenging for women to inherit from their own kin group. This same development would privilege the nuclear family to the detriment of the larger kinship group common with parallel descent.

Marriage patterns were also affected because indigenous women formed relationships, some forced but many consensual, with European males. Many of these unions were viewed as permanent marriages by Indians. However, some Spaniards denied the validity of these marriages because the ceremonies had not been officiated by a Christian priest. These unions also led to the creation of *mestizos*, individuals of European and Native ancestry, who initially were seen as either Spanish or Indian. By the late sixteenth century, colonial officials decried the growing number of mestizos, seeing them in a negative light. They would be categorized officially as a separate ethnic group along with mulattos (people with African and European ancestry) and other racially diverse individuals, all of whom who were referred to by the general term *castas*. Thus, these marriages and sexual alliances, regardless of their permanency, and the resultant children, had a profound impact on demography.

Along with these changes in marriage patterns, the arrival of the Europeans brought a different moral code regarding gender relations and expectations, sexual practices, marriage, and family customs. Spanish and Portuguese mores were different and far more patriarchal than indigenous traditions. European legal codes and Christian values regarding gender relations would severely weaken gender parallelism. Indigenous women became legal minors, subject to fathers and then husbands. But independent (widowed) women with property continued to administer and dispose of that property as individuals.

Indigenous ideas about sexuality ran afoul of Christian ideas about sin and chastity. European priests emphasized that desires of the flesh were temptations that led to sin and the damnation of the soul. These clergymen labeled premarital sex and any sexual activity for pleasure rather than procreation as sinful. Virginity for women before marriage and fidelity after marriage was touted as the ideal, although European attitudes were far more lenient toward male infidelity. However, to the frustration of many Christian priests, these Old World ideas about sexuality did not immediately resonate with all Native Americans, many of whom continued to hold onto their beliefs about sexuality for many years. In general, the emphasis on female virginity was not easily understood or adopted until the eighteenth century except among highly acculturated Natives such as those who lived in the Indian barrios of Mexico City. In some Andean communities, trial marriage continued into the early twentieth century. In addition, Natives tended to be less rigid regarding sexual practices; for example, their ideas about homosexual acts were not as fixed as those of Spaniards until the later colonial period.

Although ideas about chastity and premarital sex would not be immediately accepted, one of the most immediate consequences of the Conquest would be the demise of polygamy among the Native elite. High-ranking indigenous leaders actively fought against monogamy during the sixteenth century because polygamy had been a symbol of status. Such multiple marriages represented political and economic alliances that directly impacted a nobleman's power in his community. However, in order to continue their high-ranking positions as part of the Spanish imperial system, indigenous noblemen had to at least appear to accept Catholicism, a part of which was accepting Christian marriage to one wife. Thus, noblemen had to select among their wives and concubines. Those women not chosen were essentially abandoned under the law, and their children were designated as illegitimate, no longer heirs to important positions and wealth. As commoners had always had one wife, Christian monogamy did not completely threaten the social fabric of indigenous life. However, the Spanish had very strict rules about consanguinity between marriage partners. Cousins could not marry, nor could in-laws. For example, a man could not marry his deceased brother's wife. To do so was considered incest. Consanguinity rules impacted and disrupted indigenous endogamy and further fragmented kinship rights and traditions.

Even with the changes and dislocations of the sixteenth century, marriage remained the foundation of society during the colonial period. Almost everyone regardless of ethnicity sought to marry and create a family. Race, wealth, and occupation defined a person's position in society, but the nuclear family and larger kinship groups (extended family) still could and did mitigate and complicate that position. For many individuals, especially the elite, marriage impacted lineage, public reputation, business ventures, and educational opportunities. Given the importance of marriage to the individual, the larger family, and society, many factors played a role in choice of spouse: ancestry, ethnicity, economic potential or accomplishments, compatibility, and romantic love. Arranged marriages were not uncommon for both Spanish and Native American elite during the era; however, the majority of individuals appeared to have quite a bit of say in spousal choice.

Regardless of compatibility and romance, marriage could and did constitute an economic alliance between two families, and this was particularly the case for the wealthy. For example, young women were expected to bring a substantial dowry to the marriage. The dowry was designed to insure the wife's welfare upon the death of her husband. The husband could and usually did administer and invest the dowry but was obligated to make provisions so that the value of the dowry could be recovered if needed. Unfortunately, there were many instances when husbands squandered or otherwise lost the dowry of their wives. In theory, however, upon the dissolution of the marriage, the dowry had to be returned in full to the wife's family. Dowries of wealthy women were indeed substantial and included farms, ranches, and other real estate, as well as jewels and costly clothing, slaves, art objects, and expensive furniture. In addition to the dowry, the groom provided his bride with a gift of 10 percent of his assets. Known as the *arras*, this gift provided for the wife upon the death of the husband and belonged to her heirs after her demise. Once married, a woman was placed under the legal protection of her husband, and technically she needed his permission to enter into any business transactions or contracts. Many upper-class and middle-class husbands gave such permission, and some wealthy women did administer their own dowries and the arras.

Most wives of merchants and tradesmen worked with their husbands in workshops and stores as well as on farms and ranches. The middle and poorer classes did not have dowries per se, but women did bring household items and clothing to the marriage. Women who had a particular skill in sewing, weaving, or cooking were highly valued as spouses because they aided the family economically. Religious organizations or rich patrons provided dowries to certain young women in an effort to secure a prosperous future for them. It was feared that, without a stable marriage and home life, these women would succumb to ruin. In some cases, these organizations sought out suitable grooms, promising the men that the young ladies were hardworking and pious. However, as the eighteenth century progressed, dowries fell out of fashion.

In addition to economic issues, ethnicity impacted spousal choice. Based on official marriage records, most Spaniards and Natives living in traditional communities married within their own ethnic and class group. However, poor Spanish males were very likely to seek partners among other ethnic groups and cross caste lines. Individuals of mixed ancestry (mestizos, mulattos, or *pardos*—individuals of mixed African and indigenous heritage) married at the same level or above in the caste system. Rates of official marriage among African slaves depended on several variables such as the ratio of males to females on any given plantation or farm and the discretion of the slave owner, many of whom discouraged marriage among their slaves. Enslaved women tended to marry more frequently than their male counterparts primarily because there were fewer slave women and many eligible males.

Ethnicity also impacted the age at which individuals married. Spanish women tended to marry at a young age; most were 17–18 years old, but it was not unheard of for 15- or even 14-year-old girls to wed. Spanish males usually married in their thirties, or were at least 5 to 10 years older than their brides. Older males were more established financially and socially, and parents believed that they were better able to provide for wife and family. Older males sought out young brides because they were more likely to be chaste (an important quality in the eyes of many Spanish males). Younger women also could conceivably birth more children—something greatly desired, especially on farms and ranches. The tendency to select older husbands disadvantaged younger Spanish men; but those who were gainfully employed and perceived as financially stable, no matter the age, did find marriage partners—though not always Spanish women. However, indigenous couples married earlier, and males of mixed ancestry not only married earlier than Spaniards but were more likely to marry older women.

Gender expectations in marriage also impacted marriage choice. The ideal wife, according to moralists of the time, was shy, pious, ordered, maintained hearth and home, and sought to follow her husband's judgment in all things. The ideal husband was loyal, God-fearing, industrious, and able to provide economically for his wife and children and serve as a moral example. Obviously not all individuals lived up to these lofty ideals, and societal expectations were a bit more tempered. Most people expected their spouse to be their companion for life and hoped that their relationship would be amicable.

Although many factors impacted spousal choice, romantic and sexual attraction appeared to play an important factor for many. Courtship customs and expectations regarding romantic love were impacted by popular plays, songs, dances, and poetry. Many romantic plays were the bread and butter of theatrical houses and itinerant acting troupes. These plays included star-crossed lovers, mistaken identities, and cloak-and-dagger romantic intrigues. The plot resolution in these plays always maintained societal standards. For example, a servant girl never fell in love with and married a nobleman. Nonetheless, in almost all cases the star-crossed lovers were reunited and joined in matrimony, to the effusive applause of the extremely heterogeneous audience. During the eighteenth century, more prosperous husbands commissioned and paid for the performance of short romantic plays in the home as a gift to their wives.

Poetry was also extremely popular in colonial society and not solely a pastime for the elite literati. Individuals commissioned poetry for birthdays, saint days, and anniversaries that were dedicated to their loved ones, especially a beloved spouse (usually husbands wrote or commissioned poetry for their wives). Poetry was also utilized in courtship, and again it was men who either wrote or commissioned poems. In some cases, local (less famous) poets had a portfolio of ready-made poems for all occasions and for a small fee would copy the poem, inserting the name of the beloved where appropriate. Such commissioned and purchased poems tended to laud the face and eyes, beauty, and gentle nature and personality of the beloved.

Lyrics to popular songs almost invariably were about romance: love found, scorned, or lost. Many songs were catchy ditties with highly suggestive lyrics that alluded to sexual acts or the apparent sexual prowess of tailors or bakers. For example, songs about bakers included lyrics equating the act of putting a loaf of bread in the oven to impregnating a woman. Dance steps to accompany the lyrics also could be suggestive but depended on how risqué the dancers wished to be in public. Taverns offered food and drink and nightly or weekly music with dancing and were the sites of the most licentious dancing, according to local officials.

Religion also played an important role in marriage choice. Although individuals were introduced to possible spousal candidates through family connections, local priests were often asked to investigate and ascertain the worthiness of a suitor or to persuade reluctant parents of a suitor's stellar character. Women also hosted special rituals and devotions to Saint Anthony in which particular men (the hoped-for fiancés) were invited to participate. Desperate women also concocted potions that included menstrual blood, locks of hair, bits of clothing, or herbs placed in hot chocolate drinks, in an effort to bind a disinterested lover to them. Women recited charms and cast spells to make men love only them; but some women also sought to make men sexually impotent with all females except themselves. Conversely, some men used magic for increased virility and "staying power" or for the ability to seduce as many women as possible.

Both sexes sought methods to seduce the other for marriage, love, and sexual gratification. Women were more likely than men to seek permanent relationships, although not necessarily official marriage. The seventeenth century in particular was defined by a culture of seduction or Don Juanism. Musical lyrics, dancing, and poetry all played a role in seduction as well as body language. A "language of eyes" developed in which couples attempted to express interest and talk to each other via facial expressions. Women also utilized hand fans and cleverly placed shawls to attract the attention of men sexually. The *tapadas* of Lima, Peru, were especially scandalous in the eyes of local authorities. These women covered their heads with shawls all except for their eyes and under guise of anonymity sallied forth to chat and flirt with their lovers or potential lovers. A woman who lifted her skirt to show a man a bit of her stockings was also demonstrating her willingness to engage in sexual activity. In Mexico, if a woman agreed to wash a man's hanky, she was accepting his sexual advances.

Once mutual attraction and interest were established and reciprocated, individuals sought ways to be alone, not an easy task, especially for heavily protected young women. Suitors regularly visited the homes of their beloved while a parent, sibling, relative, or servant served as a chaperone. Nonetheless, even within the home, lovers found time alone to steal a kiss or more. Others made assignations to meet at a church, at the home of a friend, or some secluded public location. Servants and friends delivered verbal messages, written notes and letters, and served as lookouts, facilitating these clandestine rendezvous. Poorer women were not protected nor confined to the home because they needed to earn income to aid their families. Although they were usually accompanied in their duties by female friends or relatives, they had more opportunities to interact with their suitors.

Whether wealthy or poor, seduction was most often accomplished through conversation and words and phrases designed to titillate and excite. In many cases, a man promised not only his undying devotion but marriage if a woman agreed to have sexual intercourse with him. Into the eighteenth century, the promise of marriage made as part of seduction was legally binding upon a man, particularly if witnesses were present to hear his pronouncements or he left written evidence such as a note or letter. The women's family would demand that he marry or pay some kind of financial indemnity to compensate for her loss of honor. Even if the marriage did not take place, his confirmed intention to marry, no matter how insincere, could keep social stigma at bay for many years. Such promises to marry did prove problematic as time wore on. In some cases, when marriage was about to take place, past lovers appeared, claiming that the groom had given them his marriage promise. Litigation could go on for years as the court sought to ascertain who the groom should marry.

Just as in the romantic theater so popular at the time, young lovers who desired to marry found their intended marriage threatened by the racial and social norms, questions of legitimacy, and socioeconomic aspirations of their parents. Until the age of 25, young people lived under the *patria potestad*, or rule of the father, which legally viewed them as minors. Therefore, parental consent for marriage was necessary. Many young people never questioned their parents' choice of spouse. However, young couples could "force" a recalcitrant parent to accept their desire to marry by secretly running away and consummating their love. Rather than risk familial dishonor and the risk of illegitimacy of a child born out of wedlock, the parents acquiesced and approved the marriage. More adamant parents, however, had the authority to "imprison" young adults (in their own bedrooms and homes) or move them from town to thwart romances or force their compliance to marry someone supposedly more suitable. The truly desperate and legally savvy lovers sent word of their imprisonment to the ecclesiastical court via hurriedly scribbled notes delivered by servants or reports provided by sympathetic relatives or even innocent bystanders persuaded to come to the aid of the star-crossed lovers. The Church's doctrine of free will granted all individuals the right to choose between good and evil. Granted by God, free will could not be wrought asunder by parents even in the case of spousal choice. Church officials, upon receiving notification, accompanied by civil militia, would "liberate" the imprisoned individuals and marry them to their choices above the objections of the outraged parents. Marriage under these circumstances could lead to disinheritance or disgruntled resignation on the part of the offended parents.

In 1776, the *Real Prágmatica de Matrimonios* decree was issued, transferring jurisdiction over spousal choice disputes to the civil courts. The law essentially sought to prevent interracial marriage and deprived children of their inheritance, property, and titles if they wedded over the objections of their parents. The royal court also consistently ruled in favor of parents who objected to the spousal choice of their children. The law was particularly important to the elite, who actively sought to protect their lineage and maintain ethnic and socioeconomic purity.

No matter the circumstances, once married, all couples were expected to have children and usually welcomed the new arrivals with great enthusiasm. Religious teachings emphasized that sex within marriage was primarily for procreation purposes. Sexual positions that did not lead to procreation were frowned upon by the Church. Oral sex, mutual masturbation, and positions other than the traditional "missionary" (with the man on top) within marriage were considered unacceptable; regardless of Church strictures, couples engaged in these activities as well as anal sex, although the latter was more socially taboo. Many of these sexual behaviors and positions fell under the Church's definition of sodomy, although rarely were heterosexual couples prosecuted for their sexual activities. Other than nonprocreational sexual behaviors, no reliable forms of birth control existed at this time other than abstinence. Some women did utilize herbal concoctions and teas in an effort to abort unwanted pregnancies. However, many more women sought the intervention of the saints, especially St. Anthony or St. Gertrude, to become pregnant. Infertility could have tragic effects in a society in which family and children were highly valued for economic needs, social status, and personal fulfillment. Barring serious illness or the early death of a spouse, it was not unusual for a couple to have at least nine children, although perhaps only five would survive until adulthood.

Although marriage was a sacrament in the eyes of the Catholic Church, perhaps close to 40 percent of individuals did not marry within the Church, although the number of individuals marrying officially increased as the centuries progressed. Such common-law unions were viewed as legitimate marriages by the community, although state and ecclesiastical authorities viewed the children of such unions as illegitimate. Local priests and ecclesiastical courts sometimes ordered individuals who were known to be cohabiting to marry; however, it appears as though only a small percentage of those couples followed the Church's directive. Some individuals in unofficial marriages sought to legalize their union years later because, having acquired property and some wealth, they wanted to recognize their legitimate heirs.

Not all marriages proceeded harmoniously. Husbands had the right to discipline their wives physically and correct what they considered to be disrespectful or unseemly behavior. Criminal records demonstrate that on many occasions violence led to serious injuries and fatalities. The nature of domestic violence in the home depended on several factors, including the severity and egregiousness of the violent acts, the ethnicity of the couple, the willingness of male relatives to intervene on behalf of the abused wife, and the strength of the patriarchal system in any given location. Indigenous marriages were less likely to resort to violence in order to solve disputes because the tradition of pre-Columbian gender complementarity granted women a stronger public position in society. In addition, male relatives and indigenous leaders in traditional communities were more likely to intervene and mitigate disputes before they reached fatal levels. Large urban centers, with a shifting anonymous and very diverse population, also allowed for more freedom of movement and contact with employers and co-workers who could serve as support for a distraught wife. Although women were usually the victims of spousal abuse, some men were victims as well. Such incidences of female-on-male violence may have been underrepresented because society mocked any male who allowed a woman to physically abuse him. Such a situation would have seriously injured his public reputation.

Obviously not all unhappy marriages resorted to violence. Many individuals simply ended their marriage and went their separate ways, reaching unofficial agreement about the dispensation of property, care for the children, and even financial arrangements (a kind of colonial alimony). Such ad hoc divorces were not recognized as such by religious and civil authorities, and in some instances the courts would arrest individuals and order them to cohabit and resume married life together. However, the dissolution of the marriage was not always mutual, and it was not uncommon for one spouse, usually the husband, to abandon the family. This left a wife to struggle to provide for her family, facing financial destitution from the loss of spousal income.

A small percentage of individuals sought an official separation from their spouse. Legal separation entailed a long-drawn-out process before judges in which witnesses attested to the claims and counterclaims of the petitioner and defendant, resulting in much public scandal and gossip. In the majority of cases, the parties were from the more propertied class; and most plaintiffs were women who had familial backing of some sort. Women generally resorted to the court system in order to procure alimony and child support and the return of the dowry and the arras. It was a costly endeavor and, even when a separation was granted, did not allow for remarriage for either party. Successful female petitioners returned to their family accompanied by any small children. Boys who were over 12 years of age might be given in custody to their father and his family. Alimony payments would be negotiated and determined by the court. However, even if the petitioner succeeded and was granted separation, there was no guarantee that compliance would occur in regard to alimony.

In all cases, the plaintiff, upon whom the burden of proof fell, would be granted legal separation only if her case was deemed justified and extreme in the eyes of the judges. Some individuals sought to prove that their spouse was religiously incompatible. The petitioner was forced to prove the heretical tendencies of the defendant while demonstrating her own religious orthodoxy and avoiding the attention of the Inquisition. Most individuals sued for legal separation on the grounds of physical abuse, abandonment, or adultery. Women usually lodged the charge of physical abuse and had to prove that the abuse was consistent and extreme by society's standards. Abandonment was the easiest to prove; however, a wife had to demonstrate that she had had no contact or received no payments from her husband for 5 consecutive years. Adultery was the most difficult charge to prove, because most adulterous affairs occurred in secret. Male adultery was much more common and socially expected; therefore, the adultery charge against a wayward husband had to be truly scandalous and notoriously public. Having a known mistress, even maintaining a second household, was not sufficiently egregious. However, if that mistress consistently taunted the wife in front of a large number of witnesses, then the case for adultery could be made more effectively.

Even under ideal circumstances, marriages did not last long for many individuals. The average life expectancy during the colonial period was approximately 50 years, although it was higher for the upper class, who had better nutrition. Life expectancy of males was also lower than that of females, although women risked their lives with each pregnancy. Many women found themselves as widows. In the case of the upper class, family members would exert substantial pressure on the widow to remarry, particularly if she was still young (under 25). Poor widows sought a second husband for companionship, a father for their children, and for the added income. Older recent widows with several children found it difficult to remarry. Those women with property or steady employment might consciously chose not to remarry. However, well-off older women had "legal freedom," the right to administer their and their deceased husband's wealth. They also had tutorship of their children. Many women continued to work the family business, later sharing that responsibility with their male children when they reached their majority. Financially secure and prosperous widows who chose not to remarry were sometimes viewed with suspicion and were accused, unsuccessfully, of witchcraft by jealous neighbors and business competitors. Most men sought to remarry upon the death of their wives, particularly if they had small children. A propertied widower who sought to remarry did not have a hard time finding willing and interested females.

Men, no matter their marital status, also could turn to prostitution to fulfill their sexual needs and desires. Prostitution was viewed by society as a necessary evil, and many believed that having prostitutes available somehow protected more honest and pious women from men's sexual aggression. Many citizens believed that sex with a prostitute or for remuneration was not a sin, a popular belief that, as Church authorities actively sought to point out, was not in keeping with Catholic doctrine. Most large cities in the colonial period had known houses of prostitution. In Mexico City in the eighteenth century, an anonymous satirical poem lauded the virtues of the capital's ladies of the evening, and the verses indicated their specialties and fees. Religious and civil authorities sought to redeem prostitutes by sometimes placing them in *recogimientos* (special reform houses) that functioned like a combination of workhouse/school and prison for a specified time period. Some prostitutes voluntarily entered these recogimientos in an effort to reform their lives. Courtesans, the most famous being María Micaela Villegas Hurtado (La Perricholi) in Lima and Josefa Ordoñez in Mexico City, were usually accomplished actresses. They took several lovers, including highly placed government officials. These actresses led scandalous lives, dressing and behaving above their social station. The actual number of full-time prostitutes and courtesans was probably limited, but some poverty-stricken single women engaged in occasional sex for remuneration as a survival strategy, especially during the years of economic stagnation and high inflation of the late eighteenth century.

Homosexuality existed during the colonial period, although it was not initially conceptualized as a lifestyle or established sexual identity. Individuals might engage in a variety of sexual acts that would not necessarily fix their sexual identity. Moralists viewed homosexuality as one of a series of sexual practices that the Church deemed reprehensible and against nature. For theologians of that time, oral and anal sexual activities were the greatest sexual sins because they positively excluded procreation. As time progressed, differentiations were made between men who penetrated others and men who were penetrated. The latter was considered particularly offensive and connected to developing notions about effeminate men who acted and dressed as females. Although the Inquisition sometimes prosecuted cases of homosexual activity, civil authorities held specific jurisdiction over the crime of sodomy (a generic term that included anal and oral sexual acts regardless of the gender of the participants). Concerted prosecutions occurred rarely but with dramatic and tragic results. The majority of males found guilty of the "nefarious sin" (homosexual acts) were executed by burning at the stake. They were also more likely to be tortured even after they had confessed. Young men deemed to have been innocents corrupted by older unscrupulous men sometimes escaped the death penalty but still had to endure 250 lashes of the whip as punishment. During 1657–58, in Mexico City, over 125 men were tried and executed by viceregal authorities who claimed that the accused had founded dens of sin that promoted sodomy and provided venues for nefarious parties and orgies. Authorities were stunned to learn that such gatherings had been taking place for 20 years. They were shocked that several men regularly dressed and acted like women. Officials considered these male relationships to constitute a concerted attack on Spanish society, morality, and masculinity. Lesbianism was also viewed as a crime against nature, but it rarely appears in colonial documents. Women were not executed, although officials were most scandalized when they learned that some women penetrated others with the use of a leather baton that simulated a penis. Most instances of homosexual activity were private acts that rarely appeared to catch the eye of civil authorities. Local officials might very well ignore sexual activity if citizens were discreet and appeared to embody contemporary notions of Spanish masculinity and femininity. Effeminate behavior on the part of males, however, raised suspicion and led officials to investigate.

## CONTEMPORARY LATIN AMERICA

The 1800s were a particularly challenging period, as Latin American nations began the century with violent struggles for independence from Spain and other European colonial powers. With a few exceptions, independence, once achieved, did not lead to political and economic stability. New leaders often disagreed over the type of government and the nature and pace of economic development. Civil wars broke out repeatedly in many nations, and regional strongmen came to power to fill the political vacuum generated by such civil unrest. It was not until the late nineteenth century that political and economic stability became the norm. The cycle of wars, dictatorships, and resultant economic chaos shattered families.

### Changes in Gender Roles

With peace, however, came concerted efforts to define these new modern nations. Commensurate with the times, new policymakers placed an emphasis on such values as individual and property rights. However, gender relations and married life were essentially unaffected by these larger political discussions and policies. Latin American nations upheld the power of husbands and fathers that had been accorded during the colonial period. According to the new national legal codes promulgated in the nineteenth century, men had "marital power" that allowed a husband to continue to control and discipline his wife and supervise and manage her property. Wives required their husbands' consent to enter into business transactions, sign contracts, and engage in financial activities. Husbands retained the custody of minor children, and divorce was prohibited. The laws merely codified the traditional ideology that held that women's roles were as mothers and homemakers, obedient to their husbands. Men, in turn, were guided by a definition of masculinity that prized virility, repressed emotion, and encouraged competition. Women drew strength from the private sphere, while men exercised political and economic power in the public sphere. This traditional ideology served as the basis of society and the foundation for gender inequality.

Although laws reiterated colonial practices and norms, beginning in the latter quarter of the nineteenth century Latin American society experienced substantial change that would affect marriage and gender relations. Education in particular became a major concern of national policymakers. Already in the eighteenth century, officials had become more interested in educational opportunities for all, including girls and women. This trend continued into the nineteenth and twentieth centuries as more government revenues were invested in educational programs in major urban areas. Increasingly women were seen as an integral part of the economy, even if they did not work outside of the home. Nineteenth-century policymakers believed that homemakers required an education to be able to run their household more effectively. In addition, because women were entrusted with the care of children, who were seen as the future of these new nations, it was their patriotic duty to be a good wife and mother. Thus leaders came to believe that an educated woman would raise better citizens.

This emphasis on maternal "patriotic duty" opened new fields of endeavor for women. For example, women increasingly became the primary educators of children, marking their entrance into the professional career of public school teacher. They also entered into the health fields such as nursing, an occupation that was a logical choice for women seen as the caretakers of others. With industrialization (starting in the late nineteenth century), more women entered the official workforce as factory laborers and as clerical staff. Industrialization also fueled migration from rural to urban areas, which opened even more educational and job opportunities for both men and women. These economic and educational changes were particularly welcomed by middle- and upper-class women, who lauded the moral superiority of women and began to promote social reform and engage in charitable works on a much larger scale.

With attitudes and socioeconomic changes taking place, many nations, between the 1880s and the 1930s, altered their laws regarding marriage issues. Women now shared custody of minor children with their husbands. They controlled their independent income, although in many nations they were still required to obtain their husbands' authorization to work in the first place. Additionally, women inherited a more equitable portion of the estate upon the death of their husbands. Signatures of both spouses were now required in order to dispose of important marital properties such as the familial residence.

## Modernization, Family Life, and Women's Rights

In addition to the promulgation of new laws, increasing modernization had an impact on family life. Families now had to grapple with dislocations caused by migration from a small village to a large metropolitan area. In many cases, families had to survive and flourish without the benefits of the extended family. Urban life was anonymous, more fast-paced, and cosmopolitan, incorporating new modes of thinking from abroad that altered local perspectives. These new ideas championed individual rights, autonomy, and increased political participation. It is therefore understandable that the early twentieth century saw the advent of Latin America's suffragette movement, which sought to garner the vote for women. Most feminists emphasized women's intellectual capabilities and moral contributions as a means to demand increased political participation. Many believed that their potential for achievement was curtailed by archaic laws and mores. Beginning in 1929 with Ecuador, women would be successful in obtaining the right to vote. It would be a long fight, however, as some nations would not legislate female suffrage until as late as 1961 (Paraguay). It is unclear how the suffrage movement affected individual families and gender roles; however, it encouraged women to become more active in political causes and parties. This in turn caused a new generation of men and women to advocate for more changes.

Latin America's second wave of feminism marshaled a tremendous amount of this political energy and came to fruition under the dictatorial regimes of the late 1960s and 1970s with most lasting until the economic crisis of the 1980s. Women organized and entered into the political sphere to both fight against oppression and provide for their families during increasingly harsh economic conditions. Men and women worked together to champion human rights and create neighborhood organizations such as communal kitchens and health committees. Such social activism helped to create, from the bottom up, the pro-democracy movement in many Latin American nations. Working and struggling side by side allowed men and women to develop different types of working relationships that countered the traditional patriarchal model.

Even without political activism, the economic crisis caused more and more women to enter the workforce, a trend that continues in Latin America. More than ever before, wives now contribute their salaries to the financial viability of the household. They are perceived as more independent, with their own career interests and their own unique presence in the public sphere. The prevalence of women even in traditionally male occupations has had profound impact in the workplace, although it has exacerbated problems such as sexual harassment on the job. Nonetheless, women have reached management-level positions in many professional occupations, supervising both male and female employees and associates. Husbands, who have historically defined their role as the provider for their family, now find themselves adjusting to a different work and familial arrangement.

This new view of a more egalitarian marriage had always existed in some sectors in Latin America, but now it is more openly championed and more thoroughly articulated in popular culture. Today, gender expectations are understandably complex but do include marrying for love and companionship, the expectation of children, and a stable family life in which men and women are partners and seek to create an enjoyable home environment and interact with their children. Reproductive health programs that provide for easier access to contraception have led to a dramatic decline in birthrates in Latin America in general; not only are couples having fewer children, births are spaced more widely apart. In some nations such as Argentina, Uruguay, and Chile, individuals are marrying later, in their late twenties or choosing to remain childless.[1] Thus, increasingly, many couples have more disposable income and can better plan their own future and the education and care of their children; also, many men have been forced by circumstances to redefine their roles.

Certainly patriarchy still exists in Latin America, as it does in other parts of the world, including the United States and Europe. Many men struggle between traditional views of masculinity and the changes in gender roles and expectations. In addition, the new egalitarianism is largely urban; traditional gender ideology is slow to change in rural areas, particularly poor areas characterized by subsistence agriculture. No matter the location, women are still expected to be the primary caregivers and responsible for the home. For those women who work outside the home, the burden is tremendous. Upper- and middle-class women hire household staff so that they can fulfill their duties to family and career. Unfortunately, working-class and poor women do not have the resources. A man's willingness to share in household chores and childcare depends upon the individual and, in many cases, his age, race, class, and stage in the life cycle. Young men and middle-class males are more likely to play an active role in childcare and household duties because they have been socialized to do so by society, their mothers, and their girlfriends and wives. This has led to new views on fatherhood and its importance to definitions of manhood.

Unemployment and the lack of stable employment also affect family dynamics, causing some males to become very active participants in childcare and household duties; in other cases, however, it leads to the dissolution of the family unit. Providing for one's family is still a defining characteristic for masculinity in Latin America, and the inability for care for the welfare of the family has a negative impact on the self-image of many males.

Regardless of these challenges, the more egalitarian marriage is hailed as natural and desirable in Latin America societies. Children learn from an early age to desire marriage and to have children of their own. Particularly girls are socialized to see marriage and a family as the most important part of their future, although education is highly valued. Young people are encouraged to date within their peer group at school or church. Traditionally, young women have sought to date older boys. Courtship tends to be more formal than in Europe or the United States, but the level of

## WORKING FATHERS AND MIGRATION

Many males migrate (mostly to the United States) to find work due to economic necessity and the desire to provide for their family. Although they send remittances to their family on a regular basis, their partners still must work and shoulder the burden of childcare alone. Psychologists, sociologists, and policy-makers have only begun to analyze the impact on the family, children, and society-at-large of the large number of absent fathers due to migration. Male children, in particular, are negatively affected and become more prone to acting out in school, skipping school, and engaging in other antisocial behaviors. In Ecuador, a new disease, called *nervios*, has been defined to explain these behaviors among boys with absent migrant fathers.

parental leniency depends on a number of factors such as class, ethnicity, and rural versus urban environments. Most dating begins as activities shared with other couples, such as dancing with a larger group of friends. Young people are active consumers of popular culture media, from television shows to music, which also influence their expectations regarding love, sexuality, and marriage.

## Popular Culture and Latin American Women

Popular culture emphasizes romantic love and marriage as the ideal, and a necessary ingredient for a contented life. Popular music, from ballads to rock 'n' roll, is overwhelmingly dedicated to issues of romantic love. Women's magazines encourage and portray middle- and upper-class values and lifestyles that present a new Latin American woman. She is characteristically beautiful, stylishly dressed, educated, and a professional, and she very much desires to wed and have children. These magazines offer dating advice, although they provide somewhat less explicit sexual information than their counterparts and parent magazines in the United States and Europe do.

*Telenovelas,* extremely popular evening soap operas of limited duration, provide a similar approach to gender relations. More than duplications of print media, they are an updated, more daring version of colonial romance plays. Telenovelas are incomplete without star-crossed lovers, malicious gossips, vengeful villains, and mistaken identity. They also demonstrate that the virtuous person, whether female and male, no matter the socioeconomic status, always manages to capture the heart of his or her beloved. Generally, however, telenovelas present middle- and upper-class views of family life and love and therefore show men and women working in the professions, attending university, and living in elegant surroundings.

Telenovelas focus on the intimate, emotional states of the characters and show gender relations as more egalitarian than they may be for most viewers.

Latin American filmmakers since the late 1980s have begun to examine gender relations and sexuality in more controversial ways than as shown in the telenovelas. This new cinematographic trend coincided with the arrival of female directors and screenwriters on the film scene. Films such as Mexico's *Entre Pancho Villa y una mujer desnuda* or Brazil's *Eu, Tu, Eles* use humor to depict gender relations in a state of flux, individuals caught between individual ideas and new modes of thinking and traditional concepts of family inherited from previous centuries. Familiar scenarios are upended, and viewers are left to question their own views on gender roles. However, as in the case of magazines and telenovelas, marriage is still held up as desirable. Films, telenovelas, and magazines not only represent these changing attitudes; they also influence individuals, presenting them with different lifestyles and possible personal choices that may differ from those of their parents. This is not to say, however, that such depictions of modern marriage are not found in Latin American reality.

## Marriage and Divorce

Religion has also altered conceptualizations about traditional gender roles in the twentieth century. With the decisions of the Second Vatican Council of 1961–65, the Catholic Church articulated very clearly a more progressive view of gender relations and emphasized in its writings the equality that exists between spouses. The Church posited "mutuality" for men and women in all spheres and stated that marriage enhanced and sheltered the personal dignity of the husband and wife. The Church supported reforms to legal codes that gave equal rights to husbands and wives. Liberation theology, a progressive movement within the Catholic Church popular in Latin America, encourages both male and female participation in religious and political matters. Its "base communities" focus on literacy and discussion of the Bible and raise the consciousness of participants and encourage cooperation between the sexes. Evangelical Protestantism, especially Pentecostalism, has also affected gender relations. It emphasizes clean living, thriftiness, hard work, and dedication to family. This has strengthened the households of converts and even led to limited socioeconomic advancement. In general, both the Catholic and Protestant churches seek to fortify and support the family, but view gender relations in a more egalitarian light. All seek to discourage some of the more stereotypical qualities of *machismo* such as philandering, carousing, and the squandering of household funds on unhealthy habits such as drinking or gambling.

Religious institutions and much of popular culture seeks to bolster the institution of marriage. For many citizens and policymakers, marriage has been (and is) seen as sacred and indissoluble. This particular belief, bolstered by Catholic authorities, for whom marriage is a sacrament, made it particularly difficult to legalize divorce in Latin America. The inability to effectuate a legal divorce led many individuals to separate and de facto divorce. Although many marriages may have ended amicably, individuals were not guided or mandated by law in terms of the disposition of property, child custody, alimony, and child support. This in turn had an overall negative effect on the lives of women, who still tended to be lower wage earners than their husbands, and of the children, who usually came to reside with their mothers. Many proponents of legalized divorce viewed changes in the law as not only a means to ensure that laws represented lived reality but also as a means to aid women as single heads of households.

Individuals separated from their spouses also entered into consensual unions with new lovers but were never able to regularize that union, because they were legally married to another. Many consensual unions were tantamount to a second marriage and produced offspring that were viewed as illegitimate. This in turn led to legislation that recognized the legitimacy of children although they were produced outside of wedlock. The indissolubility of marriage also led some individuals to join consensual unions even when there was no impediment to legal marriage. Before divorce was legalized, legal codes had to be altered to protect partners of consensual unions in terms of property rights. Ironically, women had more rights in consensual unions than as married women. The number of children born out of wedlock grew to be quite high. For example, during the 1980s, 50 percent of children in Argentina were born to parents not legally married.[2]

In some nations, middle- and upper-class individuals traveled abroad, obtained a divorce, and then remarried, returning home to a country that recognized neither the divorce nor the second marriage. Such "foreign" divorces and marriages, although illegal, gave social legitimacy to their actions and were preferable to openly living in sin. In Chile, where divorce was not legalized until 2004, individuals utilized a loophole in the legal code to annul their marriages regardless of how many years they had been married. Witnesses (falsely) swore that at the time of the marriage ceremony, the individuals were not residing in the district where the marriage was officially registered. Therefore, the marriage was invalid. The "fraudulent" annulments were costly, requiring the services of attorneys, but they allowed for a legal type of divorce for the middle and upper classes.

Even though divorce is legal today in Latin America, most nations have strict laws stipulating the circumstances under which individuals can sue for divorce. For instance, most nations list adultery as acceptable grounds for divorce. Some states in Mexico, however, give preferential treatment to husbands who can prove that they were "forced" into adultery because their spouse refused to have sexual relations with them. Women who are unfaithful have no such avenue of justification for their actions. Obtaining a divorce is generally still time-consuming and expensive for many. With the exceptions of Puerto Rico and Cuba, where divorce is much easier and quicker to obtain, the cost and difficulty of obtaining a divorce are reasons why the divorce rate in Latin America is low. These same factors account for the continuation of ad hoc dissolutions of marriages. Single-parent families, usually headed by women, have increased and represent on average 30 percent of households in most nations.[3] Nonetheless, many people in Latin America believe in the indissolubility of marriage and seek to reconcile or endure rather than divorce, and this too affects the divorce statistics.

Another factor impacting the divorce rates and the dissolution of consensual unions in Latin America is the problem of domestic violence. To date, almost all Latin American nations have enacted laws against spousal abuse. However, effective enforcement of these laws remains a major concern. A large percentage of cases consist of women who have been physically assaulted by their male partners. Police often fail to respond to calls for assistance or are hostile towards the victims and downplay the seriousness of the situation. To ameliorate this aspect of the problem, many nations have instituted special domestic violence police units composed of female officers; however, these special units are often understaffed and lack psychological support personnel. In addition, many nations require women to undergo a medical examination before they file a formal complaint. Medical examiners frequently underreport the nature of the injuries, which then determines whether a crime is considered a misdemeanor or a felony. Thus, a victim can be severely bruised and permanently scarred, but her assailant will only spend 2 years in jail. In other instances, prosecutors and judges emphasize reconciliation rather than punishment, even for serious repeat offenders. In some instances, male judges are sympathetic to husbands to can prove mitigating circumstances to the physical abuse such as their wife's infidelity. This "crime of passion" defense can influence judges even in cases of homicide. However, activists in Brazil and Costa Rica in particular are having some success with raising awareness and demanding changes in how authorities view and prosecute such assaults between partners.

## Increasing Openness in Sexual Information

The changing nature of gender relations in Latin America has created a public space in which discussion about marriage and spousal rights and protections are openly discussed, creating impetus for more change and social advocacy. This is especially true of sexuality, which is talked about more openly than even in the 1970s. Sexual imagery is very common in marketing and advertising, and films, telenovelas, and magazines present sexual themes. A growing segment of the publishing industry consists of sexual manuals and guides to improving sexual relationships between partners. Many are published as marital advice books; but more and more are strictly focused on sexuality and increasing sexual pleasure. There has also been an increase in shops (both on-line and businesses in large urban areas) that specialize in sexual aids, lotions, and lingerie that are clearly targeted to women and couples. These establishments are in addition to the traditional male-centered and fast-growing pornography industry. It is understandable, then, that many individuals expect people who are romantically involved to engage in sexual relations before marriage, although ideally many share religious taboos against such relations.

## Reproductive Issues

The popular media's emphasis on sexuality and individual interest in sexual exploration have made the lack of affordable and accessible birth control a central issue in Latin America. Although modern contraception is much more accessible, especially in urban areas, it still represents substantial cost to many poor and working-class couples. Condoms, highly recommended to avoid sexually transmitted diseases and the spread of HIV/AIDS, are not always readily available. In addition, many males refuse to wear condoms, although concerted public anti-HIV/AIDS campaigns have impacted such views, especially in Mexico and Brazil. All of these factors combined have led to a rise in adolescent pregnancies among the poor, even though the overall fertility rate in Latin America is declining. Yet there is still a stigma attached to having children out of wedlock, and many women turn to abortion as a means to end the pregnancy.

Abortion is illegal in most Latin American countries; it is readily available only in Cuba, although some nations (for example, Brazil) make exceptions for women who have been raped or when the mother's life is in danger. Nonetheless, abortion is widespread, and Latin America has a higher rate of abortion than any other part of the world. With the exception of El Salvador, abortion laws are not enforced. Upper- and middle-class women visit private clinics where they have safe procedures. Poor women can only afford clandestine abortions or resort to chemicals such as the ulcer medicine Cytotec, which they believe will cause an abortion. These unsanitary and dangerous conditions have resulted in a high mortality rate. Some claim that 5,000 women annually die from complications of clandestine abortions.[4] The legalization of abortion laws has become a polarized issue, pitting pro-choice and public health forces against the Catholic Church and its activists. Most public opinion polls show that the average person is opposed to abortion but makes exceptions for cases of rape, if the mother's life is in danger, or in the case of fetal abnormality.

## Gays and Lesbians

Sexuality, gender relations, divorce, and reproductive rights have become and continue to be openly debated topics in Latin America. With the exception of abortion, individual and societal perceptions revolving around the family as an institution and relations between men and women are dramatically different from those of 100 years earlier. Views about homosexuality are also in the process of change. Intolerance of gays and lesbians is still the norm in most Latin American nations. Nonetheless, homosexuality today is more likely to be seen as a lifestyle choice, not a crime or psychological disorder. Gay organizations hold rallies and organize marches to present their views on a variety of issues concerning sexual rights. Legal codes, however, do not grant homosexuals in partnerships the same rights as married heterosexuals.

The fight against HIV/AIDS in Latin America has allowed activists the means to discuss homosexuality and to inform discussions and debates about sexual identities in Latin America. Two million people are infected with HIV/AIDS in Latin America, more than the United States, Canada, Western Europe, Australia, and Japan combined. Half of all victims of the disease reside in Brazil, Mexico, Colombia, and Argentina, although nations such as Haiti and Belize have the worst epidemics. The spread of HIV/AIDS is facilitated by poverty, massive migration, homophobia, and church/state disagreements regarding how to best stop the spread of the disease. In nations such as Mexico, HIV/AIDS is mostly spread by men who have sex with men and women, while in the Caribbean the disease is spread primarily through female sex workers who do business with both locals and tourists. Injecting drug users also still play a role in the spread of the disease. Some governments have been more active than others in launching a major campaign against HIV/AIDS. The Catholic Church is vigorously opposed to condom use to prevent infection, which greatly complicates public service campaigns. Brazil has effectively contained the spread of the disease through television, print, and radio announcements, successful collaboration between nongovernmental agencies and public health authorities, and pioneering treatment programs that include free antiretroviral drugs for all those diagnosed with HIV/AIDS. The Brazilian government also is actively seeking to produce nationally new treatment drugs for the disease, thus sidestepping the large cost of importing drugs from international pharmaceutical companies.

In addition to open discussion of HIV/AIDS within Latin America, there is also increasing attention being given to transgender and bisexual lifestyles. For example, there are men who may engage in sexual acts with another male as well as with women, but they consistently reject the label of homosexual and do not consider themselves gay or bisexual. This only emphasizes the complexity of sexual identities that are being discussed in the public forum. Some of these men refuse the terms "homosexual" or "bisexual" because they hold traditional views regarding masculinity and machismo. Others do so because they do not wish to categorize their diverse sexual identity. The discussion of nonheterosexual lifestyles, however, continues to collide with official views held by religious authorities and much of their congregations.

Activists continue to advocate for change and work to liberalize divorce, legalize abortion, or increase the conditions under which a legal abortion can take place, to make birth control more accessible, and to encourage family planning. However, traditional gender roles still serve as the foundation for marriage and family for many individuals. Policymakers tend to be conservative when discussing such social issues, because their constituents share their views or because they are influenced by religious teachings. Nonetheless, values continue to change and are not static. Today, young people have more opportunities and possibilities to express themselves. However, young couples must negotiate between tradition and changing perceptions about gender roles that encourage individual goals and desires.

# RESOURCE GUIDE

## PRINT SOURCES

Arriagada, Irma. "Changes and Inequality in Latin American Families." *CEPAL Review* 77 (2002, August): 135–153.

Brusco, Elizabeth. *The Reformation of Machismo. Evangelical Conversion and Gender in Colombia.* Austin: University of Texas Press, 1995.

Chant, Sylvia H., with Nikki Craske. *Gender in Latin America.* New Brunswick, NJ: Rutgers University Press, 2003.

Craske, Nikki, and Maxine Molyneux, eds. *Gender and the Politics of Rights and Democracy in Latin America.* London: Palgrave, 2002.

Deere, Carmen Diana. *Empowering Women: Land and Property Rights in Latin America.* Pittsburgh: University of Pittsburgh Press, 2001.

Forero, Juan. "Push to Loosen Abortion Laws in Latin America." *New York Times* (2005, December 3).

Garza Carvajal, Federico. *Butterflies Will Burn. Prosecuting Sodomites in Early Modern Spain and Mexico.* Austin: University of Texas Press, 2003.

Gutierrez, Ramon. *When Jesus Came, the Corn Mothers Went Away. Marriage, Sexuality and Power in New Mexico, 1500–1846.* Stanford, CA: Stanford University, 1991.

Gutmann, Matthew C. *Changing Men and Masculinities in Latin America.* Durham, NC: Duke University Press, 2003.

Higgins, Kathleen J. *"Licentious Liberty" in a Brazilian Gold-Mining Region. Slavery, Gender and Social Control in Eighteenth-Century Sabara, Minas Gerais.* University Park: University of Pennsylvania Press, 1999.

Htun, Mala. *Sex and the State: Abortion, Divorce and Family under Latin American Dictatorships and Democracies.* New York: Cambridge University Press, 2003.

Hutchison, Elizabeth Q. *Labors Appropriate to Their Sex: Gender, Labor and Politics in Urban Chile, 1900–1930.* Durham, NC: Duke University Press, 2001.

Johnson, Lyman, and Sonya Lipsett-River, eds. *The Faces of Honor. Sex, Shame, and Violence in Colonial Latin America.* Albuquerque: University of New Mexico Press, 1998.

Joyce, Rosemary A. *Gender and Power in Prehispanic Mesoamerica.* Austin: University of Texas Press, 2000.

Kellogg, Susan. *Weaving the Past: A History of Latin America's Indigenous Women from the Pre-Hispanic Period to the Present.* New York: Oxford University Press, 2005.

Lavrin, Asuncion. *Sexuality and Marriage in Colonial Latin America.* Lincoln: University of Nebraska Press, 1989.

Molyneux, Maxine. *Women's Movement in International Perspective: Latin America and Beyond.* New York: Palgrave, 2001.

Parker, Richard. *Beneath the Equator: Cultures of Desire, Male Homosexuality and Emerging Gay Communities in Brazil.* New York: Routledge, 1999.

Powers, Karen. *Women in the Crucible of Conquest: The Gendered Genesis of Spanish American Society, 1500–1600.* Albuquerque: University of New Mexico Press, 2005.

Schroeder, Susan, Stephanie Wood, and Robert Haskett, eds. *Indian Women of Early Mexico.* Norman: University of Oklahoma Press, 1997.

Seed, Patricia. *To Love, Honor and Obey in Colonial Mexico. Conflicts over Marriage Choice, 1574-1821.* Stanford, CA: Stanford University Press, 1988.

Shaw, Lisa, and Stephanie Dennison, eds. *Latin American Cinema: Essays on Modernity, Gender and National Identity.* Jefferson, NC: McFarland, 2005.

Sigal, Pete. *From Moon Goddess to Virgins. The Colonization of Yucatecan Maya Sexual Desire.* Austin: University of Texas Press, 2000.

Stern, Steve J. *The Secret History of Gender: Women, Men and Power in Late Colonial Mexico.* Chapel Hill: University of North Carolina Press, 1995.

Twinam, Ann. *Public Lives, Private Secrets: Gender, Honor, Sexuality and Illegitimacy in Colonial Spanish America.* Stanford, CA: Stanford University Press, 1999.

## WEBSITES

Continental Network of Indigenous Women. http://enlacemujeresindigenas.org.

Center for Reproductive Rights. http://www.crlp.org.ww_lac.html.

World Bank. *LAC Gender Database*. http://www.devdata.worldbank.org/genderstats/home.asp.

Sexual Citizen. *Sexuality, Health and Human Rights in Latin America*. http://www.ciudadaniasexual.org. University of Peru Cayetano Heredia website dealing with sexual identities, reproductive rights, and such issues.

Latin American Network Information Center, Women and Gender Resource List. http://lanic.utexas.edu/la/region/women.

Latin Zone Media and Marketing. http://www.zonalatina.com. Search the site for many articles on women, gender, and machismo.

*Brazzil* Magazine. http://www.brazzil.com. Search the site for many articles on women and gender issues in Brazil.

## VIDEOS/FILMS

*Between Light and Shadow: Maya Women in Transition* (United States, 1997). Produced by John McKay and Kathryn Lipke Vigesa.

*Central Station* (Brazil, 1998). Directed by Walter Salles.

*Danzon* (Mexico, 1991). Directed by María Navarro.

*The Double Day* (United States, 1975). Directed by Helena Solberg-Ladd.

*Entre Pancho Villa y una mujer desnuda* (Mexico, 1996). Directed by Sabina Berman.

*Eu, Tu, Eles* (Brazil. 2000). Directed by Andrucha Waddington.

*Fresa y chocolate* (Cuba, 1994). Directed by Tomás Gutiérrez Alea.

*Hasta Cierto Punto* (Cuba, 1993). Directed by Tomás Gutiérrez Alea.

*Hour of the Star* (Brazil, 1986). Directed by Suzana Amaral.

*Madagascar* (Cuba, 1994). Directed by Fernando Pérez.

*Telenovelas: Love, TV and Power* (United States, 2001). Directed by Alexandre Valenti.

*To Be a Mother in Latin America* (United States, 1997). Directed by Carmen Sarmiento.

*Women of Latin America* (series) (United States, 1995). Directed by Carmen Sarmiento.

# NOTES

1. Arriagada 2002 (in Resource Guide, Print Sources), p. 142.
2. Htun 2003 (in Resource Guide, Print Sources), p. 97.
3. Arriagada 2002 (in Resource Guide, Print Sources), p. 143.
4. As quoted in Forero 2005 (in Resource Guide, Print Sources).

# MUSIC

PETER MANUEL

Latin America and the Caribbean have been the sources for some of the world's most dynamic and internationally beloved styles of popular music. In the 1920s the Argentine tango had become the rage in Paris and other European cities, and in the mid-century decades the Cuban *son* became the dominant dance-music genre in much of urban Africa. A few decades later, music emanating from tiny Jamaica took the world by storm—first in the roots reggae of Bob Marley and others and then in the ardent and provocative dancehall music of Buju Banton and his contemporaries. Today Latin American and Caribbean music styles such as reggae and *salsa* are enjoyed throughout much of the world. They are also cultivated worldwide, whether in the form of cover bands that reproduce hits produced in the Americas, or in the form of local adaptations, such as singers in Central Africa who chant dancehall in the style of Jamaican stars but in their own local languages.

Although the reasons that Latin America and the Caribbean have been such a vital crucible of popular world music styles may be difficult to explain, the region's creativity may have something to do with the felicitous syntheses of African-derived and European-derived musical features. Some contend that the uniquely modern and expressive power of the region's musics has derived from their inherently creole nature, as the product of peoples at once liberated from Old World traditions—both African and European—but able to draw extensively from them.

Latin American and Caribbean popular music styles have also benefited from relative proximity to metropolitan centers in the United States and elsewhere and from the active involvement, starting in the early twentieth century, of record companies eager to market local music both internationally and in their countries of origin. By the 1960s or so, when many developing-world countries had barely begun to generate distinctive local popular music scenes, countries such as Cuba and Argentina had already been through several stages of popular music styles, all enjoying substantial international marketing and appeal. If popular music is understood to be a music whose style has evolved in connection with its dissemination as a commodity via the mass media, some Latin American popular music styles emerged in the latter 1800s, as marketed via sheet music and player piano rolls.

Many Latin American and Caribbean genres overlap international borders and thus the region-by-region format of this chapter runs the risk of obscuring their transnational character.

## MEXICO AND THE AMERICAN SOUTHWEST

Mexico, by far the largest country in the Spanish-speaking world with a current population of 105 million, hosts a correspondingly diverse and active popular music scene, with a vast music industry whose products are consumed and enjoyed internationally. Much of Mexico's population is at least partially indigenous in terms of racial heritage, and many Mexicans are monolingual speakers of Indian languages such as Zapotec. Nevertheless, as in the Caribbean and several other Latin American countries, Amerindians do not seem to have contributed to the stylistic evolution of popular music genres, which can be better characterized as primarily European, rather than African or Indian, in original derivation.

In the nineteenth century, the urban music forms that were popular in Mexico were primarily Hispanic in origin. Many were regional variants of the strophic narrative *corrido*. Italian influence was evident in the operatic *bel canto* style being used to render sentimental urban *canción*, a term in Mexico and elsewhere denoting a sentimental, amatory song, in slow tempo, not associated with dance. The canción has remained vital in its way as a result of the compositions of Agustin Lara (1897–1970) and, more recently, the songs of vocalists such as José José.

In the 1920s the Cuban *bolero* took root in Mexico, where, in tandem with Lara and other composers, groups such as Los Calaveras and the New York–based Los Panchos refined the genre and standardized the trio style, with smooth, sophisticated harmonies and guitar playing. For urbanizing Mexicans in the subsequent decades, the bolero became a symbol of modernity and urban expression, in contrast to the unpretentious rural folk styles left behind. Emerging and flourishing alongside the bolero, although in different contexts, was *mariachi* music, with its distinctive ensemble of violins, trumpets, and guitar and guitar-variants. The mariachi repertoire draws from a variety of regional genres (including *son jalisciense, son jarocho*, and *son huasteco*). Because mariachi music is quintessentially performed live (for example, at restaurants) rather than via the mass media, it fits somewhat uneasily into the category of commercial popular music.

### Norteño Music

Perhaps the most fertile region for the creation of a stylistically distinctive Mexican music has been northern Mexico (the *norteño* region) and the U.S. Southwest (which was part of Mexico until seized by the United States in the 1840s). By the 1930s the accordion, earlier introduced by German and Czech immigrants, had become the basis of a *conjunto* ensemble format also featuring the *bajo sexto* bass-chordal guitar, contrabass (later electric bass), and percussion. In the 1930s through the 1950s, many commercial Mexican films starred singer-actors—especially Jorge Negrete and Pedro Infante—whose norteño-based swashbuckling *charro* image was linked to their renditions of *canción ranchera*. These songs were characterized by a virile, melodramatic vocal style (often harmonized in parallel thirds) and the use of a polka rhythm—in either fast or slow tempo—and could be accompanied either by a mariachi ensemble or an accordion-based *conjunto*.

From the subsequent decades, norteño music and its Texas-Mexican counterpart developed along parallel, albeit somewhat distinct lines, although both retained the accordion-based conjunto ensemble and favored polka-style rhythms. In norteño music, the dominant genre continued to be the corrido, with its narrative text often celebrating colorful characters such as bandits or revolutionary heroes such as Pancho Villa. Many songs from the 1980s, especially by groups such as Los Tigres de Norte, sang of drug dealers (*narcotraficantes*) or of illegal immigrants to the United States. Although, in some sense, rooted in northern Mexico, norteño became the quintessential music of the border experience, of undocumented Mexicans living throughout the United States, and of many Mexicans in the hinterland who enjoyed its colorful lyrics, bouncy rhythms, and quasi-outlaw associations.

For its part, Tex-Mex, or *tejano* music, became more reflective of the tastes and sensibilities of the assimilated, settled Mexican Americans, many of whom no longer spoke much Spanish. The text-driven corrido gave way to dance-oriented songs with short, catchy refrains and with flashy accordion playing by virtuosos such as Santiago "Flaco" Jiménez (b. 1939). Alongside the conjunto format, to some extent associated with working-class Mexican Americans in the United States, were larger, horn-based ensembles called *orquestas*, which played a mixture of *rancheras*, Colombian-derived *cumbias*, and other genres. Texas-Mexican pop singer Selena Quintanilla (1971–95) was extending her audience well beyond the tejano market until her untimely death.

Meanwhile in the 1990s a new instrumental format called *banda* emerged, featuring one or more singers accompanied by acoustic brass band (or, in the case of *techno-banda*, supplemented with electric instruments). Most of the banda repertoire consists of rancheras, cumbias, and songs in polka rhythms.

At present a variety of popular music styles are heard throughout Mexico, including norteño, pop ballads (*balada*), cumbias, banda, Dominican *bachata*, the provocative, idiosyncratically feminist music of Gloria Trevi (b. 1970), and Spanish-language rock, which has flourished in Mexico since around 1970. "Tropical" music styles such as salsa and *merengue* are especially popular in the Caribbean port of Veracruz. Mexican music—especially mariachi music and norteño—also tends to dominate popular tastes in El Salvador, Honduras, and Nicaragua. Further down the coasts, in Panama and Costa Rica, the tropical sounds of salsa and cumbia are more often heard, alongside the current *reggaetón* hits. Panama itself is the home of salsa star Ruben Blades—who became that country's Minister of Culture—and of proto-reggaetón vocalist El General.

## THE CARIBBEAN

Although all regions of Latin America have been dynamic musical centers in their own way, the Caribbean has been especially vital. The international influence and appeal of Caribbean genres such as reggae and the Cuban son are especially remarkable in view of the relatively small populations involved. Caribbean countries are also culturally diverse, being divided according to colonial history into Spanish, French, English, and Dutch sectors, with descendants of East Indians also figuring prominently in some countries. Nevertheless, most Caribbean music cultures have been shaped by similar general conditions. Most prominent among these is the syncretism of African-derived and European-derived elements, in an effervescent process of *creolization*, implying the development of dynamic new cultural forms through the encounter of two or more parent cultures.

The indigenous Tainos and Caribs of the region do not appear to have contributed in any significant or verifiable way to the development of modern popular music styles. Far more important is the African input, which pervades the Caribbean and accounts for much of the region's dynamism and distinctive features. Many elements of African culture, from kinship networks to specific songs and dances, were lost in the brutal Middle Passage and in the hostile New World experience. However, transplanted Africans and their descendants were able, to varying degrees in different locales, to perpetuate many of their ancestral traditions, especially aspects of music culture. These surviving features include some specific elements such as drums, rhythms, and lyric fragments, and also more general characteristics, such as the emphasis on rhythm, the use of short, repeated phrases or rhythmic patterns (called *ostinatos* in the European tradition), call-and-response singing, and rhythmic syncopation. Most of these features figure prominently in contemporary Caribbean popular music styles. Equally prominent and crucial are elements derived from the European heritage, including chordal harmony, melodic instruments, European languages and verse forms, dance styles, and other features.

## Cuba

Cuba (population 11.3 million) has been the single most influential crucible for popular music in the Caribbean. Cuba's musical dynamism derives not only from its size, relative to other Caribbean islands, but from its even balance of African- and European-descended peoples and a social history that facilitated their dynamic interaction. In the mid-1800s an Afro-Caribbean-inflected parlor music, the *contradanza habanera* (or, outside Cuba, simply *habanera*), became popular in Europe—disseminated on sheet music, via music theater groups that crisscrossed the Atlantic, and through contexts such as Georges Bizet's opera *Carmen* (1876). Some piano contradanzas were Chopinesque light classical works, but many were produced as tuneful dance pieces that, marketed on sheet music, constituted incipient commercial popular music styles.

More akin to urban popular music was the *danzón*, which emerged in the 1870s in the music of Afro-Cuban composer and bandleader Miguel Faílde in the town of Matanzas and soon spread to Havana and elsewhere. Like the contradanza, the danzón was primarily instrumental and most typically played by a small wind and percussion ensemble. Although this form was built on a European-derived rondo pattern with a repeating first section (e.g., ABABACAC), the use of a lively syncopated ostinato (called the *cinquillo*, sounding like *one*-and-*two*-and-*three*-and-*four*-and-repeated) gave the danzón a distinct—and controversial—Afro-Caribbean flavor.

After independence was achieved in 1902, the growing sense of cultural nationalism invigorated local music styles but was mitigated by racist ambivalence toward the Afro-Cuban aspects of these emerging styles. In the subsequent years, 78 rpm records started to be produced and mass marketed in Cuba, marking the true emergence of commercial popular music styles. Recordings gave new life to the danzón, whose old-fashioned, horn-dominated *orquesta típica* gave way to a new ensemble called *charanga*, which featured flute, two violins, piano, bass, and percussion. The danzón continued to acquire a more Afro-Cuban flavor, especially in the addition of a final section based on a static, syncopated ostinato or vamp. Another genre emerging around this time was the bolero, which (having nothing in common with its Spanish namesake) developed as a romantic dance song, in a moderate or slow rhythm with a subtle Afro-Cuban syncopation.

However, the most seminal and important Cuban music genre to emerge in the early 1900s was the son. The son appears to have commenced as an urban folk genre in the towns of eastern Cuba (Oriente), combining vocals with syncopated ostinatos played on the guitar-like *tres* and percussion instruments. In the years following independence, the son traveled west to Havana, where it grew in richness, sophistication, and range of dissemination. It also came under the influence of the *rumba*, a lower-class, Afro-Cuban, voice-and-percussion party music. From the rumba, the son acquired the use of the *clave* sticks and the structurally important basic patterns they played (also called clave); also from rumba came the essentially two-part song structure, consisting of an initial verse section and a second, longer section called *montuno*, featuring call-and-response singing (and sometimes instrumental solos) over repeated chordal ostinatos. By the 1920s Havana and nearby Matanzas featured dozens of son ensembles, especially septets using tres, guitar, bass (of some sort), clave, bongo, and trumpet. The most popular groups, such as the Sexteto Habanero, Septeto Nacional, and the Trío Matamoros, also made many commercial recordings still known today. Most of the son musicians were black or mulatto, and the son's lyrics were rooted in Afro-Cuban street life and slang.

The 1940s and 1950s were especially dynamic years for Cuban popular music. Havana hosted a lively entertainment scene, with many cabarets and ballrooms for tourists and the local bourgeoisie and a network of humbler dance clubs for working-class Afro-Cubans. Records and radio stations proliferated, and musicians were able to cultivate, draw from, and synthesize a variety of local genres as well as American music styles such as big-band jazz.

The music scene encompassed a variety of new genres and modernized versions of older ones. Boleros could be heard in various contexts and forms, but especially in the guitar-and-voice trio format popularized by Mexican groups in the 1940s and 1950s. By this time the bolero was a thoroughly international genre, flourishing in Puerto Rico, Mexico, and elsewhere. With their romantic lyrics, boleros have been especially popular with women.

By the 1940s the danzón had come to be regarded as old-fashioned by most Cubans, despite the extension of and new emphasis on the syncopated, "funky" coda section (which came to be called *mambo*). But before expiring entirely, the danzón contributed to the birth of two new genres. One of these was the *chachachá*, fashioned in the early 1950s by charanga bandleader Enrique Jorrín. Jorrín's innovation was essentially to add sung lyrics and chordal progressions to the rhythm of the coda of the danzón, retaining the medium tempo and the use of the flute-and-violins charanga format. In the 1950s the chachachá enjoyed a faddish popularity in Cuba and even the United States, in more or less diluted forms.

An ultimately more dynamic development was the emergence of the big-band mambo. The use of the big-band format in Cuba, as in Puerto Rico, Haiti, and the Dominican Republic during this period was inspired by the swing bands of Duke Ellington, Count Basie, and others. In the days before amplification, the big-band format allowed a group to fill a large dance hall with sound. It also offered opportunities to exploit the practice of sectional arrangement, whereby contrasting ensemble textures could be formed by juxtaposing different sections (i.e., trumpets, saxophones, trombones, and the rhythm section of piano, bass, and percussion). Caribbean big-band leaders successfully applied these practices to local rhythms, especially as adapted from the son and the coda of the danzón. Despite its Cuban parentage, the big-band mambo itself flourished most outside of Cuba, especially in New York clubs such as the Palladium and Savoy Ballroom, as played by the bands of Cuban-born Machito (Frank Grillo, 1912–84) and the Newyorican (i.e., New Yorker of Puerto Rican descent) Tito Puente (1923–2000).

In Cuba itself in the 1950s, especially outside of the upper-class ballrooms, the rapidly evolving son served as the most popular dance music genre. Although some elders preferred the quaint, somewhat folksy sextet sound, more in vogue was the conjunto, using a band of two or three trumpets, piano, bass, and percussion, all playing tight patterns combining to make a hard-driving composite rhythm that could keep dancers on their feet for hours. The Conjunto Casino and Sonora Matancera were two popular Cuban bands of the period, but most dynamic and seminal was the music of Arsenio Rodríguez (1911–70), a blind bandleader, tres player, and composer. Arsenio penned many tuneful songs, standardized the rhythmic patterns and the use of the conga drum, and proudly reaffirmed the son's links to Afro-Cuban grassroots culture, especially via lyrics portraying vignettes of barrio life. In the 1950s Arsenio settled in New York, where he had to struggle to make ends meet and died in relative obscurity, even as a new generation of salsa musicians was studying his music and finding inspiration in it.

In Cuba, the lively music scene of the 1950s masked acute social tensions rooted in poverty, illiteracy, racism, the Mafia presence, and the corruption of the United States–backed dictator Fulgencio Batista. Hence, when charismatic guerrilla leader Fidel Castro put Batista to flight and seized power in 1959, the sense of optimism and expectation was widespread. The subsequent effects of the Revolution on Cuban music were mixed. With the nationalization of the entire music industry (along with the rest of the economy), many musicians acquired steady full-time employment with full benefits and vacations. At the same time, however, the United States imposed an embargo that cut off American tourism, crippling the club and cabaret scene. Many musicians went into exile, especially to nearby Miami. As the Cuban government offered relatively little support to dance music and the nationalized record industry stagnated, many young people lost interest in Cuban music.

In the early 1980s the popular music scene revived and received greater state support. Particularly dynamic were the salsa-style Son 14 of Adalberto Alvarez, Van Van (a sort of horn-enriched charanga group), and Irakere, a brassy supergroup that offered both straight-ahead dance music and eclectic, avant-garde fusions of jazz, son, and other Afro-Cuban genres.

One distinctively new genre that emerged in the Revolutionary period was *nueva trova*, a Cuban efflorescence of the pan-Latin American *nueva canción* (new song) movement. Emerging in the latter 1960s, nueva trova performers, including Silvio Rodríguez and Pablo Milanés, were primarily inspired by progressive American singer-songwriters such as Bob Dylan and Joan Baez. The songs dealt variously with love (while avoiding commercial clichés) or else voiced progressive political sentiments, generally in favor of the goals of the Revolution. The Cuban government eventually came to support the movement, and nueva trova singers went on to enjoy much popularity in Cuba and elsewhere in Latin America, especially among progressive students during the Cold War period, when Cuba was seen as an attractive alternative to the United States–backed military dictatorships that dominated the hemisphere.

In 1990, in the wake of the breakup of the Soviet Union and the cutoff of its aid to Cuba, the Cuban economy collapsed and has yet to recover. The effects on the music scene have been dramatic. State funding for the arts in general has been slashed, and the local record industry has effectively disappeared. Most Cubans find mere survival to be a daily struggle, and they have little disposable income for nightlife or recordings. At the same time, the government has belatedly revived tourism, so many musicians have been able to find work performing in tourist hotels, restaurants, and clubs. The state has also relaxed bureaucratic controls on musicians: many have been able to tour and even reside abroad and make their own deals with foreign record companies. Many Cubans aspire to join the ranks of the numerous professional musicians who have been able to find work abroad or who have managed, even if they stay in Cuba, to earn sums exponentially larger than even the best-paid doctors and engineers.

Despite such vicissitudes, the so-called special period has been, in some ways, a fertile one for music. Its most dramatic musical product has been *timba*, which flourished in the 1990s as a sort of avant-garde modernization of salsa and son. As popularized by groups such as Charanga Habanera and NG La Banda, timba featured brassy, dazzlingly virtuosic horn lines; long montuno sections with multiple choral refrains; great textural variety, with bass, percussion, and other instruments dropping in and out; and lyrics that often commented wryly on the entire urban scene of hustling tourists for dollars. Also emerging in this period has been a lively local rap scene, selectively supported by the state; particularly prominent is the group Orishas, whose members now reside in Paris. Especially popular among Cuban youth today are local and imported versions of reggaetón, which has taken the Spanish Caribbean by storm in recent years.

Another curious development resulted from the extraordinary international popularity of Ry Cooder's 1997 *Buena Vista Social Club* recordings and Wim Wender's subsequent film by the same name, in which the American guitarist Cooder collaborated with ("discovered") a set of aging performers of 1920s-style son and bolero. Although most Cubans themselves may have felt bemused by the faddish foreign vogue of this rather old-fashioned music, the octogenarian performers enjoyed superstardom in their twilight years, and Buena Vista–style groups have proliferated in hotels and clubs in response to tourist demand.

## Puerto Rico

Puerto Rico (population 3.8 million), despite its relatively small size, has hosted one of the Caribbean's most dynamic music cultures. Because the island was a sister colony to Cuba until 1898, many aspects of its music culture evolved as adaptations and reinterpretations of Cuban imports, from the danza of the late colonial era to the bolero and even salsa. These, however, have traditionally flourished alongside purely local genres such as *plena*, the Afro-Rican *bomba*, and the more Hispanic-derived *jíbaro* (peasant) music. Since the 1980s, Puerto Ricans have also become skilled performers of the Dominican-derived merengue and of local adaptations of rap and dancehall reggae (Spanish-language reggaetón). With two-thirds of people of Puerto Rican descent living in the mainland United States (especially in New York City), Puerto Rican music culture must be seen as a transnational entity, especially inseparable from Newyorican culture, which itself overlaps with black and other Latino subcultures in New York and elsewhere.

Commercial Puerto Rican popular music can be said to have emerged in the early decades of the twentieth century when local performers and composers of Cuban-style bolero and son began to make 78 rpm records. Two particularly gifted, prolific, and internationally beloved composers of boleros were Rafael Hernández (1892–1965) and Pedro Flores (1894–1979). Because the state of the music scene in Puerto Rico was underdeveloped until the 1950s, both composers were obliged to reside in New York and elsewhere abroad for extended periods in order to further their careers. During this period, recordings of Puerto Rican music were made less often on the island than in New York City, with its media infrastructure and the presence of a steadily growing Newyorican population. From the 1940s, although the island's music scene grew, the trickle of migrants to New York turned into a torrent, so much of Puerto Rican music culture evolved as an entity straddling the easily traversed "blue pond" of the Atlantic.

If the bolero as a genre originated in Cuba, the plena was a purely homegrown Puerto Rican genre, emerging in the early twentieth century as an unpretentious, often irreverent, topical verse-and-refrain song, most typically sung by lower-class islanders in informal gatherings. In the 1920s and 1930s, plenas started to be recorded and commercially marketed in New York City, especially as sung by New York–based vocalist Manuel "Canario" Jiménez. In such recordings, the tambourine-like *pandereta*—the trademark of the genre—would typically be supplemented by other dance-band instruments. In the 1940s, a glamorous big-band version of the plena was popularized by Cesar Concepción, who performed mostly in ritzy hotels and ballrooms for the local elite.

In the 1950s, a more dynamic version of the dance-band plena flowered, popularized by the bands of Mon Rivera and, especially, Rafael Cortijo (1928–82) and his singer, Ismael ("Maelo") Rivera (1931–87). Cortijo's band was a Cuban-style conjunto, and much of their repertoire consisted of *sones* in more or less standard Cuban style. However, he was also celebrated for his dance-band versions of plena, which reasserted the genre's proletarian earthiness via their vigorous style and their lyrics portraying vignettes of Afro-Rican barrio life. Another genre that Cortijo adapted to dance-band format, in a fairly Cubanized style, was the Afro–Puerto Rican bomba, which in its traditional style consisted of voices and percussion, accompanying a solo dancer.

In the 1960s Cortijo's band splintered and public tastes shifted from plena toward salsa. In the 1970s, salsa flourished with great vigor in both New York and Puerto Rico, with the long-lasting groups El Gran Combo and Sonora Ponceña becoming virtual institutions in island culture. Although salsa became an international entity, with its style deriving mostly from the Cuban son, Puerto Ricans, who have cultivated it with such energy and creativity, have justifiably regarded it as one of the hallmarks of island culture.

Despite salsa's status, in the 1980s its popularity became rivaled by that of the merengue, initially brought from the neighboring Dominican Republic by inexpensive touring bands. Although some hard-core salsa fans regarded the merengue as a foreign menace, Puerto Rican performers such as Olga Tañón and Elvis Crespo were soon turning merengue into a genre not only enjoyed, but also performed and reinterpreted by islanders.

The 1990s saw the successful cultivation of two more imported genres in Puerto Rico. One was rap, which, as performed in Spanish by artists such as the New York–born Vico C (b. 1971) and Eddie Dee (b. 1940), has come to occupy a small but recognized niche in island music. Another such genre has been rock (or rock *en español*), rendered by groups such as Puya and Fiel a la Vega. Some critics initially regarded local rappers and *rockeros* as wanna-be Yankees, but many such performers are ardent advocates of Puerto Rican cultural nationalism; indeed, rock and rap have become so international in character that there need be no contradiction in singing a rock song about Puerto Rican pride, for example, or about the need to reclaim the island of Vieques from the U.S. military.

In the new millennium, although salsa and merengue have been holding their own, the most popular youth music in the island has been reggaetón, a distinctive Spanish-language reinterpretation of Jamaican dancehall reggae. Although originally inspired by Jamaican deejays, reggaetón—also cultivated in Cuba, New York, and elsewhere—has acquired its own distinctive flavor, with its particular standardized rhythm, its stentorian yet often tuneful choruses, and its infectious, unpretentious anthems to dancing and partying.

## Salsa

Salsa is an international genre that cannot be regarded as the unique patrimony of any particular place, much less a Caribbean island. Although its style derives originally from Cuba, it arose primarily in New York City, especially as performed by Puerto Ricans, and some of its hottest performers have been Colombians and Venezuelans.

Salsa arose in the 1960s and 1970s from the spirit of cultural ferment, ethnic pride, and creative energy among New York Latinos—primarily first- and second-generation Puerto Ricans. Although the mambo craze had passed and Puerto Rican genres such as plena and bomba were relatively unknown in the city, Newyorican bands started reinterpreting and reinvigorating the style of Cuban son from the 1950s to 1960s, which was familiar to several musicians via the presence of Arsenio Rodríguez. A crucial catalyst was provided by

Fania Records, run by bandleader Johnny Pacheco (b. 1935) and entrepreneur Jerry Masucci, who successfully marketed New York and Puerto Rican bands as the voice of Latinos throughout the Americas. Fania also coined the term *salsa* as a rubric for the style.

Flourishing with great dynamism in the 1970s, salsa encompassed a certain range of styles, all of which retained the basic rhythmic patterns, two-part (verse section followed by montuno) formal structure, and instrumental styles of the modern Cuban son. On the conservative or *típico* end was the music of Pacheco, modeled on that of 1950s son groups such as the Sonora Matancera, and of Newyorican bandleader and *timbales*-player Tito Puente (1923–2000) and Cuban-born singer Celia Cruz (1924–2003). Insofar as the term *salsa* implied a new genre, it was more appropriate for the music of innovators such as Ruben Blades (b. 1948) and Eddie Palmieri (b. 1936). Blades's songs of the 1970s, particularly those produced with bandleader Willie Colon, were lively and tuneful, and many of their lyrics presented colorful and sensitive snapshots of or commentaries on barrio life; others were politically outspoken and progressive enough for right-wing Miami Cubans to ban his music from local radio stations. A prominent handful of songs by Colon and others incorporated distinctive Puerto Ricanisms, such as singing "le lo lai" or the use of the mandolin-like *cuatro*. Perhaps what most distinguished salsa from the Cuban son was its links—made explicit in several 1970s song texts—with the spirit of idealism, sociopolitical commitment, and ethnic pride that invigorated Latinos in New York and much of the Americas. Salsa soon came to be the voice of the barrio, not only in New York and Puerto Rico, but in Venezuela, Colombia, and elsewhere, serving both as a marker of Latino pride and an accompaniment to creative dancing.

A typical salsa band consists of a lead singer; two or three others who sing the *coro* (chorus) during the montuno and perhaps also play percussion; piano and bass; four or five horns—typically two trumpets and two trombones; conga; and a percussionist who plays bongo during the first section of the song and switches to cowbell during the montuno. All of the instrumental parts adhere to standardized patterns (deriving from the son) that constitute cogs in the driving, kinetic, composite group rhythm.

In the 1980s, hard-core salsa (*salsa dura*) seemed to be losing steam; as the sociopolitical zeal of the 1970s dissipated, the genre lost ground to merengue in popularity, and a softer, more sentimental and pop-oriented style called *salsa romántica* came into vogue. Although disparaged by fans of the hard-driving 1970s sound, salsa romántica attracted legions of female fans and represented a new kind of departure—albeit in feeling rather than structure—from the 1950s Cuban son. At the same time a new crop of singers emerged, including the crossover vocalist (who also records in English) Marc Anthony (b. 1969) and the idiosyncratically feminist Linda "La India" Caballero (b. 1969). In the late 1990s, the New York–based band DLG (Dark Latin Groove), under the direction of innovative producer Sergio George, popularized an eclectic mix of salsa, contemporary R&B, and dancehall, and since then it has not been uncommon to hear such styles juxtaposed in a single song. Salsa, indeed, has exhibited remarkable durability, as commercial popular music styles go. Although some older fans may complain that the vitality of the 1970s has not been matched, the genre has been holding its own against the competition of newer styles such as rap, *bachata*, and reggaetón.

## The Dominican Republic

Despite its troubled history, the Dominican Republic (population 8.8 million) has hosted a vigorous local popular music scene, whose main constituents—merengue and bachata—have enjoyed international appeal in recent decades. Many aspects of the origins of the most renowned Dominican music form, the merengue, remain obscure. In the nineteenth century the word merengue (whether of French or African origin) was applied in Puerto Rico and the Dominican Republic to a creole dance music genre deriving from the Caribbean contradanza family. Such music could be played by wind ensembles or, in more rustic contexts, on guitar, the metal *güira* scraper, and a double-headed drum called the *tambora*. By the turn of the century the button accordion had largely replaced the guitar, promoting simpler chord progressions, and a lively and quite distinctive style of merengue evolved in the densely populated Cibao valley, with its major town of Santiago de los Caballeros. In the early decades of the twentieth century, the basic elements of the Cibao style crystallized: especially its crisp, frenetic, but tightly controlled composite rhythm—produced by the staccato pyrotechnics of the accordion, the hissing and scratching güira, and the rollicking tambora pattern, with its distinctive roll leading up to the downbeat of each measure. Atop this intricate rhythm, a vocalist (often the accordionist) would sing topical verses, segueing to a call-and-response section (formerly called *jaleo*, and now more often referred to as mambo). This style, called *merengue típico cibaeño* (traditional Cibao-style merengue) or *perico ripao* (ripped parrot), was further modernized, often coming to accommodate a saxophone, in the music of Tatico Henríquez (d. 1976).

Until the 1930s, the merengue was largely shunned by the bourgeoisie of the country's capital city, Santo Domingo. However, the merengue's status changed after Rafael Trujillo seized power in 1930 in a coup d'état and commenced his thirty-one-year dictatorship. Trujillo, while running the country as if it were his private ranch, was an ardent lover of the merengue, especially as played by larger ensembles with horn sections. He effectively declared the merengue to be the country's national music. Merengue bands accompanied him on his speaking tours, elite clubs were required to play merengues, and radio stations broadcast merengues singing his praises. Trujillo brought the leading dance band of Santiago, Orquesta Alberti, to the capital, renaming it Orquesta Trujillo (just as he renamed the city Ciudad Trujillo). Soon the modernized merengue became popular throughout the country, especially in the form of hits such as "El compadre Pedro Juan." Thus the merengue prospered, in its way, during the dictatorship, while other aspects of cultural and intellectual life were stunted. Dance bands with horn sections performed on the radio and in urban clubs, while the merengue típico still thrived in Cibao and, especially, in Santiago, a city which took on a status akin to that of Nashville in the United States, as the center of country music.

In 1961, after the U.S. Central Intelligence Agency abetted the assassination of Trujillo and U.S. Marines invaded the island a few years later, power passed to the hands of Joaquin Balaguer (1907–2002), Trujillo's right-hand man, who went on to dominate the country's political scene almost until his death. The Balaguer period constituted a new chapter in the country's cultural and musical history, characterized in part by massive urbanization and emigration. In the 1970s Johnny Ventura (b. 1940), bandleader and later progressive politician, further modernized the merengue and perfected a stage "combo show" with uniform-clad band members performing flashy choreography. As the Dominican record industry belatedly got under way, the merengue continued to evolve, with the talents of bandleaders such Wilfrido Vargas (b. 1949).

The modern merengue, as codified by Vargas, Ventura, and others, retains the Cibao folk merengue's basic rhythm, and the use of güira and tambora. A section of two saxophones effectively perpetuates the accordion's role, playing fast, staccato riffs throughout much of the song, often punctuated and answered by riffs played by two trumpets. A crisp, disco-style bass drum beat and a similarly staccato bass guitar pattern add the lower end to the merengue's frenetic but tight and intricate composite rhythm.

One result of Balaguer's economic policies was massive emigration: from the 1980s several hundred thousand Dominicans, out of desperation or ambition, emigrated to nearby

Puerto Rico and the U.S. mainland, especially New York City. Merengue bands accompanied them, and the merengue's popularity soon extended to Puerto Ricans and Newyoricans enthralled by its sizzling rhythms and simple choreography.

In the 1980s, Dominican popular music was enlivened by the emergence of a new genre called bachata. Bachata derives from a guitar-based bolero tradition brought to the cities by rural migrants in the Balaguer period. Although it was initially disparaged by urbanites as crude, by the early 1990s bachata had grown in popularity, sophistication, and legitimacy and become a major commercial pop entity. It also acquired a distinctive style, with its bouncy rhythm, quite different from the bolero. By the 1990s the country was experiencing a belated cultural awakening, in which an important role was played by music in general and, especially, by eclectic bandleader, composer, and singer Juan Luis Guerra. Meanwhile, a modernized form of merengue típico cibaeño continues to flourish today in the Cibao and among emigrant communities in New York.

## The French Caribbean

The French Caribbean primarily comprises independent Haiti and the French *départements* of Martinique and Guadeloupe. However, Franco-Caribbean musical influence extends well beyond these islands because of the vibrancy of French creole culture in the colonial period and the exodus from Haiti during that country's revolution (1791–1804).

In the early twentieth century, the most popular form of creole music in Haiti was the *mereng* (merengue), a syncopated dance music that could be rendered on guitar, piano, or urban dance band. Although the mereng is historically related to the Dominican *merengue*, their modern versions are quite distinct. Also gaining popularity during this period was the Cuban son and bolero and the Dominican merengue. In the 1950s, an urban, horn-based, dance-band style called *konpa* (*compas*) crystallized in the ensembles led by Nemours Jean-Baptiste and his rival Weber Sicot. In the 1960s, groups such as Tabou Combo popularized a modernized form of konpa, sometimes called "mini-jazz," using electric guitars in place of large horn sections.

Haitian cultural life suffered under the prolonged dictatorships (1957–86) of François "Papa Doc" Duvalier (d. 1971) and his son Jean-Claude "Baby Doc." Nevertheless, during the years preceding Baby Doc's ouster, konpa bands based in Haiti, New York, Montreal, and Paris displayed much vitality and served as vehicles, however circumscribed, for distraction from and, occasionally, protest against the dictatorship. The post-Duvalier years failed to provide stability; as a result, in some respects, Haitian popular music has been able to flourish more outside the country than within. In the 1980s a more pop-oriented, ballad-like style called *nouvel jenerasyon* came into vogue, although modernized konpa has continued to dominate dance music scenes.

In Martinique and Guadeloupe from the 1930s to the 1950s, the *biguine* had flourished as a lively local dance music, performed by various ensembles at dance halls, tourist clubs, church parties, and other affairs. In the subsequent decades, Haitian-style konpa enjoyed greater popularity, but around 1980 a new local style developed, called *zouk*. As popularized especially by the group Kassav, zouk features lyrics in local creole, set to a tight, medium-tempo beat rendered on synthesizers, drum machines, and other instruments.

## Jamaica

The popular music of Jamaica (population 2.7 million) has enjoyed worldwide fame quite incommensurate with the island's small size and population. Such fame is also surprising in view of the fact that Jamaica had little popular music of its own until the early 1960s. By that decade, a younger generation had emerged that had lost touch with Afro-Jamaican religious music styles, such as those of *kumina*, and had little interest in the old-fashioned creole folk songs called *mento*. Instead what appealed to young urban Jamaicans was African-American rhythm & blues, via records played by mobile sound systems at neighborhood dances. The sound systems, with their own equipment, record collections, and mike-wielding deejays, have remained core institutions in Jamaican popular music.

Around 1960, as Afro-American music tastes shifted from R&B to soul, Jamaican deejays were finding themselves unable to get new records with the sound their patrons liked. Sound system owner Clement (Coxson) Dodd (1932–2004) took the crucial step of hiring studio musicians to record songs locally for his use as a deejay, but he and others soon found that there was great public demand for the records they produced. Within a few years, a distinctive style, called *ska*, had emerged, with its jerky offbeat syncopation constituting a Jamaican twist on R&B. Many ska songs, such as the 1964 hit "My Boy Lollipop," were simply syncopated cover versions of African-American songs, but many others were originals, produced in small Jamaican record studios that arose during this period.

In the subsequent years, the development of Jamaican popular music can be seen to reflect a set of interrelated processes. One was a form of internationalization: starting with "My Boy Lollipop" and moving through reggae to dancehall, Jamaican music acquired extraordinary global popularity. Accompanying this internationalization was a growing sophistication, as urban musicians mastered and developed original approaches to studio recording, live performance, and song composition. Also related was a process of indigenization, as unpretentious cover versions of R&B songs gave way to artful original compositions. Many songs were distinctively Jamaican in the orientation of their lyrics, which sang ambivalently of rude boys (lumpen hoodlums), of ghetto life, of the struggle for human rights, or of Rastafari, the local Afrocentric religion that proclaimed Ethiopian Emperor Haile Selassie to be God and idiosyncratically reinterpreted Old Testament beliefs.

By 1970, ska had largely given way to reggae, with a slower, syncopated beat that showed how far Jamaican had moved from its R&B roots. At the same time, reggae, like ska, remained largely a studio recording art, brought to the people primarily by sound systems rather than by live performances of bands. The tuneful, impassioned songs of Bob Marley (1945–81), Jimmy Cliff, and others spread evocative messages of love, spiritual redemption, and a utopian vision of Africa. The idealism and fundamental optimism of roots reggae cohered with the mood of the country in the mid-1970s, as many believed that the progressive socialist government of Michael Manley, in cooperation with other developing countries, could redistribute Jamaica's wealth and challenge imperialist domination.

However, the deterioration of the economy and law-and-order situation in the late 1970s led to widespread disillusionment and a change in national mood and musical tastes. Although Marley had become an international superstar, youth interest shifted to a new generation of deejays, who—whether at sound-system dances or on recordings—chanted verses in simple, repetitive tunes over familiar, independently produced *riddims*, or instrumental tracks. As popularized in the early 1980s by deejay singers such as Yellowman, dancehall (as the new style came to be known) focused not on fantasies of Africa, but on the vicissitudes of ghetto life: guns, machismo, dancing, the struggle for survival, sex, and more sex. The sound systems remained central to the scene, whether featuring deejay records, live deejays chatting over records of riddims, or surrealistic, radical, "dub" remixes of current songs. The sound systems' use of records and turntables as musical instruments prefigured similar developments in the rap scene around 1980.

By the latter 1980s dancehall had matured into a distinctive and mature genre, with stars such as Buju Banton, Ninja Man, and Shabba Ranks all popularizing their own styles. In the 1990s, together with deejays such as Sean Paul, Beenie Man, and Bounty Killer, they made dancehall the most popular music throughout the English-speaking Caribbean and enjoyed considerable stardom throughout the English-speaking world as a whole. Several dancehall deejays (as vocalists are called) have collaborated with Afro-American rappers.

Unique to dancehall is the practice of recycling riddims; at any given time, a dozen or so riddims are popular and in use, such that both established and up-and-coming deejays voice their lyrics over the same familiar set of accompaniment tracks, rather than recording them fresh in the studio. Another unique institution is the "sound clash," in which two or more sound systems duel with each other, taking turns playing excerpts from their exclusive collections of "dub plates"—short recordings made by deejays especially for the sound system, using the tune of a current song but substituting lyrics praising the system.

Dancehall, like many popular music styles, has been controversial; many older fans of roots reggae disparage dancehall's frequent machismo, sexism, and lewdness; its defenders, for their part, point to its driving rhythms, its artful use of Jamaican patois, and the way that it celebrates female sexuality. Another controversy has involved the obsessive homophobia of deejays, who sing innumerable songs that explicitly incite hatred and violence against gay people. Since around 2000, several leading deejays have found their international tours canceled because of outcry against such diatribes.

## Trinidad and the Calypso World

Although Trinidad (population 1.1 million) is, like Jamaica, an English-speaking former British colony, its cultural character is in many ways distinct. Nearly half the island's population is ethnically East Indian, and there is a stratum of French Creole and even Spanish cultural heritage that is not found in Jamaica. As in Jamaica and elsewhere in the Anglophone West Indies, Afro-American rap and R&B are perennially popular, existing alongside local genres.

The most renowned local popular music is *calypso*, which has been linked since its inception to pre-Lenten Carnival. This celebration was introduced by the white French creoles who immigrated with their slaves to the island in the late 1700s. After British conquest in 1797, Carnival continued to grow, especially as an occasion for rowdy street processions of Afro-Trinidadians—slaves or, after 1838, free men and women. Carnival processions featured drumming until 1881, when a prohibition of drums led to the adoption of bamboo-based "tamboo-bamboo" ensembles with responsorial singing. In the years after 1900, the rehearsal sites for masquerade groups ("mas bands") became lively places to socialize. A few entrepreneurs set up tents where listeners could pay a small fee to hear amateur singers, accompanied by a humble, string-based house band, sing topical, often humorous and satirical songs, in a creole folk style that came to be called calypso. By the 1930s the calypso tents were fixtures of the Carnival scene, with performers competing for prizes and their songs (several of which were commercially recorded) serving as vehicles for the expression of grassroots Afro-Trinidadian male attitudes.

In 1957, the government decided to organize the Carnival events, forming a National Carnival Commission, which, among other things, replaced the local tent contests with a nationwide competition. This period also saw the emergence of Francisco Slinger (b. 1935), the "Mighty Sparrow," who proved to be the genre's most outstanding exponent, with a career lasting until the present millennium.

The calypso season starts around December, when singers begin composing or otherwise acquiring songs, many of which may comment on recent local events. The calypsonian must also hire an arranger to compose ensemble parts for the band. The singer then auditions to perform his or her song(s) regularly through January and February at a "tent," most of which are now clubs or theaters. Demonstration tapes of the songs are also broadcast on radio and TV, so the country gets saturated with the season's calypsos in the pre-Lenten months. (Sales of calypso recordings, however, are low and are mainly for tourists.) A panel of judges selects a set of singers to perform as semi-finalists and then selects a "Calypso Monarch" from finalists on "Dimanche Gras," the Sunday preceding Ash Wednesday. At that point calypso activity in Trinidad largely ceases until the following Carnival season, and radios and dances revert to rap, modern R&B, and Jamaican dancehall. However, calypso singers often attend festivals in other locales, such as Barbados's summertime Crop-Over, Toronto's Caribana, and New York's Labor Day Parade.

Recognizing the need for a local dance-music style, in the latter 1970s calypsonian Lord Shorty (1941–2000, subsequently Ras Shorty I) came up with a bouncy syncopated rhythm which he called *soca*. Soca quickly took root as a national dance music, accompanying a dance style based on pneumatic pelvic thrusting ("wining"). Soca lyrics, unlike those of calypso, are generally short and light, often consisting of calisthenic-type commands (e.g., "Get something and wave!"). With its infectious rhythm, soca was threatening to marginalize calypso in the tent competitions until the National Carnival Commission created a separate Soca Monarch competition in 1993.

Another distinctive Trinidadian idiom, which has spread to many other locales, is steel band music. Steel bands evolved in the 1940s as Afro-Trinidadian mas band members found that they could get distinct pitches on the head of a discarded oil drum if it were properly dented. Ingenious innovators quickly learned how to make ensembles of such instruments (called "pans"), which then replaced the tamboo-bamboo street bands. After initially repressing the bands for the violent brawls the street processions often provoked, the government turned to supporting them. The art form grew rapidly in sophistication and legitimacy: today there are over a hundred steel bands on the island, with the "Panorama" competition constituting one of the main attractions of Carnival. The steel bands, which may number over a hundred players, mostly perform arrangements of contemporary soca and calypso tunes.

Although Trinidad has been renowned as the land of calypso, Carnival, and steel drum, these cultural products have always been associated primarily with creoles, or Afro-Trinidadians. Nearly half the country's population, however—and over half that of neighboring Guyana—are descendants of indentured laborers who came from India between 1845 and 1917. Although the first generation of Indians tended to remain in their isolated farming communities, Indians in recent decades have increasingly urbanized and asserted their rightful place in their nations' political and artistic culture. Indians have also contributed a distinctive pop style to the region's music culture, in the form of chutney and chutney-soca.

Chutney derives from the lively, often humorously bawdy folk songs and dances that Hindu women would perform, with no men around, at weddings in Trinidad, Guyana, Suriname, and the Bhojpuri region of India. In Trinidad, Hindu women starting taking these songs and dances out of the closet in the 1960s and 1970s. By the mid-1980s public chutney "fêtes" were being held every weekend, in which men and women would dance energetically, in a modified Bhojpuri style, to chutney songs provided by a band consisting of a singer with harmonium (akin to an accordion), *dholak* barrel drum, and a metal rod called a *dantal*. In the next decade, a drum machine playing a soca beat was added, and English lyrics tended to replace verses in Hindi (which few Indo-Caribbeans outside of Suriname speak). The result was called chutney-soca, which is now a major pop phenomenon and also a new Carnival competition category (with both black and Indian contestants). Trinidad is already being referred to as the land of calypso, Carnival, and chutney.

## COLOMBIA AND OTHER CARIBBEAN BASIN COUNTRIES

Colombia, with its regionally and ethnically diverse population of 42 million people of African, European, and Native American descent, hosts an impressive diversity of popular music traditions whose evolution has been conditioned by the country's turbulent history. As in countries such as Cuba and Brazil, the most dynamic of Colombia's popular music forms have been associated with black and mulatto performers and communities, posing a certain sort of challenge to the conceptions of national identity traditionally favored by the white bourgeoisie.

The most important Colombian popular music genre with the largest international audience has been the cumbia. Cumbia was originally a folk song and dance form of the Atlantic coastal region, especially of black and mulatto communities (as its African-derived name suggests). In the 1940s and 1950s it was made into an urban popular genre by mambo-influenced, horn-based bands such as those of Lucho Bermúdez, and reached a peak of local popularity in the 1960s via Los Corraleros de Majagual and other groups. Its trademark is the moderate-tempo chick-chicka-chick-chicka-chick beat and an accordingly simple basic choreography. Many cumbia bands resemble Cuban-style son or salsa conjuntos, except for the frequent use of two clarinets, which are not popular in the Caribbean. During this period, the cumbia spread throughout Mexico and the rest of Spanish-speaking South America, where it is cultivated in different styles. It is arguably the single most widespread music genre in all of Latin America.

More unique to Colombia is *vallenato*, which originated as a folk genre of the northeastern region (especially around Valledupar), traditionally associated with cowboy culture. In the 1960s and 1970s vallenato assumed a more modern and broadly popular form, especially as rendered by accordion-based ensembles of Alejo Duran (d. 1989), Lisandro Meza, and others. Basic to the vallenato repertoire are the cumbia, the *puya*, and the son and merengue (which share nothing in particular with their Caribbean namesakes). By the 1980s the genre had become thoroughly associated with the drug dealers whose activities were bringing money and devastating corruption and violence into Colombian society. Many bands have been patronized by cocaine dealers and even sing their praises. In recent years, vallenato acquired a new sort of local legitimacy and international visibility through the neo-traditional music of Carlos Vives (b. 1961).

Another local genre has been *porro*, a rather loose category of songs traditionally played on brass bands but since heard in a variety of formats. Porro songs, in accordance with their association with railroad workers and other working-class men, abound in thinly veiled erotic puns and metaphors.

Cosmopolitan styles such as rock, rap, and Latin pop are also well entrenched in Colombia, and local crossover singer Shakira has had a string of international pop hits in both English and Spanish. Other international Latin genres have also been popular in Colombia, with the tango enjoying particular appeal in the twentieth century. From the 1980s, salsa also became a presence in the Colombia scene, especially as rendered by performers such as Grupo Niche and Joe Arroyo, who have enjoyed international appeal. Neighboring Venezuela has also been a dynamic center for the consumption and production of salsa; its most popular star has been singer, bandleader, and bassist Oscar d'León (b. 1943).

A curious phenomenon since the 1980s among the black communities of Cartagena and other Atlantic coast towns has been the vogue of African popular music (especially from the Congo), as disseminated by sound systems, in a format called *picó* (evidently from "pick-up").

Mention should be made of two other Atlantic coastal countries, which, although geographically South American, are in other respects distinct. Guyana (population 700,000), with its English-speaking population of mostly East Indian and African descent, has the character of a West Indian rather than a Latin American country. As in Trinidad, chutney, soca, and reggae are popular, although the country has not been able to support a viable popular music infrastructure. Chutney is also popular among the substantial East Indian community of neighboring Suriname (population 436,000), existing alongside a remarkably diverse and dynamic set of syncretic genres cultivated by that country's black population, including *kaseko*, *kawina*, and *aleke*.

## The Andean Countries and the Southern Cone

The Andean nations of Peru, Bolivia, and Ecuador are populated mostly by Indians, Spanish descendants, and mestizos. Indian language and traditional music styles remain widespread despite centuries of subjugation by whites. However, urban popular music styles, as elsewhere in the hemisphere, are more derivative of Afro-Latin and international genres. Hence, salsa, cumbia, tango, and rock are popular and cultivated in these countries. A distinctive variant of the cumbia in Peru is *chicha*, which emerged in the 1960s as a favored genre of lower-class urban migrants from the Andes region. Some chicha melodies have a markedly Indian flavor. Peru was also a center for *nueva canción*, the "new song" movement that flourished, despite state repression, in the 1960s to 1980s, especially among politically progressive students. As in Chile (population 16 million) and elsewhere, several nueva canción groups made self-conscious use of Andean Indian musical instruments and styles, partly to express solidarity with these otherwise downtrodden people. In Chile itself, nueva canción was repressed with particular ferocity by the dictatorship (1973–88) of Augusto Pinochet, who seized power in a CIA-supported coup.

In neighboring Argentina (population 39 million) the most renowned popular music by far has been the *tango*. The tango originated in the slums of Buenos Aires, which were populated by migrants from the countryside—black and mulatto descendants of slaves and legions of Italian immigrants. Musically, the early tango shared affinities with the Cuban habanera (or contradanza habanera), as disseminated especially by music-theater troupes that criss-crossed the ocean between Havana, Spain, and Buenos Aires. (The term *tango*—itself of uncertain origin—was applied to theatrical versions of the habanera and various duple-metered genres in Spain and elsewhere.)

In Buenos Aires, the tango during the "old guard" period (roughly 1885–1913) was performed mostly in the lumpen underworld of brothels and bohemian cafes. Although originally an instrumental genre played on violin, flute, and harp, in the years after 1900 the tango came to be more typically played by piano, violin, and the concertina-like *bandoneón* and increasingly included sung lyrics. Its texts, full of local slang called *lunfardo*, typically dramatized the macho, knife-wielding, womanizing dandy who, despite his tough exterior, was suffering the wounds of romantic betrayal. Other lyrics described brothel life, preached fatalism, or cursed the cruel indifference of society. Tango was also dance music and soon developed its own distinctive choreography, with partners executing closely coordinated, often picturesque steps while embracing each other intimately. Embedded as it was in the seamy underside of society, tango during this period was scorned by the bourgeoisie.

From the second decade of the twentieth century, the tango, in suitably packaged form, came to enjoy a faddish vogue both as a social dance and a stage art in Paris, filling the role of an exotic, passionate dance that was at once urbane and naughty. In the wake of this foreign legitimization, and as the Argentine tango itself became more professional and sophisticated, the Buenos Aires elite belatedly embraced the genre and made it its own. In this second stage of tango history, the genre "donned a smoking jacket" and entered the domain of the bourgeois cabaret, the ballroom, and even the concert hall. The standard ensemble became an *orquesta típica* of two violins, two *bandoneones*, piano, and string bass. The tango evolved rapidly through the artistry of composer-arrangers Julio De Caro and Osvaldo Fredo and vocalist Carlos Gardel (1887–1935), whose silky voice and suave urbanity epitomized the sophisticated, yet passionate image of the genre in its heyday. During this period, tango, while still rooted in Buenos Aires, effectively became the national music of Argentina and was widely disseminated throughout Latin America and even the United States via records and cinematic musicals, many of which starred Gardel. Argentine intellectuals have written extensively on the complex and contradictory class and gender dynamics of their cherished national genre.

In the 1950s and 1960s, the tango's most creative and dynamic period as a popular music genre waned, although it took on a new life as a stage dance idiom and, in an avant-garde form, as a concert style in the music of composer Astor Piazzolla (1921–92). Since then, the tango has remained vital, but mostly in a revivalist fashion.

Other genres of foreign stylistic origins have taken root in Argentina. In the city of Córdoba and its environs, a local variant of cumbia has flourished in the form of *cuarteto* music, which is typically played by an ensemble of synthesizer or keyboard, electric guitar, bass, and percussion. Perhaps more popular on a national level, especially among younger generations, has been rock, which Argentines have imported and avidly cultivated locally since the 1970s. In the years of dictatorship that ended in 1983, despite censorship of overt protest lyrics, *rock nacional* enjoyed a special sort of urgency as the focus of a progressive youth counterculture. Since then, the Argentine rock scene has remained vital in its way, although without the sense of sociopolitical importance and with a new level of competition from imported music styles.

The music culture of neighboring Uruguay resembles in many respects that of Argentina. Tango was long popular, especially in Montevideo, as is rock today, while in the rural areas the cumbia is pervasive.

## Brazil

Brazil (population 185 million), as the only Portuguese-speaking and the largest country by far in Latin America, constitutes a musical universe unto itself. As in Cuba, the late ongoing importation of slaves, the fluid racial mixing, and presence of large communities of free blacks throughout the colonial period facilitated the emergence of a dynamic variety of syncretic and urban popular music styles. In the latter 1800s, these comprised rowdy Afro-Brazilian voice-and-percussion genres (such as the early *lundu*) and also creolized salon music and dance forms, such as the *maxixe, modinha*, and the *lundu-canção*.

In the second decade of the twentieth century, the samba emerged as a distinctive and widely popular urban song form. The samba has gone on to flourish in various forms, including those associated with pre-Lenten Carnival, especially as celebrated in Rio de Janeiro. In Rio's Carnival, each Carnival procession group (or "school") selects an original samba composition as its theme song, which is performed as the group proceeds during Carnival, on the mass media, and at other occasions. These songs, including *samba de morro* (hill samba) or *samba-enredo* (theme samba), are ultimately judged in a competitive contest.

The samba itself consists of a vocal melody with instrumental accompaniment. The choral refrains are generally sung in unison, often with the wide melodic range, chromatic melodies, and jazz-influenced chordal harmonies characteristic of much Brazilian music.

By 1920 a different, but related kind of samba had emerged as an urban, popular, mass-mediated song genre. The *samba-canção* ("samba-song") shared several musical features with the Carnival samba, especially its downbeat-accented rhythm, but also evolved in a parallel direction as a studio entity, especially as performed by Noel Rosa (1910–37), Jose Luis "Caninha" de Morais (1883–1961), Pixinguinha (1898–1973), and Ary Barroso (1907–64). In the late 1950s, a reaction against the increasingly "sweet" ballroom samba developed, resulting in a greater diversity of styles.

Around 1960 the *bossa nova* emerged as a somewhat controversial but durable and dynamic new style. Although to some extent an extension of the earlier "sweet" samba-song style, its leading performers—João Gilberto (b. 1931), Antonio Carlos Jobim (1927–94), and Baden Powell (1937–2000)—incorporated sophisticated, yet smooth-sounding jazz harmonies and melodies, along with a nonpercussive, often guitar-based instrumental accompaniment and a soft, almost whispery vocal style. Bossa nova songs such as "Girl from Ipanema" and "Desafinado" became familiar to North American audiences via their popularization by Sergio Mendes, jazz saxophone player Stan Getz, and others.

In the mid-1960s, the acronym MPB—for *música popular brasileira* or Brazilian popular music—came to denote the wide variety of styles flourishing in the ever-expanding music industry. Some of these styles reflected the influence of rock, as Brazilian musicians self-consciously "cannibalized" cosmopolitan sounds in order to enrich their own stylistic palette. Hence, MPB includes the diverse music styles of Chico Buarque (b. 1944), Gilberto Gil (b. 1942), Milton Nascimiento (b. 1942), Caetano Veloso (b. 1942), and others. Self-conscious eclecticism became especially overt in the late 1960s musical movement called *tropicália*, led by Veloso and Gil.

Since the 1950s, as rural migrants continue to pour into Brazil's cities, urban stylized versions of country music came to be cultivated, as under the term *música sertaneja*. Many songs in this style sing of the migrant experience, retaining elements of rural music adapted to urban studios. A distinctive style associated with northeastern Brazil is *forró*, whose accordion-led ensembles became popular throughout the country, especially among the working classes. Like other genres, *forró* was often combined with rock elements, resulting in a style called *forrock*.

Brazilian music has enjoyed a wide international dissemination, and modern singers do not need to adulterate their music for Hollywood audiences, as songstress Carmen Miranda (1909–55) is sometimes regarded as having done in the 1940s and 1950s. Although in the past, Latin Americans have sometimes complained of a "cultural imperialism" that inundated the hemisphere with films and music from the United States, nowadays Brazil, with its well-developed entertainment industry, is a massive exporter of music and television shows (translated or subtitled as needed).

# RESOURCE GUIDE

### PRINT SOURCES

Austerlitz, Paul. *Merengue: Dominican Music and Dominican Identity.* Philadelphia: Temple University Press, 1997.

Averill, Gage. *A Day for the Hunter, a Day for the Prey: Music and Power in Haiti.* Chicago: University of Chicago Press, 1997.

Berrian, Brenda. *Awakening Spaces: French Caribbean Popular Songs, Music, and Culture.* Chicago: University of Chicago Press, 2000.

Boggs, Vernon, ed. *Salsiology.* Westport, CT: Greenwood, 1992.

Bradley, Lloyd. *This Is Reggae Music: The Story of Jamaica's Music.* New York: Grove Press, 2000.

Carpentier, Alejo. *La música en Cuba.* Mexico City: Fonda de Cultura Económica, 1946. Translated by Alan West-Duran as *Music in Cuba,* edited by Timothy Brennan. Minneapolis: University of Minnesota Press, 2001.

Castro, Donald. *The Argentine Tango as Social History, 1880–1955: The Soul of the People.* Lewiston, NY: E. Mellon Press, 1995.

Collier, Simon. *The Life, Music, and Times of Carlos Gardel.* Pittsburgh: University of Pittsburgh Press, 1995.

Cooper, Carolyn. *Sound Clash: Jamaican Dancehall Culture at Large.* New York: Palgrave/MacMillan, 2004, and Durham, NC: Duke University Press, 2000.

Díaz Ayala, Cristobal. *Música cubana del areyto a la nueva trova.* Hato Rey, PR: Editorial Cubanacan, 1981.

Evora, Tony. *Orígenes de la música cubana: los amores de las cuerdas y el tambor.* Madrid: Alianza Editorial, 1997.

Florine, Jane. *Cuarteto Music and Dancing from Argentina: In Search of the Tunga-Tunga in Córdoba.* Gainesville: University Press of Florida, 2001.

Guilbault, Jocelyne, Gage Averill, Édouard Benoit, and Gregory Rabess. *Zouk: World Music in the West Indies.* Chicago: University of Chicago Press, 1993.

Hill, Donald. *Calypso Callaloo: Early Carnival Music in Trinidad.* Gainesville: University Press of Florida, 1993.

Loza, Steven. *Tito Puente and the Making of Latin Music.* Urbana: University of Illinois Press, 1999.

Malavet Vega, Pedro. *Del bolero a la nueva canción.* Ponce, PR, 1988.

Manuel, Peter. *Popular Musics of the Non-Western World: An Introductory Survey.* New York: Oxford University Press, 1988.

———. *East Indian Music in the West Indies: Tan-Singing, Chutney, and the Making of Indo-Caribbean Culture.* Philadephia: Temple University Press, 2000.

Manuel, Peter, Kenneth Bilby, and Michael Largey. *Caribbean Currents: Caribbean Music from Rumba to Reggae,* 2nd edition. Philadelphia: Temple University Press, 2006.

Mason, Peter. *Bacchanal! The Carnival Culture of Trinidad.* Philadelphia: Temple University Press, 1998.

Mauleón, Rebeca. *Salsa Guidebook for Piano and Ensemble.* Petaluma, CA: Sher Music, 1993.

McGowan, Chris, and Ricardo Pessanha. *The Brazilian Sound: Samba, Bossa Nova, and the Popular Music of Brazil.* New York: Billboard Books, 1991.

Moore, Robin. *Music & Revolution: Cultural Change in Socialist Cuba.* Berkeley: University of California Press, 2006.

Pacini Hernandez, Deborah. *Bachata: A Social History of a Dominican Popular Music.* Philadelphia: Temple University Press, 1995.

Perna, Vincenzo. *Timba: The Sound of the Cuban Crisis.* London: Ashgate, 2005.

Perrone, Charles. *Masters of Contemporary Brazilian Song: MPB 1965-85.* Austin: University of Texas Press, 1989.

Perrone, Charles, and Christopher Dunn, eds. *Brazilian Popular Music and Globalization.* New York: Routledge, 2002.

Reuter, Jas. *La música popular de México: origen e historia de la música que canta y toca el pueblo mexicano.* Mexico City: Panorama, 1981.

Rohlehr, Gordon. *Calypso and Society in Pre-Independence Trinidad.* Port of Spain: G. Rohlehr, 1990.

Rondón, Cesar. *El libro de la salsa.* Caracas, Venezuela: Ediciones B, 1980.

Schreiner, Claus. *Musica Brasileira: A History of Popular Music and the People of Brazil.* New York: M. Boyars, 1993.

Steumpfle, Stephen. *Steelband Movement: The Forging of a National Art in Trinidad and Tobago.* Philadelphia: University of Pennsylvania Press, 1995.

Steward, Sue. ¡Música! The Rhythm of Latin America: Salsa, Rumba, Merengue, and More. San Francisco: Chronicle Books, 1999.

Stolzoff, Norman. Wake the Town and Tell the People: Dancehall Culture in Jamaica. Durham, NC: Fordham University Press, 2000.

Sublette, Ned. Cuba and Its Music: From the First Drums to the Mambo. Chicago: Chicago Review Press, 2004.

Wade, Peter. Music, Race, and Nation: Música Tropical in Colombia. Chicago: University of Chicago Press, 2000.

Waxer, Lise. The City of Musical Memory: Salsa, Record Grooves, and Popular Culture in Cali, Colombia. Middletown, CT: Wesleyan University Press, 2002.

———. Situating Salsa: Global Markets and Local Meaning in Latin Popular Music. New York: Routledge, 2002.

Zolof, Eric. Refried Elvis: The Rise of the Mexican Counterculture. Berkeley: University of California Press, 1999.

## WEBSITES

Bailyn, Evan. Music of Puerto Rico. 2005. The Penn Group. http://www.musicofpuertorico.com.

Blaya, Ricardo García. Todo Tango. 2005. http://www.todotango.com.

CliqueMusic: A Música Brasileira Está Aqui. 2006. http://www.allbrazilianmusic.com.

DancehallReggae.com. 7 July 2006. DancehallReggae Productions. http://www.dancehallreggae.com.

Dancehall Reggae Music—The Internet Resource. http://rudegal.com.

Descarga.com. 29 July 2006. Descarga. http://www.descarga.com.

Island Mix: Strictly Soca/Calypso. http://www.islandmix.com.

Tambora y Güira. 2 October 1999. http://mindspring.com/~adiascar/musica/index-e.htm.

## VIDEOS/FILMS

Bachata: Music of the People (United States, 2003). Directed by Giovanni Savino.

Bomba: Bailando el tambor [Bomba: Dancing the Drum; 56 minutes] (United States, 2000). Directed and photographed by Ashley James, produced by Roberta Singer, City Lore, the New York Center for Urban Folk Culture.

Bossa Nova: Music and Reminiscences (Barre, VT: Multicultural Media, 1993). Directed by Walter Saslles.

The Buena Vista Social Club (Germany, 1999). Directed by Wim Wenders.

Mas Fever: Inside Trinidad Carnival (United States, 1989). Directed by Glenn Micallef and Larry Johnson. Filmsound, Portland, Oregon.

Pan in A Minor: Steelbands of Trinidad (France, 1987). Directed by Daniel Verba and Jean-Jacques Mrejen. Iskra Films.

Roots Rock Reggae: Jamaican Music (United States, 1988). Beats of the Heart series. Produced and directed by Jeremy Marre. Shanachie SH-1202.

Routes of Rhythm, with Harry Belafonte (vols. 1–3) (United States, 1990). By Eugene Rosow and Howard Dratch. Cultural Research and Communication.

Salsa: Latin Pop in the Cities (United States, 1983). Beats of the Heart series. Produced and directed by Jeremy Marre. Shanachie SH-1201.

Shotguns and Accordions: Music of the Marijuana Regions of Colombia (United States, 1983). Beats of the Heart series. Produced and directed by Jeremy Marre. Shanachie SH-1205.

The Spirit of Samba: Black Music of Brazil (United States, 1983). Beats of the Heart series. Produced and directed by Jeremy Marre. Shanachie SH-1207.

Tan-Singing of Trinidad and Guyana: Indo-Caribbean "Local-Classical" Music (United States, 2000). Produced by Peter Manuel.

Tex-Mex: Music of the Texas-Mexican Borderlands (United States, 1982). Beats of the Heart series. Produced and directed by Jeremy Marre. Shanachie SH-1206.

## RECORDINGS

*A Carnival of Cuban Music: Routes of Rhythm vols. 1 & 2.* 1990, Rounder CD 5049.

*Arsenio Rodríguez.* 1959–60. Ansonia ALP 1337.

*Astor Piazzolla: Octeto Buenos Aires.* 1995. ANS Records ANS 15276-2.

*Bossa Nova: Sua história, sua gente.* 1991. Philips/Polygram 848 302-2.

Boukman Eksperyans. *Vodou Adjae.* 1991. Mango Records 162-539-899-2.

———. *Kalfou Danjere* [Dangerous Crossroads]. 1992. Mango 162-539 972-2.

*Brazil Classics 3: Forró, Etc.* 1991. Luaka Bop/Warner Bros. 9 26323-2.

*Brazil: Forró: Music for Maids and Taxi Drivers.* 1989. Rounder 5044.

*Calypso Awakening from the Emory Cook Collection.* 2000. Smithsonian Folkways SFW40453 2000.

*Calypso Callaloo: Early Carnival Music in Trinidad.* 1993. Compiled by Donald Hill. Gainesville: University Press of Florida. Book and CD.

*Calypso Carnival 1936–1941.* 1993. Rounder 1077.

*Caribbean Revels,* edited by Verna Gillis and Gage Averill. 1991. Smithsonian Folkways C-SF 40402.

*Carlos Vives: La Tierra del Olvido.* 1996. Sonolux/Polygram 314 528 531-2.

*Conjunto! Texas-Mexican Border Music.* Vols. 1-6. 1994. Rounder Records.

*Cuba Classics 2: Dancing with the Enemy.* 2005. Luaka Bop 9 26580–2.

*Cuba Classics 3: Diablo al infierno.* 2000. Luaka Bop 9 45107–2.

*Cuban Counterpoint: History of the Son Montuno.* 1994. Rounder CD 1078.

*The Cuban Danzon: Its Ancestors and Descendants.* 1982. Smithsonian Folkways FW04066.

*Cumbia/Cumbia 2: La epoca dorada de cumbias colombianas.* 1993. World Circuit WCD 033.

*Haiti Kanaval Konpa.* 2002. Metrosonik 002.

*Haiti: Rap & Ragga (match la rèd).* 1994. Déclic Communication 319-2.

*Konbit: Burning Rhythms of Haiti.* 1989. A&M CD 5281.

*Merengue: Dominican Music and Dominican Identity.* 1997. Rounder.

*Planet Zouk: The World of Antilles Music.* 1991. Rhythm Safari CDL 57165.

*Rough Guide to Cuban Son.* 2001. World Music Network. RGNET 1046CD.

*Rough Guide to Cumbia.* 2000. World Music Network RGNET 1043CD.

*Rough Guide to Latin Jazz.* 2003. World Music Network RGNET 1089CD.

*Rough Guide to Mambo.* 2004. World Music Network RGNET 1136CD.

*Rough Guide to Merengue and Bachata.* 2001. World Music Network RGNET 1039CD.

*Rough Guide to Salsa de Puerto Rico.* 2003. World Music Network RGNET 1030.

*Rough Guide to Salsa Colombia.* 2003. World Music Network RGNET 1112CD.

*Rough Guide to Ska.* 2003. World Music Network RGNET 1083CD.

*Rough Guide to the Music of Argentina.* 2004. World Music Network.

*Rough Guide to the Music of Brazil.* 2004. World Music Network RGNET 1021CD.

*Rough Guide to the Music of Haiti.* 2002. World Music Network RGNET 1067CD.

*Ruben Blades: The Best.* 2001. Globo/Sony CDZ-907.

*Say What? Double Entendre Soca Music from Trinidad.* 1990. Rounder 5042.

*Steel Drum Party.* 1995. EDIS 9020.

Tabou Combo. *The Music Machine.* 1978. Mini Records MRSD1070.

# PERIODICALS

ROBERT T. BUCKMAN

## HISTORICAL OVERVIEW

The story of the Latin American popular press has not been a happy one. A region historically blemished by poverty, illiteracy, and dictatorship did not prove fertile ground for newspapers and magazines. Despite these obstacles, some periodicals did take root and they and their publishers and writers have played a leading role in the cultural and political developments of their respective countries.

Colonial Latin America had no Benjamin Franklins, John Peter Zengers, or Thomas Paines. The few printing presses that were shipped to the Spanish and Portuguese colonies remained tightly under the control of the viceregal governors. The only periodicals were official gazettes, called *gacetas,* in both the Spanish realm and in Portuguese Brazil, which published official decrees for the few elite, educated males who could read them. During the period of Spanish colonial rule in the New World, the Inquisition still held sway.

The situation was only slightly better in Brazil. Rather than enslave the indigenous Indians as the Spanish had done, the Portuguese drove them into the interior and imported black slaves from Africa. In both realms, racial hybridization was to shape the popular cultures that exist today.

The French Revolution of 1789 and the Declaration of the Rights of Man did not extend rights to the black residents of Haiti, who revolted and made Haiti the first Latin American republic to achieve independence in 1804. Napoleon's conquest of the Iberian Peninsula in 1808 contributed directly to the eventual independence of the Spanish colonies and Brazil. Because of their scarcity, printing presses played a lesser role in the independence movements in Latin America than in the English colonies, but they did play a role.

In 1810, Father Camilo Henríquez, one of the agitators for Chilean independence, was given possession of the printing press belonging to the Santiago government after the collapse of Spanish authority. He published Latin America's first independent newspaper, *La Aurora de Chile,* which would be an intellectual beacon in Chile's independence movement. After independence in 1817, the concept of an independent press took root in Chile, and the idea spread eventually to other newly independent republics. Latin America's two oldest dailies are *El Mercurio* of Chile (1837) and *El Comercio* of Peru (1839).

In most countries, however, the principle of one-man rule was simply transferred from a Spanish king to a succession of absolute dictators. Chile's climate of enlightenment attracted exiled writers and intellectuals from throughout Latin America, most notably Andrés Bello of Venezuela and Domingo Faustino Sarmiento of Argentina. Sarmiento, who had fled the dictatorship of Juan Antonio de Rosas, became editor of *El Mercurio*. Later, he returned to Argentina to edit the Buenos Aires newspaper, *El Nacional,* and was elected president in 1868.

Latin American periodicals lacked the technological advances of the U.S. press and literate populations, except in Argentina, Brazil, and Uruguay. The few newspapers and magazines remained economically viable through notoriously low wage scales, which has not changed.

Early Latin American newspapers were primarily dull mercantile sheets, aimed at a tiny audience of businessmen, or vehicles for political opinion, aimed at intellectuals. Yet, weekly or monthly periodicals were influential enough among the privileged elite that dictators would frequently close an offending periodical and jail its editor or force him or her into exile.

Periodicals also played a vital role in the cultural development of Latin America, making their pages available to the poetry and short prose of writers such as Sarmiento, who would become some of Latin America's greatest literary figures. This tradition continues today, in both high and popular culture. For example, the novelist Gabriel García Márquez of Colombia, the Nobel Laureate in literature in 1982, began his career as a journalist and continues to write for newspapers and magazines; he is the board chairman of a news-feature magazine.

By the twentieth century, labor-saving technologies brought down the cost of publishing. Newspapers and magazines proliferated as central governments, political parties, the Catholic Church, labor movements, and other entities, as well as capitalist publishers, produced periodicals for newly literate and increasingly affluent audiences, especially in Argentina, Brazil, Chile, and Mexico. Photographic reproduction and the tabloid format (and sensational journalism) were borrowed from the United States. Offset printing was introduced to Latin America in the 1960s. Computerized word processing and typesetting spread rapidly in the 1970s and 1980s, which led to a proliferation of low-budget, desktop-published periodicals. Of course, these periodicals had difficulty surviving in such a competitive marketplace unless they were backed by subsidies from the government, the Catholic Church, or political parties.

## Struggle for Freedom of the Press

The U.S. concept of freedom of the press, which serves a critical watchdog function against governmental abuse and corruption, proved to be both elusive and dangerous in Latin America in the nineteenth and twentieth centuries. A new generation emerged of personalist autocrats who wielded absolute power, some of them for decades. Only Chile and Uruguay enjoyed almost uninterrupted democratic rule and free expression during the first seven decades of the twentieth century.

During the Cold War, personalist dictators were replaced occasionally by elected civilians but more often by military juntas, some right-wing, some left-wing. By 1973, only three of the region's republics—Colombia, Costa Rica, and Venezuela—still had pluralist democracies.

What all these dictatorial regimes—*personalista* or juntas, right-wing or left-wing—had in common was a lack of tolerance for independent publications that criticized their actions or exposed corruption, and they employed a variety of draconian measures to suppress these writings.

The most overt suppression was through outright expropriation or closure, which was employed by Brazil's Getulio Vargas (1930–45), Argentina's Juan Perón (1946–55), and Cuba's Fidel Castro (1959–), among others. Expropriation, in which the government assumed the role of publisher, was rare; most dictators opted to keep periodicals in line through intimidation. Closure of newspapers, temporarily or permanently, was more common, although it still was employed as a last resort.

Thin-skinned dictators occasionally imposed prior censorship. The most infamous example was that imposed by the military junta that ruled Brazil from 1964 to 1985. Newspapers were encouraged to practice self-censorship, but those that refused were required to submit their page proofs in advance to government censors. The country's most prestigious daily, *O Estado de São Paulo,* and its evening sister paper, *Jordal da Tarde,* were subjected to prior censorship from 1971 to 1975. Eventually, the junta found censorship to be more of an embarrassment than it was worth, and abandoned it in 1978.

A more subtle, more insidious, and arguably more effective form of control has been self-censorship. Periodicals are theoretically—even constitutionally—free to publish what they wish without prior restraint, but they do so knowing that critical editorials or cartoons and embarrassing investigative reports could result in any number of legal or extra-legal sanctions. These sanctions include withholding government advertising for state-owned enterprises, such as utilities or public transit; tax audits or the threat of them; implementation of a *colegio* system, which requires a professional license to practice journalism, a license that a government can revoke at whim; accusations of labor or safety law violations, often trumped up; denial of import permits for newsprint; and defamation lawsuits under the archaic Spanish legal principle of *desacato,* by which a government official can sue for damages if he or she has been offended by an article, even if it is true.

Most Latin American journalists contend that prior censorship is preferable to self-censorship because the government states what it finds objectionable; with self-censorship, it is a guessing game, and information the public needs is often suppressed by fear of reprisals.

For decades Mexico maintained a newsprint monopoly. The government, controlled from 1929 until 2000 by the Institutional Revolutionary Party, or PRI, touted itself as a benefactor to struggling periodicals by supplying newsprint at subsidized prices. However, publications that proved too critical of the PRI suddenly found themselves denied newsprint.

Finally, dictators regularly imprisoned journalists, exiled them—or murdered them. This was especially true during the brutal right-wing military regimes in Argentina, Brazil, and Chile of the 1960s, 1970s, and 1980s. As recently as Castro's crackdown on dissent in April 2003, more than twenty independent Cuban journalists were arrested and sentenced to prison terms of up to 27 years.

Probably the highest-profile journalistic murder during this period was that of Pedro Joaquín Chamorro, editor of the anti-Somoza newspaper, *La Prensa,* in Nicaragua. He was gunned down in an ambush in January 1978. Somoza denied instigating the murder, but middle-class citizens, who had remained neutral in the Sandinista rebellion against Somoza, turned against the dictator after Chamorro's murder. In July 1979 Somoza fled to Paraguay, where he himself was to die in an ambush a year later.

In the late 1970s and throughout the 1980s, a wave of democratization swept Latin America as military governments began to surrender power, willingly or unwillingly, beginning with Ecuador in 1978 and ending with Haiti in 1991. Mexico, too, experienced dramatic political reform beginning in 1989, leading to political pluralism, the end of the newsprint monopoly, and greater tolerance for journalistic opposition to the PRI. Currently, Cuba is the only Latin American republic with an unelected ruler.

Nonetheless, some civilian governments sought to exert the same tools of intimidation against the opposition press as did the dictators, especially defamation suits, tax audits, labor and immigration laws, licensing, and even physical violence. Domestic and international pressure, through such organizations as the Inter American Press Association (IAPA), the Committee to Protect Journalists, and Reporters Without Borders, has sometimes stymied these attempts to curtail freedom of the press. The seeming lack of commitment to freedom of the press by these fledgling democracies was serious enough that in 1994 the IAPA promoted the Declaration of Chapultepec, which reasserts the rights of a free and independent press and condemns violence against journalists. However, representatives of only twenty-two of the nations of the hemisphere signed the declaration in Mexico City. Despite the lofty language of the Declaration of Chapultepec, repression by democratically elected civilian presidents, such as Venezuela's Hugo Chávez, has continued.

Physical violence against journalists also continues. According to the IAPA, 298 print and broadcast journalists were slain in the Western Hemisphere between October 1988 and April 2006, including 118 in Colombia, 51 in Mexico, 29 in Brazil, 19 in Guatemala, 18 in Peru, and 14 in El Salvador. Many were investigative reporters or photographers; others had regularly written critical editorials or columns. Most of these murders go unsolved because of suspiciously lack-luster investigation. Many other journalists have been wounded, beaten, or received death threats. This issue appeared on the agenda of the Second Summit of the Americas in Santiago, Chile, in 1998. The leaders of the thirty-four countries represented (Cuba was excluded) agreed to establish an office within the Inter-American Commission for Human Rights, a subsidiary of the Organization of American States, to investigate attacks against journalists. Despite this high-profile initiative, attacks against journalists in Latin America continue.

Each year, the New York–based Freedom House, a sixty-year-old nonpartisan, nonprofit organization, rates freedom of the press in each of the world's countries on a 100-point scale, factoring in the degree of government pressure and threats from nongovernmental sources. In 2006, only three of the Latin American republics were rated as "Free": Costa Rica, Chile, and Uruguay, in that order (see Table 1).

## CURRENT TRENDS: NEWSPAPERS

As Latin America developed technologically and economically, especially since the 1980s, most countries witnessed the rise of a middle class with an appetite for a wider variety of periodicals. Literacy figures, however, should be viewed skeptically. The standard for what constitutes a "literate" person varies from country to country. A government may consider people literate if they can write their names. Thus, in a country with a declared literacy rate of 86 percent, such as Brazil, the statistic does not mean that 86 percent of Brazilians are capable of reading the average daily newspaper. UNESCO's newspaper circulation figures, now a decade old, show that newspaper readership in Latin America was still lagging far behind that in the more developed countries. Still, there is a statistically significant correlation between literacy and newspaper circulation, and many daily and nondaily newspapers of the twenty-first century are being tailored to this growing mass of newly literate but relatively unsophisticated readers.

Latin American newspapers tend to be modeled after their North American or European counterparts in format, content, and style. In the twenty-first century, this similarity has become more pronounced as computerization has facilitated the use of color graphics.

Daily newspapers can be divided roughly between the elite and the popular press, which may be subdivided in some countries into capital city and provincial newspapers. As in

| Country | Rating | Status |
|---|---|---|
| Costa Rica | 18 | Free |
| Chile | 26 | Free |
| Uruguay | 28 | Free |
| Bolivia | 33 | Partly Free |
| Dominican Republic | 37 | Partly Free |
| Brazil | 39 | Partly Free |
| Peru | 39 | Partly Free |
| Ecuador | 41 | Partly Free |
| El Salvador | 43 | Partly Free |
| Panama | 43 | Partly Free |
| Nicaragua | 44 | Partly Free |
| Argentina | 45 | Partly Free |
| Mexico | 48 | Partly Free |
| Honduras | 52 | Partly Free |
| Paraguay | 57 | Partly Free |
| Guatemala | 58 | Partly Free |
| Colombia | 61 | Not Free |
| Haiti | 68 | Not Free |
| Venezuela | 72 | Not Free |
| Cuba | 96 | Not Free |

Ratings: 0–30 = Free, 31–60 = Partly free, 61–100 = Not free

Source: Freedom House, New York, 2006.

Table 1   Press Freedom in Latin America

Europe, almost all the prestige papers are based in the capitals and circulate nationally, a legacy of the Spanish colonial practice of centralization. Brazil, however, has a bipolar media concentration between Rio de Janeiro (the capital until it was moved to Brasilia in 1960) and São Paulo. Bolivia, Ecuador, and Honduras also have a division of political and media power and influence between the capital and larger cities.

The elite dailies are usually multisection broadsheets like major U.S. dailies or *The Times* of London. Typically, at least four basic sections offer a comprehensive agenda of world, national, and local news, business and economic news, sports, and cultural and entertainment news; often, a fifth section is devoted to local news. The opinion-editorial pages normally are included in one of the news sections. The Sunday editions are usually huge and contain well-written literary and other cultural supplements, continuing the legacy of Latin American newspapers as manifestations of a country's culture. The reporting is journalistically "respectable" and generally reliable. Consequently, these elite dailies serve as a country's newspaper of record. In smaller or less developed countries, such as Guatemala and Paraguay, the elite dailies have a tabloid rather than a broadsheet format.

Some elite dailies are over a century old and have established global reputations for journalistic excellence. Some of the more venerable are *La Prensa* (1869) and *La Nación* (1870) of Buenos Aires, Argentina; *O Estado de São Paulo* (1875) of São Paulo, Brazil; *Jornal do Brasil* (1891) and *O Globo* (1925) of Rio de Janeiro, Brazil; *Listín Diario* (1889) of Santo Domingo, Dominican Republic; *El Mercurio* (1900) of Santiago, Chile; *El Comercio* (1839) of Lima, Peru; *El Universal* (1916) and *Excélsior* (1936) of Mexico City; *El Tiempo* (1911) of Bogotá, Colombia; *El Universal* (1909) and *El Nacional* (1943) of Caracas, Venezuela; *El Telégrafo* (1884) of Guayaquil *and El Comercio* (1921) of Quito, Ecuador; *El Diario* (1904) of La Paz, Bolivia; and *La Prensa Libre* (1889) and *La Nación* (1946) of San José, Costa Rica.

Other prestigious dailies of record, such as *El Imparcial* of Guatemala City, *El Espectador* of Bogotá, and *La Prensa* of Lima, became victims of the marketplace and changing tastes and ceased publication or became weeklies as younger, aggressive competitors—as well as television—cut into their readership and advertising bases.

A new generation of prestige dailies arose in the second half of the twentieth century, newspapers that have distinguished themselves with reliable, aggressive, and often courageous investigative reporting. These include *Reforma* (1993) in Mexico City, *Prensa Libre* (1951) and *Siglo Veintiuno* (1990) in Guatemala City, *La República* (1982) in Lima, *ABC Color* (1967) in Asunción, Paraguay, *La Prensa* (1980) in Panama City, and *Página/12* in Buenos Aires (1987).

The newspapers of the popular press normally employ the tabloid format and differ sharply from those of the prestige press in both style and content. They are aimed at a working-class readership, devoting more attention to sensational crime stories and to sports. Their circulations are usually greater—sometimes far greater—than those of the elite dailies. They focus more on popular culture and less on high culture.

Three success stories among the newspapers of the popular press include *Folha de São Paulo* (1921), which boasts the largest circulation in Latin America, 1,200,000; *La Tercera de la Hora* (1950) in Santiago, Chile's largest circulation paper, which claims 180,000 readers compared with 120,000 for *El Mercurio;* and *Clarín* (1945), Buenos Aires's and Argentina's largest paper, with a reported circulation of more than 600,000. Although these newspapers employ more glitz and sensational headlines than do their elite competitors, their reporting remains journalistically mainstream and generally accurate.

Other working-class daily tabloids aim at an even lower-brow audience and are characterized by oversized photos of quasi-nude bathing beauties—sometimes topless—and grisly crime scenes. They have far less hard news or editorials, and what news they report is usually in the form of vignettes. Truth and accuracy are often overlooked in the interest of a good story. In-depth or interpretative reporting is virtually nonexistent, except for personality profiles of glamorous cinema or television personalities and soccer stars. Still, their circulations—and advertising revenues—indicate that they have found willing audiences, and they fill an important journalistic niche by their emphasis on popular culture: soccer, beauty contests and contestants, and entertainment events and personalities, particularly from *latino* music, cinema, and the ubiquitous *telenovelas,* the Latin American version of soap operas, which enjoy a passionate following.

Provincial dailies also fill an important niche by reporting local events that the capital-based press may ignore, but few of these papers have achieved much journalistic distinction. Probably the region's most respected provincial daily is *El Norte* of Monterrey, Mexico, which enjoys national prestige; it is owned by *Reforma* in Mexico City.

The nondaily press has long had a major political and cultural influence, especially since the rise of democracy, which coincided with the era of desktop publishing. Because of the expense of the technology of printing daily newspapers and the vigorous competition in the marketplace, weekly, semiweekly, and biweekly newspapers operating on a shoestring have carved out specialized audiences for themselves.

As one example, provincial cities and towns that lack the advertising base for a daily newspaper may support a nondaily, which provides a source of information that the community would otherwise lack. However, these papers lack the professional and technological resources of the dailies.

Low-budget, low-circulation nondailies in major capitals also give voice to various political movements, and their investigative reporting and iconoclastic editorials and cartoons bring to light information and opinions that may not appear in the dailies. These gadfly publications, which have proliferated in such capitals as Caracas and Santiago, serve the classic watchdog function of a free and independent press and have proved a thorn in the side of many a president. *La Razón* in Caracas and *The Clinic* in Santiago are two of the best examples. However, they are characterized by slanted reporting rather than objectivity and, consequently, lack the credibility of the mainstream dailies. Other nondailies eschew political controversy to specialize in sports, business, or entertainment reporting.

The newest trend in Latin American newspapers—and magazines—is online editions. Virtually every prestige daily, and most of the popular tabloids, now have Websites. Access to computers is still relatively restricted in Latin America, just as newspaper readership was confined to the wealthy elite in the nineteenth century. But countries such as Mexico, Haiti, the Dominican Republic, and El Salvador have huge émigré populations in the United States that enjoy greater affluence, and these online editions provide a vital link to the news at home. Some daily publications, such as *Clave Digital* of the Dominican Republic and *El Faro* of El Salvador, are exclusively online and have proved highly popular with the émigré communities. Other online publications are weekly. The economic advantage of online newspapers is that there is no capital expenditure for a printing press, paper, and ink.

Ownership and competition patterns in Latin America differ sharply from those in the United States, where chain ownership and local monopolies have become the norm. In part because of more lenient inheritance tax laws in Latin America, many major newspapers have remained in the same families for generations. The most illustrious are the Mitre family of *La Nación* and the Gainza and Paz families of *La Prensa* in Argentina; the Edwards family of *El Mercurio* in Chile; the Miró and Quesada families of *El Comercio* in Peru; the Cano family of *El Espectador* and the Santos family of *El Tiempo* in Bogotá; and the Mesquita family of *O Estado de São Paulo.*

Chain ownership has manifested itself in Latin America, however. One of the largest and best known is the *El Sol* chain in Mexico, which was forced into receivership in the 1970s. It was taken over and operated by the Mexican government for a time until it was purchased by media magnate Mario Vásquez Raña.

It is more common to see elite dailies branch out to publish sister newspapers, evening or working-class morning papers. The Edwards family of *El Mercurio* in Chile established *Las Ultimas Noticias,* an evening tabloid, in 1902, and *La Segunda,* a working-class (but politically conservative) tabloid, in 1931. *El Mercurio*'s only serious competitor, *La Tercera,* also began publishing a more sensational working-class daily, *La Cuarta,* in 1990, and it now claims a circulation greater than *La Tercera*'s.

A similar situation occurred in Guatemala, where two fiercely competitive mainstream dailies, *Prensa Libre* and *Siglo Veintiuno,* both began publishing low-brow, working-class papers in the late 1990s, *Nuestro Diario* and *Al Día,* respectively. *Nuestro Diario* now claims the largest circulation in Central America, double that of its parent newspaper. *Prensa Libre* also publishes a provincial nondaily in Quetzaltenango.

A few national governments still publish daily newspapers, which print legal notices as well as news in the tradition of the old *gacetas* and serve as faithful editorial mouthpieces for whichever party is in power. Examples are *Diario de Centroamérica* in Guatemala, *El Peruano* in Peru, and *La Nación* in Chile. Government-owned papers predictably suffer from a lack of credibility and a corresponding lack of readers.

Although few U.S. cities still have competing daily newspapers, Latin American capitals and even some provincial cities may support a multitude of competing dailies. Even though Los Angeles, California, a city of 4 million, has only one major daily, Guatemala City, with a population of about 1 million, supports six, including a government-owned daily. Lower wage scales are one reason for this phenomenon; Latin American newspapers also rely heavily on part-time stringers. Costly home-delivery distribution is rare in Latin America; readers normally buy newspapers from hawkers at intersections on major thoroughfares or from ubiquitous newsstands.

## CURRENT TRENDS: MAGAZINES

Latin American magazines have been far less prevalent than daily and nondaily newspapers. Their development in most countries was hampered by the following obstacles: poverty, because magazines are more expensive for readers than newspapers; illiteracy, because magazines are generally aimed at a better-educated and more specialized audience; competition with newspapers (and later the broadcast media) for advertising revenue; and far greater production costs for slick magazines than for newspapers printed on relatively inexpensive newsprint.

Magazines arose fairly early in the more populous, literate, and affluent countries, such as Argentina, Brazil, Chile, and Mexico; some were on a par with U.S. and European magazines in quality of production and writing. A few were exported, and still are, to less affluent countries. But for several decades of the twentieth century, some of the most successful magazines were Spanish or Portuguese editions of major U.S. magazines, which transcended national borders. Two of the most widely read were the Spanish editions of *Reader's Digest* (*Selecciones*) and *Good Housekeeping* (*Buen Hogar*). Time-Life (now Time Warner) still publishes Brazil's most popular feature magazine, *Manchete*. Even today the poorer countries, such as Bolivia, Nicaragua, and Honduras, cannot support a magazine industry, and the titles available on their newsstands are imports from the United States, Spain, or other Latin American countries.

As in the United States and Europe, Latin American magazines are categorized roughly by content and audience. The most common are general interest, news, and women's magazines, according to the selection available at the average newsstand. Circulation figures for Latin American magazines are difficult to verify. The newsmagazines are usually published weekly; the others are monthly.

Some women's magazines, such as *Buen Hogar* and *Vanidades,* headquartered in Mexico, enjoy a region-wide readership, but others are primarily for domestic consumption, such as *Para Ti* in Argentina and *Paula* in Chile. They are characterized by glossy paper, full-color photography, and generally professional writing. Their content is roughly comparable with U.S. women's magazines: personality profiles of female celebrities, fashion trends, women's health issues, childrearing, sex and marriage, cooking and recipes. Some are aimed at young professional women, others at traditional housewives.

Newsmagazines usually resemble *Time* and *Newsweek* in size and format. Some are several decades old and, like newspapers, often had to struggle against censorship and intimidation during the era of dictators. Two of the oldest are *Siempre!* in Mexico (1954) and *Veja* in Brazil (1968), both politically conservative, whose economic success spawned aggressive, left-wing competitors, *Proceso* in Mexico (1977) and *Isto É* in Brazil (1969). Some general interest magazines, such as *Cromos* in Colombia, are difficult to categorize because they blend political reporting with cultural topics, such as sports, literature, art, and entertainment. Like newspapers, the leading magazines also have online editions.

Popular culture in Latin America is centered on several major topics: sports, especially soccer throughout the region and baseball in the countries of the Caribbean; cinema, which dates to the 1920s and 1930s in Argentina, Brazil, and Mexico and has flourished in recent decades in Chile, Peru, Colombia, and Cuba; television, especially the hugely popular *telenovelas*, whose stars become national and regional icons because they transcend national boundaries; traditional and popular music, including the tango in Argentina, the samba in Brazil, ranchero in Mexico, salsa along the littoral of the Caribbean, and the newer *latino* sounds that also transcend frontiers and create regional megastars such as Shakira of Colombia and José Luis Rodríguez of Venezuela.

Photographs and articles about the celebrities of popular culture are ubiquitous in Latin American newspapers and magazines, but they are the grist particularly for the general-interest feature magazines. Popular cultural figures in the United States, Europe, and, especially, Spain also have traditionally fascinated Latin American magazine readers, from Frank Sinatra and Julio Iglesias to Britney Spears and Antonio Banderas. But the trend in the past two decades has been to place more emphasis on domestic popular culture icons or those from neighboring countries. Coverage of U.S. popular culture figures also has become more focused on U.S. Latino stars, such as Ricky Martin of Puerto Rico, or on Latin Americans who have become successful in the United States, such as Mexican actress Salma Hayek and Dominican baseball great Sammy Sosa. Without question, popular culture icons sell magazines, which is critical in a highly competitive marketplace, and the magazines in turn have become mirrors and chroniclers of Latin American popular culture.

Comic books have been popular in Latin America since at least the 1940s, and not only with children. Just as the most popular magazines were translations of major U.S. magazines, the Walt Disney Company once dominated the Latin American comic book market with translations of its Mickey Mouse and Donald Duck monthly comics. This dominance even became a political issue of the *dependentistas*, who saw U.S. comics as an insidious capitalist plot to corrupt Latin American children into embracing U.S. cultural values and consumerism. The Chilean writer Ariel Dorfman made that argument in the book *Como leer el Pato Donald* [How to Read Donald Duck], coauthored by the Belgian Armand Mattelart and published in 1973 during the aborted presidency of the Socialist Salvador Allende. They charged that the comics were laden with capitalist symbolism and subtle propaganda.

Meanwhile, another Chilean created a uniquely Chilean comic book character, which is embraced throughout Latin America and even Spain: Condorito. The cartoonist, René Ríos, who went by the *nom de plume* of Pepo, explained that he was inspired by the 1945 Disney cartoon movie *The Three Caballeros,* which "starred" three birds: Donald Duck from the United States; José Caricoca, a parrot from Brazil; and Panchito, a red rooster from Mexico. Ríos said he decided Chile needed its own cartoon character and so he chose the condor, the country's national symbol. Condorito is a lovable ne'er-do-well with an eye for the ladies, and his sometimes risqué humor is clearly aimed more at adults than at children. Ríos created Condorito in 1945, and by the 1950s his monthly comic books had spread throughout Latin America. In 1983, the Mexican telecommunications conglomerate Televisa acquired the rights and began publishing a Mexican edition, with Mexican rather than Chilean slang and vernacular usage, which circulates throughout Central America as well.

Condorito remained politically neutral during the turbulent 1960s and 1970s. Ríos continued to draw Condorito into his eighties, eventually training successors to continue drawing after he retired in the mid-1990s. Ríos died in 1999. Condorito still can be found on newsstands in every Latin American country except Cuba and Haiti. The publisher claims 82 million readers annually.

Another cartoon character that has obtained a regional audience is Argentina's Mafalda, created in 1964 by Joaquín Salvador Lavado, who draws under the pseudonym Quino. Mafalda is a little girl about the age of Dennis the Menace or the *Peanuts* characters. The humor is often quite profound and is clearly aimed at adults as well as children. The strip originated in newspapers and was featured in the weekly magazine *Siete Días,* but soon Mafalda began appearing in comic books as well. She is syndicated in newspapers throughout Latin America.

Despite the trend toward regional transnationalization of information and culture, each country retains its own discrete culture, and its periodical press consequently retains a distinct individuality, which requires that each country be examined separately. Circulation figures published in such sources as the *Editor and Publisher Yearbook* and the *Europa Yearbook* vary greatly and should be considered estimates at best, because newspaper sales in Latin America are almost exclusively through street vendors rather than home delivery.

## MEXICO AND CENTRAL AMERICA

### Mexico

The largest Spanish-speaking country in the world, with 100 million people, Mexico is a potentially huge market for periodicals, but it was hampered by illiteracy until after the bloody Revolution of 1910–20. Newspapers and magazines have flourished for a century, although their circulations remain small for such a populous country.

Freedom of the press is ostensibly guaranteed by the Mexican Constitution of 1917, the oldest in Latin America, but it was long considered a qualified privilege. From 1929 to 2000, the presidency and most other governmental posts in Mexico were monopolized by the Institutional Revolutionary Party (PRI). Under this system, party and government were intertwined. The government controlled the supply of newsprint through a monopoly called Pipsa, which supposedly was a benevolent means of providing independent publications with paper that cost below market value and thus fostering development of the print media. However, editors and publishers discovered that their paper supply could be jeopardized by overly critical editorials or aggressive investigative reporting. Self-censorship was the norm in Mexico for decades.

The PRI also ensured favorable coverage, and discouraged criticism or exposés, by paying bribes, called *fafas,* to underpaid journalists, who came to rely on the supplemental income. The extent of this system came to light after the opposition Party of the Democratic Revolution (PRD) came to power in the Mexico City municipal elections of 1997. The new government discovered that dozens of journalists working for independent media were also on the city's payroll.

President Carlos Salinas de Gortari, who was sensitive to charges that the PRI had rigged his 1988 election, undertook unprecedented democratic reforms during his six-year term of office. He ended the newsprint monopoly and showed greater tolerance toward criticism by the press, with the result that newspapers that were formerly submissive became more aggressive and the few iconoclastic publications that had dared to challenge the system became bolder still. In 2000, Vicente Fox of the conservative National Action Party (PAN) won the presidency, ending the PRI's 71-year grip on the office. Although he faced his share of criticism by the press, Fox showed more forbearance than his predecessors. He also enacted Mexico's first public records law, which opened the doors to investigative journalists.

In this new climate of openness, the Mexican press now faces its greatest threat—not from government but from drug traffickers. In 2004, more journalists were killed in Mexico than in Colombia, previously the most dangerous country in the Americas for journalists. Dozens of journalists have been killed, wounded, or threatened with death by drug traffickers, especially along the U.S. border.

## Newspapers

Mexico has about 220 daily newspapers, although the number continually fluctuates in such a large and competitive market. Circulation figures in Mexico are estimates at best. Mexico City alone has about eighteen dailies, including various business newspapers and the English-language *The News,* owned by the O'Farrill family that owns the powerful television network, Televisa. It has a circulation of about 30,000.

The two dailies considered Mexico's newspapers of record are *El Universal* and *Excélsior,* both broadsheets founded in 1916 and 1917, respectively, at the height of the Revolution. Of the two, *Excélsior* showed greater allegiance to the PRI, which wielded great power on its editorial board. As a result, *Excélsior* lost much of its journalistic credibility during the reform period of the 1990s, whereas *El Universal* took advantage of its new freedom to engage in aggressive investigative reporting. Nonetheless, the PRI still has enough loyal followers to give *Excélsior* a reported circulation of 200,000. *El Universal* is close behind, with 180,000. *El Universal* also owns a sports daily, *La Afición* (1930), which has 85,000 readers.

Mexico's most powerful newspaper baron has long been Mario Vásquez Raña, whose Organización Editorial Mexicana owns about forty-five dailies, including the chain of thirty *El Sol* newspapers. He acquired the chain in the 1970s from the government, which took it over when it went into receivership. Some of the provincial *El Sol* papers are the circulation leaders in their cities, but others have languished in recent years.

Vásquez Raña acquired control of *Excélsior* in 2005, and he also owns Mexico City's two other most-read dailies, *La Prensa* (1928, circulation 275,000) and the sports daily, *Esto* (1941, 400,000). *El Sol de México* in the capital (1965) has a circulation of only 76,000.

Two newspapers belonging to the new generation of opposition to the PRI are *Unomásuno,* founded in 1977 by Julio Scherer García as a daily companion to his left-wing weekly news-magazine *Proceso,* and the more conservative *Reforma,* launched in 1994 by Alejandro Junco de la Vega, who also owns the prestigious *El Norte* in Monterrey. *Unomásuno* has lost much of its popularity since Scherer García's retirement, and its circulation is now only about 40,000. *Reforma,* however, has established itself, along with *El Universal,* as one of the country's most respectable and reliable sources of information. A morning broadsheet, it is characterized by its color masthead and its aggressive reporting. Its circulation estimates vary from 94,000 to 126,000.

Other major dailies in the capital are *El Heraldo de México* (1966, 200,000); *Ovaciones* (1947, 130,000 morning and 100,000 evening), which also is owned by Televisa; *La Jornada* (1984, 100,000); *Diario de México* (1948, 76,000); *Novedades* (1936, 43,000); and *El Día*

(1962, 50,000). The two business dailies are *El Financiero* (1947, 147,000) and *El Economista* (1989, 20,000).

Unlike the United States, many of Mexico's interior cities still have competitive dailies; many provincial morning dailies still have evening sister papers. Probably the most respected provincial daily is Junco de la Vega's *El Norte* in Monterrey, Mexico's third-largest city. It dates to 1938 and has a circulation of 133,000. It has an evening companion, *El Sol* (1922), which has 45,000 readers.

Guadalajara, Mexico's second-largest city, has four general-interest dailies and one business daily. The most venerable is *El Informador* (1917), which is locally owned and claims 46,000 readers. Vásquez Raña owns its morning competitor, *El Occidental* (1942), which has a circulation of 49,000, and an evening paper, *El Sol de Guadalajara* (1948), which has an unreported circulation. The Autonomous University of Guadalajara publishes a successful newspaper, *Ocho Columnas,* founded in 1978 and with a circulation of 40,000. A five-day morning business daily, *El Financiero,* has 12,000 readers.

Nondaily newspapers have carved out an important niche in Mexico, both before and since the press reforms of the 1990s. Some of the most strident opposition to the PRI came from both right-wing and left-wing weekly or fortnightly newspapers, which learned to survive without subsidized newsprint. Weekly newspapers along the northern border also have exhibited the most courageous reporting on the activities of drug traffickers, with the result that many of their journalists have been killed or wounded. Probably the most illustrious is *Zeta*, a weekly in Tijuana, on the border with California, founded in 1980 by Jesús Blancornelas, who exposed local political corruption and the activities of the notorious Tijuana drug cartel of the Arellano Félix family. *Zeta* editors were murdered in 1988 and 2004, and Blancornelas was critically wounded in an assassination attempt in 1997.

## Magazines

Mexico has one of the best developed magazine industries in Latin America, and many of its magazines enjoy circulation in neighboring countries. Mexican magazines also have become increasingly specialized; many are the Spanish-language equivalents of their U.S. counterparts, such as *Selecciones,* or *Reader's Digest* (1940), which claims a circulation of 611,000 in Mexico and Latin America, and *Mecánica Popular,* or *Popular Mechanics* (1947), which has a circulation of 248,000.

U.S. women's magazines are especially popular in Mexico. There are Spanish editions of *Cosmopolitan* (1973, 260,000 readers), *Marie Claire* (1990, 80,000), and *Vogue* (1999, 208,000). A Mexican women's magazine that is now found throughout Latin America is *Vanidades* (1961), published fortnightly rather than monthly, which has a circulation of 290,000.

Mexico's three established weekly news-political magazines are *Impacto* (1949), *Siempre!* (1954), and *Proceso* (1976). Scherer García launched *Proceso* after he was fired as editor of *Excélsior* for his editorial criticism of then-President Luis Echeverría. When he applied for and was denied subsidized newsprint for the new magazine, he bought paper at full price on the open market. Fierce competitors, *Siempre!* and *Proceso* resemble *Time* and *Newsweek* in size and format, both average about 98 pages per issue, and both have a circulation of about 100,000. *Siempre!* is somewhat more conservative in its editorial slant. *Impacto* focuses more on politics, whereas the other two have a broader selection of international and national news and sections on business, sports, entertainment, and culture. *Impacto* has about 80,000 readers.

Other leading magazines are *Tele-Guía* (1952), a Mexican version of *TV Guide,* which has a circulation of 375,000, and *Conozca Más,* a scientific magazine that sells 80,000 copies.

## Guatemala

Central America's most populous country, with a population of 14 million, Guatemala is also one of the least literate countries of Latin America. Widespread illiteracy (more than 50 percent of the population), compounded by grinding poverty, decades of dictatorship, and a 36-year-long guerrilla war that killed 30,000 people, many of them journalists, stunted newspaper circulation and precluded development of a magazine industry.

Guatemala has experienced only two periods of political democracy and anything resembling freedom of the press: 1944–54 and 1986 to the present. For several decades, the country's newspaper of record was the staid but reliable *El Imparcial,* which was founded in 1922. Another daily of that period was *Nuestro Diario.* In 1951, during the first democratic period, a group of five disaffected reporters abandoned *Nuestro Diario* and launched *Prensa Libre,* a respectable tabloid, which by 1958 had eclipsed *El Imparcial* in circulation and prestige. *El Imparcial* ceased publication in the 1980s.

In 1963, the Carpio Nicolle brothers launched Latin America's first offset newspaper, *El Gráfico,* which proved highly competitive with its use of color photos and graphics. It also was used as a political vehicle for the presidential aspirations of one of the brothers, Jorge, who ran unsuccessfully in 1986 and 1991 and was killed under mysterious circumstances in 1993. With the loss of its publisher as well as its credibility, *El Gráfico* folded in 1999.

In 1990, a group of businessmen with a conservative political agenda began *Siglo Veintiuno,* which quickly rivaled the also conservative *Prensa Libre* in journalistic prestige if not in circulation. *Prensa Libre*'s circulation is placed at 110,000, *Siglo Veintiuno*'s at 22,000. The two papers launched sensational working-class tabloids in 2002 that quickly surpassed the circulations of their more traditional sister papers. *Prensa Libre* publishes *Nuestro Diario,* which claims a circulation of 200,000, the largest in Central America. *Siglo Veintiuno,* meanwhile, publishes *Al Día,* which is believed to have about 35,000 readers. *Prensa Libre* also launched a high-brow daily, *El Periódico,* with a circulation of about 10,000, edited by the respected José Rubén Zamora, former editor of *Siglo Veintiuno,* who was fired under political pressure. *Prensa Libre* has relinquished control of *El Periódico.*

Guatemala's only evening paper is the tabloid *La Hora,* owned by the Marroquín family, which dates to 1944 and has a small but stable circulation of 18,000. The government has long published its own daily, *Diario de Centroramérica,* which reflects the editorial slant of whichever military or civilian group happens to hold power. It consequently lacks any credibility and has a tiny readership.

The only major provincial newspaper is *El Quetzalteco* in Quetzeltenango, published three days a week; it is owned by *Prensa Libre.*

Guatemala lacks a magazine industry but has between 15 and 20 nondaily periodicals, including weekly supplements in the daily newspapers.

The Guatemalan press suffered terribly during the years of military rule from 1954 to 1986 and the overlapping civil war of 1960–96. Dozens of journalists across the political spectrum were killed, either by the military or by left-wing guerrillas. Among them were Izidoro Zarco, co-publisher of *Prensa Libre,* who was kidnapped by guerrillas in 1970, held for ransom, and then slain, and Mario Ribas Montes, a columnist *with El Imparcial,* who was also slain by guerrillas.

The so-called democracy since 1986 has not brought true freedom of the press. The second elected president, Jorge Serrano, attempted to suspend the constitution and rule by decree in May 1993. He sought to impose prior censorship, but the fiercely competitive dailies collaborated to thwart the censors and to ensure that each other's newspapers reached the streets. Massive public protests and the withdrawal of the military's support for Serrano forced him to flee into exile.

The interim president, Ramiro de León Carpio, respected freedom of the press, even hiring a *Prensa Libre* editor as his press aide, but the next president, Alvaro Arzú, narrowly elected in 1996, proved supersensitive to press criticism. He used the threat of tax audits to force *Siglo Veintiuno* to fire its internationally respected editor, José Rubén Zamora, effectively muting its criticism. He succeeded in persuading wealthy friends to obtain control of Guatemala's only weekly newsmagazine, *Crónica*. Its staff was fired, and, not long afterward, with its credibility gone, it ceased publication.

The next president, Alfonso Portillo (2000–04), proved to be even worse. He was a surrogate for former military strongman Efraín Ríos Montt. During his presidency, death threats against critical journalists became commonplace. Security personnel stormed the home of Zamora and terrorized him and his family. During a violent demonstration by pro-Ríos Montt partisans in July 2003, several journalists were beaten and one died of a heart attack.

With the election of Oscar Berger in late 2003, the climate changed dramatically for the better, and Freedom House moved Guatemala from the "not free" to the "partly free" category. Ríos Montt was indicted for complicity in the death of the journalist who died in the 2003 disturbances.

## Honduras

Honduras is another of the quintessential banana republics where generations of dictatorship and dependency on the one export commodity resulted in a largely poverty-stricken and illiterate society. A relatively small population also inhibited development of the press. What newspapers have managed to survive are low in circulation, owned by wealthy interests, read by members of the establishment, and supportive of one of the two political parties, Liberal and National.

There are only four dailies in Honduras, two in the capital, Tegucigalpa, and two in the larger city of San Pedro Sula. The oldest are both in San Pedro Sula: *Tiempo* (1960), with a circulation of 30,000, and *La Prensa* (1964), which claims 62,000. In the capital are *La Tribuna* (1976), owned by former President Carlos Flores, with a circulation of 45,000, and *El Heraldo* (1979), also with 45,000. There is no magazine industry.

## El Salvador

El Salvador's press was caught up in the violence of the late twentieth century, and many journalists perished as targets of assassinations or were caught in the crossfire. The warring factions signed a peace accord in 1992, but economic growth and social justice have been slow.

The press remains highly politicized. Two well-established and competing dailies, both politically conservative, have dominated the field for decades: *La Prensa Gráfica* (1915), generally regarded as the newspaper of record, with a reported circulation of 112,800; and *El Diario de Hoy* (1936), which claims 115,000 readers. Both have tabloid formats but are serious, general-interest, family-oriented papers. Both support the right-wing ARENA party, which has controlled the presidency since 1994. *El Mundo* (1967) is the only daily that can be considered left of center; it has a circulation of 40,000. The oldest daily is *Co Latino,* which dates back to 1890 but has a circulation of only 15,000. A relatively new online newspaper is *El Faro* (http://www.elfaro.com).

## Nicaragua

Nicaragua ranks with Haiti at the bottom of the per capita income scale in Latin America, the legacy of decades of self-serving dictators and exploitation by foreign fruit companies.

Like several other countries in Latin America, political power was contested by the rival Liberal and Conservative parties. Two daily newspapers sprang up in the twentieth century, largely in order to editorialize in favor of one of the parties. *La Prensa,* owned by the Chamorro family, dates to 1926 and supported the Conservatives. The Liberals' champion was *Noticias,* which served as a mouthpiece for the Somoza dynasty that ruled Nicaragua from 1934 to 1979. *La Prensa* became the only outspoken opposition to the dictatorship, and it was frequently closed as a result.

The Sandinista revolution arose during the rule of the last of the Somozas, Anastasio, who came to power in 1967. In January 1978, Pedro Joaquín Chamorro, editor of *La Prensa,* was gunned down in an ambush on his way to work. Somoza vehemently denied complicity in the murder, but Chamorro's death so galvanized the public opposition to Somoza that he was forced to flee the country in July 1979.

The victorious Sandinistas expropriated *Noticias* and converted it into a daily organ of the Sandinista National Liberation Front, called *Barricada. La Prensa* continued to enjoy prestige under the Sandinistas because of Chamorro's martyrdom and because his widow, Violeta Barrios de Chamorro, initially served on the three-member ruling junta. But soon *La Prensa*'s criticism of the Sandinistas' antidemocratic tendencies drove it into outright opposition. The Sandinistas allowed it to continue publishing, but *La Prensa* was closed repeatedly and the staff constantly subjected to intimidation.

Ironically, Xavier Chamorro, brother of the slain editor and himself pro-Sandinista, launched a competitor to *La Prensa* in 1980: *Nuevo Diario.*

After the election upset that brought Violeta Chamorro to the presidency in 1990, the Sandinistas' fortunes went into eclipse. Meanwhile *La Prensa,* published by another of Pedro Chamorro's brothers, Jaime, regained its position as Nicaragua's undisputed newspaper of record. In 1998, *Barricada,* deprived of further government subsidies, ceased publication, although it later reemerged temporarily as a weekly. Now the weekly Sandinista organ has a less combative name: *Visión Sandinista.*

Today, *La Prensa* and *Nuevo Diario,* both general-interest broadsheets, remain Nicaragua's only dailies. They are still published by Jaime and Xavier Chamorro, respectively, and are still political rivals. *La Prensa* has a reported circulation of 30,000–37,000; *Nuevo Diario*'s circulation is from 30,000 to 45,000.

## Costa Rica

Costa Rica has a long tradition of political democracy and freedom of the press and enjoys a high literacy rate and relatively high per capita income for Latin America, but its small population of 4 million has prevented the development of more than a handful of daily newspapers.

The oldest daily, *La Prensa Libre,* was founded in 1889 and still claims 56,000 readers. For several decades, however, the country's newspaper of record has been *La Nación,* founded in

1946 and editorially aligned with the National Liberation Party, one of the country's two dominant political parties. Its reported circulation is 125,000, followed closely by the far less prestigious *Diario Extra,* with 120,000. Other dailies are *Al Día* (1992, 65,000), *El Heraldo* (1994, 25,000), and *La República* (1950, reborn in 1967, 61,000). All the dailies are published in the capital, San José, and circulate nationally. There is an English-language weekly, *The Tico Times,* in the capital, with a circulation of 15,000.

There are about fourteen nondaily periodicals, including a general-interest weekly magazine, *Rumbo* (1984, 15,000). A weekly Catholic magazine, *Eco Católico,* dates to 1931 and claims 20,000 readers.

## Panama

Small in area and population (3.2 million), Panama is something of a cultural anomaly in Latin America. Once a province of Colombia, it was the last Latin American country to gain independence, through a U.S.-engineered movement in 1903. Yet it boasts one of Latin America's oldest daily newspapers, *La Estrella de Panama,* which was launched in 1853 when Panama was a way station for U.S. prospectors crossing the isthmus en route to the California gold fields. The large English-speaking element led *La Estrella* to launch an English edition, *The Panama Star,* which continued to publish for well over a century.

The economic impact of the Panama Canal, completed in 1914, gave Panama one of the highest standards of living in Latin America and, consequently, one of the highest literacy rates. However, political turbulence and periodic episodes of military rule were not conducive to press freedom.

For much of the latter twentieth century, *La Estrella* was owned by the intermarried Altamirano and Duque families. Its chief rivals were the sister newspapers owned by the politically influential Arias family, *Crítica* (1925) and *El Panamá América* (1958). Arnulfo Arias was three times elected president and three times deposed by the military. After the third such coup d'état, in 1968, the military government under Brigadier General Omar Torrijos expropriated *El Panamá América* and *Crítica* from Arias's brother, Harmodio. It turned those two papers and a small morning tabloid, *Matutino,* into government mouthpieces for Torrijos and his efforts to negotiate a new canal treaty with the United States. Torrijos permitted *La Estrella de Panamá* to remain in the hands of Tomás Gabriel Altamirano Duque, but only after he blackmailed Altamirano Duque with the threat of prosecution for corruption while he was administrator of Panama's social security system. Thus, *La Estrella de Panamá* followed a slavish pro-Torrijos editorial line. Torrijos's grip on Panama's press was absolute.

However, in return for President Jimmy Carter's support for a new canal treaty in 1977, Torrijos grudgingly promised to respect human rights, including freedom of the press, and repealed the infamous Law No. 11 (*Ley Once*), which imposed strict media controls. A wealthy anti-Torrijos businessman, Roberto Eisenmann, took advantage of this thaw to launch a new daily, *La Prensa,* in 1980, which quickly eclipsed the pro-government papers in circulation. *La Prensa* relentlessly exposed government corruption and human rights abuses and lampooned Torrijos in editorial cartoons. After Torrijos's death in a plane crash in 1981, *La Prensa* proved equally nettlesome to his less tolerant successor, Manuel Noriega.

Noriega ordered *La Prensa* closed from 1984 to 1986. When it was reopened, the staff found the offices had been vandalized; acid had been poured into the computers and the printing press. *La Prensa* gradually resumed publication and was as strident in its criticism as it had been. Meanwhile, an anti-Noriega tabloid, *El Siglo,* began publication in 1985. Noriega closed both *La Prensa* and *El Siglo* in a general crackdown on dissent in 1987.

*La Prensa* and *El Siglo* did not resume publication until shortly after the U.S. invasion that removed Noriega from power in December 1989. The new civilian government of President Guillermo Endara, whose 1989 election victory had been nullified by Noriega, restored *El Panamá América* and *Crítica* to the widow of Harmodio Arias, who renamed the latter paper *Crítica Libre,* or "Free Criticism." Ironically, Arnulfo Arias's widow, Mireya Moscoso de Arias, served as president of Panama from 1999 to 2004.

The new period of democracy did not mean an end to government hostility toward the press, however. Endara once unsuccessfully sued an editorial cartoonist for libel. His successor, Ernesto Pérez Balladares, sought to revoke the work visa of a Peruvian national working as an editor at *La Prensa* because of his aggressive investigative reporting, but international criticism forced him to relent.

Today, *La Prensa, El Panamá América, Crítica Libre,* and *El Siglo* continue to compete for the small market of daily newspaper readers. Although circulation figures fluctuate, all four papers are believed to have circulations in the 40,000 range. *La Estrella,* which lost virtually all of its journalistic credibility during the dictatorship, has a circulation of about half that range. It still enjoys a readership among the political party identified with Torrijos and Noriega. Torrijos's son, Martín Torrijos, was elected president in 2004. The newest daily, *El Universal,* launched in 1995, claims 16,000 readers. All circulate nationally; there are no provincial dailies.

There is only a handful of nondaily periodicals. The most popular is a weekly satire magazine, *El Camaleón,* which has a reported circulation of 80,000. There is also a thrice-weekly newspaper, *Sucesos.*

## THE CARIBBEAN AND VENEZUELA

### Cuba

The last Spanish colony to achieve independence, in 1898, Cuba is also an anomaly as one of the world's few remaining Marxist-Leninist states. Ironically, Fidel Castro's revolution succeeded in a country that had enjoyed a relatively high standard of living by Latin American standards. However, the inequality between the upper and middle classes and the lower classes was stark, and Cuba was plagued by intermittent dictatorships after the United States relinquished control of the island in 1903.

Newspaper readership was well developed in Cuba, although it was controlled by the elite social class and followed a conservative line. Self-censorship was practiced during the various dictatorships, notably that of Fulgencio Batista (1933–40 and 1952–59).

Within two years after his overthrow of Batista, however, Castro had expropriated all independent media, including the venerable daily *Diario de la Marina,* and turned them into organs of the government or the Communist Party.

Since 1961, Cuba's official daily organ, a legacy of the old Spanish *gazetas,* has been *Granma,* published by the Communist Party and named for the boat that brought Castro and his band of eighty revolutionaries to Cuba from Mexico in 1956. Cuba's economic reversals since the collapse of the Soviet Union have taken their toll on the number of pages in *Granma,* which reports sanitized versions of international and national news, government propaganda on the editorial page, and generous reportage of sports and culture. With no competition and with government funding, *Granma* has a reported press run of 400,000, making it one of the largest dailies in Latin America.

Other periodicals include *Verde Oliva,* the monthly organ of the armed forces (100,000), and *Juventud Rebelde,* aimed at Cuba's youth (250,000).

Several magazines were published before the revolution, but they, too, were either closed or expropriated and renamed. One popular feature magazine that was expropriated but retained its name was *Bohemia,* which focuses on cultural stories, both Cuban and foreign.

In the 1990s, a handful of so-called independent journalists began challenging the control of media and of thought by sending freelance articles to newspapers abroad and, in some cases, by attempting to publish crude periodicals. Their efforts were met with harassment, physical attacks, imprisonment, exile—or all four. During Castro's infamous crackdown on dissent in April 2003, seventy-six people were arrested for various "crimes against the state," including twenty-five dissident journalists. They were sentenced to prison terms of up to 27 years. The best known was Raúl Rivero. Under intense international pressure to release the prisoners of conscience, Castro freed some of them in 2005, including Rivero, who went into exile in Spain.

## Dominican Republic

Dominican newspapers suffered for more than a century from dictatorship, illiteracy, and poverty. The brutal 31-year dictatorship of Rafael L. Trujillo gave way after his assassination in 1961 to a period of political turbulence that resulted in an "elected dictatorship" under Joaquín Balaguer, who maintained power through rigged elections until 1978. He later would serve two more terms and remained the dominant political force until his death in 2002. He followed what could best be called a strained tolerance toward opposition media. Today the Dominican press is generally free, and it benefited from an economic boom from 1996 to 2001, when the country had the fastest-growing economy in Latin America.

The dean of Dominican newspapers is *Listín Diario,* founded in 1889 and still the most-read newspaper in the country, with a reported circulation of 88,000. Known for its independence and left-of-center editorial line, the paper suffered closure during the Trujillo era. In 2003, the government expropriated *Listín Diario,* not for its criticism but because its current owner, Ramón Baéz, was arrested for fraud involving a bank he owned. In 2004, a judge ruled that the newspaper was not involved in the fraud and ordered it returned to Baéz's family, but its reporting and editorials are less partisan than before.

For 40 years, *Listín Diario*'s primary competition was from *El Caribe,* founded in 1948, which provided a conservative counterbalance. Today *Listín Diario*'s reported circulation is only 32,000. Another daily, *Ultima Hora,* appeared in 1970 and now claims 40,000 readers. Two younger dailies were established in 1981: *Hoy* (40,000) and *El Nuevo Diario* (10,000). There is only one daily outside the capital, Santo Domingo: *La Información* in Santiago de los Caballeros, established in 1915. Its reported circulation is 15,000. A free-circulation daily, *Diario Libre,* began publishing in 2003 and has proven successful.

An interesting journalistic phenomenon in the Dominican Republic is a new online newspaper, *Clave Digital,* which was begun by disgruntled staff members of *El Caribe* who reportedly were unhappy over being kept from covering major stories more aggressively. It claims 1 million hits a month, no doubt in part to the large Dominican émigré community in the United States.

The leading Dominican magazine is *Revista Dominicana,* a weekly, which follows the standard format of combining news, business, sports, and features with full-color photography. Another popular weekly is *Ahora!*

## Haiti

The most destitute and least literate nation of the Americas, Haiti also has been plagued by dictatorship for all but the past few years of its existence, and even under civilian control it has been characterized by violence and corruption. The seeds of a viable periodical press never took root in Haiti, and what periodicals there were were read only by the tiny elite social class. Freedom House rates Haiti "Not Free." Because of the poverty and illiteracy, radio is the only true mass medium in the country.

Haiti has two small but venerable dailies: *Le Nouvilliste* (1898), which is believed to have a circulation of 6,000, and *Le Matin* (1908), believed to have a circulation of 5,000.

There are about a dozen nondaily periodicals, including the government's official gazette, *Le Moniteur,* which dates to 1845. Two successful weekly newspapers are *Haiti Observateur* (1971) and *Haiti en Marche* (1987). *Le Nouvelliste* and *Haiti en Marche* operate popular Websites aimed at the Haitian émigré community in the United States.

## Venezuela

Long handicapped by dictatorships and grinding poverty that inhibited growth of a free and independent press, Venezuela experienced a liberal social revolution during 1945–48, which coincided with the oil boom that made the country one of the world's leading petroleum exporters. Democracy took root after the overthrow of the dictatorship of Marcos Pérez Jiménez in 1958, and periodicals representing a broad array of political thinking quickly flourished. Venezuela's stable two-party democracy was widely hailed as a model for Latin America. However, the oil wealth did not trickle down to the lower classes, and the two traditional political parties that alternated in power both fostered corruption on a massive scale.

The election of a maverick former army officer, Hugo Chávez, to the presidency in 1998 on a left-wing platform that stressed greater social and economic equality has largely polarized the people and the press into passionate pro-Chávez and anti-Chávez camps, with the result that journalistic objectivity virtually ceased to exist. Chávez has denounced both print and broadcast media owned by what the calls the "oligarchy," which often has led to physical attacks on those media or their journalists by pro-Chávez elements. Chávez also imposed a restrictive new press law and has harassed opposition publishers with defamation suits. The climate of intimidation is such that Venezuela is one of only four Latin American countries whose press is rated "not free" by Freedom House.

There are eighteen dailies in Caracas, but many are political, religious, or business publications rather than general-interest. The country's newspaper of record is the venerable *El Universal,* founded in 1909. It has a reported circulation of 120,000 daily and 250,000 on Sunday. Its leading competitor for mainstream readers is another broadsheet, *El Nacional* (1943, 100,000). But the most-read newspaper during the week is the morning tabloid, *Ultimas Noticias* (1941, 200,000), owned by the influential Capriles family, which owns numerous other media. A small English-language daily, *The Daily Journal,* has operated since 1941. All three of the major papers are anti-Chávez.

Three other successful dailies carved out their niches after the establishment of democracy: *Meridiano* (1969, 100,000), *2001* (1973, 100,000), and *El Globo* (1990, 68,000).

The remaining dailies in the capital have much lower circulations than the six major papers and tend to have defined political agendas. One, *Tal Cual,* launched in 2000 by Teodoro Petkoff, is known for its aggressive exposés and editorial attacks against the Chávez government.

There are about forty-five provincial dailies, but none is believed to have more than a five-digit circulation. The most established are *El Impulso* (1904) in Barquisimeto, *Panorama* (1914) and *La Columna* (1924) in Maracaibo, and *El Carabobeño* (1933) in Valencia.

There are about twenty-five nondaily magazines and newspapers, but the number keeps changing in the politically and economically volatile marketplace. The most established is *Venezuela Gráfica* (1951), a weekly illustrated news and entertainment magazine. The other mainstream, and conservative, weekly newsmagazines are *Bohemia* (1966) and *Zeta* (1974).

There are weekly and fortnightly newspapers that operate on a shoestring to support various political agendas. One of the best known is *La Razón,* a weekly, whose editor, Pablo López, faced a criminal defamation suit by a wealthy Chávez supporter. López fled into exile in Costa Rica in 2000 when the judge in the case refused to allow him to prove in court that the newspaper's article was true.

## THE ANDES
### Bolivia

Hampered by poverty, illiteracy, and decades of dictatorial rule, the Bolivian press has largely been confined to the country's elite. Bolivia has been democratic since 1982, which has not ended its political turmoil and violence, in which the media play an influential role.

The country's newspaper of record is *El Diario* in the capital La Paz, founded in 1904. Its circulation is estimated at 55,000, believed to be the greatest in the country. The capital supports four other, younger dailies: *Hoy* (1968), *Jornada* (1964), *La Razón* (1990), and *Ultima Hora* (1929), but circulation figures are either unobtainable or unreliable. *La Razón* is thought to be in second place, with 35,000 readers. The Catholic Church began publishing a daily newspaper, *Presencia,* in La Paz in 1952, but it folded about 2000.

Santa Cruz, the country's largest city and its most affluent, supports four competing dailies: *La Estrella del Oriente* (1864), *El Deber* (1955, 35,000), *El Nuevo Día* (1987), and *El Mundo* (1979, 15,000); *El Mundo* is published by the chamber of commerce. Cochabamba also has two dailies, *Los Tiempos* (1943) and *Opinión* (1985), as does Sucre, *Correo del Sur* (1987) and *Página "20"* (1993). Oruro has one venerable daily, *La Patria* (1919).

Bolivia has never developed a significant magazine industry. A weekly newsmagazine, *Aquí,* launched in 1979, has perhaps 10,000 readers. Two other weeklies are *Actualidad Boliviana Confidencial* (1966, 6,000) and *Notas* (1963). Readers rely largely on imported magazines, especially from neighboring Argentina. Radio is the country's most pervasive and influential mass medium. There are approximately 270 radio receivers per 1,000 population.

### Colombia

With a long tradition of violence and periodic dictatorships, Colombia still has one of the worst climates for the functioning of a free and independent press. The climate of danger led Freedom House to rate Colombia "Not Free." The Colombian press also has a reputation as one of the most politicized in Latin America, with newspapers and magazines being affiliated with one of the two major parties, the Liberal and Conservative. Several presidents of the twentieth century have published politically oriented Bogotá dailies, including the Liberals, Alfonso López (1934–38), publisher of *El Liberal,* and Eduardo Santos (1938–42), publisher of *El Tiempo,* and the Conservative, Laureano Gómez (1950–53), publisher of *El Siglo. El*

*Tiempo* and *El Liberal* represented rival factions within the Liberal Party, which were almost as strident in their attacks on each other as they were in their attacks on the Conservatives.

## Newspapers

The Liberal-Conservative conflict erupted into civil war in 1948, a 10-year conflict known as *La Violencia,* which cost an estimated 200,000 lives. The newspapers were caught up in the violence; the offices of *El Tiempo, El Siglo, El Espectador,* and *El Liberal* were all burned. As president, Gómez imposed censorship on the Liberal newspapers. Gómez was overthrown in 1953 in a coup led by Gustavo Rojas Pinilla, who also imposed prior censorship on Liberal and Conservative newspapers alike; some were closed. *El Tiempo* and the venerable *El Espectador,* founded in 1887 by Fidel Cano, changed their names during this period to *Intermedio* and *El Independiente,* respectively, refusing to associate their names with censored newspapers.

Rojas Pinilla, Colombia's last experience with dictatorship, was deposed in 1957. In 1958, the Liberals and Conservatives reached a power-sharing accord by which they would alternate the presidency between them for 16 years, until 1974. However, a new conflict began in 1964 in the form of a leftist insurgency that has continued for more than 40 years and claimed hundreds of thousands of lives. In the 1980s, drug-related violence wrought by the powerful Medellín cartel, among others, and the rise of right-wing paramilitary forces to counteract the guerrillas exacerbated the situation.

Journalists have been frequently caught in the crossfire, or targeted for death, because of what they write or broadcast. Probably the highest-profile journalistic martyr was Guillermo Cano, director of *El Espectador,* assassinated in 1986 by the Medellín cartel led by Pablo Escobar for his reporting on the cartel.

Colombia has a population of more than 40 million, the third largest in Latin America. Despite the potential for this large market, a combination of poverty, illiteracy, and violence has hampered development of the print media; economic factors have also taken a toll.

*El Espectador* was forced to convert from daily to weekly in 2001 to remain alive. It still enjoys a respectable circulation of 200,000. In 2004, Fidel Cano, grand-nephew and namesake of the founder, became director.

*El Siglo,* originally founded in 1925 as the Conservative organ, faded from the scene for a time and then reappeared as *El Nuevo Siglo,* although its circulation is minor, about 68,000.

*El Tiempo,* founded in 1911, is still owned by the Santos family and is still a Liberal organ. Nonetheless, it provides balanced and reliable coverage of events and is the country's newspaper of record. Its reported circulation is 265,000 daily and 536,000 on Sundays.

Outside the capital there are about twenty-six dailies. The oldest and possibly the largest is *El Colombiano* in Medellín, founded in 1912. Another old and successful provincial daily is *El Heraldo* in Barranquilla, published since 1933.

## Magazines

Despite the obstacles, some magazines have been hugely successful and are read throughout Latin America. The oldest and best known is *Cromos,* which dates to 1916. For decades it has combined the elements of a weekly newsmagazine and a glossy, full-color feature magazine with stories on entertainment, culture, and sports. It is larger in dimension than the standard newsmagazine and sometimes exceeds 200 pages. *Revista Cambio,* founded in 1950, follows a similar format and averages about 100 pages each week. Its chairman of the board is now Gabriel García Márquez, the 1982 Nobel laureate in literature. The third leading magazine, *Semana,* is the youngest, and it adheres to the same successful format. There are a handful of specialty magazines, but these three dominate the market and exercise considerable political influence.

## Ecuador

Since Ecuador's return to democracy in 1978, its press has become among the most politicized in the region, editorializing and slanting coverage in favor of one of a multitude of political parties. For a poor country, Ecuador supports a surprising number of dailies, even in provincial cities, a phenomenon explained by low wage scales and support from political parties and the wealthy advertisers who belong to them.

One of the oldest continually published dailies in Latin America is *El Telégrafo,* in Guayaquil, the major port and the country's largest city. It is still regarded as one of three newspapers of record; its circulation is 45,000 daily and 55,000 Sundays. The others are *El Universo* in Guayaquil (1921), with a circulation of 174,000 daily and 290,000 Sundays, and *El Comercio* in the capital, Quito (1906), with a circulation of 106,000. All three are broadsheets.

The other dailies in Guayaquil are *Expreso* (1973, 60,000), *El Extra* (1975, 200,000), and *La Segunda* (1983, 60,000). In Quito, *El Comercio* has an evening sister paper, *Ultimas Noticias* (1938, 60,000). Two postdemocracy dailies are *La Hora* and *Hoy,* both established in 1982. *Hoy*'s reported circulation is 72,000; *La Hora*'s is unknown.

The city of Cuenca has three dailies: *El Mercurio* (1924), *El Tiempo* (1955), and *El Austral* (1987). Quevedo also has three dailies: *Ecos de Quevedo* (1963), *El Planeta* (1979), and *La Palabra* (1989). Other provincial dailies are *El Heraldo* in Ambato (1958); *La Verdad* (1944) and *Diario del Norte* (1987) in Ibarra; *Crónica de la Tarde* (1979) and *El Siglo* (1982) in Loja; *El Nacional* (1964) and *El Correo* (1983) in Machala; *El Mercurio* (1924) in Manta; *El Diario* (1934) in Portoviejo; and *El Espectador* (1972) and *El Libertador* (1984) in Riobamba.

Ecuador lacks a significant magazine industry. The country's best established and most widely read magazine is *Vistazo,* a glossy, full-color biweekly that dates to 1970 and has 85,000 readers. It is a peculiar mix of news and glamour, politics and entertainment, culture and cheesecake.

## Peru

Few Latin American countries display more disparity between the creole and mestizo elites and the majority Indian underclass than does Peru. For more than a century, the Indian majority languished in illiteracy and poverty until a liberal social movement came to power in 1945 and the left-wing military junta ruled from 1968 to 1980. Peru also experienced an economic boom that helped foster cultural development in the nineteenth century from the export of bird guano for fertilizer.

Latin America's first periodical was probably a literary journal, *Mercurio Peruano,* which was published briefly at the end of the eighteenth century. Peru has had an established press since just after independence, beginning with *El Peruano,* the official gazette, which was established as a weekly in 1825 and is still in daily publication. Unlike other surviving *gacetas,* *El Peruano* carries a diverse selection of news, sports, and cultural and economic news in addition to the usual dull official decrees.

Latin America's second-oldest daily is *El Comercio* in Lima, founded in 1839. This broadsheet, owned for several generations by the Miró and Quesada families, remains Peru's newspaper of record and has the country's greatest circulation, 150,000 daily and 220,000 on Sunday. Lima boasted another of Latin America's prestigious dailies for much of the twentieth century, *La Prensa,* which had a reformist agenda. It was published by the Beltrán family from 1903 to 1984. *La Prensa* also had an evening sister paper, *Ultimas Noticias,* which once boasted a circulation of about 100,000, but it too has folded.

Two other established Lima dailies are *Expreso* (1961), which has a circulation of 100,000, and its evening sister paper *Extra* (1964), which has 80,000. Another pre-junta daily, *Ojo* (1968), has 100,000 readers.

Like *El Comercio, Expreso* and *Extra* represent interests of the conservative elite. In 1974, they, *La Prensa,* and four other dailies were expropriated by the military junta and were turned over to various so-called social sectors, such as labor unions, schoolteachers, and peasants. The once-respected papers lost any semblance of credibility, and the previous owners began publishing weekly or fortnightly newspapers, which enjoyed large readerships. When democracy was restored in 1980, newly elected President Fernando Belaunde Terry—the same president the generals had deposed in 1968—restored the dailies to their rightful owners in his first official act.

*La República,* founded in 1982 after the return to democracy, follows a more leftist editorial course and has established a reputation for aggressive investigative reporting that brought retribution from President Alberto Fujimori, an elected autocrat who governed from 1990 to 2000. During Fujimori's third election campaign in 2000, security forces invaded the home of a *La República* reporter who was in possession of a potentially embarrassing videotape and sawed his arm to the bone. The paper's circulation is between 50,000 and 60,000.

The newest Lima daily is *Gestión* (1990), which is now the second-largest paper, with a circulation of 131,000. A sports daily, *El Bocón* (1994), sells 90,000 copies.

Peru has fifteen provincial dailies, including three in Arequipa. The oldest, *El Pueblo* (1905), has a circulation of 70,000.

There are approximately twenty magazines and nondaily newspapers. The dean of the weekly general-interest magazines and still the most widely read is *Caretas,* founded in 1950. Aggressive but even-handed in its reporting, it was closed three times during the military government and its director was exiled twice. It also faced intimidation from Fujimori. Its circulation is placed at 90,000. It averages 100 pages a week and combines serious news coverage with glossy pin-up photos.

Another popular weekly magazine is the more conservative *Oiga,* which has 60,000 readers. *Gente* (1958), which focuses on culture, entertainment, and personalities, has 25,000.

## THE SOUTHERN CONE AND BRAZIL

### Chile

As the birthplace of the Latin American independent press, with the appearance of Father Camilo Henríquez's *La Aurora de Chile* in 1810, Chile enjoyed a full century of uninterrupted political democracy and freedom of expression after independence in 1817 and attracted intellectuals and writers from less fortunate Latin American countries, who provided even greater cultural enrichment. Chile's emphasis on education and freedom of thought gave it a journalistic and literary tradition out of proportion to its population. It is not coincidental that Chile is the only Latin American country to have produced two Nobel laureates in literature: Gabriela Mistral in 1945 and Pablo Neruda in 1971.

## Newspapers

Dozens of independent newspapers flourished in this climate of freedom, representing a broad spectrum of political thought. Latin America's oldest continuously published newspaper, *El Mercurio,* was founded in Valparaiso in 1827 and became a daily 10 years later. It was purchased in 1900 by Augustín Edwards, who moved it to Santiago, where his heirs continue to publish it. It is Chile's newspaper of record.

This tradition of a free marketplace of ideas continued well into the twentieth century, when Socialist and Communist publications appeared, and has been interrupted only twice: the dictatorship of Carlos Ibáñez (1925–31) and the military government under Augusto Pinochet (1973–90). The unfettered expression of sometimes volatile opinions contributed to the turmoil of the 1960s and 1970s that was marked by the election of the minority Socialist-Communist government of Salvador Allende in 1970 and the bloody military coup that truncated it and brought draconian controls over the media in 1973. All pro-Allende publications were closed, and mainstream newspapers, such as *El Mercurio* and its also conservative chief rival, *La Tercera,* were trusted to practice self-censorship. Some publications attempted to practice independent journalism, such as Emilio Filippi's weekly newsmagazine *Hoy,* or the Catholic magazine *Mensaje,* but their staffs were harassed and sometimes the magazines were closed temporarily.

In 1988, Pinochet lost a plebiscite that would have continued his rule until 1997, and he called free elections the following year. A Christian Democrat, Patricio Aylwin, was sworn in as president in March 1990, ushering in a new era of freewheeling journalism. Chile's post-Pinochet press has been strengthened by a robust economy that has been the envy of Latin America, although some newspapers established during the Pinochet era, such as *Fortín Mapocho* and Filippi's *La Epoca,* folded in the 1990s.

*El Mercurio* and *La Tercera,* the latter founded in 1950 by the Picó family, remain the dominant newspaper forces in Santiago. *La Tercera*'s daily circulation is reported to be 200,000. *El Mercurio*'s is 120,000 daily and 280,000 on Sunday. *El Mercurio* also publishes two tabloids, *La Segunda* (1931, 40,000) and *Las Ultimas Noticias* (1902, 150,000). The chain also continues to publish the original *El Mercurio* in Valparaiso, as well as other provincial dailies in Antofagasta, Arica, Iquique, Osorno, and Temuco.

In 1991, a media conglomerate, Compañía Periodística, S.A. or Copesa, owned by Alvaro Saieh, bought *La Tercera* from the Picó family and began publishing a sensational working-class daily tabloid, *La Cuarta,* which has been a phenomenal success, reportedly eclipsing *La Tercera* in circulation, although exact figures are not available.

There are at least thirty provincial dailies and a proliferation of iconoclastic weeklies and bimonthly newspapers that engage in investigative reporting and seek to slaughter sacred cows left untouched by the mainstream papers. Among the most widely read are *El Periodista* and *The Clinic.* Another, *Plan B,* launched in 2003, lasted only 18 months.

## Magazines

Chile's strong literary tradition has given it a magazine industry far out of proportion to its size. Chile's strong economy has not guaranteed viability in a fierce and glutted market, however. The once-popular news weekly, *Hoy,* folded a few years after its founder, Emilio Filippi, sold it in order to begin a daily newspaper.

The dean of Chilean magazines is *Ercilla,* a news weekly in the style of *Time,* that dates from 1936. It ceased publication in 1991 and later reappeared as a bimonthly with a circulation of 28,000. The most successful newsmagazine now is *Qué Pasa,* a conservative organ founded in 1971 during the Allende presidency. Copesa acquired it in 1991. It claims 30,000 readers. A more recent newsmagazine is *Asuntos Públicos.*

*Vea,* a general-interest weekly illustrated magazine, may be the most popular magazine, with 150,000 readers.

Women's magazines have traditionally been popular in Chile. The oldest and still most popular is *Paula,* founded in 1967; its circulation is 85,000. Another leading women's magazine is *Caras,* a high-quality publication that circulates outside Chile as well. Copesa publishes a women's supplement, *Mujer,* in *La Tercera.*

Because of Chile's high degree of sophistication as a result of the traditional emphasis on education and the affluence from an expanding economy, the magazine industry has become more specialized than in most Latin American countries. Magazines now cater to computer lovers (*ComputerWorld* and *Mouse*), law (*La Semana Jurídica*), and the environment (*BioPlanet*). As always, there is an assortment of feature and opinion magazines, including the venerable *Mensaje. Conozca Más,* a science magazine launched in the waning days of the Pinochet era, claims 90,000 readers.

## Argentina

Traditionally one of Latin America's most prosperous and literate countries, Argentina also has consistently boasted a large array of periodicals. Under the liberal constitution of 1853 that followed the brutal dictatorship of Juan Manuel de Rosas, Argentina experienced a "golden age" of democracy, public education, economic expansion, and literary expression; at the turn of the twentieth century, its per capita income exceeded that of the United States.

Argentina's two most famous newspapers were established during this period: *La Prensa,* founded by José M. Paz in 1869, and *La Nación,* founded the following year by Bartolomé Mitre, who was president from 1862 to 1868. Through much of the twentieth century, journalism scholars ranked both newspapers as among the world's best, and both were known for resisting the repression of both elected and military governments between 1943 and 1983.

The constitutional dictatorship of Juan Domingo Perón of 1946–55, and the even more draconian military regime of 1976–83 that followed Perón's second presidency, had a chilling effect on Argentine journalism, which did not improve appreciably during the 10-year administration of the elected President Carlos Menem (1989–99). Periodic economic crises, and the debt crisis and economic meltdown of 2001–02, made it difficult for any but the hardiest publications to survive. Despite two decades of democratic government, an atmosphere of intimidation still exists in which the government uses many of the same tactics once used by Perón to discourage aggressive editorial criticism and investigative reporting. Threats and physical attacks against journalists, which Menem once dismissed as "part of their job," are commonplace.

### Newspapers

Many Buenos Aires newspapers circulate nationally, even internationally to Uruguay and Paraguay. *La Prensa*'s circulation has dwindled to about 42,000 as it has suffered from a loss of credibility. *La Nación,* although no longer owned by the Mitre family, remains Argentina's newspaper of record, with a circulation of about 200,000. For years, however, it has been eclipsed in circulation by such working-class tabloids as *Clarín* (1945), the country's circulation leader with 600,000, and *Crónica* (1963), which in the 1960s was the circulation leader with 700,000 but has since dropped to 450,000. Another venerable tabloid that has survived is *La Razón* (1905, 62,000). Buenos Aires also has two business dailies, *El Cronista* (1908, 65,000) and *Ambito Financiero* (1975, 115,000). The English-language *Buenos Aires Herald* dates to 1876 and claims a circulation of 20,000. A successful newcomer is *Página/12,* which was established in 1987 and was one of the few papers that exposed corruption during the Menem administration. Owned by *Clarín,* it claims 280,000 readers.

The dominance of the Buenos Aires dailies suppressed the circulation of provincial dailies. Nonetheless, there are about eighty provincial dailies, a few of which are more than a century old, such as *La Capital* in Rosario (1867, 65,000) and *El Día* in La Plata (1884, 55,000). Many others date to the first half of the twentieth century. Probably the most prestigious is *La Voz del Interior* in Cordoba (1904, 100,000).

Nondailies flourished after the return to democratic rule in 1983, representing a broad spectrum of political thinking or specializing in coverage of sports or entertainment, but not all could survive in Argentina's sometimes volatile economic climate.

## Magazines

Argentina has long supported a thriving magazine industry, but economic turbulence, political repression, and changing tastes have all taken a toll. Nonetheless, Argentina now publishes dozens of magazines, both general interest and specialty. At present, the media group Atlántida publishes four of the country's most-read magazines: *Gente, Biliken, Para Ti,* and *Pararazzi.* All are slick feature magazines in the style of *People* and *Us* in the United States. *Biliken* began as a humor magazine in the 1960s. *Para Ti* is a women's magazine that can be found on newsstands throughout Latin America.

Weekly newsmagazines have come and gone in Argentina. *Siete Días Ilustrado,* a combination news and feature picture magazine in the style of *Life,* has survived since 1967. The most widely read weekly newsmagazine currently is *Revista Noticias,* which began in 1984. It generally follows the format of the U.S. newsmagazines, with sections on national politics, economy, culture, customs, personalities, science, sports, and international news. It contains about 120 pages.

The *Forbes*-like business magazine *América Economía* circulates throughout Latin America.

## Uruguay

By virtue of lucrative cattle and wheat imports, Uruguay has long been Latin America's most affluent and consequently most literate nation. It also has been its most democratic, and its press has traditionally been politicized by loyalty to the Colorado or Blanco parties.

For more than a century, the dean of the Uruguayan press and the newspaper of record was *El Día,* founded in 1886 by the leader of the Colorado Party, José Batlle y Ordóñez, who also served as president of the republic from 1903 to 1907 and from 1911 to 1915. It was he who gave Uruguay its European-style social welfare system, which is still in place today, and his photo appeared on *El Día*'s masthead. At its zenith, *El Día* had a circulation of 100,000, but by the time it ceased publication in 1996, it had dwindled to 10,000. It attempted to keep the name alive with a Website, but that too disappeared in 2001. Another pro-Colorado paper is *La Mañana* (1917), which has 50,000 readers.

The organ of the rival Blanco Party is *El País,* founded in 1918 and the current circulation leader with 106,000. Other established dailies in the capital are *El Diario Español* (1905, 20,000) and *El Diario* (1923, 12,000).

A new generation of dailies arose during and after the military government of 1973–85, including *Ultimas Noticias* (1981, 25,000), an evening tabloid; *La República* (1988, 20,000);

and *El Observador* (1991, 26,000). The newer parties have been less supportive of the two traditional parties and more supportive of the left-wing Progressive Encounter coalition, which came to power in the 2004 presidential election.

There are provincial dailies in Florida (*El Heraldo,* 1919, 20,000), Minas (*La Unión,* 1877, 2,600), Maldonado (*Correo de Punta del Este,* 1993, 2,500), Paysandú (*El Telégrafo,* 1910, 8,500), and Salto (*Tribuna Salteña,* 1906, 3,000).

There are approximately 17 nondaily periodicals in Uruguay, including the magazines *Búsqueda,* a nonpartisan newsmagazine founded in 1972, which has a circulation of 25,000; *Brecha* (1985, 8,500); and *Aquí,* the Progressive Encounter organ.

## Paraguay

Isolated and landlocked Paraguay was governed under a long succession of dictators who showed little interest in the country's social or cultural development. Moreover, a majority of the population were Indians who spoke not Spanish but Guaraní, which also became a written language. What newspapers that were published were controlled by wealthy interests loyal to the country's governing elite. Since 1947, Paraguay has been governed by the Colorado Party, a longevity in power exceeded only by the Communist Party of North Korea. Most of that period was under the dictatorship of Alfredo Stroessner from 1954 to 1989. The party has published a daily, *Patria,* since 1946.

For several decades, the country's newspaper of record was *La Tribuna,* a dull, gray government mouthpiece that is replete with official decrees in the tradition of the Spanish *gacetas.* In 1967, a wealthy businessman, Aldo Zucolillo, launched a general-interest tabloid, *ABC Color,* which took its name from a popular tabloid in Madrid, adding the word "Color" to tout its introduction of color photography and graphics to Paraguay. It quickly became the country's most-read paper, and its popularity spawned two copycat competitors, *Hoy,* owned by Stroessner's son-in-law, Humberto Dominguez Dibb, and *Ultima Hora,* the country's only *vespertino,* or evening paper, launched by Demetrio Rojas.

By the 1970s, Paraguayan journalism was experiencing growing pains. *ABC Color* and *Ultima Hora* engaged in increasingly aggressive reporting and criticism of the dictatorship and of Paraguay's notoriously entrenched corruption. However, they carefully avoided criticizing Stroessner by name, which would have resulted in immediate reprisals. When Dominguez Dibb's marriage fell apart, even *Hoy* joined the chorus of criticism. In 1979, Stroessner attempted to squelch this growing freedom of the press by having his interior minister close down *Hoy* and *Ultima Hora* for 30 days as a warning.

Because of its large circulation and financial strength, *ABC Color* temporarily escaped such retribution. But as Zucolillo's criticism and investigative reporting became increasingly nettlesome, Stroessner ordered the paper closed permanently in 1984. Not coincidentally, Nicolás Bó, a wealthy automobile dealer and political ally of Stroessner, launched a new daily, *Noticias,* which followed an editorial line predictably loyal to Stroessner and the Colorado Party.

Stroessner was overthrown in a military coup in 1989. His successor, General Andrés Rodríguez, won an open presidential election and allowed *ABC Color* to reopen. In the post-Stroessner era, the Colorado Party broke into rival factions, and the newspapers, always politicized, chose sides. *ABC Color* remains the country's newspaper of record, although its image has become tarnished by its identification with the Colorado faction of the cashiered army general, Lino Oviedo, who instigated an unsuccessful coup attempt in 1996 and is accused of masterminding the assassination of Vice President Luis Argaña, of a rival party faction, in 1999. A sensational working-class tabloid, *Diario Popular,* tapped into the market of low-income readers and has proved successful. It was once owned by Juan Carlos Wasmosy, Oviedo's arch rival, who served as president from 1994 to 1998.

This growing competition in Paraguay's limited market of readers, as well as the new political realities, began to claim casualties. *Hoy* folded not long after Dominguez Dibb's death in the 1990s. His brother, Osvaldo, launched a new daily, *La Nación,* in 1995. *La Tribuna* also folded in the 1990s. *Noticias,* its credibility tarnished by its association with the dictatorship, ceased publication in January 2005.

Circulation figures for the country's 5 dailies, all published in Asuncion, are rough estimates. *ABC Color* is deemed the leader with about 32,000, followed closely by *Ultima Hora* with 30,000, *Diario Popular* with 29,000 and *La Nación* with about the same, and *Patria* with 8,000. *Noticias* had a circulation of about 20,000 when it folded. *Ultima Hora* is now owned by Antonio J. Vierci, Paraguay's first cross-media owner; he also owns a television station, Telefuturo, and FM Radio La Estación, as well as a supermarket chain.

Paraguay never had a magazine industry until well after the fall of Stroessner. Two popular magazines are *Zeta,* owned by Zuni Castiñeira, a former model turned media executive, and *Tveo.* Both focus on entertainment and personalities.

## Brazil

The exiled Portuguese royal family brought the first printing press to Brazil after the Napoleonic invasion in 1808. It published a dull official organ, *A Gazeta do Rio de Janeiro.* Soon, privately owned presses joined in the chorus clamoring for independence.

Ironically, freedom of expression in Brazil during the constitutional monarchy of Emperor Dom Pedro II (1831–89) often exceeded that in democratic republics such as Argentina. Dom Pedro, an enlightened intellectual who abolished slavery in the 1870s, did not even suppress publications that called for establishment of a republic, which came to pass in 1889. However, Dom Pedro did not place the same emphasis on public education as did the Argentines and Chileans; thus, Brazilian literacy lagged behind that of many of the Spanish-speaking countries—and still does. Although a plethora of newspapers were established during the nineteenth century—some of which are still published today, such as *O Estado de São Paulo* and *Jornal do Brasil* in Rio de Janeiro—the papers were limited to the elite ruling class and had limited circulations.

Democracy and freedom of expression thus took root firmly in Brazil, which has had only two experiences with dictatorial rule: Getulio Vargas and his quasi-fascist Estado Novo (1930–45) and the military regime that overthrew the left-wing President João Goulart in 1964 and ruled until 1985.

Vargas closed numerous critical publications and expropriated *O Estado de São Paulo* from 1940 to 1945. Vargas returned to power in 1951 following a democratic election, but his antipathy toward freedom of the press proved his undoing. In 1954, Carlos Lacerda, an anti-Vargas editor and well-known radio and television commentator, was wounded in an assassination attempt that killed an air force officer in the crossfire. The shooting was linked to the presidential guard, which led the press to clamor for Vargas's resignation. Instead, Vargas shot himself to death.

The military regime of 1964–85, peculiar for its rotation of soldier-presidents every four years, closed left-wing publications and imposed moderate controls on the remaining media through a series of edicts, the most notorious being Institutional Act No. 5 of 1968. It provided the media with a fourteen-point list of guidelines and encouraged the print media to practice self-censorship. The government employed only ninety censors nationwide. In most cases of actual prior censorship, page proofs were required to be transmitted to the capital, Brasilia. In some cases, such as with the satirical weekly magazine *O Pasquim* [The Broadside], authorities confiscated entire press runs when a publication tried to evade censorship.

The most celebrated case involved the venerable *O Estado de São Paulo,* which was conservative and supportive of many of the policies of the military regime. As it had under Vargas, the Mesquita family chafed at governmental restrictions. In August 1971, Julio Mesquita informed the government he would no longer censor his own paper. Thus, government censors came every day for three and a half years to *O Estado* and to its evening sister paper, *Jornal da Tarde.* The prior censorship of the two respected papers made the government the object of national and international ridicule, and a new president withdrew the censors in January 1975. Censorship was lifted altogether in 1978.

The period of self-censorship led to a homogenization of news content, which had the effect of depriving each publication of any uniqueness. Unable to compete effectively in a crowded market, marginal publications went bankrupt. This happened even to the 73-year-old daily *Correio da Manhã* of Rio de Janeiro and to the highly critical weekly newspaper *Opinão.*

With the restoration of democracy in 1985, newspapers and magazines resumed their aggressive reporting and their biting commentaries; newer newspapers and magazines also arose to take advantage of the new atmosphere of freedom. The marketplace remains fiercely competitive, however.

## Newspapers

With a population of more than 170 million, Brazil has the ninth-largest newspaper circulation in the world, about 8 million. However, because of high functional illiteracy and poverty, daily newspaper circulation per 1,000 remains relatively low for a major industrialized country, about 40, compared with 123 in neighboring Argentina. Nonetheless, the country has more than eighty dailies, although about a fifth of them are concentrated in and around Rio de Janeiro or São Paulo. Two claim the largest circulations in Latin America, *O Estado de São Paulo* and *Folha de São Paulo,* about 1.2 million each, although figures vary widely from source to source. *O Estado*'s sister evening paper, *Jornal da Tarde,* has a reported circulation of about 700,000.

In Rio de Janeiro, *O Globo,* cornerstone of the media conglomerate that includes the dominant Globo television network, is the largest daily with a circulation of perhaps 400,000. Its Website claims it is the largest paper in Brazil but offers no figures to substantiate that claim. *O Globo* was founded in 1925 by Irineu Marinho, and the empire of newspapers, magazines, radio, and television is now run by his son, Roberto Marinho. The Marinho empire also owns *Diario de São Paulo. Jornal do Brasil,* considered Rio's most prestigious daily, has about half *O Globo*'s circulation.

Both Rio de Janeiro and São Paulo have business dailies. *Jornal do Comercio* in Rio, probably the country's oldest newspaper, was established in 1827 and has a reported circulation of 19,000. *Gazeta Mercantil* in São Paulo was established in 1920 and has a reported circulation of 106,000. The *Jornal dos Sports* in Rio claims a circulation of 150,000.

The provincial dailies tend to have much smaller circulations, as the country's major dailies circulate nationally as chroniclers of major national and world events. The largest is *Zero Hora* in Pôrte Alegre, with a reported circulation of 727,000.

There is an abundance of nondailies in Brazil, all with relatively small circulations. Many are provincial newspapers reporting local news; others are political and specialty newspapers in the major metropolitan areas.

## Magazines

Brazil has had a thriving magazine industry since the early twentieth century, although magazines have faced the same obstacles as newspapers. An example was *O Cruzeiro*, a weekly news-photo magazine in the style of *Life*, owned by the Assis Chateaubriand family. At the time of the military dictatorship, it claimed a circulation of 1 million in Brazil and another 500,000 for its Spanish-language edition, making it the second most-read magazine in Latin America. When its owner died in 1968, family squabbles, mismanagement, and self-censorship all contributed to its demise in the 1970s. The weekly newsmagazine *Visão* also folded.

A similar fate did not befall the still-popular *Manchete*, also a news-photo weekly, launched in 1956 and owned by Time-Life. It is largely a popular culture vehicle, focusing on entertainment and sports, especially soccer and racecar driving. Its circulation is estimated at 110,000.

Brazil has three popular news weeklies that follow the format of *Time* and *Newsweek* and have survived both censorship and economic upheaval: *Veja* and *Isto é*, which date to the late 1960s and struggled for editorial independence during the dictatorship, and the younger *Época*, part of the Globo empire. The three weeklies provide Brazilian readers with a diverse diet of national, international, business, sports, and cultural news. The only one with a reported circulation is *Veja*, with 1.2 million.

Brazil's most popular monthly women's magazine is *Claudia*, which dates to 1962 and has a circulation of 460,000. *Marie Claire*, owned by Globo, claims 273,000 readers. The Brazilian edition of *Elle* has 100,000.

Brazil also has specialty magazines in such area as automobiles, gardening, and health.

Brazilian magazine publishing is seeing a trend toward chain ownership similar to that in the United States and Europe. Besides *Época*, Globo also publishes a feature magazine, *Quem*, which focuses on celebrities, like *People* in the United States. Editora Tres owns *Isto é*, as well as a feature magazine, *Gente*, which competes with *Quem*, and a business magazine, *Dinheiro*.

A tawdry aspect of Brazilian periodicals is the thriving, and legal, pornography industry. It is not unusual for pornographic magazines to outsell the mainstream publications, although reliable figures are unobtainable.

# RESOURCE GUIDE

## PRINT SOURCES

Alisky, Marvin. *Latin American Media: Guidance and Censorship.* Ames: University of Iowa Press, 1981.

Buckman, Robert. "Cultural Agenda of Latin American Newspapers and Magazines: Is U.S. Domination a Myth?" *Latin American Research Review* 25 (1990): 134–155.

Chaffee, Steven H., et al. "Mass Communication Research in Latin America: Views from Here and There." *Journalism Quarterly* 67 (1990): 1015–1024.

Cole, Richard R., ed. *Communication in Latin America.* Wilmington, DE: Scholarly Resources Inc., 1996.

*Editor and Publisher International Year Book.* New York: Editor and Publisher Co., 2005.

Fox, Elizabeth. *Media and Politics in Latin America.* Beverly Hills, CA: Sage Publications, 1988.

Montgomery, Louise. "Images of the U.S. in the Latin American Press." *Journalism Quarterly* 65 (1988): 655–660.

Pierce, Robert N. *Keeping the Flame: Media and Government in Latin America.* New York: Hastings House, 1979.

Salwen, Michael, and Bruce Garrison. "Press Freedom and Development: U.S. and the Latin American Views." *Journalism Quarterly* 66 (1989): 87–92.

*Statesman's Yearbook and World Gazetteer.* New York: St. Martin's Press, 2005.

## WEBSITES

Committee to Protect Journalists, The Americas: http://www.cpj.org/regions_06/americas_06/americas_06.html.

Inter American Press Association: http://www.sipiapa.com.

Freedom House. http://www.freedomhouse.org/template.cfm. Map of press freedom and country reports.

Zona Latina: http://www.zonalatina.com.

# LOVE, SEX, AND MARRIAGE

**LOVE, SEX, AND MARRIAGE:** Mexican race car driver Adrian Fernandez and his new wife, Colombian model Catalina Maya, listen to a guitar player after their wedding ceremony in the Caribbean sea town of Cartagena, in northern Colombia, March 11, 2005. AP Photo.

**LOVE, SEX, AND MARRIAGE:** Antonio Medina, right, and Jorge Cerpa kiss for photographers after receiving their official marriage documents during a ceremony in Mexico City, March 16, 2007. The sign behind says in Spanish "your right to choose." An economist and a journalist became the first couple united under Mexico City's new gay civil union law. AP Photo/Gregory Bull.

# MUSIC

**MUSIC:** Puerto Rican bomba musicians and dancer. Courtesy of Shutterstock.

**MUSIC:** Banda Dida performs during Carnival, in Salvador da Bahia, Brazil. Courtesy of Shutterstock.

# PERIODICALS

**PERIODICALS:** A vendor hawks newspapers in front of the "Angel of Independence" in Mexico City, August 15, 2002. Mexican President Vicente Fox had just announced that he would cancel his visit to Texas from August 26 to 28 as a sign of protest after Texas ignored his pleas and put a Mexican-American drug smuggler to death for killing a Dallas police officer. AP Photo/ Eduardo Verdugo.

**PERIODICALS:** Brazilian supermodel Gisele Bündchen gestures during an event to celebrate her 10 years of modeling with *Vogue Brasil* magazine during the São Paulo Fashion Week in 2005. In the background, her first cover with the magazine. AP Photo/Victor R. Caivano.

# RADIO AND TELEVISION

**RADIO AND TELEVISION:** Mario Kreutzberger, in his role as Don Francisco, gestures during taping of *Giant Saturday*, or *Sabado Gigante*, in Miami. The variety show marks 20 years in the U.S. in 2006, and in 2007 will hit 45 years in Chile, where it originated. AP Photo/Lynne Sladky.

**RADIO AND TELEVISION:** In this picture released by Canal 13, Argentine soccer legend Diego Maradona dances with Brazilian television star Xuxa Meneghel during Maradona's weekly television show in Buenos Aires. AP Photo/HO/ Canal 13.

**SPORTS AND RECREATION:** Brazilian soccer fans during the World Cup match. Courtesy of Shutterstock.

**SPORTS AND RECREATION:** Cock fights are very popular in parts of Mexico. Courtesy of Shutterstock.

**SPORTS AND RECREATION:** A rack of luchador masks, used in Mexican wrestling. Courtesy of Shutterstock.

# THEATER AND PERFORMANCE

**THEATER AND PERFORMANCE:** A woman in a costume for El Día de los Muertos, the Day of the Dead celebrations. Courtesy of Shutterstock.

**THEATER AND PERFORMANCE:** A typical dancer in the Fiesta Pentecostes (a Christian Pentecost festival) in the Incan village of Ollantaytambo (Sacred Valley), Peru. © Rfoxphoto / Dreamstime.com.

# TRANSPORTATION AND TRAVEL

**TRANSPORTATION AND TRAVEL:** A ship transiting Panama Canal at the Gatun Locks. Courtesy of Shutterstock.

**TRANSPORTATION AND TRAVEL:** The Temple of the Great Jaguar in Tikal, Guatemala, a spectacular Mayan temple built around 600 AD. Tikal's Mayan ruins are a popular tourist and study site. Courtesy of Shutterstock.

**TRANSPORTATION AND TRAVEL:** Cusco, Peru, a much-visited center of Incan culture. Courtesy of Shutterstock.

# RADIO AND TELEVISION

LEONARDO FERREIRA

If journalism as an activity in the Western Hemisphere did not begin with New Spain and its importation of the printing press in the mid 1530s, but rather with Native American chronicles in books, stelae, and other writings in Middle America (and perhaps even with ancient Incan runners and their knots—*quipu*—telling stories in the Andes), then radio broadcasting in Latin America did not originate with inventive and avid merchants and media professionals who mimicked foreign powers. Dictatorial ambitions, war pressures and propaganda, national security concerns, imperialistic business goals, party and official agendas—and, occasionally, some educational campaigns—had as much or more to do with this new and revolutionary medium than did local commercial entrepreneurship.

Eventually, by the late 1920s and early 1930s, the U.S. broadcast model would defeat both the British Broadcasting Corporation (BBC) and the USSR's Marxist-Leninist models throughout Latin America. As scholars Elihu Katz and George Wedell explained, "The absence of significant broadcasting developments in either Spain or Portugal, coupled with the pan-American links established since independence, caused them to be greatly influenced by the United States in the institutionalization of their broadcasting systems. The majority of the [Latin] American countries were already within the sphere of influence of the United States both politically and economically when broadcasting technology became commercially available. The South American countries were among the first after the U.S. to introduce radio broadcasting on a commercial basis."[1]

## THE RISE OF MASS MEDIA IN LATIN AMERICA

Contrary to what voice radio pioneers envisioned in the early 1900s, Latin American broadcasting has not been an industry of "one to many" but mostly "many to one"—that is, large and fragmented audiences dedicated to a system of commercialized airwaves for the ultimate benefit of one powerful family, one greedy company, or one ambitious leader or tycoon. Combine the ongoing and mighty corporate media concentration with the fragile state of public broadcasting, in addition to the historic politicization of the political spectrum, and both market and nonmarket electronic media structures can be easily described throughout the Americas. For decades, activists have been defying the region's unfair communications structures by using community radio and grassroots, often pirate, television stations, not to mention printed publications; however, alternative outlets have been no match for the hegemony of mainstream media, their news, their entertainment, and above all, their advertising revenue.

Online information is exciting for freedom of expression, but in a complex geography where "over a billion people around the globe [are] living [on] under $1 dollar a day" (half of the world lives on less than $2 a day), the Internet in Latin America is also a limited and privileged medium—although various contents and uses (e.g., blogging, Internet radio, online video, and alternative publishing) remain promising avenues for challenging the oligopolistic plutocracy of conventional mass communications.[2] Unfortunately, the average Internet penetration in Latin America and the Caribbean barely reaches 15 percent of the total population, and that is an optimistic figure compared to sobering World Bank statistics (slightly over 10 percent in 2005).[3] In fact, according to current 2006 global development indicators from the World Bank, Latin American countries with the highest Internet access range from Chile's 267 Internet users per 1,000 people and Costa Rica's 235 to as low as Bolivia's 39, Honduras's 32, Paraguay's 25, and Nicaragua's 23 Internet users per 1,000 individuals. As a whole, Latin America and the Caribbean are probably averaging about 11.5 percent Internet access, or about 115 users per 1,000 people.[4] The big three—Mexico, Argentina, and Brazil—reported only 135, 133, and 120 Internet users per 1,000 persons, respectively.

Thus, because of the high costs involved, ongoing mass media users tend to be found in rich neighborhoods, cosmopolitan strata, and urban areas. Serious and concerted efforts are being made in some countries to universalize the Internet; however, because of the strong pressures of poverty in multiple places, in addition to scarce resources in funding sustained new media projects, well-intentioned online programs face monumental difficulties. Much speculation exists about the United States and other developed countries helping in the diffusion of Internet services to developing nations, but the United States, for instance, spends about thirty times as much money for military aid as it does for actual social development assistance, an amount far below the GDP levels of other smaller industrialized economies. Nevertheless, average U.S. citizens think their government invests a great deal more in helping others than it actually does: merely $20 billion a year in international assistance from a $2 trillion-dollar economy.

The World Bank no longer reports radio set availability; it reports the number of Internet users and the number of daily newspapers sold per 1,000 people, as well as the percentage of households with television (although most of Central American and several Latin American nations go unreported). Eighty-eight percent of Latin American and Caribbean homes have television, according to a World Bank development report, relying on International Telecommunication Union (ITU) data. The countries with the highest penetration are mostly in South America: Argentina (97 percent), Chile (95 percent), Colombia (92 percent), and Brazil (90 percent). Mexico and Costa Rica, 92 and 91 percent, respectively, also report high levels of access to television.[5]

Latin America's eight decades of broadcast transmissions demonstrate how a market concept of media democracy finally benefited private conglomerates over government censors: a notable victory, especially for the elites, although less significant for impoverished people in need of effective rights and channels to express their opinions. Instead of having to endure the moralistic hypocrisy of former dictators and their allies, ordinary Latin Americans now confront the equally inhibiting pressures of self-censorship, socioeconomic and technological inequality, personal discrimination, access constraints, and other hurdles caused by information monopolies, a system primarily inspired by the commercial broadcast model and the marketplace of ideas in the United States.

For disadvantaged people, this weakened, if not empty, media democracy is not exclusive to Latin America and the Caribbean. Since the mid-1980s, media plutocracies and their transnational businesses have moved to decisively dominate communications worldwide, prompting the collapse of the Berlin Wall while choking developing nations and their people through globalization and a so-called liberalization process. Not surprisingly, the majority in the Latin American region have little regard for institutional democracy and its formal freedoms and institutions. "They are *democracias líquidas* (liquid democracies)," wrote Argentine journalist Mariano Grondona in the late 1990s, weak sociopolitical and media systems that have little if anything to do with the robust democracies that founding fathers fought for and envisioned.[6]

Latin America and the English-speaking Caribbean are simply two more examples of the unnerving "fewer voices, one world" of present times. Thus, it is instructive and imperative to reassess how multinational broadcasters built their power during the late twentieth century in this part of the globe, so that ordinary citizens in this vast region will one day discover the path toward a truly free and democratic society working for all, not just for a self-selected and self-appointed elite.

Sadly, many professionals and observers are infatuated with the triumph of the Latin American "free" presses over military dictatorships and are unwilling to discuss the serious flaws in the contemporary media marketplace. Arguing that new technologies, notably the Internet, offer unprecedented levels of competition and choice in present-day communications, many believe that ownership concentration of the mass media is either a nonissue or not much of a threat. Such views are actually reviving and fueling authoritarian reactions against open-communication societies. Describing the Southern Cone, primarily Argentina, Uruguay, and Paraguay, at the dawn of the new century, a conventional Latin Americanist recognized that "the return of democracy in [these countries] has not opened wide possibilities for media democratization, but, instead, has been the backdrop for increased concentration of media and information resources."[7]

Critic after critic concurs with this evident problem in other parts of the continent, from the Andean community to Central America to the Caribbean islands. "Much of the [Central American] media are reflective of a commercial history tied to ruling oligarchies of the region," commented another respected scholar, while experts on Caribbean media affairs agree that both government authorities and the concentrated, advertisement-based, and conservative media owners have been responsible for most of the censorship and social control in these impoverished islands, most of which have faced a steady exodus of their populations to Europe and the United States since the early 1960s.[8]

In the Andean region, not only in Colombia, Ecuador, and Venezuela but also in Peru and Bolivia, most people have also endured a slanted globalization that benefits rich individuals and conglomerates, forcing a rushed and chaotic "communications revolution in poverty" that does little to provide basic necessities and meet the expectations of the poor.[9] President Hugo Chávez of Venezuela, the leader who had captured the world's and his country's public attention as he partially demystified the Western powers and their formal democracies with messages designed to shock, especially against the United States, is a vivid example of the new threats societies, the mass media, and individual expression face every day in the western hemisphere: political paternalism, ideological intolerance, and state intrusion into the right to be let alone. All of these are fueled by an obtuse opposition, especially in the broadcast media, which refuses to understand that

Venezuelans and other Latin Americans need solutions far beyond mainstream U.S. market or consumer models.

## THE RADIO CORNER

By the turn of the twentieth century, the European news media model had already been suffering from a poor image. Civil liberties, particularly freedom of expression, were not particularly well respected in Europe, which "detest[ed] the idea of a free press" so much that aristocrats considered it "the greatest and most urgent evil, the most malignant and formidable enemy to the constitution."[10]

Regulation of the European press had been in full force since the late 1800s, notably in Spain, France, Germany, Russia, Serbia, and Austria, and much of that legal spirit was eventually transferred to the emerging Latin American broadcasting industry. France and Spain, in addition to England, Germany, and Italy, became the most legally influential nineteenth-century models in Hispanic America. A reflection of this legal dependence is the continuous tendency of Latin American countries to replicate the media policy frameworks of leading European nations. Evidently, the United States represented an interesting alternative to European models, but it was also a social and legal system full of major contradictions and internal struggles.

For thirty years (1902–32), Oliver Wendell Holmes Jr., the charismatic associate justice of the U.S. Supreme Court, delivered repeated liberal rationales in freedom of the press and free speech cases. He stood up against monopoly powers, the abuse of workers, and the blind reliance on laissez-faire dogmas espoused by Spencerian legal theorists. A modern advocate of the free marketplace of ideas as borrowed from John Milton's *Areopagitica*, Holmes favored the public interest and the protection of the weak whenever the balance of competition had been broken.[11] Based on the tradition of Milton's defense of a free press and the commerce clause of the U.S. Constitution (Article 1, Section 8, Clause 3), this influential justice formulated two major ideas that would eventually impact the entire continent: the "clear and present danger" standard and the marketplace-of-ideas concept. However, his ideas ended up being misused in a series of unanimous convictions against speeches and publications of working-class leaders (some of them socialists), turning his doctrines into repressive "bad tendency" tests that sentenced politicians such as Eugene V. Debs for their political beliefs. Eventually, Latin America would not only pay close attention to the First Amendment debates in the United States but would also employ the Amendment's principles, especially, although not exclusively, during the last quarter of the twentieth century.

The Mexican Revolution, along with World War I and Anglo-America's redefinition of freedom of speech and of the press, occurred just before the arrival of broadcasting in Latin America. These events also linked the liberty to express opinions and other fundamental guarantees to social prerogatives such as the right to work, to receive an education, and to have the means for production and for community participation.[12] Statutory laws regulated the broadcast press on the basis of free but responsible communications. All malicious expressions, for example, that might damage an individual's reputation, privacy, or the social peace would be punished according to the revolution's Ley de Imprenta (Press Law of 1917). Malicious information could come in the form of verbal communications, signs, or other means such as writing, printing materials, drawings, photographs, lithographs, or any other form of public dissemination or transmission via mail, telegraph, telephone, radiotelegraph, or any messaging system.[13]

Radio broadcasting in Mexico, for instance, dates back to the early 1920s during the presidency of General Alvaro Obregón. In August 1921, as part of the state of Veracruz's festivities to commemorate the Tratados de Córdoba (the Cordoba Treaties that sealed Mexico's independence), President Obregón hailed one of the country's first experimental radio broadcast transmissions. There was also a celebration accompanied by military marches, car races, aviation demonstrations, theatrical performances, and film exhibitions. One month later, from the first floor of the Teatro Ideal in Mexico City, brothers Adolfo and Pedro Gómez-Fernández also experimented with a brief broadcast of two songs in which tenor José Mojica interpreted Paolo Tosti's "Vorrei." Using a De Forest transmitter, with the financial support of businessman Pedro Barra Villela, the Gómez-Fernández brothers operated a local radio station that lasted nearly four months (September 1921 through January 1922).[14]

There are so many emerging, simultaneous, and intertwined radio developments in Latin America and the Caribbean that, according to Mexican journalism historian Fernando Mejía Barquera, it is often difficult, if not arbitrary, to identify someone as "the first radio broadcaster" in this or that country, or in this or that region.[15] Over time, nation-states gradually introduced and expanded radio broadcast services, beginning with amateur or government (usually military) experimenters and ending with major media magnates. The same process occurred in the United States, fueled by the efforts of inventors, engineers, merchants, aficionados in industrial cities, and the Navy research conducted in the Great Lakes.[16]

An educational and entrepreneurial initiative involving public and private actors introduced radio broadcasting in the United Mexican States. Unlike newspapers and, later, television, this country's radio industry did not emerge as a centralized and mostly metropolitan medium. Provincial locations such as Pachuca, Cuernavaca, Morelia, San Luis Potosí, Chihuahua, and Ciudad Juárez were broadcasting pioneers, along with the Federal District, Guadalajara, and Veracruz. In Monterrey, Nuevo León, Constantino De Tárnava established regular late-night transmissions of classical music featuring soprano María Ytirría, pianist Carlos Pérez, tenor Aubrey Saint John Clerke, and poetry reader Audoxio Villarreal. Engineer De Tárnava's station TND (Tárnava Notre Dame) was inaugurated on October 27, 1921, and his first experimental transmission can be traced back to the end of World War I.[17]

Another engineer, Salvador Francisco Domenzáin, was also a key figure in the early days of Mexico's radio industry. Not only did he contribute to pioneer radio broadcasting by inaugurating a station in the Federal District in 1922, but he also helped the country to organize the Liga Central Mexicana de Radio (Mexican Central League of Radio) on March 6, 1926. Actually, the previous year, engineer Domenzáin had founded the Liga Nacional de Radio (National Radio League), paving the way for the subsequent merger of the Center of Engineers and the Mexican Central Club of Radio. Around that time, Domenzáin also assisted federal authorities in setting up a transmitting/receiving station at the Cancillería (Foreign Relations Secretariat).

On March 19, 1923, with the support of the secretary of war and the navy, Colonel José Fernando Ramírez and engineer José de la Herrán launched the JH radio station, named after the engineer's initials. It transmitted late-night programs between 10:00 PM and midnight for nearly eight months. Almost simultaneously, Francisco C. Steffens inaugurated a shortwave station in the Federal District, which featured classical music programs every Sunday. Radio competition instantly increased with the arrival that same year of Raúl Azcárraga's La Casa de la Radio (House of Radio) on May 8 and the French-funded CYB, La Estación de El Buen Tono (Good Sound Station), on September 15.

Within a few months, Azcárraga's station, operating from his store for electronic appliances, merged with Félix F. Palavicini's prestigious newspaper, *El Universal*. Its musical programming included high-profile artists such as the famous Spanish guitarist Andrés Segovia, the

Mexican composer Manuel M. Ponce, pianist Manuel Barajas, and poet Manuel Maples Arce, who read his poem "Radio." Proud of their deal, *El Universal* wrote on its front page that "as the great U.S. newspapers do, *El Universal* [also] has a powerful broadcast radio station. It is set up in the nation's capital."[18] In response, the *Excélsior* also acquired a broadcast station half a year later.

These broadcast-newspaper combinations came to be known as the CYL and CYX radio stations, respectively. Their nomenclature, initially accepted by the ITU's Berne Conference of 1924, had to change to identifications beginning with the call letter X following agreements signed at the 1929 International Telecommunication Union conference in Washington, D.C. However, the *El Universal*–Casa de la Radio venture ended in 1928.

On April 26, 1926, president and revolutionary leader Plutarco Elías-Calles (1924–28) signed into law the Ley de Comunicaciones Eléctricas (Electrical Communications Act) that obviously included broadcasting. Adopted even before the U.S. Radio Act of 1927, Article 12 of the Mexican electronic media statute prescribed that radio transmissions could neither threaten the state's national security nor attack, in any way, legitimate government authorities. Elías-Calles had made his political reputation as an anticlerical man who firmly believed in order, laws, and institutions.[19]

Mexico's radio broadcast industry experienced an exponential growth in the 1930s and in the subsequent two decades. On February 5, 1930, Radio Mundial-XEN (World Radio) introduced one of the hemisphere's first all-news radio stations. Its owner and director was the media giant Palavicini, founder of *El Universal* and former member of the 1917 Constitutional Assembly. An entrepreneur well acquainted with U.S. media formats and practices, Palavicini had purchased his equipment from General Electric. By then, communications-related multinationals from the United States were active in Latin America and the Caribbean, looking for and exploiting media business opportunities.

In the 1920s, with the arrival of broadcasting, RCA made concerted efforts to shape not only Mexico's but Latin America's broadcasting along North American patterns. The aim was "to open the region's radio systems to direct United States corporate investment and commercial development with minimal oversight."[20] Commercialization, as opposed to radio's educational, scientific, and cultural origins, clearly dominated the Mexican radio enterprise by the early 1930s. On September 18, 1930, Emilio Azcárraga Vidaurreta, father of Emilio Azcárraga Milmo, a media mogul who later founded the broadcasting corporation Televisa, inaugurated La Voz de América Latina-XEW (Voice of Latin America), a five-kilowatt broadcast station with national and cross-border audience ambitions. This dream, a Spanish-speaking broadcast service across the continent, would be the central theme of his family. To finance it, Azcárraga Vidaurreta initiated the use of strategies to attract advertisers, persuading product manufacturers of the benefits in joining the news and entertainment radio bandwagon.[21]

Not surprisingly, the Mexican government came up with incentives as well as controlling regulations on licensing and advertising in the first half of the 1930s. In 1931 the use of broadcast permits was replaced with long-term concessions of up to fifty years, asserting the government's duty to protect the broadcast spectrum as a national public resource by creating favorable conditions for foreign investment. Chapter VI, Book V, of the 1933 Law of General Means of Communications (Ley de Vías Generales de Comunicación, July 10) ordered that broadcast stations could devote only 10 percent of their time to commercial announcements (Article 17).

This same statute guaranteed federal authorities free access to all commercial frequencies, for which purpose the government created the so-called Press and Advertising Autonomous Department (Departamento Autónomo de Prensa y Publicidad—DAPP). Charged with managing the state's radio stations and the government's social communication policy, the DAPP was also organized to monitor and regulate the use of advertising in commercial and cultural broadcasting. In coordination with the National Revolutionary Party (Partido Nacional Revolucionario or PNR) and the Public Education Secretariat, the DAPP set out to promote government programs for national development. During Lázaro Cádenas's presidency (1934–40), radio stations from the above governmental entities (XEFO, XEUZ, XFX, XEDP, and XEXA) were expected to work together for the same goals, primarily national unity, social progress, and public information.

In 1933 the federal government donated radio sets in rural villages, hoping to lure peasants into listening to development programs produced by the Secretaría de Education Pública (SEP) while enjoying the wonders of a new technology. The principal goal then was to foster harmony, public order, and cultural and political unification. But peasants did not listen, for there were no transmissions of popular songs such as the revered *rancheras*—although recipients loved the radio sets. Eventually, development agencies incorporated popular themes from folk melodies and the *charro* spirit (Mexico's cowboy), successfully standardizing and spreading a simplified message of national pride and unity.[22]

By 1939 the DAPP no longer existed, and its activities had moved to the secretary of government. Production of the *Hora Nacional* [the National Hour], however, initiated by the DAPP two years before, went on until the 1990s, maintaining the philosophy of national unity and the tradition of Latin America's oldest broadcast program. Nevertheless, there was a significant hesitation over the scope of this show. In sixty years, the program's title changed from *The National Hour* (1937) to *The Hour of the Mexican Republic's Government* (1949) to *The Hour of Mexico* (1977) and then back to its original title.

In the end, Mexico, as the rest of Latin America, abided by the European principle that broadcasting was ultimately a public service, destined to serve and realize social goals beyond private industry or individual ambitions. At the 1924 Inter-American Conference on Electrical Communications held in Mexico City, the nationalistic, Europeanized, and public-service model defeated the evolving U.S. commercial broadcast format.[23] Officially, Mexico endorsed any free-market competition consistent with the government's political and developmental ideals. In practice, the profit-oriented philosophy would quickly absorb the Mexican and Latin American broadcast systems. In fact, by 1940, the Mexican government had virtually stepped out of radio broadcasting, leaving most of the business to the already powerful entrepreneur Azcárraga Vidaurreta.

Network radio and subsequently television fell into the hands of a private oligopoly and monopoly in Mexico, heavily influenced by and dependent on U.S. technology, manufacturers, advertisers, training, program formats, and marketing. During the late 1930s and early 1940s, Mexican radio networks grew around XEW, Azcárraga's mother station, his fourteen regional affiliates, and his Mexican Music Company, an RCA subsidiary. A second network of his property was built on XEQ-Mexico City, making Azcárraga Vidaurreta the first president of the Radio Broadcasting Industry National Chamber (CIR) in 1942.[24]

With somewhat more or somewhat less private competition, the introduction of radio broadcasting in Argentina (1923), Brazil (1923), Chile (1923), Peru (1925), Cuba (1925), Colombia (1929), and other Latin American nations followed essentially the same Mexican pattern. As mentioned earlier, they all fell under the programming spell, organizational structure, and overall commercial influence of Anglo-America. But there are some special features across the Latin American broadcasting systems in terms of policy, economics, political structure, and foreign influence.

In Cuba, for instance, before Fidel Castro's revolution, the influence of the U.S. broadcasting system was overwhelming. The Mestre brothers and their CMQ network created an overly commercialized broadcast system, turning the island into an experimental site for the U.S. broadcasting empire in Latin America. In fact, in the mid-1960s, Goar and Abel Mestre (known as the Czar) toured the region and acquired stations on behalf of the NBC-owned Cadena Panamericana de Televisión (Pan-American TV Network).

This began an expansion trend that was accelerated by RCA radio in 1940, when it launched shortwave rebroadcasting arrangements in twenty Latin American countries. CBS's Cadena de las Americas (Chain of the Americas) and Crosley Broadcasting's Cadena Radio Interamericana (Inter-American Radio Chain) followed suit within a few months. Clearly, radio broadcasting expanded rapidly in the Americas, and by 1943, there were at least sixty-eight radio stations in Mexico, fifty-seven in Chile, fifty-two in Cuba, forty-two in Brazil, forty in Argentina, and thirty-five in Uruguay, to name the most radio-seduced countries. Apparently, half of the radio receivers available in Latin America could pick up shortwave radio signals.[25]

Concerned about the Nazi, Fascist, and Falangist broadcast operations of the German, Italian, and Spanish dictatorships—which enjoyed considerable sympathy in Latin America, whether out of nostalgia for lost empire, a tradition of authoritarian values, or fear of the advance of Marxism-Leninism—the United States decided to launch a Pan-American crusade of hemispheric friendship. Privately and governmentally, U.S. authorities and entrepreneurs embarked on a concerted propaganda campaign supporting freedom of the press, freedom of choice, and freedom of enterprise in the Americas. Although posting mixed results in the beginning, this U.S. imperialistic venture eventually became triumphant after World War II. Not a single Latin American country was able to resist the temptation and domination of the economic, political, and cultural paradigms of Anglo-America, particularly in media affairs.[26]

Since the late 1920s, Brazil had also introduced radio broadcasting as a private yet noncommercial enterprise, with stations owned and run by clubs or associations of listeners. In fact, until the presidency and civil dictatorship of Getúlio Vargas (1930–45), the government had discouraged advertising, fostering education and culture over the airwaves instead of entertainment and profitability. By the late 1960s, though, following an even more repressive military era (1964–85), the Brazilian federation was fully immersed in the U.S. broadcast model of commercialization, painfully twisted toward monopolization and political persecution.[27]

Chile is perhaps the most interesting case in the general struggle between commercialization and educational interests in both radio and television broadcasting—that is, until General Augusto Pinochet's dictatorship (1973), which fractured the media and social history of this South American country. The Chilean broadcast radio, introduced as a purely private venture in the early 1920s, gradually grew more balanced in favor of public, educational, and community constituents because of governmental pressures. Political parties, religious groups, universities, and workers' unions received licenses to compete with commercial radio stations. Similarly, in Colombia, the first radio station (HJN) was created by the government to promote education (August 7, 1929). Yet, in the end, broadcast radio in Colombia as well as in Argentina, Peru, Venezuela, and most of the non-English-speaking nations of Latin America and the Caribbean became purely commercial, modeled on the mercantilist spirit of the United States. Soon after, and in some places even before World War II, the region's radio stations and networks became heavily Americanized and were ultimately controlled by profit-oriented, oligarchic, and politically partisan groups.

Although Brazil had a media history of roughly 150 years before World War II, this sleeping giant did not truly awake in world and Latin American contexts until Nazi submarines showed up at its shores—four centuries after colonization.[28] During the fifteen years of Vargas's regime, a modernizing although repressive era comparable to the Porfiriato in Mexico, the Brazilian press and society prospered both economically and technologically along the lines of Anglo-America but in hemispheric isolation.

Pre–World War II media developments also made history in Brazil, although they were usually little known beyond her borders. In 1938 Assis Chateaubriand led the country's pioneer and most influential radio network of the time, Diários e Emissoras Associadas, formed by twelve newspapers, five radio stations, and one magazine.[29] Radio broadcasting in Brazil also emerged with strong political, cultural, and educational tones. Government reactions to broadcasting resulted in authoritarian, conservative, and paternalistic regulations, affected by public-interest expectations. But, remarkably, unlike the predominantly commercial start in various Latin American nations, notably Argentina, Peru, Colombia, and Venezuela, Brazil launched her radio industry as an educational, community-owned, and not-for-profit venture. Member-supported associations, such as the pioneer club established by educator Roquette Pinto and astronomer Henry Moritze in 1923, characterized the early days of Brazilian broadcasting.[30] This was true until a federal law in 1932, introducing the use of advertising for commercial broadcasts, effectively killed the private community spirit and initiative.

Government regulation, rather than industry dynamics, focused on censoring content, particularly after the Constitutionalist Revolution of 1932, when students in São Paulo used a radio station (Radio Record) to demand liberty for Brazil.[31] For that purpose, following his coup and the new constitution of 1937, President Getúlio Vargas organized the Departmento de Imprensa e Propaganda (DIP) in 1939 to control news and information and to promote his concept of Brazilian culture, order, and morality.[32]

Persecution and assassination attempts against journalists and laws imposing foreign investment, public order, government access, right of reply, and antidefamation rules dominated the press during the World War II years (see Article 12, Clause 14 of the 1937 Political Constitution of Brazil).[33] In fewer than nine months in 1943, the DIP reported "2,256 incidents of censorship of the words of songs and 1,088 cases of censorship of recordings of radio programs."[34] The only regulations on the new broadcasting technology were decrees 20,047 in 1931 and 21,111 in 1932, prescribing national interest and licensing obligations, respectively. As often occurred with new technologies, radio broadcasting activities remained mostly unregulated, especially after permitting advertising in 1932.

Radio competition turned into a virtual war in various places as individuals, stations, and companies looked for profits and political gains through advertising and propaganda. With rare exceptions, such as in Chile, education consisted only of ephemeral rhetoric in Latin America. Radio characters ranged from gifted musicians and popular figures (e.g., the guitarist Andrés Segovia, the singer Carlos Gardel, and the boxer Jack Dempsey) to dull and imposing politicians, many of them military dictators. In Colombia, for instance, Gardel's accidental death fueled a new radio genre—news—after half a decade of classical music, sports talk, radio readings, patriotic scores, and religious programming.[35] Technology, geopolitics, blood, presumed social impacts, local and alien commercial ambitions, and political manipulation mixed erratically in this *salpicón* (cocktail) of emerging Latin American broadcasting. In most countries, politics and the radio business were "as unpredictable as Popocatepetl."[36]

In celebration of the sixty years of the Radiodifusora Nacional de Colombia (founded on February 1, 1940), the daily *El Tiempo* published an interview with Gustavo Samper, director of the National Institute of Radio and Television (Inravisión), the Colombian public broadcasting enterprise. Thanks to the Radio Nacional, as it is popularly known, ordinary Colombians learned about news immediacy, communication power, and even popular repression. Indeed, during the tragic Bogotazo, when the people's leader Jorge Eliécer Gaitán was assassinated in downtown Bogotá on April 9, 1948, several radio stations were taken over by members of the Liberal and Communist parties, calling for a national revolt against the ruthless Conservative Party government of President Mariano Ospina Pérez. When asked what to do with this historic network, Samper responded with another question: "Why can't an educational text go with an advertisement reading Coca-Cola? What's the problem? Commercialize National Radio is his solution."[37]

During the Bogotazo, "comrades" and other rebels took over the frequencies, including the Radio Nacional, under the Gaitánist motto of *a la carga* (charge), commented witnesses in *9 de Abril 1948*, a video also featuring Gloria Gaitán, the caudillo's daughter.[38] Immediately, according to the historian Hernando Téllez, Colombian authorities suspended all operating licenses and checked the records of each station and news announcer to determine whether or not to reestablish the respective licenses.[39] Following this decision, "the government forced the creation of the National Association of Broadcasting (*Anradio*), demanding the obligatory affiliation of all stations to the new organization and giving licenses only to those which became Anradio affiliates."[40] When choosing its membership, Anradio received instructions from the Colombian Ministry of Communications, "effectively discriminating against anti-government ones."[41]

More than finding out who steered what and when in the history of Latin American and Caribbean broadcasting, it is far more challenging and interesting to uncover how and why prominent broadcasting events occurred the way they did, and who benefited from them. That would be another chapter in itself, but some authors have addressed the subject with considerable success in their publications, notably Elizabeth Fox and her well-known *Latin American Broadcasting: From Tango to Telenovela* (1997).[42]

In one memorable case in Argentina, "the state was interested in radio for geopolitical and nationalizing purposes in the early days," but soon after, "private interests became more dominant," according to Dr. Waisbord, formerly at Rutgers University and more recently with the Academy for Educational Development in Washington, D.C. In his view, "the commercial development and structure of broadcasting cannot be understood [in Argentina, Uruguay, and particularly Paraguay] without addressing the close relations between governments and media owners."[43] An obvious beneficiary was Juan Domingo Perón, who used broadcasting—especially television—for self-promotion, adding "this medium to [his] propaganda arsenal of newspapers and radio stations."[44]

In Venezuela radio became possible once Luis Roberto Scholtz and Alfredo Moller had persuaded the "dictatorial trinity" of the Gómez family—in particular the three-time president, general, and army inspector Juan Vicente Gómez and his son, General José Vicente Gómez—of the benefits of broadcasting to the country. In this way, Venezuelans began their broadcasting history with a military radio station. Another member of the Gómez family, General Juan C. Gómez, had been assassinated (in the presidential Palace of Miraflores) shortly before the launching of AYRE, the first broadcast station, in May 1926, according to the Venezuelan Chamber of the Broadcasting Industry (CVIR). Moller, the station's presenter, "had to be extremely prudent in not broadcasting anything that could be interpreted as a criticism of the regime."[45]

As with Getúlio Vargas's modernization and censorship machine, the Gómez dictatorship virtually wiped out any possibility of dissent. Every morning for two years, AYRE newscasters read the official news handed out by the pro-government *El Nuevo Diario* [New Daily], while Harry Wilson, the North American engineer who had been hired to set up the station in the corner of El Tejar and the Nuevo Circo building, sneaked in evening news received from foreign lands. As in Brazil, leftist young people who had organized into a student federation were the only vocal and courageous opposition to the tyrants, including the Venezuelan leaders and subsequent presidents Raúl Leoni and Rómulo Betancourt.[46] Then, on December 9, 1930, Broadcasting Caracas, today Radio Caracas, became the government's mouthpiece.

In the Caribbean, people have known all too well about criminal dictators and human rights abusers. Writing for the *Listín Diario* in the Dominican Republic, professor and author Andrés L. Mateo warned the region, and the hemisphere, not to forget Rafael Trujillo's *Era del Miedo* [Age of Fear], a long period of terror (1930–61) built on top of authoritarian tradition and historic violence imposed as an inexorable fate. The dictator dominated all public and most private life with his slogan "in this house the boss is Trujillo." In other words, Trujillism, noted Mateo, "was bigger than Trujillo. Thus, not even twenty Vargas Llosas writing twenty more novels [like the *Danza del Chivo*] could barely describe the frightening reality lived in [the Dominican Republic] at that time." Nothing would be more ludicrous than to expect freedom of thought, speech, or the press in a dictatorial regime of that sort.[47]

Professor Joseph D. Straubhaar, a reputable Latin Americanist currently at the University of Texas–Austin, summarized the development of the region's radio industry by arguing that it "set a pattern for broadcasting in most of South America: a predominance of entertainment over education or cultural programs, a clear dominance of advertising-supported stations, a tendency to import a good deal of materials and well as program ideas, and [a] countervailing tendency to use a great deal of national and local material as well. [C]ommercial radio was widely successful because it fit well into the developing South American developing markets."[48]

Recognizing the wisdom of "several researchers who make a strong case that the activity of U.S. radio networks" helped draw Latin American nations toward commercialization in the 1930s and 1940s, Straubhaar also highlighted the presence of U.S. advertising agencies; U.S. advertisers and corporations; and U.S. technologies, programs, and approaches as basic components of the Latin American consumer media system. Although removed from definite dependency conclusions, this scholar contributed relevant ideas regarding cultural proximities and reversed competition roles, accounting for developing-country gains in international markets and counteracting actions against excessive foreign program imports in ways that dependency researchers could not immediately explain.

An expert on *telenovelas*, Straubhaar explained *radionovelas* as the origins of drama in Latin American broadcasting, a fascinating fusion resulting from multiple influences coming from France, Cuba, Mexico, and Argentina, among others. Particularly important, he observed, "were scripts imported from Cuba, where *radionovelas* were first developed as a Latin American form of the U.S. soap opera, sponsored by Colgate, the U.S. corporation which wanted to sell soap in Latin America with the same advertising vehicle that had proved successful in the United States."[49]

Gaitán would probably have leaned toward a simpler but equally powerful explanation of the essential character of Latin American mass media. As Professor Gonzalo Soruco at the University of Western Ontario in Canada has pointed out, "The early days of the [Latin American] republics saw the press turned into an organ of political parties used mostly to vilify opposition politicians. Beginning in the twentieth century, the press has become the organ of the elites and the rich, often used as a party organ espousing the political ideology of the owners—at times turning into a product that entertains rather than informs the readers."[50] Ana María Miralles would be even more succinct: the Latin American news media moved from the early gazettes and the confrontation against absolute colonial powers to a republican party press, a depoliticized or commercialized news industry, and finally became a mostly concentrated or monopolized communications media.[51]

## TELENOVELAS: A STAPLE OF LATIN AMERICAN PROGRAMMING

Perhaps the most dramatic difference between North American and Latin American programming is the television telenovelas. Begun early in the history of Latin American television, these continuing hour-long dramas were usually shown every week night for a period of three to four weeks. The plots in the early years were often similar: A young couple wanted to marry, but circumstances worked against them. It was only after much discussion, anger, and crying that they were able to wed and live happily ever after. Beginning in the late 1960s, the telenovela came into its own. Now they sometimes run a full year, and the plots are considerably more urbane and contemporary. The production quality has also increased with onsite production as well as better lighting and camera work.

Perhaps the most famous early telenovela was *Beto Rockfeller*. An instant hit, this program dealt with a young man who posed as a rich man and ended up becoming alternately involved with both high society and the working-class world. *Simplemente Maria*, a mix of *Pygmalion* and "Cinderella," is another famous telenovela that tells the story of a poor girl who, after much tribulation, was accepted into wealthy society. This program was popular all over Latin America.

The telenovelas of Mexico and Brazil have some differences in tone and style. Generally speaking, Mexico's telenovelas tend to be more romantic and more puritanical than Brazil's. Some of the more famous Mexican telenovelas include *Los Ricos También Lloran*, *Maria Mercedes*, *Topazio*, and *Miramar*. Among the well-known actors are Verónica Castro, Lucia Ménedez, and Thalia Sodi. Brazilian telenovelas are more contemporary, more political, and often deal with social issues. Some of the better-known Brazilian telenovelas are *A Escrava Isaura*, *A Próxima Vítima*, *Em Busca de Felicidade*, *Angel Malo*, and *O Rei de Gado*.

*John Bratzel*

## THE TELEVISION BALLROOM

More than a remarkable economic, political, or institutional revolution, Latin American television emerged as a notable technological event with lasting cultural implications. Television stations simply replicated and exacerbated what radio broadcasting had done twenty to thirty years earlier.

Television advertising, to name one important feature, was more ambitious, sophisticated, and alienating than advertising had been during the radio days. Naturally, radio advertising revenue suffered greatly once television came about. Commercial television programming, appealing and entertaining as it was thanks to its novel images and sounds, showed little innovation in formats and themes. Radio and film audiences in Latin America could easily associate the U.S.-imported television productions with old, local, and foreign-influenced radio programs. In Latin America, as elsewhere in this hemisphere, sports, comedies, radionovelas, live musicals, sponsored talks, trivia contests, and practically all other shows were not an invention of television.[52]

Although not very creative, children's programming probably constituted the only genuinely innovative TV format, for radio and newspapers paid little or no attention to younger audiences before the arrival of television technologies. The English-speaking rock and roll and the U.S.-styled disc jockey that eventually seduced millions of Latin American adolescents and children did not firmly take hold until the first half of the 1960s. Alfonso Lizarazo, for example, a popular South American disc jockey of the late 1960s, introduced the practice of moving from radio to television musical entertainment in Colombia—a sort of homegrown *Ed Sullivan Show*.[53]

In the same way, television was organizationally and managerially almost identical to broadcast radio, following even more tightly the internal structure, ownership patterns, profit motives, commercial spirit, and social and political roles of radio networking. With television, unlike radio, the U.S. broadcast model became fully dominant. In addition, being more capital intensive, television turned even more elitist, concentrated, and discriminatory than radio, favoring urban, white, and higher-income populations. For nearly two and one-half decades, that is, until the early 1970s when big sports such as the Olympics and World Cup soccer brought million of viewers, television was a technology of limited access and coverage both in rural and in densely populated, impoverished urban areas. In many countries and numerous settings, this continues to be the case in spite of the Internet excitement.

## XUXA: UNLIKELY ICON OF CHILDREN'S PROGRAMMING

One of the best-known popular culture stars in Latin America is the Brazilian Maria da Graça Meneghel, much better known as Xuxa and now one of the wealthiest people of Brazil. Xuxa's career tends to defy easy description. She began as a model and night club performer, posed for a Brazilian gentleman's magazine, was the girlfriend of soccer star Pelé, and hosted a highly successful children's show, among other things. Broadcast all over the western hemisphere in Spanish and then in English, the show was enormously popular. Each show began with Xuxa arriving in a pink spaceship, followed by singing, dancing, and games that provided a frenzied atmosphere. Eventually, the show folded, but Xuxa's career, before and after the program, is a fascinating part of Latin American popular culture.

*John Bratzel*

The true revolution of television was technological, as is now the case with the Internet in Latin America. Other dominant features such as media economics, media diplomacy, and media politics and censorship, including most notably the dominance of U.S. private and commercial operations and practices, were simply transferred from radio to television. And these same patterns are being transferred once again into the new technologies of this century, even more insidiously dominated by monopolistic interests and multinationals operating primarily though not exclusively from the United States. Overall, the technological impact of television has resulted in damaging perceptions of cultural inferiority, intellectual dependency, social inequality, political manipulation, misinformation, alienation, lack of access, distortion of values, and polarized conflicts.

Similar to the path followed in the broadcast radio industry in Mexico and most of Latin America, television stations emerged with variations of public interest, educational, and state goals and controls. Within a few years, however, the domestic television scene was usually dominated by private commercialization, cosmopolitism, and elitism. A vertical and often manipulative synergy among closed monopolies, U.S. imports, and nepotism at the highest levels of private and governmental media entities and authorities dominated the new and supposedly promising television industry. In Mexico, to cite a revealing case, President Miguel Alemán introduced television in a state of the union speech in 1950 after the National Institute of Fine Arts made a comparison between two broadcast systems: the

## THE UNIQUE FLAVOR OF LATIN AMERICAN TV

The production of television programming in Latin America historically has been dominated by two nations: Brazil and Mexico. In Brazil, the most populous Portuguese-speaking nation, the dominant broadcaster is Globo. Similarly, Televisa prevails in Mexico, which is the largest Spanish-speaking nation. Both entities were started early in the creation of television programming. Recently, Venezuela and Argentina have been creating new programming, and Colombia, Chile, and Peru are also producing their own shows. The other Latin American states generally acquire their programming from the program-producing nations. Yet another important broadcaster is Univision in the United States, which produces entertainment for the Latino population of the United States and also sells its programming to Latin America.

Generally speaking, the television productions of Spanish and Portuguese America have many similarities in style and content to those of the United States. Variety shows, early morning news programs, soap operas, quiz shows, and sports tend to predominate. In an increasingly global world, countries do not hesitate to borrow styles and themes from other nations. It would be wrong, however, to say that the programming is the same in the United States and in Latin America. Latin America has both unique shows and a unique style.

*John Bratzel*

BBC and the commercial models from the United States. Naturally, considering the history and status of Mexico's radio industry, the latter was chosen as the most convenient and comparable.[54]

Initially, Alemán favored his friend Rómulo O'Farrill in the licensing process, giving this newspaper publisher the honor of inaugurating the first television concession in Latin America. XH-TV, Canal 4 (Channel 4), began its official transmissions on August 31, 1950, nine months after being granted a license by the Mexican communication authorities. Brazil's TV Tupi and Cuba's Union Radio-TV followed suit in September and October 1950, respectively. In Mexico, Emilio Azcárraga Vidaurreta had to wait until July 1950 for license approval; in March 1951 he launched XEW-TV, Canal 2, learning that only media loyal to the president would do well in business. O'Farrill had faithfully supported the earlier presidential candidacy of Manuel Avila-Camacho (1940–46), led by campaign manager Alemán, in his newspaper, *Novedades*. Azcárraga Vidaurreta had supported the opposition.[55]

By 1955, eventually with Alemán on board, O'Farrill and Azcárraga merged their operations to form a powerful television monopoly, the Telesistema Mexicano (TSM), which would reign unchallenged in Mexico for the next forty years. Through it, the Azcárraga family obtained the upper hand and took revenge for not being first into this business. This network, later called Televisa (Televisión Vía Satellite), would also turn into a hemispheric media empire that controlled dozens of radio and TV stations, satellite facilities, print publications, an international news service (ECO), and dominant interests in the U.S. Univision chain, formerly known as the Spanish International Network (SIN). In the first few years of the twenty-first century, Televisa also produced 35,000 hours of television broadcasts a year, exported programming to fifty countries, covered the world with more than 100 correspondents, and transmitted satellite signals to forty-seven countries on three continents.[56]

The Mexican government, with the timid exceptions of presidents Luis Echeverría-Alvarez (1970–76) and José López Portillo (1976–82), traditionally and often enthusiastically nurtured this monopoly. Presidents Adolfo Ruiz-Cortines (1952–58), Adolfo López Mateos (1958–64), and Gustavo Díaz-Ordaz (1964–70) were especially supportive of a television monopoly that plunged Mexico into a manipulative regime of self-censorship in broadcast news, dominated by large corporate, party (PRI, Institutional Revolutionary Party), and state interests that lasted until the mid-1990s. Relaxing the nationalistic and public service philosophy defined by the Law of Communication of 1940, which banned any licensing to foreign stations, the Mexican federal government enacted the Federal Broadcasting Law of 1960, giving Televisa the necessary space to expand its business across borders via microwave and satellite communications.

Leading Latin American countries, namely Brazil (September 1950), Cuba (October 1950, nearly a decade before the revolution), and Argentina (1951), tried to match Mexico's early start. Early adopters, following the big three pioneers and Cuba, were Venezuela (November 1952), the Dominican Republic (1952), Colombia (June 1954), and Uruguay (1955). The first Central American nations to inaugurate television stations were El Salvador, Guatemala, and Nicaragua (all in 1956); Peru introduced the service in 1958, followed by Chile, Ecuador, Honduras, and Panama in 1959. Relative latecomers were Costa Rica (1960), Trinidad and Tobago (1962, the first English-speaking country with an operational TV channel), Jamaica (1963), Barbados (1964), Paraguay and Antigua (both in 1965), St. Lucia (1967), Surinam (1968), and Bolivia (1969). By 1984 only a few Caribbean states—Anguilla, Guyana, Dominica, Granada, and Belize— were without a television transmitter in their territories. In 1986, Belize was one of the last to set up a TV station.[57]

In the spread of television, even more so than in the development of radio, the region presented patterns of a hemispheric transnational diffusion and domination, resulting in common features of TV development in the most media-influential Latin American countries. To begin with, the adoption of television came as a result of the political ambitions of exclusive, modernizing elites under either restrictive civilian authority or military rule. Indeed, the PRI's dominance of Mexico imposed a style of vertical, commercial, and state-controlled television that many Latin American nations replicated, particularly in terms of domestic security, national sovereignty, and profitability interests and values. In addition to creating a virtually unregulated advertising industry, Mexico's Federal Broadcasting Law of 1960 synthesized the state expectations for radio and television, focusing on the promotion of public order, state propaganda, and private gain, and the suppression of critical views.

In fact, dictators General Juan Domingo Perón (1946–55 and 1973–74) in Argentina, General Marcos Pérez-Jiménez (1952–58) in Venezuela, and General Gustavo Rojas-Pinilla

## U.S. INFLUENCES ON LATIN AMERICAN PROGRAMMING

Latin American television dubbs many U.S. shows. *Baywatch* and the *Simpsons* have been particularly popular in Latin America. Beauty pagents of all types also do well. Quiz-show formats are also often used and can be seen in Mexico's *100 Mexicanos Dijeron*, which is equivalent to *Family Feud*. The same is true for *Wheel of Fortune*. Other formats such as *American Idol* have also been adapted by Latin American nations to match local culture. Perhaps the most famous "adapter" of programming is Brazil's Silvío Santos, one of that country's most famous and richest citizens.

U.S. influence can be seen in other forms of programming as well. *Sabado Gigante*, a production of Univision, is a mixture of a music and entertainment coupled with a game show. Hosted by Don Francisco (Mario Kreutzberger), the show features singers from all parts of Latin America and the Caribbean and is popular all over Latin America. The program is produced every Saturday night in Miami and then made available to Latin American networks. In some countries, the show is presented in four one-hour programs, and in other nations in two two-hour programs. Another Univision offering is *Primer Impacto*. This show provides news and human interest and is hosted by Barbara Bermudo and Fernando Del Rincón.

*John Bratzel*

(1954–57) in Colombia introduced television for government and ruling party propaganda purposes. In Brazil, army general and president Eurico Gaspar Dutra (1946–51), who had actively participated in the construction of dictator Getúlio Vargas's Estado Novo, also launched television for obvious political gains and motives. In all these cases, and including that of Mexico's Alemán administration, the agenda had been technological progress and modernization (more a myth than reality at that time), internal order, and a desire for territorial sovereignty and national security.[58]

Once the early dictatorial rhetoric of public service and state-controlled television enterprises faded, the television industry in most Latin American countries became easy prey for voracious U.S. television expansionism. For slightly over a decade, both Chile and Uruguay stood out as two significant exceptions to the fully dominant U.S. commercial broadcast model. In Chile, for instance, the government of President Jorge Alessandri (1958–64) bravely resisted the modernization course, refusing to grant licenses for what the president considered to be the banal, mediocre, and superfluous commercial television industry, unnecessary for a poor country in need of resolving serious socioeconomic problems.[59]

Unlike most states in Latin America, the Chilean government believed in a strong broadcasting system that supported the public functions of culture and mass education. Following a television decree issued by the Carlos Ibañez administration (1952–58), which banned the licensing of foreign stations, the Alessandri presidency authorized Chilean universities to set up television channels to foster education, the arts, technology, political independence, and pluralism. The first stations began to operate in 1959. With a rare but interesting coalition of Christian democrats, conservatives, socialists, communists, and radicals, the country "rejected private commercial television on the grounds that it would favor big business and encourage mass audiences at the expense of educational and cultural programming."[60]

Even so, for more than a decade, Alessandri's Television Law of 1958 was repeatedly violated by TV stations that raised funds through commercial advertising without any legal punishment. This anomalous situation was corrected in the Television Statute of 1970, which also sought to give television stations greater private control and economic independence before the inauguration of President Salvador Allende (1970–73). The center-right and Chilean conservatives, rallying behind the elderly former president Alessandri, feared that Allende and his leftist front organization, Unidad Popular, would disrupt the balance of power that had "smoothly" run the country during the last two decades. The military was especially outraged that a socialist president had been elected by the narrow margin of less than 40,000 votes. Curiously, twelve years earlier, Allende had lost the presidency to Alessandri in a similarly close election. Afraid of potential manipulation of universities and television stations by the left, retiring President Eduardo Frei (1964–70) sanctioned the above-mentioned Television Law of 1970, taking various executive powers in broadcasting away from the presidency.[61]

In any case, Chile's educational television philosophy was one of the most significant attempts to build a broadcast system separate from the private, commercialized, and free-market model imposed by the United States in Latin America. In another example, Channel 5 in Uruguay, a television station created in 1963 under the Servicio Oficial de Difusión Radio Eléctrica (SODRE, Official Service of Radio Electric Diffusion), advocated a public broadcasting monopoly similar to that of the BBC in Great Britain. Colombia's efforts to create an alternative broadcast structure also resulted in a hybrid or mixed system, where government authorities owned and administered television frequencies and studios. Through the Instituto Nacional de Radio y Televisión (Inravisión, National Institute of Radio and Television), the government granted concessions to private programmers for commercial exploitation. In the end, every educational television endeavor in Latin America succumbed to the new and inflexible patterns based on commercial market laws and dominated by monopolistic groups, U.S. program imports, and both hard- and soft-sell advertising campaigns.[62]

In Brazil, before the noted media takeoff of the mid-1960s, the U.S. commercial model visibly seduced the Brazilian print and broadcast press. A corporate, sensational, monopolistic, and apolitical format gradually set out to dominate the practice of conventional journalism, with authorities supervising and, if necessary, repressing civil rights based on national integrity and security grounds. The presidency of Juscelino Kubitschek was a significant exception, but its liberal achievements were reversed by a U.S-supported and regionally damaging military coup (1964) that led to the Southern Cone's "Dirty War" of the 1970s.[63] For the next two decades, the Brazilian press lived a dual life of liberal constitutionalism in media and economics and a fascist authoritarianism in mass media politics and regulation.

## TELEVISION NEWS

News programs have always been a staple of television, and they are prominent throughout Latin America. Government pressure and a lack of resources have often hindered quality reporting, but these programs are still popular. In Mexico, the most famous news program was *24 Horas*. Hosted by Jacobo Zabludovsky for twenty-seven years, the show ended when Zabludovsky stepped down. Another well-known news show is *Las Noticias por Adela*, which mixes both hard and soft news. Local television stations broadcast news in ways similar in format and style to those of local news shows in the United States, with anchor people sitting at a desk and reporters in the field.

*John Bratzel*

Eventually, this dualism made possible the growth, concentration, and expansion of the powerful Rede Globo. Currently, the Globo Network consists of at least eight wholly owned television stations, seventy-four affiliates, and 1,500 satellite rebroadcasting antennas. Other holdings include one of the country's four largest dailies (*O Globo*), one of the two main national cable networks, dozens of radio stations, and magazines (e.g., *Marie Claire*, *Criativo*, *Globo Ciéncia*, and *Globo Rural*).[64]

In the mid-1950s, in violation of the supreme Mexican law, the Adolfo Ruiz Cortines administration (1952–58) also approved the merger that created the Telesistema Mexicano (TSM). The Mexican telesystem combined the Azcárraga family concessions, XEW-TV (Channel 2) and XHGC-TV (Channel 5), with the O'Farrill family's XH-TV (Channel 4), Mexico's television pioneer. Channel 4, inaugurated on August 31, 1950, had also emerged as Latin America's first operational television station, three weeks before TV Tupi of Brazil and two months ahead of Union Radio-TV of Cuba.[65]

The antimonopoly exemption for television, invented by the government, revolved around the legal fiction that the Mexican channels noted above were separately licensed, operated, and administrated, when, in practice, Emilio Azcárraga Vidaurreta effectively controlled the three concessions. During the next four decades, television would be a puppet of the state; conversely, to a significant degree, every president would also be a puppet of television. President Miguel Alemán Valdés (1946–52) and his political and economic interests in O'Farrill's television venture constituted an obvious example of the latter.[66] In 1993 satellite communications expanded the list of strategic areas exempted from the antimonopoly clause of Article 28, but two years later, as part of the dominant privatization efforts of the late twentieth century, both railroads and satellite communications were taken off the rolls to promote those industries' competition and commercialization.[67]

Long before receiving imported television series and news, Latin America received live sports transmissions via satellite. Just as the 1964 Tokyo Olympiad had allowed the United States to test the efficacy of its emerging geosynchronous satellite program, the 1968

## THE POPULARITY OF SPORTS PROGRAMMING

Sports shows are a staple of Latin America, a fact that is particularly true in Brazil. In that nation, it seems impossible to turn on a television set without being able to find a soccer match or a show with men sitting around discussing soccer. When the World Cup matches are played, other programming is put aside: soccer is king in Brazil. Baseball is strong in Mexico but does not have the national following that soccer has in Brazil. The Liga Mexicana de Beisbol broadcasts programs, but interest tends to be regional. Besides soccer and baseball, professional wrestling, with all of its dramatics, is also popular in Latin America. NASCAR is gaining an audience in Latin America; although there is some interest in United States football, it maintains only a limited audience.

*John Bratzel*

Olympic Games in Mexico City served as the vehicle for Mexico to try out NASA's ATS (Applications Technology Satellite) series in the Americas. As the first country in the region to use an Applications Technology Satellite (ATS-3), Mexico delivered televised and other satellite signals about the Olympics to Western Europe and the United States.[68] Later in 1968, Brazil also relied on this spacecraft to run an experimental study on the reception of telephone calls and text. Ten years later, this same VHF artifact was still being used in the Caribbean, linking Jamaica, Barbados, and St. Lucia in an educational project, even though the satellite had been planned to last only eighteen months.[69]

What sealed the term "via satellite" in the minds of millions of Latin Americans, however, was not the intercontinental televised transmission of the 1968 Olympics, Pope Paul VI's visit to Colombia (also in 1968), or Neil Armstrong's landing on the moon (July 20, 1969). The key event, especially for marketers and advertisers, was the live television coverage of the 1970 soccer World Cup: *Fútbol México-70*. For three weeks that summer, millions of homes followed live scenes of Pelé and his Brazilian team winning the legendary Jules Rimet cup, an event that tangibly represented the debut of international television in Latin America both technologically and economically.

This sports-satellite symbiosis played a determinant role in Mexico's decision to launch a domestic satellite system in 1985. In fact, some Latin American scholars are convinced that international competitions such as the Olympic Games and the World Cup soccer matches have been ideal occasions for fostering media technology invasions worldwide.[70] Technology sellers and their buyers, usually state agencies, often defend new technologies as beneficial to the adopting country by definition. Following the 1986 version of the World Cup—once again in Mexico—local officials justified the acquisition of the Morelos satellite system as a great image tool. In their view, thanks to the massive audience of this popular event, "2.8 billion people around the globe could watch, via-satellite, how Mexicans overcame crises and natural tragedies," including a devastating earthquake killing nearly 100,000 people months before the championship.[71]

Similar claims surfaced in South America during the early stages of the same tournament, originally offered to Colombia. As a Colombian minister of education noted, events such as the World Cup represent unique opportunities for countries in need of a better image abroad.[72] Government officials of the Liberal Party's Turbay administration (1978–82) favored the Satélite Colombiano (Satcol), assuring people there would be innumerable benefits to the country from a national satellite network in orbit. But Colombian president Belisario Betancur (1982–86) rejected both the Satcol project and the World Cup *Colombia-86* immediately after taking office (September to October 1982).[73] His decision brought as much praise as condemnation, with Betancur arguing that it was far better to say "*yes* to Gabriel García Márquez's Nobel Prize (1982), *no* to the via-satellite World Cup."[74]

Despite the enormous popularity of this sport in Colombia, critics, including the Betancur administration, feared an economic disaster similar to what had happened in Argentina in 1978, when the World Cup reported huge losses. Still, officials in both Mexico and Argentina had few misgivings regarding the implications World Cup satellite television events would pose and offered no reservations to the modernization pressures applied by the powerful FIFA (Fédération Internationale de Football Association).

In sum, beyond the telenovela phenomenon and major sports transmissions, television broadcasting has been an arid land for over half a decade in Latin America.

# RESOURCE GUIDE

## PRINT SOURCES

Cabrujas, José Ignacio. *Y Latinoamérica inventó la telenovela*. Caracas: Alfadil Ediciones, 2002.

Cole, Richard R. *Communication in Latin America: Journalism, Mass Media, and Society*. Wilmington, DE: SR Books, 1996.

Fernández, Claudia, and Andrew Paxman. *El Tigre: Emilio Azcárraga y Su Imperio Televisa*. Mexico, D.F.: Editorial Grijalvo S.A. de C.V., 2000.

Fox, Elizabeth. *Latin American Broadcasting: From Tango to Telenovela*. Luton, UK: University of Luton Press, 1997.

Fregoso, Gilberto. "Fútbol México-86: Así Se Hizo el Mundial." *Chasqui* 34 (1990, April/June): 70–79.

Hayes, Joy Elizabeth. *Radio Nation: Communication, Popular Culture, and Nationalism in Mexico, 1920–1950*. Tucson: University of Arizona Press, 2000.

Johnston, Donald H. *Encyclopedia of International Media and Communications*. New York: Academic Press, 2003.

Mariscal, Judith. *Unfinished Business: Telecommunications Reform in Mexico*. Westport, CT: Praeger, 2002.

Mattelart, Michéle. *The Carnival of Images: Brazilian Television Fiction*. Translated by David Buxton. New York: Begin and Garvey, 1990.

Mejía-Barquera, Fernando. "Historia Mínima de la Radio Mexicana (1920–1996)" [Minimal History of Mexican Radio]. *Revista Mexicana de la Comunicación*, 1–50. Mexico City: Fundación Manuel Mejía, 2000. Accessed July 20, 2006. http://www.fundacionbuendia.org.mx.

Menéndez Alarcón, Antonio V. *Power and Television in Latin America: The Dominican Case*. Westport, CT: Praeger, 1992.

Pareja, Reynaldo. *Historia de la Radio en Colombia*. Bogotá: Servicio Colombiano de Comunicación Social, 1984.

Pasquali, Antonio. *El orden reina, escritos sobre comunicaciones*. Caracas: Monte Avila, 1991.

Pasquali, Antonio, and Armando Vargas-Araya. *De la Marginalidad al Rescate: Los Servicios Públicos de Radiodifusión en América Latina*. San José, Costa Rica: Editorial Universidad Estatal a Distancia, 1990.

Rockwell, Rick, and Noreen Janus. *Media Power in Central America*. Champaign: University of Illinois Press, 2003.

Salwen, Michael Brian. *Radio and Television in Cuba: The Pre-Castro Era*. Ames: Iowa State University Press, 1994.

Simpson, Amelia. *Xuxa: The Mega-marketing of Gender, Race, and Modernity*. Philadelphia: Temple University Press, 1993.

Sinclair, John. *Latin American Television: A Global View*. New York: Oxford, 1999.

Skidmore, Thomas E., ed. *Television, Politics, and the Transition to Democracy in Latin America*. Washington, DC: Woodrow Wilson Center Press, 1993.

Skidmore, Thomas E., and Peter Smith. *Modern Latin America*. New York: Oxford University Press, 1992.

Straubhaar, Joseph D. "Brazil." Pp. 65–80 in Alan B. Albarran and Silvia M. Chan-Olmstead (eds.), *Global Media Economics*. Ames: Iowa State University Press, 1998.

Villamil, Jenaro. *La Televisión que Nos Gobierna: Modelo y Estructura desde sus Orígenes*. Mexico D.F.: Grijalbo, 2005.

## WEBSITES

*IPOBE.* http://www.ibope.com. IBOPE is a television industry rating service and has material on many Latin American nations in Portuguese, Spanish, and English.

*Rede Globo de Televisão.* http://redeglobo.globo.com/. Globo is the dominant media outlet in Brazil.

*Televisa.* http://www.televisa.com/. This is the main Website of Mexico's Televisa broadcasting.

*Univision.* http://www.univision.net/corp/en/index.jsp. Univision Communications. Univision produces programs in the United States, which are also broadcast in Latin America. The URL is for the English-language Univision Website.

*Telenovelas in Latin America.* http://www.zonalatina.com/Zldata70.htm. This is a good guide to telenovelas and includes many shows' Websites.

# NOTES

1. See Elihu Katz and George Wedell, *Broadcasting in the Third World: Promise and Performance* (Cambridge, MA: Harvard University Press, 1977), p. 70.
2. See *The Poverty Trap: A Conversation with Bill Clinton*, CNN (September 2, 3, 2006). See also video streaming in *Clinton Global Initiative*, http://clintonglobalinitiative.org/home.nsf/pt_home.
3. See Iscar Blanco, *La Realidad de la Brecha Digital en América Latina*, Final Project, Spanish-Language Journalism Program (Coral Gables, FL: University of Miami, 2006).
4. See "The Information Age," Table 5.10 in World Bank, *World Development Indicators*, Data, Information Technology, accessed August 1, 2006. http://devdata.worldbank.org/.
5. Ibid.
6. See "Democracias líquidas," *El Nuevo Herald* (March 25, 1998), p. 13A.
7. See Silvio Waibord, "Argentina, Uruguay, and Paraguay, Status of the Media In," in Johnston 2003 (in Resource Guide, Print Sources), vol. 1, p. 46.
8. See Rick Rockwell, "Central America, Status of the Media In," in Johnston 2003 (in Resource Guide, Print Sources), vol. 1, p. 212; Edward S. Herman, and Robert W. McChesney, *The Global Media: The New Missionaries of Global Capitalism* (Washington DC: Cassell, 1997), p. 176.
9. See Leonardo Ferreira, "Colombia, Ecuador, and Venezuela, Status of the Media In," in Johnston 2003 (in Resource Guide, Print Sources), vol. 1, pp. 235–246.
10. See Robert J. Goldstein, "Freedom of the Press in Europe (1815–1914)," *Journalism and Mass Communication Monographs* no. 80 (February 1983), pp. 1–23.
11. See Arthur M. Schlesinger Jr., *The Almanac of American History* (New York: Barnes & Noble Books, 1993), pp. 408–409, 412.
12. See Jorge Carpizo, and J. Madrazo, "*El Sistema Constitucional Mexicano*," in *Los Sistemas Constitucionales Iberoamericanos*, edited by D. García-Belaúnde, F. Fernández Segado, and R. Hernández-Valle (Madrid: Editorial Dyckinson, 1992), pp. 559–611.
13. See Jairo E. Lanao, *La Libertad de Prensa y la Ley* (Miami: Sociedad Interamericana de Prensa, 1999), pp. 400–406.
14. See Mejía-Barquera 2000 (in Resource Guide, Print Sources), p. 2.
15. Ibid., p. 1.
16. See Sidney W. Read Head, Christopher H. Sterling, and Lemuel B. Schofield, *Broadcasting in America* (Boston: Houghton Mifflin, 1984), pp. 27, 31, 265.
17. Ibid., pp. 2–3.
18. Ibid., p. 4.
19. Ibid., p. 5.

20. Hayes 2000 (in Resource Guide, Print Sources), p. 7.
21. See Mejía-Barquera 2000 (in Resource Guide, Print Sources), pp. 5–6.
22. Hayes 2000 (in Resource Guide, Print Sources), p. 6.
23. Ibid., pp. 7–8.
24. Ibid., p. 19.
25. See Michael B. Salwen, "Broadcasting to Latin America: Reconciling Industry-Government Functions in the Pre–Voice of America Era," *Historical Journal of Film, Radio, and Television* 17 (1997): 67–89.
26. See Fred Fejes, "The U.S. in Third World Communications: Latin America 1900–1945," *Journalism Monographs* no. 86 (1983), pp. 1–29.
27. See Salwen, Michael B., Bruce Garrison, and Robert T. Buckman, "Latin America and the Caribbean," in *Global Journalism*, 2nd edition, edited by John C. Merrill (New York: Longman, 1991), pp. 267–310.
28. See Paleologo, Constantino, *Brazil en América Latina: una experiencia en Periodismo Internacional*, translated by U.S. Gelsi (Rio de Janeiro: Ediçoes O Cruzeiro, 1960), p. 12.
29. See Straubhaar 1998 (in Resource Guide, Print Sources), p. 74.
30. See Fox 1997 (in Resource Guide, Print Sources), p. 54.
31. Ibid.
32. See Skidmore and Smith 1992 (in Resource Guide, Print Sources), p. 169.
33. See Gustavo A. Otero, *El Periodismo en América* (Lima: Empresa Editora Peruana, S.A., 1946) p. 226.
34. See Fox 1997 (in Resource Guide, Print Sources), p. 55.
35. See Hernando Téllez, *Cincuenta Años de Radiodifusión en Colombia* (Bogotá: Editorial Bedout, 1974), pp. 14–15.
36. See Felipe Gálvez, "Voice and Rider of the Air," *México en el Tiempo* 23 (1998, April): 1. México Desconocido Online. Accessed July 15, 2006. http://www.mexicodesconocido.com.mx/english/historia/siglo_xx/imprimir.cfm?idsec=4&idsub=23&idpag=710.
37. See "Sesenta años con la misma frecuencia" [Sixty Years with the Same Frequency], *El Tiempo* (February 1, 2006): 2, accessed February 2, 2000, http://www.eltiempo.com/hoy/vih_a000tn0.html.
38. See *9 de Abril 1948* (2001), directed by María Valencia Gaitán, Instituto Colombiano de la Participación Jorge Eliécer Gaitán (Bogotá, Colombia/New York, NY: Distributed by Latin American Video Archives).
39. See Téllez 1974.
40. See Leonardo Ferreira and Joseph D. Straubhaar, "Radio and the New Colombia," *Journal of Popular Culture* 22.1 (Summer 1998): 135.
41. Ibid. See also Pareja 1984 (in Resource Guide, Print Sources).
42. See Fox 1997 (in Resource Guide, Print Sources). Other important works to review are Fox 1988; and *Latin Politics, Global Media*, edited by Elizabeth Fox and Silvio Waibord (Austin: University of Texas Press, 2002).
43. See Johnston 2003 (in Resource Guide, Print Sources), vol. 1, p. 37.
44. Ibid., p. 38.
45. See "Cámara Venezolana de Industria Radiodifusión (CVIR)," p. 7 in *Historia de la Radiodifusión en Venezuela* (2006).
46. Ibid., p. 10.
47. See Andrés L. Mateo, "El miedo en la era de Trujillo," *Listín Digital*, pp. 1, 2. Accessed July 18, 2001, http://www.listin.com.do/opinion/opi1.html.
48. See Johnston 2003 (in Resource Guide, Print Sources), vol. 4, p. 221.
49. Ibid.
50. See Gonzalo Soruco, "The Cocaine Paranoia: Another Peril to Freedom of the Press in Bolivia," in *Encounter's 88*, edited by Andrew MacFarlane and Robert Henderson (London: University of Western Ontario, 1988), p. 24.
51. See Ana María Miralles, *Voces Ciudadanas: Una Aldea de Periodismo Público* (Medellín, Colombia: Universidad Pontificia Bolivariana, 2000), pp. 25–35.
52. See Pareja 1984 (in Resource Guide, Print Sources), p. 141.
53. Ibid., p. 84.

54. See Fox 1997 (in Resource Guide, Print Sources), p. 39.

55. See Fernández and Paxman 2000 (in Resource Guide, Print Sources), p. 53.

56. See Fox 1997 (in Resource Guide, Print Sources), p. 37.

57. See Pasquali and Vargas Araya 1990 (in Resource Guide, Print Sources), p. 27.

58. See Pasquali 1991 (in Resource Guide, Print Sources).

59. See Fox 1997 (in Resource Guide, Print Sources), p. 118.

60. Ibid., p. 119.

61. Ibid.

62. See Pasquali and Vargas-Araya 1990 (in Resource Guide, Print Sources), p. 35.

63. See Skidmore and Smith 1992 (in Resource Guide, Print Sources), p. 178.

64. See Roberto Amaral and Cesar Guimaraes, "Media Monopoly in Brazil," *Journal of Communication* 44.4 (Autumn 1994): 26–38; Straubhaar 1998 (in Resource Guide, Print Sources), pp. 69–70.

65. See Fernández and Paxman 2000 (in Resource Gude, Print Sources), p. 54.

66. Ibid.

67. See Roberto Rives-Sánchez, "*La Constitución Mexicana hacia el Siglo XXI* (Mexico D.F.: Plaza y Valdés Editores S.A. de C.V., 2000), pp. 111–112.

68. See Héctor Schmucler, *Los Satélites en la Expansión Transnacional: El Caso de América Latina* (Mexico D.F.: ILET, 1983), p. 26.

69. See Agency for International Development, *AID Rural Satellite Progam* (Washington, DC: AID/Academy for Educational Development, June 1981), p. 52.

70. See Michael Real, "Comunicación, Publicidad y Deportes," *Chasqui* 34 (April/June 1990): 59.

71. See Fregoso 1990 (in Resource Guide, Print Sources).

72. See Cristina de la Torre, "Que Pasó con el Mundial?" in *Las Cinco Maravillas Millonarias de Colombia* (Bogotá: Editorial Oveja Negra/FESCOL, 1982), pp. 11–64.

73. See Jaime Niño, "El Satélite SATCOL o el Precio de la Soberanía sobre la Orbita Geoestacionaria," in *Las Cinco Maravillas Millonarias de Colombia* (Bogotá: Editorial Oveja Negra/FESCOL, 1982), p. 153.

74. See Fregoso 1990 (in Resource Guide, Print Sources), p. 70.

# SPORTS AND RECREATION

JOSEPH L. ARBENA

To suppose that soccer is the only sport that matters in Latin America (defined here as everything in the western hemisphere south of the United States) is to ignore two fundamental facts: that in several countries soccer is far from being the number one sport, and that even in those places where soccer predominates, participants or spectators support numerous other sports in differing degrees. Such variety was observable even before 1492.

## PRE-COLUMBIAN GAMES AND SPORTS

### Mesoamerica

One of the innovative culture zones in pre-Columbian America, Mesoamerica ranges between roughly 25° and 13° north latitude, encompassing central and southern Mexico, the Yucatán peninsula, Belize, Guatemala, and western portions of El Salvador and Honduras, with influence outward both north and south.

One trait that helps define the region is *ulama* (or *ulamaliztli*), "America's oldest sport," played generally with a natural-rubber ball, slightly smaller than a bowling ball and weighing about nine pounds, that may be hit by just a few body parts—hips, knees, elbows—depending on time and place. Over 3,000 years, ulama has been played by the Olmec, Toltec, Zapotec, Mixtec, Aztec, Maya, and their descendants on permanent or movable courts—the former associated with monumental stone structures of varying design—with scoring based on hitting the ball through a high hoop or across a marked line. It once had deep ritualistic and political meaning, was accompanied by gambling, and at times was followed by human sacrifice.[1]

Less structured and even less like modern sports among Mesoamericans were such activities, at times competitive, as swimming, boating or canoeing, running, pushing, and archery. Widely popular was *patolli*, the objective of which was to move six pebbles around a cross-shaped "board" painted on a portable mat, using two-sided bean dice to determine the appropriate moves. With strong religious/mystical meaning and linked to extensive gambling, patolli has been compared to ancient Hindu parchisi, modern Parcheesi, and backgammon.[2]

Seeing in these games and sports strong ritualistic and religious meaning, the Spanish sought to suppress them as subversive challenges to Madrid's cultural and therefore political hegemony. Such efforts were not entirely successful, and remnants of these activities persisted into the twentieth century, though without their original religious and political overtones. In fact, a few practices, such as the Tarahumara races in northwest Mexico, were periodically highlighted as a way to promote simultaneously Mexico's indigenous past and sporting future.[3]

## Caribbean and South America

Nowhere else in pre-Columbian Latin America did a single game have the spatial dispersion and permanence of ulama. In Patagonia different groups played *chueca*, a stick-and-ball game that resembles field hockey. Elsewhere the most common games involved running, swimming, and activities associated with hunting or warfare.[4]

## COLONIAL ERA

Iberian conquerors and settlers after 1492 brought their own games and premodern sports. These included animal sports such as cockfighting, equine events such as horse racing, bullfighting, ball games, and table games. All of these usually involved high levels of gambling. As in many parts of Medieval Europe, the Latin American colonial era was marked by tensions between the sporting values and styles imposed from the top and the preferences of the folk below, especially in areas with a strong indigenous heritage or imported African populations.

British colonial rule in Latin America started somewhat later and continued through the late twentieth century, a few territories still governed from London after 2000. In those formal colonial realms the principal athletic legacy is cricket, carried by the colonial lords for their own enjoyment and, along with schools and churches, as a means to turn at least a portion of the subordinate Afro-Caribbean population into Englishmen, especially after the end of slavery in the 1830s.[5]

## MODERN SPORTS

### Origins and Diffusion

The sports most played and watched today first appeared in their structured yet still formative phase in the mid-nineteenth century on both sides of the North Atlantic. What mainly distinguished these so-called modern sports from earlier premodern forms was their break from religious ritual, their standardization of rules across time and space, their acceptance of participants based on ability more than race or class or wealth, their periodic modification or rationalization to improve performance or safety or marketability, their ties to expanding bureaucracies, their use of ever-more precise statistics, and their obsession with records.[6]

The sources of these sports fall into various categories: (1) those that evolved out of centuries-old European folk games such as the stick-and-ball games that produced field hockey, cricket, and baseball; the kickball games that became rugby, soccer, and American, Canadian, and Australian rules football; kegels, which inspired bowling; and track and field events and wrestling derived from the ancient world and even earlier primitive play; (2) sports inspired by farming or military activities, such as equestrian events, archery, and fencing; (3) sports such as basketball and volleyball invented to fill specific needs in specific places; (4) sports developed around new technologies such as roller skating, cycling, and auto racing; and (5) traditional activities from non-European societies that were imported and Westernized, such as polo and the Asian martial arts.

Almost all these modern sports have spread or diffused from their places of origin to Latin America. This process of diffusion has progressed in various ways: formal imperial/colonial control, informal imperial influence, military bases, commercial contacts, migration flows, educational institutions, missionaries, students returning from study abroad, and, more recently, the media—radio, film, television, and the Internet.

Why some sports caught on more in some places than others is a result of their differing intrinsic (internal) and extrinsic (outside or contextual) qualities. The former refers basically to the structure and nature of the game/sport: rules, equipment, playing area, methods of scoring, officiating, and physical requirements. The latter refers to historical sources, ethnic connections, economic ties, religious symbolism, global political implications, and bureaucratic structures.[7] Resistance to modern sports, in the form of traditional games or the Turnen gymnastics movement, was soon either reduced to marginal areas or totally overwhelmed in Latin America as in Europe and elsewhere.[8]

## MAJOR SPORTS

### Soccer

A variety of ball games using exclusively or partially the feet and lacking uniformity, some with names like *le soule* or *calcio*, were played for centuries across medieval and early modern Europe. But what we know today as association football or soccer (*fútbol* in Spanish,[9] *futebol* in Portuguese) took shape in England. Although school boys had been playing the dribbling game for several decades, codification awaited the creation of the Football Association in 1863; the popular Challenge or FA Cup started in 1871. The Scots experienced organized association football first in 1867, then accelerated the passing game and developed working class support and professionalism. They also aided the external diffusion, first to the continent and then elsewhere. The name *soccer*, a slangy British contraction of *association football*, appeared in print in 1891.

In 1904, trying to impose a degree of stability and uniformity to this rapidly evolving game, seven European countries founded the International Federation of Association Football (FIFA). By 1914 it had grown to 24 members, including Argentina and Chile. It has gone on, of course, to become the sport's principal international governing body, with 200-plus national associations and six regional confederations (CONCACAF and CONMEBOL cover Latin America).

Soccer's arrival in Latin America was part of that larger process of British cultural diffusion during the nineteenth century. Merchants, bankers, sailors, teachers, missionaries, diplomats, and engineers all carried their sports to overseas posts and practiced them among themselves and taught them to the locals. In Argentina, for example, Britons were playing soccer and forming the Buenos Aires Football Club in 1867, but major credit for spreading the game falls on Alexander Watson Hutton, who arrived in 1882 and later founded the English High School, source of the legendary Alumni squad. Hutton's name now graces the library of the Asociación del Fútbol Argentino (AFA).

The Brazilian story is similar. No doubt British sailors had played some soccer in Rio and other ports by the 1880s. The real jump came after 1894 in São Paulo thanks to Charles Miller—son of a British father and a Brazilian mother—who returned from schooling in England and helped found soccer clubs at several local businesses. Even with the drafting of a few Brazilians, for more than a decade the game remained very British and very elitist. By 1910, however, clubs had sprung up over much of the country and through much of the working class, though Rio and São Paulo remained dominant.

The 1920s saw significant changes in Latin American soccer, especially in the far south. First, the game had diffused outward geographically from major cities with large foreign communities and socially to local populations on all socioeconomic levels. Second, as a result of both intrinsic and extrinsic factors, many locals became fiercely dedicated players and fans, developing skills and styles often different from those of the English. In Argentina, for example, the creative dribbling and fancy footwork became marks of *el pibe*, or free-spirited youth, as opposed to the more methodical Englishmen.[10] Third, whereas in Britain professional soccer began as early as the 1870s, in Latin America no professionalism appeared until after World War I, and then fitfully and amid controversy. In an effort to improve their teams, clubs began paying some players, particularly those with no independent incomes, under the table—so-called brown money. Open professionalism came to Argentina in 1931, Uruguay in 1933, and Brazil between 1933 and 1936. Other countries lagged behind; Colombia, for example, where British influence was much weaker, went professional only in the late 1940s, aided by the arrival of numerous Argentines who left their homeland over a labor dispute with the Peronista government. Professionalism not only caused divisions among the bureaucrats who managed national soccer but raised questions about participation in the Olympics, where the amateur rule was still enforced.

In international soccer, the 1920s belonged to the Uruguayans. They won Olympic gold in both 1924 and 1928 and numerous friendlies with European squads. In the South American Cup competition, begun in 1916, played twelve times through 1929 and later renamed the Copa América, Uruguay finished first six times and second twice. As evidence of Southern Cone preeminence, Uruguay, Argentina, and Brazil combined finished first twelve and second ten times; only Paraguay managed two runner-up slots.

By 1928 little Uruguay, its population less than two million, was a relatively stable, limited democracy, with a progressive social consciousness, good public education, and a flourishing economy, even if too heavily dependent on agriculture. These conditions, combined with growing interest among other countries to hold a truly open international tournament, led the Uruguayans to offer to host a soccer World Cup (*Mundial* in Spanish) for the first time in 1930.[11]

Latin America's performance at the World Cup has been positive. Host Uruguay won in 1930, defeating Argentina in the final. In 1934 neither of those two competed in Italy. By 1938 Brazil had caught up with its neighbors and took third. In 1950 host and highly favored Brazil lost to Uruguay in a final that provoked a spike in Brazilian suicides.

In total, Brazil—the only country to qualify for all eighteen World Cup final sites—has five world titles, Uruguay and Argentina two each, plus several runner-up slots. On the European side, Italy has four titles, Germany three, and England and France one each.

Latin America's global position following Mundial 2006 is somewhat contradictory. Eight Latin American teams qualified to go to Germany; four made it to the second round, but only one, defending champion Brazil, got to the quarterfinals . . . then lost. Before 1982, the only years in which no Latin American team finished in the top four were 1934 and 1966. In the new FIFA classification—still imprecise but more realistic than the previous system—Brazil still ranks first and Argentina third in the world; however, only 5 of the top 19 and 12 of the top 50 are filled by Latin American countries. This somewhat diminished status results in part from the breakups of the Soviet Union and Yugoslavia and the rise of numerous African nations into their second generation of independence. Perhaps there is hope for the future, as Brazil won the 2003 FIFA World Youth Championship and Argentina the 2005.

Major soccer countries have similar professional organizations. AFA, for example, administers a system with a premier First Division, followed by Divisions B, C, and D, and several special classifications. Each group has around 20 clubs; each year the top teams move up one division (*acenso*), while the bottom clubs are relegated down (*decenso*). The premier division goes through a two-stage tournament: opening (*apertura*) and closing (*clausura*). From 2004 through 2006 the top clubs were Boca Juniors, Vélez Sarsfield, and River Plate.

The Confederação Brasileira de Futebol (CBF)—founded in 1914, affiliated with FIFA in 1923—similarly operates on three levels or Séries A, B, and C; A and B have twenty clubs and compete between April and November/December. Recently the top Série A clubs have been São Paulo, Internacional, and Corinthians. In 2005 four bottom clubs were relegated. The CBF also directs the Copa do Brasil and annual state championships. The only Latin American president of FIFA has been João Havelange (b. 1916), who competed on the Brazilian Olympic team in 1936 (swimming) and 1952 (water polo) and served as president of the Brazilian Sports Confederation (CBD) and member of the Brazilian Olympic Committee. He was FIFA president from 1974 to 1998.

The Asociación Uruguaya de Fútbol was founded as "League" in 1900, later changed its name, and affiliated with FIFA in 1923. It today administers a First Division of sixteen clubs with opening and closing phases, a Second Division with eight clubs, and a Metroplitan League with seven clubs. The top clubs as of 2006 are Peñarol, Nacional, and Danubio.

The Federación Mexicana de Futbol Asociación (FMF or FEMEXFUT) was founded in 1927 and affiliated with FIFA in 1929. It currently has four professional divisions. The First Division, with eighteen teams, plays two seasons, apertura and clausura, each ending with a playoff tournament (*Linguilla*) to determine the champion; this expansion of games is finance driven. Each year one team is relegated. The champs from 2003 through 2005 were Pachuca, Toluca, América, and UNAM (the Pumas of the national university).

As the region's leading sport, soccer has produced far more "stars," or "cracks" as they are known, than we could mention here. Names such as Alfredo Di Stéfano (Argentina) and Obdulio Varela (Uruguay) live on in national memories. More recently, of course, appears Edson Arantes do Nascimento, much better known as Pelé (b. 1940), the man many consider the greatest of all time. He played his first professional game with Santos in 1956, joined the national selection in 1957, and marked six goals in helping Brazil win its first World Cup in 1958. After three Cup triumphs he left the national team in 1971, retired from Santos in 1974, then played two seasons with the New York Cosmos. Over his career Pelé, also called "the King" or "Black Pearl," was credited with 1,284 goals in 1,363 games; yet it was his style more than his numbers that captivated his admirers. He later served as Minister of Sports; his countryman, FIFA President Havelange, never had good relations with him, however.

For most observers the only challenger to Pelé's supremacy is Diego Armando Maradona (b. 1960), known as El Pibe. He played for Argentina Juniors, won a senior league title with Boca Juniors, a title with Barcelona, and multiple trophies with Napoli, Italy. He led Argentina to its second World Cup in 1986, when his infamous—"Hand of God" goal—scored by a motion that appeared to involve a slap of the ball by Maradona's raised hand—was followed by perhaps the most magnificent individual goal in Mundial history. El Pibe's ability and durability were incredible, but his eventual abuse of cocaine and other drugs cost him the later years of his career and perhaps his historical reputation; he was expelled from the 1994 World Cup and never recovered his skills. A recent abdominal operation may have helped him conquer his weight problem; a television program has enhanced his public image.

Other stars of a slightly earlier generation include (1) Hugo Sánchez (b. 1958), considered to be Mexico's greatest player and a member of the FIFA 100 and named in late 2006 coach of the national team; (2) Colombia's Carlos Valderrama (b. 1961), who played for numerous Colombian teams as well as in France, Spain, and three teams in the U.S. Major League Soccer; and (3) José Luis Chilavert (b. 1965), Paraguayan goalkeeper but also a free kick specialist who scored numerous goals (62 in his career), played in Argentina, Uruguay, Spain, and France, retired in 2004, but marred his image with an, at times, hot-headed and irascible personality.

As of 2006 within the Latin American soccer community, the numerous standouts include Brazil's Ronaldo, Ronaldinho, and Kaká; Argentina's Maxi Rodríguez and Juan Ramón Riquelme; Mexico's Francisco Fonseca (or Kikín) and Jared Borgetti; and Uruguay's Alvaro Recoba, Paolo Montero, and Diego Forlán.

Apart from the annual struggles for league leadership, most countries feature at least one traditional club rivalry—based on history, location, or class—that raises emotions and attracts attention even when neither team is in contention for the championship. These "Classics" include Boca vs. River Plate in Argentina, Fluminense vs. Flamingo ("Flu-Fla") in Brazil,[12] Colo Colo vs. Universidad Católica in Chile,[13] Alianza Lima vs. Universitario in Peru, Peñarol vs. Nacional in Uruguay, Millionarios vs. Santa Fe in Colombia, and América vs. Cruz Azul in Mexico.

In addition to the qualifying rounds for the Mundial, Latin Americans participate in two major regional competitions: Copa América and Copa Libertadores. The oldest national teams tournament in the world, the former began as the South American Championship and was held erratically through 1967. It was revived and renamed in 1975 by the Confederación Sudamericana de Fútbol (CONMEBOL). Since 1993 it has invited the traditional ten South American countries, plus two others, to create three groups of four. These others have included Mexico, Costa Rica, Honduras, the United States, and Japan. The 2004 tournament was played in Peru, the final won by Brazil over Argentina on penalty kicks. The 2007 Cup will be contested in Venezuela.

Copa Libertadores is an annual competition begun in 1960, also by CONMEBOL, which features the top club teams from South America. At first only the national champions of the nine major South American federations participated, but over the years the qualifiers have increased, including the champions and high finishers of several leagues per country, such that, in 2006, 38 teams from 11 countries played 138 games to decide the champion—Internacional of Porto Alegre, Brazil. Argentine clubs hold 20 titles, Brazilian clubs 13, Uruguayan clubs 8, 3 others no more than three.

From 1960 the winner went on to play the European club champion in the Intercontinentel Cup. In 1980 Japan, with corporate sponsorship, offered to revive sagging enthusiasm by hosting the Toyota Cup. Twenty years later FIFA set out to create a true Club World Cup when eight teams met in Brazil; Corinthians defeated Vasco da Gama for the title. But the tournament floundered until FIFA got the Japanese to merge the Toyota Cup with the new Cup. In 2005, out of 6 teams, São Paulo defeated Liverpool to give Brazil the first two Cup titles.

Less prestigious so far is the CONCACAF Gold Cup, or North and Central American and Caribbean championship, played, more or less, every 2 years since 1991, always in the United States (alone or, twice, shared with Mexico). Mexico has won it 4 times, Canada one, and the United States three, including at the eighth in 2005; the ninth is set for U.S. cities in June 2007. The current format matches the Copa América—three groups of four—requiring that teams be invited from outside the zone. Countries have declined invitations, have not always sent their best teams, or have excluded star players.

The global growth of soccer has meant more media attention and more money for media moguls, select clubs, and elite players. One expression of this is an international money-driven migration of talent, similar to relationships in baseball, basketball, and cricket. The best Bolivian, Paraguayan, and Peruvian soccer players wind up in Argentina or Brazil, and the best players from the small clubs in Argentina, Brazil, Colombia, Mexico, and Uruguay wind up playing at the larger clubs. In turn, the best players from those countries wind up playing in the cash-laden European countries such as Spain, England, France, and Italy.

One downside of this is that the clubs in the talent-exporting countries are weakened. In addition, the national teams are weakened because their players have less time to practice and play together in their homeland. And the proliferation of extra-league and post-season games has only exacerbated the situation.

Most of the Latin American countries with strong soccer traditions also play *futsal* (*fútbol sala* in Spanish, *futebol de salão* in Portuguese), a five-player-per-team indoor game sanctioned and governed by FIFA since 1989. Paralleling the organization of regular soccer competitions, there is a Futsal Copa América, won by Argentina over three-time champ Brazil in 2003, a FIFA Futsal World Championship, won by Spain over Brazil in 2000 and Italy in 2004—Brazil having won the three titles before 2000—and an Intercontinental Futsal Cup, won by a Spanish club over a Brazilian one in both 2005 and 2006.

## SOCCER VIOLENCE

Although riots and deaths occasionally marred soccer games beginning in the 1920s, the massification and commercialization of soccer have contributed to a rise in rowdiness, even violence, in and around stadiums. While this is true in almost all those countries where soccer is the dominant sport, it may have reached its extreme in Argentina, where the exuberant fan clubs or *barras bravas*, Argentina's version of British hooliganism, have been responsible for the beatings and murders of fans of opposing clubs; the worst group is generally thought to be that of Boca Juniors. Since 1924 Argentine soccer violence has caused the deaths of slightly over 200 victims, about 95 percent of them males. Even in Uruguay there were nine fan deaths related to soccer between 1957 and 2006, when a man was fatally stabbed and his son severely beaten following a match. That same year a match in La Plata, Argentina, was suspended when hundreds of fans surrounded the teams' hotels and would not allow them to move to the stadium, which was to be closed to spectators as a means to end the violence of the barras bravas. Such rowdy fans are increasingly responsible for stadium injuries, even if not fatal ones.

In Brazil these groups are known as *torcidas organizadas* and, by the 1990s, had contributed to a serious decline in attendance at some of the country's major stadiums; at least six persons died in the last half of 1994 alone. Efforts by the police and the clubs themselves have reduced the violence to some degree, and attendance has similarly recovered. But the situation remains delicate.

Another increasingly popular variant played in over 170 countries, many in Latin America, is beach or sand soccer. Rules for this fast-moving professional game were set out in 1992: 5 players, unlimited substitutions, three 2-minute periods. Brazilians organized the first World Championship at Copacabana in 1995, hosting every year after. In 2005 it became the FIFA World Cup of Beach Soccer, played in Rio that year as was the second in November 2006. Of the eleven championships, Brazil has won nine and finished third once;

Uruguay has finished second five times, Peru once, and Argentina third once. Other powers are France, Portugal, and Spain.

## Baseball

After soccer, the "king of sports" in more Latin American countries than any other is, no doubt, baseball. Railroad and mining workers carried the evolving American game into northern Mexico in the 1880s, while henequen plantation workers carried it to the Yucatán peninsula, where they found that Cubans had already planted baseball along with other expressions of Cuban culture. U.S. occupational forces also facilitated baseball's spread to Nicaragua, Panama, Puerto Rico, and the Dominican Republic, where it especially appealed to migrants from the Anglo-Caribbean with cricket experience. Other, often English-speaking, Caribeños carried it to eastern Costa Rica and to Panama, fusing with the Yankee influence in the Canal Zone. Japanese immigrants added to the small baseball community in Brazil.

Since World War II, baseball's place in Latin America has changed only slightly. It remains "the King" in Cuba, the Dominican Republic, Puerto Rico, and parts of Mexico; it shares top billing with soccer in Venezuela, Panama, and Nicaragua. It is visible but secondary in Colombia, in Costa Rica, and on several islands. It is played, but hardly matters, in Brazil and Argentina. Consequently, professional leagues are viable mainly in those four countries that annually send their champions to the post-1970 Caribbean Series: Puerto Rico, Venezuela, Mexico, and the Dominican Republic. No doubt baseball, like cricket in the Anglophone Caribbean, has lost some of its dominance due to the diffusion of basketball.

Mexico was at the center of an interesting sidebar in major league baseball history. In 1946 Jorge Pasquel (1907–55), wealthy entrepreneur, president of the Mexican League, and ardent nationalist, attempted to raise his league's status by buying top U.S. and Latino players. His efforts failed, but he shook the major leagues enough to initiate a few changes in racial attitudes and in the treatment of players.

Cuba is a special case. Imported in the 1860s by students returning from the United States and reinforced by U.S. military and commercial personnel, baseball became part of the Cuban nationalist movement in opposition to Spanish culture and colonial rule. Partially professional league competition started in 1878–79 and remained vibrant till Fidel Castro banished all professional sports in 1962; Havana had had a franchise (Sugar Kings) in the International League, 1954–60.

Since the 1960s Cuba has been an amateur power, winning numerous Olympic (gold in 1992, 1996, 2004, silver in 2000) and Pan American medals. The defection of players seeking political, economic, and athletic goals has only marginally weakened the national team; it finished second to Japan in the inaugural World Baseball Classic (WBC) in 2006. At the Pre-Olympic Baseball tourney held in Havana, August–September 2006, Cuba qualified for the 2008 Games in Beijing and, along with Mexico, Venezuela, Panama, and Nicaragua, also for the 2007 Pan Am Games. Cuba and three others are also set for the 2007 WBC. Mainly for economic reasons, attendance at its often fanatically partisan six-team league games has been erratic in recent years, though it appears to be recovering. Cubans also remain informed and excited about the U.S. major leagues.

In the United States, writing on Cuban baseball is almost limitless. This reflects both the long U.S. involvement in Cuban politics, economics, and culture and the number of sterling players Cuba sent to organized white baseball and the Negro leagues during the twentieth century. The post-1959 years, despite the alteration in those ties, has only deepened the fascination.[14]

A few fair-skinned Latin Americans played in U.S. major league baseball before 1947, including Armando Marsans, an olive-skinned Cuban who played for Cincinnati in the early

1910s, and Baldomero Melo Almada, a very light Mexican who hopped around the majors through the 1930s. But the larger influx awaited the game's racial reintegration. Such has been the shift of U.S. athletes to other sports and the intense Latino dedication, encouraged by U.S.-operated youth academies, that by opening day 2006, despite U.S. immigration quotas, 190 (23.4 percent) of the 813 players on major league rosters were born in Latin America: eighty-five Dominicans, forty-three Venezuelans, thirty-three Puerto Ricans, fourteen Mexicans, six Cubans, four Panamanians, two Colombians, and one each from Nicaragua, Aruba, and Curaçao. The number under contract in the minors was even higher.

This Latin American presence in the U.S. national pastime means numerous black and brown foreign players in major league baseball (MLB) and more high-salaried heroes back home. Certainly individuals have seen their economic situations improve dramatically, but this exploitation of a rich Latin American resource has arguably left the exporting societies much poorer, as seen in the decline of the winter leagues; stars who reach the majors are reluctant to play in the off-season for fear of getting injured.[15] There have also been accusations of corruption, abuse, and exploitation in the scouting-recruitment process in Latin American countries: inadequate treatment of injuries, poor food and sanitation at the academies, and insufficient clarity regarding the contracts and reciprocal obligations.[16] Even where there are no abuses, many Latino aspirants wash out after a few weeks at the academies and are returned to society with no hope of ever playing professionally and inadequate education to prosper locally.

Over the years, the organization of professional baseball in the leading countries has been unstable, teams and leagues unpredictably rising and falling. The Mexican League in summer 2006 had 16 teams divided into northern and southern zones, reflecting the historical patterns of diffusion and popularity. Except in the far north there are no teams along the west coast, and, except in the capital (the Tigres and Diablos), no teams in the densely populated center. While the central area concentrates on soccer, in the north and the Yucatán baseball is "king."

In the Dominican Republic in the 2005–06 winter season six teams competed over fifty games: two from Santo Domingo (León del Escogido and Tigers del Licey, eventual champion), two from San Pedro de Marcorís, and one each from La Romana and Santiago. Similarly, in Venezuela eight teams divided into east and west competed through sixty-two games. The postseason tournament, and thus the championship, was won by the Leones of Caracas. In Puerto Rico six teams played a 28-game season, the ultimate winner being the Carolina Gigantes. Those three, plus 2005–2006 Mexican Pacific League champ Mazatlán, met in Maracay, Venezuela, in February 2006 for the Caribbean Series, a double round-robin. The hosts won with a 6–0 record, their first Series triumph in 17 years. Mazatlán was likewise host champion in 2005; Puerto Rico hosts in 2007.

Where it is prominent, baseball has produced an array of heroes comparable to soccer stars elsewhere, and the number is growing. Since 1900 over 1,200 Latinos have played MLB: roughly 438 Dominicans, 259 Puerto Ricans, 192 Venezuelans, 153 Cubans (marking a dramatic drop after 1959), and 99 Mexicans (a consequence of Mexico's restrictive player contract system). Past Latino stars who have not made the Hall of Fame include Fernando Valenzuela (Mexico), the Alou brothers (Dominican Republic), Luis Tiant, Jr. (Cuba), Vic Powers (Cuba), and Chico Carrasquel (Venezuela). Among the numerous stars in the first decade of the twenty-first century, standouts include Pedro Martínez, Miguel Tejada, and Vladimir Guerrero, all from the Dominican Republic, Edgar Rentería (Colombia), Andruw Jones (Curaçao), Mariano Rivera (Panama), and Sandy Alomar (Puerto Rico).

Though killed in a plane crash on the last night of 1972 while on a humanitarian mission to Nicaragua, which had recently hit by a devastating earthquake, Puerto Rico's Roberto Clemente Walker, the first Latin American elected to the Hall of Fame, remains a virtual living icon, especially for rising players from all the circum-Caribbean countries. "His memory kept alive as a symbol of action and passion,"[17] Clemente represents what young players can become. MLB's annual award to the player who best exemplifies community service is named in his honor, and his career and service were again recognized at the 2006 All-Star Game in Pittsburgh's new PNC park; the winner of the 2006 Clemente Award was Carlos Delgado (Puerto Rico).

Since Clemente, Cooperstown has welcomed from Latin America Martín Dihigo (Cuba; selected by the Veteran's Committee, also a member of three other baseball halls of fame), Juan Marichal (Dominican Republic; later his country's Minister of Sports), Luis Aparicio (Venezuela), Rodney Carew (Panama; born in the old Canal Zone), Orlando Cepeda (Puerto Rico), and Tony Pérez (Cuba).

## Boxing

Sailors, Young Men's Christian Association (YMCA) teachers/coaches, and gentlemen's club members all helped spread boxing. Despite charges of brutality and corruption, the sport remains popular everywhere. Prominent Latino boxers took stage early in the twentieth century, and their heirs remain celebrities today. There are so many weight divisions and sanctioning bodies today that it would be impossible to cite all the champions who have come out of Latin American countries. In the early twenty-first century there are four established sanctioning bodies: International Boxing Federation, World Boxing Association, World Boxing Organization, and, perhaps strongest in Latin America, the World Boxing Council, headed for thirty years (1976–2006) by Mexican José Sulaimán Chagnon; a fifth, the World Boxing Foundation, is trying to muscle in. Typically they administer seventeen weight classifications.

Among the numerous past greats the following can be mentioned: Argentines Luis Angel Firpo, José María "El Mono" Gatica, and Carlos Monzón; Colombians Rodrigo Valdés and Kid Pambelé; Panamanians Al Brown and Roberto Durán; Cubans Kid Chocolate, Kid Gavilán, and "Mantequilla" Nápoles, who switched his nationality to Mexican; Mexican Julio César Chávez; and Puerto Rican Félix Trinidad. Deserving of special mention is Cuban heavyweight Teófilo Stevenson, who won three Olympic gold medals, two Pan Am golds, and three world championships, but refused to leave Cuba to fight as a pro. He was followed by Félix Savón, who built a similar record.

Today, among Brazil's few heroes outside soccer is Acelino "Popo" Freitas (38-1, 32 KOs), who in 2006 won his fourth world title in the WBO light heavyweight division. Mexicans have a wider choice: Marco Antonio Barrera (b. 1974) and Erik Morales (b. 1976) have, as of 2006, each won eight world titles covering different weights and federations, have fought evenly three times, and hate each other. Nicaraguans might stop cheering for Ricardo "El Matador" Mayorga (b. 1973) after he lost his title to Oscar De La Hoya in May 2006 and tested positive for diuretics. Even if still on the amateur level, Cuban boxers surely pleased their countrymen in winning five gold and eight total medals at the Athens Olympics in 2004. (They also won five medals in judo and three in wrestling.)

## Cricket

Evolving out of centuries of medieval stick-and-ball games, cricket was one of the earliest modern sports to be codified and bureaucratized—London's Marylebone Cricket Club (MCC) dates from 1787—and was carried by British businessmen, government officials, and diplomats to overseas posts in both Britain's formal empire and areas more informally influenced by the British.

Tradition holds that cricket was first played in Buenos Aires in 1806 by British officers taken prisoner during an ultimately abortive invasion of the Río de la Plata; the two-hundredth anniversary of that event was celebrated by a visit of a team from MCC in February 2006, when the Argentines defeated the British for the first time ever. The first cricket club was formed in Buenos Aires in 1831; the more prestigious Buenos Aires Cricket Club, which played at Palermo Park, was inaugurated in 1864. The Argentines began international matches against Uruguay in 1868, Brazil in 1888, and Chile in 1893. The Argentine Cricket Association dates from 1913. It became an Associate Member (unique among Spanish-speaking Latin American countries) of the International Cricket Council (ICC) in 1974.

Among non-English-speaking Affiliate Members of the ICC, Brazil's Rio Cricket Club was founded in 1872 and its São Paulo Athletic Club in 1882; the game was carried as well to Santos, Recife, Minas Gerais, and elsewhere by enthusiastic Englishmen. In Valparaíso, Chile, crews of two Royal Navy ships played cricket in 1829; thirty-one years later a cricket club was founded in that port city. From there the game spread to Santiago and Concepción. However, after World War II the sport declined at the schools in favor of rugby. It has enjoyed a minor revival at the turn of the twenty-first century but depends mainly on expatriates from England and Australia. In Mexico cricket enjoyed some popularity during the Porfiriato (1877–1911) but has long suffered from lack of players and a suitable venue. Here it has been expatriates from India who, grouped as the Tigres de Bengala (Bengal Tigers), have injected new life into the game. Costa Rica, Cuba, and Panama are likewise members of the ICC, all, like Brazil and Chile, joining only in the twenty-first century.

In all of these countries today, cricket remains a marginally commercial sport played mainly by and for a social elite, many with long family or business ties to England. None of these are capable of competing with the ten Full Members of the ICC and thus not qualified to play official Test matches.

The story is notably different in the English-speaking Caribbean, including the islands, Belize (British Honduras), and Guyana (British Guiana). Here the British had a larger numerical presence, direct political and economic control, and markedly greater cultural influence. In an effort to Anglicize, and in a sense control, the Afro-Caribbean population they offered them schools, the church, and cricket, and many of these people took advantage of the offer.

By the mid-twentieth century some of the best West Indies (WI) cricketeers were the nonwhite locals who had earned spots on the Test team. The issue became not one of integration but of the selection of the team captain. Finally, in 1959, the West Indian Board gave in to pressure and named Barbadian Frank Worrell the first black captain, initiating an era of West Indian global supremacy.

During the early 1960s and, after a slight drop off from the late 1960s till the mid-1970s, again from the mid-1980s till the mid-1990s, the West Indies Test team set the pace. Worrell was joined by Clive Lloyd, Learie Constantine, George Headley, Everton Weekes, Clyde Walcott, and all-rounder Garfield Sobers on a list of WI heroes whose images and World Cup titles (1975 and 1979, 1983 second place, 1996 third) live on in public memory.[18]

Since the mid-1990s or before, however, the West Indies have failed to produce superstars comparable to those of the previous generations, and their performance has been erratic at best. The lists of batsmen, fast bowlers, spinners, and wicketkeepers are almost devoid of international stars. This decline has been attributed to urbanization, which has reduced the space available for youth to play street cricket, to a postindependence bourgeoisie's belief that other careers are as good as cricket for advancement, to rising illegal drug use among the youth, and to an Americanization of Caribbean culture as a result of media penetration of the islands and easier access to the mainland United States, reducing ties to Britain and promoting other sports such as golf, tennis, and, above all, basketball.[19]

The lone significant exception to this has been Brian Lara, "The Prince of Port-of-Spain." A native (b. 1969) of Trinidad and Tobago, at an early age Lara showed exceptional talent, especially at producing runs. Working his way up through youth cricket, he became captain of the West Indies B team in 1990, the same year in which he made his Test debut. Since then he has captained the Test team three times and set records for highest individual score in both first-class and Test cricket; he also holds the record for highest total number of runs in a Test career, scoring 20 percent of his team's runs, third on the all-time list. On defense, he ranks fifth all-time in the category of most career catches by a non-wicketkeeper.

## Tennis

Tennis entered Latin America in the mid to late nineteenth century mainly as an elite sport played first at country clubs administered by communities of foreigners—mostly British, French, and North Americans—then at clubs founded by and for the emerging professional classes and the lingering old aristocracy. Only gradually and in limited places did tennis facilities become more accessible to the middle class.

Over the years only a few Latin Americans have entered and remained for long among the world's tennis greats. A native of Guayaquil, Ecuador, Francisco "Pancho" Segura (b. 1921) moved to the United States, played at the University of Miami, became a very good amateur, turned pro in 1947, and was named No. 1 among pros in 1952, though was a notch below Jack Kramer and Mexican-American Pancho Gonzales. Mexican Rafael Osuna (1938–69) won the U.S. Championship in singles in 1963 and combined with Antonio Palafox to win two Grand Slam doubles. Another Ecuadorian, Andrés Gómez (b. 1960), never matched Segura but did win the French Open singles title in 1990, defeating Andre Agassi in the final. He was a better doubles player, with two Grand Slam titles.

Argentine Guillermo Vilas (b. 1952), a left-handed baseliner, was the first South American male to win a Grand Slam event, eventually taking four; he was also runner-up four times. He, with another top-ten player, José Luis Clerc, took Argentina to its first Davis Cup finals and was named to the International Tennis Hall of Fame in 1991. Often moody, rude, and insulting, Chilean Marcelo Ríos (b. 1975) never won a Grand Slam event but, in 1998, became the first Latino male to be ranked No. 1. He retired from the Association of Tennis Professionals (ATP) tour in 2004 but played some seniors events in 2006.

Two other Chileans brought their country Olympic glory at Athens in 2004: Nicolás Massú (b. 1979) and Fernando González (b. 1980) combined to win the doubles gold; later the former won the singles gold and the latter the bronze. Both have been ranked in the ATP top ten in singles. Gonzáles finished second to Roger Federer in the Australian Open of January 2007.

## Golf

Golf courses are increasingly conspicuous across Latin America, though their principal target is the tourist market, not local hackers. A few Latin American golfers have gained international stardom and thus national hero status, notably Roberto DiVincenzo (Argentina), Juan "Chi Chi" Rodríguez (Puerto Rico), and, stretching the boundaries,

Tex-Mex Lee Treviño, a native of Dallas, Texas, who starred on the regular and senior PGA circuits.

As of the early twenty-first century no male Latin American golfers have international premier status. On the women's tour, by contrast, several Latin Americans have risen above the horizon. María Isabel Baena, native of Pereira, Colombia, developed enough at her local club to earn a scholarship to the University of Arizona, where she won ten matches and the National Collegiate Athletic Association (NCAA) individual championship in 1996. From there she went on to play on the Ladies Professional Golf Association (LPGA) tour, rising twice to third-place finishes in 2001. In 2005 she won the HSBC World Match Play Championship of the LPGA Tour and was named Colombia's athlete of the year by Bogotá's *El Espectador*.

Four years younger and still peaking is Lorena Ochoa, native of Guadalajara and eight-time Mexican national champion. As a student at the University of Arizona she was named NCAA freshman of the year in 2001, set a record with eight consecutive wins in 2001–02, and emerged as NCAA golfer of the year in 2002. In 2001 she became the first golfer and the youngest recipient of the National Sports Award presented by Mexican President Vicente Fox, an honor she garnered again in 2006, when she won six tournaments (bringing her LPGA total to nine) and almost US$2.6 million, was named Associated Press Female Athlete of the Year, and replaced Annika Sorenstam as LPGA Player of the Year (although she lost the ADT championship and its million-dollar prize by two strokes to Paraguayan Julieta Granada).

The countries most aggressively pursuing foreign visitors to their designer links are Mexico, Puerto Rico, and the Cayman Islands. Cuba's earlier interest in golf was dampened by post-1959 anti-elitist policies and the virtual disappearance of country clubs. More flexible tourism programs over the last decade, expected to be even more so after Fidel Castro's departure, suggest that Cuba might again become a center of golf tourism.

## Track and Field (Athletics)

Track and field events trickled into Latin America by various means: foreign schools, local schools and clubs run by trained physical educators and coaches, YMCA, students returning from studying abroad, the impact of the Olympic movement. Consequently, all countries now exhibit those sports on some level, with amateur youth and occasional pro meets. And almost all have had some individual performers who have gained international recognition, even if they have had to go abroad for advanced training.

The careers of runner Alberto Juantorena and javelin thrower María Caridad Colón in the 1970s gave evidence of the potential for Cuban track and field success under INDER (discussed later in this chapter in the section on Sports and Politics). International medal counts prove the point. At the Pan American Games of 1999 Cuban won twenty-eight track and field medals, Brazil seventeen, Mexico fourteen, Jamaica nine, the other Latin Americans mere dribbles. The same story was told in 2003: Cuba, twenty-six; Brazil, sixteen; Mexico, thirteen; and Jamaica, ten. At Athens, Cuba tied Jamaica with five total medals; Mexico and Brazil only one each. At the 2006 Central American and Caribbean Games Cuba garnered almost half the gold medals (twenty-one of forty-four) and 45 of 132 total medals. The closest after that was Colombia with nineteen and Mexico with fourteen total.

The most recent International Association of Athletics Federation (IAAF) overall ranking of individual men and women lists only sprinter Veronica Campbell of Jamaica among its top ten. Still, Brazilian Marilson Gomes dos Santos became the first South American to win the New York Marathon in November 2006.

## Basketball

If basketball is not "king" in any individual country, in terms of participants and spectators collectively it may be the realm's true second sport in the twenty-first century. Since the early 1900s it has been spreading as a recreational and scholastic activity, and as a semi-professional club sport. Even if it has not challenged soccer where that dominates, it has become more visible everywhere and has made inroads into baseball's and cricket's domains in the circum-Caribbean.[20]

Invented by James Naismith in 1891 at Springfield College in Massachusetts, home today of the Basketball Hall of Fame, the game was carried globally by the YMCA and other educators and later by both American travelers and Latino visitors to the United States. Though somewhat more complicated than soccer, basketball likewise benefits from relatively simple rules and a need for minimal equipment. By mid-century rudimentary outdoor courts were frequently constructed at schools and public parks in even the smallest communities. Except at the highest levels of competition, people of all ages and sizes can play. In recent decades television has served to accelerate the diffusion further.

Such intensity has produced greater success for Latin American teams in international competition. Brazil won the Pan American Games gold medal in 2003; the Dominican Republic won silver and Puerto Rico bronze. Brazil also won the 2005 FIBA Tournament of the Americas (Copa América); Argentina finished second, Puerto Rico third. Mexico, which has had its own professional league (LNBP) for seven years, defeated Costa Rica to win the 2006 Centro America Championships. At the Under-18 FIBA Americas Championship, Argentina captured the silver and Brazil the bronze. Two years before at the Under-21 Tournament of the Americas, Puerto Rico won second and Argentina third. Argentina, the reigning Olympic champion, finished fourth at the World Championship in 2006, after finishing second in 2002. The FIBA final rankings for 2006 have Argentina fourth, Brazil seventeenth, Panama twenty-first, and Venezuela twenty-fourth.

Latin American players, many cited below, also participate in the National Basketball Association (NBA) Basketball without Borders program, hosted in Buenos Aires in 2005 and in 2006 at the Coliseo Roberto Clemente in San Juan, Puerto Rico. Players serve as camp coaches for hundreds of youth, searching for talent but also teaching about friendship and healthy living, especially emphasizing HIV/AIDS awareness and prevention.

As with baseball, internationalization of basketball has also witnessed a rise in global talent and a foreign invasion at the highest professional levels. Non-natives of the United States now constitute 18 percent of NBA rosters. While 60 percent of those are from Europe, Latin Americans have also left their mark. Since the turn of the century, perhaps no Latin American has impacted the NBA more than Emanuel "Manu" Ginóbili (b. 1977), who led his native Argentina to the 2002 Basketball World Championship silver medal and 2004 Olympic gold medal and the San Antonio Spurs to two NBA titles (2003 and 2005).

Manu's career path is similar to that of other Latin American players. After scholastic experience, he played three years in the Argentine professional league. In 1998 he moved to Italy and led Kinder Bologna to Italian and Euroleague titles, becoming an All-Star and popular hero. In 2005 he became the second Latin American named to the NBA All-Star team.[21]

Ginóbili was preceded by and is now accompanied by other Latin Americans in the NBA. Rolando Blackman, Panamanian (b. 1959) but raised in New York, was All-American at Kansas State, drafted by Dallas, and an NBA All-Star four times. Mexico has sent two players to the NBA: Horacio Llamas (b. 1973), after leaving Pima Community College, played sparingly for two seasons with the Phoenix Suns (1996–98). Eduardo Nájera starred at the University of Oklahoma before doing backup work with Dallas, Golden State, and Denver. Brazil likewise has two sons in the NBA: Leandro Barbosa, "Leandrinho" (b. 1982), a guard with Phoenix since 2003, and Maybyner Rodney Hilário, or Nené (b. 1982), drafted by the Knicks in 2002 but a member of the NBA All-Rookie first team with Denver, has worked to promote youth sports and the NBA in Brazil. Uruguay's only NBA entrant is Esteban Batista (b. 1983) who played the 2005–06 season with Atlanta. Adonal Foyle (b. 1975) is an honors graduate in history from Colgate University and has played since 1997 as a backup center with Golden State; he hails from the little Caribbean islands of St. Vincent and the Grenadines.

Argentina's national team has provided Manu with three NBA friends: Andrés Nocioni (b. 1979) has been a part-time starter and leader of the Chicago Bulls since 2004–05; named to the All-Sophomore team in 2006. Carlos Delfino (b. 1982) followed a path similar to Ginóbili's, playing at home, then in Europe, then being drafted by Detroit of the NBA. Fabricio Oberto (b. 1975) also played at home and in three European countries before signing with San Antonio in 2005. It is interesting that the biggest Argentine basketball stars are mainly from interior provinces, not from the national capital.

Puerto Ricans have made notable contributions to U.S. collegiate and professional basketball. "Butch" Lee was born (1956) of American parents in Santurce, speaks fluent Spanish, coached several Puerto Rican teams, and is considered a Puerto Rican national. He played college ball at Marquette, was Naismith College Player of the Year (1978), and played for three NBA teams before injuries ended his career. José Ortiz (b. 1963) played at Oregon State and briefly with the Utah Jazz, but his greatest successes came in Spain and Puerto Rico's pro leagues and national team. Ramón Rivas (b. 1966) played four years at Temple, then had a short stint with the Boston Celtics. Like Ortiz he achieved more in Spain and on the island.

More recently, Ricky Sánchez (b. 1987) played pro ball at home, skipped college, and signed with Denver in 2005. Since then he has played with Denver in the NBA Summer Pro League and with Idaho in the Continental Basketball Association. José Juan Barea (b. 1984) may have a more promising future. He was a high-scoring four-year letterman at Northeastern University and played extensively in the highest Puerto Rican pro league (BSN). He helped Puerto Rico win gold at the 2006 Central American and Caribbean Games. He is currently under contract with the Dallas Mavericks. Barea is helped on the Puerto Rican team by more experienced Carlos Arroyo (b. 1979), a four-year star at Florida Atlantic, now with NBA experience at Toronto, Utah, Detroit, and Orlando.

## Volleyball and Beach Volleyball

Like basketball, volleyball was invented by a YMCA instructor, William Morgan, in 1895 in Holyoke, Massachusetts, and was initially spread to Latin America (and elsewhere) mainly by that YMCA: Cuba (1905), Puerto Rico (1909), Uruguay (1912), Brazil (1917), and so on.

Although volleyball for both men and women was introduced at the second Pan American Games (1955) and the summer Olympics in 1964, the beach version (first played in 1930, first tournament in 1948) reached the Olympics only in 1996 and arrived at Winnipeg in 1999. Cuba has won the most Pan Am gold medals in the traditional game (twelve), Brazil the most total medals (twenty). On the beach at Winnipeg, Canadian men won the gold,

Brazilians both the silver and bronze; Brazilian women won the gold, the United States the silver, and Mexicans the bronze. At Santo Domingo (2003) Cuban men won the gold, Brazilians again silver and bronze; Cuban women also took gold, Mexicans silver, and Brazilians bronze.

At the Athens Olympics in 2004 Brazil took gold in the men's traditional, silver in the women's; on the beach Brazilian men garnered the gold, Cuban women the bronze; the Brazilian women were fourth.

## Swimming and Diving

While recreational swimming in Latin America dates back to pre-Columbian times and is enhanced by so many miles of beautiful beaches, competitive aquatic events were limited until recently by a lack of facilities. Only a few persons of greater economic means could get the training or practice time needed to compete; Jeanette Campbell, discussed later in this chapter in the section on Women in Sports, was clearly a rarity.

With more public and scholastic pools available, a few Latinos are making a modest splash in international chlorine waters. Brazilian Gustavo Borges (b. 1972) is a freestyle specialist who studied and trained at the University of Michigan and won silver in the 100-meter at Barcelona and the 200-meter at Atlanta and bronze (100-meter) at Atlanta and Sydney (relay). Another Brazilian and butterfly swimmer is Kaio de Almeida (b. 1984), who competed at Athens but has done best internationally in short-course events (25-meter pool). Argentine José Meolans (b. 1978) is another freestyle short-course champion, with presence in three summer Olympics.

Divers are rarer than swimmers. Two Mexicans are most visible: Fernando Platas (b. 1973) has represented his country in four Olympics, winning silver on the 3-meter springboard in 2000; he finished fifth at Athens. He holds gold medals from the Central American and Caribbean Games and the International Swimming Federation (FINA) world championships. His teammate Rommel Pacheco (b. 1986) finished tenth at Athens. Platas and Pacheco also performed in synchronized diving at the 2003 Pan American Games, earning a silver medal. The only other Latino in sight of a medal at Athens was Brazilian Cesar Castro (b. 1982), who has also begun to compete in synchronized diving.

## Horse Racing

Horse racing may have been the first modern sport in Latin America and offers an interesting lesson in patterns of cultural diffusion. In Southern Cone countries horses race British style, clockwise on grass; in the circum-Caribbean they race North American style, counterclockwise on dirt. This reflects the differing degrees of foreign influences in the late 1800s and early 1900s and roughly parallels the relative strength of soccer in the south and baseball to the north.

One consequence of horse racing's popularity in Latin America has been the success of Latino jockeys on North American tracks. Leading examples include (1) Puerto Rican Angel Cordero (b. 1942), who won three Kentucky Derbies, two Preakness Stakes, one Belmont Stakes, and four Breeders Cups and rode a total of 7,057 winners over a 22-year career; (2) Panamanian Laffit Pincay (b. 1946), who won one Kentucky Derby and three Belmont Stakes and broke Bill Shoemaker's record for career wins before retiring after 38 years of racing in the United States; (3) Peruvian Edgar Prado (b. 1967), who has won two Belmont Stakes and one Kentucky Derby (on ill-fated Barbaro in 2006), and in 1997 became the fourth rider to win 500 races in one year. Another Panamanian, Fernando Jara, though just

18 years old, won the 2006 Belmont aboard Jazil and the Breeder's Cup Classic aboard Invasor. Cordero and Pincay are members of the racing hall of fame.

As for the horses, Cañonero II was bred in Kentucky but raised and initially raced in Venezuela, native land of his owner. After a mediocre beginning, in 1971 he won the Kentucky Derby and Preakness and finished fourth at Belmont. The following year, however, he set the track record at the same track in winning the Stymie Handicap. Invasor, bred in Argentina, was Uruguay's Horse of the Year in 2006 even before he won the Breeders' Cup.

## Auto Racing

Almost all classifications of auto racing, including open road, dirt track, stock car, Kart, Formula Three, and Formula One, are run in Latin America, and several Latin American drivers have ranked among the world's elites. Juan Manuel Fangio (Argentina), considered by some "the king of the steering wheel" and his country's greatest sportsman of all time, moved from open road racing on the Argentine pampa and neighboring Andes to join the Formula One Grand Prix circuit in 1948. Before his retirement in 1958 he had won 102 international races and five Formula One World Drivers' Championships (WDC) (1951, 1954–57). A popular Argentine successor to Fangio, though never a world champion, was Carlos Reutemann, who in eleven seasons won twelve Grand Prix races.

Three Brazilian drivers captured a total of eight WDC: Nelson Piquet (1981, 1983, 1987), Ayrton Senna (1988, 1990–91), and Emerson Fittipaldi (1972, 1974). All are national heroes, but perhaps Senna generated the most emotion in Brazil and around South America because of his flamboyant personality, his patriotic loyalty, and his tragic death on Lap 7 of the 1994 San Marino Grand Prix.

In the new millennium Brazil maintains its visibility in Formula One circles. The leading veteran is Rubens Barrichello (b. 1972), who, like his mentor Ayrton Senna, is a native of São Paulo and who was nearly killed in a violent crash during a practice run at San Marino just two days before Senna died on the same track. Barrichello has nine Grand Prix victories since he moved to that level in 1993. He twice finished second to Ferrari teammate Michael Schumaker (2002 and 2004) in World Championship rankings. His switch to Honda in 2006 has not brought the success he sought.

Another São Paulo native, Felipe Massa (b. 1981), moved triumphantly through classifications from karting to Formula 3000 Euro-Series. In 2002 he joined the Sauber team and raced in his first Grand Prix. In 2006 he moved to Ferrari and gained his first victory at the Turkish Gran Prix in August. Schumaker's announced retirement raised Massa's hopes for 2007.

Cristiano de Matta (b. 1973) also raced Formula One in 2003–04 for Toyota after moving up the ladder from karting to Formula Ford to Formula 3000 to Indy Lights and more. But twenty-eight Grand Prix starts produced no wins and few points, so in 2005 and 2006 he raced Champ Cars and achieved greater success. He was seriously injured in a test accident in August 2006, putting his racing future in question.

Hélio Castroneves (b. 1975, São Paulo) has gained his greatest fame in North American open-wheel racing, winning the Indianapolis 500 in 2001 and 2003 and finishing second to countryman and Penske teammate Gil de Ferran in 2003. He finished third in the Indy Racing League (IRL) 2006 14-race season; another Brazilian, Vitor Meira (b. 1977, Brasilia), finished fifth.

Given its proximity to the United States, it is perhaps not surprising that Mexico is experiencing a growth of stock car racing. NASCAR held Busch Series races there in 2005 and

2006, with plans to continue, and manages a variety of stock car competitions, including the fourteen-event Desafío Corona, administration and marketing of which is handled by NASCAR Mexico, whose objective is to expand live racing, media broadcasts, and the sale of sponsors' products.

Since 1967 Mexico's Baja California has been home to "the oldest and most well known of all desert races," held annually in November—under a full moon if possible— and called since 1975 the Tecate SCORE Baja 1000. Sixty-eight racers entered the first running; in 2005 almost 300 entrants competed in twenty-seven pro and five sportsman classes for cars, trucks, motorcycles, and ATVs. Most races have begun in Ensenada. Some years they end farther down the peninsula; in others they loop around to or near the starting point and are designated the Baja 500. Drivers as well as spectators arrive from all over the world.

Other successful Latin American drivers include, for IndyCars®, Adrián Fernández (Mexico), who previously drove in the CART division, and Roberto Guerrero (Colombia), and for Champ Cars, Mario Domínguez (Mexico). Juan Pablo Montoya (Colombia), who moved from Champ Cars to Formula One in 2001 and eventually won seven races, switched to NASCAR Nextel Cup in 2006-07, apparently frustrated and bored by the condition of his McLaren cars and by Schumaker's dominance of the field with seven WDC.[22]

A few women have also been entering the field. For example, Juliana González (b. 1991, Medellín, Colombia) piloted a Go Kart at age twelve and, by 2006, was racing in both the Panam GP Series and Formula Ford. Her idol is Ayrton Senna; her dream is to compete in Formula One. María Isabel Cajiao (b. 1973), whose husband also races, won at least once driving a Renault Clio in the street vehicle category.

## Less Common Sports

### American Football

For various cultural, environmental, and economic reasons (i.e., its heavy and expensive equipment, its physicality, and its links to American historical evolution and culture), this sport has raised only limited enthusiasm in the region. It was played by American youth in the Panama Canal Zone until the Zone's disappearance and the reduction in size of the American community in the 1980s. There has also been a slight spread of enthusiasm for Super Bowl Sunday even among people who do not understand or play the game, but that is more a social than an athletic event.

Only in Mexico do we see a significant expression of this twenty-first-century manifestation of an American postindustrial sport. In truth, the sport in Mexico dates back to the 1920s and continues today in several ways. Several Mexican universities have sponsored teams and helped stock national teams to play in the American Football World Cups of 1999 and 2003, where Mexico finished second to Japan both times; the 2007 tournament is set for Japan, and the 2011 site was still undetermined as of the beginning of 2007. NFL teams sporadically play preseason exhibition games in Mexico, and a number of Mexicans and Mexican Americans have succeeded on U.S. collegiate and professional teams. These include place kickers Rafael Septién, who played for the St. Louis Rams and Dallas Cowboys, and Raúl Allegre, who starred with the Baltimore Colts and New York Giants. Others were Jim Plunkett, Oakland Raiders quarterback, and Tom Flores, successful coach in both Oakland and Seattle.[23] In Mexico a few young females also compete in organized American football programs.

As of 2006, several Mexicans were working with NFL teams after careers at American universities. Rolando Cantú already had two years of experience as offensive guard with the Arizona Cardinals. Previously he played for Tec de Monterrey in the highest league of the Organización Nacional Estudiantil de Futbol Americano (ONEFA). Another native of Nuevo León and former teammate of Cantú in Monterrey, Luis Berlanga, was aiming for the San Francisco 49ers after holding the NCAA record in all divisions for converting 73 consecutive extra points in the same season while playing for Division II Northwest Missouri State. In January 2007 the Kansas City Chiefs signed a two-year contract with huge offensive lineman Ramiro Pruneda, who led Monterrey Tech to four Mexican national championships.

Non-Mexican Latinos with some NFL connection are Salvadoran José Cortez, who kicked for Oregon State and several NFL teams over seven seasons, and defensive lineman Luis Castillo, of Dominican origin, a graduate of Northwestern who starts for San Diego. Four Puerto Ricans have played in the NFL. The first, Ron Rivera, won a Super Bowl championship ring with the Chicago Bears. Marco Rivera (Packers and Cowboys) has played in three Pro Bowls. O. J. Santiago and Glenn Martínez played for Atlanta and Detroit, respectively.

## Rugby

Rugby is a spin-off from the same ball game heritage that produced soccer. The split between Association football and Rugby football (which permits running with the ball in the hands) evolved between 1830 and 1860, leading to the Rugby Football Union in 1871; Scotland, Ireland, and Wales followed in the same decade. As with soccer, cricket, and polo, a variety of Englishmen carried the game to Argentina, the first match being played in 1873. In 1899 four Buenos Aires clubs combined to form the River Plate (later Argentine) Rugby Football Union, laying the basis for international play in 1910.

Since 1965 the international team has been called The Pumas, with mixed results. They have qualified for five World Cups (1987, 1991, 1995, 1999, 2003), but only in 1999 did they move on to the quarterfinals. In 2006 they counted over 300 amateur rugby clubs, with some 57,000 registered players. Their International Rugby Board (IRB) ranking is eighth and they have already qualified for the 2007 Cup. Uruguay is the only other Latin American country ever to qualify (1999).

## Polo

Played in China and Persia two thousand years ago and spread throughout Eurasia by the Mongols (known as Mughals or Moguls in India), polo is one of the world's oldest games and likely the oldest ball and team game. From Persia it moved to India and was extremely popular by the sixteenth century. It was quickly adopted by British colonialists, who founded the Calcutta Polo Club in 1862. From there it moved to Mother England, where John Watson drafted the basis of the modern polo rules, the London Hurlingham Club arose in 1874, and the first Champion Cup was contested in 1876.

English and Irish merchants, bankers, engineers, and educators carried it to Argentina, where it fitted perfectly into the physical atmosphere of the pampa and the long tradition of equestrian sports. The first official game was played there in 1875 and the Flores Polo Club was founded in 1880, the legendary Argentine Hurlingham Club six years later. The River Plate Polo Association began in 1893, the year of the first open tournament. In 1922, at

Hurlingham, representatives of the sport's major clubs founded the Asociación Argentina de Polo (AAP), which has remained first among international teams. From its polo complex in Pilar north of Buenos Aires, the AAP administers a program that covers some 30,000 players in Argentina, among some eighty countries around the world.

After Argentina, the only Latin American country with a visible international polo program is Mexico, where polo, like cycling, was encouraged by the pro-European mindset of the Porfirian elite between the mid-1870s and 1910, although polo is played at lower levels in almost all Latin American countries.

Polo was an Olympic sport five times: 1900, 1908, 1920, 1924, and 1936; Mexico, riding on that tradition, took third place in 1908 and 1936. Once the Argentines built their own polo culture, they gained premier status, winning the gold in both 1924 and 1936. The Argentines have been uninterrupted world champions since 1949, and their annual Palermo Polo Open is the world's most prestigious international tournament.

Only in 1951 was polo a medal sport at the Pan American Games: host Argentina won the gold; Mexico the silver; and Peru the bronze. The failure to continue polo at these Games no doubt reflects both the sport's limited presence in the hemisphere and the cost involved in transporting the ponies to the competition venue.

## Jai Alai

The Basque region of northeastern Spain spawned a family of ball games that today we know as handball, squash, and jai alai. The first two are seen now scattered thinly all over the western hemisphere, though they are most common as amateur sports in the Southern Cone. Jai alai, professional and linked to heavy gambling, with its long three-sided court, hard ball, and curved basket or *cesta*, has prospered most in Havana (especially before 1959), Mexico, and Florida, mainly around Miami and Tampa.

## Cycling

In the late 1800s, from France and later Italy, the new sport of cycling crossed the Atlantic to the mountainous tropical regions of Latin America, most visibly Mexico, Costa Rica, Colombia, and other Andean countries. Clearly the sport matched nicely with the terrain, but it also appealed to those elements who sought to connect with *fin de siècle* Parisian social behavior. In the Mexico of President Porfirio Díaz (1877–1911), this atmosphere led to Sunday outings in the city's green spaces or in the nearby countryside.[24] The appeal of bicycling survived the Revolution and soon also supported amateur as well as professional racing, giving rise to such competitions as La Vuelta a Colombia (now Pilsen), begun in 1951 (the fifty-sixth was won in August 2006 for the fourth time by José Castelblanco, who had been sanctioned in 2004 for taking testosterone), and La Vuelta a Costa Rica, begun in 1965.[25] The forty-third Vuelta a Venezuela was run in September 2006.

Similarly, qualified Latin Americans began racing on the European circuit. Colombian Luis Herrera (b. 1961) is the second rider to win "King of the Mountain" jerseys in all three grand tours: France, Spain, Italy. Santiago Botero (b. 1972, Medellín) was World Time Trial Champion in 2002. Victor Hugo Peña (b. 1974) in 2003 became the first Colombian to wear the *maillot jaune* (yellow jersey) in the Tour de France. Raúl Alcalá (b. 1964) was the first Mexican to participate in the Tour de France, finishing eighth in 1989 and ninth in 1990, also winning two stages.

Beginning in the late nineteenth century, women have been attracted to cycling, even if not in competition at first. Certainly it was fashionable and, with proper attire, socially acceptable. But in Mexico and other countries it contributed, however slightly, as did golf and tennis, to women's sense of freedom and liberation, a small part of changing gender relations in Latin America.

## Bullfighting

In the nearly two centuries since the breakup of the Spanish American Empire, bullfighting has lived an erratic existence. In part as a rejection of things Spanish, in part in pursuit of things modern, most former colonies banned it by 1900. Even Mexico temporarily suspended *la corrida de toros*. Where it is celebrated today, vocal critics continue to denounce its brutality.

*Taurismo* remains significant today in Mexico, Colombia, Venezuela, Ecuador, and Peru, which respectively boast thirty-eight, fifteen, eleven, eight, and nine principal bull rings. In addition, many towns have small rings that function on holidays or during fairs, usually with matadors on the rise and younger and smaller bulls.

While in those five countries the traditional organization and method of the bullfight is dominant, lesser-known variations are practiced to varying degrees. For example, *pegas*, *forcados*, and *rejoneo* are types of bullfighting on horseback that date from medieval Spain.[26]

It must be borne in mind that bullfighting is not a contest between the matador and the bull. Rather, like figure skating and gymnastics, it is competition against a subjective standard. In principle, the matador, the picadors, and the banderilleros should perform with the bull in a spontaneously choreographed ritual, culminating in the kill. When that happens, not only does the matador earn praise, but so do the bull and the ranch that raised him.

## Other Equestrian Sports

In addition to bullfighting, Iberian colonial domination generated equestrian activities associated with farming and ranching, which gradually evolved into more structured festivals and competitions and ultimately games and sports. In Mexico, the best known of these is *charrería* and its romanticized cowboy/horseman figure, *el charro*. Emphasizing style more than speed, it embodies many of the events associated with American rodeo: roping steers and horses, riding bulls and broncos, wrestling bulls.[27]

Similar to charrería is the Chilean rodeo, performed by *huasos* or Chilean horsemen, organized under the Federación del Rodeo Chileno in 1961, and declared a national sport the following year. Evolving out of colonial ranching practices, the rodeo is now an organized, stylized competition conducted in an outdoor arena called a *medialuna* ("half moon"); moves by both men and horses are uniquely Chilean. Nationally today there are some two dozen associations and almost 200 clubs performing in 200 medialunas. The huasos and their partners, or *chinas*, have both work clothes and elegant dress outfits. The weekend long festivals also involve typical music and dance, especially the *cueca*, and wine and food.

## Oddities

Sprinkled across Latin America are games and sports popular in limited geographical areas, the products of unique historical and environmental circumstances.

### Tejo

In June 2000 the Colombian Congress declared *tejo* a national sport. Called *turmequé* by indigenous groups, it involved the tossing of a gold disk. In the colonial era, the Spanish substituted a stone disk, which later became metal. Played outdoors, the object now is to toss the disk a set distance, about the length of a bowling lane, into a metal receptacle lined with small packs of blasting powder or caps; the player or team that explodes the most packs is the winner.

Centered mainly in the departments of Cundinamarca and Boyacá, the game has diffused to a few other areas of Colombia's Eastern Cordillera and to neighboring Ecuador and Venezuela. Though considered a farmer/working class sport, it is played in some upper-class clubs and by some prominent politicians, and by both men and women. At the highest level the sport is regulated by the Federación Colombiana de Tejo. Competitions may last for hours and typically are linked to loud music and the consumption of huge quantities of beer.

### Pato

Played since the 1930s and directed by the Federación Argentina de Pato (FAP) since 1941, this is a rationalized revival of a rough game practiced on the pampa by gauchos since the early seventeenth century and partially suppressed in the nineteenth. Originally men on horseback tussled over a duck tied in a leather bag. Now teams of four use a heavy leather ball with six metal handles, which they try to toss into raised baskets at each end of the field.

On a smaller scale, modern pato, like polo, is a sport of the elite, its matches a time for socializing. Still, in 1953 President Juan Perón decreed pato the sport most representative of national culture. After years of promoting pato at home and abroad, the FAP held the first World Championship of Pato-Horseball in April 2006; the hosts finished second to Portugal.

### Cockfighting

One of the legacies of the colonial era is cockfighting, especially popular among men in rural or marginally urban areas. Like bullfighting it is often attacked by opponents of blood sports, yet it survives into the twenty-first century in almost all countries, though mainly in Mexico and Central America—principally Nicaragua and Puerto Rico, where it is popular, legal, and accompanied by lots of gambling.

### Capoeira

This Afro-Brazilian male activity is a fusion of dance, acrobatics, and martial skills, often tied to black and slave resistance movements and gang behavior in the nineteenth century. At times classified a sport, it is best viewed as a stylized music/dance form.

### Professional Wrestling

Although for a half century undeniably more theater than sport, professional wrestling, like professional boxing, began as a legitimate spin-off of a truly amateur sport, the evolving freestyle wrestling included in the modern Olympic Games in various forms since 1904 and later in the Pan American Games. Today both the amateur and professional varieties are practiced in almost all Latin American countries.

But it is the professional variety that attracts the most attention and paying customers. Known as *lucha libre* or free fight, it is seen almost everywhere but is apparently most popular in Mexico, where it began in the 1930s, and tag-team is the primary match type. Most wrestlers wear masks and represent good-guy and bad-guy personalities. Among the best known and loved/hated are the Blue Demon and the Son of the Saint, the late Saint having been a special figure.[28]

## Bowling and Billiards

Modern indoor bowling—called *boliche* in most areas—is available in virtually all countries, though the number of alleys is relatively low. The sport is mainly for amateurs and semi-professionals. Only one or two Latin Americans belong to the Professional Bowlers Association and have qualified for the PBA tour. Across the region there may be more regular participants in billiards—not much pool—though again this is social and amateur, often limited to smoky bars or gentlemen's clubs.

## Roller Skating

Although roller skating—now including inline skating—has long been an international sport in Latin America, few Latin Americans have gained recognition outside the hemisphere. Two exceptions are Argentine Nora Alicia Vega (b. 1961), who won numerous South American, Pan American, and world titles, and Brazilian Fabiola da Silva (b. 1979), multiple winner in Aggressive Inline Skating competitions, including ESPN Summer X Games.

## Sport Fishing, Sailing, and Power Boat Racing

Virtually all the islands and countries with coastlines have participants in these activities for recreation or in competition, up to the Olympic level. As minimal examples, Puerto Rican sailor Enrique Figueroa has represented his nation at Barcelona, Sydney, and Athens, and in August 2006 the Mexican Costa Maya witnessed the twenty-second Gran Carrera Motonáutica Río Hondo–Bacalar for seven categories of power boats.

## Skiing

Recreational and competitive skiing is confined almost exclusively to mountainous mid-latitude Chile and Argentina, where climate and terrain are most suitable and where immigrants from Germany, Austria, and Switzerland have promoted the sport in areas with a conspicuous Alpine touch, though a few small resorts are also located in other Andean countries. Consequently, Chile and Argentina benefit from tourism during the northern hemisphere summer and are the only Latin American countries to enter seriously international winter sports competitions, though victories are rare. Argentina, Brazil, Chile, and Venezuela participated in the 2006 Winter Olympics in Torino, Italy, but failed to win Latin America's first medal. Peru was scheduled to make its Winter Olympic debut, but its athletes never arrived.

Not surprisingly, attempts to hold winter Pan American Games faltered miserably. Lake Placid, New York, tried to hold them in 1959, but too few countries were interested. Originally scheduled for 1989 but canceled, such an event was eventually held in Las Leñas, Argentina, in 1990 and drew 97 competitors from only eight countries, including the United States and Canada—which combined to win all eighteen medals awarded in the three alpine skiing events that were staged; other events were canceled because of a lack of snow. Santiago, Chile, was set to host the second Pan Am Winter Games in 1993 but gave up, again because of insufficient snow and support. The idea has been dormant since.

### Archery

Although indigenous peoples used bows and arrows for hunting and play, modern archery is derived from the imported European sport, and it is not seen widely outside private clubs. At the 2006 Olympic Games only three Latinos—all Mexicans—competed; the best, Juan René Serrano (b. 1984), won his first match, lost in the second round, and finished twentieth overall.

## SPORTS ORGANIZATIONS

Consistent with Allen Guttmann's characterization of modern sports, Latin American sports are awash in organizations and bureaucracies, even if terribly underfunded and grossly inefficient. Each country has, at least on paper, a federation tied to every sport practiced and linked to the appropriate international organization, by sport, region, or competition. Some of them are cited in this chapter. All of them have Websites (see the Resource Guide).

### International Sports Competitions

Small numbers of Latin Americans were involved in the modern Olympic movement almost from its beginning. Cubans won two medals at Paris (1900) and ten at St. Louis (1904), all in fencing. A Chilean competed at Athens in 1896, but Chile did not win its first medal till Amsterdam (1928) or its first gold till 2004, the same year the Dominican Republic won its first championship. Off the field as well, Latin Americans were drawn early into Olympic affairs, as modern Olympics founder Pierre de Coubertin sought to broaden the movement's appeal and base. Of the thirteen members of the original International Olympic Committee (1894), one was Argentine José Zubiaur. Of the 115 IOC members in 2006, there are thirteen regular members from Latin America (as defined in this chapter), plus three honorary members.

Latin American leaders, athletic and political, learned early the advantages of hosting international sporting events: Hosting justifies expenditures on sporting infrastructure, usually inspires local athletes to perform better, and gains domestic and foreign attention, hopefully positive. If a country cannot display progress in athletic competition, it can partially compensate through efficient hosting of such competitions.

By the 1920s Coubertin and the IOC leadership set out to expand the Olympic spirit and Olympic-type competitions. Aided in places by the YMCA, these efforts led to the 1922 South American Games held in Brazil. That competition attracted four national teams (Brazil, Argentina, Uruguay, and Chile) and continued only erratically afterward. In 1978 eight countries sent teams to La Paz, Bolivia, for the first Southern Cross Games. When the third games, organized by the South American Sports Organization (ODESUR), convened in Santiago, Chile, in 1986 they were renamed the South American Games. The eighth in this new series was destined for La Paz (2006), but domestic instability in Bolivia led ODESUR to move the Games to Buenos Aires, with some events in Mar del Plata.

At the Paris Games of 1924 the Mexicans were pushed by the IOC to initiate similar games and for various reasons they found the idea appealing, leading to the 1926 Central American and Caribbean Games held in Mexico City.[29] Originally called just the Central American Games, this gathering fielded only three teams (Mexico, Cuba, and Guatemala) and some 269 athletes, but it eventually became a major event held every four years, adopting its current name for the fourth edition held in Panama in 1938. The twentieth Central American and Caribbean Games, held mainly in Cartagena, Colombia, in July 2006, brought around 8,000 competitors from the 32 member countries of the Organización Deportiva Centroamericana y del Caribe (ODECABE), which administers the games. As has been the pattern, Cuba harvested the most total (285) and gold (138) medals, with Mexico (275 total, 107 gold) a respectable second. Colombia (219 and 72) and Venezuela (263 and 49) formed another tier; Puerto Rico (96 and 24) and Dominican Republic (97 and 22) another. No other country won more than forty-eight total medals (Guatemala) or nine gold (Jamaica); three countries won no medals at all.[30] The 2010 games will be held in Mayagüez, Puerto Rico; Veracruz, Mexico, is a strong candidate for 2014.

Reviving an older name and an event held in Guatemala in 1921, smaller Central American Games were begun in 1973, as the weaker isthmian countries felt overwhelmed by Mexico and Cuba; 1,095 athletes representing seven countries competed in twenty sports at the Eighth Central American Games, held in Antigua, Guatemala, in November 2006.

Other subregional games include the Bolivarian Games, initiated at Bogotá in 1938 to celebrate the four hundredth anniversary of the city's founding, with 694 athletes from six countries competing. The fifteenth edition was held in Armenia, Colombia, in 2005; the 2009 Games are slated for Sucre, Bolivia.

Five Latin American countries have hosted a total of six soccer World Cups: Uruguay (1930), Brazil (1950), Chile (1962), Mexico (1970 and 1986), and Argentina (1978). Colombia was originally awarded the 1986 Mundial but withdrew because of its confessed inability to provide adequate infrastructure and security. Mega-wealthy narcotics traffickers had invested heavily in soccer teams, leading to the bribing, beating, and killing of players, coaches, and game officials, reducing confidence in the sport. Under FIFA's rotational hosting system, 2014 returns the Mundial to South America. Brazil is the clear favorite to get the nod. Nevertheless, based on Colombia's successful organization of the Central American and Caribbean Games in 2006, President Alvaro Uribe reports that his country, supposedly free of the problems of the 1980s, is prepared to submit a strong bid, just as Brazilian President Luiz Inácio Lula da Silva predicts that the first-class hosting of the fifteenth Pan American Games in Rio in 2007 will strengthen his country's bid to host the 2016 Olympics. Brazil is also hosting the women's World Championship of basketball in 2006.

No doubt the premier multisport events exclusively within the western hemisphere are the Pan American Games. Again encouraged by the IOC, especially at the 1932 Los Angeles Olympics, the original plan was to start the games in Argentina in 1942, but as with the Olympics and soccer Mundial, World War II disrupted the schedule. With the Olympics resuming in London in 1948 (eight Latin American countries won medals) and Brazil hosting the Mundial, won by Uruguay, in 1950, Argentine President Juan D. Perón, an avid sports fan and accomplished fencer, perceived the political benefits in reviving the idea for 1951.

Those inaugural Pan Am Games drew 2,513 athletes from twenty-one nations, competing in nineteen sports. Host Argentina dominated, grabbing 152 medals, including 68 gold. The United States was well behind at 47 gold of 99 total, winning gold in basketball but not, surprisingly, baseball.[31] The 2003 Games, held in Santo Domingo, Dominican Republic, saw 5,500 athletes from forty-two nations compete in thirty-five sports.

Through those fourteen Games, the United States has dominated the medal count (1,651 gold, 3,679 total), Cuba has risen to second (309 gold, 1,658 total), and Canada third (309 and 1,439). Then come Argentina, Brazil, and Mexico, after which there is a noticeable drop to Venezuela, Colombia, Chile, and Puerto Rico.

The fifteenth Pan American Games are scheduled for Rio de Janeiro, Brazil, July 14–29, 2007, and should again draw some 5,500 athletes from forty-two countries, playing the twenty-eight Olympic sports plus others, including futsal. For the first time, the Para Pan American Games, the third such competition, will be held at the same site as the regular games; 1,300 athletes and 600 officials are expected in Rio, August 12–19. In October 2011 the Games will play out to the beat of mariachi rather than samba in Guadalajara, Mexico.

Capping Latin America's international hosting may have been the summer Olympic Games held in Mexico City in 1968. In recognition of its apparent stable political environment, its rich blend of indigenous and European cultures, and its status as an emerging economic force, Mexico became the first so-called Third World country to be so honored. Unfortunately, during the weeks before the Games began, student and labor unrest led to repressive government action that culminated in the Massacre at Tlatelolco, where several hundred protestors were killed by army and police.

But the Games and related cultural activities went on, as 5,531 athletes (14 percent female) from 113 countries competed in 182 events. Mexican reactions to the rulings party's brutality would build over the coming decades. However, except for some complaints about the effects of the high altitude, the overall impression of Mexico's administration of the festival was most positive.[32] The major political action during the Games involved black U.S. athletes protesting race relations back home.[33]

In the Anglophone Caribbean, occasional cricket Test Matches and visits by club teams from abroad have served the same purposes: to gain international recognition and to raise popular spirits and loyalty at home. West Indies is scheduled to host the cricket World Cup in 2007.

One visible consequence of hosting international athletic competitions is the construction or renovation of some of Latin America's largest and most famous sporting venues, most still in use. Uruguay inaugurated its Estadio Centenario at the 1930 World Cup, and Brazil its mammoth Maracanã, with capacity for 200,000, in 1950. Guatemala built most of what remain its national sports facilities also in 1950, while Mexico upgraded the stadium at the national university (UNAM) for the 1968 Olympics and raised the Estadio Azteca for the 1970 FIFA Mundial. Hosting has also often stimulated improvements in communications, especially television transmission and global connections.[34]

## SPORTS AND POLITICS

Several of the events described in the preceding section had unquestionable political overtones, some matching even those of the 1968 Mexico Olympics. As noted elsewhere, Mexico's hosting of the first Central American and Caribbean Games in 1926 was aimed at building domestic and international legitimacy. Guatemala's hosting of those same Games in 1950 brought calls for nationalistic support of the populist/reform government of Juan José Arévalo. Cuba's hosting of the 1991 Pan American Games likewise served to lift domestic morale in the midst of a difficult economic period and to show foreigners that Fidel Castro's regime had ability and legitimacy.

Politically charged to an extreme was the 1978 soccer Mundial held in Argentina, by then under the control of the military in heavy pursuit of its *Proceso* or "Dirty War," which ultimately led to an estimated 30,000 deaths. The generals and admirals apparently hoped that the successful conduct of the tournament and, as it turned out, the eventual Argentine victory would cause jubilant Argentines to forget or forgive their excesses and failures. That may have been true for a few weeks, but the Mundial effect dissipated rapidly, and in four years the military tried a seizure of the Falkland/Malvinas Islands as another diversion, also ultimately a disaster.[35]

But the links between sports and politics go far beyond hosting international competitions. Carlos Salvador Bilardo, coach of Argentina's World Cup winning team in 1986, notes that soccer has always been inextricably linked with politics, and Ariel Scher concludes that "the political-sporting history of Argentina is, in some sense, the history of learning to use sport as a political resource."[36]

As noted, Juan Perón sought political benefits from sponsoring the 1951 Pan Am Games. He also hoped to boost his popularity by tying himself to such national sports heroes as Juan Manuel Fangio (auto racing) and José María "El Mono" Gatica (boxing), by organizing sports competitions for students—the Eva Perón Games—and by channeling funds to select soccer clubs. But Perón was not unique among Argentine presidents before or after, including Carlos Menem (1989–99), who delighted in donning the national soccer team shirt and playing a vigorous game before the cameras.[37]

Leaders in other countries have also used sporting events and personalities to boast their political status. The military in Brazil, which had seized power in 1964, linked its regime to the 1970 Mundial triumph of the national soccer team. Leading candidate and eventual winner Carlos Salinas made public appearances with top-ranked boxer Julio César Chávez during the Mexican presidential campaign of 1988. In Brazil political figures at all levels gain favor by supporting soccer teams and facilities.[38]

Then there is Fidel Castro. Besides participating in games (usually wearing his trademark fatigues), and embracing victorious athletes, he abolished the pre-1959 sports system, including professional sports, and replaced it in 1961 with the Instituto Nacional de Deporte, Educación Física y Recreación (INDER). Those changes, combined with the U.S. embargo and broader boycott, cut Cuba off from many of its traditional sources of sports equipment, technical assistance, and player exchanges. So while they learned to produce much of their own equipment, they sought technical and coaching aid from the Soviet Union and other Eastern Bloc countries with strong sports programs. INDER officials scout and coach children from an early age, guide them to the sports that suit them, separate out those with the greatest potential, send those to special schools for more intense training, and finally move the best up the line to national and international competition. After a short generation Cubans had learned so well that their international performance level was superior and their own coaches so well-prepared that they are being invited to prepare athletes in both developed and less developed countries.

The results are impressive. Not only, as already noted, does Cuba dominate the Central American and Caribbean Games and, among Latin American countries, the Pan Am Games, but at the Summer Olympics since the 1980s it is the top Latin American gold and total medal winner and, based on per capita national population, perhaps number one in the world. At Moscow in 1980, with the United States and others boycotting, Cuba finished sixth, with eight gold and twenty total medals. They skipped Los Angeles (1984) and Seoul (1988) for political reasons, but left Barcelona (1992) in fifth (fourteen gold, thirty-one total), Atlanta (1996) in ninth (nine and twenty-five), Sydney (2000) in eighth (eleven and twenty-nine), and Athens in eleventh (nine and twenty-seven).

But there have been costs. In the decade since about 1995, virtually every time a Cuban sports team travels abroad, especially in the western hemisphere, one or more athletes or coaches defect. Others take the riskier route by sea. Baseball players, such as Liván and Orlando "El Duque" Hernández, are the most publicized, perhaps because of the importance of baseball in Cuba, perhaps because they often get big dollars for signing professional contracts. Consequently, Cuban baseball administrators have banned selected players from the national team for fear they might defect.

## WOMEN IN SPORTS

Undeniably, females in Latin America have not enjoyed the social and economic support historically provided to males. Beginning in the first half of the last century some women did become celebrities for their national athletic achievements and rare international marks. In Argentina: Freestyle swimmer Jeanette Campbell (b. 1918), after numerous domestic victories, became the first Argentine female to compete in the Olympics and the only one at Berlin in 1936, where she took the silver. Jockey Marina Lezcano (b. 1957) won the quadruple crown of horse racing in 1978, though her achievement was belittled by traditional male sportswriters.

But until late in the twentieth century the females who gained ongoing recognition for their international athletic prowess were usually members of successful teams (such as the Peruvian volleyball team that won five silver and two bronze medals at the Pan Am Games between 1959 and 1991) and a few individuals in special situations such as tennis players Maria Bueno (Brazil), Gabriela Sabatini (b. 1970, Argentina),[39] Gigi Fernández (b. 1964, Puerto Rico),[40] and several Cuban revolutionaries such as María Caridad Colón, who threw the javelin for gold at Moscow in 1980, and sprinter Ana Fidelia Quirot, multiple international champ at 400 and 800 meters, a personal favorite of Fidel Castro and vocal defender of the post-1959 Revolutionary system.

In the last twenty years a new generation of female athletes has earned national hero status for their accomplishments in the world, gradually overcoming popular stereotypes, obstacles to their training, and barriers to their acceptance. These include Olympic gold weightlifters (Sydney 2000) María Isabel Urrutia (Colombia) and Soraya Jiménez (Mexico). Thanks to injuries, charges of doping, and the pressures of celebrity the latter retired from competition in June 2004; her apparent heir is Carolina Valencia, who won three golds at the 2006 Central American and Caribbean Games.[41]

Swimmer Georgina Bardach (b. 1983, Argentina) won gold at the 2003 Pan American Games and bronze in the 400-meter individual medley at Athens. Also in 2003 Brazilian Juliana Veloso won bronze in 3-meter springboard, one place ahead of Mexican Laura Sánchez. Two other Mexican women, Paula Espinosa and Jashia Luna, are likewise competing at higher levels.

Another Mexican in the spotlight is Ana Gabriela Guevara (b. 1977, Nogales), a natural athlete who began seriously training for track in 1997. Racing mainly in the 400-meter and 4 × 400 relay, she has won gold at World Championships 2001, Pan American Games 1999 and 2003, Central American and Caribbean Games 2002 and 2006, and Goodwill Games 2001, and silver at the Athens Olympics. She is sophisticated beyond her sport, with a personal Website administered by her cousin Alvaro in Tucson, featuring a tribute song composed by him. At its 2006 Youth Awards, Univision named her Most Electrifying Female Athlete.

Since the early 1990s women have also begun to compete openly in organized soccer, challenging one of the region's most traditional perceptions and barriers to gender equality: that soccer is a man's sport, played in a man's world. Within Latin America few countries have fielded teams in serious competition. Mexico and Argentina have modest aspirations. But only Brazil, also despite inadequate financial support and popular recognition, has shown that it belongs among the elite, finishing second to the United States (2–1 in overtime) at the summer Olympics and fourth at the FIFA Under-19 World Championship both in 2004. The others cannot match the North Americans, Europeans, and Asians.[42]

Although their teams have not always reached the highest levels, individual players have gained wider recognition. Mexicans Maribel Domínguez (b. 1978), whom FIFA denied the right to play for the Celaya men's team with which she had signed a contract, played briefly in WUSA (2003–2004), was ranked seventeenth best footballer in the world in 2004 and led Mexico to the quarterfinals at the 2004 Olympics, and Patricia Pérez played 2004–2005 and just 2005, respectively, with highly regarded FC Barcelona in Spain. Compatriot Monica Gonzales earned All-American honors at Notre Dame. Appropriately, several Brazilians play in Europe: Milene Domingues (b. 1979) in Italy and Marta Vieira da Silva (b. 1986) in Sweden. (Note that Brazilian women, like the men, frequently go by just one name.)

Perhaps indicative of the reluctance to grant women equal sports status was the acceptance by the Pan American Games of men's soccer starting in 1951 but not offering women's soccer medal status till 1999. In general, these delays and eventual adjustments are reflections of attitudes and practices in the larger society. Sports may help either to maintain or to change social behavior, but rarely do they follow a path totally distinct from the larger society. Sports, like music, dress, architecture, and even food, do not function in isolation; they are in an almost constant state of interaction. (For women linksters, see the earlier discussion of golf).

It is worth noting that women are not the only athletes to suffer occasional harassment or neglect for breaking certain taboos. Two Mexicans, Raúl González Rodríguez and Daniel Bautista, who won multiple Olympic medals, world championships, and Pan American titles in the 1970s and 1980s, both complained that in their country "walkers" did not receive much respect, press coverage, or financial aid.

## SPORTS PUBLICATIONS AND THE MEDIA

A quick perusal of newsstands and bookstore magazine racks in any Latin American city reveals an impressive range of periodicals devoted to sports. Depending on location one can expect to find weekly or monthly publications, in addition to daily newspaper sports sections, reporting on everything mentioned in this essay and more, from archery to water polo. Most are domestically printed, though many are imported; most are in the local language, though some are in English, a few even in French or Italian. Among the best known across the region are Argentina's *El Gráfico,* Brazil's *Placar,* and the United States' *Sports Illustrated,* which is considering a Spanish language edition.

With cable and satellite technology, television transmission of sporting events is almost unlimited. Univision, Televisa, and Rupert Murdoch's complex empire mean that any sporting event anywhere in the world can be viewed anywhere in Latin America.

## LATIN AMERICAN SPORTS IN MUSIC, FILM, AND LANGUAGE

Sports topics and personalities have been the subjects of songs and films across Latin America: Pelé, "El Mono" Gatica, Irineo Leguisamo, Fernando Valenzuela, and Juan Manuel Fangio have appeared in scripts or lyrics. A recent Chilean film, *Barras bravas*, explores the cultural and psychological roots of this youth group violence tied to soccer.

Different writers and scholars have tried to measure the impact of sports vocabulary and images on host languages and speech styles. On one level the concern has been that the use of foreign words or phrases corrupts the dominant idiom. Another focus has been on the way that sports metaphors and analogies have become a part of daily conversation and political discourse.[45]

## SPORTS IN OTHER CULTURAL FORMS

### Writing about Sports

In 1968 Eduardo Galeano—Uruguayan historian, social commentator, and a self-proclaimed "beggar for good soccer"—lamented that, given its sheer joy and its historical significance, soccer in Latin America suffered from a lack of serious writing by both scholars and men of letters: "The bulls had their Hemingway; soccer awaits the great writer who will come to its rescue." To help correct this failing, he compiled a small collection of writings about the game.[43] Thirty years later he published his own commentary on the game he loves, still lamenting the sparseness of good writing as well as the decline of the sport from beauty and creativity too often to duty, industry, and boredom.[44] This last sentiment is echoed by Mexican Rafael Pérez Gay, who decries the beginning of a new era of soccer when efficiency, the cool capability to achieve a determined effect, triumphs over romanticism, that joyous imagination that releases the emotions of the spirit.[46]

Surely Galeano's critique is partially correct: Latin American soccer lacks its great novel. Yet, as Mexican Juan Villoro suggests, it may be that soccer, although it is an affair of words and demands words, carries codified references so wrapped up in the emotions contained in its own epic, tragedy, and comedy that it does not leave much room for an author's inventiveness. Since soccer arrives already narrated, its unpublished mysteries tend to be brief. Novelists, not content to be mirrors, prefer to look elsewhere. By contrast, chroniclers, interested in recounting what has happened, find unending inspiration.[47] In support of this are numerous anthologies of short stories centered on soccer themes: fans, players, goals, the mystique of the soccer ball.[48]

Looking specifically at Brazil, as early as 1978 Milton Pedrosa noted that soccer, the most popular sport of Brazil's national passions, is a topic that, especially after 1940, became a subject of novels, poetry, and painting, though as the central theme it probably does not appear in fictional works as much as might be expected. He offers thirteen prose and poetry selections that feature soccer prominently, plus a list of over fifty Brazilian authors who have written about soccer.[49]

This is not to say that there have been no novels, even good (though not great) ones, built around soccer themes. Renowned Peruvian Mario Vargas Llosa has soccer function as the principal means of socialization for 11-year-old boys in a middle-class school.[50] Another Peruvian, Isaac Goldemberg in *Play by Play,* considers soccer as a way for individuals and countries to gain recognition and status. Argentine humorist-cartoonist Roberto Fontanarrosa weaves his novel of intrigue around soccer. Fernando Niembro and Julio Llinás attribute the problems faced by Diego Maradona and the Colombian team at the 1994 World Cup (held in the United States) to a CIA conspiracy. Even retired star Pelé is the nominal coauthor of a murder mystery related to soccer.

Other sports have also been the subject of much good Latin American literature, injected into the works of some of the most acclaimed authors. Argentine Julio Cortázar focuses on boxing, as does Mexican playwright Vicente Leñero, both noting the beauty and pain of the sport. Chilean Antonio Skármeta uses soccer in one story but tennis in another to highlight the emotional crises often confronting youth. The always pensive Jorge Luis Borges finds solace in chess (which is also regarded as a sport in Latin America). Argentine Osvaldo Soriano, though an avid fan of soccer and the San Lorenzo de Almagro club, also uses boxing to display human brutality. Nicaraguan Sergio Ramírez comments on political and family issues in baseball settings. Peruvian Abelardo Sánchez León, who has also written about soccer and volleyball, uses swimming to raise questions about the meaning of life and love.[51] And, as noted, C. L. R. James's portrayal of Anglo-Caribbean cricket, though not a work of fiction, is an intellectual and literary masterpiece.

A few North American fiction writers have likewise composed around Latin American sports themes. As two examples, Mark Winegardner looks at Mexican culture and nationalism through the events and personalities surrounding the Mexican League's attempted upgrade in 1946,[52] and Tim Wendel looks at the Cuban Revolution and Fidel Castro's alleged baseball skills.[53]

# RESOURCE GUIDE

## PRINT SOURCES

The endnotes of this chapter contain numerous citations that lead to materials regarding Latin American sports themes and personalities. The following titles offer additional options.

Alabarces, Pablo, ed. *Hinchadas.* Buenos Aires: Prometeo Libros, 2005. Fans and fandom.
Arbena, Joseph L., comp. *An Annotated Bibliography of Latin American Sport: Pre-Conquest to the Present.* Westport, CT: Greenwood Press, 1989. Cites 1379 titles, mainly in English, Spanish, and Portuguese.
———, comp. *Latin American Sport: An Annotated Bibliography, 1988–1998.* Westport, CT: Greenwood Press, 1999. Cites 1,098 titles mainly in English, Spanish, and Portuguese.
Arroyo, Eduardo. *"Panama" Al Brown, 1902–1951.* Paris: Editions Jean-Claude Lattes, 1962. The rise and sad decline of a Latino boxer; typical of others of his era.
Bjarkman, Peter C. *Baseball with a Latin Beat: A History of the Latin American Game.* Jefferson, NC: McFarland Press, 1994. Focuses on Latino players in the United States. Lots of stats.
Burns, Jimmy. *Hand of God: The Life of Diego Maradona.* London: Bloomsbury, 1996. Rather sensationalist, but a good introduction.
Burton, Richard D. E. *Afro-Creole: Power, Opposition, and Play in the Caribbean.* Ithaca, NY: Cornell University Press, 1997. Lays out provocative theoretical framework for understanding the tension between control and resistance through play/sports.
Mangan, J. A., and Lamartine P. DaCosta, eds. *Sport in Latin America.* London: Frank Cass, 2002. Nine essays on aspects of modern sports in Latin America.
Maradona, Diego. *El Diego: The Autobiography of the World's Greatest Footballing Genius.* London: Yellow Jersey Press, 2005.
Mason, Tony. *Passion of the People? Football in South America.* London: Verso, 1995. Author's British bias at times shows through.
Mitchell, Timothy. *Blood Sport: A Social History of Spanish Bullfighting.* Philadelphia: University of Pennsylvania Press, 1991. Helpful background to the Latin American corrida.

Mordillo, Guillermo. *Mordillo football*. Barcelona: Lumen & Tusquets, 1981. One of many collections of cartoons related to soccer; this one in honor of Pelé. The cartoonist is Argentine. Want a laugh? Check his Website, http://www.mordillo.com.

Morelli, Liliana. *Mujeres deportistas*. Buenos Aires: Editorial Planeta, 1990. Sketches of 17 female Argentine athletes and the obstacles they overcame to achieve success.

Pelé. *Pelé: My Life and the Beautiful Game*. Garden City, NJ: Doubleday, 1977.

Porter. David L., ed. *Latino and African American Athletes Today: A Biographical Dictionary*. Westport, CT: Greenwood Press, 2004.

Regalado, Samuel O. *Viva Baseball! Latin Major Leaguers and Their Special Hunger*. Urbana: University of Illinois Press, 1998. Why Latinos are so driven to play MLB and who has succeeded.

"Suggested Readings." Pp. 233–241 in Joseph L. Arbena and David G. LaFrance (eds.), *Sport in Latin America and the Caribbean*. Wilmington, DE: Scholarly Resources, 2002. Overlaps with two Arbena bibliographies, but contains additional titles; only in English.

## WEBSITES

As noted above, virtually every sport in every country has its own Website and almost every team and every athlete can be found by a search engine such as Google or Ask. A few of the principal ones that in turn can lead to others include:

*CaribbeanCricket.com*. http://www.caribbeancricket.com. Get into West Indies cricket.

*EFDeportes.com*. http://www.efdeportes.com. Administered in Argentina, includes articles about sports and physical education across all of Latin America; also covers conferences and new publications. Issue no. 100 distributed in September 2006.

Fédération Internationale de Football Association. *Fifa.com*. http://fifa.com. History, organization, activities of the world's governing body of soccer; data on World Cups past and future.

INDER. *Sitio Oficial del Organismo Central I.N.D.E.R.* http://www.inder.co.cu. Site of the Cuban sports and recreation institute.

International Olympic Committee (IOC). http://www.olympic.org. Provides access to National Olympic Committees and International Sports Federations.

*Latin Basket*. http://www.latinbasket.com. This site and the next provide entry to basketball leagues, tournaments, and other activities across the hemisphere.

Latino Baseball Players Website. http://www.latino-mlb-players.com/. Even more direct line than MLB's site to Latin American big league players.

Major League Baseball. http://www.mlb.com. Through MLB's site, you can gain access to international competitions and other leagues.

*OCESA*. http://www.desafiocorona.com. One entry into NASCAR in Mexico.

*The Official Formula 1 Website*. http://www.formula1.com. Search for Latin American Formula One drivers and races.

World Boxing Council. http://www.wbcboxing.com. One of the leadings sanctioning bodies. Others can be found by entering names in search engine.

# NOTES

1. For technical studies of the game, see Vernon L. Scarborough and David R. Wilcox, eds., *The Mesoamerican Ballgame* (Tucson: University of Arizona Press, 1991). For a brief popular description of a surviving form of the game, see John Fox, "Students of the Game," *Smithsonian* 37.1 (2006, April): 110–117.

2. Román Piña Chan, *Games and Sport in Old Mexico* (Leipzig: Edition Leipzig, 1969).

3. Richard V. McGehee, "The 100 Kilometer Tarahumara Race, 1926," *Track & Field Quarterly Review* 93.2 (1993, Summer): 60–61.

4. Veerle van Mele and Roland Renson, *Traditional Games in South America* (Schorndorf, Germany: Verlag Karl Hofmann, 1992).

5. C. L. R. James, *Beyond a Boundary* (London: Stanley Paul & Co., 1963). Some observers consider this analysis by a renowned Trinidadian scholar and essayist the best social history of any sport ever written.

6. Allen Guttmann, *From Ritual to Record: The Nature of Modern Sports* (New York: Columbia University Press, 1978).

7. Allen Guttmann, *Games and Empires: Modern Sports and Cultural Imperialism* (New York: Columbia University Press, 1994).

8. Ibid., and Wolf Krämer-Mandeau, "Gymnastics Systems and Turnverein Movement in Latin America," in *Turnen and Sport: The Cross-Cultural Exchange*, edited by Roland Naul (New York: Waxmann Münster, 1991), pp. 21–49.

9. In Mexico and countries around the Caribbean, *futbol* is printed without the accent over the *u*; in most of South America it carries the accent as shown here. There is no change in pronunciation.

10. Eduardo P. Archetti, *Masculinities: Football, Polo, and the Tango in Argentina* (Oxford: Berg, 1999). More directly focused is Archetti's article "El potrero y el pibe: territorio y pertenencia en el imaginario del fútbol argentino," *Nueva Sociedad* 154 (1998, March–April): 101–119.

11. For a good general introduction to soccer's history, see Bill Murray, *The World's Game: A History of Soccer* (Urbana: University of Illinois Press, 1996).

12. Surveys suggest that Flamengo has the largest fan base of any Brazilian club.

13. In some Latin American countries universities, functioning as businesses, sponsor soccer teams. These are strictly professional, as are the players, and are not part of extra-curricular student activities.

14. Two of the most comprehensive and reliable among the numerous books by journalists and academics are Roberto González Echevarría, *The Pride of Havana: A History of Cuban Baseball* (New York: Oxford University Press, 1999) and Peter Bjarkman, *A History of Cuban Baseball, 1864–2006* (Jefferson, NC: McFarland Press, 2007).

15. Alan M. Klein, *Sugarball: The American Game, the Dominican Dream* (New Haven, CT: Yale University Press, 1991).

16. For one case of alleged abuse, see Arturo J. Marcano Guevara and David P. Fidler, *Stealing Lives: The Globalization of Baseball and the Tragic Story of Alexis Quiroz* (Bloomington: Indiana University Press, 2002). The same authors summarize their critique of MLB's treatment of Latino recruits in "Baseball's Exploitation of Latin Talent," *NACLA Report on the Americas* 37.5 (2004, March–April).

17. David Maraniss, *Clemente: The Passion and Grace of Baseball's Last Hero* (New York: Simon & Schuster, 2006).

18. Michael Manley, *A History of West Indies Cricket* (rev. ed.; London: André Deutsch, 1990).

19. Keith A. P. Sandiford, "Apocalypse? The Rise and Fall of the West Indies," pp. 82–98 in Boria Majumdar and J. A. Mangan, eds., *Cricketing Cultures in Conflict: World Cup 2003* (London: Routledge, 2004).

20. For basketball's rise in the Anglophone Caribbean, see two books by Jay R. and Joan D. Mandle: *Grass Roots Commitment: Basketball and Society in Trinidad and Tobago* (Parkersburg, IA: Caribbean Books, 1988) and *Caribbean Hoops: The Development of West Indian Basketball* (Langhorne, PA: Gordon and Breach, 1994).

21. Daniel Frescó, *Manu: el cielo con las manos* (Buenos Aires: Aguilar, 2005); Jack McCallum, "How to Own Your Own Country," *Sports Illustrated* (October 27, 2003), 78.

22. Biographies are available in English for Fangio, Fittipaldi, Senna, and Montoya.

23. Luis Amador de Gama, ed., *Historia gráfica del fútbol americano en México, I: 1936–1945* (México, D.F.: Olmeca Impresiones Finas, 1982); Mario Longoria, *Athletes Remembered. Mexicano/Latino Professional Football Players, 1929–1970* (Tempe, AZ: Bilingual Press/Editorial Bilingüe, 1997).

24. William H. Beezley, *Judas at the Jockey Club and Other Episodes of Porfirian Mexico* (Lincoln: University of Nebraska Press, 1987).

25. Rafael Duque Naranjo, *Los escarabajos de la Vuelta a Colombia* (Bogotá: Editorial Oveja Negra, 1984); Parmenio Medina Pérez, *Veintiún años de la Vuelta a Costa Rica* (San José: Editorial Costa Rica, 1986).
26. Arturo Combe Ayala, *La magia del toreo a caballo* (México, D.F.: Olé-Me-xhic-co Editores, 1994).
27. Kathleen M. Sands, *Charrería Mexicana: An Equestrian Folk Tradition* (Tucson: University of Arizona Press, 1993).
28. A magnificently illustrated book with some useful text is Alfonso Morales Carillo et al., eds., *Lucha Libre: Masked Superstars of Mexican Wrestling* (New York: D.A.P., 2005).
29. The promotion of Mexican involvement in national and international sports activities as a means to better Mexico's image and stimulate its economic and social modernization paralleled a similar push for the tourist industry; see Dina Berger, *The Development of Mexico's Tourist Industry: Pyramids By Day, Martinis By Night* (New York: Palgrave Macmillan, 2006).
30. For political reasons Cuba did not participate in the 2002 games held in El Salvador, leaving the door open to easy Mexican medal dominance.
31. Steven Olderr, *The Pan American Games: A Statistical History, 1951–1999/Los Juegos Panamericanos: Una historia estadística, 1951–1999* (bilingual edition; Jefferson, NC: McFarland & Co., 2003).
32. Joseph L. Arbena, "Mexico City 1968," in *Encyclopedia of the Modern Olympic Movement*, edited by John E. Findling and Kimberly D. Pelle (Westport, CT: Greenwood Press, 2004), pp. 175–83.
33. Amy Bass, *Not the Triumph but the Struggle: The 1968 Olympics and the Making of the Black Athlete* (Minneapolis: University of Minnesota Press, 2002).
34. Mexico hosted the Olympics in 1968, the soccer Mundial in 1970, and the volleyball World Championships in 1974, and with each event there was an upgrade in communications technology, domestic or international.
35. Abel Gilbert and Miguel Vitagliano, *El terror y la gloria: la vida, el fútbol y la política en la Argentina del Mundial'78* (Buenos Aires: Editorial Norma, 1998).
36. Ariel Scher, *La patria deportista: cien años de política y deporte* (Buenos Aires: Planeta, 1996).
37. Ibid., for an informative summary of the connection between modern sports and Argentine presidents as well as "Che" Guevara.
38. Alex Bellos, *Futebol: The Brazilian Way of Life* (New York: Bloomsbury, 2002).
39. Sabatini won the U.S. Open in 1990 and was elected to the International Hall of Fame in 2006; since retiring she has run a successful women's perfume business.
40. Fernández was a singles and doubles NCAA All-American at Clemson University in 1982–1983 and won doubles gold medals at the 1992 and 1996 Olympics. She won 17 Grand Slam doubles titles, retired in 1997, and was named Puerto Rico's Female Athlete of the Century in 1999.
41. Joseph L. Arbena, "In Search of the Latin American Female Athlete," in *Sport in Latin America and the Caribbean*, edited by Joseph L. Arbena and David G. LaFrance (Wilmington, DE: Scholarly Resources, 2002), pp. 219–32.
42. A somewhat humorous commentary on women and soccer in Argentina is found in María Rita Figueira, *¡Sí, sí, señoras! El fútbol y las mujeres* (Buenos Aires: Editorial Sudamericana, 2002). An older study of Brazilian soccer culture is Janet Lever, *Soccer Madness: Brazil's Passion for the World's Most Popular Sport* (Prospect Heights, IL: Waveland Press, 1995; reissue, with new Preface, of 1983 publication).
43. Eduardo Galeano, ed., *Su majestad el fútbol* (Montevideo: Arca Editorial, 1968).
44. Eduardo Galeano, *Soccer in Sun and Shadow*, translated by Mark Fried (2d ed., New York: Verso, 2003 [1st ed., 1998]).
45. Joseph L. Arbena, "Sports Language, Cultural Imperialism, and the Anti-Imperialist Critique in Latin America," *Studies In Latin American Popular Culture* 14 (1995): 129–41.
46. Rafael Pérez Gay, *Sonido local: piezas y pases de futbol* (México, D.F.: Ediciones Cal y Arena, 2006), p. 53.
47. Juan Villoro, *Dios es redondo* (México, D.F.: Editorial Planeta, 2006), pp. 20–21.
48. Eighteen Argentine examples of this mix of soccer and fiction are found in Roberto Fontanarrosa, ed., *Cuentos de fútbol argentino* (Buenos Aires: Alfaguara, 1997). A former starting member of the Argentine national soccer team turned author, Jorge Valdano edited two volumes comprising forty-seven stories about soccer, including works by such renowned writers as Mario

Benedetti, Manuel Rivas, Augusto Roa Bastos, Osvaldo Soriano, Alvaro Cepeda Samudio, Humberto Costantini, and Vicente Verdú; see *Cuentos de fútbol* (Madrid: Alfaguara, 1995) and *Cuentos de fútbol 2* (Madrid: Alfaguara, 1998). More recently the Uruguayan ambassador in Italy, an author and news reporter, published eight of his soccer short stories in Carlos Albin, *Colgado del travesaño* (Montevideo: Ediciones Santillana, 2006). Also, Juan José Reyes and Ignacio Trejo Fuentes, eds., *Hambre de gol: crónicas y estampas del futbol* (México, D.F.: Cal y Arena, 1998).

49. Milton Pedroza [*sic,*], "Presencia del fútbol en la literature brasileña," *Revista de Cultura Brasileña* 46 (1978, June): 53–88.

50. Mario Vargas Llosa, *Los cachorros* (Barcelona: Lumen, 1967).

51. See entries in the two bibliographies edited by Arbena listed in the Resource Guide. Also check Arbena, "Sport and Sport Themes in Latin American Literature: A Sampler," *Arete: The Journal of Sport Literature* V.1 (1987, Fall): 143–59.

52. Mark Winegardner, *The Veracruz Blues* (New York: Viking, 1996).

53. Tim Wendel, *Castro's Curveball* (New York: Ballantine Books, 1999).

# THEATER AND PERFORMANCE

KRISTEN McCLEARY

Theater and performance were essential aspects of the cultural fabric of Latin America preceding the arrival of Europeans in 1492. For indigenous Latin Americans, theatrical traditions were inextricable aspects of their religious practices. With the arrival of the Europeans, theater was extricated from the holistic worldview of the Native Americans and became used as a tool of colonialism: Spaniards and Portuguese used theater as one way in which they could meld indigenous beliefs into a Christian framework. Contemporary popular theater and performance in the Americas has evolved along two trajectories: (1) live-action theater that tends to follow European or Western entertainment traditions and (2) festivals, celebrated from a few days to a month, which retain religious underpinnings of Catholic, African, and Native American beliefs. What signifies "popular" aspects of these traditions, however, varies dramatically depending upon national context and historical era.

Popular theater often merges with commercial theater in urban capital cities, a few of which maintained regular theatrical circuits (Buenos Aires, São Paulo, Rio de Janeiro, Santiago, Lima, and Mexico City) throughout much of the twentieth century and into the current century. What is "popular" in these locations can often be measured in numerical terms based on the price range of plays and attendance rates. Popular theater in capital cities has historically been viewed as any stage entertainment that is not opera or lyrical theater, the preferred entertainment forms of the bourgeoisie and/or elite classes. As a result, "popular" genres here range from musical-revue theater to light comic opera to burlesque to stage hits from the United States and Europe. Currently, a great deal of Latin American performance art embraces these "low" forms of theater to explore social and political issues ranging from sexuality to the impact of an authoritarian government.

What is most commonly defined in Latin America as "popular" theater, however, emerged in the 1960s and 1970s as a form of political resistance and empowerment. Referred to as "New Theater" or "Popular Theater," this tradition emerged after the 1959 Cuban Revolution to address a "new" proletariat and peasant audience. This theater, in general, is designed to advance and support the interests of socially marginalized groups—Latin America's majority poor population, who tend to live in the area's rural regions. Augusto Boal (b. 1931) is the most famous practitioner of this tradition of theater; he defined its goals, objectives, and methods in his internationally influential book, *Theatre of the Oppressed* (1979). In Boal's view, theater could easily play a large social role in the world by embracing a nonhierarchical format that included close ties to the popular classes through community participation. This grassroots theater draws from daily life themes that impact the community in which it is performed. Plays chosen to be performed often have political themes. Actors, stage technicians, and directors are amateurs. Audiences engage in dialogue with the actors. The production of a play is not about entertainment as much as it is about educating and empowering those members of society who are politically, economically, and socially disenfranchised. Many of these performances take place outside of regular theater venues and on temporary stages in the work spaces of the community members, including factories and agricultural fields. This form of popular theater is linked to numerous community organizations, which often sponsor public outreach in the form of social networking through theater festivals.

In general the popular theater described above developed on a grassroots level, without governmental support. A strong tradition of state-organized popular theater has existed in those Latin American countries that, either through the bullet or the ballot box, have chosen leftist-leaning or outright socialist governments. The postrevolutionary eras in Nicaragua (1979) and Cuba (1959), for example, resulted in the rise of governments that placed cultural dissemination at the center of the tools they used to transform society, emphasizing community-based but government-sponsored theatrical productions. Populist governments in many Latin American countries fomented theatrical activities in order to promote literacy, general education, and political awareness among the poorer social sectors.

Popular theater has also been a means by which intellectuals, scholars, and artists voiced their dissent from the military dictatorships that threatened much of South America in the 1970s and 1980s. Here, popular theater developed out of independent theater to merge with leftist political movements in the urban centers and with religious festivals and traditions in the rural and/or more indigenous areas of the region. Theater provided one of the most consistent forms of and forums for resistance during the years of authoritarian regimes.

Popular performance art in Latin America can be seen in the numerous annual festivals that take place in largely nonurban and non-Europeanized regions. In general, performance art differs from the more traditional stage theater productions in that it disregards boundaries between the arts, blending together music, theater, and dance. Performance art in popular festivals has been one of the most important ways in which indigenous and African traditions have been kept alive in the region. These festivals, however, are also living examples of the syncretic relationship that has taken place for over five hundred years as people from Africa, Europe, and the Americas have interacted, exchanged, modified, and invented new cultural traditions. Religious festivals continue to be one of the most prominent forms of popular performance in the Americas.

Carnival is the most notable incarnation of these popular festivals. Originally a Catholic festival, carnival lasted from three to five days prior to the forty days of Lent that precede Easter. Since historically Lent for many was a time of self-sacrifice and self-reflection, often involving the forgoing of certain carnal pleasures such as eating red meat, the days before the start of Lent focused on indulging the desires that one soon would have to give up. Over time, carnival has evolved dramatically in Latin America and takes on different shapes in each of the countries where it is celebrated. In countries like Mexico and Peru, carnival has been absorbed into pre-Columbian indigenous festivals, while in other countries, like Brazil and Cuba, popular carnival celebrations reflect African cultural traditions. While carnival celebrations have evolved over the years in each of these countries, their persistence in the face of numerous attempts to restrict non-European elements shows a remarkable legacy of cultural resistance, transformation, and adaptation.

## ARGENTINA

Argentina (population 40 million) has an extremely rich popular theater tradition even though it was dominated by foreign plays and acting troupes until the early twentieth century. To this day, Argentina has more theatrical activity than any other Latin American nation. The most Europeanized of all Latin American nations, Argentina supports a popular theater not related to "ethnic" theater but rather to theater that reaches across social class lines. Many of its popular formats are related to European theater. For example, at the end of the nineteenth century, the most widely attended form of theatrical entertainment was the Spanish zarzuela (a light comic opera or operetta specific to Spain) performed by singers, dancers, and actors from Spain. Spanish acting troupes traveled extensively throughout Latin America, with an especially strong presence in Buenos Aires, the capital city, which was home to a large number of Spanish immigrants. The zarzuelas were performed in hourly sections, much like movies arc today, so that theaters could accommodate several audiences a night and even schedule some matinees. Zarzuelas were known to be a cheap, affordable, and lively entertainment that greatly appealed to the city's working and middle classes especially because they were affordable. The popularity of this entertainment cut across social class lines as well, and many members of the elite also attended zarzuelas.

The dominance of Spanish entertainment fare in Buenos Aires inadvertently resulted in a burgeoning sense of national identity on the part of *criollo* (native born) audiences, actors, and writers. Indeed, it was inevitable that over time *porteños* (inhabitants of the city of Buenos Aires) would demand entertainment fare that reflected their own habitat rather than that of Madrid, including plays performed by actors who used Argentine accents and manners. For a time, out of the culture of the zarzuela performances, there appeared a hybrid form of play that combined the general short format of the zarzuela with events transformed to specific Argentine settings. In addition to these kinds of plays, theatrical activity in Buenos Aires ranged from European companies at the city's elite opera houses to a variety of popular performances in inexpensive theaters, including circus acts, puppet shows, and vaudeville performances.

### Creole Circus and Gaucho Dramas in Argentina

Argentina also boasted a rich tradition of outdoor and rural circus performances, which included plays in addition to horseback riding, acrobatics, juggling, and storytelling. One of the biggest hits of the circus circuit was the gaucho drama *Juan Moreira*, written by Eduardo Gutierrez. First published as a serial in the newspaper *La Patria Argentina* between 1879 and 1880, spoken dialogue was added to the play in 1886, and it became a hit when it was performed by the Podestá family, who were well-known circus performers. José Podestá, a comic actor from Argentina's most famous acting family, personified an Italian immigrant, Cocoliche, who spoke his lines in a comedic blend of Spanish and Italian. Since then, the term "cocoliche" has referred to Italian immigrants who speak an Italianized Spanish. Although the character is comedic, he also represents the sympathetic, hard-working immigrant who was embraced in Argentina.

Most native-born Argentine actors began in the circus. For example, the Podestá family had come to prominence in Argentina as circus performers. Before playing in *Moreira*, José had risen to fame in Buenos Aires playing the famous Pepino the clown, a hugely successful solo act. In addition to the Podestá family, there were many other circus performers in Argentina, including the Carlo brothers and Alejandro Scotti. These performers traveled throughout the interior of Argentina but also entertained audiences from the stages of

Buenos Aires—a few of which had removable floors to accommodate performers on horseback. Circus performances included a wide variety of entertainments—acrobatic acts, tricks on horseback, pantomimes, plays, and short vaudeville pieces—in addition to acts of magic and even séances. The most famous clown in Buenos Aires was from England. Frank Brown (1860–1943) appealed to a broader audience than did the rural circus performers, but his performances mainly targeted children. He drew the wrath of the city's elite when he tried to erect a circus tent in downtown Buenos Aires for the nation's centennial celebration in 1910. Despite the fact that the city had given Brown a permit to put his tent there, a group of upper-class young men burned down the structure before the celebrations opened. They thought the tent was an eyesore that introduced the remnants of a rural Buenos Aires into an event that many elites hoped would convince the world that the nation's capital was as European and urban as any of those on the continent across the Atlantic.

Out of the disparate elements of rural circus dramas and urban zarzuelas, a new national form of popular theater emerged known as the *sainete*. These short comedic plays were less dependent on musical numbers than were zarzuelas, although music continued to be an important component of the plays. Sainetes were increasingly penned by native-born authors, almost always second-generation immigrant men. They dealt with everyday themes and character types generated by the rapidly changing urban milieu of Buenos Aires where, by 1910, every three of four adults were foreign born. The plays involved stereotypical relationships among Italian landlords, English businessmen, Middle Eastern peddlers, Jewish traders, and *Gallegos*—the name which, in theory, referred to Spaniards from Galicia but was actually a term which in popular usage referred to any Spanish immigrant. Sainetes depicted everyday life concerns and characters, including a rich depiction of the daily milieu of the lower classes in early twentieth-century Buenos Aires.

The most emblematic sainete play is by Alberto Vacarezza (1886–1959) titled *Tu cuna fue un conventillo* [Your Cradle Was a Conventillo]. Vacarezza's plays were often set in *conventillos*, or tenement apartments of the immigrants, where action unfolded in the building's central patio. He wrote over sixty sainetes in his life. The popular Argentine tango was introduced into sainetes in 1918 with José González Castillo (1885–1937) and Alberto T. Weisbach's (1883–1929) play *Los dientes del perro* [The Teeth of the Dog]. From that time on, tangos were frequently included in sainetes.

While sainetes usually were comedies of errors, a group of playwrights evolved out of this genre who tackled heavier themes relating to issues of social justice of the time. Among these was the playwright Nemesio Trejo (1862–1916), whose body of work addressed many of the hot topics of the day, including the tenement strike of 1907: *Los Inquilinos* [The Tenants] showed the rift between the city's elite, who claimed that Buenos Aires was the "Paris" of Latin America, and the city's recently arrived immigrants, who faced unsavory and unsafe living conditions in many of the city's centrally located conventillos. Rent increases resulted in a tenant strike as occupants fought for a 30 percent decrease in rents. Trejo's play opened during the height of the strike in October 1907, reflecting the rapidity with which many playwrights were able to respond and comment on the current events of the day.

Florencio Sanchez (born in Uruguay) was a social anarchist influenced by works of Tolstoy, Ibsen, and Chekhov. Much of his work was political and confrontational, causing his work to be banned from time to time. One play, *La gente honesta* [Honest People] (1902), was a comedy about the customs of Rosario, Argentina's second largest city; it was banned at the last minute since it ridiculed public figures, one of the few areas where censorship was in place at the time. Not all of Sanchez's plays, however, were overtly political. His most famous play, *M'hijo el dotor* [My son, the doctor] (1903), told the story of a young man from Montevideo,

Uruguay, who changes his habits after several years in the city of Montevideo. He returns home to the countryside and alienates family and friends by having picked up city manners.

Other famous playwrights of the era included Roberto J. Payro (1867–1928), who examined the problems of a rapidly transforming society in *Marco Severi* (1905) and *El Triunfo de los otros* (1907), and Gregorio de Laferrère, who was a master of farce and caricatures of popular types. *Jettatore* (1904), *Locos de verano* (1905), and *Bajo la garra* (1906) are among his most famous works.

The 1920s were an era when musical revue theater and sainetes continued to draw in large crowds, and popular theater merged with commercial theater at the box office as critics disparaged the quality of plays being performed to full houses. The 1930 military coup, which brought the dictator José Félix Uriburu to power, occurred at a time when theater was in decline. Nonetheless, an important independent theater group, Teatro Popular, was formed in 1930 by Leónidas Barletta. The primary goals of the group were to combat the star system of actors that prevailed at the time, and to reclaim theater from the clutches of profit-driven producers. Teatro Popular, thus, introduced independent theater to Argentina.

Theater did not flourish under the populist regime of Juan Domingo Perón during the 1940s and 1950s. Perón focused his attention on electronic forms of mass media such as radio, motion pictures, and music. Theater became very active once again in the 1960s when a number of independent theatrical groups emerged. For example, Libre Teatro Libre was a theatrical collective that included both Chilean and Argentine members and was part of the New Popular Theater movement that emerged in the 1960s and 1970s.

## Theater under Dictatorships

During the Dirty War (1976–1982), when a military junta brutally ruled the country and roughly 30,000 Argentine citizens disappeared, theater practitioners faced a number of difficulties including the loss of financial support on the one hand, and the threat of disappearing and/or being arrested for staging any spectacles that were deemed to be critical of the government. As a result, many playwrights and actors left the country. Most went into self-imposed exile in Spain or Mexico. Rodolfo Walsh and Fernando Urondo were "disappeared," a status that entered the lexicon denoting the fact that people whom the military government deemed as "subversive" would often disappear at night, never to be heard from again. In addition to threats to theater performers, some theater houses were even burned down during this era of cultural, political, and social repression. The years under the military dictatorship clearly took their toll on theater: attendance rates dropped from 2.9 million to 2.2 million the year after the military coup. Most of the drop in attendance occurred in those theaters that produced Argentine texts and experimental works. However, it is notable that people continued to attend theater even during the years of military clampdown, which attests to the "staple" role theater continued to play in the Argentine cultural diet.

Playwrights, however, found it too dangerous to address the regime explicitly during the height of the dictatorship in the 1970s. Beginning in the 1980s, however, a cultural thaw took place that allowed for some theater groups to begin producing plays. The most important of these was the Teatro Abierto (Open Theater) movement (1981–85), which brought together over 100 playwrights, actors, and groups to overtly respond to the declining military dictatorship. Many of Argentina's best known playwrights had been excluded from government-sponsored theater earlier in this era, including Osvaldo Dragún (1929–99), Roberto Cossa (b. 1934), and Griselda Gambaro (b. 1928). Teatro Abierto brought together these and other playwrights, actors, and technicians who had been blacklisted under the dictatorship. Arising during the decline of the military era, Teatro Abierto produced political plays that challenged the military government about its responsibility for the disappearance of thousands of Argentine civilians. Gambaro's play *Decir sí* [Saying Yes] (1981), for example, takes place in a barbershop where the barber and client play reverse roles and play out scenes of aggression and sadism. At the end, the barber slits the client's throat; this action operates as a condemnation of the severe violence of the military regime. Diana Raznovich was another important playwright from Teatro Abierto. Her 1981 play *El desconcierto* [Disconcerted] explores the role of the audience in keeping silent during the military regime. The theater where it was to be staged was burned to the ground on opening night. Osvaldo Dragún's (b. 1929) work is well known throughout Latin America and the United States. His most-performed plays, including *Historias para ser contadas* [Stories to Be Told] (1957), *Historia de mi esquina* [My Corner's Story] (1957), and *Historias con cárcel* [Jail Tales] (1973), mix local color with song, dialogue, and pantomime. His plays deal with both social and political themes, including, for example, *La peste viene de Melos* [The Plague Comes from Melos] (1956), which recounts the story of the CIA-backed coup against Guatemala's democratically elected president, Jacobo Arbenz, in 1954.

After democracy returned to Argentina in 1983, there was a resurgence in noncommercial theater with several new theatrical movements, including *teatro joven* (youth theater) and *teatro underground*. Many of these new theater groups provided multimedia presentations combining theater with music, buffoonery, improvisation, puppetry, dance, and video games. Even today, these theater groups operate at unusual hours (often the first show begins at 1:00 AM or later, reflecting the nocturnal cultural mores of Argentina), and in unusual venues such as subways, nightclubs, warehouses, and on the streets.

The Mothers and Grandmothers of the Plaza de Mayo, political groups that arose during the military dictatorship to protest the death and disappearance of their loved ones, have also used theater to continue their political work. The Grandmothers, for example, organized Theatre for Identity, which put on a production entitled *About Doubt* in 2000 that showed the dilemma of young people adopted during the Dirty War who do not know if they are being raised by their biological parents or by the people responsible for "disappearing" their parents. Eduardo Fanego directed the production, which was performed in commercial and fringe theaters. In 2001 the Grandmothers of the Plaza de Mayo brought together forty-one playwrights to write plays about identity. These were performed by hundreds of actors and presented over three months in thirteen different theaters. This and other types of experimental theater have continued to grow in Buenos Aires. Danile Veronese is the most established contemporary playwright and director, known for his plays *Monteverdi, Método Bélico*, and *Mujeres sueñan caballos* [Women Dream of Horses]. Since 2000 a number of small theaters have been opened by companies that run cooperatives. Some of these spaces hold no more than twenty audience members and are decidedly noncommercial. Theater has also benefited from the Festival of the Southern Cone, in the province of Córdoba, which began with the return of democracy in 1984. The festival joined the International Festival of Buenos Aires in 1999 and 2001.

## Performance

Indeed, the military dictatorship expanded the notion of "performance" and gave rise to performances that were and are strictly political in nature. One of the most prominent of these is known as the *escrache* (to expose), acts of public shaming developed by political activists who were opposed to granting immunity to members of the security apparatus and the military who had participated in crimes against humanity during the Dirty War. Escraches came to prominence with the group H.I.J.O.S. (Children of the Disappeared). Their main goal is to draw attention to the perpetrators of crimes; they do so by stressing public performances, which include singing and chanting slogans, dancing, and parading. Escraches are meticulously planned out and involve hundreds of people. Demonstrations include theatrical elements involving stage settings using giant puppets and huge photos of the disappeared. Before an escrache takes place, H.I.J.O.S. members canvas the neighborhood that is the focus of their campaign where specific perpetrators live and work. They go door-to-door informing people about the crimes perpetrated by their neighbors, and they also hand out flyers and post photos of the perpetrators in public locales.

More recently, street performances have merged with the political dramas that unfolded when the economy crashed in Argentina in 2001. *Piqueteros* (picketers, literally referring to the unemployed poor of Argentina) first emerged in June 1996 in the small town of Cutral-Có, Neuquén Province, when workers were laid off by the state oil entity, and their neighbors blocked National Route 22, a key road linking the city to Patagonia. The numbers of piqueteros exploded after 2001, and they have emerged as important political actors for the working classes in Argentina. Known publicly for their ability to set up devastating road blocks as forms of protest, piqueteros also create a strong social network for Argentina's increasingly large poor population. Often arising out of *villas misérias* (poor neighborhoods), piqueteros have developed strategies to share their meager resources by pooling their incomes, communally preparing food, sharing childcare duties, and organizing political actions.

## De la Guarda

This avant-garde performance group came together at the end of 1994 as a merger between the street performance group La Organización Negra and the vanguard dance group El Descueva. These groups emerged at the end of the military government in 1983 and focused on performances that explored and reenacted the violence of the military regime. De la Guarda achieved national and international success in 1990s with its show *Período Villa, Villa*. The show involved a series of aerial acts and broke the bounds of traditional spectator-ship with acrobatics, the play of light and shadow, and the breaking away from traditional stage boundaries. Over the heads of a standing audience, performers swoop on long tethers, yelling as they whiz by. The performers run up the walls, dance in midair, or swing down, acting out images of pursuit, teamwork, and domination to loud rock music, evoking the feel of a mosh pit. The show debuted in Argentina, where it ran for six months in a temporary tent, and it has played London, Las Vegas, Athens, and New York. The troupe deliberately makes its show popular by trying to reach large audiences. It performed a second show, *Doma*, in 1998 in the Velódromo of Buenos Aires to 70,000 people, and the group has some-times offered free shows. De la Guarda is considered to be at the international forefront of redefining performance and theater with its blend of dance, acrobatics, music, and light show.

## Carnival in Argentina

At the end of the nineteenth century, Argentina had a carnival that rivaled that of Brazil. Unfortunately, carnival in Buenos Aires continued to embrace the practice of throwing objects onto passersby, which at times resulted in injuries and interfered with the daily comings and goings of the city dwellers who worked in the downtown business districts.

As a result, city council members began to overregulate theater and zealously enforce the regulations. Eventually, carnival evolved from a popular street activity into one that was designed more for the upper and middle classes: events took place inside theaters and required entrance fees. Many Porteños began to travel to Uruguay to celebrate carnival, combining their summer vacations with carnival celebrations that remained more popular on the other side of the Río de la Plata. Buenos Aires remains a unique example of how carnival practices have faded away in certain nations. While a small carnival celebration persisted throughout the twentieth century, the military government (1976–83) banned public holidays during carnival. Noting that important economic revenues were generated by carnival's ability to attract tourists, the city council of Buenos Aires recently has tried to rejuvenate the celebrations by sponsoring *murgas* (carnival groups) and by establishing a two-day holiday for city employees during carnival. Up to 800,000 people have enjoyed carnival in recent years, with 75,000 people participating in murgas.

## URUGUAY

Much of theatrical practice in Uruguay has merged with that of its neighbor, Argentina, since the body of water that separates the two nations, the Rio de la Plata, has been easily traversed over the years by playwrights, actors, and audience members. As a result, much of the same theatrical activity that took place in Buenos Aires also occurred in Montevideo, Uruguay's capital city. Playwright Florencio Sánchez (1875–1910), for example, who found a great deal of success in Argentina in the early twentieth century, was Uruguayan by birth.

In the early twentieth century, modernization and European immigration transformed the Rio de la Plata region and heralded a golden era of comedic popular theater. Most of this, however, flourished in Buenos Aires, which had a population about four times that of Montevideo. In addition to Sánchez, Uruguayan playwrights such as Carlos Mauricio Pacheco, Alberto Weisbach, and Alfredo Duhau generated one-act hits for the stages of Buenos Aires. Between 1920 and 1947, many theaters were shut down in Montevideo as the city turned toward movies. The city did not have a large enough population to sustain its own theatrical activity, and a number of actors and playwrights moved to Buenos Aires, contributing greatly to the still-booming theatrical era there. Theater began to boom again in Uruguay after 1947, when Juan Domingo Perón's nationalist policies prevented Uruguayans from continuing theatrical work in Argentina. Renewed efforts were made to create a unique Uruguayan theater. One of the most well-known of these groups was Teatro El Galpón (Warehouse Theater), co-founded by director Atahualpa del Cioppo (1904–93), and Nelly Goitiño, among others. The group was committed to linking theater with the community and to promoting noncommercial theater. They created collaborative theater and even went door-to-door asking for financial support so they would not be beholden to the government or commercial interests. Del Cioppo has received the most credit for El Galpón's formation since he was responsible for the company's collaborative commitment. By the end of the 1950s, over twenty independent theater groups existed. The umbrella group FUTI had its own portable tent and used it for performances that housed over 600 people. More than 700,000 people attended theater annually in 1959.

Unfortunately, the boom of theatrical productions was greatly diminished as a result of the military dictatorship (1973–83). During these years, many well-known actors and playwrights were censored and particular works were prohibited. The government's view that it was waging war with subversive elements of society forced most public performances into private spaces to avoid conflict. In 1979 censorship was imposed on all theaters in Uruguay.

The bureaucratic requirements of cultural control virtually strangled most popular productions. The military closed Teatro El Galpón, for example, in 1976. Members of the group, however, were at the forefront of organizing resistance to the dictatorship, continuing to organize performances even while in exile.

During the last decade, Uruguay has suffered from high unemployment rates and an economic downturn, which have taken their toll on popular theater practices, and theaters have struggled to find government financing and audience support. The Comedia Nacional (National Theater) is the country's only fully subsidized theatrical company. Since 2000, about 40 to 50 theatrical shows are performed in Montevideo each weekend, including both classical and popular theatrical productions. The government launched a Socio Espectacular (Show Partnership) system in 1998 to try to buttress falling attendance rates by offering discounts to films, football games, and theaters. Popular and independent theater has continued to be performed. Nelly Goitiño continues to direct Teatro El Galpón and staged Ariel Mastandrea's *El hermano olvidado* [The Forgotten Brother] in 2001. Puerto Luna is a younger theater group that performed Antonio André's play *El Cerdo* [The Pig] in the same year. As in Argentina, experimental theater has been the most current trend, especially with younger theatrical practitioners. New theater directors such as Mariana Percovich, Alberto Rivero, Ruben Coletto, and María Dodera dispense with traditional and textually based theater to play with the use of space, discursive speech, and linear timelines to explore subconscious impulses and new means of expressions. Roberto Suárez's *Una cita con Caligula: crónica de una conspiración* [An Appointment with Caligula: Chronicle of a Conspiracy] (1999), for example, uses excessive bloodshed and features bodies that appear torn and abused to challenge the relationship between actors and audience members and to explore the impact of violence and power struggles in contemporary society. Mariana Percovich's *Cenizas en el corazón* [Ashes in the Heart] (1999) takes a more light-hearted approach to experimental theater as it plays with the image of Uruguay's famed tango singer, Carlos Gardel. Just as with much of contemporary theater, it was performed in a nontraditional theatrical space, the newly renovated Cervantes Hotel restaurant. In general, contemporary performances have created a new audience of young people, who support their favorite directors and actors, and have developed in stark contrast to the traditional theater that tends to stage realistic dramas.

## Carnival in Uruguay

For such a small country, Uruguay has a very popular and well-attended annual carnival celebration, a tradition that dates back to the nineteenth century. Carnival in Uruguay draws far more visitors than it does in neighboring Argentina, albeit far less than its other neighbor, Brazil. In 1987, for example, 2.8 million tickets were sold to carnival in comparison to 400,000 theater tickets and 1.5 million movie tickets. Carnival in Uruguay is known for the large number of murgas and *tablados*, or stages that are erected in neighborhoods where murgas perform. Murgas are carnival groups affiliated with particular neighborhoods. Most of their songs and dances reflect the customs of their particular locales. Each murga consists of between fourteen and seventeen members. They perform for about a half an hour on stages where they often compete for prizes with other groups. Lyrics to murga songs mix comedy with social and political criticism. *Candombes*, groups linked historically to masked dancers, are also popular during carnival here. Candombes are rooted in African drumming and dancing rituals that date back to the arrival of the first Afro-Uruguayans in about 1750. As elsewhere, carnival in Uruguay generates a great deal of economic activity in the region, and many people devote months of work to carnival preparations. The state finances some prizes and oversees parades. Carnival is largest in Montevideo, the capital city, consisting of a variety of events that take place throughout the city, organized by neighborhoods, and receiving both state and corporate sponsorship. Categories of carnival include murgas, comedy shows, *comparsas* (musical groups) of *negros lubolos* (black-face performances), review shows, magicians, and skits. Carnival is celebrated over most of the month of February and sometimes part of March.

## Puppet Theater in Uruguay

Puppet theater has also been an important form of popular expression in Uruguay. Groups of independent puppeteers arose in the 1940s, attempting popular education campaigns through the use of theater. Puppets took many forms, including the giant-headed puppets that appeared during carnival. Jaime Urrutia (1919–85) was one of the most famous puppeteers of the era. Puppeteers continued to merge their entertainment with that of popular education in the 1960s, and puppet shows were performed in streets, during public meetings, and in independent theaters. This growth came to a standstill during the military dictatorship, and one puppeteer and teacher, Gustavo Sosa Zerpa, was even arrested and imprisoned. In 1985, after the return of democracy, El Galpón opened Uruguay's only school of puppetry.

## CHILE

The majority of Chileans (population 16 million) are in the central valley where Santiago, the capital city, is located. Much of the nation's theatrical traditions have focused on this urban center. Armando Moock (1894–1942) is Chile's most famous playwright even though most of his theatrical production centered in Buenos Aires, Argentina, where he moved in 1918. His most famous play, *Pueblecito* (1918), was performed over 2,000 times. It was a comedy that depicted cultural differences between urban and rural dwellers in Chile, providing a detailed view of life in Chile's small towns.

Popular theater thrived in Chile during the 1960s and early 1970s as a result of the presidencies of Eduardo Frei (1964–70) and Salvador Allende (1970–73), who were both interested in integrating the rural and urban poor into the national fabric. Theater became a way to achieve these goals. In the years before the military coup of 1973, Chile witnessed a great deal of growth in amateur theater groups arising out of protest movements in the late 1960s and fostered by Allende's Popular Unity government. Universities played a central role in teaching and supporting drama. The Union of Actors, Cinema, Theater, TV, and Radio (SIDARTE), founded in 1968, worked closely with community groups to perform plays in working class districts and in rural areas. Theater themes focused on those related to the audience, including alcoholism, gender and family relations, and poverty. Before the 1973 coup, a number of universities organized with amateur theater groups and other popular organizations to further increase and promote grassroots theater.

The advent of the military regime under General Augusto Pinochet in 1973 resulted in a "cultural blackout." As a result of theater's close ties with universities that were centers of leftist opposition to Pinochet, many intellectuals and writers left the country in exile. Some, however, stayed behind and used theater as a means to defy Pinochet's regime (1973–89). The coup wiped out amateur theater since Pinochet saw theaters as organizations that had supported Allende, the president who had died during the military coup. Popular theatrical activity focused on independent theater groups. For example, Taller de Creación Teatral de la Universidad Católica (ICTUS), which was founded in 1959, emerged as one of the most active theatrical groups during the era of military rule. It faced challenges from the Pinochet government, including censorship and withdrawal of financial support. One of the most well-known plays produced by the group was written by Sergio Vodanocic: *Cuántos años tiene un día?* [How Many Years Does a Day Have?] (1978). Another important independent theatrical group of the era was Teatro La Feria, which presented its first work, *Hojas de Parra* (1977), in a circus tent, deliberately recalling earlier eras of popular theater. Most of these groups used theater to open up alternative spaces for dialogue during the years of dictatorship.

Egon Wolf (b. 1926) was a playwright who produced anti-bourgeoisie plays in the 1960s. One of his most well-known plays, *Los invasores* [The Invaders] tells the story of an industrialist who dreams that his house has been invaded by a group of poor people. Once inside, they organize a socialist government. In the play, dream and reality soon blend together, and the play operates as a warning to the middle classes that their comfortable way of life comes at the expense of many of the nation's poor.

During the era of the Pinochet dictatorship, most popular theater was political in nature. After Pinochet stepped down from power in 1989, theater opened up to become more experimental. In the 1990s, several groups tried to recreate Chilean theater by developing a new national culture in open spaces, with large audiences, in a festival-like atmosphere. Andrés del Bosque explored circus techniques and created *Las siete vidas del Tony Caluga* [The Seven Lives of Tony Caluga] as part of this new movement. New generations began to explore emotions and intimacy through theater as they emphasized performance art over textually based performances.

The government also returned to supporting some theatrical productions, which allowed theater to grow in the post-Pinochet era. In recent years, theater productions have drawn anywhere from 3,000 to 60,000 audience members, depending on the nature of the entertainment. Students and young people are frequent supporters of theater and are able to purchase tickets at reduced prices. Amateur or grassroots theater also grew throughout the 1980s and 1990s, and about 250 such groups work with school theaters to promote theater performances. The Escuela de Teatro de la Universidad Católica hosts a national theater festival every year held outside during the country's summer month of January.

# CARIBBEAN

## Cuba

Cuba (population 12 million) had a rich tradition of politically ideological theater before the revolution. Theater was one of the main forms of entertainment for all social classes dating back to the colonial era.

Most theatrical activities were dominated by acting troupes from Spain throughout the nineteenth century. In addition to the fact that Cuba remained a colony of Spain until 1898, the island also received a large wave of immigration from Spain into the mid- to late nineteenth century. Spanish acting troupes and performers were so dominant that in 1915 an organization was formed to promote the work of Cuban playwrights in the repertoire of foreign acting companies.

One of the first truly popular formats of theatrical entertainment at the time was the zarzuela (Spanish light opera), a form of musical theater still popular in Cuba. The musical format quickly began to absorb and reflect Cuban-related themes. For example, Cuban zarzuelas typically had plots that dealt with racial issues, featuring both Spanish immigrants and members of the Afro-Cuban population. The very popular zarzuela *Cecilia Valdés* (1932), written by Gonzálo Roig (1890–1970) and based on Cirilo Villaverde's 1882 novel, provided a particularly Cuban interpretation of the exploration of race relations between a Cuban planter family and their slaves. This zarzuela also dealt with an interracial relationship between a *mulata* and a young man of the elite class. It remains one of the most popular zarzuelas in Cuba. Indeed, zarzuelas were more popular here than in any other Latin American country. Many artists left Cuba for the United States during the era of the revolution and formed local associations that continued to present zarzuelas in cities with large Cuban populations.

Another form of popular comedic tradition in Cuba is known as the *Bufo Cubano,* a version of the minstrel show. This type of show, originating in the United States, had traveled to Cuba at the end of the nineteenth century. Spanish revues imitated the format of these shows with whites in blackface playing Afro-Cubans and singing well-known songs. *Bufos Habaneros* were set in Cuba's capital and featured black characters from a milieu specific to Havana's working classes. The *teatro bufo* became famous for developing music and dance that combined Spanish and "African" rhythms, such as the *danzón.* This genre of theater also developed a number of stock theater characters such as the mulata and the *negrito.* These figures were originally developed as racist depictions of Afro-Cubans, but they came eventually to symbolize the nation's racial mixture. Raimundo Cabrera (1852–1923) was a popular writer of the bufo genre. His *From the Park to the Moon* ran for over 100 performances in Havana. Federico Villoch (1866–1954) was another famous Cuban playwright from this period.

After Cuba's independence in 1898, Cuban theater began to embrace nationalistic themes, contained native songs and dances, and were performed by Cuban actors. Much of this theater was comedic and generally popular in that its audience members cut across all social classes. Cuban "vernacular" theater reached its peak of popularity in the 1920s with the performances of the Alhambra Theater Repertory Company.

In the 1940s popular theater was promoted under the development of the Teatro-Biblioteca del Pueblo (People's Theater Library). The 1940s witnessed an explosion of organizations that focused on grassroots theater productions in local high schools and vocational schools. In the 1950s a number of new playhouses were established for the middle classes and performed European and U.S. dramas of the era. However, Cuban artists also opened a number of dramatic workshops in the provinces of Camagüey and Oriente. In 1954 the Cuban Ministry of Education supported performances of plays at popular prices in the auditorium of the Museum of Fine Arts. Cuban theater was also very receptive to the theater of Bertolt Brecht in the 1950s with many troupes from East Germany giving seminars about his theatrical theories in Cuba.

The 1959 Cuban Revolution dramatically impacted the shape of Cuban theater. Art and culture were placed at the forefront of the new government's attempts to foster social change throughout the nation. To do so, it established a National Theater of Cuba in 1959; this included a Department of Folklore to promote Cuban regional and national arts in contrast to entertainment spectacles, which had previously been targeted to a foreign, largely U.S., audience. Many of the plays and performances that were staged drew from specific Afro-Cuban culture such as *santería* and other Afro-Cuban religions. The performers were not professionally trained. Many of them were from the lower classes, whose cultural practices had been hidden, not celebrated, by the state until this time. By the mid-1960s, however, the government's strident move toward more orthodox Marxism ended its support of Afro-Cuban religious traditions: the government issued controls and restrictions on santería that were eventually lifted in the 1970s.

The government also instituted the Consejo Nacional de Cultura (National Council of Culture), which was used to promote the revolutionary goals of Fidel Castro's government.

The cultural reorganization included the organization of amateurs in labor centers or schools all over the island in order to reach as many people from the popular social sectors as possible. In addition, the School of Art Instructors was developed, which had theater as a component. The mission of an art instructor was to develop interest in the arts among Cubans who did not have a formal education and to promote the work of amateur artistic and theatrical groups. In 1962 a group was founded to promote lyrical theater, including zarzuelas. The government also supported the revival of Cuban vernacular plays from the early part of the century.

Close governmental supervision of theater, however, backfired, and there was a decline in theatrical production beginning in 1963, largely as a result of the declining numbers of audience members: the middle classes were leaving or had already left the island, and the popular classes were not yet sufficiently convinced of the entertainment merits of the "educational" theater promoted by the government. The revolution's early years, nonetheless, promoted the work of Cuban playwrights.

A group of practitioners began to perform and work in the Escambray, a region in the center of the island that had been one of the counterrevolutionary holdouts until 1965. Sergio Corrieri (b. 1938) formed Teatro Escambray (1968) in an effort to take theater out of culturally rich Havana and into the countryside where theater was not commonly found. In addition, this was an attempt to put theater to use as a weapon of the revolution by selecting an area of resistance to Castro's new society. They developed a "discover-action-debate" formula that allowed the audience to transform the play as it was taking place. One play, *La vitrina*, was performed from 1970 until 1978. It always ended with a debate with the audience that led to revisions in the play. Teatro Escambray became popular with researchers, writers, artists, and critics, and its productions were increasingly performed at international festivals. The group built theaters and cultural centers where rural workers organized regional theater groups. They worked closely with the Communist Party and with mass organizations, including the Committee for the Defense of the Revolution and the Cuban Women's Federation, to organize communities and explore the issues that most affected local inhabitants.

## Carnival and Festival in Cuba

Cuba also has a strong carnival tradition, which has become intricately linked with both the revolutionary state of Fidel Castro and with Afro-Cubans. Carnival, an annual celebration originating in Europe and held in the days preceding Lent, developed strong African traditions in Cuba. Carnival was widely celebrated in the 1800s, with groups from various African nations competing in drumming ceremonies and dancing contests. Carnival also allowed the popular classes a moment to turn the tables on the upper classes—by pelting them with water, rotten eggs, and even small stones. As happened elsewhere in Latin America, many regulations in the nineteenth and early twentieth centuries tried to prohibit celebrations closely linked to the African-descended population and the popular classes. In the twentieth century, carnival was increasingly regulated and was relegated to being an indoor activity affordable only by the upper classes of society.

Carnival often focuses on the crowning of a carnival king and queen—a practice dating back to the early eighteenth century among Afro-Cubans but with roots that extend all the way to the sixteenth century. These celebrations are reflective of the blending of African and European religious traditions and derive from the role Afro-Cubans played in festivities honoring Catholic saints. Afro-Cubans had organized in *cabildos de nación*, a phrase that originally denoted the organization of African slaves by their presumed locations of origin but eventually came to refer to festive groups. In addition to carnival, a number of popular religious ceremonies have served to retain African elements that contributed to an Afro-Cuban identity, despite many attempts to prohibit the practice of African-derived cultural expressions. For example, Afro-Cuban carnival celebrations in the mid-twentieth century originated with the historic Day of the Kings holiday, which was celebrated as early as January 6, 1573. The celebration coincided with Epiphany as celebrated by the Catholic Church. This day was historically a "free" day for African slaves: they were allowed to celebrate the holiday on the streets, where they embraced African cultural practices, including dance, costume, and music. Between 1880 and 1940, a series of governmental regulations were established in an attempt to banish all traces of Afro-Cuban traditions from carnival, Day of the Kings, and other popular festivals as the Cuban elite, like elites in Latin America at large, embraced a cultural ideology of "whitening" that stressed European over non-European traditions and peoples. Since the 1940s there has been more governmental recognition and promotion of Afro-Cuban traditions, and carnival celebrations currently flourish in Cuba, especially in the provinces of Santiago de Cuba and Camagüey.

Women play an important role in carnival celebrations, especially in Santiago de Cuba. One of Santiago's most famous carnival groups, La Placita, has existed since 1950. Each year, the group chooses a topical theme for carnival celebration: for example, *American Tourism* in 1950, *Campesinos* [Peasants] in 1952, and *Cuban Fantasy* in the year of the revolution. Since the revolution, La Placita has devoted its carnival theme to some aspect of the revolution, including the *Stalin Fantasia* theme in 1960. Carnival groups deliberately develop Afro-Caribbean and nationalistic themes in an attempt to rescue the national folklore and popular culture of the nonelite.

## Performance

Cuban-born Coco Fusco (b. 1960) is one of the most well-known performance artists of Latin American heritage. Much of her performance art deals with issues that impact Latinos/Latinas in the United States. Her work explores issues such as gender, globalization, and intercultural theory and practice. Fusco is well known for her promotion of performance arts internationally as well as through academic publications. She has collaborated with Guillermo Gómez Peña on the 1992 performance piece *Two Undiscovered Amerindians Visit the West,* performed during the 500-year anniversary of Columbus's "discovery" of the Americas. The two also developed and performed *Mexacane International* (1994–95), which was performed in shopping malls and presented a fake agency looking to export "foreign talent." Both pieces were controversial in that many people observing them did not see them as performances but as real events. Fusco is an associate professor in the Visual Arts Division of Columbia University's School of the Arts, and most of her work is centered in New York even though it deals with Latin American themes.

## Colombia and Venezuela

Popular theater in Colombia merged with that of Enrique Buenaventura (b. 1925) who, with his group Teatro Experimental de Cali (TEC), introduced the New Theater method in 1955. Drawing from the ideas that the Brazilian theater practitioner Augusto Boal had developed, TEC developed a unique relationship between the theater, performers, and the local working class, and included the audience in a critical role as participants and spectators who, as a result of the grassroots theater productions, have begun to question their relationship

## MASKS

The use of masks in social rituals has a long history in Latin America. Masks played an important role in Aztec ceremonies preceding the arrival of the Europeans, for example. After the conquest, Spanish religious leaders built on pre-Columbian religious festivals to convert the indigenous peoples. Christian morality plays were played out by actors who used the pre-Columbian tradition of performing ceremonies with masks.

Popular festivals, including the tradition of carnival, have generated cottage industries throughout Latin America that produce the many costumes, musical instruments, and, especially, masks worn for religious ceremonies. Masks are made from a range of materials including papier-mâché and wood which are then painted with bright colors. Other elements, as well, contribute to mask design including leather, wax, clay, cloth, and wired mesh. More recently, manufactured rubber masks have become accepted into Latin American festivals, threatening to damage the artisanal craft-making enterprise.

Masks come in a variety of shapes ranging from human to animal to a combination of the two. In many countries, carnival includes devil dances and these are some of the most spectacular masks crafted. In Mexico, the jaguar is a dominant figure, and is often an ambivalent deity capable of being simultaneously good and evil. Many other animals common to Mexican iconography include bats, lizards, serpents, and snakes. In Puerto Rico, *vejigante* (a word that derives from *vejiga* or bladder; *vejigante* signifies monsters that roam the streets during carnival) masks and costumes represent both animal and devils who take on playful, or prankish, characteristics, and whose actions are free of socially-restrictive traditions.

Symbolically, the mask means many different things depending on the context. Masks figuratively help the wearers hide their own identities, while at the same time the individual, by putting on a mask, can fuse his identity with that of the community. Sometimes dancers who have no masks put on dark glasses, which indicate that the person is no longer his or her everyday self.[1]

to the larger society. While concentrating on the working class districts of Cali, Buenaventura also reached out to the middle classes. The group's plays usually tackled overtly political themes. The play *Soldados* [The Soldiers] (1966) by Carlos Reyes (b. 1941), for example, is based on a novel about a strike on Colombian banana plantations in 1928. The play was performed to different audiences, including workers, peasants, and university students, who discussed the play and helped to shape it into its final form. This play was transformed over the years as a result of audience feedback, and it was eventually performed under the title *La Denuncia* [Denunciation] (1973), which depicted a polarized world between the oppressors, represented by the Colombian government and the United Fruit Company, and the oppressed, represented by the workers. The TEC disbanded in 1990. Santiago García's (b. 1929) company, La Candelaria, continued to promote New Theater. The play *El paso* (1990), for example, deals with problems such as drug-related violence that faced Colombia in the late twentieth century.

Colombia also has a rich festival tradition commemorating important religious events. Indigenous festivals in Colombia include performance rituals as well as traditional forms of music. Two of the most well-known festivals are the Sedan Chair Parade and the Founders' Parade, where various trades are remembered and represented, including woodcutter, muleteer, farmer, and domestic worker. Colombia's most famous carnival celebration takes place in Barranquilla. The festival has been deemed a "Masterpiece of the Oral and Intangible Heritage of Humanity" by UNESCO. Located on the Caribbean coast and at the mouth of the country's largest river, Barranquilla was historically Colombia's busiest trading center. Each year during the last four days before Lent, carnival reflects the blending of indigenous, African, and European traditions through dance, musical genres, and folk instruments. Carnival music is generally performed by drum ensembles or by groups playing a variety of wind instruments. Carnival is also full of handcrafted objects, including floats, costumes, head ornaments, and animal masks. Groups of extravagantly masqueraded dancers, actors, singers, and instrumentalists delight crowds with theatrical and musical performances based on historical as well as current events. Contemporary political life and figures are satirized through mocking speeches and song lyrics that lend a burlesque atmosphere to the carnival. The Colombian government proclaimed the carnival of Barranquilla a "National Cultural Heritage" in 2001 in order to help preserve the celebration's folk elements, which were being lost as a result of the commercialization of the festival. Street performers who study popular art forms, like carnival celebrations, perform in the country's most popular carnivals. In addition to the carnival in Barranquilla, the Carnival of the Devil in Riosucio and the Black and White Carnival in Pasto are well attended. These actors wear masks and perform on stilts and poles to musical accompaniment. The Papayeras, for example, is a musical group that performs with street theaters such as the Teatro Taller de Colombia and *P'a lo que sea* (For Whatever). The Teatro Taller was formed in 1972 by Jorge Vargas and Mario Matallana to promote street theater. They sponsored a week-long symposium on street theater in Bogotá, the nation's capital, in 1968.

Colombia also boasts a number of secular festivals in the form of beauty pageants, which have become almost as popular there as the Super Bowl is in the United States. On average one new beauty queen is crowned somewhere in Colombia each week. The national beauty pageant is followed as closely as a major sporting event; most citizens become aware of the main candidates, who frequently appear in Colombian newspapers. Colombian novelist Gabriel García Márquez's story "The Funerals of Mama Grande" lists a few of the more than 300 beauty contests that are held in the country: "There is a queen for mango, for pumpkin, for the green pumpkin, for the green banana, for the yellow banana, for the cassava just to mention a few."[2]

Theater has faced many obstacles in Venezuela, and it has struggled to develop a strong presence there. Most theatrical activity takes place in Caracas, the capital city. The Ateneo de Caracas, founded in 1931, promotes Venezuelan culture, including supporting the work of many theater companies. The Ateneo also sponsored the Caracas International Theater Festival in 1975. El Nuevo Grupo (The New Group) was formed in 1967 by Isaac Chocrón and two other playwrights, Román Chalbaud (b. 1931) and José Ignacio Cabrujas (b. 1937). The group focuses on textual over experimental performances and promotes the works of national authors. Two organizations in Venezuela deal with theater for social change: the Asociación Venezolana de Teatro Popular (Venezuelan Association of Popular Theater) and the Teatro para Obreros (Workers' Theater). In recent years, theater for young people and puppet theater have become especially active areas of production. Puppetry was first introduced to the country by an Italian puppet troupe in 1939. In 1948 the puppet group El Tamborón was founded, and members have organized workshops and classes to develop puppetry throughout the country. Federico Reyna is the best-known puppeteer, whose creations (characters named Juan Bimba, Juan Barrigón, and Calicio) became extremely popular throughout the nation. A national puppet organization was created in the 1970s. One professional theater group, Tilingo, incorporated puppetry into theater performances. The company also organized an International Puppet Play Competition in 1981, which drew over 100 productions from throughout Latin America. Puppetry is commonly taught in Venezuelan schools: children learn how to make puppets and then how to make their creations perform.

Perhaps Venezuela's most popular performance, however, belongs to the tradition of beauty pageants that inundate the nation. The Miss Venezuela contest has been held annually since 1952. The level of competitiveness required for women to make it through the rigorous demands of Venezuela's national contests has resulted in this country having more national beauty contest titles to boast of than anywhere else in the world. The country has had four Miss Universe, five Miss World, and four Miss International winners. A sizeable "beauty industry" has developed here to support the pageants. Young girls may enroll in finishing schools and often take a four-month crash course to prepare for a particular pageant. Sometimes success in beauty has led to success in unexpected areas for Venezuelan women. In 1996, for example, fifteen years after Irene Saez became Miss Universe, she was elected mayor of Chacao, the richest part of Caracas, Venezuela's capital city, with 185,000 residents.

## Brazil

Brazil (population 188 million), the largest Latin American country in terms of geographic territory and population, has a diverse ethnic population and broad geographical spread, both of which have impacted the forms of popular theater and performance that have developed there. In urban areas, for example, popular theater might refer to vaudeville and burlesque shows; in the rural areas, theater more likely relates to religious festival processions. In northeast Brazil, one finds traditions that relate to both an African and an indigenous cultural heritage, while plays and performances in Rio de Janeiro and São Paulo, large urban centers, retain a more European cultural heritage.

Historically, theater has not been at the forefront of Brazil's cultural traditions, despite the fact that European theatrical practices were introduced there upon the arrival of the Jesuits in the sixteenth century. One of the oldest theaters is in Ouro Preto, and some of the first actors on its stage were mulattos, people of mixed African and European descent. In the early 1900s through the 1920s, Brazilian *revista*, or dance-hall theater, was especially popular. Arturo Azevedo (1855–1908) was one of the best-known playwrights of this tradition. These plays focused on contemporary themes and issues faced by ordinary citizens in Brazil. They also focused on the culture clash between urban and rural life. Similar to vaudeville, revista theater comprised a variety of sketches, songs, and dance numbers. Moreira Sampaio (1851–91) was another important author of revistas and comedies from that period.

Theater in Brazil was dominated by foreign acting troupes until the early twentieth century. It was not until the 1930s and 1940s that a unique Brazilian popular theater, based on local customs, began to develop. Martins Pena (1815–48) is considered the father of Brazilian comic theater. Comedies of manners, which focused on the development of stock characters (stupid Portuguese immigrants, pretentious mulattos/mulattas who mixed in French with their Portuguese, and screaming mothers-in-law, for example), dominated in the early twentieth century. The acting troupe Procópio Ferreira was one of the best known in this genre.

Theater was notably absent in the country's nationalist-inspired Modern Art Week of 1922. In the 1930s, Getúlio Vargas's government, known as the New State, actively censored Brazilian stage plays, and theater began taking up themes that could be seen as subtly criticizing the government. For example, in 1939 the Olga Delorges Company staged the play

*Tiradentes*, based on the eponymous figure who is the father of Brazilian independence and who symbolizes the struggle against a tyrannical state. Needless to say, theater, popular or otherwise, did not flourish during this decade.

Popular theater became increasingly contrasted with commercial theater in Brazil beginning in the 1940s when the group Teatro do Estudante do Brasil (TEB or Brazilian Student Theater) emerged. Paschoal Carlos Magno formed the group in an attempt to revitalize national theater. Another group, Os Comediantes, followed; this was an amateur organization that was the first to stage Nelson Rodrigues's (1912–80) work *Vestido de Noiva* [Bridal Gown] in 1943, which brought national attention to all involved—many heralded this moment as the beginning of the Brazilian national stage. Os Comediantes transformed Brazilian theater by modernizing acting techniques, giving directors creative control, and doing away with the star system by stressing ensemble productions.

São Paulo began to emerge as the center of theatrical activity in Brazil in the 1950s and 1960s. A number of amateur groups were consolidated under the Teatro Brasileiro de Comédia (TBC), which became nationalized and radicalized in the 1960s. The TBC focused on avant-garde and foreign theater, dismissing the use of the star system to produce ensemble plays. Charges that it was increasingly elitist resulted in the creation of alternative models of theater that were more popular based. From this emerged Augusto Boal's Teatro de Arena, which focused on plays depicting lives of the common people in Brazil. In addition, Teatro de Arena sought to include Brazilian Portuguese and nationally themed texts in its productions. Boal saw theater as a tool to empower marginalized social "actors." The theater structure promoted awareness of one's social situation, and participation did not hinge on an individual's artistic talent.

The rise of Teatro de Arena and the prominence of Augusto Boal were closely linked to the military coup that affected Brazil in 1964. Boal's theater became a powerful independent movement in opposition to the military regime. He developed a new form of theater that emerged out of his experiences living abroad and from his own interest in the theatrical works of Bertolt Brecht. Boal wrote *Theatre of the Oppressed*, the seminal text in nonhierarchical grassroots theater throughout the developing world. This form of theater helped communities to become politically aware and to transform the experiences of the marginalized in Brazil and elsewhere in the world. He was greatly influenced as well by the Brazilian pedagogue Paolo Freire, who also used grassroots educational tools to empower the disenfranchised population. After 1964 Boal's work was restricted and censored. Boal himself became imprisoned and tortured by the military dictatorship for three months in 1971 because of his outspoken criticism of the regime. He went into exile in Argentina and Portugal. Boal's ideas about the empowering nature of theater continue to be taught in over seventy countries.

## *Augusto Boal and* Theatre of the Oppressed

The Brazilian Augusto Boal has been at the forefront of theories about popular theater ever since he published *Theatre of the Oppressed* in 1979. Often referred to as a body of theatrical techniques, Boal's ideas have been innovative in world popular theater for over forty years. The title of his book pays homage to the Brazilian educator Paulo Freire's 1970 book, *The Pedagogy of the Oppressed*, which had reinvented literacy training by emphasizing the importance of consciousness-raising among adult students. Freire's educational techniques were based on the premise that students were adults and required material that matched their own intellectual and reasoning skills. Educational tools were redefined to include items and themes that related specifically to the community and included such instruments as crops, tools, social customs, and traditions.

Augusto Boal adapted Freire's ideas about education by incorporating literacy training with theatrical practices. Boal developed a literacy campaign, *Integral Literacy Operation*, while working for the revolutionary Peruvian government in the 1970s. The goal of the campaign was to eradicate illiteracy in four years. The project was complicated by the fact that most Peruvians they were working with did not speak Spanish as their first language. Indeed, Peruvians spoke over forty dialects of the principal indigenous languages, Aymara and Quechua, in addition to forty-five other languages.

Boal employed theatrical tactics in the campaign. His practices were based on the belief that theater had been co-opted by the elite sectors of society, who then had built a wall between them and their audience members. In Boal's view, the wall should be torn down, and theater should arise from the audience, from the popular sectors of society. He believed that everyone could be an actor and theater practitioner. Boal was jailed in Brazil for his political activities. Once released, he went into exile first in Argentina and then in Europe. Boal returned to Brazil after the end of the military government. He was elected to the city council of Rio de Janeiro in 1992. Boal's theater is revolutionary in the sense that it does not allow spectators to remain passive.

Boal's techniques have been adopted throughout the world. Since 1976 his work has been disseminated largely through his Center for Techniques of Expression in Paris. In Latin America, his influence can be seen most clearly on Nicaragua's Alan Bolt and Colombia's Enrique Buenaventura.

## Rural Brazilian Theater

In contrast to indoor urban theater discussed above, Brazil also has a strong festival tradition of performance, which takes place especially in the "backlands" of the northeast. *Autos*, or medieval Portuguese mystery plays, were transplanted to Brazil by the Portuguese colonizers and used by Jesuits to try to convert Indians into Christians. These dance-dramas persist to the current day. They are usually composed of two parts: the first is a procession in which participants parade through a town or village; the second part is the actual performance of a dramatic narrative. Most of these performances are linked to an important day on the Christian calendar, such as Christmas or Easter.

One of the longest-lasting rituals, *Bumba-meu-boi*, represents a synthesis of Iberian, African, and indigenous traditions. The main action of the play revolves around the death and resurrection of a dancing ox (*boi*)—clearly reminiscent of Christian themes. Usually performed on January 6, the celebration retains elements of native and African traditions that celebrate the death and resurrection of nonhumans. The ox, however, is also symbolic of the economy of rural colonial Brazil, where much life in the hinterlands depended on the curing and selling of hides. At one time, this ritual was attended by all social classes, but now the playing out of Bumba-meu-boi is largely relegated to the working classes and peasants. In the city of Maranhão, the ritual has been commercialized, and its annual performance takes place in a special stadium. Audiences are required to pay, and the performers have become more professional—both signify the ritual's transformation into the broader capitalist economy.

There has been much discussion of the decline of Brazilian theater, in general, with the return of civilian government in 1985. Indeed, theater receives less attention from the foreign press than it had during the era of dictatorship when it was written about as a form of protest and resistance to political oppression. However, a vibrant theatrical movement arose in Brazil in the 1980s and 1990s, and a new generation of directors and producers began to exert total control over their productions. The most well-known figure of this post-modern theatrical movement was Gerald Thomas, whose theater company—opera seca (dry opera)—is centered in Rio de Janeiro. Thomas studied theater in London and was active in Amnesty International; he worked in the Brazilian section that documented human rights abuses during the dictatorship. Thomas returned to Rio in 1985, and he has worked internationally since, becoming a promoter of contemporary Brazilian avant-garde theater. His 1989 play, *Mattogrosso*, received international attention because of the participation of the famous minimalist musical composer Philip Glass.

Rio de Janeiro and São Paulo, Brazil's large southern cities, remain the centers for theatrical activity of all types in the nation. Even in those cities, theater audiences have remained relatively small. In São Paulo, a city of 37 million inhabitants, only 300 productions were staged in 2001, and most had short runs.[3] There has been very little federal subsidizing of cultural events, which has contributed to the lack of resources for theatrical productions. Nonetheless, there continue to be theatrical companies that promote popular theater throughout the nation. One of the most important groups is Grupo Galpão (Warehouse Group), an ensemble based in Belo Horizonte, which has performed at festivals throughout South America and Europe. Galpão's acting style grows out of the popular early-twentieth-century circus and street-theater tradition of rural Brazil. The group is known for its originality, wit, physicality, and highly visual work. Parlapatões, Patifes e Trapalhões (Braggarts, Rogues and Fumblers) also draws on circus techniques and folk traditions in their performances. The Brazilian Comedy Theater has sponsored the group's recent work, which was a series of plays based on the works of Rabelais that opened in 2001. The Teatro União e Olho Vivo (Union Theater and Sharp Eye), which has operated since 1967, is devoted to promoting folk theater; it tours community centers and diverse neighborhoods of São Paulo, performing plays with strong social themes like *João Cândido do Brasil—A revolta da chibata* [João Cândido from Brazil— A Slender Whip Uprising] (2001).

One of the most well-known Brazilian theater festivals takes place each March in Curitiba, capital of the state of Parana and Brazil's seventh largest city. Launched by students in 1992, the festival had become the premiere showcase for new Brazilian theater and performance. The first festival's opening play, Caca Rosset's controversial staging of *A Midsummer Night's Dream*, was previously banned in São Paulo. Festival organizers include Leandro Knopfholz, Cassio Chamecki, and Victor Aronis. The festival provides the most important meeting place for Brazilian theater artists and a growing number of their international colleagues who journey to see the work on display. Contemporary Brazilian theater is dominated by directors, and all the leading directors have participated in the festival: Antunes Filho, Jose Celso, Martinez Correa, Ulysses Cruz, Aderbal Freire Filho, and Enrique Diaz, among others. Grupo Galpão performed *Street of Sorrows* at Curitiba in 1995. The play tells the familiar Passion of Christ story, accompanied by evocative dances and music that mixes Western soundtracks with liturgical hymns. The piece was originally staged in a circus tent.

## Carnival in Brazil

In Brazil, carnival has taken many forms and shifted in size throughout the years. At the turn of the nineteenth century, carnival was often denoted more by the practice of *entrudo*, which consisted of revelers throwing water, rotten eggs, and other objects onto passersby from windows high above city streets. In the twentieth century, carnival in Brazil has been transformed into one of the most well-known festivals in the world. Carnival, however, takes many different shapes throughout the country. Two of the most important destinations for celebrating carnival in the Southern Hemisphere's summer months are Rio de Janeiro and Salvador, Bahia, both former capitals of the nation. Carnival in Brazil has been transformed from a European celebration into one that celebrates and is shaped by its large population of those of African descent. Afro-Brazilians make up about 40 percent of the population. Carnival is also closely linked to the musical form of samba unique to Brazil, which is a musical form that borrows from African rhythms and is also influenced by jazz.

The importance of the samba to carnival in Rio de Janeiro is evident in the name given to the open-air stadium wherein carnival contests take place: the Sambadrome. The origin of carnival in Rio is closely tied to the evolution of the samba—a form of music unique to Brazil that stresses African-based rhythms. The musical form of the samba, common to a popular neighborhood of the city, evolved in the 1920s into a form that was ideal for parading. The first samba school was developed in 1928 in Rio de Janeiro. Soon after, other musicians began to formalize their sambas as well, forming competitive schools of their own. Since then, samba schools have dominated the organizational structure of Rio's carnival. Many samba schools are located in the poorer parts of the city, providing community outreach to neighborhoods that otherwise might not have it. As many as 60,000 people participate in Rio's samba school processions, which take nineteen hours and two nights to cross the 700 yards of the Sambadrome.

Salvador, Bahia, Brazil's first capital, retains one of the most important carnival traditions of the city. Salvador retains a largely Afro-Brazilian population, and its carnival reflects these African cultural traditions. The internationally renowned Brazilian singers Gilberto Gil and Caetano Veloso are from the Bahia area and are integral figures in the carnival celebrations there. This carnival differs from that of Rio de Janeiro, which focuses largely on events in the indoor and regulated Sambadrome. In Salvador, carnival celebrations focus on slow-moving *trio elétricos*, flat-bed trailers that carry performing bands throughout the city. Each trio elétrico carries its own sound equipment and is usually brightly decorated. These vehicles form the nucleus of the *blocos* (carnival groups). Participants pay a fee to belong to a bloco and are visually identified by the use of similar costumes known as *abadá*. Members of a bloco parade inside the roped area that surrounds the trio. Bahian carnival, which emphasizes Afro-Brazilian culture, draws a large international audience that is primarily white and North Atlantic. Bahian carnival has grown greatly over the last few years into a commercial phenomenon that exports carnival music and imports tourists. The leading *bloco afro*, Olodum, even performed a music video with Michael Jackson and Spike Lee. Carnival here has become locally and globally "popular," as folklore has merged with consumerism.

Salvador's carnival celebration has become synonymous with the celebration of Afro-Brazilian culture. For example, the well-known Afro-Brazilian samba group, Ilê Ayê, developed here in 1974 during the military dictatorship as the first bloco afro in Brazil. This group hosts pageants including a "Black is Beautiful" evening when an Afro-Brazilian queen is chosen to preside over carnival. The finalists and the queen wear specially designed outfits that draw from African design traditions, often including cowrie shells that are used for divination in the Afro-Brazilian religion, Candomblé. The blocos afro were created as community associations but have evolved to contain some of the same commercial elements of the blocos. These blocos are often associated with an Orixa, or god, in Candomblé. In general, these groups promote an Afro-Brazilian consciousness. They had begun to contest the commercialization that was taking place with the trio elétrico. Another famous bloco afro,

Olodum, was founded in 1979 as a carnival club for the Pelourinho area in Bahia. The Pelourinho is the central market of the city; it was also a slave market until the end of slavery in Brazil in 1888. Olodum has grown as an organization: in addition to performing during carnival, its group is involved in issues of cultural heritage, art, health, and finance. The group runs a theater company, dance group, and school for local youth; it also publishes a journal. Olodum has about 100 full-time employees and 400–500 band members.

## Paraguay

Popular theater in Paraguay is either theater spoken in Guaraní, the primary indigenous language of the region, or independent, noncommercial theater that began to be developed in the 1960s. In 1964 Oscar Wespel, an Argentine actor and mime, founded the Teatro Popular de Vanguardia (Avant-garde Popular Theater). Most of Paraguay's most well-known independent theater playwrights emerged from this group. Rudi Torga began to change the group's style by producing the work of national authors. In 1970, he founded Teatro Estudio Libre (Free Studio Theater or TEL), which regularly toured the country, promoting popular theater through their repertoire of plays in Guaraní and Spanish. In 1980 the Centro Paraguayo de Teatro (Paraguayan Theater Center) was founded, which promoted theatrical activities of all sorts. In 1989 Lucio Sandoval, Teresita Pesoa, and Fermín Martínez formed the Actores Asociados in an attempt to produce popular theater in Guaraní and Spanish. They produced a number of such plays, including Julio Correa's well-known play *Yvy Yara*, which toured the country. In addition to Guaraní-language productions, other popular forms of theater in Paraguay have merged with musical forms such as the polka, *guaranías* (native music), and the Paraguayan zarzuela.

## CENTRAL AMERICA

Theater has not been at the forefront of cultural development in Central America, a region that encompasses Latin America's poorest countries, many of which were torn by civil wars in the 1980s. In El Salvador (population 7 million) the Spanish-born Edmundo Barbero (1899–1985) promoted theater as head of the national Center of Fine Arts and the director of Teatro Universitario (University Theater) in the 1950s. Barbero is credited with promoting a new generation of writers in El Salvador, including Walter Bénecke (1930–80), Walter Chávez Velasco (b. 1932), and Roberto Armijo (1937–87). Guerrilla groups sponsored theatrical performances during the 1980s, but there was little theatrical expression during the civil war (1980–92). A few theatrical groups have helped encourage theater since the 1980s (Hamlet, Vivencias, Artteatro), and universities continue to promote theater. In 1999 the actress Dorita de Ayala was awarded the National Prize for Culture, which has also helped to invigorate theater here.

National theater in Costa Rica (population 4 million) came of age in the decade of the 1970s. Until then, most theater had been dominated by outside acting companies, which flourished especially during the 1920s and 1930s when dramatic companies from Spain and other parts of Latin America made stops in Costa Rica. In 1970 the government created the Ministry of Culture, Youth, and Sports and began to subsidize national theatrical productions. The country also founded a National Theater Company, two university theater schools, and a national theater workshop during this decade. Independent theater also developed, with the assistance of exiled writers and actors from South America, especially from Uruguay,

Chile, and Argentina. During the 1980s and 1990s, commercial theater predominated here, with shows based on sexual innuendo and comic situations. Contemporary popular theater can best be seen in the rise of small groups of theater enthusiasts that develop noncommercial theater and are self-supporting. Among these groups are Quetzal, Núcleo de Experimentación Teatral (NET or Nucleus of Theatrical Experimentation), and Skene. Rubén Pagura directs Quetzal, a group that puts on one-man shows using a minimalist approach. In 2001 they performed Alonso Alegría's *El cruce sobre el Niágara* [Crossing the Niagara]. NET has presented a number of theater shows outside of traditional theatrical venues in San José. Most theatrical activity takes place in the national capital, San José (population 1 million), which has about twenty theatrical venues. Finally, children's theater is especially rich here, with a number of groups (Contraluz, Giratablas, Ticotíteres) providing entertainment.

## Nicaragua

Nicaragua experienced a theatrical golden age between 1951 and 1978, which corresponded to the development of an improving economy and growing population. A number of experimental theater groups emerged at this time in Managua, the capital city. Among those was Teatro Experimental de Managua, which was attached to the Fine Arts school. During the 1970s many Catholic base communities were developed throughout the country as a result of the Catholic Liberation Theology movement arising out of Vatican II in 1968. These communities included theatrical performances as an important component of their political and religious work. These structures served as the base for a popular theater movement that took root after the ouster of long-term dictator Somoza in 1979.

With the Nicaraguan revolution (1979–90) won by the FSLN, Sandinista leaders promoted dialogue about the use of art in everyday life. Since the 1970s the Sandinistas had used theater as a way to organize and promote their political ideology. The Teatro Estudio Universitarito (TEU) was a student group formed in the 1970s that served as a base for Sandinista cultural work. After the revolution, theater collectives were formed under the Movimiento de Expresión Campesina Artística y Teatral (MECATE). Along with the Association of Cultural Workers (ASTC), this group led a series of workshops that helped mobilize large segments of the population to develop theater performances linked to social empowerment agendas. Alan Bolt developed two theater collectives in 1979, Teyocoyani and Nixtayolero, both drawing from Augusto Boal's ideas of theater as a way to raise the political consciousness of the popular classes. Bolt was a Sandinista in the 1970s, and he used theater to promote social change. He and his group of theater practitioners went to live in the poorest parts of Nicaragua, sharing the people's lifestyle and exploring the reasons for oppression. Bolt's theater movement was only loosely connected to the Asociación Sandinista de Trabajadores de la Cultura (Sandinista Association of Cultural Workers or ASTC) after the triumph of the Sandinista revolution in 1979. He helped to develop theater for use in the extensive National Literacy Campaign that followed. Theater performances stressed local identities and traditional cultures, trying to rescue indigenous traditions as well as value them. He also emphasized exploring the ways in which the colonization process had become accepted and reinforced by those who were colonized. Most of this Communitarian Theater Movement took place on agricultural cooperatives. Plays dealt with a variety of themes, ranging from domestic violence to geopolitical issues. One play, *Juan y su mundo* [Juan and His World] (1986), for example, presented the dilemma of a peasant caught between the Sandinistas and the antirevolutionaries, reflecting current realities that took place during the war against the U.S.-backed Contras. Involvement in theater troupes was widespread:

there were up to 70,000 members of theater brigades during the Sandinista–Contra war that developed out of literacy campaigns in the countryside.

A popular form of theater in Nicaragua has traditionally been the Güegüense theater, a form in which indigenous peoples mock Spanish conquistadors. These satirical narratives account the humorous adventures of a hero, who tricks and outwits his masters. Güegüense drama, as a result, has dialogue that is encoded with double meanings. It also draws upon the indigenous tradition of a trickster. The plays retain strong traces of indigenous culture, including the silent roles of female characters, repetition of dialogue, and the personification of animals through mask wearing. The plays also blend Spanish and Nahuatl languages. During the Somoza dictatorship (1937–79), Güegüense theatrical performances were restricted. After the collapse of the Somoza regime, this popular folkloric tradition was revived.

## Guatemala

Guatemala has not historically had a strong theatrical tradition. Theater began to emerge in the late 1950s, largely as part of the wave of popular theater taking place throughout Latin America that emphasized the consciousness-raising of the region's marginalized citizens. Here, such theater was closely linked to the nation's universities. Rubén Morales Monroy headed the Compañía de Arte Dramático of the Universidad Popular, which has been an important component of national theater. Since 1962 the nation has hosted a Guatemalan Theater Festival linked to the Universidad Popular. Morales Monroy studied theater in Mexico between 1960 and 1961, where he developed a form of theater referred to as "popular realism" that uses theater to recreate the daily life situations of the nation's poor and working classes. His theater company has produced the works of national authors, who develop political themes as well as *costumbrista* theater. These authors include Manuel Galich, Manuel José Arce, Hugo Carrillo, and María del Carmen Escobar. The "Group of Ten" was an important theatrical group that formed in 1971 and produced theater in El Gadem, the only theater devoted exclusively to live performances, between 1972 and 1994.

One of Guatemala's most famous literary authors, Miguel Angel Asturias (1899–1974), known for the novels *El señor presidente* [Señor President] and *Hombres de maiz* [Men of Corn], wrote four plays that explored popular characters and local themes. *Soluna* (1955), for example, combines mystic elements with Mayan religious motifs; it centers on a Chamá Soluna mask, which represents a mythic combination of deities of the Sun and the Moon.

Festivals are an extremely important component of nonurban cultural practices. In Guatemala, an estimated 56 percent of the population is mestizo (mixed European and Native American), and 44 percent are predominantly indigenous. Festivals that link to the indigenous cultural traditions are commonly practiced, including rituals related to the cultivation of maize, which date back to the ancient Mayans of pre-Columbian times. There are also commonly "house feedings" rituals that take place after a house has been build. They contain syncretic elements that combine indigenous traditions with the symbols of Catholicism. The cross frequently used in indigenous communities during the ritual of the sowing of maize has a double meaning: it represents Christ's death, yet it also represents the concept of the four corners of the universe within Mayan belief.

## Mexico

European theatrical traditions began to merge with pre-contact indigenous religious festivals from the moment the Spaniards first conquered Mexico in 1521. Theater became an important tool through which the Spanish conquerors attempted to convert natives to Christianity. Theater appealed to the Nahuas, whose traditional ceremonies shared much in common with European scripted theater.

As elsewhere in much of Latin America, theater in Mexico focused on foreign productions of plays, usually dominated by genres and their actors touring from Spain, notably zarzuelas (Spanish light opera).

At the end of the nineteenth century, popular theater in Mexico City, the primary focus of theatrical activity, included *teatro frívolo* (a type of music hall theater), which included a series of short pieces of entertainment broken up by musical numbers. Urban theater at the end of the nineteenth and early twentieth century was heavily commercialized. *Tanda*, or theater shows performed every hour, kept theaters in Mexico City full from 4:00 PM to 1:00 AM. Theater tickets were often oversold, causing chaos to ensue inside of theaters.

In addition to urban theater, Mexico also had a strong tradition of theater in *carpas*, or tents, usually performed by circus troupes in rural areas, which grew substantially after the Mexican revolution. Canvas tents were mobile theaters that could be easily carried and erected throughout the Mexican countryside. Circus performances drew from European notions of circus life, including the use of white-faced, painted clowns, but they soon incorporated Mexican entertainment forms as well. One of the most well-known international figures of Mexican film and theater, Mario Moreno (1911–93), better known by the sobriquet Cantínflas, arose out of the carpa tradition of theater. Moreno's best-known character arose accidentally. Asked to fill in for the theater's announcer at the last minute, Moreno mumbled and garbled his speech so much that someone referred to it as "cantínflas," a nonsense word. The verb *cantinflear* has become part of Mexican Spanish, meaning to use a lot of words to convey nothing. By 1937, Cantínflas was the headline entertainment at the Folies Bergères in Mexico City. He also moved on to make almost fifty movies. He donated a good deal of his income to social causes in Mexico, including building hospitals and housing for Mexico City's underserved population.

Puppet performances were also popular forms of entertainment. The most famous puppeteer was Don Soledad "Chole" Aycardo, whose entertainments drew people from all social classes.

Lightweight comedic theater remained the staple of Mexican entertainment throughout the revolution that swept the country between 1910 and 1920. Current events, nonetheless, became intertwined with theater performances, and eventually musical comedy gave way to more serious drama incorporating themes reflecting social issues. Marcelino Dávalos was one of the most prolific playwrights of the era; he was known for plays that were also social critiques, such as *Guadalupe* (1903), *El Crímen de Marciano* [Marciano's Crime] (1909), and *Aguilas y estrellas* [Eagles and Stars] (1916).

With the consolidation of the revolution, most of the new government's interest in cultural production was devoted to the plastic arts and public murals. José Vasconcelos (1881–1959) served as the head of education and culture for the Mexican government between 1921 and 1924. Vasconcelos spearheaded a number of cultural programs designed to unify all parts of Mexico after the revolution, emphasizing the role of culture in transforming the traditional ways of life of rural Mexicans. In terms of theater, Vasconcelos initiated the Misiones Culturales (Cultural Missions) program, which involved sending teachers out to rural areas of Mexico; these teachers included dramatic theater as part of their educational outreach.

There also arose a tradition of folkloric theater exemplified by Rafael M. Saavedra's Teatro Regional Mexicano, which opened in 1921. This theater inspired the construction of an open-air theater in Teotihuacán for the reenactment of preconquest rituals. Regional theater was also strong in the Yucatán region of Mexico where Mayan theater flourished. During the 1920s a number of small plays featuring indigenous or mestizo protagonists were performed in the region, using a mix of Spanish and Mayan dialects.

A number of small, independent-oriented theater groups emerged in the 1920s; these focused on the promotion of avant-garde theater in Mexico and the reorientation of Mexican acting styles and dramatic material away from Spain and toward Mexico. Antonieta Rivas Mercado (1900–31) started Teatro de Ulises in 1928, which promoted conceptual theater. The Group of Seven promoted nationalistic themes. Celestino de Gorostiza (1904–67) developed Teatro de Orientación, which operated from 1932 to 1939. In 1943 Gorostiza and Xavier Villaurrutia (1903–50) founded the state-subsidized Teatro de México, which produced primarily Mexican plays.

One of Mexico's most prominent playwrights and theater critics, Rodolfo Usigili (1905–79) was active in promoting national history. He translated and directed plays for the Teatro de Orientación and founded the Teatro de Medianoche (Midnight Theater) in 1940 to promote national works. Usigli's play *El gesticulador* [The Impostor] (1937) remains one of the most well-known and often-performed plays of the era.

Experimental theater groups arose out of the protest movement of the 1960s in Mexico. CLETA (Centro Libre de Experimentación Teatral y Artística) was an umbrella group organized primarily by theater students from Universidad Nacional Autónoma de Mexico (UNAM), the large free public university located in Mexico City. CLETA became an organization that promoted class consciousness for students and the working classes through popular theater. Other popular theater initiatives were government sponsored. Some of these were promoted through the Instituto Nacional de Bella Artes (INBA), which has had a school of theater art since 1947. In 1963 INBA founded a theatrical group that promoted theater in the provinces, much like Vasconcelos's Misiones Culturales. From 1972 to 1976, the governmental program Compañía Nacional de Subsistencias Populares (CONASUPO) steered Mexico City–trained actors and directors toward working in the countryside. This work was carried out by a different governmental organization, El Taller de Arte Escénico Popular, between 1977 and 1982. The Asociación Nacional "Teatro-Comunidad, A.C." (TECOM) was founded in 1987 and remains active in promoting local theater productions. TECOM sponsors annual theater festivals, which bring together as many as 150 theater groups.

This strong tradition of rural theater cooperatives resulted in the development of the Laboratorio de Teatro Campesino e Indígena (Farmworker and Indigenous Theater Laboratory or LTCI), which departed from earlier efforts to promote rural theater with its lack of a didactic purpose. This group was organized in 1983 in the state of Tabasco and is currently headed by theater director Alicia Martínez Medrano. Instead of performing overtly political works, the group performs versions of well-known Mexican and Spanish plays adapted for local indigenous audiences. For example, the group staged García Lorca's *Blood Wedding* set in the cornfields of Tabasco rather than in Spain. The production attempted to recover local history that had been erased by the postrevolutionary government's attempt to "Mexicanize" all indigenous peoples. The LTCI has sponsored similar adaptations of plays throughout Mexico, including a version of *Romeo and Juliet* in the State of Sinaloa. The adaptation was set in the year 1908, and Juliet was a native Mayan of southern Mexico, while Romeo was from a group of Mayos of northwestern Mexico, who were immigrating to the region. The production was set in a henequen plantation, reflecting the actual local history of the state.

In the 1990s there was an emergence of many female playwrights in Mexico who contributed new images of male and female characters to popular theater that break the mold of traditional views of Mexican society performed on stage. Sabina Berman, who won the National Institute of Fine Art National Theatre Prize in 1979, 1981, 1982, and 1983, is one example. Her play *Entre Villa y una mujer desnuda* [Between Villa and a Naked Woman] (1992) was a hit in Mexico in 1993, a year when four women had six plays in Mexico's theaters, and two others were finalists in the playwriting competition sponsored by Sociedad General de Escritores de Mexico (SOGEM), the Mexican writers' union.

## Mayan Theater

Theater is also used in Mexico to contest political oppression and to create a space for an indigenous identity in the larger Mexican state. Growing out of Harvard professor Evon Z. Vogt's cultural work in the region, the Chiapas Indigenous Cultural Society was formed in 1981. Writers affiliated with the society attempt to retain cultural control over the written and oral expressions of their cultural heritage. Work pertaining to theater began in 1985 with a traveling puppet theater that dramatized local folktales that had previously been captured only in oral forms. Performed in local Mayan dialects, plays were performed in connection with the publication and dissemination of bilingual texts in an effort to encourage literacy in the region. The theater group Lo'il Maxil (Monkey Business) performs most of the plays produced here in Tzotzil and in Spanish. The group performs about twelve plays, which publicly address and preserve Mayan cultural norms, mythology, and the pre-Hispanic past.

Mexico also has a strong history of performance artists who continue to challenge social norms by combining traditional and nontraditional theatrical forms. One of the most well-known Mexican performance artists, Guillermo Gómez Peña (b. 1955), born in Mexico but working in the United States since 1978, focuses on themes that explore the cultural relationship between the United States and Mexico, especially in regard to border cultures. He explores themes that arise from his own experiences of being a Mexican performer in the United States and someone who does not fit neatly into any ethnic or national category. He often works in collaboration with other artists, such as Coco Fusco and the Chicano performance artist Roberto Sifuentes. His performances pieces include *Border Brujo* (1988, 1990), *Friendly Cannibals* (1996), *Dangerous Border Crossers* (2000), and the works with Coco Fusco, including *Two Undiscovered Amerindians Visit the West* (1992) and *Mexacane International* (1994–95). He was a founding member of the Border Art Workshop/Taller de Arte Fronterizo and the editor of the experimental arts magazine *The Broken Line/La Linea Quebrada*. In 1991 he was the recipient of the prestigious John D. and Catherine T. MacArthur Fellowship.

Jesusa Rodriguez (b. 1955) is another well-known performance artist in Mexico who contests mainstream commercialized culture. Her performances often tackle taboo subjects in Mexico, such as the role of women in society and religion. In particular, she has performed pieces about abortion that have brought her the ire of the Catholic Church as well as that of the Mexican government.

One of the most popular performers in Mexico who does not operate on a stage is the figure Superbarrio, who emerged in the 1980s as a spokesperson for the marginalized urban communities in Mexico City. A high-school dropout with a humble upbringing, Superbarrio has become one of Mexico City's greatest folk heroes. Arising out of the aftermath of the 1985 Mexico City earthquake, which killed more than 8,000 and left countless without homes, he has stood as the champion of the working class, the poor, and the homeless. Superbarrio invokes superheroes of the past at the same time as he plays jokingly with the image: Superbarrio is a superhero with a moral conscience, political acumen, and often a physical paunch, which is highlighted in his formfitting leotard costume. Superbarrio also invokes the appearance of Mexican wrestlers, and his masked appearance allows him anonymity, which lends itself to his serving as the representative for the faceless urban poor. Rather than fight crime and corruption with violence, he uses his unique image to organize labor rallies and protests and to file petitions.

## Festivals in Mexico

Annual rituals that included dances, processions, and masked pageants were common in Mexico before the arrival of the Spaniards in the sixteenth century. All of these rituals had a religious component, since pre-Columbian indigenous peoples lived in a world where religion permeated all aspects of life and death. Rituals and festivities were seen as integral parts of life; they usually celebrated religious deities who, in turn, were believed to bestow gifts on the population by providing rain, harvests, and good health. After the Spanish conquest in 1521, Catholic priests tried to convert indigenous communities to Catholicism. They encouraged the celebration of important Catholic holidays such as Holy Week, Christmas, and Corpus Christi. Catholic beliefs soon merged with indigenous pre-Columbian traditions, and festivals tended to include traditions and rituals of both cultures. Festivals were usually sponsored by elite rulers, but some were also supported by local communities outside of a larger political framework. Generally, families rotated responsibilities for hosting these smaller festivities. Festivals contained a number of elements, including theater, dance, and processions. They were usually followed by a large feast.

## Carnival

Carnival, the pre-Lenten celebration with European origins, was introduced by Europeans, and it remains one of the most popular celebrations in Central Mexico. Carnival is especially popular in Tlaxcalan communities, which celebrate it with dances, masks, and feasting. Carnival is celebrated by at least thirty-eight of these communities during a week-long period beginning the Sunday before Ash Wednesday. Until the 1970s, most carnival participants were male. The more recent inclusion of women and girls as dancers began to challenge traditional notions of carnival. Most of these carnival celebrations include masquerades that typically represent *charros* (Mexican ranchers), generic Caucasian men, and vassals. Costumes clearly mark differences between social classes and genders.

Carnival has become an important component of local governments in these communities. City councils regulate regional festivals and oversee village processions. Most of the dances are organized within neighborhood associations. One or two community members volunteer to sponsor a group of dancers. Dancers rehearse for a few months preceding carnival. The sponsors seek out assistance from family members and friends in terms of financial support and help with food preparation and costume design. The celebrations are locally organized, and they are seen as important Catholic rituals that will promote the well-being of the community. They still include many historical and pre-Columbian elements in addition to European ones.

## Day of the Dead

Mexico has countless local popular festivals, but the most widely celebrated is the annual November 1–2 Day of the Dead celebration. This day is aptly named, for it serves as a day on which people honor and celebrate the souls of the dead through a ritual that also defies death in the very liveliness of the festivities. It is celebrated with figures of skulls and skeletons everywhere and has also turned into an international tourist event, especially in Mexico City. The holiday is celebrated at the same time as the Christian feast of All Saints' or All Souls' Day, showing syncretic links between pre-Columbian indigenous and postconquest Catholic religious rituals. The tradition of honoring the dead in a festive tradition is traced back to the Aztec heritage of Central Mexico, where ceremonies were held during the Aztec month of Miccailhuitontli, ritually presided over by the "Lady of the Dead" (*Mictecacihuatl*) and dedicated to children and to the dead. With the arrival of the Spaniards, new concepts of the afterlife were added to the Mexican cosmogony, in particular ideas of heaven, hell, angels, and devils. The cyclic view of the Aztecs, which understood death as a passage from life, fused with Catholicism's All Souls' Day (November 2) and All Saints' Day (November 1) to become Day (or Days) of the Dead.

The holiday is celebrated between October 31 and November 2; during this time, households offer food and drink for the dead, often set out on grave sites. Cemeteries are also tended to and gravesites decorated on these days. However, in certain areas, such as Oaxaca in southern Mexico, Day of the Dead extends from mid-October until November 30, San Andreas Day, when the gates of heaven are closed after all the souls have returned.

Day of the Dead rituals vary from locality to locality, but most share similar traits. Most people spend a great deal of time and effort preparing for the ceremonies. There is an emphasis on having everything made new for the day, requiring outfits, pottery, and incense vessels to be made, and fresh food to be prepared. Goods for the offerings are gradually collected throughout the year. At the end of October, families set up small *ofrendas*, altars holding offerings to the dead, which are decorated with flowers, candles, and brightly colored paper with cutout designs on them. Portraits of saints and of deceased members of the family are set out on the tables. The celebrations begin on the last two days of October. It is widely believed that the souls of children return first, and then the adult dead will come to receive their offering.

These festivities have become popular draws for international tourists. In some areas of Mexico, Day of the Dead festivities have become increasingly regulated and commercialized, with competitions held to judge the best ofrenda in the community. In general, however, Day of the Dead celebrations are private family affairs. Potters and craftspeople produce ceramic skeletons and skulls that depict skeletons engaged in everyday activities, ceramic vessels, and a number of paper products used to decorate the ofrendas. Special flowers are cultivated to commemorate the dead as well. Marigolds and *veruche*, a wild yellow flower known as the *flor de los muertos* (flower of the dead), are the most commonly used. Because Day of the Dead festivities are held to honor, remember, and celebrate deceased ancestors and relatives, the day is a festive one throughout the country.

## ANDEAN REGION

The Andean region stretches from northern Chile to southern Colombia and centers on the highlands of Bolivia and Peru—countries with large indigenous populations. Historically, Peru, in addition to Mexico, was a primary focus of the Spanish conquest. The Andean region is very diverse, and there is no one unifying cultural heritage even though many traits are shared amongst the indigenous peoples who originally formed part of the Inca Empire. As a result, conquest plays still resonate here, and they are currently performed in many locations. In general, many popular festivals of the region celebrate aspects of pre-Columbian religions, including rituals for Wiracocha (Father Sun) and Pachamama (Mother Earth), both Andean divinities. Festivals relate to the planting and harvesting of crops as well as to the preparations for branding cattle. Rituals that combine Andean song, dance, and music are also prevalent in this area, often commemorating seasonal changes.

## Peru

Theater was an important component of elite life in the capital city of Lima in the late nineteenth century; popular theater largely occurred in the countryside where it attracted mainly indigenous peoples who staged their own plays. Indigenous theater was especially prominent in the south of Peru in Cusco and Ayacucho. Many local popular plays include themes related to local history in addition to the conquest. Plays depicting the Spanish conquest are frequently performed, often in a manner that favors mestizo or Spanish culture. In Ancash the play is performed so that there is a reaffirmation of Spanish culture and victory. The festival ends with a bullfight, symbolizing the important place attributed to Spanish culture here. Other historical themes are also present in these plays. For example, many depict the famous Túpac Amaru rebellion against the Spaniards in 1781. The small town of Toqroyoq, in southern Cusco, also draws dramatic themes from local histories. People here commemorate a peasant rebellion in 1921, which took place amid a number of similar uprisings in the countryside. Performances take place on June 29 each year on the Day of Domingo Warka, named for the leader of the rebellion. The dramatic rendering of the event borrows from historical events that occurred during the rebellions of Túpac Amaru I and II (1572 and 1781). Folklore festivals began to be heavily promoted here in the 1930s and 1940s. The Inca solstice festival for Inti Raymi, for example, was first developed in Machu Picchu in the 1940s.

In 1968, after a military coup, the government enacted a number of social and cultural reforms. In terms of theater, all subsidies were pulled and reallocated to the state-sponsored group, Teatro Nacional Popular (National Popular Theater or TNP). Alonso Alegría was the director, and he became a driving force for popular theater during the 1970s. The Brazilian-born theater practitioner Augusto Boal developed his "Theater of the Oppressed" in two Peruvian cities, Lima and Chiclayo, in the 1970s. Theater developed alongside the Peruvian government's quest to eradicate illiteracy in the nation in 1973, when it was estimated that almost one-fourth of the population was illiterate.

Popular theater exploded in the decade of the 1970s, focusing largely on Peru's most urban areas, Lima and Callao. Just as elsewhere in Latin America, theater was seen as a means to an end in that it offered a way for social activists and politicians to incorporate the nonelite into civic society. Amateur theater flourished in workshops and small cultural groups that practiced and performed on weekends in neighborhood auditoriums to audiences averaging about 100 members. One of the most important popular theater groups was the Yuyachkani Cultural Group, founded by Miguel Rubio and Teresa Ralli in 1971. Like many other groups of the time, this one focused on collective theater where practitioners developed collaborative stage plays rather than presenting the work of an individual author. One of the first plays, *Puño de Cobre* [Fistful of Copper] (1971) was based on a real strike that the Federation of Miners waged against a foreign corporation. Based on Augusto Boal's theatrical methods, this play toured through mining centers in Peru. The Yuyachkani Cultural Group continues to be a vital force for popular theater in Peru. The group is well known for creating deeply symbolic repertoires that combine different types of theater arts, including drama, song, and dance. They have created works that are at once revolutionary and oddly familiar, paying perfect homage to the culture that fostered them. One of the group's most popular pieces, *Músico Ambulante* [Traveling Musicians], focuses on four different animals as they journey through

Peru. Each represents a cultural faction. The donkey, for example, represents the people of the Andes; the cat, the people of the jungle; the dog, the people of the northern coast; and the chicken, those of African origin. In addition to producing stage plays, Yuyachkani teaches seminars and workshops for people of all ages and runs a library specializing in theater and popular culture. In 2000 Yuyachkani won Peru's National Human Rights Award.

In the 1990s *teatro de guerrilla* developed, a term defined by the Maoist-inspired revolutionary group Sendero Luminoso (Shining Path), responsible for a great deal of violence during this decade. The group used theater to spread its political message and presented songs, dance, mime, and music to audiences largely composed of their ideological companions and the poor. Over the last fifteen years, the Instituto Cultural Peruano Norteamericano (ICPNA or Peruvian North American Cultural Institute) has supported a number of international festivals in dance, theater, and music. The Movimiento de Teatro Independiente (MOTIN or Independent Theater Movement) unites most of the noncommercial theater groups of the country and sponsors a national theater convention that takes place every two years in different parts of the country. Theater has grown not only in urban areas but also in the poorer countryside where open-air theaters dominate.

In the early 1990s about 100 plays were performed annually, reaching a total audience of about 15,000. Most theaters do not hold more than 150 spectators. Despite a limited audience, more than 2,700 people defined themselves as actors in 1992.

## Ecuador

Theater in Ecuador has not been as pervasive as in other parts of Latin America. In the 1930s a popular form of what is called sketch theater emerged. These plays were comedic representations of Quito's urban lower-middle classes, rooted in local customs. Ernesto Albán, one of Ecuador's most famous actors, developed a character, *el chulla quiteño*. The character uses his wits to climb up the social ladder. Ironically, a military government that came to power in 1963 helped promote theater by hiring Fabio Paccioni, an Italian theater professor, to teach in Quito. Paccioni formed two theater groups, Teatro Ensayo (Experimental Theater) and Teatro Popular (Popular Theater); the latter tried to provoke social change among the poor and disenfranchised. After this, however, theater in Ecuador declined, and one scholar has referred to it as the performing arts' Cinderella. Partly in response to the lack of funding, Ecuador developed a strong street theater tradition in the 1970s, with groups holding performances in all types of public spaces, including city plazas. Most of the entertainment focused on Quito, the capital city.

A lack of funding from the state has also impacted the theatrical community, which, at times, has responded innovatively to such challenges. The group Malayerba, for example, has staged plays using sparse sets. In *Nuestra Señora de Las Nubes* [Our Lady of the Clouds], written by Arístides Vargas, two characters, Bruna and Oscar, are immigrants, and the only stage props consist of two suitcases that accompany them on their journey. The play was voted "Best of Latin American Theater" in 1999 by Nicaragua's press during the Fifth Managua Monologue and Duologue Festival, and it has toured throughout Latin America. Malayerba has operated since 1980. Ecuador has recently hosted a number of performance festivals, including the International Festival of Manta, a festival hosted by the Guyaquil-based troupe Sarao, and another by the acting troupe Humanizarte, based in Quito. Held from August to October 2001, the festivals hosted troupes from Spain, Mexico, Peru, and Colombia in addition to Ecuador. Quito has also sponsored an International Puppet Festival, organized by the company Tintintero, directed by Yolanda Navas.

## Bolivia

Bolivia has a strong tradition of popular performances of plays that take the Spanish Conquest of the region as their main theme. The plays present the indigenous version of events and center on the figure of Atahuallpa, the Inca ruler who was killed by the Spaniards in Cajamarca. The main plot points of the play are the killing of Atahuallpa and the appearance of the Spanish king, who, at the end, punishes Francisco Pizarro, the Spanish conquistador of the region, for killing a legitimate ruler. The play is staged with indigenous peoples playing Spaniards and Incans.

Bolivia was one of the most important centers of the Spanish empire during the colonial era as a result of its gold and silver mines. Theater flourished during this era, but it was largely entertainment for the elite classes. Popular theater in Bolivia, outside of a tradition of ritual and festivals, begins in the 1920s with an expansion of publications of all sorts. It was during this decade that the first popular, nationalist theater groups began. El Grupo Gesta Bárbara, for example, performed popular dramas that reflected local types such as native miners, *cholos* (acculturated indigenous peoples), and white company owners and foremen. Social-class conflicts were often the focus of these dramas. The Chaco War (1932–35) resulted in negative economic consequences for Bolivia, and cultural entertainment declined almost totally. In the 1940s Raúl Salmón developed a popular theater that addressed the problems of the country and performed largely for the working classes and veterans of the Chaco War. The 1952 Bolivian revolution altered the social order of the country dramatically. In terms of theater, the new government attempted to develop a national theater style and focused its efforts on bringing the life of agricultural laborers to the stage. This form of theater placed the customs and music of the indigenous peoples at the forefront. The group Teatro al Aire Libre put on presentations in Quechua and Aymara. Two of the most important groups from this era were Grupo Tupiza, directed by Líber Forti, an Argentine, and the Brigada Cultural de la Paz that toured throughout the country. Notable playwrights from this era include Guillermo Francovich (1901–90), Luis Llanos Aparicio, and Robeto Cuevas.

During the 1960s and 1970s, community theater groups expanded greatly. The Taller de Teatro (1979) presented *teatro carpa* (theater performed in tents), which provided entertainment to small towns and rural communities. Folkloric theater also grew under the direction of Jaime Sevillano and his group Nairakhata. Sevillano worked among indigenous groups, developing performances from local indigenous customs performed by the community.

### Carnival

Current-day carnival in Oruro, Bolivia, is one of the largest festivals in South America. The carnival combines pre-Columbian forms of ritual and performance with Catholic religious festivals. Oruro is located in the high plateau region of Bolivia and is an important mining center dating back to the colonial era. Carnival dates back to the late 1700s, when Spanish chroniclers feared that these large celebrations might turn into rebellions against their dominance in the area. The Spaniards asserted more control over these popular festivities and encouraged the indigenous peoples to venerate the Virgin of the Mineshaft, the patron saint of the carnival. The indigenous population also included homage to the pre-Columbian deity, Supay, whom they viewed as the patron of the mines. In attempting to convert indigenous peoples, the Catholic Church told them Supay was a devil, and thereafter the indigenous peoples who impersonated him dressed up as devils. Thus began the tradition of the "diablada" costumes and conquest plays about the Spanish defeat of the Incas that persist as part of carnival here. Through the veneration of the Virgin Mary, who was referred to as Virgin of the

Mineshaft, and Supay, carnival celebrations pay homage to both Christian and pre-Columbian religious figures.

In the nineteenth century, two carnival celebrations were carried out here, one for the elites and the other for indigenous peoples. The Indians and cholos performed the same type of conquest plays and dance dramas they had performed since the era of contact between Bolivia and Spain; in the early twentieth century, they began to celebrate a new dance drama called the *morenada* (black man), which included dances, performances, masks, and costumes that reflected elements of African slavery in the nation's past.

Carnival was once again transformed in the decade of the 1940s, coupled with the development of a socialist political movement in the nation that began to value indigenous cultures and ways of life as an authentic socialist past. Indigenous festivals began to be promoted as expressions of Bolivian national identity. Elites were part of this cultural transformation, and the two distinct carnival traditions for different social classes merged into one. In addition, the morenada groups grew in size and number. The morenada groups were comprised largely of miners who worked in the region; these groups formed their own carnival societies and were known for some of the most lavish costumes of the festival. In the 1950s other groups began performing as blacks (known as *sayas*) from the Bolivian tropical lowlands. Afro-Bolivian music and dance forms have increasingly become incorporated in modern-day carnival celebrations as a result. In addition, carnival in the mid- to late twentieth century also celebrated Andean Indian themes, including the llama herders who twirl their slings while dancing. *Kullawada* groups represent village weavers.

Festivals take place in many different locations in Bolivia at different times of the year. As a result, some craftspeople work full time making costumes and masks for the celebrations. Because some of the costumes are so expensive to buy, many revelers choose to rent them from year to year. Preparations usually begin community wide in November, four months before carnival. About three square miles in a town are reserved for the carnival parade. Carnival takes place over a week-long period that coincides with the pre-Columbian harvest season. As a result, it still contains many traditional indigenous forms in the variety of activities that take place. For example, people celebrate the harvest season and honor Pachamama, the earth mother. They also provide *ch'allas*, offerings of food, drink, and coca to deities. The carnival has recently been recognized by UNESCO as a "Masterpiece of Oral and Intangible Heritage of Humanity."

# RESOURCE GUIDE

## PRINT SOURCES

Armstrong, Piers. "Songs of Olodum: Ethnicity, Activism, and Art in a Globalized Carnival Community." Pp. 177–191 in Charles A. Perrone and Christopher Dunn (eds.), *Brazilian Popular Music and Globalization*. New York/London: Routledge Press, 2002.

Bettelheim, Judith, ed. *Cuban Festivals: An Illustrated Anthology,* New York/London: Garland, 1993.

Boal, Augusto. *Theatre of the Oppressed.* London: Pluto, 1989.

———. *Legislative Theatre: Using Performance to Make Politics.* London/New York: Routledge, 1998.

Bryan, Susan. E. "The Commercialization of the Theater in Mexico and the Rise of the *Teatro Frívolo* [Frivolous Theater]." *Studies in Latin American Popular Culture* 5 (1986).

Carmichael, Elizabeth, and Chloë Sayer. *The Skeleton at the Feast: The Day of the Dead in Mexico.* Austin: University of Texas Press, 1991.

Castro, Donald S. "The Sainete Porteño, 1890–1935: The Image of Jews in the Argentine Popular Theater." *Studies in Latin American Popular Culture* 21 (2002).

Castro, Ruy. *Rio de Janeiro: Carnival under Fire.* New York/London: Bloomsbury, 2003.

Cordry, Donald. *Mexican Masks.* Austin/London: University of Texas Press, 1980.

de Costa, Elena. *Collaborative Latin American Popular Theater.* New York: Peter Lang, 1992.

Frischmann, Donald H. "New Mayan Theatre in Chiapas: Anthropology, Literacy, and Social Drama." Pp. 213–238 in Diana Taylor, *The Archive and the Repertoire: Performing Cultural Memory in the Americas.* Durham, NC: Duke University Press, 2003.

Fuente, Alejandro de la. *A Nation for All: Race, Inequality, and Politics in Twentieth-Century Cuba.* Chapel Hill/London: University of North Carolina Press, 2001.

García Márquez, Gabriel. "Big Mama's Funeral." In *No One Writes to the Colonel.* New York: Harper & Row, 1968.

George, David. *The Modern Brazilian Stage,* Austin: University of Texas Press, 1992.

Graham-Jones, Jean. *Exorcising History: Argentine Theatre under Dictatorship.* Lewisburg, PA: Bucknell University Press, 2000.

Guillermoprieto, Alma. *Samba.* New York: Vintage Books, 1991.

Haley, Shawn D., and Curt Fukuda. *The Day of the Dead: When Two Worlds Meet in Oaxaca.* New York/Oxford: Berghahn Books, 2004.

Kaiser, Diana. "Escraches: Demonstrations, Communication and Political Memory in Post-dictatorial Argentina." *Media, Culture & Society* 24 (2002): 499–516.

Lane, Jill. *Blackface Cuba, 1840–1945.* Philadelphia: University of Pennsylvania Press, 2005.

Larson, Catherine, and Margarita Vargas, eds. *Latin American Women Dramatists: Theater: Texts and Theories.* Bloomington: Indiana University Press, 1998.

Leclercq, Nicole, and Ian Herbert, eds. *The World of Theatre 2003 Edition: An Account of the World's Theatre Seasons 1999–2000, 2000–2001 and 2001–2002.* London/New York: Routledge, Taylor and Francis Group, 2003.

Londré, Felicia Hardison, and Daniel J. Watermeier. *The History of North American Theater: From Pre-Columbian Times to the Present.* New York: Continuum, 1998.

Matas, Julio. "Theater and Cinematography." Pp. 436–442 in Carmelo Mesa-Lago, *Revolutionary Change in Cuba.* Pittsburgh: University of Pittsburgh Press, 1971.

Mauldin, Barbara. "Ritual and Play: Carnaval in Nahua Indian Communities of Tlaxcala, Mexico." Pp. 145–175 in Barbara Mauldin (ed.), *Carnaval!* Seattle: University of Washington Press, 2004.

———. *Carnaval!* Seattle: University of Washington Press, 2004.

———. *Masks of Mexico: Tigers, Devils, and the Dance of Life.* Santa Fe: Museum of New Mexico Press, 1999.

McCleary, Kristen. "Elite, Popular, and Mass Culture? The Spanish Zarzuela in Buenos Aires, Argentina, 1880–1920." *Studies in Latin American Popular Culture* 21 (2002).

McFarren, Peter. *Masks of the Bolivian Andes.* La Paz: Editorial Quipus, 1993.

Perales, Rosalina. *Teatro Hispanoamericano Contemporaneo, 1967–1987,* vol. I. Mexico D.F.: Grupo Editorial Gaceta, S.A., 1989.

Rowe, William, and Vivian Schelling. *Memory and Modernity: Popular Culture in Latin America.* London/New York: Verso Press, 1991.

Ruétalo, Victoria. "From Villa to Village: Situating Argentina's Theatrical Coordinates on the Global Map." *Studies in Latin American Popular Culture* 21 (2002).

Salvador, R. J. "What Do Mexicans Celebrate on the Day of the Dead?" Pp. 75–77 in J. D. Morgan and P. Laungani (eds.), *Death and Bereavement in the Americas. Death, Value and Meaning Series,* vol. II. Amityville, NY: Baywood, 2003. Available online at http://www.public.iastate.edu/~rjsalvad/scmfaq/muertos.html.

Samaké, Cynthia Le Count (historical sections by Barbara Mauldin). "Dancing for the Virgin and the Devil: *Carnaval* in Oruro, Bolivia." Pp. 173–202 in Barbara Mauldin, *Carnaval!* Seattle: University of Washington Press, 2004.

Shaw, Lisa, and Stephanie Dennison. *Pop Culture Latin America! Media, Arts, and Lifestyle.* Santa Barbara, CA/Denver/Oxford: ABC-CLIO, 2005.

Soria, Mario T. *Teatro Boliviano en el siglo XX.* La Paz: Editorial Casa Municipal de la Cultura, 1980.

Sturman, Janet. *Zarzuela: Spanish Operetta, American Stage.* Urbana/Chicago: University of Illinois Press, 2000.

Taylor, Diana. *The Archive and the Repertoire: Performing Cultural Memory in the Americas.* Durham, NC: Duke University Press, 2003.

Underiner, Tamara L. *Contemporary Theater in Mayan Mexico: Death-Defying Acts.* Austin: University of Texas Press, 2004.

Weiss, Judith A., and Leslie Damasceno. *Latin American Popular Theater: The First Five Centuries.* Albuquerque: University of New Mexico Press, 1993.

Wilson, Richard. *Maya Resurgence in Guatemala: Q'eqchi' Experience.* Norman: University of Oklahoma Press, 1995.

## WEBSITES

*BrazilMax.* May 15, 2006. http://www.brazilmax.com/. This travel Website focuses on cultural and historical events related to Brazilian society and culture. It provides information on the country's carnival celebration with in-depth articles in English.

CELCIT. June 10, 2006. http://www.celcit.org.ar/. The Website for CELCIT (Centro Latinoamericano de Creación e Investigación Teatral) offers essential information for anyone interested in or working on contemporary Latin American theater and the performing arts. It offers up-to-date news on significant productions and practitioners across Latin America, including reviews.

*Coco Fusco's Virtual Laboratory.* June 1, 2006. http://www.thing.net/~cocofusco/. The performance artist Coco Fusco's Website shows some examples of her live work and written texts.

*Dramateatro Revista Digital.* May 15, 2006. http://dramateatro.fundacite.arg.gov.ve/. Published in Venezuela, *Dramateatro* is an online journal devoted to the theater, with particular emphasis on Latin America. It publishes critical articles and essays on all aspects of the theater, including text and performance, across the centuries.

*LANIC.* June 10, 2006. http://lanic.utexas.edu/la/region/performing/. The best general Website for theater and performing arts listings in Latin America; found at the University of Texas-run Website LANIC (Latin American Network Information Center). The Website organizes further Web resources by country. Most of the resources listed are not in English. Most themes related to popular theater are found in the performing arts category of the humanities section.

*Perucultural.org.pe.* May 30, 2006. http://www.perucultural.org.pe. A Website sponsored by the Peruvian government about Peruvian cultural events and practices.

*Revista Telón.* May 23, 2006. http://www.telon.cl/editorial.htm. *Telón* is an online magazine dedicated to Chilean theater and cinema. It offers up-to-date information on notable theatrical performances as well as detailed information about Chilean theater companies, offering brief biographies and summaries of their work.

## PERIODICALS/MAGAZINES

*Drama Teatro.* This is an electronic journal from Venezuela that contains up-to-date information on theatrical activities throughout Latin America. The journal includes scholarly essays, critical reviews, events, and pedagogical resources. http://dramateatro.fundacite.arg.gov.ve/.

*Gestos: Teoría y práctica del teatro hispánico.* GESTOS is a multilingual journal devoted to critical studies of Spanish, Latin American, and U.S. Latino theater. Articles are published in English, Portuguese, and Spanish. Each issue includes four main sections: essays, performance reviews of Hispanic texts from around the world, book reviews, and an unpublished play text by a prominent dramatist from the Hispanic world.

*Latin American Theatre Review.* The primary scholarly journal that focuses on Latin American theater in the United States, LATR contains both historical and contemporary articles about the role of theater in the region. It is published by the Center for Latin American Studies at the University of Kansas.

*Studies in Latin American Popular Culture.* This annual interdisciplinary journal publishes articles, review essays, and interviews on diverse aspects of popular culture in Latin America. It primarily publishes articles in English.

## VIDEOS/FILMS

*Black Orpheus* (Brazil, 1959). Directed by Marcel Camus. This retelling of the Orpheus and Eurydice Greek legend is set against Rio de Janeiro's madness during carnival. Orpheus, a trolley-car conductor, is engaged to Mira but in love with Eurydice. A vengeful Mira and Eurydice's ex-lover, costumed as Death, pursue Orpheus and his new paramour through the carnival night. *Black Orpheus* earned an Oscar for Best Foreign Language Film in 1959. Also of interest is *Orfeu*, written and directed by Carlos Diegues (Brazil, 1999). This is a retelling of the same story set in the slums of Rio de Janeiro.

*Death and the Maiden* (1994). Directed by Roman Polanski, starring Sigourney Weaver and Ben Kingsley. This play is based on Chilean playwright Ariel Dorfman's account of what happens when a woman previously imprisoned by a military dictatorship thinks she has stumbled across the man responsible for torturing her many years after she has been released.

*Grupo Cultural Yuyachkani: Persistencia de la Memoria* (Peru, 1996). Directed by Andrés Cotler. This documentary celebrates the twenty-fifth anniversary of the Peruvian theatrical group that was founded in 1971. The group, whose name means "I am remembering" in Quechua, works to preserve national indigenous dance, music, folk traditions and performance through theater. The video, however, is only available in Spanish.

*Papeles Secundarias* (1989). Directed by Orlando Rojas. Awarded best film in 1990 at the New York Festival Latino. A theater group in crisis is the setting for this story. Its aging actors, on stage as in life, confront their fears and failures.

*Sacred Games: Ritual Warfare* (Mexico, 1988). Every year in San Juan Chamula, Chiapas, in southern Mexico, thousands of Mayan Indians gather to celebrate carnival, which they call Festival of Games. This award-winning documentary, which shows the merger of Catholicism and ancient Mayan rites, captures the passion and mystery of the event and demonstrates how the Mayan symbolic world is renewed each year in the celebrations.

*Wylancha* (1991). Directed by Gisella Canepa Koch. In the Andes, the time for celebrating propitiatory rituals coincides with the carnival season. One such ritual is the *wylancha*, in which members of the community of Molloko, in the Acora district of Puno, offer their alpacas to the mountains and the earth, their protecting divinities. Documentary.

## EVENTS

Curitiba Festival. Annual festival in Brazil since 1992. It showcases contemporary Brazilian theater as well as international theater. Since its inception, 747 shows have been performed to over 700,000 audience members. http://www.festivaldeteatro.com.br/site/index.asp.

Carnival in Brazil. Carnival celebrations usually fall in the month of February but sometimes start in January and end in March. The Website gives information on carnival in Brazil: http://www.ipanema.com/carnival/dates.htm.

Day of the Dead. November 2 is the official date for Day of the Dead, although it is celebrated between October 31 and November 2 throughout Mexico. See author Mary J. Andrade's Website about Mexico's celebration, which includes information on different regions of Mexico, photographs, and recipes: http://www.dayofthedead.com/.

## ORGANIZATIONS

International Theatre Institute. UNESCO, 1 rue Miollis, 75732 Paris CEDEX 15 France. Tel: +33 1 45 68 48 80; fax: +33 1 45 66 50 40; Secretariat: iti@unesco.org; Webmaster: web@iti-worldwide.org; Internet Services: j.sosnowski@iti-worldwide.org. The International Theatre Institute (ITI), an international nongovernmental organization (NGO), was founded in Prague in 1948 by UNESCO and the international theater community. ITI sponsors annual international theater festivals and conferences that take place all over the world. http://www.iti-worldwide.org/.

National Theater Museum, Argentina. Museo Nacional del Teatro, Teatro Cervantes. Avenida Córdoba 1199, Buenos Aires, Distrito Federal 1055, Argentina. Argentina is one of the few Latin American countries to have a theater museum. Exhibits include the gaucho suit worn by famous Argentine singer Gardel for his Hollywood film and the *bandoneon* (accordion-type instrument) belonging to Paquita Bernardo, the first musician to play such an instrument. http://www.teatrocervantes.gov.ar/sitio/site/home/default.php.

CELCIT, Bolívar 825, 1066 Buenos Aires, Argentina. Telephone: (5411) 4361-8358; email: correo@ celcit.org.ar. Another important organization for theater in Latin America is Centro Latinoamericano de Creación y Investigación Teatral, which began in Venezuela in 1975 but has been located in Argentina since 1979. The organization serves as a regional theatrical resource, providing information on recent plays, workshops, and classes on theater in Latin America, Portugal, and Spain. It also gives information on upcoming festivals in the region and provides a list of theater practitioners and investigators. See http://www.celcit.org.ar/sec/index.php.

# NOTES

1. Ruth D. Lechuga, and Chloë Sayer, *Mask Arts of Mexico* (San Francisco: Chronicle Books, 1995), p. 14.
2. García Márquez 1968 (in Resource Guide).
3. Leclercq 2003 (in Resource Guide), p. 43.

# TRANSPORTATION AND TRAVEL

JOHN F. BRATZEL

Latin America is extremely large. Seven thousand miles separate the northern border of Mexico from the southernmost point of land, Tierra del Fuego. At the equator, where South America is widest, the distance from the Atlantic to the Pacific Ocean is 3,200 miles. Within this huge land mass, the terrain is extremely variable, from the Atacama Desert of Chile to the rainforests of Brazil. Broad plains, such as the Pampas of Argentina, contrast with the high peaks (Aconcagua reaches 23,000 feet) of the Andes. These huge distances and difficult topography make transportation and travel very difficult in Latin America. Nevertheless, by one means or another, it is still possible to travel to almost every part of Latin America.

## MEXICO

The indigenous peoples of Mexico, including the Olmecs, Toltecs, Tarascans, Mayans, and Aztecs, were not noted for their road building. A principal reason was the difficult terrain, but perhaps a more significant reason was the lack of draft animals such as horses or oxen. The arrival of Hernán Cortés and the Spanish did not immediately change this situation. Disease killed a high percentage of the indigenous inhabitants, and as a result, labor became an expensive commodity. The Spanish did not see road work as the best place to use their Indian labor. In cases where roads were built, they generally radiated out from Mexico City. The Spanish Crown wanted to maintain control of the whole society and economy, and the road system, such that it was, supported this end.

Mexican independence from Spain (1810) did not bring about change, however. What followed were sixty years of unsettled government, which did not foster infrastructure development. It was not until the rule of Porfirio Díaz, from 1876 to 1910, that transportation seriously improved. Railroads led this transformation.

### Train Travel

Porfirio Díaz wanted to build a modern Mexico, and he saw railroads as a significant factor in this transformation. When he took over, only 700 miles of track existed; this increased

345

to 12,000 miles by 1900 and 15,000 miles by 1910. New lines were built to the U.S. border that opened up Mexico to new markets and new products. In Mexico City itself, residents also could enjoy new travel conveniences, including trolleys.

The heavy fighting that marked the Mexican Revolution (1910–20) destroyed some of the railroad infrastructure that had been so laboriously built during the time of Díaz, but rather than quickly rebuilding, subsequent governments invested very little funding in maintenance, improvements, and new building projects. In 1993, with further changes occurring in 1997, most of the railroads in Mexico were privatized, with companies purchasing fifty-year concessions.

Despite this, there is still almost no regular passenger rail service in Mexico. Tourist trains aimed at sightseers, however, are available. Representative of this type of travel is the famous Chihuahua-Pacific (Chepe) Railroad's "Train Ride in the Sky." This popular, 405-mile trip travels through the State of Chihuahua to Los Mochis in Sinaloa State on the Pacific. The fourteen- to sixteen-hour trip passes through the famed Copper Canyon region, offering a spectacular view of the natural wonders of northern Mexico.

A better-known and even more popular line is the Guadalajara-Amatitan rail trip known as the Tequila Express. Running every Saturday, this train leaves Guadalajara for the relatively short trip to the tequila production region of Mexico. Passengers enjoy mariachi music, food, and of course, an open bar. Upon arrival in Amatitan, travelers tour tequila production facilities, have lunch and dinner, and board the train for a return ride to Guadalajara.

In the future, Mexico plans to build a bullet train or high-speed train, the *Tren Bala*, between Guadalajara, Mexico's second city, and Mexico City. The plans have moved past the discussion stage and, as of 2006, tracks are being laid. Slated for completion in 2011, this train will significantly cut congestion and make travel between the two major cities of Mexico considerably easier.

## Highway Travel

Most of the important highways radiate from Mexico City, west to Acapulco and Guadalajara, east to Puebla and Vera Cruz, south to Oaxaca and then Chiapas, and north to Monterrey and Nuevo Laredo. Three other significant highways connect Tijuana through Baja California to Cabo San Lucas; another branches out from Tijuana, paralleling the U.S. border to Matamoros; and a third follows the Pacific Coast of Mexico from the U.S. border to Guatemala.

The majority of the estimates suggest that there are approximately 217,000 miles of road in Mexico, ranging from superhighways and freeways to merely improved surfaces. Although the road mileage may seem sufficient, the number of cars in Mexico is growing at a fast pace and outstripping the nation's ability to build new highways. This has created significant road congestion and traffic jams, problems compounded because roads are not always in the best of repair. To deal with these problems, Mexico has allowed private contractors to construct toll roads. These expressways are of high quality, but they are also relatively expensive to use. The high tolls limit traffic, which makes using these roads convenient for those who can afford them, but it has not done much to solve the congestion problem.

Road traffic has also created pollution. This, coupled with manufacturing, has left Mexico City and Guadalajara with serious smog problems. As a remedy, Mexico City adopted a system in which cars may not be driven in the city one weekday a week, based on the last number of the car's license plate. Unfortunately, this idea has not significantly improved either pollution or congestion.

Driving in Mexico is not like driving in the United States and Canada. The culture in Mexico is one of personal space and personal rights. Mexicans, for example, generally ignore lane lines. Speed laws do not have a history of being seriously enforced. Drivers do not expect other drivers to let them into lines of traffic. Driving slowly in Mexico, when speed is possible, risks being hit from behind, and traffic lights seem to be treated as suggestions rather than as rules.

All this is exacerbated by impediments found in the roadways. One problem is the *tope* or speed bump. These are intended to slow down traffic, but drivers often detour around them, which causes problems, or slow down, only to step on the gas after passing over the bump. In addition, topes are hard to see at times, and many cars have been damaged by hitting these obstacles. The obstacles presented by topes are supplemented, chiefly in the more rural areas but even in cities, by farm animals, which are often allowed to roam free. Considerable damage can be done by hitting animals, and it behooves drivers to watch carefully for them.

There are other, seemingly unwritten, rules as well. For example, on a narrow bridge, the driver who flashes his or her lights first is considered to have the right of way. Mexico has put forward a number of initiatives to try to temper the "personal rights" nature of Mexican driving. Whether these will succeed or not is unclear: Mexican popular culture defines all drivers as kings of the road, but in this case, there are more kings than there are roads.

## Automobiles

As noted previously, the number of automobiles is increasing rapidly in Mexico. In 1996 Mexico had 8.6 million cars; by 2000, that number had grown to 10.44 million, an increase of 21 percent. When the number of trucks is added to the number of cars, the total number of vehicles on Mexico's highways in that year jumps to 15.37 million. Current sales of cars and trucks, over 1 million per year, suggest that this increase will continue. Compared to wealthier countries, the percent of adults owning vehicles is still low, but a stable economy and increased manufacturing, coupled with oil revenues, means that the ownership percentage will grow, further clogging Mexican roads.

For many years Mexicans had a choice of cars made by General Motors, Ford, Chrysler, Volkswagen, and Nissan. To a great extent, this is still true today because these manufacturers sell the most cars, but Jaguar, Mercedes Benz, and a host of other manufactures now have showrooms in Mexico.

All this has added to a surging automobile culture in Mexico. Magazines about cars, such as *Sobre Ruedas*, the most important Spanish-language automobile magazine, are must reads for car enthusiasts. *Sobre Ruedas*, with a circulation of over 600,000, is a glossy magazine that analyzes and comments on cars and describes the latest trends. Like many auto magazines all over the world, it gives out a series of awards to cars in a variety of categories and offers detailed arguments explaining its choices.

For many years, the most popular car in Mexico was the Volkswagen Beetle, called the Volkswagen Sedán in Mexico. It is also known colloquially as the *Vocho*. The car appeared on the market in 1954 and sold so well that Volkswagen built a plant to produce it in Puebla. So popular was the car that Mexico continued to produce the Beetle long after other plants in other countries had ceased production. It was not until 2003 that the last Beetle was produced in Mexico. The reason for its continued success was that it was cheap and reliable.

Perhaps Volkswagen should have changed sooner, since by that time it had lost its lead to General Motors and its small, relatively cheap Opel Corsa. The Corsa was considerably more up-to-date than the Vocho. It was also regularly updated and redesigned to keep up with the changes in the market. The Corsa is being marketed today as the C2, the "C" being a reference to the Corvette. The linkage between these vehicles is somewhat obscure, but the car is selling well.

The Corsa's reign as the top-selling car did not last long: Nissan knocked it from the top spot. The first car Nissan produced was the 160J, which enjoyed some success but was not a best seller. In 1984 Nissan began producing the Nissan Sentra, called the Tsuru in Mexico after a type of Japanese bird. A variety of redesigns coupled with quality advertising eventually brought the Sentra to the top spot in Mexico in 1998, and the car enjoyed that position until 2005.

Volkswagen was slow to act, but when it did, it was successful. In 1998 the company brought out the Pointer, which slowly rose to be the most popular car in Mexico in 2006. Volkswagen also markets the Jetta, which is a cut above the Pointer in quality but also much more expensive.

The top sellers have much in common in that they are all small and relatively inexpensive. These kinds of cars are ubiquitous on the streets of Mexico. Although the venerable Beetle is still very much in evidence, cars with more modern styling and engineering are replacing it. Mexicans with more money want larger, more prestigious cars. SUVs, sports cars such as the Ford Mustang, and large European cars are also very much in evidence.

Gas is not particularly cheap even though Mexico is a major oil producer. Generally speaking, gas prices are about 15 to 20 percent lower than they are in the United States. However, since personal income is significantly below that of the United States, gas is not really cheap for Mexicans. Still, in an increasingly car-dependent culture, the sacrifice seems justifiable to car enthusiasts.

## Taxis

Taxis in Mexico, particularly in Mexico City and in other large metropolitan areas, can be an experience. Drivers are often quite pleasant, and interesting conversations are fairly common for Spanish speakers. Taxi rides sometimes lead to rather exciting trips since some drivers have more in common with race drivers than with anyone else. Driving fast, and darting in and out of traffic, can be both exhilarating and dangerous. Drivers have been known to back up for two or three blocks to get to the right road, and some find ways to get to a destination by using neighborhood streets in a dizzying panoply of turns.

Mexican taxicab riders have to be concerned not only about traffic accidents but also about robberies. Mexico City has about 86,000 legal taxis and about 26,000 unlicensed cabs. The bulk of these are still safe, but caution should be exercised.

Fares vary. Some are flat fees based on zones, and others are based on miles driven and time used. Flat fees are much preferred in the congested cities, where traffic tie-ups are common. Taxis in smaller cities often do not have meters or any discernable system of determining the fare.

## Bus Travel

Intercity bus travel in Mexico is convenient, pleasant, efficient, and relatively inexpensive. The most difficult problem is finding the bus station and choosing the level of bus travel. Mexico has many bus companies, and although some are quite large, there is no single company that covers the whole country, Nevertheless, about fifteen companies dominate the intercity bus routes. Service is divided into multiple categories, and figuring out which level is which is not always easy. One company's designations do not always match another's, so, for example, Diamante, Executive, Primera Plus, and Primera sound as if they are different classes of service; in reality, however, they may be quite similar.

At the higher levels of service, the buses are modern, have reclining seats, show videos, and are maintained by a professional staff. Food, often a variety of sticky, sugary confections, is served along with soft drinks. Some even have two restrooms. The highest classes have only three seats in a row and only about twenty-four seats per bus. Riders enjoy considerable space and a very pleasant experience. These buses usually take the toll roads, which speeds up the trip. But even at slightly lower levels of service, buses are comfortable and well appointed. For journeys under four hours, it is much more convenient to take the bus than to fly.

This is not true, however, for the second-class bus systems, which often feature older, well-used buses, including school buses. These buses tend to stop at every town and are regularly flagged down on the road by prospective riders. Individuals get on with all manner of items; indigenous languages can often be heard. Seating is not usually assigned, but finding a seat is not difficult because people get on and off regularly. In Mexico, although there are no signs or other form of announcement, it is generally understood that the seats behind the driver are usually available only to the friends of the driver.

These buses never take the toll roads; they often use highways that are not in the best of repair. This, coupled with the lack of high-quality springs under the bus, can make for a somewhat jolting ride. In many cases, however, everyone on the bus seems to know each other, and ongoing conversation usually shortens the ride.

Second-class buses often have complex religious displays on the dashboards and sometimes on the outside of the buses as well. A picture or stature of the Virgin of Guadalupe is always displayed, but flags, sports team emblems, and other saints' images are also usually present.

Bus travel within cities is readily available. Many of the buses used within the cities are school buses. Where the bus is going is usually written on the front, and travel is generally quite cheap. City buses can often be so full that riders have to stand until a seat becomes available. Some have pull cords that signal the driver when a passenger wants to get off, but many lack that amenity. In those cases, passengers simply bang on the ceiling of the bus when they need to get off.

## Ships

Mexico has become the leading cruise destination in the world. In 2004, 7.6 million passengers traveled to Mexico. On the Caribbean coast, the top destination is the island of Cozumel, famous for its nature and nightlife. A number of other ports have been developed to compete with Cozumel, including the ports of Morelos and Calica. These ports emphasize Mexican culture and nature, and support diving and snorkeling.

On the Gulf of Mexico, two ports that are visited are Vera Cruz and Progresso. Vera Cruz, from which Hernán Cortés launched his expedition against the Aztec empire, is an old city with considerable history. Progresso was a little seaside town and port for Merida, Yucatán, for many years. In the last twenty years, however, it has grown considerably and now offers all manner of shopping and restaurants.

In 2004, 140 ships docked at Cabo San Lucas in Baja California Sur on the Pacific coast of Mexico. Puerto Vallarta, south of Los Cabos, received 210 cruise ships carrying 420,000 passengers. Mazatlán was not far behind, receiving 176 ships carrying 370,000 people. All these cities offer restaurants, high-quality hotels, and most importantly, long, beautiful sandy beaches.

Acapulco, historically the center for American West Coast vacations in Mexico, has been eclipsed by the ports to the north and south. Nevertheless, Acapulco received 109 ships in

2004. Aging facilities, combined with regular freight traffic, have made the area somewhat less desirable for tourists.

Ixtapa and Zihuatanejo are south of Acapulco and are well-established cruise line stops. A new entrant is Huatulco, which is now being developed for those wanting a little less hustle and bustle and more scenery and solemnity.

## Air Travel

Mexico's air transport system is large and sophisticated. In 2003, 498,000 flights flew 32.76 million passengers domestically in Mexico. Most international flights, except those going to a tourist destination such as Cancún, land at Mexico City's Benito Juárez airport. This sprawling airport sits right in the city, and passengers can easily believe they are landing on a city street, only to discover at the last second—much to their relief—that they are landing at an airport. The Mexico City airport is effectively landlocked by development all around it, and so expansion, which is obviously needed, would be expensive. Attempts by President Fox in 2002 to develop an airport on the outskirts of the city were stymied by environmentalists and local landholders. Nevertheless, visitors find Mexico City's airport to be efficient, if somewhat overcrowded.

In an effort to relieve the overcrowding at the Mexico City airport, direct international flights land at a variety of other airports. Guadalajara and Monterrey both have important international airports. There are also direct flights for the tourists. Cancún, for example, has a large number of U.S. and other airlines landing at its airport. Other resort cities have similar methods to provide easy quick service for tourists.

Although Mexico has smaller internal airlines and 93 regional airports, it is difficult to go from one regional airport to another. The problem is that many of the flights go through Mexico City, with the attendant costs and increase in travel time. An individual flying from Oaxaca to Merida, for example, must go through Mexico City. Moreover, these flights are quite expensive. Internal travel, if it is not too far, should be made by bus.

## CUBA

Cuba is unique because its history has been so different from that of the rest of Latin America for the last forty-five years. This is to the result of the socialist dictatorship of Fidel Castro, who assumed power in 1959, and the U.S. trade embargo that followed. One result for Cuba has been a transportation system that has stagnated in some cases and adapted in others.

## Ground Transportation

Railroads played an important role in the early history of Cuba. Railroad construction began early in Cuba, and by the last half of the nineteenth century, railroads had reached most parts of Cuba. Passenger service was begun at this time, but the main goal of the railroads was the transport of sugar, derived from sugar cane, to Havana for shipment.

Today, parts of the railroad system have been abandoned, but the main railroad down the center of the island still operates. Using equipment often purchased secondhand, trains run twice a day between Havana in the west to Santiago in the east. Often seen as the last resort compared to other forms of travel, these trains are often late, badly kept, and frequently cancelled. Tourists, who usually must pay in hard currency, are normally assigned to special cars with considerably more amenities than the cars used by the Cubans themselves.

Long-distance buses have taken up the slack from trains, but just as with train travel, the Cuban population, for the most part, uses a different system from the tourist population. Cubans use the Astro buses, which are often very crowded. Tickets are not always readily available, and both Cubans and those tourists who would like to use the more-typical Cuban system should buy tickets in advance. Tourists generally use the Viazul buses, which are modern, air-conditioned, and on time. The main roads the buses travel in Cuba are well maintained, including the highway running down the spine of Cuba (Carretera Central), but secondary roads are often in poor repair.

In Havana, Cubans have been very clever in devising means of getting around the city. Bicycles, for example, are ubiquitous; so are buses. *Guaguas*, as these buses are called, come in all shapes and sizes. Most have been purchased secondhand from Canada or Europe and are quite old. Service is fairly good, however, when there are no breakdowns. An unusual response to the embargo and Cuba's economic difficulties is the creation of the *camello*, or camel bus. These conveyances consist of a semitruck cab pulling a specially built trailer used for moving people about. The trailers are immense, and camellos can carry up to 400 people at a time. It is a difficult and generally uncomfortable way to travel.

The Cubans also move people around using bicycle carriages, rickshaws, and egg-shaped contraptions powered by motorcycle engines called coco-taxis. With bodies shaped like eggs, and a look more suited to a Dr. Seuss book than to anything else, the coco-taxis will take passengers around the city for nominal fees. Another means of transport is by converted truck. Most have benches running along each side of the back for passengers to sit on and are informal in their schedules and routes. Finally, Cuba fosters and supports hitchhiking. Drivers are expected to stop, pick up all those they can reasonably accommodate, and take them along.

Perhaps more than anything else, the most distinctive feature of Cuban transportation is its automobiles. Shortly after Fidel Castro came to power, the United States stopped shipping cars or car parts to Cuba. Nevertheless, the Cubans were able to keep cars running, and today Havana is almost a living museum of pre-1960 automobiles. Parts have been scavenged from all makes and models to keep the cars running, which testifies to the cleverness of the Cuban people and the effectiveness of the embargo.

Few new cars exist in Cuba, although Russian Ladas as well as small Fiats built in Poland can be seen. Currently, the number of individuals owning cars in Cuba amounts to less than 1 percent of the population. Moreover, the government has shown no interest in increasing that percentage and makes it virtually impossible to purchase a car. The cost to Cuba's foreign exchange would be high, but the resulting demand for more gasoline is the critical factor in Cuba's desire to discourage car ownership.

## Air and Sea Transportation

Traveling to Cuba by air is much more difficult than going to other Latin American nations. The continuing embargo prohibits U.S. citizens from legally traveling to Cuba unless they have the correct license. Licensing rules continue to change as events and administrations change, so the likelihood of being able to obtain permission to travel varies over time. Travel to Cuba is expensive because of limited competition. Cubana Airlines, which hosts many of the flights, has a reputation for using old Russian planes and having a weak safety record. In the last few years, however, Cubana has started using planes made by Airbus and has attempted to improve service. It is possible to fly to Cuba from Canada, Mexico, Europe, and Central America.

Water travel is not an important part of the Cuban transportation structure. However, ferries do take passengers to the Isla de la Juventud (Island of Youth), formerly known as the Island of Pines.

## Destinations

The Cuban people have relatively few outlets for vacations: gaining permission to leave Cuba and having the funds to do so are unlikely events for most individuals. Moreover, Cubans cannot take advantage of the tourist hotels reserved for foreigners. Cubans, however, do benefit from their access to the Caribbean and to various clubs and camps.

## HAITI

Haiti is among the poorest and least developed countries in the world. It does not have a public transportation system in the usual sense, but the Haitians have been able to develop informal arrangements that allow people to move around. The most important means of conveyance is the "taptap." These vehicles are mostly converted pickup trucks with seats in the back. Some taptaps have regular routes, but this is not standard for all of them. Taptaps often are stuffed with people, but the Haitians believe there is always enough room for at least one more passenger.

The very poorly maintained roads of Haiti, along with the overloading of the trucks, make travel in taptaps dangerous. Moreover, taptap drivers show little restraint when it comes to speed. The same is true for the drivers of private automobiles.

The main airline that flies to Haiti is American Airlines, although Air France also has flights. A number of smaller Caribbean airlines also make stops in Port-au-Prince.

## DOMINICAN REPUBLIC

The Dominican Republic was the site of the first city established by Christopher Columbus. The gold and silver that were so desired by the Spanish were in Mexico and Peru, however, and as a result, the Dominican Republic languished. Following independence, the Dominican Republic was marked by considerable factionalism, military coups, and the long-lasting dictatorship of Rafael Trujillo. Despite political problems and topographical difficulties, the Dominican Republic has developed a transportation system.

## Ground Transportation

The Dominican Republic's railroad system was developed to serve sugar cane growers, and in the last twenty years, it has deteriorated considerably. There is effectively no passenger service. Instead, buses ply the roads, taking people to all parts of the country. From Santo Domingo, the capital, it is possible to take first-class buses to all the major cities. Prices are cheap, and the service is good. Lower classes of buses are available as well. These stop frequently and are not particularly comfortable.

The most-often-seen forms of transportation are the guaguas, old buses, minibuses, or vans that pick up and drop off passengers wherever is most convenient. Each guagua has a conductor, who hangs out the bus looking for passengers and collecting fares. These buses are often overcrowded, so riding in them can be a painful experience. In a similar unregulated fashion, *caros publicos*, which are privately operated cabs, collect and drop off passengers as they move between and within cities. Riders share space because the more riders, the more money the drivers and companies make, and stuffing a vehicle is not unusual. Finally, there are motorcycles set up to seat passengers behind the driver. Called *motoconchos*, these conveyances weave in and out of traffic and are quite dangerous to passengers as well as to pedestrians. No helmets are provided.

All these forms of transport must use the road system, which is in fairly good shape based on the standards of the region. The main roads are quite good, but once off them, it is useful to have a four-wheel-drive vehicle or at least one with high ground clearance. Roads have huge potholes, and even where there are no potholes, the road surface is often uneven.

## Air and Sea Transportation

It is not difficult to fly to the Dominican Republic since the country is served by a number of large international carriers. Internal flying is also common, and a system of in-country airlines can fly people to most parts of the nation.

While it is possible to find fishermen to take passengers to other islands, there is no well-developed system of sea transport. Cruise ships, however, regularly call at Santo Domingo.

## Destinations

While most Dominicans can take advantage of the nation's beautiful sea coast, it is usually foreign tourists who fly to resort areas such as Puerto Plata. Located on the north side of the country, Puerto Plata has first-class resort hotels, complete with sandy beaches, water sports, adventure tourism, shopping, and entertainment.

## GUATEMALA

Guatemala is a country with a rich history and rich culture, a true combination of the pre-Columbian world and contemporary society. It has the largest population of any country in Central America at 12.3 million; the capital, Guatemala City, and the surrounding area have 2.7 million residents. The nation has had a turbulent history with considerable internal conflict, but currently it is rather stable. Despite problems, Guatemala's transportation infrastructure is relatively strong.

## Ground Transportation

Railroads have never played an important role in Guatemala. Built mainly by the United Fruit Company to haul bananas, Guatemalan trains fell into disuse as trucks took over freight hauling. In 1999 a Pittsburgh, Pennsylvania–based company bought the rail concession between Guatemala City and the Atlantic coast at Puerto Barrios and now ships freight between the two. Currently, however, there is no passenger train service except for specially chartered trains. These steam trains, specially chartered for tourists, are not offered on a regular basis.

The road network is fairly strong, although many roads are not paved. The most important road is the Pan American Highway, which runs from Comitán, Mexico, through Huehuetenango and Guatemala City and then on to San Salvador.

The bus has a special place in the popular culture of Guatemala. There are first-class buses with air conditioning and reclining seats, but these conveyances tend to be similar from one nation to another. Guatemala has the "chicken bus," so named because invariably someone will be transporting chickens. Chicken buses are really school buses; they tend to be old, and they tend to be jammed with people. The amount a rider pays is low, but then so is the comfort. Often, three or even four people will squeeze into a seat. The people on the buses are diverse, and many indigenous languages can be heard. Drivers often entertain their passengers with games, and Guatemalan music can always be heard in the background. Brave tourists searching for local color and a real experience often take these buses and are seldom disappointed. There are, however, some dangers: the buses are occasionally stopped and the passengers robbed. Nevertheless, it is possible to go almost anywhere in Guatemala by bus, if not by first-class bus.

## Air and Sea Transportation

Guatemala City is served by numerous airlines including American, Continental, Delta, Iberian, United, TACA, and a number of others. The airport is efficient and well run. The interior is served by a subsidiary of TACA, Tikaljet—as its name implies, it will fly you to the ruins at Tikal or to other cities in Guatemala.

Cruise ships dock in Guatemala, and the flood of tourists can often dwarf the population of the area. The Caribbean coast is the most usual destination.

## Destinations

Antigua and the various Maya ruins are principal destinations for tourists. Antigua was the historic seat of the government of Guatemala during the colonial period and, as such, offers a view of the past unsurpassed in Central America. It is easy to get to Antigua, usually by minibus from any of the hotels in Guatemala City. It is more difficult to see Tikal, one of the most spectacular of the Maya ruins. Those wishing to visit there fly to the town of Flores in the north of Guatemala. From there, it is easy to find transportation for the half-hour ride to the ruins.

## HONDURAS

Honduras is located in the north-central part of Central America and has a population of approximately 7.5 million people, about 1.5 million of whom live in the capital, Tegucigalpa. It has both an Atlantic and a Pacific seacoast. The per capita income is low, and poverty and underdevelopment have marked the nation. As a result, the transportation infrastructure is not well developed.

## Ground Transportation

In the early 1900s, Honduras granted significant land concessions to foreign companies such as United Fruit and Standard Fruit to build railroads. The plan was that ultimately a national railroad system would result, which would include service to Tegucigalpa. The companies, however, built railroads only for their own benefit in order to ship bananas and other products. These railroads were all in the north, on the Atlantic Ocean side of the country.

In the 1970s and 1980s these railroads were taken over by the government, but they have not been significantly refurbished. It is not possible to travel from the Atlantic side of Honduras to Tegucigalpa or to any other country. Although tourist train trips have been tried, a major effort in that direction has not been accomplished.

The result has been that roads are forced to carry most of the freight and all the passengers. The main road runs from the Gulf of Fonseca to Tegucigalpa and then north to San Pedro Sula and Puerto Cortez. There are also secondary roads along the Caribbean coast. On the whole, the roads are not in particularly good repair. The situation was considerably exacerbated by Hurricane Mitch in 1998. Fully 70 percent of Honduran roads were damaged, and many bridges were destroyed. Much of the system has been rebuilt, often on higher, more stable ground, but because of the rebuilding, new construction was slowed considerably.

Bus service is available and reasonably priced within Honduras; buses also run to neighboring countries. First-class buses are available from companies such as Hedman Alas, which also operates buses in Guatemala. At times bus ridership expands, such as during holiday periods, and in these cases, it is useful to make reservations ahead of time. Within Tegucigalpa, inexpensive bus service is also available. Bus stops are often not marked, and bus routes are not as clear as they might be. Tourists must get help from local people to be able to navigate successfully in the capital city.

Taxis are also plentiful, but they have no meters. In some cases, a flat rate applies, while in other situations, the cost of the ride has to be negotiated before the trip starts. Generally speaking, the white-colored cars with a rooster logo, the "radio cars," are the safest and best choice.

## Air and Sea Transportation

Tegucigalpa's airport is called Toncontin. It has a storied history of offering wonderful views as a plane lands as well as providing considerable terror because of the short runway and approach. Planes coming to Toncontin have to circle below the mountains and then quickly drop to a runway that is just over one mile long. Any mistake can be tragic, and the airport has had a number of accidents. Still, quite a few airlines fly to Tegucigalpa, including American Airlines, Continental Airlines, and TACA. In 2000 Toncontin served 364,000 passengers. Within the country, there are a number of smaller airlines that offer good service to surrounding cities, including the city of San Pedro Sula, which has a runway over 9,000 feet long.

Cruise ships stop on the Caribbean coast of Honduras but not in great numbers. There are, however, ferries that take people to the Bay Islands in the Caribbean, and there is also ferry traffic up and down both coasts.

## Destinations

The number one destination, other than the sun and sand of the Caribbean coast, is Copán, the famous Maya ruin. Called the "Paris" of ruins because of its intricate stone work, it draws many tourists. Visitors normally fly to San Pedro Sula and then take a bus ride, lasting about two and a half hours, to the Copán ruins. The city of Santa Rosa de Copán is hospitable to tourists, with good restaurants and hotels.

## EL SALVADOR

El Salvador is the smallest Central American country and the only one without an Atlantic outlet. It has a comparatively large population, and fully 32 percent of the land is arable. As a result of topography, El Salvador has a fairly well-developed transportation system. The problem has been ongoing violence and governmental confusion since the 1970s, both of which have hampered development.

### Ground Transportation

The plight of the railroads exemplifies this problem. Built initially by the British, the railroads were the envy of Central America, but a lack of reinvestment, guerrilla activity, and a competing road system led to the suspension of all rail traffic, both freight and passenger, in 2002. As of 2006, attempts to reopen the system have been made, but these attempts have offered little hope of permanence.

The roads in El Salvador are quite good. The Pan American Highway goes right through El Salvador from north to south. A second road from San Salvador runs closer to the coast and is also a first-rate thoroughfare. Unfortunately, banditry and guerrilla activities have made road travel quite dangerous.

As in other regions of Central America, bus travel is important and is the easiest way to move around in the country. First-class buses ply the major arteries and are comfortable and efficient. The second-class buses do not have the amenities, but they do have considerably more charm and local culture. In El Salvador, in particular, buses take on the personalities of their owners and are often decorated with paintings, religious art, sports-team memorabilia, and similar items. Colors also vary depending on company and driver preference.

### Air and Sea Transportation

Using air service to El Salvador is easy. San Salvador has a modern airport, which is served by many of the major North American and European carriers as well as by TACA. Although there are 138 airports in El Salvador, only 5 have paved runways. Flying within the country is possible, but given the short distances, road travel by bus is usually easier.

Sea transport is not a major part of El Salvador's transportation services. El Salvador has two major ports, but the country does not host many cruise ships.

### Destinations

Because of the history of crime and guerrilla activity, tourists are not drawn to the country. Perhaps that will change over time. One the most interesting places to visit is the village of Joya de Cerén. The village was destroyed by a volcano much as Pompeii, Italy, was, and thus the world of the Maya at an early stage in its development was preserved. Bus trips can easily be made from San Salvador. Visitors and Salvadorans alike can also enjoy the Cerro Verde National Park, with its volcanoes and mountains, and the beaches of the Costa del Sol.

## NICARAGUA

Like so much of Central America, Nicaragua (population 5.6 million, of which 1.4 million live in the Managua area) has suffered considerable internal strife. Today the country is calm, but the previous years of fighting and bloodshed have hurt the economy and the transportation system as well. The transportation that does exist is on the Pacific side of Nicaragua; the Caribbean coastal region has very poor transportation.

## Ground Transportation

Although railroads exist, they are nonfunctional because tracks and bridges have been destroyed by a combination of guerrilla activity, lack of maintenance, and natural forces. There is no effective railroad traffic in Nicaragua.

The highways of Nicaragua carry the bulk of the people and freight and are located mainly on the western side of Nicaragua. The principal road is the Pan American Highway, which runs from Honduras, between Lake Managua and Lake Nicaragua, through Managua, and then to Costa Rica. This highway is generally fairly good; other roads are not as well maintained. Many of the highways are not paved. There is also no road to Bluefields on the Caribbean coast. Considerable discussion exists regarding building a road from coast to coast. Dubbed the "dry canal," the hope is that it will become an alternative to the Panama Canal for shipping freight.

Driving can be difficult because of the quality of the roads, but for visitors, a bigger problem is a shortage of road signs. Within Managua, for example, it is difficult to find a house number even for a place that has one. Since the city sprawls, knowing the destination and exactly how to get there is a requirement.

The most popular cars in Nicaragua are made by Toyota, Nissan, and Hyundai. Most of those purchased are the smaller, four-cylinder autos produced by these manufacturers. People in the countryside, in particular, want the larger SUVs because of their four-wheel-drive capability and higher ground clearance to use on the often rough roads.

Most urban buses are school-bus style, but Nicaragua also has buses made from pickup trucks and stake trucks. Owners add seats and an awning and go into business. Bus stops are only loosely marked, but buses will often have their routes listed on their sides.

For interurban travel, many people travel by minibus or fifteen-passenger vans. These are more comfortable than are second-class buses, which are described as "chicken buses," although drivers are known to pack in extra people, making travel uncomfortable.

## Air and Sea Transportation

The Managua airport is up-to-date and hosts a number of airlines including American, Continental, COPA, TACA, and Delta. Domestic airlines include Atlantic Airlines and La Costeña. In addition to the airport in Managua, Nicaragua has ten other airports with paved runways.

Although there are other seaports on the Pacific, the most important is Corinto, about one hundred miles northwest of Managua. On the Caribbean side, Puerto Cabezas and El Bluff are the most significant ports, but they do not approach the volume at Corinto.

## Destinations

Besides Managua and the Pacific coast beaches, one important destination in Nicaragua is Ometepe Island in Lake Nicaragua. With its two volcanoes, the island is a wonderful place to visit. The best way to get there is by boat from Rivas (port of San Jorge). Another location is Bluefields on the Caribbean coast. Visitors can enjoy the world of La Mosquitia, along with spectacular beaches and rich coastal rain forests.

## COSTA RICA

Costa Rica is distinctive in Central America in that it is democratic and stable. While relatively low in percentage of arable land, Costa Rica has made the most of its situation by setting aside its wilderness as national parks and using them to bring in tourists. As a result, its transportation system is considerably better developed than those in other areas in Central America.

### Ground Transportation

As is the case in much of Central America, Costa Rica's railroad system is old and not financially sound. Trains exist along the Atlantic coast, and Costa Rica has developed passenger service at various times, but train travel is not a mode that passengers can rely on to move about Costa Rica.

Travelers find that it is much better to use taxis or buses. Taxi service in Costa Rica is convenient and relatively inexpensive. Taxis at the airport are orange, and passengers usually buy tickets from a kiosk before taking one of these taxis. Other licensed taxis are red and sport a gold triangle. These all have meters—even so, it is important for the traveler to make sure the meter is turned on. Costa Rica also has many "pirate" cabs, which operate as taxis. These do not have meters, and it is important to negotiate the price before beginning any trip. In outlying areas away from the capital of San José, many taxis are the four-wheel-drive automobiles needed to negotiate the difficult roads in the region. As with unmetered cabs, fees have to be set before travel.

Costa Rica has the highest number of traffic deaths per mile driven in the Western Hemisphere. Ticos (the usual way to refer to Costa Ricans) are mild mannered until they get into cars. Wild lane changes, pulling out directly into traffic, and a disregard for pedestrians are common. Exacerbating this situation is an inadequate road system. Although some of the major highways are very well kept, many roads have hairpin turns, huge pot holes, and no signage.

The major road in Costa Rica is the Pan American Highway, which runs the length of the nation from Nicaragua to Panama, through San José. Roads tend to run from the Pan American Highway to towns on the Pacific coast. The roads along the coast are often fairly treacherous. There is also a road from San José to Puerto Limón on the Caribbean coast, but that coast does not have a fully developed net of roadways.

Buses are popular, cheap, and common in Costa Rica. Although there are numerous first-class, air-conditioned travel buses, most buses are school buses. Still, these are often in better shape than in other parts of Central America. Even these buses tend to hold to a schedule (although the schedule is not always displayed), leave on time, and are relatively comfortable—as long as the traveler does not have large amounts of luggage. There is a distinct lack of storage on these buses. Ticos travel a great deal on the weekends. Within San José, buses run everywhere and are cheap to ride. Finding the correct bus can be difficult, but the drivers are helpful in overcoming this problem.

### Air and Sea Transportation

The San José airport is modern, well run, and about twenty minutes from town. Many major airlines fly into the airport, including American, Continental, and Delta airlines as well as KLM. Internal air transportation is very well developed, with four airlines—Nature Air, Travel Air, Sansa, and Lacsa—offering flights to tourist areas. On these flights, passengers should plan on being in a small plane and having restrictions on baggage weight. This can be an enjoyable and somewhat thrilling way to travel. Outlying airports are sometimes little more than dirt strips. Not all have terminals, but those that do tend to have an open building with one agent and a cooler of pop.

Both pedestrian and car ferries are found in Costa Rica; some of them substitute for bridges across rivers, while others move up and down the coast. Three different companies operate ferries from Puntarenas, across the Bay of Nicoya, to the tourist beaches further south.

## Destinations

Costa Rica is a major tourist center. Over 500,000 tourists from North America visit the nation every year. Most are drawn to the beaches along the Pacific Ocean, including Tamarindo, Manuel Antonio, and Dominical, which are some of the most beautiful in the world. Besides exploring the beaches and the ocean, sports people can enjoy fishing for sailfish and surfing. Near San José is the famous Arenal Volcano, which is spectacular by itself. In addition, tourists can also enjoy a walk through the adjoining forest, which includes hundreds of different varieties of orchids that live in the sulfur-laden atmosphere of the area. River rafting is also popular on the Pacuare River. On the Caribbean coast, Tortuguera, the home of the green sea turtle and an abundance of plant life, is a favorite destination. Finally, in the southern part of Costa Rica, visitors can enjoy Corcovado National Park. Noted for its amazing plant and animal life, this unspoiled region is one of the most popular destinations for travelers.

## PANAMA

Panama has been defined by transportation. The shortest distance between the Atlantic and Pacific is across this nation, and this fact has dominated the country's history. Panama's transportation saga begins in 1513 when Vasco Nuñez de Balboa led Spaniards across the isthmus to "discover" the Pacific Ocean. The conquest of the Inca Empire and the discovery of precious metals in Peru and Colombia made Panama the gateway to these riches. Products from Spain and Europe were shipped across Panama to the prosperous colonies on the Pacific.

For hundreds of years, these goods followed the Camino Real, the Royal Road across the isthmus, but the road's name does not define its characteristics. Crossing Panama was difficult and very dangerous. Yellow fever and malaria were endemic, and many people died on the way or shortly afterwards. This situation was not rectified until a railroad was completed in 1855. Spurred on by the California gold rush and the demand for goods on the Pacific coast, the railroad was relatively short, covering about fifty miles, but it had to cross major swamps and rivers, which made its building a major accomplishment for the period.

Building the railroad also allowed for the construction of the Panama Canal. Originally, Panama was part of Colombia, but so determined was President Theodore Roosevelt to build a canal that he inspired and supported an independence movement that made Panama a separate nation and the eventual site of the canal. In 1914 the Panama Canal was finished and was designated one of the engineering marvels of the world. Ships that previously required months to go around Tierra del Fuego now crossed the isthmus in days, significantly shortening time and distance.

## Ground Transportation

The previously mentioned railroad continued to function until the 1970s, but eventually it fell into disrepair. As ships increased in size and could no longer use the canal, other means of transshipping were required. In 2001 a rebuilt Panama railroad opened to carry containers and passengers across the country. Both Panamanians and tourists make use of the train, which travels alongside the canal for most of its distance, offering amazing views of the jungle and lowlands as well as of the canal itself. Two versions of the train are available: a tourist excursion train (currently about $35 for a round-trip ticket) and what amounts to a commuter train. Many people travel between Colón on the Atlantic and Panama City on the Pacific, often on a daily basis. The trip is comfortable, safe, and quick.

Most Panamanians, however, want to drive their cars, and the intercity road system supports such travel. Although there are a number of highways, two main roads dominate. The first is the Pan American Highway, which runs from Costa Rica to Panama City and then on to Yaviza, where it ends. It does not connect to highways coming from Colombia. The second major road parallels the canal from Colón to Panama City. These highways are well cared for, but drivers still have to be vigilant. One problem, for example, is that signs are not erected to alert drivers to road construction.

City driving is an altogether different experience. Panamanian drivers are noted for their quest for speed and for ignoring most traffic rules. Horn blowing seems endemic and is a constant part of city life. The streets are old and narrow in some parts of the cities, so slowly inching a car ahead into traffic is the system drivers use. There are not always traffic lights at major intersections. Buses are particularly dangerous since their drivers seem to believe a bus's size means it always has the right-of-way.

Bus service between towns is similar to that in other Central American countries: there are two levels of service, and it is easy to make connections. In towns, however, the intracity buses, or *chivas* as they are known, pay little heed to traffic laws: they stop to pick up and let off passengers wherever they want. Although bus stops are designated, they do not necessarily indicate where the bus will be. Riding in a chiva is the experience of a lifetime. Blasting music, drag-racing starts, screeching brakes, and wild turns typify chiva travel. Panamanians are used to it, but for anyone else, a strong constitution, a sense of humor, and the bravery of a lion are prerequisites.

## Air and Sea Transportation

Air transportation is easy since Panama City is served by numerous international carriers. Forty-one airports have paved runways, so internal air transportation is also fairly easy. A number of services will fly passengers and cargo within Panama and to other nations in Central America.

Sea transportation is obviously critical to Panama. Currently, there are numerous ports, and many cruise ships dock in Panama. The largest attraction is the canal itself. While relatively few Panamanians travel through the canal by boat, numerous cruise ships do transit the isthmus. Private tours can also be arranged easily in Colón and Panama City to take ships through the canal for under $150.

## Destinations

Most of the destinations in Panama are associated with adventures into the jungle, such as to the Embera Indian village; to pleasant beaches, such as those found at Taboga Island (a short

## THE PAN AMERICAN HIGHWAY

The Pan American Highway is usually credited as beginning in Circle, Alaska, and traveling approximately 16,000 miles south to Puerto Montt, Chile. Since no road in the United States or Canada bears that name, the actual distance is not definite. Moreover, a portion of the highway is not completed: a fifty-four-mile stretch of the road is not finished in the Panamanian Darien.

The first proposals for a Pan American highway were actually for a Pan American railroad, but these suggestions were more fanciful than real. Serious discussion began at the Fifth International Conference of American States held in 1923, and delegates passed definite proposals during the 1936 Maintenance of Peace Conference in Buenos Aires.

World War II spurred the construction of the northern part of the road, from the continental United States to Alaska, but it was not until the 1950s that Latin American countries began to plan and build the southern section. A source of confusion was that the highway from the U.S.-Mexican border to Panama was dubbed the Inter-American Highway, but many maps and people simply refer to the entire road from Alaska to Chile as the Pan American Highway.

Despite the many years that have gone by, the road is still not finished. The Darien, a portion of southern Panama and northern Colombia, still has no road. The major problem is that the region is remote and a morass of bogs and swamps. Building is very expensive and difficult. A larger issue, however, is growing opposition to disturbing the ecology of the region. As roads have been built, development has quickly followed, leading to a history of environmental destruction. It is possible the Pan American Highway may never be completed.

In addition to the road that follows the western coast of South America, a number of spur lines also have the name Pan American Highway. Venezuela, Paraguay, Argentina, Uruguay, and Brazil all have segments of the road.

The building of the road has been a major achievement and has helped the commerce of the nations through which it travels.

boat ride from Panama City); or to the historical forts and buildings of the Spanish colonial empire, such as Fort San Lorenzo. A wonderful attraction is the San Blas Islands off the Caribbean coast of Panama. This excursion can be a fascinating visit to various islands, which are populated by indigenous peoples who have to a large extent maintained their culture.

## COLOMBIA

Colombia is a rich and beautiful country, but a country whose history has been marked by considerable violence. Even before becoming a major supplier of illegal drugs, Colombia suffered from a decade of political killings (1948–58), resulting in the deaths of approximately 200,000 people and a great deal of property destruction. With the advent of the drug trade, violence has continued, and the Colombian government does not have full control over the country. As a result, many Colombians have been forced into exile. The transportation sector also has not prospered during the last few decades.

Exacerbating the political situation is the difficult mountainous terrain of Colombia. Despite having four major population centers—Bogotá, Medellín, Cartagena, and Cali—travel between cities, except by air, can be time consuming and difficult. Colombia has a very low ratio of road mileage to population.

## Ground Transportation

As in many Latin American nations, passenger rail travel has declined in favor of roads over the last twenty years. Various governments have vowed to rebuild the railroads, but action does not always follow the rhetoric. The city of Medellín does have a light rail system that bisects the city both from north to south and from east to west, but Colombia does not have a high-quality system of passenger train service. Colombians generally use buses or travel by air between major population centers.

The intercity bus system is well developed, with modern buses and regular schedules, but road conditions prevent taking full advantage of the capabilities of these buses. Moreover, travelers find that it is inadvisable to go through certain areas of the country: bandits and guerrilla forces will not hesitate to stop and rob the passengers on a bus. Travelers also face military checkpoints, at which documentation has to be produced. In other areas of the nation, guerrilla groups have their own checkpoints.

Within Bogotá, and increasingly in other cities, new articulated buses are providing excellent service, but most Colombians travel on *busetas*, or little buses. These are mostly vans although the term is often used to refer to school-bus-style buses as well. These services are private, and the buses are decorated based on the whims of their owners. Sports icons and religious symbolism abound, as do statements of dedication to the owner's girlfriend or spouse. Prices are low, but service is erratic. Still, many of the passengers are regulars, and the atmosphere can be almost family-like.

In the cities, road building and repair have simply not kept pace with existing needs. Traveling from one side of Bogotá to the other can take hours, whether by taxi, which is relatively inexpensive, or by private car. Signage is poor, and intersections that should have traffic lights often do not, which engenders aggressive tendencies in drivers. Luckily, given the number of accidents, the most popular cars in Colombia are small, four-cylinder cars from Japan and Europe.

Despite being inadequate and often in disrepair, there are two main north–south roads in Colombia, one on either side of the central mountain range. The eastern road runs from Santa Marta to Bogotá, and the western road runs from Barranquilla, through Medellín and Cali, to the Ecuador border. There are two highways that join these two main roads at Bogotá. Other major highways run along the Caribbean coast, but there is no road service to the southeastern, or Amazon, area of Colombia.

## Air and Sea Transportation

The rugged terrain of Colombia that makes road and rail traffic so difficult also spurred the growth of air travel. Air transportation, both internationally and domestically, is very well developed. Besides a variety of U.S. and European carriers, Avianca, Colombia's national airline, flies internationally as well as domestically. For domestic business, five or six other airlines compete for passengers.

Colombia is blessed with the Magdalena and Cauca river system, which is navigable for 850 miles. Both freight and passengers are carried on a wide variety of river craft. The Atrato

River and the rivers in the Orinoco system are also navigable for considerable distances. The use of the rivers has declined because of air and road service, but it is still an important option.

## Destinations

As noted previously, the violence and instability of Colombia have led to many Colombians leaving their nation and going elsewhere. It is not unusual then, that Colombia is not a center of tourism. Cruise boats, nevertheless, regularly dock at the main Caribbean ports, such as at Cartagena, Santa Marta, and Barranquilla.

The main vacation spot for Colombians is the Caribbean coast near Santa Marta, an area noted for its palm-shaded beaches and warm, tropical water. Cartagena, which is not far away, is the walled city where much of the early history of colonial Colombia took place. For the more adventurous, the Amazon region of Colombia offers a jungle setting.

## VENEZUELA

Venezuela is a diverse land with open prairies, mountains, and lovely beaches. It also has huge amounts of oil, a fact that has dominated Venezuelan history for the last fifty years and has enabled the construction of a modern transportation network.

## Ground Transportation

As in most nations of the hemisphere, Venezuela's rail system has been eclipsed by the development of the highway system. Although the train service that does exist still carries passengers, its major purpose is to support mining in the west and agriculture in the east. As of 2006, however, plans exist to build more railroads, including a north–south line south of Caracas.

Bus travel is easy and relatively inexpensive, largely as a result of the low cost of gasoline—under twenty cents a gallon. The more modern, first-class buses are called *rapidos*, but as in most countries, a second tier of school buses supplies the needs of rural areas. Many people prefer to take the *expresos* at night. These are comfortable buses, but passengers must bring their own food and warm clothing. It can be very cold at night; sleeping bags are not unheard of. Buses in Venezuela do not usually make stops along the road but go from terminal to terminal. Often the bus stations themselves are a little seedy and can be dangerous. Riders find that it is best to travel with someone else.

While Caracas has a full set of urban buses, the best way to travel is by the excellent subway system. Designed by the French, this system is continually expanding, which makes travel easy and convenient. Each subway stop is an architectural statement, and simply getting off at every stop to look at the structures is a worthwhile endeavor.

The highway system of Venezuela is large and sophisticated in comparison to those of many other Latin American nations. The most important expressway was built in the early 1950s to connect Caracas with its port, La Guaira, on the Caribbean. Previously, traveling the twenty miles had taken several hours and had been a harrowing experience. With the highway, the time was cut to less than an hour, and driving that distance became very easy. Recently, the highway suffered a bridge collapse and was closed in January 2006, which required travelers to return for part of the journey to the old roads, resulting in considerably increased travel time.

The two most developed highways travel from the border of Colombia to Caracas and then along the Caribbean coast. Another north–south road that runs between Barcelona and northern Brazil travels through the agricultural regions of Venezuela and is part of the Pan American Highway. With the exception of the road on the east, the Amazon region of Venezuela effectively has no roads at all.

Cheap gas and good roads have led to the development of a true car culture in Venezuela. Venezuelans prefer big, powerful American cars with large engines. In fact, the sales of cars by manufacturer mirror the sales in the United States: General Motors is first, followed in order by Ford, Toyota, and Chrysler. The current government of President Hugo Chavez, however, has welcomed Chinese automobiles to Venezuela. Most of these autos are the smaller, four-cylinder variety, but it is not clear whether they will catch on.

The wealthy buy the finest cars in the world, and all types can be found on the streets of Caracas. Over the years, these have been passed down to those who are less well-to-do, so the streets of Caracas can be likened to a museum showcasing car production of the last fifty years. The streets seem to contain every make and model ever built. Moreover, many cars have been fixed using parts from other cars, and owners do not always paint the parts to match. A single green fender on a white car or a different-color hood is not unknown.

Driving in Venezuela is easier than elsewhere because the roads are laid out better, but having lots of powerful cars in a limited space can lead to bad accidents. Drivers are aggressive, and those who are timid or uncertain behind the wheel should not drive in Venezuela.

## Air and Sea Transportation

Caracas is served by numerous international carriers and has a well-developed system of internal airports serving outlying areas. The Caracas airport, Maiquetia, is modern and attractive, but it is known as being a dangerous place. Recently, robbery has been a problem. Although transportation to Caracas is easy to find, Venezuelans and foreigners alike have to be vigilant.

Venezuela has a well-developed port system, with La Guaira the largest. Other ports, particularly those west of Caracas, are cargo ports handling petroleum and minerals. Within Venezuela, a number of the rivers, such as the Orinoco, are navigable for part of their lengths, but river traffic does not play a major role in transportation for the majority of Venezuelans.

## Destinations

For many Venezuelans, the easiest trip is to the Island of Margarita. Although individuals can fly there, the least expensive way is to take a ferry from La Guaira or one of the other cities farther east. The island is glorious and known for having sunny weather 340 days of the year. The beaches are white and long, and accommodations include those established for the very wealthy to those designed for campers.

Venezuelans also go to Angel Falls, at 2,650 feet the highest cataract in the world. Located in a remote spot in the southeastern region of Venezuela, the falls are not easy to get to. The simplest way is to fly. Once there, helicopter rides are available, or for the intrepid, native canoes can be paddled into the continuous mist that envelopes the bottom of the falls.

## ECUADOR

Ecuador is a small in size, but its topography makes inexpensive, easy travel difficult. Adding to this difficulty has been continuing political turmoil and an ongoing shortage of funds that has made the transportation system of this nation only adequate.

## Ground Transportation

Indicative of the transportation difficulties of Ecuador was the building and maintenance of the railroad system. Guayaquil, the port of Ecuador, is only about 170 miles from the capital, Quito, but for many years travel was difficult and time consuming. A railroad was the answer, but the rugged terrain and a variety of political developments delayed the railroad's construction. It was not finished until 1908. The northern section, between Quito and San Lorenzo on the coast, was not completed until 1957. The line, however, was often closed because of washouts and maintenance problems. In 1998 El Niño's effects washed out significant sections, and as of 2006, it had not been completely repaired.

Nevertheless, passenger travel is available in the sections that are open. While Ecuadorians take advantage of the service, it is the tourists who often ride the railroads because the views are truly spectacular. The most famous section is between Riobamba and Quito. Travelers climb the "Devil's Nose" in a series of switchbacks and then traverse the Avenue of the Volcanoes (so dubbed by the famous geographer Alexander von Humboldt) to arrive in the city of Quito. Trains do not run every day, but steam excursions are possible for those wanting such an experience.

Other parts of the railroad are also still in use, and passenger travel is possible, but currently there is no strong, national system of train travel in Ecuador. Plans are in the works to rejuvenate the rail system, but progress is slow.

One reason for the lack of progress is the existing highway system. The most important road is the Pan American Highway which runs from Tulcán on the Colombian border, through Quito, and on to the Peruvian city of Tumbes. Important spur highways go to Cuenca and Guayaquil. These roads are maintained better than are other roads in Ecuador.

Buses travel to virtually every city that has a road leading to it. First-class buses offer comfort, while second-class buses go everywhere. Tickets are relatively cheap and are usually no problem to purchase. Weekend tickets and tickets for days during religious festivals, however, are best purchased a day or two ahead. Buses are often overcrowded; it is not unusual for ticket sellers to fill the bus considerably over the number of seats.

## Air and Sea Transportation

Air transportation is popular and fairly inexpensive in Ecuador. A number of internal airlines supply services between cities, a development partially spurred by the lack of any other viable transport system. International service is readily available at both Quito and Guayaquil. Other cities in Ecuador have access to international flights as well.

Water transportation is important in Ecuador, especially in rural areas where the river may be the only highway. Boats, from modern craft to dugout canoes, pick up and drop off passengers much like a bus would. For passengers, these trips are often fascinating, both for the flora and fauna and for the people along the way.

## Destinations

The most important sea travel is to the Galapagos Islands. All manner of boats make the 550-mile trip. These include luxury cruise ships, tall ships, small yachts, and cargo ships. Many of these voyages include stops at multiple islands and extend over a week in length. For those wishing to fly, top-quality accommodations are available.

Ecuadorians and tourists alike take advantage of the Ecuadorian Amazon. Numerous boats ply the Amazon River, and trips can easily be arranged.

# PERU

Peru has a rich heritage dating back before the Inca Empire. Large settled societies flourished and grew, only to ultimately fall. When the Spanish arrived, they discovered a well-ordered Peruvian society based upon a pyramidal structure of social control. In order to maintain power and facilitate growth, the Inca Empire constructed a sophisticated road system. Two roads ran north and south from present-day Quito, Ecuador, to Santiago, Chile. There were also numerous connecting roads. Since these thoroughfares traversed difficult mountainous terrain, the Inca built steps and switchbacks to negotiate mountains and bridges to cross rivers. Rest centers were placed at regular intervals along the roads.

Following the Spanish conquest of the Inca, the Spanish did little to preserve the road system, and time and natural factors slowly worked to erode what the Inca had so painstakingly built. Spain's goal was easy contact with the areas of great mineral wealth, but Spain did not support contact between colonial centers that might diminish Spanish control. By 1821, when Peru gained its independence, the road system was in poor shape. Unfortunately, the new national government of Peru had neither the funds nor the control to reinvigorate the transportation systems.

## Ground Transportation

It was not until railroad construction became possible that a serious effort was made to build a high-quality transportation system, but as in other nations, cost, political bickering, and terrain made this difficult to accomplish. Despite these problems, Peru slowly developed a comparatively extensive railroad system. The system, however, declined from the 1930s through the 1960s. Today, significant portions of the system are no longer accessible. Of the two main railroad lines, the northern line goes from Callao on the coast to Lima, and then to Huancayo and Huancavelica. Some parts of this line are out of service, owned separately, or operate on a different gauge of track, all of which hampers traffic. The southern line, which also has portions out of service, runs from Arequipa in the south to the Lake Titicaca region, and then to Cusco and Machu Picchu. This road also allows access to the Pan American Highway running to La Paz, Bolivia.

Most of the railroad operations in Peru deal with freight. Although there is passenger service, much of it is limited to tourist excursions. The northern line is famous for being the highest railroad in the world. The southern line brings tourists to Cusco and Machu Picchu, the much-visited centers of Inca life and culture.

A significant reason for the decline in train service was the rise in highway availability. The Pan American Highway starts in the very north of Peru, travels along the coast through Lima, and then splits into two parts. The western road follows the coast into Chile. The eastern arm goes to La Paz, Bolivia, and from there into Argentina. These roads are generally well maintained.

Other roads do not receive the same treatment, but in the last ten years, the government has tried to pave internal, secondary roads to open up the frontiers. Nevertheless, while there are exceptions, the eastern portions of Peru generally have no, or very poor, roads. The Amazon region can only effectively be reached by air.

Travel between cities is generally easy because of the bus system. A variety of service levels are offered, and first-class buses tend to leave and arrive on time. As riders move inland and off the main roads, service quality drops because buses are older, highways are less well maintained, and washouts and landslides close roads for periods of time.

Within cities, there are various styles and sizes of buses, but all are known for their aggressive drivers. The larger buses are called microbuses to distinguish them from *cambis*, or *micros*. Cambis are vans rigged to take passengers. Many operate up and down the longer streets, but actual routes may change depending upon the driver and passengers. Since earnings are based on how many people are in the bus, the cambis race up and down the street, cutting each other off in order to load passengers. Often passengers seem to encourage daring traffic moves, which increase the already well-developed aggressive impulses of the drivers.

## Air and Sea Transportation

Reaching Peru by air is easy. Many international airlines fly to Lima, and within Peru a full complement of airlines makes internal travel relatively inexpensive. One of the major destinations is Cuzco. Tourists often prefer taking the plane to experiencing a difficult bus trip. Other regional centers also have regular air service.

Water transportation in Peru is significant. Particularly in the eastern portion of the nation, the Amazon River and Marañón River are major highways. Ocean-going ships can transit from the Atlantic Ocean up the Amazon to Iquitos and, depending on the water levels, as far as Pucallpa. Access to the Atlantic is important economically for Peru.

## Destinations

For travelers, the number one destination is the Inca heartland, including Machu Picchu, Cusco, and the region around Lake Titicaca, which is the highest navigable lake in the world at an altitude of 12,500 feet. Another archeological site, this one in the north near Trujillo, is Chan Chan. Built by the Chimor people, this city was large and sophisticated. It was conquered by the Inca prior to the arrival of the Spanish. Although built of adobe rather than stone, it still demonstrates to the visitor the splendor of the city.

## BOLIVIA

At its zenith, Alta Peru (later Bolivia) was central to the Spanish colonial empire. Within what would become Bolivia's borders was literally a mountain of silver near the city of Potosi. Indeed, for most of the eighteenth century, Potosí was the largest city in South America—until the silver ran out. At much the same time, independence movements began in Latin America. While many thought that Bolivia would be part of Peru, in the end Bolivia became a separate nation.

What followed was a series of events and wars, all of which worked to diminish the country. The Pacific coast region was lost in a war with Chile, a province that produced natural rubber went to Brazil, another province went to Argentina to gain support against Chile, and still more of the nation (as claimed by La Paz) was lost to Paraguay in the Chaco War. Fighting wars and losing them did little to support effective government, and this, added to very difficult, high terrain, has led to a poor transportation system.

## Ground Transportation

As part of the settlement of the War of the Pacific (1879–83), Chile agreed to build a railroad from Arica on the Pacific Coast to La Paz. Construction took many years and was finally completed in 1912, giving Bolivia a rail outlet to the sea and direct international commerce. Until that time, another railroad from Antofagasta, Chile, to Oruro and later La Paz had fulfilled that need. During the first half of the twentieth century, more railroads were built going north and south from La Paz, including a rail line to Lake Titicaca.

These railroads are all in the Bolivia's west. On the eastern side, railroads have been constructed to Brazil from Santa Cruz. The problem is that these roads do not connect with the western system. Discussion is ongoing about connecting the two systems by laying track between Cochabamba and Santa Cruz.

Despite the separation of the two rail networks, the Bolivian railroad system is operational, and it is possible to travel in comfort from La Paz to Peru, Brazil, Argentina, and Chile. Passenger traffic is significant, and three levels of service are available. Travelers also enjoy breathtaking scenery and a fascinating experience.

One reason why the railroads are so heavily used in Bolivia is because roads are relatively poor. The Pan American Highway runs from the Lake Titicaca region to La Paz, then to Oruro and Potosí, and then to Argentina. Other major roads go from Uyuni to Antofagasta and from Santa Cruz to Brazil. While roads may be paved, drivers should not assume that there will be shoulders on the road or good signage. Most of Bolivia's roads are not well maintained. At times, they decrease to one lane, and no guard rails have been built. It is very scary for the uninitiated to take a Bolivian mountain trip, whether in a bus or a car.

Buses go between major cities and small towns. As in other nations, there are levels of service, and at the highest level, all efforts are made to provide the passenger a pleasant time.

## Air and Sea Transportation

As a landlocked nation, Bolivia has no sea transportation itself but does make use of port facilities in other countries. Argentina, Brazil, Chile, and Peru all allow Bolivia rights under a variety of negotiated agreements. Travel by water, however, is also possible on many of the rivers in the Bolivia. Parts of these rivers, however, are often fast, run through rapids, or dry up, decreasing the utility of water transportation.

All the problems with distance and terrain have helped the air industry. La Paz is easy to reach by air from other countries. Various local carriers fly people to the smaller cities in the region.

## Destinations

Bolivia, despite spectacular scenery and a strong indigenous culture, has not attracted tourists, both because of political instability and high altitude. Many people do not want to travel to places at 12,000 feet because of the difficulties of terrain and altitude. The tourism that does exist focuses on adventure tourism for the young.

# CHILE

Chile is unusual in that it is about 2,700 miles long and only about 150 miles at its widest. It is a long, ribbon-like nation between the Pacific Ocean and the Andes. From north to south, the climate and vegetation change dramatically, from the deserts of the north, to the rich central valley, to the cold, forbidding climate of Tierra del Fuego.

Chile was not central to the Spanish empire and, as such, was allowed more self-government than were other areas. The result was that following independence, Chile was considerably less turbulent politically and was able to develop a form of elite-based democracy. Democracy, however, was shattered in 1973 when the army seized the nation and ruled until 1990. Developments during this period hurt Chile, but today it is one of the most prosperous countries in Latin America, and it has one of the best transportation systems on the continent.

## Ground Transportation

Initially, the proximity of the sea allowed for relatively easy water transportation, but the last half of the nineteenth century ushered in a railroad-building boom. Railroads were built from the port of Valparaiso to the capital and main city, Santiago. Subsequent railroad building pushed lines north and south, allowing for easy and quick travel to most parts of the nation. Today, the railroads have deteriorated. The railroad north of Santiago is effectively gone. The southern railroad still operates, but service is not as reliable as it once was. Many of the travelers today are tourists.

Trains have been replaced by a well-developed system of roads. The most important is the Pan American Highway (Route 5), which runs the whole length of the country. Supporting this highway are roads running east and west to Concepción and other population centers. Paved roads also cross the mountains and connect the Chilean cities of Santiago, Antofagasta, and La Serena with Argentina. Another road runs from Iquique in the north to Bolivia. Roads are well maintained. Many sections have been privatized and rebuilt over time and have become toll roads. Traveling is not cheap, but those using toll roads receive value for their money.

Buses, as in other areas of Latin American, are ubiquitous. First-class buses travel highways on time and in safety. In the cities, buses are also available and are considerably less ad hoc than in other areas in the region. Moreover, the bus system is being centralized and upgraded in Santiago with the use of new articulated buses. Finally, Chilean drivers tend to be considerably less aggressive than in other nations, which makes driving considerably easier.

An alternative to buses is the Santiago Metro which is modern, clean, and fast. There are three main lines and over eighty stations. Moreover, new lines and stations are being added. Santiago is also working to integrate the Metro with the bus system so that one fare can take a person to almost anywhere in the city.

## Air and Sea Transportation

Chile has full-service airports at all its important towns. Chile also has a first-class airline, Lan Chile, which flies in Latin America and to the United States. It is affiliated with the "One World" airline consortium, so travelers can earn frequent flyer miles on American Airlines as well as on other major carriers.

Despite the road system, sea transport is still viable, but mainly for cargo. In the south, however, from Puerto Montt southward, where the road system is not as good as further north, small ships and ferries move cargo and people to the more remote cities.

## Destinations

Chileans and visitors enjoy skiing in the southern part of Chile. Different levels of ski resorts are available, and many of the valleys boast first-rate skiing, with all the amenities one would expect to find at the finest ski resorts anywhere. Prices are comparatively reasonable, and since Chile's seasons are the reverse of those in North America, a visit to Chile can provide year-round skiing.

Much the same is true of fishing in Chile. In the southern Puerto Montt region, trout fishing at its best is available; remote, seldom-fished streams yield large trout. It is an angler's dream. And again, as in skiing, the reverse seasons allow for summer fishing during the North American winter.

The most spectacular trip, however, is to Easter Island, which is famous for its massive stone heads. Lan Chile flies directly from Santiago to the island, and accommodations are available. The best way to travel around the island is by taxi, although bicycles are becoming more popular.

## GUYANA, FRENCH GUIANA, AND SURINAME

Three nations occupy the northern coast of South America, bordered by Venezuela on the west, Brazil on the south and east, and the Atlantic to the north. These three nations, Guyana, French Guiana, and Suriname, have a combined population of less that 1.5 million people; of the three, Guyana has almost half the population.

All three nations are marked by poverty, made worse by the lack of a developed transportation system. For example, effectively all railroads in the region are dedicated to transporting single crops or products. And while roads run along the coasts, roads to inland areas are virtually nonexistent. Those that do exist are often gravel roads and subject to washout.

Within the various cities, all three nations maintain bus systems. Most rely on small buses rather than on large ones, and routing can be chaotic. The bus system is increasingly suffering from increasing fuel prices, which drain operating funds and strain the system.

All three nations can be reached internationally by air, but service is not necessarily daily. Smaller planes can be found to fly individuals to other destinations. The rivers of the region are important because in many cases they substitute for roads, carrying both passengers and goods.

## BRAZIL

Brazil is the largest country in Latin America and has a population approaching 200 million. Rather than breaking away from the mother country as the Spanish colonies did, Brazil remained under Portuguese imperial control, but that imperial control was centered within Brazil. Eventually, the Brazilians adopted a republican form of government, which has generally controlled the nation except for the periods 1937–45 and 1964–85.

Although the country was named after a dyewood—Brazil wood, whose color is extracted and used for dyeing cloth—Brazil's first significant product, and the product that shaped its early history, was sugar. With the importation of thousands of African slaves, the Brazilian northeast became the world center of sugar production. Later, other products would become significant, such as minerals in the state of Minas Gerais and coffee in the south.

As each area was settled, the Brazilians had to develop transportation to and from the area, and the easiest answer was coastal shipping. As a result, the Brazilian population hugged the sea, and the interior was not developed.

## Train Travel

In the nineteenth century, railroads seemed to be the answer. Most of the rail lines, however, followed the coast and, compared to the size of Brazil, penetrated inland only a relatively short distance. The northeast had a well-developed train system, but as the economy developed and moved southward, train trackage became centered in the south from the state of Minas Gerais to Rio Grande do Sul. Railroads were at their zenith in the early 1940s and have declined since then. Various governments have indicated that they plan to rebuild the rail system, but the cost of doing so is enormous.

Today, many railroads still operate, but the service is becoming increasingly unreliable except on specific runs. Good service, for example, exists between São Paulo and Rio de Janeiro. Trains have dinning cars and all the traditional amenities. The most famous trip is between Curitiba and Paranaguá, which is known for its wonderful views and vistas. Another important rail line runs to Santa Cruz in Bolivia, and still others connect Brazil to Paraguay and Uruguay.

## Highways

One of the reasons railroads are declining is the rise of highways. Brazil has a well-developed highway network, but maintenance is a constant problem. The government seems more inclined to build new roads than to fix the old ones. Much like the railroad system, most of the roads are within a hundred miles of the coast, but considerable effort is being made to open up western Brazil with the construction of new highways.

Not everyone is supportive of this decision. As roads move into the Amazon regions, cattle ranching quickly follows, and with it comes the general destruction of the native vegetation. Not all of these new roads are paved, and many suffer from washouts and landslides, but prior to this construction, the only way to reach some of the western areas was by plane or small boat.

Within the cities, modern freeways exist, but traffic congestion is still monumental. It can take hours to go short distances, and despite Brazilian drivers making use of side streets, and occasionally sidewalks, commuting is not easy or quick. Pedestrians do not have the right of way in Brazil. São Paulo, in particular, is not for drivers who are easily frightened. Trucks, buses, and cars aggressively compete to use the road, and unless one is nimble and alert, no progress can be made. As a result of this aggressiveness, traffic accidents are a serious problem.

## Automobiles

Volkswagen vehicles are the most popular cars in Brazil, especially the Volkswagen Beetle. The traditional Beetle is no longer produced in Brazil, but the car is still ubiquitous, as is the Brasilia, a station wagon–style Volkswagen. Over time, both types have been modified by Brazilian drivers, and many now have larger engines or are equipped with unusual parts, such as the hood of a more expensive car. But underneath, the Volkswagen still reigns. More and more, other manufacturers are trying to challenge Volkswagen, all producing varieties of small, four-cylinder cars. General Motors is particularly aggressive in this regard, but it has to compete with Honda and Toyota. The Chinese are also trying to establish a presence in the nation with their automobiles.

What makes Brazil unique, however, is its use of ethanol to power its cars. After sugar is extracted from sugar cane, there is little use for the remaining plant, called *begasse*. For years, it was mostly discarded. Beginning in the mid-1980s, Brazil decided to convert the begasse into ethanol to power cars. Today, all cars must run on a mixture of gas and at least 25 percent ethanol. In fact, many cars operate on 100 percent ethanol. By the end of 2007, all cars produced in Brazil must use 100 percent ethanol.

Producing and using ethanol has been an enormous savings to Brazil because the country does not have to import expensive gasoline. Moreover, as oil increases in price, the decision to use ethanol seems increasingly propitious. Currently, plans are underway to use heavier plant oils as additives to diesel fuel, with the goal of creating a renewable fuel to substitute for diesel.

The effect of these laws has meant that automakers must design their cars differently and allow for different engine settings. It has also meant that rather than the smell of gas around "gas" stations, there is the sweet smell of ethanol. Relatively inexpensive fuel encourages more frequent driving, however, and there are lots of cars on a road system that is simply not adequate for the volume. Moreover, parking is very difficult in the major cities of Brazil. Cars fill every niche, and one cannot count on finding parking at one's destination.

## Bus Travel and Subways

The Brazilian bus network is fully developed. Buses are available in a variety of classes for intercity travel, and finding a comfortable, fast bus with all the amenities is not difficult. It is best to buy tickets in advance, but passengers traveling during the week can normally walk up and buy tickets. Runs are frequent. For example, a bus leaves every fifteen minutes between São Paulo and Rio de Janeiro.

City buses operate in all the major cities, but bus service suffers on the congested roads. Buses often seem to crawl along as they try to negotiate city traffic. This is particularly true in São Paulo. An alternative is the various subways of Brazil. The São Paulo Metro that serves the region offers four main lines and is complemented by train lines that are coordinated with the Metro. The system is well laid out, modern and clean, and has a high ridership. It can be hot in the summer, however.

Rio de Janeiro and Recife have subway systems as well. The Rio de Janeiro system is not as large as the São Paulo system, but it is adequate. Clearly, a larger system is needed. Recife's system is unusual in that most of it travels above ground. Both the Rio de Janeiro and Recife systems are easy to use and relatively inexpensive.

## Sea Travel

Rio de Janeiro and Santos (the port of São Paulo) are the largest ports in Brazil, but there are many others up and down the coast. Ferry and passenger service is still available along the coast, but bus travel has displaced most of the passenger service. Virtually all of the major cruise lines regularly make calls on the ports of Brazil, including the Amazon river port of Manaus.

Most of the river traffic can be found on the Amazon and its tributaries. From fairly large ships to dugout canoes, all manner of craft travel the waters of the region, making it possible to go to almost any destination by water. Tourists, in particular, have taken to using small boats to travel the region, but local traffic is still the backbone of this brown-water fleet.

## Air Travel

Flying to Brazil is easy and relatively inexpensive. In addition to the major international carriers, VARIG, a major Brazilian airline, flies internationally. Within Brazil, VARIG and TAM provide excellent, first-class service. With such a large area to cover, quite a few smaller, private airlines make it possible to go just about anywhere. These airlines often have scheduled flights, but depending upon passenger demand, special flights can easily be arranged. Since the planes are small, baggage and passengers must be weighed and situated carefully in the plane to ensure safety.

## Destinations

Brazil has just about everything. The bright lights of Rio de Janeiro and São Paulo compete with the warm, sunny beaches of the northeast. The strong German influence can be found in the south, where the topography begins to look like Bavaria. But, clearly, the best destination for Brazilians is the Amazon River and all the mysteries it holds. From fishing to bird watching to simply enjoying the unique flowers and vegetation, a trip up the Amazon is a wonderful event. The trips are easy to arrange, and the amount of adventure can be dictated by what the traveler purchases.

## PARAGUAY

Asunción, Paraguay's capital, was one of the first Spanish settlements in the New World. It was intended as an entry point into the continent, but it quickly became an outpost. While the Paraguay and Paraná rivers offer Asunción access to the sea, the distance of approximately 1,000 miles between the capital and the South Atlantic is simply too far to allow strong commerce to develop. Besides distance, Paraguay also had a history of political isolation in its early years following independence. This did not stop the nation from fighting the disastrous War of the Triple Alliance with Argentina, Brazil, and Uruguay, and in the process losing a large portion of its population and a considerable amount of its land.

Politically, control in Paraguay has been assumed by a number of strong leaders, who ruled the country as dictators. The last was Alfredo Stroessner, who controlled the nation from 1954 to 1989. While brutal, his regime did provide the stability that allowed for some infrastructure development. Since his departure, Paraguay has had a variety of leaders, but lack of funds has made it difficult for the various governments to modernize Paraguay.

## Ground Transportation

Water transportation was the key to getting to Paraguay and to traveling within the nation. Unfortunately, droughts occur, and at times river travel becomes difficult. In the nineteenth century, the answer seemed to be the railroad. It was not until the early part of the twentieth century, however, that a line was finished joining Asunción with Buenos Aires,

but like so many other railroads in Latin America, this line has closed down. A lack of maintenance and the high cost of rebuilding the track and roadbed led to its downfall. For a number
of years, steam trains still ran along segments; at times, these trains have been resurrected for
tourists, but currently there is no passenger rail service in Paraguay.

Road building has helped spur the demise of trains. In the last quarter century, new roads
have been built or modernized between Asunción and Ciudad del Este, roughly at the junc-
ture of Argentina and Brazil at Iguazú Falls. The road, however, continues into Brazil and the
port of Santos. Another road connects the capital with Encarnación and Argentina.
Currently, work is taking place to complete the Trans Chaco Road, which will connect Asunción
with Bolivia.

Even these major roads, however, are not particularly well maintained, and at times they
can narrow to one lane. This seldom seems to slow down Paraguayan drivers or long-distance
buses, which plough ahead regardless of the situation. Despite the daring nature of the drivers,
as in most of Latin America, the bus is the simplest and easiest way to get around. A variety
of bus classes are available from many different bus companies. It is important to learn
exactly what services a bus system is offering since these vary—and to remember that price
is not always the measure of quality.

Asunción's fleet of intracity buses is largely composed of school buses. Many seem almost
ancient, and all are very colorful. Drivers seem to take considerable pride in the motif they
select, and some of the art is quite remarkable. Much of it is graphic rather than pictures.
Inside the bus, the theme outside is sometimes repeated. In all cases, however, the buses are
uncomfortable, even when there are few passengers. Springs, which once saved passengers'
backs, surrendered to the pothole-filled roads long ago.

There are relatively few private cars in Paraguay, and those that exist seem to be of two
levels. In Asunción, it is not unusual to see very expensive European luxury autos and U.S.
sport utility vehicles costing many thousands of dollars. On the other hand, there are many
quite ramshackle vehicles from previous decades that look as if they belong in a junk yard.
Strangely, there seem to be few vehicles in between these extremes.

## Air and Sea Transportation

Flying to Asunción is not difficult, but there are no direct flights from the United States.
Most people fly to São Paulo, Buenos Aires, or Santiago and then on to Asunción. Flights
within Paraguay are not particularly easy to find. Local airlines have a history of being in
business for only short periods. In addition, flight schedules are not always maintained.

As noted, the rivers of the region are critical for travel, particularly for freight. Passengers,
however, can also use the waterways to travel between cities. The types of boats are numerous,
from old wooden scows to modern steel ships. The older boats take on the style of third-class
buses, crowded with all manner of people carrying all manner of things. Many of the boats
seem to be owned by Argentines although some owners are Paraguayan. The easiest place to
book passage is in Asunción.

## Destinations

Paraguay has not developed its tourist industry. Most travelers go to Iguazú Falls, which is
near Ciudad del Este. Other historic spots are ruins of old Jesuit missions. Other types of
visitors to Paraguay are Brazilians and Argentines looking for cheap prices on smuggled
goods.

# URUGUAY

Uruguay is one of the smallest nations in South America. Most of its land is prairie or rolling hills. The nation has generally benefited from a quasi-democratic government although there have been important interludes of military government. Since 1985, the country has enjoyed a democratic system.

## Ground Transportation

Railroads were important in the early development of Uruguay, and the government supported the growth of a sophisticated system. Over time, however, and particularly in the last twenty years, the system has deteriorated. At times steam engines are still brought out for tourist trains, but fundamentally, the rail system today is completely cargo oriented.

The highway system is large and generally well maintained. Montevideo is at the center of a series of roads that radiate out through the center of Uruguay as well as to all the neighboring countries. The most traveled highway is Route 1, which runs through Colonia, Montevideo, to Punta del Este. Traffic, however, is often heavy, which increases travel time and promotes accidents.

Traffic in Montevideo is heavy, but getting around is still relatively easy. Modernization projects and new highways and roads have promoted automobile traffic, which has allowed for calmer, safer driving than in other cities.

Bus usage dominates passenger travel in Uruguay. The bus system is known for its exceptional quality and ease of use. All intercity buses leave from Tres Cruces bus terminal and go just about everywhere in Uruguay as well as to surrounding countries. Since the country is small, most trips are short. For example, it takes about two and one-quarter hours to travel to Punta del Este. Moreover, the price is low and reasonable, considering the quality of the travel.

## Air and Sea Transportation

Much like a journey to a major city in Paraguay, the final leg of a journey to Montevideo is not direct. Most people arriving from North America will fly to São Paulo, Buenos Aires, or Santiago and then fly to Uruguay. Uruguay, however, does have a national airline, Pluna, which flies to Chile, Brazil, and Argentina, and often offers the easiest connecting flights. Pluna and Aerolineas Argentinas also fly between Buenos Aires and Punta del Este. During the tourist season, there are multiple flights each day.

Most of the population of Uruguay lives near water, whether it is the Uruguay River, the Rio de la Plata, or the South Atlantic. As a result, waterborne traffic is significant and is not just for freight. Regular passenger and car ferries run between Montevideo and Buenos Aires. These ships are modern and fast. The seats are large and plush, and depending on the level of service, quality food is served as passengers enjoy an approximately three-and-one-half-hour trip between the two cities. Ferries also leave from other cities such as Colonia, and special buses take passengers to the dock in Montevideo for passage to Argentina.

## Destinations

Uruguayans, but also many Argentines and Brazilians, make the resort city of Punta del Este their major destination. The area is reminiscent of Las Vegas in that it has large hotels, gambling casinos, golf, horseback riding, and other activities. It also has a beach and offers visitors both skiing and snorkeling. Punta del Este is expensive and is the playground of the well-to-do of the region. Other areas near Punta del Este cater to the middle class.

## ARGENTINA

Argentina is famous for its rural, gaucho culture as well as its urban tango culture, but Argentina is much more than that. It is a complex amalgam of European cultures, principally from Spain, Italy, and Germany, which has tried to create a true Argentine identity. The nation's failure to do so is attested to by its turbulent, and at times, violent politics. A world center of wealth and culture in the last half of the nineteenth century, Argentina today has lost that standing as it has struggled economically and politically. The turbulence of the last sixty years has done little to aid the nation's transportation system. Nevertheless, because of a relatively flat terrain, travel in Argentina is relatively easy.

### Ground Transportation

One of the first nations in the world to embrace railroads was Argentina. Beginning in the last half of the nineteenth century, Argentina saw a massive railroad building boom. By 1900 some observers were commenting that Argentina had overbuilt its system, but it was by far the most sophisticated system in Latin America.

Railroads all over Latin America have deteriorated in the last fifty years, and many have been closed or abandoned. Argentina has suffered from the same decline. What remains of the long-distance railroad is used almost exclusively for freight. Nevertheless, a few subsidized long-distance passenger trains still exist. While these trains do not run every day, it is possible to go from Buenos Aires to Tucumán by train. As of 2006, discussions and planning were underway within the Argentine government to revitalize the rail system in general and to build a high speed train from Buenos Aires to Rosario to Córdoba.

For train lovers, a number of tourist trains both in the Andes region and in Patagonia are available. Most of these trains are seasonal and do not run everyday. One of the most popular is the *Trochita*, which runs north and south along the Andes in northwestern Chubut province. The train gained considerable fame from Paul Theroux's book, *The Old Patagonian Express*.

Replacing the trains in Argentina are numerous highways. Argentina has a fine road system that, while not perfectly maintained, is generally quite sufficient. The major highways, in particular, are kept in good shape. The most traveled main highway is Route 9, which travels from Buenos Aires, west to Córdoba, and north to Tucumán, Salta, and Jujuy. Most roads do not have tolls, but segments have been privatized, so travelers should be prepared to pay along the way.

Buses travel to all parts of Argentina. A trip to the main bus station in Buenos Aires offers travelers a huge array of bus companies from which to select. The companies are organized by the region of the country they serve. It is also possible to bargain over the price of a ticket, particularly if traveling a long distance. Service is generally divided into three main categories: *regular*, *semi-cama*, and *cama*. *Cama* means bed in Spanish, but a better translation for these classes of travel would be regular seating, seats that are semi-reclining, and seats that recline. At the more elite levels, full, hot meals are often served, and movies are shown on closed-circuit television.

At the beginning of the twentieth century, Buenos Aires started building a complete system of trolley cars. These trams generally survived until the 1960s, when buses completely replaced them. Since then, the first buses have been replaced by more modern buses with engines in the back. Each company has buses of a different color, but these buses don't have any of the flavor of a Guatemalan "chicken bus." Rather, the bus system is completely professional and uses electronic tickets. For those wanting an upgrade even within urban transportation, it is possible to take a *diferentiales*, or a bus offering special services, including fewer stops and air conditioning.

Buses are particularly useful if going north and south in Buenos Aires: except for one line, the subway (*subte*) system in Buenos Aires goes east and west. The system is old, having been started in 1913; although it was kept updated until 1945, it generally was allowed to languish after that time. Today, the system is small for a city the size of Buenos Aires. As of 2006, plans were in place to build extensions on existing lines as well as new lines, but just keeping the old system functioning is difficult. Some of the cars are quite old, and traveling on the "A" line is a step back in time. Still, it is heavily used, efficient, and cheap.

For the citizens of Buenos Aires (called *Porteños*), another alternative is the light rail system that runs between downtown and the suburbs. Trains begin early in the morning and continue until after midnight. The trains use electric power and are quiet. It is quite a pleasant way to travel.

Of course, another possibility is driving in Buenos Aires, but given the high-quality public transportation, driving is not likely to be the best alternative. Roads are congested, lane lines and stop signs seem to mean little, and every decision a male driver makes seems to determine his manhood.

European cars are particularly popular in Argentina. Renault and Fiat both produce and sell cars in the country. Several U.S. automakers (Ford, GM, and Chrysler) also produce cars in Argentina. Generally, small four-cylinder models are the most prevalent, but large Mercedes Benz cars and powerful American-made SUVs are much sought after.

## Air and Sea Transportation

Given its size, it is not surprising that Argentina has numerous airports and airline services. Buenos Aires has two airports, Aeroparque Metropolitano Jorge Newberry (better known simply as Aeroparque) and Ministro Pistarini Airport (better known as Ezeiza after the area where it is located). Generally speaking, Aeroparque handles domestic flights while Ezeiza services international routes. Aeroparque is in town and easy to get to and use, while Ezeiza is on the outskirts of the city.

Transportation by water on the Rio de la Plata water system has been discussed in the Paraguay and Uruguay sections. It is possible to travel by boat over 1,000 miles from Buenos Aires to Bolivia, but that form of travel is dependent on the depth of water in the rivers.

## Destinations

Argentines travel to all parts of their nation a great deal, but certain places stand out. The first is Mar del Plata, Argentina's famous beach resort. Noted for its miles of beaches, this city, which is about 235 miles from Buenos Aires, offers all that one would expect, from swimming to snorkeling to shopping. Nighttime entertainment is available at various clubs.

Argentine vacationers also go to the city of Bariloche, which is nestled against the Andes and is noted for its skiing. With literally thousands of hotel rooms and many ski slopes, skiers from Argentina and the rest of the world enjoy first-quality skiing. The area is also known for its chocolate. Another area of note in Patagonia is El Calafate, in the far south of

Patagonia near the Andes Mountains. This area does not offer the bright lights and glamour of Mar del Plata or Bariloche, but it does offer unspoiled nature. Trekkers, fishermen, and duck hunters can all take advantage of the region.

# RESOURCE GUIDE

## PRINT SOURCES

Azevedo, Paulo Cesar de, Vladimir Sacchetta, and Vergniaud Calazans Concalves. *O Século de automóvel no Brasil.* Sao Caetano do Sul: Brasinca, 1989.

Federal Highway Administration. *Highways of Friendship: An Intimate Account of the Tour of the Pan American Highway Commission, Its genesis, Accomplishments and Plans for the Future.* Washington, DC: Federal Highway Administration, 1993.

Hartwig, Richard. *Roads to Reason: Transportation, Administration and Rationality in Colombia.* Pittsburgh: University of Pittsburgh Press, 1983.

Hillstrom, Kevin. *Latin America and the Caribbean: A Continental Overview of Environmental Issues.* Santa Barbara, CA: ABC-CLIO, 2004.

Howland, Joyce Elizabeth. *The Economics of Brazilian Transportation Policy, 1945–1970.* Ph.D. dissertation, Vanderbilt University, 1972.

Lande, Nathaniel, and Andrew Lande. *The 10 Best of Everything: Passport to the Best: An Ultimate Guide for Travelers.* Washington, DC: National Geographic, 2006.

Mullins, Margaret C. *Innovations in Bus, Rail, and Specialized Transit in Latin America.* Washington, DC: Transportation Research Board, 2005.

Parga, Alfredo. *Más de 100 años de automovilismo argentino: historia de una passion.* Buenos Aires: Editorial Atlántida, 1992.

Stokes, Charles J. *Transportation and Economic Development in Latin America.* New York: Praeger, 1968.

World Bank. *Meeting the Infrastructure Challenge in Latin America and the Caribbean.* Washington, DC: World Bank, 1995.

## WEBSITES

*A-Z World Airports.* http://www.azworldairports.com/airports/. Specific information about airports.

*Bus Station Argentina.* Bus Station. http://www.busstation.net/main/busarg.htm. Specific information about bus service.

*Counselor Information Sheets.* Bureau of Counselor Affairs, U.S. Department of State. http://travel.state.gov/travel/cis_pa_tw/cis/cis_1765.html#a. For tourists, a good source of information is the U.S. Government Consular information reports.

*Lonely Planet.* http://www.lonelyplanet.com/worldguide/. A good general source concerning transportation in Latin America.

*South American Passenger & Urban Transit.* RailServe. http://www.railserve.com/Passenger/South_America. Specific information about rail service.

U.S. Central Intelligence Agency. *World Factbook.* https://www.cia.gov/cia/publications/factbook/index.html. Quite a few Web pages offer information on transportation in Latin America, but most of them take their information from the *CIA World Factbook.* The *Factbook* is a good source for statistical information on road mileage, rail mileage, and similar statistical data.

*World Travel Guide.* http://www.worldtravelguide.net/country/country_guide.ehtml. A good general source concerning transportation in Latin America.

# GENERAL BIBLIOGRAPHY

Aching, Gerald. *Masking and Power: Carnival and Popular Culture in the Caribbean.* Minneapolis: University of Minnesota Press, 2002.

Arbena, Joseph L. *Sports and Society in Latin America: Diffusion, Dependency, and the Rise of Mass Culture.* New York: Greenwood Press, 1988.

Balderston, Daniel, and Mike Gonzalez. *Encyclopedia of Contemporary Latin American and Caribbean Cultures.* New York: Routledge, 2000.

Beezley, William H., and Linda A. *Latin American Popular Culture: an Introduction.* Wilmington, DE: SR Books, 2000.

Brown, Isabel Zakrzewski. *Culture and Customs of the Dominican Republic.* Westport, CT: Greenwood Press, 1999.

Casillo-Feliú, Guillermo. *Culture and Customs of Chile.* Westport, CT: Greenwood Press, 2000.

Dash, Michael J. *Culture and Customs of Haiti.* Westport, CT: Greenwood Press, 2000.

Foster, David William, Melissa Fitch Lockhart, and Darrell B. Lockhart. *Culture and Custom of Argentina.* Westport, CT: Greenwood Press, 1998.

Handelsman, Michael. *Culture and Customs of Ecuador.* Westport, CT: Greenwood Press, 2000.

Hinds, Harold E. Jr., and Charles M. Tatum. *Handbook of Latin American Popular Culture.* Westport, CT: Greenwood Press, 1985.

Ho, Christine G. T., and Keith Nurse. *Globalisation, Diaspora, and Caribbean Popular Culture.* Kingston, Jamaica: Ian Randle, 2005.

Lehmann, David. *Struggle for the Spirit: Religious Transformation and Popular Culture in Brazil and Latin America.* Cambridge, UK: Polity Press, 1996.

Lent, John A. *Caribbean Popular Culture.* Bowling Green, OH: Bowling Green State University Popular Press, 1990.

Luis, William. *Culture and Customs of Cuba.* Westport, CT: Greenwood Press, 2001.

Mordecai, Martin. *Culture and Customs of Jamaica.* Westport, CT: Greenwood Press, 2001.

Rowe, William, and Vivian Schelling. *Memory and Modernity: Popular Culture in Latin America.* New York: Vesco, 1991.

Salman, Ton. *The Legacy of the Disinherited: Popular Culture in Latin America: Modernity, Globalization, Hybridity and Authenticity.* Amsterdam: CEDLA, 1996.

Schwartz, Rosalie. *Flying Down to Rio: Hollywood, Tourists, and Yankee Clippers.* College Station: Texas A&M Press, 2004.

Shaw, Lisa, and Stephanie Dennison. *Pop Culture Latin America!: Media, Arts, and Lifestyle.* Santa Barbara, CA: ABC-CLIO, 2005.

Swanson, Philip. *The New Novel in Latin America: Politics and Popular Culture after the Boom.* Manchester, UK: St. Martin's Press, 1995.

Vianna, Hermano. *The Mystery of the Samba: Popular Music and National Identity in Brazil.* Translated and edited by John Charles Chasteen. Chapel Hill: University of North Carolina Press, 1999.

Vincent, Jon S. *Culture and Customs of Brazil.* Westport, CT: Greenwood Press, 2003.

Weiss, Judith A. *Latin American Popular Theatre: The First Five Centuries.* Albuquerque: University of New Mexico Press, 1993.

Williams, Raymond L. *Culture and Customs of Colombia.* Westport, CT: Greenwood Press, 1999.

# ABOUT THE EDITORS AND CONTRIBUTORS

## THE VOLUME EDITOR

JOHN F. BRATZEL is Professor of Writing and American Studies at Michigan State University. He has won the prestigious MSU Teacher-Scholar Award for excellence in both teaching and scholarship, the Center for Latin American and Caribbean Studies awarded him its Distinguished Faculty Award, and he has won the Popular Culture Association Presidents' Award for his work in the field of Popular Culture. Bratzel has published extensively on Latin America including two works on Latin America during World War II and two on teaching Latin American studies. He has also written articles and given papers on sports in popular culture. Currently, he is a member of the Executive Committee of the Consortium of Latin American Studies Program and the President of the Popular Culture Association.

## THE GENERAL EDITOR

GARY HOPPENSTAND is Professor of American Studies at Michigan State University and the author of numerous books and articles in the field of popular culture studies. He is the former president of the national Popular Culture Association and the current editor-in-chief of *The Journal of Popular Culture*.

## THE CONTRIBUTORS

JOSEPH L. ARBENA is Professor Emeritus of History at Clemson University. His teaching and research focus for over 40 years has been Latin America and modern sports. He previously served as editor of the *Journal of Sport History*. He twice held Fulbright Fellowships and is an elected corresponding member of the Colombian Academy of History.

ROBERT T. BUCKMAN is Associate Professor of Communication, University of Louisiana at Lafayette. He is the author of *Latin America 2006*, an annually revised reference book in The World Today Series. He served a Fulbright Fellowship in Chile in 1991. His scholarly and professional articles on Latin American media have appeared in numerous journals, and his freelance journalistic reporting on Latin American politics has been published in several major newspapers. He earned his doctorate in journalism and Latin American studies from the University of Texas at Austin in 1986.

JOHN CHARLES CHASTEEN is the Patterson Distinguished Term Professor of Latin American History at the University of North Carolina, Chapel Hill. He is the author of *National Rhythms, African Roots: The Deep History of Latin American Popular Dance* (2004).

LINDA A. CURCIO-NAGY holds a Ph.D. in Latin American Studies from Tulane University and is currently Associate Professor of History, University of Nevada, Reno. She has published on religious culture, gender issues, and festivals, including the monograph *The Great Festivals of Colonial Mexico City: Performing Power and Identity.* She is currently at work on a book entitled *Grave Sins of Sensuality: Solicitation in the Confessional in Mexico, 1564–1700.*

LEONARDO FERREIRA is Associate Dean and Director of Graduate Studies at the School of Communication, University of Miami. He studies and writes about the development of and changes within the Latin American press with particular emphasis on freedom of the press. He has published numerous articles and is the author of *Freedom of the Press? Centuries of Silence in Latin America.*

LÚCIA FLÓRIDO is Assistant Professor of French and Portuguese at the University of Tennessee, Martin. Since 2001 she has performed research on twentieth-century Brazilian literature, focusing particularly on the representation of women by male biographers. In 2006 she received a research award to conduct work in Minas Gerais, Brazil.

BRADEN K. FRIEDER is Assistant Professor of Art History at Morehead State University, Morehead, Kentucky. His research interests range from Renaissance and Baroque art to pre-Columbian America and the decorative arts. He has published book chapters and scholarly articles on art, music, and cultural history.

RANDAL P. GARZA earned his Ph.D. in Spanish Language and Literature from Michigan State University, where he also served as the Editorial Assistant of *Celestinesca,* a journal dedicated to the study of *Celestina* by Fernando de Rojas (1499). He is currently Assistant Professor at the University of Tennessee at Martin, where he teaches courses in Latin American culture, history, and film. He is currently publishing a book titled: *Understanding Plague: The Medical and Imaginative Texts of Medieval Spain.*

PETER MANUEL is Professor of Ethnomusicology at John Jay College and the CUNY Graduate Center. His numerous publications on Caribbean music include *Caribbean Currents: Caribbean Music from Rumba to Reggae* (2nd edition, 2006) and *East Indian Music in the West Indies: Tan-Singing, Chutney, and the Making of Indo-Caribbean Culture* (2000).

KRISTEN MCCLEARY is Assistant Professor of History at James Madison University. She writes about popular culture, especially theater and carnival, in Buenos Aires, Argentina in the early twentieth century. Her dissertation, "Culture and Commerce: An Urban History of Theater in Buenos Aires, 1880 to 1920," won the Conference on Latin American History's Lewis Hanke Prize in 2004.

DANIEL J. NAPPO earned his doctorate in Spanish Language and Literature at Michigan State University and is currently Assistant Professor of Spanish at the University of Tennessee at Martin. He is a García-Robles Fulbright scholar and conducts research into Latin American popular literature, especially the Mexican corrido and the Brazilian folheto. His dissertation, which he is revising for publication, examines millennial imagery in the novel of the Mexican Revolution.

PATRICE ELIZABETH OLSEN is Associate Professor of Latin American history, Illinois State University. Her book *Artifacts of Revolution: Architecture, Society, and Politics in Mexico City, 1920–1940* (forthcoming, 2007) received the Lewis Hanke Prize from the Conference on Latin American History, and the Michael C. Meyer Award from the Rocky Mountain Council for Latin American Studies. She received the University Teaching Initiative Award in 2002–03 and was named Outstanding College Teacher in 2004–05. Her current research focuses on identity, memory, and revolution in Cuba, and on on U.S. national security policy, intelligence, and hemispheric security.

JEFFREY M. PILCHER is Associate Professor of History, University of Minnesota. He earned his Ph.D. under the direction of William H. Beezley at Texas Christian University. His books include ¡*Que vivan los tamales! Food and the Making of Mexican Identity* (1998), *Cantinflas and the Chaos of Mexican Modernity* (2001), *The Human Tradition in Mexico* (2003), and *The Sausage Rebellion: Public Health, Private Enterprise, and Meat in Mexico City, 1890–1917* (2006). His current research examines the globalization of Mexican cuisine.

REGINA A. ROOT is Associate Professor of Modern Languages and Literatures at the College of William and Mary. She is editor of *The Latin American Fashion Reader* (2005) and the author of a manuscript on "Couture and Consensus: Fashion and Political Culture in Postcolonial Argentina."

INDEX

Amado, Jorge, 150
American football, 288–289
Andean cuisine
    and agriculture, 127
    cookbooks, 129
    dehydrated foods, 127
    and ethnic differences, 128
    European influence, 128
    and festivals, 130
    and geography, 126
    and government programs, 129–130
    indigenous foods, 127
    industrialization of foods, 129
    nutrition, 127
Architecture
    Brasília, 9–10
    in Cuba, 13–15
    European influences, 3
    and foreign styles, 2–4
    functionalism, 4–6
    general themes of, 2–10
    impact on society, 4–5
    international style, 6–7, 14
    in Mexico, 10–11
    postmodernism, 11
    São Paulo's Prestes Maia building, 8
    shopping malls, 8–9
    skyscrapers, 16
    and socialism, 13, 14
    and squatters, 7–8
    in university cities, 12–13
    and urban growth, 7–8
    vernacular, 1
Argentina
    art, 43–45
    automobiles, 377

carnival, 308, 313–314
dance, 68–71
food. *See* Southern cone cuisine
literature, 156–157
magazines, 242
music, 210–211
newspapers, 241–242
radio, 258
railroads, 376
soccer, 273
and sports, 297
and theater, 309–314
transportation and travel, 376–378
Argentinean cinema
    beginnings of, 105–106
    and foreign investment, 108
    and government subsidy, 107
    impact of foreign films, 106
    and national economy, 107
    during World War II, 106–107
Art
    African influence, 39, 45
    in Argentina, 43–45
    Asian influence, 37
    basketry, 38
    in Belize, 29
    in Bolivia, 37
    in Brazil, 39–41
    in the Caribbean, 45–46
    in Chile, 41–42
    in Colombia, 32–34
    during the Colonial period, 24–25, 29,
        31–32, 34, 35, 39, 43, 44, 45
    constructivism, 44–45
    in Costa Rica, 31–32
    and crafts, 39

Art (*continued*)
    and food, 28
    in French Guiana, 38–39
    in Ecuador, 35–36
    in El Salvador, 30
    European influence, 26, 29, 30, 35, 44
    in Guatemala, 29–30
    in Guyana, 37–38
    in Honduras, 30–31
    during the independence period, 29
    indigenism, 26, 36, 41
    interactive, 40–41
    in Mexico, 23–28
    modernism, 26, 37, 39–40, 43
    murals, 26–27, 31, 32, 33
    in Nicaragua, 31
    painting, 30–31, 33, 35, 36, 41–42
    in Panama, 32
    in Paraguay, 42
    in Peru, 36–37
    photography, 27–28, 33
    pottery, 28
    pre-Hispanic, 24, 28, 32
    printmaking, 25–26, 27, 40, 43
    prisoner artists, 39
    religious, 24, 36
    during the Revolutionary period, 25
    schools, 25, 29, 31, 32, 33, 34, 35, 39, 44
    sculpture, 27
    in Suriname, 38
    surrealism, 27–28, 42
    in Uruguay, 42–43, 68–71
    in Venezuela, 34–35
    and voodoo, 45–46
Automobiles
    in Argentina, 377
    in Brazil, 371–372
    in Cuba, 351
    ethanol, 372
    in Mexico, 347–348
    in Nicaragua, 357
    in Paraguay, 374
    racing, 287–288
    in Venezuela, 364
Auto racing, 287–288
Aztecs
    gender roles, 174–175
    marriage, 173
    sex, 173

Baseball
    in Dominican Republic, 279
    in Mexico, 279
    in Puerto Rico, 279
    stars, 279–280
    and U.S. major leagues, 278–279
    World Baseball Classic (WBC), 278
Basketball, 284–285
Beach volleyball, 285–286
Belize, art, 29
Boal, Augusto, 324–325
Bolivia
    agrarian reform, 129–130
    art, 37
    carnival, 338–339
    fashion, 75–76
    film, 110
    food. *See* Andean cuisine
    magazines, 236
    newspapers, 236
    railroads, 368
    theater, 338
    transportation and travel, 367–368
Bolt, Alan, 329
Boxing, 280
Brazil
    and architecture, 9–10
    and art, 39–41
    automobiles, 371–372
    carnival, 326–328
    comic books, 157–158
    dance, 65–67
    film. *See* Brazilian cinema
    food. *See* Caribbean and Brazilian
        cuisine; Southern cone cuisine
    literature, 149–151, 157–162
    magazines, 246
    music, 211–212
    newspapers, 244–246
    radio, 256–257
    soccer, 274
    television, 262, 265
    theater, 323–328
    transportation and travel, 370–373
Brazilian cinema
    beginnings of, 99
    Brasil Films, 101
    Canibalismo and Tropicalismo, 102
    censorship, 102–103
    chanchadas, 101
    Cinema Novo (New Cinema), 101–103, 104
    Collor de Mello, Fernando, 104
    Concine, 103
    contemporary, 104
    Embrafilme, 103

European influences, 100–101
Golden Age, 100
impact of foreign films, 100, 101,
    103–104
international market, 104–105
and Italian immigrants, 100
and politics, 102
Pornochanchada, 103
Vera Cruz Films, 101
and women, 104
Breccia, Alberto, 157
Bullfighting, 291

Cantínflas, 98, 331
Caribbean and Brazilian cuisine
African influences, 121, 123–124
Asian influence, 124
and festivals, 126
and foreign immigrants, 124
impact of food exports, 124
indigenous food, 122
industrialization of foods, 125
manioc, 122, 125
nutrition, 125
and slavery, 123–124
staple foods, 125–126
sugar cane, 123
Carnival
in Argentina, 308, 313–314
in Bolivia, 338–339
in Brazil, 326–328
in Colombia, 322
in Cuba, 319–320
and dance, 56–57
in Mexico, 334
in Uruguay, 315–316
Chile
art, 41–42
dance, 62
film, 109–110
food. See Southern cone cuisine
freedom of the press, 239
magazines, 240–241
music, 210–211
newspapers, 240
radio, 256
railroads, 369
television, 264
theater, 316–317
transportation and travel, 368–370
Cinema. See Film
Clemente Walker, Roberto, 279–280
Coelho, Paulo, 150–151

Colombia
art, 32–34
carnival, 322
dance, 67–68
film, 109
food. See Andean cuisine
magazines, 237–238
and music, 209–210
newspapers, 236–237
radio, 257–258
theater, 320–322
transportation and travel, 361–363
Comic books
American influence, 157, 158
Argentinian, 156–157
Brazilian, 157–158
compared to photonovels, 153
and dominicales, 153
earliest, 154
European influence, 156
and film, 155
horror, 158
and indigenous culture, 158
magazines, 225
Mexican, 154–156
origins of, 153
and publishing, 153–154
and radio, 155
underground, 158
Como agua para chocolate, 151
Condorito, 225–226
Cookbooks, 129
Costa Rica
art, 31–32
film, 108–109
magazines, 232
newspapers, 231–232
railroads, 358
theater, 328–329
transportation and travel, 358–359
Cricket, 280–282
Cuba
and architecture, 13–15
automobiles, 351
carnival, 319–320
dance, 64–65
and fashion, 84
film, 109
magazines, 234
music, 198–201
newspapers, 233–234
radio, 255–256
railroads, 350–351

Cuba (*continued*)
    and sports, 297–298
    theater, 317–320
    transportation and travel, 350–352
Cycling, 290–291

Dance
    African influence, 52–54, 62, 64, 65, 66,
        67, 69, 70
    in Argentina, 68–71
    Aztec dancing, 60
    bambuco, 67
    in Brazil, 65–67
    carnival, 56–57
    and catholic catechism, 61
    in Chile, 62–63
    collective identities, 57–58
    in Colombia, 67–68
    during the Colonial period, 52–57
    and courtship, 179
    in Cuba, 64–65
    cumbia, 67–68, 71
    Dance of Two, 52–53, 54–56, 57, 58, 59,
        62, 63, 65, 67
    danza, 64
    danzón, 64–65
    European influence, 52–53, 54–55, 70–71
    hip-hop, 68
    huayno, 62
    Inca dancing, 60
    and independence movements, 58–59,
        65–66
    and indigenous traditions, 60, 61–62, 63
    lundu, 65
    marinera, 63
    maxixe, 66
    merengue, 71
    in Mexico, 59–60, 63
    milonga, 69–70
    montonero minuet, 69
    moros y cristianos, 61
    and musical theater, 55, 69
    national dances, 51–59
    and nationalism, 59, 64–65, 66–67, 71
    nations, 53–54
    in Peru, 62, 63
    and private parties, 57
    reggaetón, 68
    and religious celebrations, 55–56
    salsa, 71
    samba, 65, 66–67
    son, 65
    tango, 69–71

    and theater, 313, 318
    venues, 57
    zamacueca, 62
De Alencar, José, 150
De Fuentes, Fernando, 97
Diving, 286
Divorce
    and domestic violence, 189–190
    laws, 189
    in the nineteenth century, 182–183
    and religion, 188
Dominican Republic
    baseball, 279
    magazines, 234
    music, 203–205
    newspapers, 234
    radio, 259
    railroads, 352
    transportation and travel, 352–353
*Doña Bárbara*, 149

Ecuador
    art, 35–36
    food. *See* Andean cuisine
    magazines, 238
    newspapers, 238
    railroads, 365
    theater, 337
    transportation and travel, 364–366
El Salvador
    art, 29
    film, 109
    newspapers, 230–231
    railroads, 356
    theater, 328
    transportation and travel, 356
Equestrian sports, 291

Fashion and appearance
    and American influence, 81
    and body image, 82
    Bolivia, 75–76
    and the caste system, 78
    during the Colonial period, 76–78
    and community festivals, 83
    in Cuba, 84
    and cultural movements, 80
    department stores, 86
    dress codes, 86
    and eating disorders, 85
    and European influence, 81
    fashion designers, 84
    globalization, 81

Hispanic designers, 81–82
and ideas of beauty, 76
and the independence movement, 78–79
and indigenous communities, 82–83
and indigenous styles, 86
influence on international fashion, 80
leisure styles, 87
in Mexico, 82
and nationalism, 79–81
and obesity, 85
plastic surgery, 85–86
in Puerto Rico, 84
and religious festivals, 83
and social groups, 78, 86
and socialism, 80
and social status, 81, 83, 86
and society, 76
textiles, 77–78
in urban centers, 84–85
western styles, 83
and women, 79
Film
animated, 106
in Argentina. *See* Argentinean cinema
in Bolivia, 110
in Brazil. *See* Brazilian cinema
in Chile, 109–110
cinematecas, 93
in Colombia, 109
and comic books, 155
in Costa Rica, 108–109
in Cuba, 109
and digital media, 94
documentaries, 95
El Salvador, 109
and gender roles, 188
and Hollywood, 93–94
impact of foreign films, 100, 106
Instituto Cubano del Arte y la Industria Cinematográficos, 109
and the Mexican corridos, 146, 147
in Mexico. *See* Mexican cinema
movie watching, 95
in the nineteenth century, 95–96, 99, 105
and photonovels, 152
piracy, 94
as a propaganda tool, 95
silent movies, 96
and sound, 96–97, 101, 106
and sports, 300
and women, 104

French Guiana
art, 38–39
transportation and travel, 370
Food and foodways
African influences, 121, 123–124
American influence, 116
in Argentina. *See* Southern cone cuisine
and art, 28
Asian influence, 124
in Bolivia. *See* Andean cuisine
in Brazil. *See* Caribbean and Brazilian cuisine; Southern cone cuisine
cannibalism, 117–118
in the Caribbean. *See* Caribbean and Brazilian cuisine
in Central America. *See* Mesoamerican food
in Chile. *See* Southern cone cuisine
in Colombia. *See* Andean cuisine
cookbooks, 129
and culture, 121
dining venues, 129–130
distribution, 120
in Ecuador. *See* Andean cuisine
European influence, 116, 118, 128
and festivals, 126, 134
food exports, 131–133
geography, 115
Iberian cuisine, 116
industrialization of foods, 119, 125, 129, 131
in Mexico. *See* Mesoamerican food
Moorish hen, 122
and natural resources, 115–116
nutrition, 120, 125, 127, 135
in Peru. *See* Andean cuisine
and political bureaucracy, 119–120
in pre-Hispanic times, 116, 117–118, 122, 127, 130
social connotations, 135
theological soup, 128
tucumán empanadas, 133
in Uruguay. *See* Southern cone cuisine
welfare program, 130
and women, 133
Fotonovela. *See* Photonovel
Fusco, Coco, 320

Gender roles
for the Aztecs, 174
during the Colonial period, 177, 179
and film, 188
gender parallelism, 172

Gender roles (*continued*)
    for the Incas, 175–176
    and music, 187
    in the nineteenth century, 184–185
    and religion, 188
    and television, 187–188
Golf, 282–283
Guadeloupe, and music, 205
Guadalupe Posada, José, 25–26
Guatemala
    art, 29–30
    newspapers, 229–230
    railroads, 353
    theater, 330
    transportation and travel, 353–354
Guyana
    art, 37–38
    transportation and travel, 370

Haiti
    and music, 205
    newspapers, 235
    transportation and travel, 352–353
Honduras
    art, 30–31
    newspapers, 230
    railroads, 354–355
    transportation and travel, 354–355
Horse racing, 286–287

Incas, gender roles, 175–176
International Olympic Committee, 294–296
Internet
    demographics, 250
    and newspapers, 223, 234
    and periodicals, 223
Iracema, 150

Jai alai, 290
Jamaica, and music, 205–207
Jeanneret-Gris, Charles Edouard. *See* Le
    Corbusier

Kahlo, Frida, 27
Kalimán, 155

*La familia Burrón*, 155
Le Corbusier, 4–6, 9, 14
*Literatura de cordel*
    artwork, 161–162
    demographic and cultural issues, 159
    and government programs, 160
    and Mexican corrido, 159

    structure of, 161
    subject material of, 160, 161
Literature
    American influence, 157, 158
    in Argentina, 156–157
    in Brazil, 149–151, 157–162
    comic books. *See* Comic books
    corrido. *See* Mexican corridos
    corruption of, 140
    definition of, 139–140
    and drug trafficking, 146–147
    effect of political revolutions, 142
    escapist, 148
    European influence, 156
    and film, 152
    first novel, 141
    and literacy, 142–143, 145, 151, 154,
        159
    literatura de cordel. *See* Literatura de
        cordel
    in Mexico, 141, 143–147, 151, 154–156
    and music, 146–147
    in the nineteenth century, 142
    nonfiction, 151
    novel. *See* Novels
    oral, 144
    photonovel. *See* Photonovel
    and politics, 145
    and publishing, 143
    purpose of, 140
    in Venezuela, 149
    in verse, 145, 159
*Los Tigres del Norte*, 147, 197
Love. *See also* Marriage; Sex
    courtship, 179, 187
    and music, 187–188
    popular culture, 187–188
    seduction, 180
Luna, Diego, 99

Magazines
    in Argentina, 242
    in Bolivia, 236
    in Brazil, 246
    and cars, 347
    in Chile, 240–241
    in Colombia, 237–238
    comic books, 225
    in Costa Rica, 232
    in Cuba, 234
    in Dominican Republic, 234
    in Ecuador, 238
    in Mexico, 228–229

news, 225, 228
in Paraguay, 244
in Peru, 239
popular culture, 225, 234
and sports, 299
in Venezuela, 236
women's, 224, 228, 241
Maradona, Diego Armando, 275–276
Marriage. *See also* Love; Sex
arranged, 178
and the Aztecs, 173–175
during the Colonial period, 176–184
divorce, 182–183, 188–190
domestic violence, 182, 189–190
dowry, 178
egalitarian, 186, 187
endogamy, 173
and ethnicity, 178–179
and family, 171, 173–175
gender parallelism, 172
gender roles, 174–175, 177, 179,
184–185
and the Incas, 176
and inheritance, 176–177, 181
and love, 179
monogamy, 176
parental consent, 180–181
and polygamy, 177–178
popular culture, 187–188
in pre-Hispanic times, 171–176
and racial diversity, 177
*Real Pragmática de Matrimonios* decree,
181
and religion, 179–180
and seduction, 180–181
and sex, 171
widows and widowers, 183
Martinique, and music, 205
Memín Pingüín, 156
Mesoamerican food
and corn, 117
culinary blending, 118–119
and cultural stereotypes, 119
European influence, 118, 121
and foreign immigrants, 118–119
indigenous cuisine, 116–117
industrialization of foods, 119
nutrition, 120
and process foods, 121
in religious celebrations, 117
tequila, 118
tortillas, 117, 119–120
and wheat, 117

Mexican cinema
American influence, 97
beginnings of, 95
Cantínflas, 98
documentaries, 95
Golden Age of, 96
and Hollywood, 96–97, 98, 99
language barriers, 94–95, 96–97
melodramas, 97–98
and the North American Free Trade
Association (NAFTA), 98
El nuevo cinema mexicano (New Mexican Cinema), 98–99
Mexican corridos, 141, 196
broad sheet, 144
and film, 146, 147
and history, 143–144
letristas, 144, 145–146
and literatura de cordel, 159
narcocorrido, 146–147
and news, 145–146
origins, 144
and politics, 145
recording of, 146, 147
Mexico
agrarian reform, 119–120
and architecture, 6–7, 10–11
art, 23–28
automobiles, 347–348
baseball, 279
carnival, 334
and dance, 59–60, 63
and fashion, 82
film. *See* Mexican cinema
food. *See* Mesoamerican food
literature, 141–142, 151, 154–156. *See also*
Mexican corridos
magazines, 228–229
and music, 196–197
newspapers, 227–228
periodicals, 226–229
radio, 253–255
railroads, 345–346
technological impact of, 261
television, 261–263, 265–266
theater, 330–335
transportation and travel, 345–350
Universidad Nacional Autónoma de
México, 12
Music
African influence, 197–198, 210
in Argentina, 210–211
big-band mambo, 199

Music (*continued*)
bomba, 201
bossa nova, 212
in Brazil, 211–212
calypso, 207
chachachá, 199
chicha, 210
in Chile, 210
chutney, 208–209
in Colombia, 209–210
contradanza, 198
and courtship, 179
in Cuba, 198–201
cumbia, 209
and dance, 195
dancehall, 206–207
danzón, 198, 199
in Dominican Republic, 203–205
forró, 212
government support, 200
in Guadeloupe, 205
in Haiti, 205
and Hollywood, 212
Indian influence, 208–209, 210
in Jamaica, 205–207
konpa, 205
and love, 187
mariachi, 196
in Martinique, 205
merengue, 203–205
and the Mexican corridos, 146, 147
in Mexico, 196–197
música popular brasileira (MPB), 212
música sertaneja, 212
Norteño, 196–197
nueva trova, 200, 210
in Peru, 210
picó, 210
plena, 201–202
and political commentary, 203
in Puerto Rico, 200–203
rock nacional, 211
reggae, 206
reggaetón, 202
salsa, 202–203, 209
samba, 211–212, 327
ska, 206
soca, 208
and social tensions, 200
son, 198–200
and sports, 300
steel band, 208
tango, 210–211

tejano, 197
and theater, 310, 318, 327, 328, 331
Trinidad, 207–208
vallenato, 209
zouk, 205

Nationalism
and dance, 59, 64–65, 66–67, 71
and fashion, 79–81
and theater, 318
Newspapers, 217–218
in Argentina, 241–242
in Bolivia, 236
in Brazil, 244–246
categories of, 220
in Chile, 240
in Colombia, 236–237
competition, 223–224
in Costa Rica, 231
in Cuba, 233–234
in Dominican Republic, 234
in Ecuador, 238
elite, 221
in El Salvador, 230–231
formats, 221–222
in Guatemala, 229–230
in Honduras, 230
and the Internet, 223, 234
and literacy, 220
in Mexico, 227–228
in Nicaragua, 231
ownership, 223
in Panama, 232–233
in Paraguay, 243–244
in Peru, 238–239
popular press, 222
provincial, 222–223
in Uruguay, 242–243
in Venezuela, 235–236
Nicaragua
art, 31
automobiles, 357
newspapers, 231
theater, 329–330
railroads, 357
transportation and travel, 356–357
Niemeyer, Oscar, 10
Novels
Brazilian, 149–151
detective, 149
genres of, 148
Mexican, 151
romance, 148–149

about sports, 300–301
    Venezuelan, 149

Oesterheld, Héctor Germán, 156–157

Panama
    art, 32
    newspapers, 232–233
    Panama Canal, 359
    railroads, 359–360
    transportation and travel, 359–361
Pan American Highway, 361
Paraguay
    art, 42
    automobiles, 374
    magazines, 244
    newspapers, 243–244
    railroads, 373–374
    theater, 328
    transportation and travel, 373–374
Pelé, 275
Periodicals
    censorship, 219–220, 230, 237, 245
    cultural development, 218
    freedom of the press, 218–220, 226,
        229–230, 239
    government intervention, 218–219, 230,
        231, 232–233, 234, 235, 236–237, 239,
        240, 241, 243, 244
    and independence movements, 217–218
    and the Internet, 223
    and literacy, 229
    magazines. *See* Magazines
    in Mexico, 226–227
    newspapers. *See* Newspapers
    and newsprint, 219
    and racism, 217
Peru
    art, 36–37
    dance, 62, 63
    food. *See* Andean cuisine
    food welfare program, 130
    magazines, 239
    and music, 210
    newspapers, 238–239
    railroads, 366
    theater, 336–337
    transportation and travel, 366
Photonovel
    compared to comic books, 153
    and film, 152
    identifying features of, 152
    and literacy, 151

    origin of, 152
    and publishing, 153
Playwrights
    Argentinean, 310–311
    under dictatorships, 311–312
    female, 332–332
    Guatemalan, 330
    Mexican, 331, 332
Polo, 289–290
Puerto Rico
    baseball, 279
    fashion, 84
    music, 201–203

Radio. *See also* Television
    in Argentina, 258
    in Brazil, 256–257
    censorship, 257
    in Chile, 256
    in Colombia, 257–258
    and comic books, 155
    competition, 257
    in Cuba, 255–256
    in Dominican Republic, 259
    European influence, 255
    and the First Amendment, 252
    government involvement, 254–255
    media democracy, 251
    in Mexico, 253–255
    news, 257
    and newspapers, 253–254
    radionovelas, 259
    and U.S. influence, 251, 254, 255–256, 259
    in Venezuela, 258–259
Railroads
    in Argentina, 376
    in Brazil, 371
    in Colombia, 362
    in Costa Rica, 358
    in Cuba, 350–351
    in Dominican Republic, 352
    in Ecuador, 365
    in Guatemala, 353
    in Honduras, 354–355
    in Mexico, 345–346
    in Nicaragua, 357
    in Panama, 359–360
    subways, 372
Recreation. *See* Sports and Recreation
Religion
    and art, 24, 36
    and dance, 55, 61
    and divorce, 188

Religion (*continued*)
    and fashion, 83
    and food, 117
    and marriage, 179–180
    and sex, 177, 181
Ríus (Eduardo del Rio), 155–156
Rivera, Diego, 26
Rugby, 289

Sanchez, Florencio, 310–311
Sex. *See also* Love; Marriage
    abortion, 190
    and the Aztecs, 173–175
    birth control, 181
    gender parallelism, 172
    HIV/AIDS, 190, 191
    and homosexuality, 172, 177, 183–184, 191
    influence of the media, 190
    and marriage, 171
    in pre-Hispanic times, 171–176
    premarital, 173, 176
    and prostitution, 183
    and religious teachings, 181
    reproductive issues, 190
    and seduction, 180
    and virginity, 173, 176, 177
Skiing, 293–294
Soccer
    in Argentina, 273
    beach or sand, 277–278
    in Brazil, 274
    clubs, 273
    club tournaments, 276–277
    and futsal, 277
    origins, 273
    professional organizations, 275
    stars, 275–276
    in Uruguay, 274
    violence, 277
    World Cup, 274
Southern cone cuisine
    and agriculture, 131
    food exports, 131–133
    and foreign immigrants, 132
    foreign influences, 130
    and industrialization of foods, 131
    and livestock production, 131
    meat, 133–134
    wine, 132
Sports and recreation
    American football, 288–289
    archery, 294

    in Argentina, 297
    auto racing, 287–288
    baseball. *See* Baseball
    basketball, 284–285
    beach volleyball, 285–286
    billiards, 293
    bowling, 293
    boxing, 280
    bullfighting, 291
    capoeira, 292
    Central American and Caribbean Games, 295
    cockfighting, 292
    during the Colonial period, 272
    cricket, 280–282
    in Cuba, 297–298
    cycling, 290–291
    diving, 286
    equestrian sports, 291
    European influence, 272–273
    in film, 300
    golf, 282–283
    horse racing, 286–287
    jai alai, 290
    and the media, 299–301
    modern era, 272–273
    and music, 300
    odd sports, 291–294
    Olympic games, 294–296
    organizations, 294
    Pan American Games, 295–296
    pato, 292
    and politics, 296–298
    polo, 289–290
    in pre-Hispanic times, 271–272
    professional wrestling, 292–293
    roller skating, 293
    rugby, 289
    skiing, 293–294
    soccer. *See* Soccer
    swimming, 286
    tejo, 292
    and television, 266
    tennis, 282
    track and field, 283–284
    volleyball, 285–286
    women in, 298–299
Superbarrio, 333–334
Suriname
    art, 38
    transportation and travel, 370
Swimming, 286

Television. *See also* Radio
    advertising, 260
    in Brazil, 262, 265
    censorship, 262–263
    children's programming, 260–261
    in Chile, 264
    demographics, 250
    educational, 264
    and the First Amendment, 252
    and gender roles, 187–188
    government intervention, 262–263
    in Mexico, 261–263, 265–266
    news, 265
    and politics, 263–264
    satellite transmission, 266
    and sports, 265–266, 299
    technological impact of, 261
    telenovelas, 260
    Televisa, 262
    in Uruguay, 264–265
    U.S. influence, 263, 264
    Xuxa, 261
Tennis, 282
Theater and performance
    African influence, 315, 318–319, 327–328
    in Argentina, 309–314
    avant-garde, 313
    beauty pageants, 322, 323
    in Bolivia, 338–339
    in Brazil, 323–328
    candombes, 315
    carnival. *See* Carnival
    censorship, 314–315, 323–324
    in Chile, 316–317
    circus, 309–310, 326, 331
    in Colombia, 320–322
    comedies, 323
    in Costa Rica, 328–329
    in Cuba, 317–320
    and the Cuban revolution, 318–319
    and dance, 55, 69, 313, 318
    Day of the Dead, 334–335
    under dictatorships, 311–313, 314–315, 316–317, 324
    in Ecuador, 337
    in El Salvador, 328
    European influence, 327
    and festivals, 308, 312, 321–322, 325, 326, 330, 334, 337, 339
    folkloric theater, 331–332, 338
    government support, 317, 325–326, 334, 336, 337, 338
    in Guatemala, 330
    Güegüense theater, 330
    and indigenous culture, 333, 335–336, 338
    and masks, 321
    in Mexico, 330–335
    and music, 310, 318, 327, 328, 331
    nationalistic themes, 318
    in Nicaragua, 329–330
    in Paraguay, 328
    in Peru, 336–337
    playwrights. *See* Playwrights
    and politics, 312–313, 329–330, 321, 337
    in pre-Hispanic times, 307
    puppet theater, 316, 322–323, 331
    revista theater, 323
    rural theater, 325–326, 332
    sainete, 310
    sketch theater, 337
    social activism, 307–308, 324, 325, 333–334
    Spanish influence, 317
    teatro carpa, 338
    teatro de guerrilla, 337
    teatro frívolo, 331
    in Uruguay, 314–316
    in Venezuela, 322–323
    and women, 320, 332–333
    zarzuelas, 309, 317–318, 331
Theater of the Oppressed, 324–325
Track and field, 283–284
Transportation and travel
    air travel, 350, 351, 353, 354, 355, 356, 357, 358, 360, 362, 364, 365, 367, 368, 369, 373, 374, 375, 377
    in Argentina, 376–378
    automobiles. *See* Automobiles
    in Bolivia, 367–368
    in Brazil, 370–373
    bus travel, 348–349, 351, 352–353, 354, 355, 356, 357, 358, 360, 362, 363, 365, 368, 369, 372, 373, 374, 375, 376–377
    in Chile, 368–370
    in Colombia, 361–363
    in Costa Rica, 358–359
    in Cuba, 350–352
    in Dominican Republic, 352–353
    in Ecuador, 364–366
    in El Salvador, 356
    in French Guiana, 370

Transportation and travel (*continued*)
    ground transportation, 345–349,
        350–351, 352–355, 356, 357, 358, 360,
        362, 363–364, 365, 366–367, 368, 369,
        373–374, 375, 376–377
    in Guatemala, 353–354
    in Guyana, 370
    in Haiti, 352–353
    highways, 346–347, 357, 360, 361,
        363–364, 365, 366, 369, 371, 375, 378
    in Honduras, 354–355
    in Mexico, 345–350
    in Nicaragua, 356–357
    in Panama, 359–361
    in Paraguay, 373–374
    in Peru, 366–367
    and politics, 361–362
    railroads. *See* Railroads
    sea travel, 349–350, 352, 353, 354, 356,
        357, 359, 360, 362–363, 364, 365, 367,
        368, 369, 372–373, 374, 375, 378
    in Suriname, 370
    taxis, 348, 355, 358
    in Uruguay, 363–364
    in Venezuela, 363–364
Trejo, Nemesio, 310
Trinidad, and music, 207–208

Uruguay
    art, 42–43
    carnival, 315–316
    dance, 68–71
    food. *See* Southern cone cuisine

    magazines, 244
    newspapers, 242–243
    soccer, 274
    television, 264–265
    theater, 314–316
    transportation and travel, 375–376

Velazquez de León, Josefina, 121
Venezuela
    art, 34–35
    automobiles, 364
    Central University of Venezuela, 12–13
    literature, 149
    magazines, 236
    newspapers, 235–236
    radio, 258–259
    theater, 322–323
    transportation and travel, 363–364
Volleyball, 285–286

Women
    and film, 104
    and food, 133
    magazines for, 224, 228, 241
    playwrights, 332–332
    political activism, 186
    roles in the nineteenth century, 185–186
    in sports, 298–299
    suffragette movement, 185
    and theater, 320, 332–333
Wrestling, 292–293

Xuxa, 261